FAMILY SYSTEMS
WITHIN
EDUCATIONAL &
COMMUNITY
CONTEXTS

*Understanding
Children Who Are
at Risk or Have
Special Needs*

THIRD EDITION

ROSEMARY LAMBIE

LOVE PUBLISHING COMPANY®
Denver • London • Sydney

 Published by Love Publishing Company
P.O. Box 22353
Denver, Colorado 80222
www.lovepublishing.com

Third Edition

Library of Congress Catalog Card Number 2007941555

Copyright © 2008, 2000, 1993 by Love Publishing Company
Printed in the United States of America
ISBN 978-0-89108-326-9

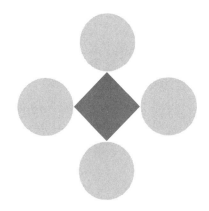

Contents

12 Family Conferences and Teacher–Student Support Teams   367

13 Family-Focused Interventions and Individualized Education Programs   395

14 Classroom and Group Extension of Family Systems Concepts   427

15 Strengthening the Possibilities for a Systems Paradigm   453

Appendix   Conceptual Frameworks of Family Systems Models   487

Preface

*T*his book provides practical information about the field of family systems. It is intended primarily for professionals in social services who work with children and youth at risk and those with special needs. Because the field of family systems is not well known outside the fields of social work and some areas of psychology, this book can serve as a basic foundation of family systems concepts for professors who teach students in university disciplines including education, counseling, and allied health fields. It will enlarge the perspective of social workers who serve children and youth in schools and the larger community. The book will be of value as well to professionals who provide on-the-job training of professionals in social services, health, and education.

At-risk students are characterized as "likely to fail at school or fail at life" (Frymier, 1992, p. 1). Because the number of at-risk children and youth continues to increase, adequate education and training for professionals who deal with at-risk children and youth is vital (Bryan, 2005). Milsom (2002) recommended that school counselors receive more preparation to serve in that capacity. The same is true for professionals who interact with children who have been found to be eligible for special education or related services in schools (Friend, 2005). This book provides specific, substantial information for general and special educators, administrators, school counselors and psychologists, clinical counselors and psychologists, nurses, occupational therapists, physical therapists, and physicians. In addition, it will be useful to professionals and parents with whom the social worker, counselor, general/special educator, and school psychologist collaborate.

You need not know family systems theory to understand this book. If you are well versed in individual psychology and explanations for behavioral and emotional problems, this book will provide you with new and different ways of looking through the lens of this background. You will not have to discard your current beliefs and opinions. Instead, you likely will add another dimension to your thinking, one that is systemic in nature. Systemic approaches consider the interconnectedness and interrelatedness of all the parts of a whole. From the family systems perspective, the interrelationships of all the members of a family are considered when dealing with any one member—in our case, a child/youth who is at risk or who has special needs.

When you have finished reading this book, you will have been exposed to extensive information on a variety of family systems concepts and methods, which will prepare you to interact in systemic ways with at-risk and special-needs children/youth and their families. Although reading this text will not make you an instant expert in the field of family systems, it will provide you with a variety of strategies and methods that you can apply in your interactions with this population.

This text addresses the strengths and resilience of children and youth as well as the challenges they face. An entire chapter is devoted to violence and bullying, to help us understand why children in general, and children with special needs in particular, turn violent and to identify the places where they experience violence, including homes, the media, the community, and schools. The text focuses on family involvement, particularly in school teams, conferences, and the design and implementation of family-focused interventions and individualized education programs. The book considers approaches to working on teams, membership on teams working with children/youth who are at risk and have special needs, and the evolution of teams over time. An appendix is devoted to explaining the conceptual underpinnings of the branch of family studies known as family systems therapy. It provides an in-depth understanding of four family systems models particularly well-suited to application to school and community contexts.

Each chapter includes extension activities for readers to explore the concepts presented. Some of the extension activities are training-related, and others are for the individual to pursue alone. The activities include recommended areas for reflection, journal assignments, discussion topics for outside class, and in-class exploratory activities and topics for those who are reading this text as part of a university or on-the-job offering.

A deeper understanding of these general ideas by community and school professionals, which I hope to foster through the content of this book, can form the foundation for knowing when, how, and why to apply these principles to families of children and youth who are at risk or have special needs. The connection between family experiences and at-risk as well as special-needs children, takes on a new meaning when viewed from a family systems perspective.

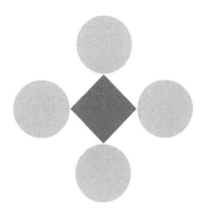

Acknowledgments

The professional influence of Dr. Debbie Bragga, coauthor of the first edition of this book, continues in this third edition. I appreciate collaborating with Drs. Joel Diambra and Daniel L. Fudge at the University of Tennessee in Knoxville. Dr. Erik Lauren, Vice President for Learning and Program Development at United Methodist Family Services in Richmond, VA, wrote a new chapter on bullying and violence prevention for this third edition. He has written a balanced and useful chapter on the prevention of bullying and violence for professionals working with at-risk and special-needs children, youth, and their families.

I will forever appreciate our former dean, Dr. John Oehler, for supporting my work in family systems that led to this book being published in its first edition. Drs. Kathy Cauley, Suzee Leone, and Sherry Sandkam at VCU revived my spirits and my belief in possibilities when needed. Dr. Tom Gumpel was a wizard at helping me laugh when I needed to lighten up. Tom also helped to keep my daughter laughing and enjoying new adventures. I thank all those people who formed a network of support surrounding me with care and encouragement at VCU. For 27 years I was richly blessed by the support of fine colleagues in many disciplines including counseling, education, nursing, psychology, social work, and special education.

I was renewed by the "village" it took to write the latest edition of this textbook. I am grateful to all who have encouraged me as I continued plodding through the third edition. Besides Dean John Oehler at VCU, there are two leaders whose presence in my life has been particularly inspiring: Greg Muzik, principal of Mary Munford Elementary School with Richmond City Public Schools, and Fred Orelove, Executive Director of the Partnership for People with Disabilities at VCU. Likewise, there are others whose inspirational lives have been part of the fabric fueling this third edition of the text. When I needed models for living a life of integrity with grace, I could easily find them among the people whose lives touch me and my daughter. They include Nora Alder; Angela and Andre Basmajian; Cory, Amy, and Grace Blake; Debbie and Rick Bragga and Kelsey Mohring; Jane Brill; Kay Brough; Lisa Callis; Debra Carlotti; Kathy Cauley; Leila Christenbury; Teresa Coburn-Joyce; Michael Davis; Victor Dempsey; Dorcas and Nathan Douthit; Trish Fetta; Paul Gerber; Rose Gordon; Jasmine Grace; Ena Gross; Cory Hall; Marcia Harrigan; Nadine Hoffman; Judy Jacob; Wendy Kliewer; Therese Kohl; Suzee and Philip Leone; Chris Lombardi; Susan Israel Massey; Alan McLeod; Jim McMillan; Donna and Mike Moore; Ann and Sarah Morck; Elizabeth Myers; John and Mary Sue Oehler; Fred Orelove and Irene Carney; Evelyn Reed-Victor; Kathie Reinhoehl; Fr. Michael Renninger; Lynda Richardson; Sherry Sandkam; Carol Scearce; Warren Snead; Sylvia Statton, Bishop Emeritus Walter F. Sullivan; Colleen Thoma; Wrenn Thompson; John Vassar; Michelle Via; Badiyyah Waajid; Beverly Warren; Cordell Watkins; Phyllis West; Jean and Wes Wilkinson; Pat Willard; Stoner Winslett; Jane Pendleton Wootton; Pam Wright; and Jackie Zich. Although no longer living, Frances G. Jones, Chris Mohring, Jim Victor, John Washburn, Msgr. Charles Kelly, and Frs. Bill Mountain and John Mullahy remain models of perseverance in the face of challenge. The task of listing names is difficult, as I fear I could inadvertently leave someone out. If your name belongs here, please know in your heart that I do value your presence and I apologize for my temporary memory lapse.

As was the case for the last two editions, my publisher, Stan Love, has been most supportive. Understanding about the overload at VCU, he waited patiently. There could be no finer publisher, and his gentle nature has kept me optimistic. Susan Warhover and Carrie Watterson, editors with Love Publishing, have been very helpful, supportive, and encouraging; they made this book far more readable than I, and our communications brightened my spirits as I kept writing. The copyeditor, Carolyn Acheson, provided attention to detail with greater formality and enhanced readability, making a significant difference in the learning of those reading this book. Debbie Bragga was not just the coauthor of the first edition. Her friendship while writing this third edition has helped me stay grounded, positive, and joined on the path. Teresa Coburn-Joyce was helpful with searches and finding errors.

As was true in the last editions, my family-of-origin and extended family have been my greatest teachers about family systems. As the sibling of a child with a severe learning disability and the daughter of a father with severe, chronic physical illnesses and a mother who was a professor of reading and language arts, I have had many opportunities for growth. My large extended family on farms in Michigan has also taught me much about family as resource. They have shared life's joys and stood beside me through the trials and tribulations of family and life. Helen Miles, my fifth-grade teacher and my mother's best friend during my childhood, affected my view of life and family at a critical time in my childhood.

My daughter, Mariah, continues to bring the value of family systems into clear focus. Each day she gives new meaning to family life, thus continuing the experience of writing another edition with greater understanding and empathy for others. Mariah was in child care and preschool when I was writing the second edition. As the mother of a fourth-grader with typical and atypical challenges, the importance of the home–school connection is riveting. Having the East Coast snipers calling on a pay phone only blocks away from Mariah's school brought home the raw fear of parents sending their children into dangerous terrain every day. I now more easily identify with parents living in urban blight who know their children may land in harm's way. I have gained a deeper appreciation for the village that supports and protects us. September 11th had this impact on parents across the country. We are aware of our vulnerability in a different way since that day. This book focuses on vulnerable children and youth and their families and communities. It is my hope that those who, prior to 9-11-01, had a sense of invulnerability can more easily imagine what it is like to grow up in an at-risk neighborhood or with special needs. The more we can relate to the vulnerable individuals in our society, the more likely it is that we will reach out with renewed understanding and in greater support of those we serve.

Murray Bowen's theory of family systems has greatly affected my professional and personal life. In 1979, reading his work started me on my journey to understanding family systems concepts and approaches. As a result, I have a deep connection to my extended family and so too does Mariah.

Virginia Satir died in 1988. I learned a valuable lesson from her: anything a human being has done can be understood, and any person can learn new ways of living with family, friends, and society. Virginia Satir did not judge people, and the tolerance she had for what others understandably see as intolerable is a fitting tribute to a woman who had the capacity to surrender, forgive, and believe in new possibilities.

Harry Aponte and Joan Winter provided six valuable years of family systems training. Without it I would not have had the depth of knowledge in family systems to begin writing this text.

Molly Dellinger-Wray, Kim Spears, Paul Rupf, Joel Diambra, Laura Robertson, and Emily Wilson allowed me to supervise their work with families, schools, and service providers, enabling me to remain in contact with the everyday challenges faced by individuals with special needs. It was a privilege to witness their dedication to and care of their clients and families.

Victoria Doughty, practitioner of acupuncture, helped me achieve greater balance as I walked the labyrinth of professorship during major structural and personnel changes. With improved balance I realized that earlier retirement would allow me to be a better mother as well as have time to write, something lacking in the previous four years.

Last, I acknowledge those who have read this textbook in any of its three editions. Thank you for using the concepts and applications so that a wider circle of at-risk and special-needs children and youth can benefit. Together, we can make a difference in the lives of those whom we serve. My hope for you is that you seldom or never lose hope. In supervising others and in my personal experience I have found hope to be essential to serving individuals, families, and our society with equanimity and courage over the span of a career. I wish you well on your journey.

Dedication

- To my daughter Mariah Rose Lambie, light of my life, and my greatest blessing and challenge
- To my mother and father, whose dedication to family enriched and crystallized my life journey—their family-first behavior forever leaves an imprint on my heart and will continue down the generations through Mariah
- To Stan Love, whose patience has been that of the Biblical figure Job—without his unwavering understanding through the repeated broken timelines, this book would not have its dedication to excellence
- To Greg Muzik, a model of dedicated and balanced leadership as well as a supporter of parental partnership and inclusion in schools—he earned his angel wings long ago
- To Richard Whelan, my doctoral advisor at the University of Kansas, who taught me the difference that taking one step at a time makes and whose personal presence, authenticity, caring, and support brought gifts of wisdom and life lessons
- To Debbie Daniels-Mohring-Bragga, coauthor of the first edition of this textbook as well as a generous and caring family friend and second mommy to Mariah
- To Kelsey Mohring, the best heart-sister Mariah could have and a model of authenticity and love
- To Frances G. Jones (Dandanny), loving life and people for 87 years and a model of "greeting each day with courage" until he died; and to his daughter, Jean Jones-Wilkinson, my closest friend
- To the Virginia Commonwealth University students who have opened their hearts and minds to me, trusting me on their journey, thus providing for a gratifying professional life filled with awe and meaning
- To the pupils I have taught and their families, especially the Hallins in Denver
- To my brothers, Tom and George; my sister-in-law, Karen; my nephew, Patrick, and his mother, Carla; and especially my extended family in Michigan who continue to support and care for us
- To Nora Alcoser Ryan, wife of my cousin Mark, a gift within our extended family and a model of tender support and charity
- To the family that has influenced my life in meaningful ways, celebrating with me the joys of life and standing by me through its challenges: Cory, Amy, and Grace Blake; Debbie and Rick Bragga and daughter Kelsey Mohring; Kathy Cauley; Wanda Charity; Michael and Connie Davis; Victor Dempsey; Dorcas and Nathan Dothuit; Joel, Trish, Nathan, and Nicole Diambra; Wilson Ellis; Tom Gumpel; Katty Inge; Helga Jack and daughter Kristina Dickey; Penne and Dan Kirkpatrick; Therese Kohl; Erik Laursen; Suzee and Phil Leone; Donna and Mike Moore; Fred Orelove; Cheryl and Allie Palmore; Maria and Vanessa Philips; Lynda Richardson and Mike Ostrander; Sherry, Melinda, Bob, and Mary Sandkam, and Brownie Tomlin; Carol Scearce; John Seyfarth; Elisabeth Stewart; Nancy, Billy, and Betsy Trimble and Sarah Pruett; Ann Waldbauer; Phyllis West; Jean, Wes, and Curran Wilkinson; Charlene Wilton; Larry Wright, Pam Oken-Wright, and Sarah Wright; Jackie and Ronnie Zich—bless you
- To Paul Kessler and his family, whose influence on my family life has been profound
- To Mariah's birth mother and all birth parents with the courage and heart to allow their children to be adopted—there is no greater gift in our world

PART ONE

Description of Family Systems

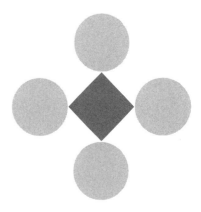

Introduction

*M*any schools of family systems therapy offer approaches that are useful with children, youth, and adults (Newsome, 2005; Nichols & Schwartz, 2005; Mullis & Edwards, 2001). Specific problems are viewed within the context of an individual's life experiences and relationships (Haley, 1987; Nichols & Schwartz, 2004). This text goes beyond the individual approaches to posit that changes in one part of an individual's life reverberate in all other areas of that person's experience, that all facets of the person's experience are inseparable parts of a whole. Research is clear, for example, that students of low socioeconomic status fall behind academically during the summer, when their parents influence their learning most (Alexander & Entwisle, 1996; Slavin, Madden, Dolan, & Wasik, 1996). This is just one of many indications of how family systems affect the lives of children and youth beyond the family into school and community.

A family systems perspective is especially appropriate for professionals who have responsibility for the care and instruction of children and youth, because the experiences of these children are determined and shaped by adults, especially their parents (Nichols & Schwartz, 2005; Abrams, Theberge, & Karan, 2005; Peeks, 1993). A family systems model does not call simply for remediation of a student's performance in school or improving a student's adjustment in either a school or community setting. It calls for attention to the child's interactions with family members and others in the community.

Although this text does not address academic programs for children and youth at risk and those with special needs, it does discuss means for understanding and working with them, their families, and communities. With this understanding, professionals in the school and community, along with the family, can address the needs of at-risk children before a problem becomes unmanageable. In this way, the overlap of family and school/community can be combined to the benefit of at-risk children and youth.

Family Systems Theories

Since the mid-1950s, professionals in the field of family studies have witnessed numerous answers to the question, "Why do things change when the family is involved?" The early description of family process was followed by experimentation and construction of theories. Family interaction was videotaped, and the data were then analyzed by sophisticated computer programs. Family theories proliferated to a point at which an article by Holman and Burr published in 1980 listed at least 18 different approaches. Clearly, it is beyond the scope of this book to discuss the content and impact of each of these theories. The three systems theories having the most impact on the field of family studies are interactionist theory, exchange theory, and systems theory. This text addresses family systems theory only.

Conceptual Models

Systems theory has been the basis for the development of most of the family treatment approaches created and applied since the 1950s. The generalizations that have arisen from systems theory are useful for understanding not only the family but also systems including the school, community, and workplace. Of the conceptual models of family therapy that emerged from this theoretical base, I have chosen to present four models in this book: the human validation process model of Virginia Satir, the multigenerational theory pioneered by Murray Bowen, the structural family systems model, and the strategic family systems approach.

Each of these models of family systems includes an approach to treatment that evolved over time and has proven effective with families experiencing problems, although, Bowen repeatedly stated his stance that he was building theory rather than using strategies for the purpose of intervening with a family system. I present these four models in particular because of their potential impact on children and youth who are at risk or who have special needs. Both the structural family systems model and the multigenerational model have individual chapters in Part One of this textbook, and the Appendix goes into detail on all four conceptual models.

A Strengths-Based Approach

A basic premise of this book is that working with families of children and youth is best approached from a positive, strengths-based perspective. Just as the word "education" stems from the Latin word that means "to draw out from" (versus filling an empty vessel), we would do well to focus on the very real strengths that all involved—the children and youth, their families, and community—bring to the challenges they face.

Professionals in community and school work within a timeframe that requires efficiency. It is easy to roll up our sleeves and focus on the perceived "problem" when in the end we would be more efficient if we were to take the time to consult our models of positive psychology (Sheridan, Warnes, Cowan, Schemm, & Clarke, 2004) and look for the resilience that lies within. Outcomes are improved immeasurably when we look within ourselves, the child or youth, family and extended family, school, neighborhood, community, faith-based organizations, and society to find the strengths that are waiting for an opportunity to bloom. Equally important is to recognize the strengths that can be built in collaboration with other professionals, the child, family, and community.

For some time the word "empowerment" has been prominent in the lexicon of social services. It communicates an alternate perspective to viewing people as incompetent. It calls forth the strengths within rather than filling needs from the outside. Still, the term suggests a hierarchy of professional facilitation rather than reaching for the strengths of those we seek to help.

Amidst poverty and broken neighborhoods, suffering, and loss, we often overlook the untapped potential of those we serve. A strengths-based perspective holds a deep recognition of the human spirit that lives in each of us and the contexts in which we live, work, recreate, love, worship, and eventually die. Respect for others is grounded in this recognition of inner strength. Within the gene structure of human nature there appears to be a "self-righting mechanism" that can help in creating positive growth (Richardson, 2002). Professionals should seek out the resources within individuals and families.

Bradley, Johnson, Rawls, and Dodson-Sims (2005) indicated that parental participation is strongly linked to student achievement. They presented eight strategies for school counselors to better collaborate with African American parents. In that article they addressed their view of Caucasian American middle class professionals' lack of experience and understanding of cultural differences and propose a metanoia, or change of heart/perspective. The authors provided nine concrete suggestions for changing one's view and broadening one's experience related to cultural differences.

Among many other writings, the strengths-based approach has been addressed in relation to families by Patterson (2002), Allison, Stacey, Dadds, Roeger, Wood, and Martin (2003), as well as Sheridan, Warnes, Cowan, Schemm, and Clarke (2004). Maton, Schellenbach, Leadbeater, and Solarz (2004) took the broader perspective, to include community in their book *Investing in Children, Youth, Families, and Communities.* Looking at families and communities from a strengths-based perspective teaches us much about what will help to bring balance amidst the conditions that favor risk and dysfunction. This perspective is woven throughout the book like connective tissue in the human body.

The following is a story of good fortune, one that allows you to see how a strengths-based perspective can be handed down by modeling.

> When I was in elementary school, my mother took me on a home-visit to a child she taught. His older brother was in my classroom and I knew the family. When we entered the home, I was surprised by the dirt floor and chickens running around the yard and

house and my mother's lack of reaction to what she saw. Mrs.
Grigsby, the mother of her student, was gracious and dignified,
and I absorbed much from this experience of being next to a collaborative process of equals.

My mother was the oldest of nine children growing up on a
farm in the Midwest and experienced extreme poverty during the
Great Depression. I had heard many stories of that time in history,
but I did not know that thirty years later people still lived in homes
with dirt floors a few blocks from my school. My mother's perspective was something that I accreted while with her on this
home-visit. That experience will be with me as one of life's
greatest gifts.

On our way home in the car, we discussed the home setting,
and my mother's focus was clearly on the positive. She talked
about the great love Mrs. Grigsby had for her children and the values she had instilled in them. When I reflected on that experience
many years later, I realized that it was one of the most important
ways that my mother taught me. She guided by modeling and was
a model of equanimity as well as respect for others. There was
reverence for all life that I heard in her voice and absorbed that
day.

Not everyone is so fortunate as to have such a model. At the same time, humans seem
to have an inner "self-righting mechanism" that we can draw upon to retrain ourselves so
we are able to see the beauty and strength within others. This capacity holds life with
profound reverence and remains balanced in the presence of pain and suffering of self and
others.

A Holistic Approach

The holistic approach stems from an ecological perspective (Abrams, Theberge, & Karan,
2005; Bronfenbrenner, 1979, 1977). This approach examines all of the various aspects of
the whole under consideration. Beyond the academic curriculum, holistic education
encompasses all of the other relevant aspects of education. Working with families is one
component of holistic education.

Further, the holistic approach, by definition, is systemically oriented. It is based on the
interrelatedness and interconnectedness of its subject, be it holistic medicine, holistic
health, holistic education, or any other related subject.

Margaret Mead is quoted as saying, "There is hope, I believe, in seeing the human
adventure as a whole and in the shared trust that knowledge about mankind sought in reverence for life can bring life."

And Komoski (1990) stated:

As the idea of holism opens new ways of approaching science, the
environment, and our health, educators are beginning to advocate
holistic approaches to teaching and learning. This trend signals a

growing appreciation of the interconnectedness of things and recognition of the truth of the adage, "the whole is greater than the sum of its parts." (p. 72)

Holistic approaches (Hendrick, 1984; Reinsmith, 1989) to education reflect a rebalancing of practice that departs from the behaviorist/reductionist view. Most of the writing on holistic education deals with systemically balanced curriculum or whole curriculum, although Byers (1992), in the journal *Holistic Education Review,* further recommends addressing the topic of spirituality in the classroom.

A number of writers in the area of counseling have addressed the spiritual dimension of working with children and youth in a special issue of *Professional School Counseling* (Sink & Richmond, 2004). Aponte (1994) has written on the spiritual dimension of families in terms of the meaning people make of life and the challenges it brings.

The text you are reading here, too, goes beyond the mainstream in proposing that working with families using family systems concepts and methods is a logical extension of holistic education. The holistic approach provides a context for increasing the breadth and depth of your interactions with at-risk and special-needs children and youth and through a holistic lens, your responsibility increases for involvement with families, especially those targeted in this book.

An Introduction to the Family and Family Systems

$\mathcal{B}$efore the 1950s, the fields of psychology and counseling concentrated on diagnosis and treatment of the individual. Psychological and behavioral problems were viewed as originating from some underlying tension or conflict within the mind and experience of the individual. Treatment typically involved psychotherapy sessions during which the therapist and the patient, through discussion and association, tried to discover the root of the problem. In addition, the individual might have been given medication to diminish depression or anxiety or to help change personal behavior.

In the middle of the 20th century, the field of family studies began to take shape (Nichols & Schwartz, 2005). Sociologists, psychologists, educators, physicians, and counselors began to think of the individual in relationship to other people, including friends, associates, and family members.

Nichols and Schwartz (2004) indicated that during the initial years of the development of family studies, "families with schizophrenic members proved to be an especially fertile area for research because their strange patterns of interaction were so dramatic" (p. 18). The first data generated regarding families were descriptive in nature (Berardo, 1980). Professionals who worked with psychiatric patients began to observe and write about their patients' involvement with and reactions to their families (Guerin & Guerin, 2002).

Professionals from various fields of mental health, primarily in hospital settings, began to notice that patients who were "cured" in the hospital and then sent home began to exhibit their symptoms again.

Educators who developed elaborate behavioral programs for use in the home discovered that what worked in the classroom did not necessarily work in the family setting. For those who worked with these patients and students, the question became, "Why do things change when the family becomes involved in therapy?"

Since the early 1980s, the family systems perspective continued to evolve, eventually moving past practitioners who identified with only one family systems theory/approach (e.g., Bowen's theory; structural family therapy) to the exclusion of other approaches. Practitioners today use several variations of the original family systems approach. At the same time, much can be learned by studying the pioneering models, as each contains gems that benefit professionals in schools and communities. As Nichols and Schwartz (2005) wrote:

> Certain problems are especially suited to the family approach, among them, problems with children (who must, regardless of what happens in therapy, return home to their parents), complaints about a marriage or other intimate relationship, family feuds, and symptoms that develop in an individual around the time of a major family transition. (p. 5)

Thus, the family systems field intersects with school professionals working with at-risk and special-needs students (Fine & Carlson, 1992). Though this book is not about training school and community professionals to conduct family systems therapy, these professionals will benefit from understanding the principles underlying family systems, to inform their practice in school and community contexts.

Principles Underlying Family Systems

The basic principle underlying family systems theory is that *no individual can be understood without looking at how he or she fits into the whole of the family*. When trying to understand a family system, one must go beyond consideration of individuals within the family to consideration of how the individuals within the family interact and how their histories have unfolded. For example, a student who looks distracted or lethargic in the classroom or hyperactive in a community setting might be viewed differently if the professional were to know that his parents were going through a divorce or that a new baby had joined her family.

A second family systems principle is that *families need rules for structure and rules for change*. Rules for structure organize the day-to-day functioning of the family. Rules for change allow adaptability to new circumstances. For example, all newly married couples have to reach agreement about how to run their household in terms of cooking, cleaning, and paying bills. When children are born, or if one or both partners become highly involved in a career, the task assignments may have to be changed. If the couple is not able to renegotiate these responsibilities, the marriage will undergo stressors that, in the extreme, could lead to divorce. The family system itself is challenged, and the children will be at greater risk for failure in school and all of life.

A third principle is that *interaction of the family with the school, community, extended family, and friendship circle is essential to the life of the immediate family*. All of these external systems need not be included in the most intimate details of family life, but family members should interact with some people outside of the immediate family to be well balanced. Families that remain reclusive and hostile toward outsiders tend to be dysfunctional in nature, and their children are at risk for failure.

Before going any further, we must define what a "family" is. The definition is not the same as it was a few decades ago and continues to evolve.

Definitions of Family

Family can be defined in a number of ways. Some people take a narrow view of mother, father, and children. Others broaden the view to include everyone living in the home. Still others include only blood relations, to the exclusion of adopted children. A few years back, Dan Quayle, vice-president under the President George Herbert Walker Bush, commented on the "negative message" sent by the main character of then-popular sitcom *Murphy Brown,* a single mother-to-be. His remark instigated a debate about single parenthood and, by extension, the definition of family.

Since the second edition of this book was written, Betty Carter and Monica McGoldrick (1999b) were editors of, and contributors to, an expanded, third edition of their textbook on the family life cycle. In the prior edition they responded to criticism in the field that the focus limited to one family form, the "White, Anglo, middle-class, nuclear family of a once-married heterosexual couple, their children, and their extended family" (p. xv). In the new edition, they changed the term from "nuclear family" to "immediate family," explaining that the new use allows for a more inclusive and realistic view, understanding, and acceptance of family life in the United States. They attribute their shift in terminology to the changes in family structure over the previous decade. In their use of "immediate family," Carter and McGoldrick include "nuclear, single-parent, unmarried, remarried, and gay and lesbian households" (p. xvi). They see commitment, rather than marriage, as the family bond.

A widely respected book on ethnicity and family therapy, in its third edition, was edited by McGoldrick, Giordano, and Garcia-Preto (2005). The concentration of *Ethnicity and Family Therapy* is on how people from various ethnic backgrounds relate to and understand family. Some ethnic groups define family narrowly, and for others, families are almost tribal in nature.

In this book, family is defined in the broadest possible sense, with the parents or caregivers defining it for themselves. If a family defines its members as everyone who lives in the house, that is the definition that should be accepted by professionals with whom they interact. Applying this definition, a teacher would welcome a grandmother at a "parent"-teacher conference, or two daddies as parents of a student. If an adult has been identified publicly as the child's birth-parent in an open adoption, the appropriate professional response is to acknowledge the birth-parent in a way that is accepting and considerate of the child. Here, a simple statement might be, "It's is good to meet you," or "Thanks, Noah, for introducing me to this special person in your life." One caveat is legal in nature: A child cannot be taken from a school or community resource unless the primary caregiver/parent who has legal custody has given written permission.

Changing Demographic Influences

To understand the changing definitions of family, we must consider changing demographics and immigration patterns. In the late 20th century, more than one million immigrants came to the United States annually, most from Asia and Latin America, according to McGoldrick, Giordano, and Garcia-Preto (2005, p.17). The U.S. Census Bureau reported, in the 2000 census, a total of 28,000,000 first-generation immigrants, or 10% of the U.S. population. With the changing face of the United States, professionals in communities and schools are being called upon to learn and understand more about diverse family values, beliefs, and practices and how to connect with those from diverse family backgrounds.

Economic and social pressures can result in increasing structural diversity among families (Entwisle, 1994). The different rates of structural change have resulted in a magnification of subcultural differences and, since 1950, major changes in the family have occurred, most of which are not immediate family in nature (Carter & McGoldrick, 1999c). These changes in the family have led to changes in how professionals view families

Family Systems Theory Related to At-Risk and Special-Needs Children and Youth

With this background on changing definitions of family, and of cultural differences in a rapidly expanding and diverse population, we will add two more considerations—families of at-risk and special-needs children.

At-Risk Children and Youth

Professionals have written and hypothesized about at-risk students from the 1980s through the 1990s (Newsome, 2005). In an early definition, Frymier and Gansneder (1989) described at-risk children and youth as those who are likely to fail either in school or in life, and pointed out that

> "at-riskness" is a function of what bad things happen to a child, how severe they are, how often they happen, and what else happens in the child's immediate environment. For example, a pregnant 14-year-old is at risk. But a pregnant 14-year-old who uses drugs is even more at risk. And a pregnant 14-year-old who uses drugs, has been retained in grade, has missed 30 days of school, and has a low sense of self-esteem is still more seriously at risk.

> Moreover, being at risk is not solely a phenomenon of adoles-
> cence. Children of all ages are at risk. A 6-year-old whose parents
> are in the throes of a divorce and who is doing poorly in school is
> at risk. A 17-year-old whose grades are good but who is deeply
> depressed because she just lost her boyfriend is also at risk. A
> 10-year-old whose brother dropped out of school a year ago and
> whose father just lost his job is certainly at risk. (p. 142)

Slavin and Madden (1989) suggested that "a practical criterion for identifying students at risk is eligibility for chapter 1, special education, or other remedial services under today's standards" (p. 4). Using 45 factors that research had linked to being at risk, Frymier and Gansneder (1989) found that between 25% and 35% of the students in their study were seriously at risk. Ralph (1989) indicated that at-risk behaviors were not growing worse but that professionals were simply identifying more students who were at risk.

Cuban (1989) offered a new explanation for at-risk students. He departed from the implication that these students are the cause of their own poor performance or that their families do not prepare them for school and do not provide proper support. In his alternative view, schools fail to meet the needs of these children

> because the culture of the school ignores or degrades their family
> and community backgrounds. Middle-class teachers, reflecting the
> school's values, single out for criticism differences in children's
> behavior and values.... The structure of the school is not flexible
> enough to accommodate the diverse abilities and interests of a
> heterogeneous student body. Programs are seldom adapted to
> children's individual differences. Instead, schools seek uniformity,
> and departures from the norm in achievement and behavior are
> defined as problems. (p. 781)

Slavin and Madden (1989) agreed with this view, indicating that the incapacity of the school to meet the needs of each pupil, rather than the incapacity of the learner, was what caused failure. They saw at-risk students as those in danger of failing to complete their education with adequate skills. They included as risk factors low achievement, retention in grade, behavior problems, poor attendance, low socioeconomic status, and attending school with a large number of poor students.

Liontos (1991) indicated that the term "at risk" had become a cliché used as a description and a prediction. Thus, when educators think of at-risk students, they often focus on school and academic failure, dropouts, the educationally disadvantaged, and underachievement. Liontos, in contrast, saw the term as one that described personal, educational, and societal ills.

Jens and Gordon (1991) suggested that when the concept of risk entered the field of education, many misunderstood its meaning. Although risk implies the potential for negative outcome, it also points to the possibility that a negative outcome can be avoided. When the negative outcome is avoided, the term *resiliency* is applied. This concept is discussed in chapter 10.

Characteristics of At-Risk Students

Westfall and Pisapia (1994) grouped factors indicated in the literature as characteristic of at-risk students into three areas:

1. Social/family background
2. Personal problems
3. School

Factors relating to social/family background include sibling/parent dropout, low socioeconomic status accompanied by poor nutrition, damage to dignity, inadequate housing, English used as a second language, dysfunctional family system including lack of structure and stability, substance abuse, physical abuse, single-parent home, lack of commitment to schools, and communication problems between home and school.

Factors relating to personal problems include having an external locus of control, learned helplessness, a distinct lack of coping skills, and acceptance of failure. Manifestation of these factors include substance abuse leading to health problems, poor self-esteem, teen pregnancy, being in trouble with the law, learning disabilities, few goals and an inability to envision options, hopelessness in looking ahead to the future, and suicidality.

Factors relating to school include behavioral problems such as acting out, absenteeism, authority problems and a sense of alienation toward school authority; failing school (particularly in the early years); failing courses; suspension/expulsion; dissatisfaction with school; having few counseling opportunities; inadequate mental health, social, and physical health services in the school; and hostile school climate for students who do not fit in. Westfall and Pisapia (1994) also reported characteristics of at-risk students who were successful in school.

Programs

Many programs are available for at-risk students. Brendtro, Brokenleg, and Van Bockern (1990) viewed this reclamation process as our hope for the future; and Slavin et al. (1996) described a successful multidimensional program for students at risk for failure that included a parent component.

In summarizing differing perspectives surrounding the term "at risk" and the areas of attention directed to those at risk, Newsome (2005) highlighted attempts in the field to reflect complexities present with those at risk; risk and protective factors found within those at risk; rating risk over a base rate (much like insurance risk studies); ecological issues such as poverty and homelessness as well as family dysfunction of those at risk; and high numbers of adolescents involved with risks such as substance abuse, delinquency, and dropping out of school.

Researchers have different views on the definition of risk, some seeing all individuals and families as well as communities as being at risk. Others (Masten & Coatsworth, 1998; Patterson, 2002) see the difference between families who meet typical stressors in life and families who face

> significant risk emerging from (a) high-risk status by virtue of continuous, chronic exposure to adverse social conditions such as

> poverty; (b) exposure to a traumatic event or severe adversity
> such as war; or (c) a combination of high-risk status and trau-
> matic exposure. (Patterson, p. 237)

This textbook draws upon these factors described by Patterson. Thus, families characterized as at risk are those living in poverty and diagnosis of chronic illness or disability, as well as other, equally significant situations that place individuals, families, and
communities at risk. For some families, significant risk creates an overload, and they
respond with higher level functioning and resilience, whereas other families do not
develop the protective factors critical for the development of resilience. In studying
those who develop protective factors, we can learn much about how to help the latter
group develop resilience in response to adversity faced in life.

Researchers (Lago-Dellelo, 1998; Montague & Rinaldi, 2001) found an interesting
relationship between at-risk status of children in early elementary grades and future determination of the designation as having learning disabilities/behavior disorders (LD/EBD).
Montague & Rinaldi stated, "Until about eight years of age, students at risk for LD/EBD
are generally unaware of their classroom teachers' negative behavior toward them and the
preferential treatment of their classmates" (p. 82). Their two studies of the same cohort of
students found that between 8 and 10 years of age, the students became aware of teacher
negativity and low expectations, followed by lowered expectations about self-competence.
These authors posited that

> ...teacher rejection is a precursor of peer rejection for students
> with behavioral problems and adversely affects students' behav-
> ioral and academic outcomes as well as development of self-
> esteem and interpersonal relationship. (p. 82)

The study of classroom dynamics and risk status for LD/BD ties together both at-risk findings and disability designation in students beginning in the third grade.

Belisto, Ryan, and Brophy (2005) validated an at-risk instrument to screen elementary level children in schools. The four main domains of the Screening for At-Risk Status
Survey included academic skills, social confidence, social cooperation, and family support. The instrument is useful in finding children early in their schooling and developing interventions to ensure their school success. The researchers concluded that, "teachers can reliably and accurately identify a group of students who are showing early signs
of school difficulty and who could benefit from a response or intervention that might not
require the full mobilization of special education resources" (p. 157).

Children and Youth With Special Needs

Like others before and after him, Skrtic (1991) suggested that schools contribute to the
problem of children and youth who fail. In his examination of schools, he focused in particular on the impact of schools on students who are, or traditionally have been, placed in
special education classes. Federal law refers to them as "children with a disability" under
the Individuals with Disabilities Education Improvement Act (IDEA) and currently cate-
gorizes them into 13 different types of disabilities. According to Dunn and Baker (2002),

the number of students with disabilities has increased every year since data were first collected in 1976–1977 (p. 278).

As required by law, 5.7 million children and youth between the ages of six and 21 receive special education services (U.S. Department of Education, 2002). This represents an increase, between 1990–1991 and 2000–2001, of 32.1% for students receiving special education and related services across disability categories served by IDEA ages birth through 21 (Friend, 2005). Friend pointed out that having a disability is a small part of each individual's identity.

The 13 disability categories specified by IDEA are as follows:

1. Specific learning disabilities
2. Speech or language impairments
3. Mental retardation
4. Emotional disturbance
5. Deaf/blindness
6. Visual impairments
7. Hearing impairments
8. Orthopedic or physical impairments
9. Other health impairments
10. Autism
11. Traumatic brain injury
12. Multiple disabilities
13. Developmental delays

Clearly, professionals working in and with schools (e.g., teachers, counselors, social workers) are asked to serve many "categories" of children and youth. What is important to the message of this book is that professionals serve the individual child or youth in the context of the family as a unit and not overly focus on disability. Also, seeing the strengths makes a substantial difference in professionals and has an impact on those with whom they work.

Special attention is given in this text to students with behavior disorders, learning disabilities, mental retardation, physical disabilities, and chronic illness. Also, this book uses the term "behavior disorders" rather than "emotional disturbance," as found in IDEA, because the former is more acceptable to parents. Further, "physical disabilities" and "chronic illness" seems more descriptive than the IDEA terminology "other health impaired" and "orthopedic impairments." In any case, the background information dealing with family systems concepts can be generalized to all families regardless of their categorization or label, and some factors are more characteristic of a family with a child having one particular disability or another.

Extension Activities

Activity 1:

Reflection: Now that you have read chapter 1, think about what you expect to learn from this book.

Journal: Begin a traditional "KWL" process by first listing what you "Know" about family systems and then what you "Want to know" about family systems. After reading the entire text, you can complete the process by writing what you "Learned." Save your original entry for later comparisons.

Log: Keep a running log of 5 or 10 key concepts from each chapter.

Activity #2:

In-Class/Training Discussion: (Leader) Lead a discussion on "Know" and "Want to know." Write the participants' comments on chart paper and save the chart for the end of the course/training for comparison with what was learned. Add to the chart what participants still want to "Learn."

Reading: Before moving on to chapter 2, read the Appendix, which presents a foundation of knowledge that allows a richer understanding of family systems. In its coverage of several conceptual frameworks that undergird unique family systems models, it is essential reading for instructors and trainers and highly useful for all others reading this book.

Survey/Question: Survey the chapters in Part One by skimming the topics one chapter at a time. After reading the topic headings for a chapter, write down three questions that come to mind. Do not censor your questions. Review your list as you prepare to read each chapter in Part One.

In-Class/Training Small-Group Discussion: Discuss some of the questions that came to mind while surveying the chapters in Part One.

Later In-Class/Training Large-Group Discussion: Select a few adjectives from the following question to use for the whole-group discussion, and add any adjectives of your own: What do you think you will find to be the most [intriguing, meaningful, disturbing, scary, unnerving, conflict-inducing, conflict-resolving, exciting, uninteresting, stabilizing, value-engendering, and quality-enhancing] topic(s) in the chapters of Part One?

In-Class/Training Discussion: If only a portion of the class/group has had professional experiences, have the professionals sit in a center circle with everyone else surrounding them in an outer circle listening while the professionals discuss the following:

Relate experiences you have had with families of students who are at risk by elaborating on challenges met, as well as lessons learned.

AND/OR

Relate experiences you have had with families of students with special needs by elaborating on challenges met, as well as lessons learned.

If both topics are covered: In your experience, how are these two kinds of families similar and different from one another?

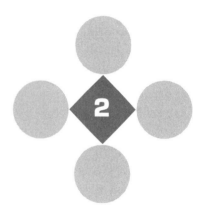

The Family Life Cycle

*D*evelopment of the child as an individual has been studied extensively from a number of perspectives. Piaget (1952) wrote about changes in cognition as the child grows. Gesell, Ilg, and Ames (1974) cataloged motor development. Freud, Jung, Adler, and other personality theorists have emphasized the importance of various periods in the psychological development of the child (Hall & Lindzey, 1978). Erik Erikson's (1963) theory of the tasks of ego development was the first to introduce the concept that psychological challenges continue into adulthood. The book *Passages*, by Gail Sheehy (1976), which was based on the work of Gould (1970) addressed the struggles and changes that adults face as we age. Sheehy's 1995 book *New Passages* addressed the stages of individual adult development. Although each of these theories acknowledges the influence of relationships upon personality development, the primary focus is on the individual, *from the inside*, and the changes and struggles during the different periods of development.

At the same time this inner development is occurring, the child is being socialized (Bronfenbrenner, 1979). Socialization implies that growth is influenced *from outside* the individual (L'Abate, 1994b). One of the primary tasks our educational and social systems face is to promote healthy development. The family life cycle concept provides an opportunity to extend this task beyond the individual to the family as well (Carter & McGoldrick, 1999b).

A Historical Perspective

Only since the 1970s, according to L'Abate (1994b), have references been found in the literature to the family as an influential factor in human development. Writers in the field of psychology continue to minimize the context in which we live and the relational aspects of our lives. Certainly, our society is individualistic in nature, and our psychology reflects a deeply entrenched orientation toward individual explanations for behavior. Seeing the individual though a systemic lens, however, enriches our understanding of human behavior and can lead to the expansion of human potential. L'Abate emphasized that both internal and external influences are important in human development, with the family as most influential.

> From a developmental perspective, the transition to a transactional, multirelational, and multidirectional paradigm allowed us to see that development takes place within a context, and that the most immediate, influential context throughout the life span, is the family. (p. 4)

Social constructionism goes outside the developmental perspective by pointing to the postmodern world in which truth and reality are seen as conceptualizations or points of view bound by both context and history. The focus of social constructionism is on the ways by which we make meaning in any social relationship, including family life (Gergen, 1991). Nichols with Schwartz (2004) stated that "our experience and our identities are partly linguistic constructions, but only partly" (p. 101).

In 1948, at the Conference on Family Life in Washington, sociologists Evelyn Duvall and Reuben Hill presented a framework for viewing development from the perspective of family that combined Burgess's (1926, 1969) concept of a developing unit with Havinghurst's (1952) and Erikson's (1963) concept of lifelong developmental task . Duvall and Hill's framework for the characteristic tasks of family life encompassed eight stages, beginning with the formation of the family by marriage. Duvall's book, first published in 1957 and now, following her death, in its fifth edition (1977), marked the beginning of a shift in emphasis from the individual to the family as the primary unit for the study of development.

Other theorists (Carter & McGoldrick, 1989b, 1999c; L'Abate, 1994a; Nichols, 1996) followed Duvall and Hill's lead, proposing models to describe predictable events and stages that occur in the development of families. These stages are collectively termed the *family life cycle*. Nichols stated, "The family life cycle is concerned with the developmental tasks of the family itself as it deals with the needs of the adult members and the development needs of the offspring" (p. 57).

Rosenberg (1992) presented an "adoption life cycle" that describes the developmental tasks of birth parents, adoptive parents, and the child who is adopted. Hajal and Rosenberg (1991) also have written on the family life cycle in adoptive families. Others (Carney & Gamel-McCormick, 1996; Turnbull & Turnbull, 2001) have focused on the life cycle of families with children who have special needs. Baber and Allen (1992) have provided guidance for families with different structures.

L'Abate (1994b) noted that

> ...development occurs along a variety of routes. Here, a delta model, much like the estuary of a large river, seems to embody the view that most individuals in most families go straight ahead, normatively following the mainstream, major flow of the river; whereas some go sideways and get lost in the marshes of life; others who go sideways come back to the mainstream; some stop altogether; some recoup; and some never recover along the path from birth to death. (Caspi, Elder, & Herbeno, 1990; J. M. White, 1991)
>
> No trajectory is like another trajectory. Yet, in the midst of all this variety, some similarities can be found. One can safely predict that most members of the same family will follow different life cycle patterns (Kreppner & Lerner, 1989; Rossi & Rossi, 1990). What similarities, if any, can we find among these differences? (p. 4)

Context and relationship are crucial to understanding children and youth who are at risk or have special needs. Imagine having a new child in your classroom or community setting who has a behavioral problem. You know nothing about her other than that she just moved into your area. By learning something about her family life cycle, you will be more likely to accept her, separating the behavior from the individual. You then will be able to direct your attention to the unacceptable behavior, which will be more understandable under the circumstances. Thus, this chapter addresses the family life cycle, which takes context and relationship into consideration and provides an important base of information for community and school professionals who work with children and youth who are at risk or who have special needs.

Stages in the Family Life Cycle

At each stage in the family's life cycle, a nodal event ushers in the next phase of development. Theorists have developed many ways of thinking about these developmental phases. Carter and McGoldrick (1999c) proposed a six-stage family life cycle model to include single adulthood prior to marriage. Turnbull and Turnbull (2001) developed a model with four stages—birth and early childhood, childhood, adolescence, and adulthood.

For purposes of exploration later in this text, this book adapts Carter and McGoldrick's six-stage life cycle model by dividing their third stage, families with young children, into two stages: young children 0–5 years old and elementary-aged children 6–11 years old. This adapted version still has six stages, but the revised stages more easily translate to the structure of schools in the United States. The adaptation also leaves out Carter and McGoldrick's initial stage of leaving home as single young adults, as this stage does not involve the school environment.

The family life cycle is a particularly useful concept for diagnosis in the family systems perspective known as *strategic family therapy* (see the Appendix), which looks at the family's stage of development as an important factor in understanding the etiology of symptoms in family members (e.g., school phobia). According to this model, family members are prone to developing symptoms at transition points in the family life cycle. When the family system is unable to adjust its interactions to accommodate changes in the life cycle, the family becomes "stuck" at a particular stage and cannot move on in its development. Interactions within the family become more and more inflexible and unproductive until one or more members of the family become symptomatic (Haley, 1980).

Nichols and Schwartz (2005) add two aspects to the family life cycle when looking at individual development: "When a son or daughter heads off to kindergarten or reaches puberty, not only must the child learn to cope with a new set of circumstances, but the whole family must readjust" (p. 74). They further indicate that the developmental movement of an individual through a transition period doesn't solely relate to the child but also to that child's parents, and sometimes the grandparents.

> The strain on a fourteen-year-old's relationship with his parents
> may be due as much to his father's midlife crisis or his mother's
> worrying about her own father's retirement as anything the boy
> himself is going through. (p. 111)

Stages in the "Normal" Family Life Cycle

Clearly, family life patterns change over time. Myriad factors contribute to the changing patterns, including differences in the roles of women and men in society, sexual orientation, family structure, assumptions about what is "normal" and what is considered "family," family members born with or developing a disability, as well as ethnic and cultural variability. For simplicity, the life cycle of an intact family, adapted from Carter & McGoldrick (1999c), is presented to be compatible with the child and youth theme of this text. The stages are as follows:

Stage 1:   The Newly Married Couple
Stage 2:   Families With Young Children (ages 0–5 years)
Stage 3:   Families With Elementary-Aged Children (ages 6–12 years)
Stage 4:   Families With Adolescents (ages 13–19 years)
Stage 5:   Families Launching Children (ages 20 and older)
Stage 6:   Families in Later Life

In this family life cycle model, the family's and the oldest child's development parallel one another. For the most part, developmental changes required of the family are determined by the age of the oldest child because that child is the first catalyst for new demands upon the family. Diagnosis of a child with special needs, however, can affect this pattern (Gargiulo, 2006; Imber-Black, 1989; Turnbull & Turnbull, 2001). So, too, can divorce and remarriage, as well as chronic or serious illness, death, alcohol problems, accidents, and the discovery of extramarital affairs (Carter & McGoldrick, 1999a, L'Abate, 1994a; Nichols, 1996).

Further, as indicated by the two chapters in Carter and McGoldrick's (1999b) book devoted to the family life cycle that discuss African American families living in poverty (Hines, 1999) and social class (Kliman & Madsen, 1999), socioeconomic status can affect the pattern and significantly impact the family life cycle. Among other factors influencing the family life cycle are adoption (Carter, 1999), alcohol problems (Hudak, Krestan, & Bepko, 1999), chronic illness (Rolland, 1999), culture (Falicov, 1999; Hines, et al., 1999), death (Walsh & McGoldrick, 2004), divorce (Ahrons, 1999; Carter & McGoldrick, 1999b; Mullis & Edwards, 2001), gender (McGoldrick, 1999c; Rosen, 1999), migration (Hernandez & McGoldrick, 1999), sexual orientation (Johnson & Colucci, 1999), siblings (McGoldrick, Watson, & Benton, 1999), and violence (McGoldrick, Broken Nose, & Potenza, 1999). Beyond these factors, the family life cycle is influenced dramatically by the era in which the family is living (Carter & McGoldrick, 1999c), their worldviews and attitudes toward transitions in the cycle, generational impact, and more.

School and community professionals working with at-risk children and youth clearly are concerned with Stages 2 through 4 of the model—Families With Young Children (0–5), Families With Elementary-Aged Children (6-12), and Families With Adolescents in Stage 4. Stage 2 is particularly relevant for schools and communities in relation to children with special needs (early childhood education). With the overwhelming amount of literature available about the importance of the first three years of life for later growth and development, schools must stay involved with families at Stage 2 (Families With Young Children Ages 0–5) in an attempt to prevent at-risk status later and to ameliorate the impact of special needs.

An emphasis of the federal government continues to be funding for birth to school age to establish training for families with children in Stage 2. The need for training parents to provide experiences that stimulate learning during the first three years of their children's lives is a particular concern. Currently, more than 830,500 children ages 0–5 receive the intervention of special education in the United States (Gargiulo, 2006).

Professional and parent collaboration is supported for families and children in the second life-cycle stage. This emphasis on parent training resulted in an increased need for professionals to be knowledgeable about family life cycle stages. Each stage of the family life cycle has plateaus, transitions, tasks, and challenges.

Plateaus

Each stage of the family life cycle includes a "plateau period" and a "transitional period" (Carter & McGoldrick, 1980; Nichols & Schwartz, 2004). Plateaus are periods of relative stability when the family operates predictably in regard to roles and functions. For example, a young married couple, having worked out the initial difficulties of living together, have settled into a lifestyle pattern in a plateau period. During plateau periods the forces of homeostasis (see the Appendix), or sameness, are in operation. School and community professionals are unlikely to spot problems related to the family life cycle during plateau periods.

Recall periods of stability in your family of origin. If your immediate family is experiencing a time of stability that reflects a plateau period in your childhood, the experience may remind you of similar times when you were growing up.

Transitions

Transitional periods occur when a life event demands changes in the structure or function of the family. Carter and McGoldrick (1999c) identified the transitions as flowing into a new life cycle stage. The six stages they defined are as follows: leaving home as a single young adult, marriage, families with young children, families with adolescents, launching children and moving on, and families in later life. Events that occur "on time," or at expected points in the life cycle, are less stressful than events that occur earlier or later than expected (Jameson & Alexander, 1994; Walsh, 1982).

For example, an unplanned teen pregnancy will be more emotionally stressful than a planned pregnancy for a couple. And the early, unexpected death of a spouse will be more stressful and require more family changes than the death of a spouse at an older age.

Problems occur when a family meets an environmental or developmental challenge and cannot accommodate its structure to the changing situation (Nichols & Schwartz, 2004). Problems are not to be considered an indication of a dysfunctional family but, rather, a family that so far has failed to readjust at one of the turning points in family life.

> Whenever someone develops psychological symptoms, the family life-cycle concept teaches us to consider the possibility that the family may simply be stuck in transition from one developmental stage to another. (p. 112)

In addition to events that usher in new life-cycle stages, events may occur that change the normal cycle of the family and precipitate a transition period. These stressors include, among others, miscarriage, marital separation and divorce, illness, disability, death, relocation, changes in socioeconomic status, and catastrophes that result in dislocation of the family unit. When these events occur, the individuals within the family must deal with their own reactions to the loss or change in circumstances (McGoldrick & Walsh, 2004) and the family as a whole must change its communication patterns, roles, and functions to deal successfully with the change (Cusinato, 1994; Patterson, 1985).

Transition periods often are marked by anxiety, uncertainty, and a sense of loss (Carter & McGoldrick, 1999c; Olson, 1988; Olson et al., 1983). Flexibility and adaptability, described in the Appendix, are needed during transition periods. Change events can be a stimulus either for successful adaptation and growth or for dysfunction (Cusinato, 1994; Walsh, 1983). Clinical or behavioral problems are particularly likely to appear at transition points in the family life cycle if the basic structure and roles of family members are not reorganized (Carter & McGoldrick, 1999c; Cusinato, 1994; Hadley, Jacob, Miliones, Caplan, & Spitz, 1974; Haley, 1980; Walsh, 1982).

Tasks and Changes at Each Life Cycle Stage

As with individual development, specific developmental tasks are required of the family at each stage of the life cycle. In addition, each stage of the family life cycle requires a change in the family's goal orientation and direction. Successful completion of tasks at early stages builds a foundation for successfully completing later stages. Like a child who must learn to stand before learning to walk, the family must learn to negotiate the tasks of rearing children before it can launch children into adulthood successfully. Failing to complete the tasks of early stages may lead to difficulties with later ones. The primary themes and developmental tasks required at each stage are as follows.

Stage 1: The Newly Married/Committed Couple

Primary theme: Intimacy (McGoldrick, 1999a)

Primary task: Realignment of relationships with friends and family to include spouse/partner and spouse's/partner's family, commitment to the new system (Carter & McGoldrick, 1999c); commonality of goals and directions for the future

An example of this realignment is the decision about where the couple will spend holidays—with which family? Successful resolution of this question is a good indicator that the individuals have made the transition to viewing themselves as part of a couple.

Individuals who marry without successfully resolving issues in their own families of origin (see chapter 4) are more likely to experience marital/partnership difficulties and adjustment problems (Bardill, 1997; Fogarty, 1976). In a classic study by Lidz, Cornelison, Fleck, and Terry (1957a) of families with schizophrenic children, the authors found that in five of the eight marriages in their study, the spouse's loyalty remained in the parental home rather than in the current immediate/nuclear family. These individuals had never made a successful transition from the role of child in their own families to the role of partner in a marital system.

Stage 2: Families With Young Children (ages 0–5)

Primary theme: Industry, developing strategies for getting things done (Kantor, 1983)

Primary parental functions: Nurturing, protecting, and caring for the infant; providing a behavioral model and appropriate limit setting (Cusinato, 1994)

Primary tasks: Realignment of marital/partnership system to include a child; changes in the couple's sexual relationship; coping with lack of privacy; developing a parenting style; realigning relationships with extended family and friends to include the child and requirements of parenting (Carter & McGoldrick, 1999c).

The companionship between couples decreases when an infant enters the family (Bardill, 1997). The presence of dependent children in the home places new demands on the couple's time, energy, and financial resources, and many couples report a decrease in marital satisfaction. Couples who had successfully negotiated the changes brought on by an infant in the home reported that children brought them closer together, by giving them a shared task and a common goal.

One example comes from a study by Pedersen (1983) of fathers' involvement with their infants. The father's role was found to be influenced by his involvement with the pregnancy and birth. If fathers were involved in anticipation of the birth, in planning for the child's space in the home, and in the actual birth, they were more likely to feel a commitment to and involvement with the new baby. Pedersen described the father's primary role as one of emotional support for the mother. He found that the more support the mother perceived from her spouse, the more she worked to include him in her relationship with the baby, and the more direct interaction occurred between the father and the infant.

Stage 3: Families With Elementary-Aged Children (ages 6–12)

Primary themes: Affiliation and inclusion, allowing others to be brought within the family boundaries; consolidating the accomplishments of family members (Kantor, 1983)

Primary parental functions: Sensitivity to the child's growth needs; providing opportunities for the child to develop independence; letting the child go and grow; vicarious enjoyment from the child's experiences (Cusinato, 1994)

Primary tasks: Being involved with peer network; establishing sibling roles; dividing family responsibilities

At this stage, parents must begin to accept the child's unique personality and the ways in which this personality is expressed both within and outside the home (Barnhill & Longo, 1978). Interactions concerning the school, extracurricular activities, and families of peers must be negotiated.

The need for parental rules is most clear during this childrearing stage. Rules provide the structure and identity for family life. In a successful training program developed by McFadden and Doub (1983) to teach parents to cope with family life-cycle changes, the following guidelines for parents regarding the responsibility for making family rules are presented in the first session (p. 143):

1. Make rules.
2. Stay in charge.
3. Stick together.
4. Make room to play with your children.
5. Change with the times.

In short, these guidelines demonstrate the needs for guidance, cohesion, and adaptability in families experiencing transitions.

For some parents, the need to share authority when their child begins school is a difficult transitional demand. Parents are accustomed to making all of the decisions about their child's well-being and may be reluctant to adhere to guidelines proposed by a teacher. Teachers would do well to keep in mind their knowledge of the life cycle and help the parents make the transition into sharing authority and by asking for input. If the teacher's attempts to elicit parental cooperation continue to fail, more severe family dysfunction may be indicated. Two of the classic signs of abusive and neglectful families are extreme family secrecy and lack of including people outside the nuclear family.

Stage 4: Families With Adolescents

Primary theme: Decentralization; loosening boundaries and changing rules for more autonomy and independence (Garcia-Preto, 1999)

Primary parental functions: Providing assistance in establishing identity; tolerating generation gap (Cusinato, 1994)

Primary tasks: Managing the child's increasing independence; refocusing on midlife career and partnership; increasing flexibility of roles

This stage of the family life cycle has become particularly difficult. As Quinn, Newfield, and Protinsky (1985) argued:

> The accelerated pace of physiological growth (of children) . . . has stretched the stage we have come to define sociologically as adolescence. . . . We have not come to a consensus on how to determine its [adolescence] onset or termination. This uncertainty obscures guideposts for defining roles and status of family members and, subsequently, family interactional patterns. (p. 102)

Often, in families, the physical maturity of children is mistaken for emotional maturity. Parents have the difficult task during this stage of developing appropriate and flexible rules for their adolescents, allowing enough room for them to experiment with independence. Parents who are extremely involved with their children often have problems with their own identities and tend to perceive adolescent rebellion as a personal affront. In addition, for the married couple, watching their children's sexual development may bring up their own unresolved sexual issues from previous stages.

School and community professionals during this stage should encourage parents to have a sense of humor about their child's rebellion. Knowing that struggles for independence are normal and necessary at this stage and that their child and family are not different in that regard can be a relief to parents who are trying to achieve a balance between control and letting go. An adolescent's perpetually messy room may not seem as important to the parent in the light of alternative forms of rebellion such as gang membership and drug abuse.

Stage 5: Families Launching Children

Primary themes: Differentiation; accepting many exits from and entries into the family (Carter & McGoldrick, 1999c)

Primary parental functions: Supporting independence; accepting and developing adult-to-adult relationship with adult children (Carter & McGoldrick, 1999c); encouraging, reassuring, and appreciating (Cusinato, 1994)

Primary tasks: Negotiating to become a couple again; renegotiating roles with adult children; realignment to include in-laws of children who marry and grandchildren; responding to disabilities and deaths of parents and grandparents (Carter & McGoldrick, 1999c)

Referred to as the "sandwich generation," many parents in this stage are caring for their parents and their college-age or recently employed offspring (Blacker, 1999). During this stage, middle and upper class women who have stayed at home with their children will likely have more time and energy to develop themselves in personal areas and perhaps find a career. Both the parents and their children are adults and, in some ways, social equals. Thus, family members must change their communication patterns to consider equality and differences of opinion among members of two generations (Hess & Waring, 1978). Women who have made a deep commitment to motherhood may experience feelings of purposelessness or lack of meaning (Bardill, 1997). Most middle- and upper-income couples, however, are in their prime (Blacker, 1999).

Stage 6: Families in Later Life

Primary themes: Letting go, dissolving ties (Kantor, 1983)

Primary parental functions: Allowing role reversals, with adult children assuming more responsibility (Cusinato, 1994)

Primary tasks: Redefining roles between aging spouses; exploring new familial and social role options (Carter & McGoldrick, 1999c); dealing with the death of friends, spouse, siblings, and peers; preparing for death

Retirement and advancing years may mean loss of income, loss of occupational status, excess time at home, and loss of accustomed roles (Aldous, 1978; Bardill, 1997). Senior citizens may face the loss of their homes and communities, their physical well-being, or their mental capacity (Brody, 1974). When one spouse/partner dies, the surviving spouse/partner must reformulate a personal identity as widow or widower and renegotiate relationships with children and extended family. If older parents are ill or disabled, children must negotiate caregiving tasks for their parents (Bardill, 1997; Montgomery, Gonyea, & Hooyman, 1985).

Walsh (1999) referred to the myth that placement in a nursing home is a frequent family choice. In reality, it usually is a last resort at a late stage of mental or physical deterioration. Research by Spark and Brody (1970) showed that three fourths of the senior citizens they interviewed lived within half an hour of at least one child, and more than four-fifths had seen an adult child in the previous week.

Lower-income families expect fewer opportunities at work. Some men, who have had jobs requiring hard labor, experience poorer health and possible early death. Some women from lower-income families continue to work more than one job in order to support their grandchildren.

Grandparenthood offers a different role and can bring generations closer. As well, it allows grandparents to relive their own experiences of childrearing. "Such reminiscence and new perspective can be valuable in coming to accept one's life and one's parenting satisfactions and achievements as well as regrets or failures" (Walsh, 1999; p. 311). Being a grandparent allows the parent/grandparent to reconnect through the new grandchild in the family. By identifying with their parents in childrearing, the new parent may develop empathy and understanding that can bring healing of wounds incurred many years ago.

The special bond of grandparent and grandchild brings opportunities for enjoying children with less obligation and responsibility. Some grandparents, though, are rearing their grand-children rather than reaping the harvest of a life's work completed.

This stage in life is impacted differently based on class and culture. The boomerang effect, in which adult children are returning home to live with their parents—sometimes with children of their own—has become fairly common in the period of time between launching children and later life. This may precipitate stress because of the rising expec-tations of less complicated lives.

We can expect continuing and greater diversity, as well as complexity in families in the later years.

> Elders can be encouraged to draw on their rich history and experi-ence to inform both continuity and innovation, as society's futur-ists.... Important in the resilience of our society is a sense of pride in age, the value of history and life experience, and the capacity to adapt courageously to change. (Walsh, 1999; p. 324)

Challenges in the Family Life Cycle

Families negotiate each stage of the life cycle with varying success. The extent of flexibil-ity and adaptability of the family contributes to how successfully the child develops in all realms. The family's past history, timing of life events, and extent of family stressors are all important in determining how the family will adapt to life-cycle difficulties. Awareness of the challenges facing a child will give school and community professionals the means to help prevent difficulties as well as respond to those that surface and affect the child's life in school and community contexts.

Stressors

All of us face stresses in life. The family is no different from the individual except that the family encounters stressors as a unit. Some stressors occur naturally and predictably in all families as they make transitions; others are related specifically to particular families, such as recurring multigenerational patterns.

Carter and McGoldrick (1999c) refer to the "vertical and horizontal flow of stress in the life cycle" (p. 5) and provide a schematic representation of the three systems that influ-ence the life cycle: individual, family, and cultural systems (see Fig. 2.1). The vertical axis brings "past and present issues to bear reciprocally on all other levels" (p.5). The horizon-tal axis is developmental and unfolds over time. In the individual system, the vertical axis "includes the biological heritage and intricate programming of behaviors with one's given temperament, possible congenital disabilities and genetic makeup" (p. 5). The horizontal axis relating to the individual system includes that person's "emotional, cognitive, inter-personal, and physical development" that has its own historical context over time. The individual's "inherent qualities can become either crystallized into rigid behaviors or elab-orated into broader and more flexible repertoires" (p.5).

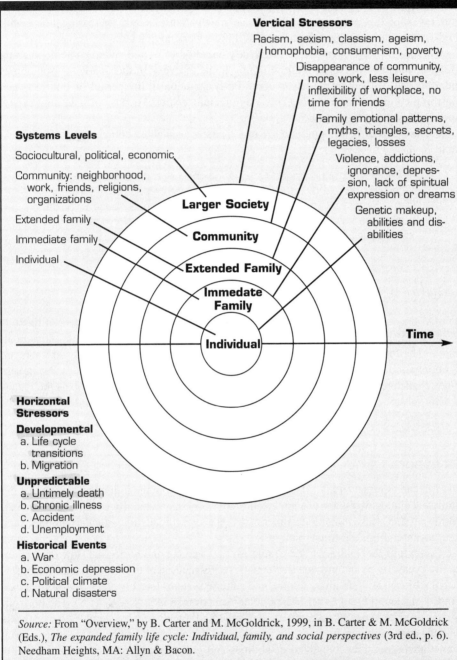

Vertical Stressors

Racism, sexism, classism, ageism, homophobia, consumerism, poverty

Disappearance of community, more work, less leisure, inflexibility of workplace, no time for friends

Family emotional patterns, myths, triangles, secrets, legacies, losses

Violence, addictions, ignorance, depression, lack of spiritual expression or dreams

Genetic makeup, abilities and disabilities

Systems Levels

Sociocultural, political, economic

Community: neighborhood, work, friends, religions, organizations

Extended family

Immediate family

Individual

Larger Society

Community

Extended Family

Immediate Family

Individual

Time

Horizontal Stressors

Developmental
a. Life cycle transitions
b. Migration

Unpredictable
a. Untimely death
b. Chronic illness
c. Accident
d. Unemployment

Historical Events
a. War
b. Economic depression
c. Political climate
d. Natural disasters

Source: From "Overview," by B. Carter and M. McGoldrick, 1999, in B. Carter & M. McGoldrick (Eds.), *The expanded family life cycle: Individual, family, and social perspectives* (3rd ed., p. 6). Needham Heights, MA: Allyn & Bacon.

Figure 2.1

Flow of Stress through the Family

The vertical axis at the family system level "includes the family history, the patterns of relating and functioning that are transmitted down the generations" (Carter & McGoldrick, 1999c; p. 5). This transmission is impacted mainly by triangulation (see Bowen Theory in the Appendix and chapter 4). Triangulation takes place out of awareness of those involved when two family members are at odds and uncomfortable with the attending anxiety. The twosome refocus their attention away from their interpersonal discomfort by drawing in a third member of the family, usually the least differentiated member and often a child, with a resulting reduction in their anxiety about differences between them. The effect is that a problem develops for the triangulated family member, such as being made overly dependent upon or smothered by one parent. At the family level attitudes include taboos, expectation, labels, and any loaded issues typical of the family's life together. Carter and McGoldrick indicate that this is the hand we are dealt. The horizontal flow at this family level refers to family movement through time and how the members cope with challenge and change during the transitions from one stage to another. Predictable stresses and unpredictable events (e.g., birth of a child with a disability, death of a baby, job loss) are part of this horizontal flow in the family.

The vertical axis/sociocultural level encompasses history of the culture and society, stereotypes, hierarchies, power patterns, and beliefs. The history of any group, particularly trauma (e.g., slavery, Holocaust, hate crimes against homosexuals), impacts individuals and families. The horizontal axis

> relates to community connections or lack of them, current events, and social policy as they affect the family and the individual at a given time. It depicts the consequences in people's present lives of the society's inherited (vertical) norms of racism, sexism, classism, and homophobia, as well as ethnic and religious prejudices, as these are manifested in social, political, and economic structures that limit the options of some and support the power of others. (Carter & McGoldrick, 1999c, pp. 6–7)

According to Jameson and Alexander (1994):

> A developmental trajectory deviating from the norm results when the stressors exceed a system's capacity to cope. Of particular interest is identification of the way in which an event or process alters "normal" developmental trajectories. The mediating/intervening systems may function as a sort of wall of defense, or immune system, when operating well, diffusing, deflecting, or encapsulating stressors and focusing adaptation. When a system or subsystem (family or individual) does not work, it can add stress to the individuals or to the system itself. The stressor may ultimately overcome normal family processes. (p. 402)

In a study of the predictable stressors that must be faced at each life-cycle stage, Olson and colleagues (1983) asked 1,140 families across the life cycle about significant stressors they experienced. The following factors were found to be the most problematic stressors reported at each stage:

Stage 1—The Newly Married Couple: Work-family (balancing changes with extended family, interacting with in-laws, and developing dual-career goals)

Stage 2—Families With Young Children (ages 0–5): Financial strains (coping with the added financial burden of young children, buying a family home, making decisions about both spouses' careers, and the cost of child-care options)

Stage 3—Families With Elementary-Aged Children (ages 6–12): Intrafamily strains (dealing with the added stress of involvement with the school, extracurricular activities, and families of children's peer group)

Stage 4—Families With Adolescents (ages 13–19): Financial strains (handling the financial demands of feeding, clothing, and entertaining adolescents)

Stage 5—Families Launching Children: Financial strains (paying for college, weddings, or helping children begin their own immediate families)

Stage 6—Families in Later Life: Financial strains (planning for the loss of income following retirement, paying medical bills, health-care costs)

Looking at the stress of having a child with a disability, Carter (1999) indicated that serious illness and disability both wreak havoc on the lives of parents. Carter and Peters (1997) found that that the death of a child doubled the rate of divorce. McGoldrick, Watson, and Benton (1999) indicated that smaller families with a child having a disability experience greater stress because fewer siblings are available to share in the caregiving. Further, sisters accept the caregiver role more readily for a brother than for a sister. Older sisters take more responsibility for caregiving the sibling with a disability than older brothers. The oldest sisters often are influenced in career and family decisions as a result of growing up with responsibility for a sibling with mental retardation (Cicirelli, 1995).

One factor that can arrest or slow the life-cycle progression is the inability to handle significant stress. Although each life-cycle stage brings a primary stressor, each stage has many additional stresses. Focusing on the six stages of the family life cycle and thinking back to your family of origin can help you identify with the stressors during the family life cycle.

Sociocultural and Multigenerational Impacts

The *sociocultural context* and the *family's generational experience* over time can influence the family's response to a normative event. The significance of a given life event, the normative timing of its occurrence, and the accompanying rituals vary with different cultures and ethnic groups.

Bowen's (1985) multigenerational theory, briefly discussed in chapter 3 and elaborated on in the Appendix, deals with the significance of various life-cycle events over many generations. For example, if a young couple is having their first child at the same time that a grandparent is dying, the birth and death will be woven together emotionally and symbolically. When the couple has another child, the feelings of joy and loss from the first event will most likely recur at the second birth. If the couple does not make the connection about how birth and death were linked at the time of the birth of their first child, they may be confused about their mixed feelings during the second birth. They may feel guilty that their feelings of anticipation and happiness are mixed with fear and sadness throughout the life cycle.

A potential problem occurs when, as Barnhill and Longo (1978) described,

> the family must continue to move on if it is to meet the new chal-
> lenges ahead. The conflicts can then become sealed over, though
> vulnerable points can be left behind. It is possible then to conceive
> that under a later situation of stress . . . the family can regress to
> previous levels of functioning. . . . Old unresolved conflicts . . . can
> become uncovered and alive again. Thus, as if it is not enough for
> the family to deal with one difficulty, an old conflict is reawakened,
> together with the old unsuccessful patterns of coping with the
> stress. (p. 471)

With this comment in mind, professionals clearly need to look at the current difficulty that a family is experiencing and also at what old issues the family possibly is reenacting. The family might have a legacy of problems from previous generations that occurred at this stage of the family life cycle. In many families, myths and stories surrounding births, deaths, and other life events are passed down from generation to generation. These myths can influence family members on unconscious and conscious levels.

For example, in many Southern families, little boys receive their first hunting gun as a rite of passage. The gift of the gun takes on a meaning and intensity born of generations of men sharing the ritual of their first hunt together. What happens in these families when a boy with a disability reaches the typical age to receive his gun? Many issues and feelings will have to be considered before reaching a decision about this boy's rite of passage. Professionals who take into account this family's culture and legacy will better understand this child. If the boy begins to play with make-believe weapons in the school or community and begins to act aggressively, the professional can have a much greater impact if he or she is aware of the cultural importance of this transition point in the child's life.

Pile-Up

Another important issue in predicting family responses to life-cycle adjustments is the concept of *pile-up* (McCubbin & Patterson, 1982). Several changes within a brief time will disrupt the family unit and influence life-cycle adjustments more severely. If the family resources are already depleted from dealing with other changes, the family may be less well-equipped to adapt to future changes.

As one at-risk adolescent girl commented to her counselor, "First, my brother gradu-ated in June, so he's looking for a job. Then my dad changed jobs in August and we had to move. My mom hates our new neighborhood. Who cares what I'm going through?"

Families With Special Needs

The diagnosis of a child with intellectual, emotional, sensory, or physical disabilities is a significant life stressor that will affect the future development of the family at all levels (Hurtig, 1994; Seltzer, Greenberg, Floyd, Pettee, & Hong, 2001; Turnbull & Turnbull,

2001). At each life-cycle stage, as the demands upon the family change, the family must once again accept the child's disability (Wikler, 1981).

A number of researchers have discussed the significant issues and challenges faced by families with children who have special needs (Blacher, 1984; Carney & Gamel-McCormick, 1996; Combrinck-Graham, 1983; Cullen, MacLeod, Williams, & Williams, 1991; Cuskelly & Gunn, 2003; Hajal & Rosenberg, 1991; Hanline, 1991; Hannah & Midlarsky, 2005; Leigh, 1987; LePere, 1988; McGrath & Grant, 1993; Patterson & McCubbin, 1983; Prosen, Toews, & Martin, 1981; Rich, Warsradt, Nemiroff, Fowler, & Young, 1991; Rolland, 1999; Shapiro, 1983; Stutman, 1984; Thorin & Irvin, 1992; Singer, 2002; Turnbull & Turnbull, 2001). Turnbull and Turnbull (2001) point out the importance of realizing that cultures are different in their responses to disability in the family. Chapter 5 speaks to ethnic differences and the importance of awareness of differences among cultures.

In the 1980s I trained Lebanese professors for the World Rehabilitation Fund on the island of Cypress. At the time, faculty members from U.S. universities were sent to help infuse competing values and approaches related to disabilities into their world, torn apart by civil strife and bombing.

Before leaving for the Middle East, I met with Lebanese immigrants to learn more about their culture. In particular, I spent time with a priest who was accustomed to hearing the family concerns, beliefs, and values embedded in that culture. I knew what to expect and found that what I had been told about their cultural response to individuals with disabilities was accurate.

As a result, I was able to offer staged recommendations for movement forward toward greater integration of individuals with disabilities into all segments of society. As well, I could embrace these colleagues without knee-jerk judgments about their cultural beliefs and heritage.

I was given a rare opportunity to be immersed in a culture of vastly contrasting beliefs, values, and ways of living. What I learned is that the Lebanese professors, many whom had risked their lives to attend the training, wanted to help their country move toward acceptance of those living with disabilities. Numerous children and youth had incurred physical disabilities as a result of the bombing and fighting, and others had significant emotional struggles.

I maintained contact with some of these professors for a number of years. One wrote to me that individuals with disabilities had been included in a parade in a large city. These people previously would have been hidden from view, but in the parade they were in full view—and being cheered by the crowds. Obviously, this was a culture undergoing change. I am grateful for the opportunity to have been a witness to these changes in cultural tradition, which shifted surprisingly quickly.

Cultural attitudes toward individuals with disabilities are as varied as differences in attitudes in any other aspect of life. Some cultures have far more positive responses than other cultures to a family member with a disability. Clearly, the way in which family members learn that their child has a disability affects their immediate response. Fortunate family members know enough to reject negativity and suspend judgment and responses. Turnbull and Turnbull (2001) shared a sad story of a mother learning from the pediatrician in the hospital that her child had Down syndrome. The pediatrician told the mom coldly that her child should be sent to an institution and even chastised the mother for having a child at her age!

The life-cycle changes facing families with special-needs children are summarized next. As you read about the challenges at each of these stages, think about how these issues may be reflected in the behaviors of children and youth with special needs as you encounter them. To begin, first-stage issues involving the effects of individuals with special needs on the marriage of their siblings are considered (McGoldrick, Watson, & Benton, 1999).

Stage 1: Challenges for the Newly Married Couple

Here, we depart from the challenges for parents to those for siblings of children and adults with special needs, who must answer a unique set of questions when they prepare for marriage and for forming their own families. Will the sibling with a disability be involved in the wedding ceremony? How will the new in-laws and extended family be introduced to the sibling with the exceptionality? Was the sibling's disability transmitted genetically? If so, what impact will that information have on the couple's future plans regarding their own family? Is genetic counseling in order? Do the partners have a difference of opinion regarding abortion? Openly talking about these potentially thorny problems in advance of the marriage can help reduce later stress and avoid pitfalls. Talking about the issue openly will avert surprises. Seeing a counselor or psychotherapist to sort out matters is helpful for some couples. Trying to negotiate these waters alone can add undue stress to already stressful times.

In the case of a planned remarriage of a parent who has a child with special needs, this child and his or her special needs should be carefully considered. Each partner's view of the situation and how to deal with it must be discussed so the child does not suffer. Blended families present a challenge, and when a child with special needs is part of the new mix, open communication can reduce the likelihood of another divorce in the newly formed family. A number of professionals (Heavey, Shenk, & Christensen, 1994; McFarland & Tollerud, 2004; McGoldrick & Carter, 1999; Nichols, 1996) have written about the remarried family and challenges affecting the family members.

Stage 2: Challenges for Families With Young Children

Most children with special needs are not diagnosed at birth, and even for those who are, the question of extent of disability often is unresolved for years. Writing about the family with a child having a disability, Seligman (1991a) reported stress factors associated with five developmental stages that were identified in 1984 by Olson, McCubbin, Barnes, Larsen, Muxen, and Wilson. During Stage 2, the primary stress factors of families with children who have disabilities include obtaining an accurate diagnosis, making emotional adjustments, and informing other family members.

The parents of a child diagnosed at birth or during the preschool years will be trying to understand the exceptionality, and some will be coping with the loss of their "dream child" (Brown, 1989; Carney & Gamel-McCormick, 1996; Featherstone, 1980). Stage 2 is a particularly vulnerable time for most couples, even when their child is born without disabilities or special needs.

When a child is born with identified disabilities, bonding and attachment between mother and infant may be delayed because of their being separated at birth (Sobsey, 1994). Parents who have dreamed of holding and feeding their baby may find themselves instead looking at their infant in an incubator or respirator attached to tubes, which doesn't allow them to hold or nurse the infant.

For some parents, the diagnosis of disability in their infant brings on depression and mourning, and this grieving process is complicated in that the child is not really dead—only the image of the dreamed-for child is dead (Blacher, 1984; Carney & Gamel-McCormick, 1996; Howard, 1978; Wikler, Wasow, & Hatfield, 1981). Postpartum depression in the mother may be significant and prolonged, and the mother's depression and anxiety can affect her attachment to the baby. McGoldrick, Watson, and Benton (1999) stated, "Parents may also shift their hopes and dreams onto their other child, which can create burden and sibling strains (Cicirelli, 1995)" (p. 157).

Schell (1981) indicated that failure of the mother to become involved in the normal nurturing rituals with her developing child, such as gazing, cooing, and smiling, makes the infant particularly at risk for abuse. Sobsey (1994), in his comprehensive exploration of abuse and violence in the lives of people with disabilities, corroborated the finding that the lack of bonding can result in a higher risk for abuse later in life.

Grieving for a "lost child" is complicated by the demands of caring for the needs of the new baby (Trout, 1983). Caring for an infant is tiring and stressful even under the best of circumstances (Carney & Gamel-McCormick, 1996). The emotional and financial strain of a child with special needs is even more extensive (Chen & Miles, 2004). Quality medical care and specialized daycare may be required. Finding a babysitter for a few hours' respite may be a monumental task.

From her interviews with 31 families with infants with disabilities, Beckman (1983) reported that the most significant stress in the families was the additional caregiving demands these children required. Cullen and colleagues (1991) found that mothers of young children with mental retardation are in need of greater support. Only half of the families in the study had child care available for respite. The mothers' concerns were directed mostly to current needs, whereas the major concerns of spouses, as reported by the mothers, was on what was lost—time, rest and relaxation, and so on.

In the face of added demands, parents may feel resentful and angry but have nowhere to express these feelings. And parents may feel guilty about their anger if they view it as directed at the child, a helpless infant, rather than at the demands placed upon them as parents.

By contrast, some have reported positive experiences of having a child born with a disability.

> A growing body of knowledge suggests that the presence of a family member with a disability may contribute to the strengthening of the entire family unit, as well as contribute positively to the quality of life of individual members of the family. In addition,

current perspectives of families question the appropriateness of applying the concept of grief to all families and of assuming that all families adapt to the birth of a child with disabilities by progressing through various "stages" of adaptation, culminating in a stage of "acceptance." (Hanline, 1991, p. 53)

Australian family therapist Michael White encourages families to shift from an oppressive worldview of being controlled by what is perceived as the "problem" to a more expansive view. Even worse is to assume responsibility for creating the "problem." In referring to White's comments, Nichols and Schwartz (1995) noted:

White isn't interested in what causes problems, but he is interested in the evolving effects of problems on families over time. His belief is that people with problems often develop what he calls "problem-saturated descriptions" of their lives: The negative events in their lives and negative aspects of their personalities are constantly in the foreground, making them feel powerless and, consequently, easy prey of problems. As family members try and fail to solve their problems, this story of failure comes to dominate the family. (p. 463)

At one time, interventions that were seen as helpful at the early stage of diagnosis of having a child with a disability included listening and offering emotional support for parents, providing information about resources in the community, and activating family and external support systems (Dunlap & Hollinsworth, 1977). Michael White suggests the concept of "restorying"—assisting family members to separate from the preceding problem-saturated stories and to externalize their problems. This intervention, he says, will help family members realize that the problem was their relationship with a "problem," which will allow them to separate themselves from what they had seen as the problem and to construct a new story. The new story will allow them to be in control of their lives and to recast old notions.

It becomes incumbent upon professionals to help families see life in a new way, to focus on possibilities, and to recognize the control they have over their own lives. Chapter 10 covers in detail the family as a resource.

Stage 3: Challenges for Families With Elementary-Aged Children

Most children with special needs who have not been recognized at birth are diagnosed during Stage 3. During this stage, the school system likely will be involved in the diagnostic process. It is imperative that school and community personnel be a support to the families, rather than an added stress. The more knowledgeable that school and community personnel are about the child's disability and the family's life-cycle stage, the more potential these professionals have to contribute positively in the diagnostic process.

McGoldrick, Watson, and Benton (1999) wrote about the relationship of siblings to a child with a disability in the family, focusing on the adjustment of the siblings. Siblings, they said, will respond to the child with a disability and also to the distress or preoccupation of the parents in terms of meeting the needs of the child with a disability (which sometimes causes stress, if parents expect siblings to be preoccupied as well or if parents want them to treat the other child as normal). They can be burdened if parents shift their hopes and dreams onto them or embarrassed at having a sibling with a disability. Older children sometimes adjust better because they are able to put the situation in perspective, but sometimes siblings with greater maturity feel distanced from peers. McGoldrick and colleagues said, "Relative birth order is also important. A younger sibling may have difficulties associated with needing to assume a crossover leadership role (Boyce & Barnett, 1993, cited in McGoldrick et al., 1999, p. 157).

Seligman (1991a) reiterated the following stress factors associated with Stage 3 (originally identified by Olson et al., 1984) for families with children having special needs:

- Clarifying personal views regarding placement of their child (e.g., inclusion versus self-contained or resource rooms)
- Dealing with reactions to the child by the child's peer group
- Arranging for both child care and after-school activities

Professionals who are aware of these stressors can make helpful suggestions to family members. They can describe advantages and disadvantages of the various delivery models and can introduce family members to other families who have been in the system for a while and have the wisdom of experience to share.

School and community personnel also should help parents and siblings learn how to talk to the child's nondisabled peers. This means giving family members the go-ahead to speak with the child's peers as well as the words to use with elementary-age children. Sometimes parents do not realize that the probing questions children ask do not require technical answers and can be handled with simple responses.

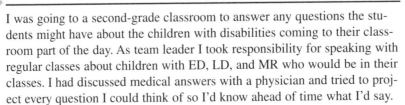

I was going to a second-grade classroom to answer any questions the students might have about the children with disabilities coming to their classroom part of the day. As team leader I took responsibility for speaking with regular classes about children with ED, LD, and MR who would be in their classes. I had discussed medical answers with a physician and tried to project every question I could think of so I'd know ahead of time what I'd say.

One question and response in particular struck me. A second-grade girl wanted to know why the children with Down syndrome "talk different."

I started off with, "Well, their tongues are thicker"… and was immediately cut off with a sigh from the group of, "Oh, I see." They didn't need a medical explanation, and I learned to tell only as much as I could see they wanted to know by the expressions on their faces.

Many different school and community personnel can assist in this learning process. It does not always have to fall on the teacher to provide this support. Often, support groups are available in which family members can discuss and role-play how to talk with the child's nondisabled peers or peers with a different disability.

In some communities, parent groups have developed resource lists for child care as well as extracurricular activities for children with disabilities. The school counselor is another good resource to promote families' networking in the community. In addition, local universities often have lists of students who are studying in the field of special education who welcome the experience of babysitting or working with children with disabilities. Some of these students have a study concentration in a certain disability (e.g., sensorial), and others are open to any kind of disability. Still others seek experience with children of specified ages.

Dyson and Fewell (1985) compared 15 families with children having disabilities to 15 families with children of the same age who had not been diagnosed with problems. Predictably, the families with children having disabilities reported higher overall stress levels and also that the experience of stress increased with the severity of the child's condition. Stress in these families seemed to stem from four primary sources:

1. Characteristics of the child, such as basic personality style and personal response to the diagnosis
2. Extent of physical incapacitation of the child
3. Parental pessimism about the child's health and future
4. Severity of the disabling condition

The researchers found that parents who reported the most social support were most able to enjoy their parenting role despite their child's difficulties. School personnel can find ways to help families search for, as well as accept, social support from extended family, neighbors, and friends.

The Dyson and Fewell study points to several important factors in family adjustment during this life-cycle stage. First, families need to have basic information about their child's special needs. The longer and more difficult the diagnostic process, the greater the potential for negative effects on the family's stability. Once the child's difficulties have been established and understood, the family can begin to move through the loss cycle toward acceptance. Support groups are invaluable resources in helping families move toward acceptance of the disability.

Second, parents need to be educated about appropriate services and school placement. The better informed the parents are, the more likely they are to become actively involved in the child's school placement and contribute to his or her positive adjustment. If parents are confused about their child's needs or have misperceptions about the limitations imposed by a specific disability, they may try to shield their child from challenges and actually may become overinvolved in placement decisions, to the detriment of the child. A sign that parents have not adequately made the transition to the childrearing life-cycle stage (Stage 3) and have not incorporated the themes of affiliation and inclusion is their expression of an "us versus them" mentality that pits the family against the school or community program.

Sherry, now in the fourth grade, had been identified with behavior problems in kindergarten. She originally was tested at 5 years of age and had an IQ in the borderline range of mental retardation. The parents did not believe that the school system heard their concerns, and they were unable to accept the diagnosis of mental retardation. When the girl entered first grade, placement in a classroom for students with mild retardation was recommended. The parents refused to agree to this setting for their daughter, so she was placed in a general classroom with resource help.

In spite of the test results that were used in the original diagnosis, the parents insisted, during their initial meeting with the psychologist, that their daughter had attention deficit disorder and learning disabilities that had never been evaluated or treated adequately. They believed that the school system had not, in 5 years, listened to their descriptions of their daughter's experiences at home. They were requesting that the psychologist assist them in pursuing a court case against the school system for failing to provide adequate services for their daughter.

The psychologist reviewed 6 years of evaluations and found that the girl, indeed, was functioning at the borderline range of mental retardation. In addition, she exhibited many behavioral symptoms of hyperactivity, attention difficulties, and areas of intellectual functioning that were within the average range. Finally, she was significantly depressed because of her continued failures at school and her perceived lack of acceptance by her parents.

In this case, the parents' failure to feel heard, to receive adequate explanations about their daughter's functioning, and to accept their daughter's dysfunctions and mourn the loss of their "perfect child" had caused the family to be stuck at Stage 2 of the family life cycle. The family had not transitioned adequately into Stage 3, with its focus on childrearing. The parents had not yet involved themselves in a partnership with the school system and in helping Sherry develop appropriate friends and activities.

During Stage 3, one of the major struggles for families with children with special needs is to balance the family's functional and emotional tasks. Parents must establish routines to take care of the specialized needs of the child with special needs while also managing the needs of the remainder of the family. An area of family functioning that is often neglected in the face of the functional demands of caring for a child with special needs is family recreation and relaxation (Shapiro, 1983). The major stress reported by families following the diagnosis of a child with chronic illness was the alteration of the family's social and recreational life (Gallagher, Cross, & Scharfman, 1981). This study revealed that the presence of a strong personal support network between spouses and with family friends made the biggest difference in the families' coping abilities. When families thought their friends understood their child's disability, did not stigmatize the family, and offered support with carpooling, babysitting, and recreational activities, their stress was reduced. Again, this recognition of the need for a strong support network points to the networking that can be accomplished by school and community professionals by helping families obtain the support that makes a difference in their level of stress.

Stage 4: Challenges for Families With Adolescents

When adolescents without disabilities successfully complete Stage 4, they emerge with adequate self-esteem, a comfortable body image, an established identity, and emotional independence. Virtually all adolescents experience adjustment problems during this stage. The presence of a chronic illness, emotional or intellectual limitations, or the struggles of a learning disability cannot help but exacerbate those problems. Added to the stresses of the adjustment for the adolescent are the struggles of the family to loosen boundaries and promote independence. Given the variability of the adolescent's special circumstances, this life-cycle stage clearly will be difficult.

Writing about siblings in the family life cycle, McGoldrick, Watson, and Benton (1999) indicated that older children "tend to make a better adjustment to disability than do younger ones because older children are better able to put the situation in perspective" (p. 157). Citing Cicirelli (1995), they indicated that adolescents may be embarrassed by the sibling with a disability; although, if their caregiving for the sibling produced more maturity, the adolescent could feel out of sync with peers because of their advanced maturity.

Seligman (1991a) reported the following stressors (originally identified by Olson et al., 1984) for families with adolescents with special needs:

- Adjusting to the chronic nature of the disability
- Dealing with issues related to sexuality, peer isolation, and rejection
- Making plans for transition from work to school

As in Stage 3, school and community personnel can help families alleviate these stressors.

During Stage 4, all adolescents begin to know their limitations and compare themselves to their peers (Patterson, 1985). The formation of a personal identity should recognize the reality of the individual's strengths and weaknesses. Of course, this will affect self-esteem. Taking personal risks, assertively dealing with peers, confronting challenges, and increasing independence are more difficult if the adolescent is starting from a base of low self-esteem or a negative identity.

In addition to the difficulties of emotional adjustments, many adolescents with special needs face issues of physical adjustment. Adolescents and parents must deal with the changes brought about by the onset of puberty and emerging sexuality. Parents who have been responsible for their child's physical well-being must now decide how much physical care to relinquish to the adolescent (Patterson & McCubbin, 1983).

If no concessions are made to the adolescent's increasing needs for privacy and autonomy, the adolescent may take control by not complying with medical treatment (Blumberg, Lewis, & Susman, 1984). For example, refusing to monitor blood sugars and overeating are common rebellious behaviors for adolescents with diabetes. Many adolescents with cerebral palsy or spina bifida stop following their catheterization procedure. Anorexia and bulimia occur in adolescents, including adolescents who seemed normal before this period. For all of these behaviors, the common theme is a lack of a feeling of autonomy and control on the part of the adolescent.

Finally, Stage 4 brings the challenges of planning for vocational development of the youth with special needs.

Questions that must be answered include the following:

- How much does the disability affect the youth's intellectual potential?
- What motivational, emotional, and financial factors, if any, must be considered?
- What are the youth's physical limitations?
- What desires and dreams for the future does the adolescent have?

The task of the family and the school and community system is to help the adolescent set realistic goals that do not underestimate or overestimate his or her potential. In developing vocational goals, the adolescent's need to feel in control and have autonomy must be kept in mind. Within limitations imposed by rules and the adolescent's abilities, the individual should be given as many choices as possible regarding future plans.

For adolescents, both with and without special needs, and their parents, the struggle between independence and dependence is heightened during this stage. The parents must try to be supportive and available while at the same time allowing for privacy and autonomy when the adolescent is ready. Adolescents may vacillate between resenting their parents' overprotection and needing their support. If some balance and resolution are not achieved, problems in communication and relationships may result.

Zetlin (1985) studied the families of 25 adolescents with mild retardation over an 18-month period, dividing family styles into supportive, dependent, and conflict-ridden. He found that members of the supportive group were least likely to experience serious behavioral disturbances during adolescence. When a disturbance arose, it usually was one of emotional confusion rather than an antisocial or rebellious nature. The adolescents who were involved in conflict-laden relationships with their parents were most likely to act out and exhibit antisocial behavior, including theft, inappropriate sexual behavior, and delinquent or violent behavior. In addition, 75% of the dependent group displayed behaviors reflecting emotional disturbance, including withdrawal, alcohol or drug use, and self-abusive or suicidal behavior. The relationships between the parents and their adolescent children that were characterized as supportive but not dependent in nature were most likely to reduce dysfunction in adolescents.

Along these same lines, Nihira, Meyers and Mink's longitudinal study of families with an adolescent diagnosed as a slow learner or diagnosed with moderate retardation (1983, 1985) found that the home environment was the most significant contributor to children's development of various social, educational, and behavioral skills. Specifically, the factors of harmony in the family and cohesive, quality parenting had a strong effect on a wide range of adjustment behaviors. Family relationships that were nonconflicting and supportive, without being smothering, were the best indicators of positive adjustment in the adolescent.

Education professionals are in a unique position to provide information about adolescent struggles to families in a nonthreatening manner. Parent information seminars can be held during high school enrollment. PTA meetings or discussions can be geared toward adolescent developmental issues and family relationships. If parents are informed, they are more likely to know what to expect from their adolescents and be able to respond with appropriate guidance and support. Educators can collaborate with community professionals in seeing that important information is exchanged with families in ways that make a difference.

Stage 5: Challenges for Families Launching Children

Seligman (1991a, p. 35) related Olson and colleague's (1984) listing of stressors in this phase of launching children as "recognizing and adjusting to the family's continuing responsibility, deciding on appropriate residential placement, and dealing with the paucity of socialization opportunities for the disabled family member."

Using data collected from 19 families having a young adult with a severe developmental disability, Thorn and Irvin (1992) found residential concerns to be prominent predictors of overall stress for family members and the young adults with mental retardation alike. Specifically, the availability, quality, and interactions with providers were the foci of the stress.

Parents and social agencies must help the young adult find a job or enroll in an appropriate vocational program. Transition programs abound, and many job coaches are funded by public funds. Depending upon the abilities of the individual with the disability, he or she might need help finding an appropriate adult residence and learning how to manage financial resources.

Socialization opportunities outside the family are particularly important at this stage. The Rehabilitation Research and Training Center (RRTC) on Workplace Supports and Job Retention, at Virginia Commonwealth University, provides an international model of working with individuals with moderate disabilities at the launching stage in the family life cycle (see www.worksupport.com).

Turnbull and Turnbull (2001) refer to three dimensions of adulthood—autonomy, membership, and change. They provide information on identifying post-secondary educational programs and supports, as well as accessing supported employment and supported living options. Particularly challenging is to find employment for individuals with severe disabilities.

According to Turnbull and Turnbull, about one-third of individuals with disabilities are employed full-time or part-time, compared to 80 percent employment of those without disabilities. Of the unemployed individuals with disabilities, 70 percent indicate that they want to be working. Two-thirds of adults with disabilities report that the disability makes finding employment and working more difficult.

Whether supported employment or supported living (e.g., group homes) meets the needs of individuals with disabilities, services are available. School and community professionals should make a concerted effort to provide this information to adults with disabilities who are looking for supported living or employment.

Another useful support at this stage is for an older mentor/sponsor with a disability to partner with the younger person with a disability. These sponsors have firsthand experience in a way that family and professionals do not. What professionals in social services can do is find these mentors/sponsors and pair them, based on what the child being launched wants and educated guesses about what pairing might be effective. The individual with a disability should be asked what kinds of characteristics he or she would like in a mentor/sponsor, what gender is preferred, whether a matching disability is desirable, and whether age or race matters. A young adult might prefer someone from the same cultural background or someone from a different background so he or she can learn from a "different set of eyes."

Launching youth with disabilities may mean packing them off to college, sheltered employment, supported employment, employment, marriage, or a number of other possibilities.

I was living and teaching well over a thousand miles away when my younger brother graduated from high school. I recall many phone conversations about what was next for him because he was dyslexic and could read little. He decided he wanted to go to college and major in fine arts and minor in geology. Our mother, a professor in reading and language arts, helped him obtain services from rehabilitation services. Mainly, readers for the blind were engaged to read his textbooks as well as tests for his classes. The rehabilitation service also paid tuition for four of his five years of college. My brother was going to the college where my mom taught, and she knew who would be a good advisor for him.

Ever since he was in seventh grade, my brother had been walking up to teachers on the first day of school and saying, "Hi, I'm Tom, and I'm dyslexic. If you don't know what that means, I can explain it to you." With that assertive background, he successfully negotiated college and earned his degree in fine arts.

When the draft for the Army was enforced, a military personnel officer flew from Washington, DC to Georgia to test my brother because they didn't believe a college student couldn't read. After testing him, the officer said, "Good luck, son, I hope you have a good life." My brother would not have been able to read the written orders he received, so he was no longer considered for any job in the military.

Our mother continued to support my brother when he was a photographer for the local newspaper, then owner of a business in their college town. Tom benefited greatly from the support of our mother until she developed Alzheimer's disease and no longer was able to help him in his career.

Few families are able to launch children without the aid of professionals in a search process by which they and their budding adult negotiate the external world beyond high school. Today, programs in secondary education provide services and support for the transition from school to work. The kinds of help needed depend on their unique circumstances and aspirations. Many individuals with disabilities need "hurdle help" throughout their lives on an as-needed basis, often during transition periods in the family life cycle. School and community personnel can help families by providing information, directing them to support groups, linking them with services that aid in transition from school to work, and encouraging them in all ways as they attempt to negotiate the adult world successfully.

Emphasis on Individuality

Clearly, each stage of the family life cycle brings different challenges to the family with a special needs child or youth. Professionals need to respect the individuality of family members as they adapt to having a child with a disability Hanline (1991). Each responds to and copes with disabilities differently, and not all parents "progress through the same predetermined stages as they adapt to having a child with disabilities" (p. 56). Hanline also indicated that families may need continued support during later transitions and critical events, as these may be particularly challenging even though they occur many years after the disability is diagnosed.

> The professional's role is to assist parents by identifying actual and potential problem areas, helping parents to carry out the tasks posed by the transition or critical event, and encouraging parents to learn skills and utilize supports that can be applied to all transitions and critical events. (p. 57)

Finally, Hanline recommended that professionals help family members make use of informal supports (e.g., babysitting, shopping, carpooling) on which they can rely during times of transition. Helping family members use these supports increases their autonomy, competence, and esteem.

Coping Strategies for Families

As a counterpart to the challenges families face is the way they cope with these challenges. Research has identified some coping strategies for families experiencing life cycle stressors, leading to some workshops that have been offered with success in addressing the needs of families under stress.

Characteristics of Coping

Figley and McCubbin (1983) identified a number of general positive characteristics that predict a family's ability to cope with life stresses. These characteristics are as relevant today as when they were identified and include

- being able to determine the cause of the stress,
- thinking systemically rather than individually,
- focusing on solutions instead of casting blame,
- tolerating differences in the family,
- openly demonstrating affection,
- using effective communication,
- showing a high level of family cohesion,
- demonstrating role flexibility,
- tapping resources internal and external to the family, and
- being free from violence and substance abuse.

These characteristics can provide a useful diagnostic checklist for the educator and community professionals involved with families of children and youth who have special needs. Whenever possible, educational programs geared toward helping families develop these characteristics should be provided. In addition, individual families may be helped to develop their own unique adaptive capacities (Reiss & Oliveri, 1980). Of course, if physical violence or substance abuse is evidenced, the family should be referred to an appropriate treatment facility. (For further discussion of chemical dependency and child maltreatment in families, see chapter 8.)

In general, functional family coping patterns seem to arise from adequate information about and understanding of the stress; supportive versus conflicting relationships within the family; and adequate social network support. From their study of 500 families with a chronically ill child Patterson and McCubbin (1983) found three predominant functional coping patterns:

1. The families preserved a sense of optimism and were cooperative.
2. They received support from others, maintained their feelings of self-worth, and were emotionally stable.
3. They gained an understanding of the chronic problem from interactions with peers and consulting with the medical establishment.

Coping Workshops

McFadden and Doub (1983) developed a series of workshops for family survival and coping that can easily be adapted for parent groups within a school setting. They begin the workshop series with a set of rules for survival during hard times. The rules encourage members to recognize when they are having a hard time; to stick together during the hard times; to slow down; and to get external help when they perceive that their family is stuck.

These rules express in basic terms some of the coping characteristics cited earlier. Professionals who are planning a family group may wish to develop, with the families, a personalized set of coping "rules."

Reflections About the Family Life Cycle Perspective

Since the first edition of this textbook was written, a number of professionals (Breulin, Schwartz, & Kune-Karrer, 1992; L'Abate, 1994b; W. C. Nichols, 1996) have pointed to the inherent limitations of the developmental family life cycle perspective. Often cited is the limitation of a static perspective that cannot take into consideration the many ways by which family structure presents itself in our culture. Indeed, many professionals in the field of psychology and family studies believe the usefulness of the concept of the family life cycle is declining.

Breulin and colleagues (1992) presented an alternative in their book, *Metaframeworks*, that attends to five levels: biological, individual, subsystemic, familial, and societal. Their orientation focuses on microtransitions and the negotiation of those changes through oscillation rather than the typical definite and discrete stages of the family life cycle literature. Alternatives to the life cycle perspective, however, have limitations as well. As William Nichols (1996) stated:

> My own speculation is that one reason some family therapists lost their interest in the family life cycle may have been an overemphasis

on the transitions between stages and on the production of pathology in relation to failures or difficulties in effecting those between-
state transitions. The other side of the overemphasis on transitions and the related spawning of pathology appears to have been
an underemphasis on the significance of normal "inside-the-stages"
developmental tasks. (p. 65)

Regardless of its real or implied limitations, the family life cycle can provide valuable
information for use by school and community professionals. Understanding the family life
cycle perspective can help professionals and families better understand and, therefore,
relate to children and their families. Empathy should be evoked more easily, and explaining the family life cycle to family members can help them gain a perspective that normal-
izes the humps and bumps of transitions, and allows them to look forward to the predictable plateaus. If problems can be diagnosed within the context of family development,
interventions are more likely to be successful.

Summary

Much of traditional psychological thought focuses on issues of development from a predominantly individual perspective. The family life cycle is a logical extension of this tradition into a family systems context. The family life cycle provides a framework for the
developmental aspect of systems theory and, as such, provides the professional with the
same tools that theories of psychosexual, cognitive, moral, and emotional development do
for the individual child or youth. The life cycle model identifies patterns of normal development for the entire family and provides a basis for judgment about dysfunction when
developmental difficulties are encountered.

Three areas in which major life-cycle problems can be generated are

1. predictable significant *stressors* that are faced at each stage, including financial
   strains, family strains, career demands, and extended family demands;
2. *cultural demands* from former generations paired with family myths that arise as
   a result of the timing of life-cycle events and the significance that an event takes
   on for the family at future stages; and
3. the *pile-up* of numerous stressors within a short period.

For the school and community professional who understands the dynamics of the family life cycle, the behavior problems of children and youth can be viewed and managed
within a context of possible extended family difficulties.

Other factors also impact family life cycle. Families with children having special
needs face some predictable situations within each stage of the family life cycle relative to
disability category. Remarriage can also bring a variation in life cycle such as two dis-
tinctly different stages occurring at the same time (e.g., young children born to a remarried couple while concomitantly launching adolescents of one or both spouses) with creativity in reducing stress important as well as professional awareness of changes in family
life of this nature. The impact on children and youth can be tempered by professional

awareness, provision of opportunity to discuss the impact of remarriage with others already lived through a parallel situation; or, a support group of similar aged individuals experiencing a recent remarriage of parent(s). Of importance to those serving families in community and school settings, means of *coping* with life cycle transitions, multigenerational impact of dysfunctional patterns from previous generations, stressors, and *pile-up* are crucial to restabilize the family whether via workshop focused on implementing simple rules (e.g., notice stressors, stick together, slow down, get help) or via training in effective communication and strategies for coping with changes in the family.

Case Example

Nancy, age 13, was brought to the attention of the school counselor and social worker by her maternal grandmother. Nancy was eligible for placement in a special education classroom for children diagnosed with mild mental retardation. Living in Germany with her parents, who were in the military, she had been receiving special education services since she was 3 years old and had adjusted well until the past 2 years.

Her parents were requesting that Nancy begin living with her grandmother because they believed she could receive better special education and recreational services in the States than in Germany, where they thought the services for special-needs students of Nancy's age in the American school in Germany were inadequate. The grandmother sought the school's recommendations about Nancy's living situation and possible placement options.

The psychologist gained a thorough family history and discovered the following timeline: When the family was living in the United States, Nancy was diagnosed with borderline mental retardation at age 3. The family began receiving early intervention services from the local school system, and the parents seemed to adjust well to Nancy's diagnosis and special needs. The maternal grandparents, who lived nearby, were actively involved in Nancy's care and adjustment.

Four years later Nancy's family moved to Germany following her father's military transfer. Nancy continued to receive special education services through the American school. The parents reported that up to this point, both they and Nancy seemed to make the necessary adjustments with few problems.

While the family was living in Germany, the mother was not required to work outside of the home. For the first time in Nancy's life, her mother was available when she got home from school. Things were going so well for the family that when Nancy was 9 years old, her parents had another child, a son. This birth was planned and was anticipated by the family with excitement. Again, the parents reported that the family seemed to make a sound adjustment to having an infant in the home. Their daughter expressed love for her brother and often helped with basic care such as bottle feeding. The parents viewed Nancy as compliant and good-natured about the changes in the family. Now in the third grade, Nancy was actively involved in school and peer activities.

During the following year, the maternal grandfather was diagnosed with cancer. Over the next 2 years, the mother made four extended trips to the United States to help with her father's care and with decisions regarding his treatment. Each time, the mother took her infant son with her but left Nancy in Germany to attend school. Nancy was very close to her grandfather, but when he died during her sixth-grade year, she was unable to attend the funeral and never got to say goodbye. Her family failed to discuss the death of her grandfather with her in any depth, partially because they did not know what she would comprehend about the death and partially because they were busy with an infant. Nancy was not given the attention she needed to grieve the loss.

At this time Nancy began to show changes in mood. Her parents reported that she was unhappy about her mother's frequent absences from home. Because of her mother's trips, Nancy was placed in an after-school daycare center, where she stayed until her father got off from work each evening. Nancy's behavior became demanding, and she was openly defiant of her parents' wishes at times. Nancy, now 12, refused to clean her room or do basic household chores that had been hers since she was 6 years old. Her school performance deteriorated, and she spent more and more time isolated in her room. When her mother was at home, Nancy reacted to her in an angry and sullen manner.

Her father finally stated that he could not handle Nancy alone and meet his military commitments. The next time Nancy's mother went to the States to settle her father's estate, she brought Nancy with her. They stayed with Nancy's maternal grandmother. After a week, Nancy's mother asked if Nancy could remain with her grandmother. This was the point at which the grandmother sought help from the school counselor, who asked the school social worker to work together on this situation.

Questions and Comments

1. *Which life cycle stages and stressors were Nancy's family able to negotiate successfully? What factors and dynamics supported positive adjustment? (Write your answers before looking at what is written below.)*

   This couple seems to have completed the transitions through Stage 1 (Newly Married Couple), Stage 2 (Families With Young Children), and Stage 3 (Families With Elementary-Aged Children) of the family life cycle with adequate adjustment. Even the diagnosis of their daughter with mental retardation at age 3 and the family's move to Germany did not seem to cause significant problems in the family.

   The couple had the support of extended family and community services. They seemed to be able to share parenting roles while both had careers. When the mother stopped working outside the home, the family made this adjustment as well. In fact, the couple made a purposeful decision to reenter the stage of families with young children when the mother's time expanded. Even after the birth of the son, the family continued to adapt and reestablish a plateau period. They included Nancy in the pregnancy and birth process and allowed her to help with the initial caregiving of their infant son.

2. *At what stage did Nancy's family become "stuck?" What contributing factors and dynamics precipitated disruption of the family life cycle?*

Not until the family reached Stage 4 (Families With Adolescents) did the failure to adapt and reorganize roles become evident. This family clearly demonstrates the concept of pile-up. Parental and marital decisions about the family were made based on the plan that the family would live in Germany, the mother would be able to stay at home with her children, and the family would have a period of relative stability.

This stability was threatened by events outside of the family's control. A short time after the baby's birth, the grandfather was diagnosed with cancer. Now Nancy's mother, in addition to her own family, became responsible for helping with her father's care. This change left her husband trying to manage his own work as well as Nancy and their home.

When the grandfather died, Nancy's mother was the only member of her family who was able to attend the funeral and experience the grief with her extended family. The family did not offer Nancy an opportunity to work-through her own grief and, further, the death of her grandfather was not even discussed to any great length. The parents were unsure how well Nancy could understand the concept of death, and much of their energy was directed toward reinvolving the mother in family life and raising an infant.

Nancy's reaching adolescence seemed to be the final factor in the pile-up of transitional demands and stresses that sent this family into crisis. The daughter's noncompliant behaviors and sullen attitude were her expression of the distress the entire family was experiencing, as well as a predictable response to her growing sense of independence and the struggles that adolescence brings. The parents felt so overwhelmed by the changes they saw in Nancy that their solution was to place her outside of the home altogether.

3. *What interventions could be used to help the family move along in the family life cycle?*

Interventions for this family involved a number of different paths. First, while together in Germany, the family was given information about the family life cycle and their pile-up was acknowledged. Nancy's development as an adolescent was discussed, and the mother was given information about the struggles faced by other families with an adolescent with special needs. The mother was invited to attend a support group for parents with children with special needs. She attended a meeting in Germany and was able to discuss the changes in her daughter with other parents who had gone through similar difficulties.

Second, the family was helped through the grief process that had hampered their ability to make an adequate transition. The mother was advised to talk to her daughter about the loss of her grandfather and to give her as much information as she wanted about her grandfather's illness, death, and funeral. The family visited the grandfather's gravesite so Nancy could say her goodbyes and have a concrete way to experience the meaning of death.

Finally, the parents were advised not to leave Nancy with her grandmother. Nancy was able to tell her mother that she didn't want to be left behind. She cried and expressed how much she had missed her mother over the past 2 years. With help from the school counselor and social worker, Nancy was able to communicate some of her turmoil and confusion about becoming an adolescent. Nancy's mother was convinced that Nancy would interpret being left in the United States as the ultimate rejection.

The mother also was advised about special education services that were available through the military in Germany. She was able to see that if, in a few years, Nancy was not happy with the situation in Germany, she could choose to return to the States at that time. By then, the grandmother would have had time to adjust to the loss of her husband and Nancy would have had time to reconnect with her family.

The counselor and social worker also advised that the parents begin to spend individual time with their daughter and time alone as a couple. The family had developed a lifestyle, when they were together, of always going everywhere and doing everything with both children. As Nancy's developmental needs were significantly different from those of her younger brother, she needed some individual attention and activities geared to her age level. The parents needed some time together to alleviate some of their stress and solidify their relationship as a couple.

With the information they received, the parents realized that even though their daughter was 13 years old, she was functioning at a much younger level because of her intellectual limitations, coupled with the family's unresolved grief and failure to make transitional adjustments. The parents then were able to provide more support and work with Nancy in managing her moods and difficult behaviors. When the parents were able to view their daughter's rebellious behaviors within the context of the family stress, they were more willing to help her through this transition.

Extension Activities

Activity #1:

Reflection: Select an age when you were in elementary school, and then later in secondary school, and focus on your family and the family life cycle at both of those life-cycle stages (i.e., Families with Elementary-Aged Children and Families with Adolescents).

Journal: How do you see the primary theme of both of these life-cycle stages affecting your family, and in what ways were the primary tasks accomplished or poorly handled? To what do you attribute any difficulties that your family of origin faced in either or both life-cycle stages?

Activity #2:

Reflection: When you were growing up, at what time(s) do you recall your family of origin facing pile-up. What was going on in your family during those times? If you can't recall any time of pile-up, think of an extended family (e.g., a cousin's family) whom you knew well who experienced pile-up at some point in their family life.

Journal: In what ways did your family cope with pile-up? Was the pile-up related to transition times or to other factors? If other factors, what were they and how have you come to understand them? If you are part of an immediate family (e.g., if you have children), in what ways have you learned to cope effectively when you face pile-up? What meaning have you learned to bring to those stressful experiences, both then and now?

Activity #3:

Discussion: If you are part of an immediate family, discuss with a member of the class group or someone else what life-cycle stage your family is in currently. What do you consider to be the primary theme and primary tasks of this stage in relation to your immediate family now? In what ways do your immediate family's experiences reflect those of your family of origin (or that of your partner, if you have one) when your family of origin was in the same family life-cycle stage?

Discussion: If you have held a professional position in which you interacted or are interacting with families, select a family with which you are well acquainted and, while maintaining the anonymity of the family, discuss what you have observed about life-cycle stages in this family. Apply what you have learned about the six stages in reading this chapter.

Activity #4:

In-Class/Training Exploration Leader Instruction: Have a member of the class/session who has worked with families of at-risk or special-needs children or youth describe one of those families through the lens of the family life cycle. After others listen to the story, have them tell how they see the family in terms of the concepts covered in this chapter.

In-Class/Training Discussion Starter: How can knowledge of the family life cycle of children and youth help professionals in communities and schools improve community and family relations?

In-Class/Training Discussion Starter: How can you, as a school or community professional, help children and youth bring meaning to stressful experiences? What value does ascribing meaning have in our lives? (Read Victor Frankl's book *Man's Search for Meaning.*)

Family Interaction Patterns

The individual's behavior is not solely dependent upon what is going on in that person's head. Rather, the behavior is maintained by a complex set of interactions that occur with regularity and can be predicted by observing the family system over time (Nichols & Schwartz, 2005). This basic systemic premise is evidenced in the work of Salvador Minuchin, a pediatrician turned psychiatrist, and his co-workers (Minuchin, Montalvo, Guerney, Rosman, & Schumer, 1967), who developed the treatment approach known as structural family therapy. The structural model is well described by Goldenberg and Goldenberg (2000, 2004) and Nichols and Schwartz (2004, 2005). In addition, Walsh and McGraw (2002) and Aponte and DiCesare (2002) have contributed to the literature on structural family therapy.

The Structural Model

Early in the development of the structural model, Minuchin (1974) noted that the primary job of the family is to "enhance the psychosocial growth of each member" (p. 51). To accomplish that task, the family must operate with some predictability and stability. For instance, children should be able to forecast that each time they misbehave, they will receive a consistent response from their parents. At the same time, the family must be able to respond to changing circumstances with some flexibility.

Structural family therapy brought order and meaning to the regularly occurring interaction patterns within the family. Nichols and Schwartz (2005) stated, "The consistent patterns of family behavior are what allow us to consider that they have a *structure*" (p.127) in a functional sense. Structural family systems therapists intervene with the structure they observe in a family. In describing structure as seen by those who adopt the structural family systems model, Walsh and McGraw (2002) stated:

> An invisible web of complementary demands and expectations regulates the family. These family transactions, which make up the family structure, determine how members relate and can be verbal or nonverbal, known or unknown. A family's uniqueness is determined by the idiosyncratic repetitive transactions that make up the family's pattern of functioning. These transactions regulate behavior in two ways: A power hierarchy exists that dictates the authority and decision making in the family, and mutual expectations formed by negotiations over time are determined and fulfilled by individuals in the family. (pp. 49–50)

Family dysfunction stems both from stress and from the family's failure to realign to cope with the stress (Colapinto, 1991). When prolonged stress occurs, if the family is not capable of changing roles and communication patterns, family conflict and dysfunctional behavior will result. Minuchin and Nichols (1993) presented case studies that painted pictures of common types of family dysfunction. Writing about family therapy, Minuchin (1992) said:

> It is a process in which therapist and family members, working together, search for and enact an alternative reality that expands the possibilities for the family and its members. (p. 14)

In structural family therapy, the role of the professional is to help families adapt to changing circumstances through changes in the structure of the family. According to this model, family members have prescribed roles and functions that set up a pattern of behaviors within the family. The trained observer can identify these patterns by watching how family members interact. The child/youth is only one member of this complex family network. Therefore, if the behavior of children and youth is to be understood, they must be observed in the context of their families' patterns of relating.

Minuchin and his colleagues observed and worked with thousands of families for more than four decades. Through their observations, they identified frequent patterns of relating in families and developed the concepts they termed *boundaries, subsystems,* and *hierarchy* to describe those patterns. In the structural family approach, problems of an individual are viewed as resulting from dysfunctional family structure in one of these three areas. The dysfunctional family patterns eventually will result in the manifestation of behavioral, emotional, or physical symptoms in a family member, usually a child or adolescent (Nichols & Schwartz, 2005).

Intensive structural therapy, as described by Fishman (1993), involves

> working with the contemporary context, the people who are key parts of the identified patient's present social environment and the social forces they represent. The social context that impinges on the nuclear family can, and usually does, include people and forces well beyond the family's bounds. To address fully the needs of the modern family, one must work to transform these outside social forces as well as the forces within the family. (p. 13)

For more information regarding the theoretical principles underlying structural family therapy, see the Appendix. The remainder of this chapter will address each of the three concepts underlying structural family therapy: boundaries, subsystems, and hierarchy.

Boundaries

In observing family structure, one aspect of importance to structural family therapists is the pattern of distance and closeness between family members (Nichols & Schwartz, 2004). How emotionally connected are family members? How openly do they communicate with one another? How well is individuality tolerated in the family? This dimension of closeness and distance is defined through boundaries, the rules that determine "who participates and how" in the system (Minuchin, 1974, p. 53).

Boundaries are described as dysfunctional if they either are blurred or are defined too rigidly. At the extremes of distance and closeness are disengaged and enmeshed family structural systems. Figure 3.1 provides a visual representation of this continuum. Families with a pattern of relating that falls at either extreme of the continuum are at risk for having a member who exhibits physical or emotional symptoms. Children tend to be at high risk for reacting to family stress and dysfunctional family patterns. If a system is functioning well, boundaries are clear and semipermeable. Everyone in the family or work group knows who is allowed to participate, when, and how.

Permeability of Boundaries

Goldenberg and Goldenberg (2004) indicated that composition within a subsystem was far less important than clarity of its boundaries, stating that "boundaries within a family vary

Disengaged Boundary	Clear Boundary	Enmeshed Boundary

Source: Adapted from *Families and Family Therapy*, by S. Minuchin (Cambridge, MA: Harvard University Press, 1974), p. 54.

Figure 3.1

Definition of Boundaries

in their flexibility or *permeability*, and that degree of accessibility helps determine the nature and frequency of contact between family members" (p. 219). With clear boundaries, a sense of "I-ness," as well as a sense of belonging to others as "we," results in each family member retaining his or her individuality but never losing a feeling of belonging within the family. Walsh and McGraw (2002) indicated that clear boundaries are midway between disengaged/rigid and enmeshed/diffuse boundaries.

In clear boundaries within a school, for example, the teacher is responsible for evaluating and managing the student within the classroom and the school psychologist is responsible for evaluating the student and meeting with families at the request of the teacher. With semipermeable boundaries, the school psychologist might observe the student within the classroom and ask for the teacher's feedback, or the teacher might meet with the family and the psychologist to discuss a student's behavior.

Assuming that both professionals are adequately skilled, if the system is operating in a functional manner, the teacher appreciates the psychologist's presence in the classroom and the psychologist values the teacher's presence at the family meeting, both professionals recognize that they are joining resources for a student's well-being. If the two professionals are communicating openly, respecting each other's domains and contributions, and working for a common outcome, the boundaries are well defined and clear.

As an example of a breach of boundaries in a school, if a parent goes to the principal before talking with the teacher about an issue, he or she has breached the boundary of functional systems. In this case, the principal must send the parent to the teacher to discuss the issue, and if they cannot jointly resolve the issue or agree to disagree, the parent and teacher may benefit from bringing in a third party, such as a department head or a grade-level lead teacher. In this example, the issue would involve the principal only if the previous two steps did not resolve the issue satisfactorily. If the principal deals with this situation by referring the parent to the teacher, the principal is establishing clear boundaries. What the parents do next is "show their cards" about whether they are from an enmeshed background or able to respond to clear boundaries.

Taking an example involving the home—if the parents are arguing a point and the child tries to get involved by taking sides or by distracting the parents, one of the parents could say, "This isn't about you. It's about your dad (or mom) and me. You're welcome to watch how we handle this and learn from it, but you don't get to participate." By observing, children can learn about how to handle boundary issues in the future.

Unfortunately, people often re-create scenes from their parents' ways of dealing with disagreements that do not demonstrate functional boundaries. In the example of the parents taking issue with something in a classroom, the principal has an opportunity to model the proper use of boundaries by first referring the parents to the teacher.

Disengaged Boundaries

At one extreme of the continuum are families or systems in which boundaries are inappropriately rigid, with excessive distance between people. According to William Nichols (1996):

> The disengaging patterns of family process are characterized by a remarkable absence of affective intensity in family attachments.

> Relationships throughout the family subsystems are marked by emotional distance, lack of sensitivity to individual needs, and a high frequency of independent activities. (p. 197)

In disengaged boundaries, communication between members is limited and collaboration within the home or with the school is difficult. Children may go to extremes of behavior such as throwing temper tantrums, setting fires, making suicidal threats, or stealing—just to get attention. Members of a disengaged family system report feeling as if they have to make decisions or handle problems alone. Family members from disengaged systems are likely to become independent and autonomous much earlier than members of families with clear or enmeshed boundaries, but the cost of the emotional loss and limiting affective ties is large (Nichols, 1996).

Disengaged Family Systems

Children and youth who come from highly disengaged families are more likely to exhibit behavior problems or problems of externalizing (e.g., stealing) versus internalizing their feelings (e.g., depression). If they do not receive appropriate intervention, they are at risk for becoming involved with legal or court systems in the future. Indications of inappropriate distance and rigidity in the family include behaviors such as speaking loudly, acting like a class clown, stealing from other children, and cursing.

School and community professionals can observe disengagement by watching the responses and interactions of family members.

> Do people in the family sit far apart from one another?
> Do the children have to repeat themselves to be heard?
> When the professional calls a parent or sends a note home, does it take a long time for the parent to respond?

Another facet of disengagement is family members' inattention to expressions of feeling:

> Do family members have to escalate their behavior to receive attention for their feelings?

Other facets of family life also may reflect disengagement. For example:

> Does the family have regular meals together?
> Does the whole family engage in any regular activities, such as church, vacations, or sports events?
> Are the parents involved in PTA/PTO activities?
> Do they attend their children's school activities when invited?

Failure of the family to be involved in these types of activities may indicate disengagement. Professionals in school and community settings should take note.

Corey (1996) shared a true story of extreme disengagement in a family. A teacher had noticed that one of her students had been absent for days, and she called the home, to no avail. Finally she called the police. When they went to the home to investigate, they found that the parents had not even noticed that their sixth-grade son had not been home in three days. This illustrates the far end of the spectrum of disengagement.

When professionals in the school or community perceive disengagement, they may have to deal more forcefully with the family. For example, if an initial note or phone call from a teacher does not elicit a response, an administrator might be called upon to co-sign the next note or to initiate the next phone call.

Professionals also should be aware that a child's lack of responsiveness may be a function of a disengaged family pattern. The child or youth may not respond until overtures of approval or nurturance are repeated several times. For example, if a child does not react to an initial reinforcing statement, the teacher might say, "Jelani, please look me in the eyes. I want you to know that I'm so proud of your teamwork with the Lego Robotics. You are a real asset to the group!"

Professionals should resist the tendency to define disengaged families as "bad" or abusive. Often, disengagement is a systemic response to extensive conflict, long-term family stress, or overtaxing of emotional resources (Goldenberg & Goldenberg, 2004; Nichols & Schwartz, 2005). The distancing may be an attempt by the family system to gain balance and continue to function in the face of these forces. Once these families recognize that something is awry, conflict and verbal reactivity may intensify. Frequently, fear of out-of-control conflict (Colapinto, 1982) or fear of engulfment (Feldman, 1992) is what leads to the initial disengagement process.

The families of a child or youth with special needs often have a long history of involvement with special educators, health care providers, and social services. At some point, they may observe disengagement between parent and child. The distance, however, may be a reaction to years or months of overinvolvement or overtaxing of the parents in trying to meet their child's needs. In these instances, knowing the historical context may be useful in understanding and changing the disengagement process.

Kevin, an 8-year-old deaf boy in third grade, was absent for 3 consecutive weeks. After the first week's absence, his speech and language teacher called Kevin's mother, a single parent, and left a message of concern on her telephone answering machine. When Kevin did not return to school after another week, the teacher contacted his mother at work and was told that Kevin had just recovered from a bad case of the flu, was being nursed back to health by his grandmother, and would return to school the next week.

After a third week of absence, the teacher asked the school counselor if she would contact the mother and invite her to the school for a meeting. Both professionals hypothesized disengagement on the part of this mother because of her failure to respond to inquiries from the teacher and the counselor about Kevin's absences. In addition, because this mother was a single parent, they believed that she might be overwhelmed with the demands of parenting and, thus, relieved by Kevin's staying at home with his grandmother.

Disengaged School and Community Systems

Disengagement also can be observed in work contexts such as schools and community. If professionals sense that they each have their own fiefdom or domain within the building or community, and if subgroups have little collaboration, disengagement is likely to be operating in that work context. In an example of disengagement within the school, if little communication flows among instruction, counseling, social work, after-school, and administration, the system is likely disengaged.

Steps toward resolving the disengagement may include identifying the fear or conflict that has led to the rigidly defined distance, increasing understanding of the various roles and functions within the school and community, and conducting team-building and collaboration exercises. If a consultant or administrator recognizes disengagement in a group, some systems take subunits or the whole system on a retreat to participate in team-building exercises.

During group activities that require communication and collaboration, the units and subunits are brought together by group leaders from outside the system who create and facilitate group processes. A ropes course is one example of a group process that helps work units to communicate effectively to accomplish tasks together. Ropes courses are similar to watered-down basic training activities in the military, using outdoor experiential exercises—such as climbing ropes, moving on a high wire from one end of two poles/trees to another, and going through challenging obstacle courses—to emphasize team encouragement, team reliance, and the functioning of the unit as a whole versus the individual. The purpose is to teach individuals to work as a group and use effective, functional communication patterns in the hope that they will use the effective communication at work in the future. If communication improves, the disengagement likely will lessen and move toward clear, flexible, semipermeable boundaries on the continuum in Figure 3.1.

Enmeshed Boundaries

At the opposite end of the continuum are families and other systems in which boundaries are blurred by excessive closeness between individuals in the system. In enmeshed systems, autonomy and independence are difficult to achieve because of the lack of privacy and intolerance for individual differences. Members of an enmeshed system may report feeling smothered or overprotected. As Aponte and Hoffman (1973) said, if one person is cut, the rest of the family bleeds.

William Nichols (1996) discussed the identifiable emotional intensity of enmeshed families related to attachment, frequency of interactions, and reciprocal dependency. At times, he said, family members speak on behalf of one another. Nichols cautioned professionals not to confuse enmeshment with emotional closeness or intimacy. Enmeshment often is evident in families with psychosomatic conditions such as diabetes and asthma.

According to Goldenberg and Goldenberg (2004):

> A psychosomatic family was found to be overprotective, inhibiting the child from developing a sense of independence, competence, or interest in activities outside the safety of the family. The physiologically vulnerable child, in turn, feels great responsibility for protecting the family. The manifestation of symptoms typically occurs

when stress overloads the family's already dysfunctional coping mechanisms. Thus, the symptoms are regarded as having a regulating effect on the family system, the sick child acting as a family conflict defuser by diverting family attention away from more basic, but less easily resolved, family conflicts. (p. 215)

Enmeshed Family Systems

Children and youth who come from highly enmeshed families are more likely to exhibit emotional problems or problems of internalizing than to act out or externalize their difficulties. Without early intervention, these children are at risk for future need of mental health services or psychiatric hospitalization. Child and adolescent behaviors such as sadness and withdrawal, identity problems, and poor social skills may be evidence of an enmeshed family environment. Nichols and Schwartz (2004) stated that "children enmeshed with their parents become dependent. They're less comfortable by themselves and may have trouble relating to people outside the family" (p. 180).

In some families, the children take the role of parents and the parents have ineffective control. In enmeshed families, a child's acting-out behaviors, such as having temper tantrums or threatening to run away, usually are in response to limit- setting, in which limits have been blurred or nonexistent in the past. This is in contrast to disengaged families, in which lack of involvement precipitates acting-out behaviors. Typically, family members from enmeshed systems place an overly high value on cohesion of the family and relinquish autonomy—leaving less time to explore and master problems in wider systems and the initiative of the child/youth is crippled (Nichols & Schwartz, 2005).

Questions that may suggest that a family is enmeshed include the following:

Do family members seem to sit too closely together or touch inappropriately?
Do younger children exhibit clingy behavior or acute distress at separation?
Do people in this family interrupt one another or speak for each other?

For example, if Johnny is asked his opinion about something, does his mother respond, "Johnny thinks _____," as if she thinks for him? If someone expresses a disagreement, is he or she ignored or talked over?

If the community or school professional observes signs of a family being enmeshed because of the child's behavior, the professional should heed certain cautions. In contrast to the disengaged system, reactivity and emotionalism are the standard in enmeshed families. A note sent home about a child's behavior to an enmeshed family may result in frantic phone calls or visits from the parents. Criticism of one family member (in this case, the child) may be perceived as a personal affront to other family members as well and may elicit a defensive reaction.

In dealing with the enmeshed family, understatement should be the rule. Rather than reinforcing the reactivity, as frequently is done with the disengaged family, the professional dealing with enmeshed systems should maintain a calm, nonreactive stance.

Professionals may find that children from enmeshed families are more clingy and attention-seeking than other children. Children from enmeshed families may have difficulty with self-direction and request frequent assistance from adults. The families may create problems for their children by hindering their development and interfering with their children's problem-solving process (Nichols & Schwartz, 2004). These children may ask the professional inappropriate personal questions or make requests for his or her time that are outside the school structure, such as requesting to go to a movie or inviting the professional to attend a recital. In instances such as these, the professional must view the child's behavior within a family context. An overinvolved, enmeshed family culture perceives these behaviors as appropriate.

I was teaching a child who was bused from another school to be in my classroom. The personnel from the school she came from had concluded that Addie's family was too close for comfort. The psychologist at that school even wondered if incest was involved because Addie's father was constantly patting and hugging her. I observed Addie in the school, and detected no problems but did not meet the family until she was transferred to my classroom.

When I met and got to know the family, I realized that the psychologist did not know much about Italian American families. I was familiar with these families because for eight years during my childhood, I was surrounded by an Italian American community and I married into a second-generation Italian American family. Calling upon my earlier observations, I concluded that the public displays of affection by Addie's father resulted in the psychologist's confusing behaviors that reflected a cultural difference, not a dysfunction.

In addition, however, Addie chose a black crayon to draw most of the time. Addie had been in my classroom only a few months before she returned to her neighborhood school. Addie was in the regular kindergarten classroom of my school most of those months, awaiting the movement from kindergarten to first grade in her neighborhood school. Addie would be in a new group in her home school when all students were experiencing the same shift the next school year.

Because professionals knew so little about family dynamics back in the 1970s, these changes posed a hardship on Addie and her family. Fortunately, Addie had a supportive family system, and she bounced back quite well. I heard from her neighborhood school that all went well for Addie throughout first grade.

As with the disengaged family, professionals must recognize that family enmeshment is a result of systemic forces. The need for intense closeness and family loyalty is often a homeostatic response to avoid extreme anxiety (Colapinto, 1982; Goldenberg & Goldenberg, 2004; Nichols & Schwartz, 2004). The family becomes enmeshed in response to chronic family stress or unfulfilled and unresolved emotional needs.

Particularly in families having a child with special needs, the parents may be fearful of allowing the child too much independence (Foster, 1986; Lusthaus & Lusthaus, 1993; Tarver-Behring & Spagna, 2004). They may think that someone who has not "walked in my shoes" cannot understand or comment on their parenting or attachment to their child. In these situations, recommendations for a family support group may be beneficial. Enmeshed parents, like other parents, often validate the opinions of other parents who have had similar experiences with their children. Keeping this in mind may help the professional in school or community maintain boundaries more clearly when dealing with enmeshed systems.

> Ranu, a 16-year-old girl with Down syndrome, had begun requesting passes frequently to leave her second-period reading class. She complained of dizziness and headaches and asked to go to the school clinic. When this pattern was repeated five times in 2 weeks, Ranu's teacher discussed the problem with co-workers and was informed that Ranu had been meeting a male student in the hall during these alleged trips to the clinic.
>
> The teacher refused to write another pass and sent a note home regarding what was going on. The following day, Ranu's parents brought her to school and went to the principal's office, requesting a meeting. The reading teacher went to the meeting prepared to face the forces of an enmeshed system.

Enmeshed School and Community Systems

The enmeshed school or community context is easily recognized by its extent of involvement and is characterized by excessive togetherness. Decisions regarding policy often are laborious because of the need to involve everyone in a consensus, whether they will or will not be affected by the decision. In these systems the agenda at staff meetings frequently is unfinished because of the emphasis on expressing feelings over accomplishing tasks. If a staff member chooses to leave a position and take another job, that behavior tends to be viewed as disloyal to the system. Peers react to the change in position as a personal affront to their workplace.

Steps in resolving an enmeshed community or school system problem may include clarifying functions and goals *for each member*, thereby taking the emphasis off the group and putting it on the individual. For example, instituting an incentive program for innovative ideas and accomplishment of goals, and focusing on solutions that minimize disagreement rather than require complete agreement from all staff members, would spotlight individual achievement rather than the system as a whole.

Subsystems

In structural family therapy the primary building blocks of family structure are the subsystems within the family. The traditional immediate/nuclear family consists of four subsystems (Minuchin, 1974):

1. Spousal subsystem
2. Parental subsystem

3. Sibling subsystem
4. Extrafamilial subsystem

Each subsystem has roles and functions that are common to all families. For example, in every family some member or members are identified as executives or decision makers for the family—the parental subsystem. Other facets of subsystem functioning are defined uniquely by each family. For example, one-parent families (e.g., deceased spouse, adoption as sole parent) have no spousal subsystem unless a second adult in the home functions as the parent's partner. As another example, the extrafamilial subsystem may consist of the biological family or extend to friends and neighbors who function in that capacity (e.g., a nextdoor neighbor who "adopts the role of grandparent" of a child whose grandparents have died).

In an intact, heterosexual immediate family, the marital partners constitute two different subsystems. As husband and wife, they compose the marital or spousal subsystem. As mother and father, they are the parental subsystem. These two subsystems have different but intertwined functions. A gay/lesbian union has a partner/spousal subsystem and a parental subsystem. Likewise, if two heterosexuals are cohabiting, they are members of the spousal/partner subsystem as well as the parental subsystem. If communication problems arise between spouses/partners, their functioning as parents will be affected.

Regardless of any innate biases, professionals in community and school should allow families to define the boundaries of family relationship and should respond to members of the parental subsystem as involving two parents. For example, both parents in a lesbian or gay partnership should be invited to conferences, meetings, and PTA in school contexts.

Spousal/Partner Subsystem

The primary tasks of the spousal/partner subsystem are to provide for the relationship, emotional, and sexual needs of the couple. Successful resolution of the first stage of the family life cycle—formation of the marital/partner system—is the framework upon which the entire future life of the family is built. Thus, the initial task of the spousal subsystem is to establish a sense of commitment and mutual trust (Framo, 1981; Nichols & Schwartz, 2004).

As was covered in chapter 1, in our postmodern age the intact, immediate family pattern has many variations (Carter & McGoldrick, 1999). As a result, the definition of the spousal subsystem may have to be expanded to address the functioning of specific families. For example, most single-parent families have no spousal/partner subsystem. In some instances, the functions of the spousal/partner subsystem may be carried out by one parent plus a significant dating or live-in relationship. In these instances, the reasons for the lack of a legal commitment and the impact upon the family must be considered. The basic premise—that the emotional well-being of parents, revolving around their primary relationship—affects their functioning within the family still holds.

Functional Support

Once the issue of commitment is resolved, the couple/partnership must work together to build a future for themselves. Basic skills in negotiating and division of labor must be developed. To function in a healthy way, the marital couple should divide chores and communicate about and resolve problems in an interdependent relationship, as well as to accomplish the tasks of daily life. Early in their life together, spouses/partners must make many decisions about how household tasks will be divided, who will earn money and how much, how the money will be allocated, how leisure time will be spent, and so on (Carter & McGoldrick, 1999c). Positive resolution of these questions comes from open, honest communication and mutual respect.

In newly blended families, (see chapter 7) having children from one or both partners, community and school personnel may notice that, until the couple/partners have resolved the functional support tasks positively, the spillover to the children/youth may be seen in their behavior and emotional health at school and the community. In knowing about this situation (new blending of families), community and school personnel can provide some extra attention, support, and encouragement to the children/youth in the newly blended family. For example, offering to play a game of checkers or chess with a child in a newly blended family provides an opportunity for relationship building.

Emotional Support

Equally important is the role that the spousal/partnership subsystem plays in providing for the marital couple's basic emotional needs (Reimers & Street, 1993). This emotional foundation is what determines psychologically healthy patterns of interaction within the family and with other systems. Friedrich (1979), from a study of mothers of children with special needs, found that reported marital satisfaction of the couple was the most accurate predictor of successful coping and family adjustment to the child's special needs.

In a follow-up study of 158 families with a child having mental retardation, marital satisfaction was found to be the best predictor of positive overall family relations (Friedrich, Wilturner, & Cohen, 1985). Turnbull and Turnbull (2001) concurred, stating, "It appears that a strong marriage can make a difference in overall family well-being. At the same time, a strong marriage is not a prerequisite for positive family outcomes; many single parents of children with an exceptionality also experience strong family well-being" (p. 112). Gargiulo (2006) supports the importance of marital integration in the spousal subsystem and listed a variety of other factors that affect how a family copes with having a child with a disability.

The happiness and stability of the primary relationship between the couple/partners contribute heavily to the partners' individual self-esteem, motivation, and mood. Particularly in modern U.S. society, in which the extended family has become subordinate to the immediate family, the partner/spousal relationship may be the couple's primary source of intimacy and sense of connectedness in the world. With a basic sense of connection as the foundation for the partnership, the couple may face many life problems more flexibly and productively.

Families With Special Needs

Spousal/partner stability is impacted by the demands of a child with special needs (Featherstone, 1980; Hodapp & Krasner, 1995). Parents who are trying to make time for their own careers, the needs of their other children, and functional household tasks may have to take time away from their relationship as a couple to meet these various demands.

The findings about divorce and marital difficulties in families having a child with a disability are contradictory (Gargiulo, 2006). In a study done more than 30 years ago, Love (1973) reported that separation and divorce in families with a child with special needs are three times as high as in the rest of the population. From their interviews with 48 couples having a child with an exceptionality and 42 couples having children without a disability, Wright, Matlock, and Matlock (1985, p. 38) reported that parents of children with handicaps were six times as likely as parents of children without handicaps to indicate that their children caused marital problems. But Longo and Bond (1984) noted that 10 studies from 1959 to 1981 reported no differences between the level of marital adjustment, parental friction, or incidence of divorce in couples having children with chronic illnesses and the control couples.

Hastings and Taunt (2002) reviewed published research about positive experiences and perceptions of families. They pointed to the "increasing recognition of the importance of asking more positive questions about the perceptions and experiences of families of children with developmental disabilities" (p. 116). Further, they recognized that this need for more positive questions had not had an impact on research trends. It will take time for the researchers to catch up on the need for positive questions regarding impact of special-needs family members on the rest of the family.

There are studies of many couples with a child with disabilities whose marriages are intact and satisfying, as well as strengthened (Scorgie & Sobsey, 2000; Scorgie, Wilgosh, & McDonald, 1998). The primary characteristics that seem to relate to healthy marital response in these cases are strong, supportive spousal relationships prior to the diagnosis of the child, and the individual personality strength of the spouses (Abbott & Meridith, 1986; Turnbull & Turnbull, 2001).

Questions that community and school professionals (including social workers and counselors) can ask themselves when diagnosing the functioning of the spousal/partner subsystem include the following:

> When was the last time the couple/partners went out on a "date" together? How does the couple make decisions?
> When conflicts arise, how are they resolved?
> Does the couple/partnership have common interests and friends?
> Do the two have a process for problem solving?
> Is communication open, direct, and honest?

Parental Subsystem

The tasks of the parental or executive subsystem are oriented primarily around nurturing and teaching or disciplining children. In the intact immediate family, this subsystem consists of a biological or adoptive mother and father. In a divorce situation, the roles of the parental subsystem may be fulfilled by a single parent, by a parent and a grandparent, by both parents not living in the same house, and by a stepparent living with one of the parents or two stepparents when both parents have remarried, or by a parent and a stepparent. When the parental subsystem is not composed of mother and father, the emotional issues involved in parenting become more complex.

Nurturing Function

For many parents of children with special needs, the nurturing and protecting functions of the parental subsystem may be particularly complicated. As was discussed in chapter 2, the feelings of shock, guilt, and grief associated with the diagnosis of a child with a disability may interfere initially with the parents' ability to bond with their infant adequately (Darling, 1991; Trout, 1983). As the child develops, parents will go through many stages of adjustment and many ambivalent feelings about the child; however, their adaptive capacity results in most parents' forming strong attachments to their infant (Darling, 1991).

In the midst of these conflicting feelings, these parents, like parents of children without disabilities, must make decisions about how much or how little freedom to allow their children while at the same time ensuring their safety. Lack of clarity about the child's developmental progress may increase the difficulty in parental decision making surrounding independence.

Disciplining Function

An issue of primary importance in all families with children is the agreement between parents about discipline. If parents divide roles rather than share them, children learn how to negotiate around their parents rather than learning to internalize values and responsibilities. A typical pattern in dysfunctional families, for example, is for the child to view one parent as a "softie" and the other parent as the "hammer." In most cases, the strong-armed parent believes that he or she has to be a strong disciplinarian to combat the partner's permissiveness. The soft parent believes that he or she has to pamper the child to make up for the other parent's harshness. The parenting subsystem has reached a homeostatic balance; however, the basic tasks of teaching and disciplining children are not being fulfilled adequately.

In the family with special needs, this parental "splitting" often is unknowingly intensified by those who offer supportive services. If the mother is the parent who attends all meetings, takes all telephone calls, and schedules all appointments involving her child with special needs, she may have a different understanding of her child than her husband does. Particularly in cases where the child's disability is not physically evident, lack of understanding on the part of one parent may lead to different disciplining styles.

For the school and community professional, a first step in joining with parents is to acknowledge their conflicting feelings and struggles. A second step may be to provide information about child development in general, and specifically about the child's level of functioning. Finally, the school/community may serve as a resource for information on parenting classes or support groups that can alleviate some of the stress of parenting. For further discussion of resources, see chapter 10 of this book.

Sibling Subsystem

Primary tasks of the sibling subsystem relate to socialization, as well as development of the children in the family. Seltzer, Greenberg, Orsmond, and Lounds (2005) stated:

> The sibling relationship constitutes the longest lasting family tie, beginning with the birth of the younger sibling and ending with the

death of one member of the sibling pair. Siblings share a common family heritage, both genetically and experientially, and perhaps for this reason, the sibling relationship is normatively characterized as egalitarian, reciprocal, and mutual. (p. 354)

As the most long-lasting and influential relationship, the sibling relationship ebbs and flows in intensity over time and has a life cycle of its own. With younger children, companionship is an everyday experience, and sharing toys, rooms, and parents helps young children develop social skills and a base for other relationships. As adolescents, siblings often rely on one another for advice and as confidants. As adults, they provide one another with support and encouragement, and as aunts and uncles, they experience new family roles and provide a network of support and love for their siblings' children. Some siblings maintain for their entire lives the same intensity as they had when they were children.

The sibling subsystem provides an identification network in which values are formed, negotiations with parents are carried out, and perceptions of the outside world are supported or clarified (Bank & Kahn, 1982; Kahn & Lewis, 1988). In addition, cross-cultural studies have characterized the sibling group as an important *in vivo* testing ground for the transmission of cultural norms, roles, and functions (Johnson, 1982; Mc Goldrick, Watson, & Benton, 1999; Weisner, 1982). Beginning at a very young age, sibling interactions can teach sharing, negotiation, assertiveness, and empathy.

Having a Sibling With Special Needs

In families having a child with special needs, the siblings must adjust to less parental time and energy (Meyer & Vadasy, 1994; Powell & Gallagher, 1993). Whereas in most families the parents tend to distribute their emotional resources somewhat evenly across siblings, in families with one child who has special problems, that child tends to receive the lion's share of parental attention.

At times, siblings may feel competitive and angry with the brother or sister who has a disability, followed by guilt about these feelings. They also may experience a form of "survivor's guilt" about being healthy when their sibling has problems (Meyer & Vadasy, 1994; Powell & Gallagher, 1993). And the siblings may feel that they can't express their emotions to their parents for fear of causing more stress (Koch, 1985).

Responses of siblings depend on family characteristics, and strong marriages predict healthy adjustment by siblings of the child with a disability. Turnbull and Turnbull (2001) relate possible positive and negative impacts of having a child with a disability in the family. They refer to negative possibilities in regard to "overidentification; embarrassment; guilt; isolation, loneliness, and loss; resentment; increased responsibility; and pressure to achieve" (p. 119). Positive impacts may include "enhanced maturity, self-concept, social competence, insight, tolerance, pride, vocational opportunities, advocacy, and loyalty" (p. 119).

Sibling relationships of children having Down syndrome were studied by Cuskelly and Gunn (2003). They looked at perspectives of the mothers, fathers, and siblings regarding the nondisabled siblings. A comparison group study matched each child with a disability with a nondisabled peer having characteristics similar to the child with Down syndrome (e.g., age, place in family constellation, gender). The researchers found no group differences in parental reports. Siblings of children with Down syndrome reported "less unkindness, and, if in same-sex dyad, more empathy than did comparison children. There were differences between same-sex and opposite-sex dyads regarding avoidance and frequency of sibling positive and negative interactions" (p. 234). The children reported no gender or group differences regarding their interactions with parents or contribution to chores. Children with a sibling with Down syndrome were involved in more caregiving activities than the comparison group. Caregiving was related to empathy and involvement.

Grissom and Borkowski (2002) studied adolescents with siblings who had and those who did not have a child with a disability. Their research related to self-efficacy, peer competence, and maternal attitudes toward and modeling of prosocial and empathic behavior. The researchers found no significant differences between the two groups of adolescents. "Females evidenced higher levels of self-efficacy than did males, regardless of siblings' disability status. For adolescents with siblings who did not have disabilities, interpersonal competence was significantly related to self-efficacy" (p. 79), whereas for adolescents having a sibling with a disability, interpersonal competence and maternal attitudes, as well as modeling, were significantly related to self-efficacy.

In the "Perspectives" section of the *Journal of Mental Retardation*, Hodapp, Glidden, and Kaiser (2005) stressed the need for comprehensive research relating to siblings of individuals with disabilities. Their view on underdevelopment increases in importance because people having disabilities are living longer. Siblings will become the most likely caregivers, as their parents either will be unable to care for their child with a disability or will have died. There is a dearth of researchers becoming identified with and carrying out research over their careers (Stoneman, 2005). Hodapp et al. made recommendations for research that spoke to: methodological, measurement, developmental and life-course perspectives, mediator-moderator variables, cultural and subcultural issues, and balanced views including both the positive and the negative.

Investigating sibling relationships and parent stress in families of children with and without learning disabilities, Lardieri, Blacher and Swanson (2000) found, with one exception, a lack of differences in those with and without a child with a learning disability in the family.

> Overall, sibling relationships in families of children with LD-only were found to be akin to sibling relationships in typical families. No significant differences were found between LD and NLD families in terms of sibling behavior, sibling self-concept, and perceived sibling impact. (p. 115)

The exception they found was in relation to parent scores. Those with a child with a behavior problem versus families of children with no behavior problems showed significant differences in relation to stress and burden. The researchers pointed to the paucity of research focused on siblings of children/youth with learning disabilities.

Some children incorporate having a sibling with special needs into a negative self-concept of their own (Meyer & Vadasy, 1994). They may feel that because their sibling has a disability, they are damaged as well. Dyson and Fewell (1989), however, found that self-concept was no different for young children who did and did not have a sibling with a disability. And Hannah and Midlarsky (1999) found, similarly, no overall difference in adjustment and competence of siblings who had a sibling with a disability. They looked at internalizing and externalizing disorders, as well as self-esteem and competence. This supports findings by Dyson and Fewell and challenges findings by Meyer and Vadasy, though Hannah and Midlarsky did find that boys with a sibling having mental retardation had challenges with school functioning; and they also found that girls with a sibling having mental retardation expressed their stress through internalization (e.g., depression) versus externalization (e.g., conduct disorder).

Awareness   Parents often are reluctant to discuss specifics about their child with special needs with their other children for fear that they will distress the children without disabilities. This does the siblings a disservice. Through overidentification, siblings may worry that they will "catch" the problem themselves (Meyer & Vadasy, 1994). Siblings seem more likely to have these worries if the disability is mild and not physically evident. Further, they may be afraid to tell their friends about their sibling with a disability for fear of being ostracized. They may withdraw from the sibling with problems, and then from their peer network, adding to the sense of isolation.

Siblings should receive information about their brother's or sister's special needs that is understandable to them. As indicated in a study by McHale, Sloan, and Simeonsson (1986), who interviewed 60 siblings of children with special needs, when siblings have a better understanding of the child's condition, sibling relationships tend to be more positive. The same need for information is true for parents (Powell & Gallagher, 1993).

Responsibility   When the home includes a child with special needs, siblings may be asked to take on more personal responsibility than usual. The oldest female sibling in these families is at particular risk for parentification (W. C. Nichols, 1996; Powell & Gallagher, 1993). Mothers who are overwhelmed with caregiving tasks for their diagnosed child may ask, either covertly or overtly, their oldest daughters to take over more parenting functions. This puts these girls at risk for not having their own emotional needs met and for developing problems in later life.

Once siblings become adults, the parents expect them to assume the parental role that they themselves can no longer take on because of the complications of aging and their assumed death earlier than their children (Hodapp, Glidden, & Kaiser, 2005). A study by Hannah and Midlarsky (2005) compared siblings of children with and without mental retardation in terms of their perceived helpfulness to siblings. Each group consisted of 50 siblings (one with and one without either a sister or brother with retardation). The comparison evidenced that siblings of a child with mental retardation perceived that they offered significantly more emotional support and custodial care. The two groups did not differ in terms of giving information or tangible aid. As perceived by the siblings, "custodial care and emotional support were associated with gender, the child's need for assistance, and self-esteem" (p. 87).

Abilities   As children develop, they may have concerns about surpassing an older sibling with special needs who is functioning at a younger age (Meyer & Vadasy, 1994; Vadasy, Fewell, Meyer, & Schell, 1984). The younger child may feel guilty about passing up his or her older sibling even though that sibling is diagnosed with special problems. Younger children may try to hide their abilities or may refuse to take part in activities in which they likely will excel.

Professionals should be particularly alert to motivational problems in children/youth with a sibling who has special needs, as the process of parentification or feelings of guilt may be operating. A discussion with the sibling and the parents about survivor guilt and the struggles of having a sibling with a disability may provide the information and support that is needed to readjust the family structure.

Positive Aspects   Dykens's (2005) study focused on the happiness and well-being of siblings and families of individuals having mental retardation, versus looking for what is wrong. Although siblings of children with special needs are at risk for various problems, the extent of these problems seems to depend, most significantly, on the adjustment of others in the home, especially the parents (Ferrari, 1984). Given adequate coping skills, open communication, and an environment of mutual support, having a sibling with special needs has some positive aspects. Siblings tend to better understand and tolerate differences in people and may become advocates for individuals with special needs (Grossman, 1972; Meyer & Vadasy, 1994). Siblings of children with emotional problems frequently show an orientation toward idealism and humanitarian interests.

Often, siblings, particularly females, choose careers that are influenced by the disability (Cleveland & Miller, 1977; Powell & Gallagher, 1993). Outlining positive frameworks, Dykens (2005) suggested operationalizing definitions for well-being and three ways to find happiness:

1. Positive emotions relating to past, present, and future
2. Involvement in work, activities, and relationships that result in engagement, flow, meaning
3. Living life in service of something greater than oneself, finding meaning in service to society

She recommended studying these frameworks when looking for positive aspects of having a child/youth with a disability as a member of the family.

Groups for Siblings of Children With Special Needs

The following are some examples of groups for siblings of children with special needs.

Workshops   Dyson (1998) surveyed 24 siblings of children with disabilities who had participated for 3 years in a support group for elementary-age children. For 6 weeks the siblings attend six 2-hour workshops that were held for 2 hours each on a Saturday afternoon in a recreation center or child development center. Components of the program were: "arts and crafts, learning about siblings' disabilities, group discussions, sharing of sibling experiences, and recreational and social times" (p. 59). The results showed that the siblings "preferred program components related to learning about their siblings' disability and methods to interact with and support such siblings. Recreation activities were equally important, as was the opportunity to socialize with others and to share experiences about disabled brothers or sisters" (p. 62).

Parent Night   The school professional may be in a unique position to provide services to the siblings of children with special needs. Daniels-Mohring, co-author of the first edition of this text, led sibling groups at a self-contained special education setting. The school served children with special needs between ages 4 and 16. In this setting, one evening a week was designated as Parent Night. Teachers and counseling staff were available during this evening to meet with families for counseling, updates on students' progress, problem-solving sessions, and goal-developing sessions.

During one quarter, a 4-week sibling group was offered. Meeting on Parent Night, this group contained eight siblings of children in the school. Activities included group discussion, sharing information, and role-playing difficult situations encountered by the siblings. Role-plays were videotaped, and at the conclusion of the group, the members elected to invite their parents to view their videotapes. After the parents were able to see their children acting out some of their concerns and problems related to their siblings, a lively and open discussion followed. Evidently, the group met a need that previously had gone unnoticed.

Sibshops   Meyer and Vadasy (1994) developed a handbook for sibling workshops, entitled *Sibshops: Workshops for Siblings of Children with Special Needs*. This format was developed from their experiences with 8- to 13-year-old siblings of children with special needs at the University of Washington. The workshops were held on Saturday mornings for 2 to 3 hours or on 2-day overnight camping trips and included both an informational and a recreational component.

Some informational activities suggested in the handbook include discussion groups using problem-focused activities; panel discussions involving adult siblings or parents of children with special needs who are willing to share their experiences; and presentations by a speech therapist, physical therapist, special education teacher, or other professionals about their experiences with children who have special needs. The handbook also includes an extensive reading list of suggested fiction and nonfiction books for siblings of individuals with disabilities.

When I taught at the elementary level, I had sibling support groups operating at the same time that the parents' group was in session. We usually met once a month, and I invited other professionals to run the sibling group while I was with the parent support group. This worked well because it gave the parents somewhere for their other children to be during the parent support group, and we often had meals prior to the concurrent support groups.

Being in a family with a child having a disability made me more aware of the needs of siblings of children with special needs. Making arrangements for the siblings was most satisfying to me, and anecdotal input from parents and siblings indicated that they thoroughly enjoyed and benefited from the arrangement of concurrent support groups. Participation in the groups was a strong indicator of satisfaction and desire for more because almost all families attended these monthly sessions. If parents had preschool children, they either kept them during the parent meeting or

arranged for child care. Although I wish we could have offered child care
for them, it was not tenable in that situation.

Anyone using a concurrent support group structure would be helped by finding a child-
care or after-school worker to care for preschool-age siblings so family members can more
easily attend groups.

Extrafamilial Subsystem

In addition to the subsystems discussed already, family systems have an extrafamilial aspect.
Not truly a subsystem of the immediate family, the extrafamilial interactions represent those
parts of the family system that interface with the outside world. Cultural differences come
into play regarding the composition of extrafamilial systems. Just as each family must define
who is considered part of the immediate family, the families served in community and school
contexts determine who is included in their extrafamilial system. With the high dispersion of
families across the country, some families include neighbors who fulfill the expected roles of
extended family and of extrafamilial members who cannot be there on an immediate basis.

For example, on Grandparents Day a lunch may be served at school, and a neighbor
or friend who assumes the functional role of grandparent for a child whose grandparents
live far way, or are deceased, will fill the role of grandparent for the child at this school
function. Some families construct their extrafamilial grouping from a circle of friends and
neighbors who act in the place of aunts, uncles, and grandparents while the children are
growing up. The child or youth can describe who in that network functions in the place of
the traditional extrafamilial subsystem.

Extrafamilial contacts provide assistance and exchange of resources, a source of social
and recreational activities, and emotional support (Turnbull & Turnbull, 2001). The extrafamilial subsystem also provides support for family and cultural values. Within each of the
other family subsystems, certain issues and functions affect or are affected by extrafamilial interactions.

Interaction With the Spousal Subsystem

One task in forming the spousal subsystem is for the couple to make decisions about interactions with extended family. If one spouse continues to be involved with his or her family of origin to the exclusion of the other spouse, problems in the spousal subsystem will
result. Likewise, if a spouse is overinvolved with his or her friendship network, the level
of intimacy within the spousal subsystem may be affected. In special-needs families, if
only one spouse participates in special functions or support groups regarding the child, it
may result in marital distance.

Interaction With the Parental Subsystem

For the parental subsystem, daycare providers, babysitters, school professionals, community resources, and extended family and friends are all extrafamilial contacts. These people interact with parents in reaching decisions regarding their children's care. They provide support and assistance to parents and also may serve as role models for appropriate

parenting skills (Kazak & Wilcox, 1984). The parental subsystem must be functioning cohesively and clearly to allow these extended network interactions to operate positively. Otherwise, the parents may send mixed messages to each other about which role models to follow in parenting. Again, in a family with special needs, if one parent is attending special parenting classes or listening to the advice of school professionals to the exclusion of the other parent, conflict in the disciplining function may result.

Interaction With the Sibling Subsystem

The extrafamilial subsystem has extensive involvement with the sibling subsystem. The family must negotiate school activities with peers, sports teams, extracurricular activities, and daily peer interactions. We often hear parents say, "It's not my child's fault—it's the crowd he [she] runs around with."

Peer relationships have a major role in children's adjustment and socialization (Abramovitch & Strayer, 1977; Cicirelli, 1995; Rubin, 1985; Sluckin & Smith, 1977). If children have positive peer relationships, they will bring home these skills to share with their sibling network. Likewise, if children feel rejected or isolated from their peers, the resulting problems with self-image and poor social skills will become a part of their sibling interactions. In families with special needs, the acceptance of peers is particularly important to the child with the disability and to the siblings alike.

Dysfunction in the Extrafamilial Subsystem

Dysfunction in the extrafamilial subsystem arises when the family is either too inclusive or too exclusive about network involvement. If family members have enmeshed and diffuse boundaries, they may not be able to make family decisions without input from the extrafamilial subsystem. At the opposite extreme, if family members have rigid or disengaged boundaries, they may isolate themselves from any social supports.

To diagnose extrafamilial functioning, school professionals may ask themselves these questions:

> Do the children ever have peers over to spend the night or go to friends' homes to spend the night?
> Are the children involved in any extracurricular activities?
> Is the family active in a church community?
> Are grandparents regularly involved with the family?
> Do the parents have their own friends?

If the extrafamilial subsystem clearly is not fulfilling the family's needs, the school or community professional may want to suggest investigating Boy Scouts or Girl Scouts, sports teams, Special Olympics, specialized summer camps, or other activities geared to the child's needs. More specific suggestions about networking resources may be found in chapter 10.

Families With Special Needs and Those With Children/Youth Who Are At Risk for Failure

Families with a child having special needs often feel isolated from their extrafamilial subsystem (Kazak, 1987). The parents may think they have few sources of support. The extended families may go through their own mourning process when a child is born with a disability. As Gabel and Kotsch (1981) argued, "Grandparents who are angry, grief-stricken, or who deny the child's handicap may become an additional burden to parents" (p. 32).

In comparing families with a child with spina bifida with matched control families, Kazak and Wilcox (1984) found that the friendship networks of the parents in the former group were smaller than were those in the latter group. The authors hypothesized that friends might withdraw support because of their lack of knowledge about the child's illness and their feelings of fear or inadequacy about providing help; also, the parents might be less receptive to support because of their own fears and anxieties.

Particularly with children who require specialized physical attention, parents may be afraid that their friends or family will not know how to respond adequately to the child's needs. In addition, parents may believe that asking for help with their child will place too great a burden on their friends.

Another potential difficulty of families with a child with special needs stems from the required interactions with outside services. Often these families must meet frequently with physicians, counselors, teachers, physical therapists, and other professionals to maintain their child's functioning. Most of these services focus on the child rather than the family (Foster, Berger, & McLean, 1981). As a result, parents often feel overwhelmed with demands from these extrafamilial systems rather than feeling a sense of support in their struggle.

In an article on strengthening at-risk families by involving extended families, Walton, Roby, Frandsen, and Davidson (2003) described the family group conference (FGC), which takes a solution-focused, strength-based approach. This manner of building assets within the family, by linking the extended family with the family having a problem with a child, has been referred to as FGDM (Family Group Decision Making), as well as FUM (Family Unity Model). The authors described an overall sense of satisfaction by most families who participated in their study. Caseworkers and facilitators also were highly supportive of the model, even 12 months later, and they preferred this option over solely state-mandated solutions. They also found judges to be optimistic about the model and expected they would be approving family plans that were produced through the FGC process.

The extrafamilial aspects of the family system are particularly important to school professionals. The most functional view of the family will include the school professional as part of the family's extrafamilial subsystem. When teachers or counselors view themselves as being joined to the family system in meaningful and positive ways, interactions that affect the system will follow. This framework lends itself to cooperation between school and family rather than to defensiveness and alienation.

Hierarchy

Minuchin used the term "hierarchy" to describe the distribution of power in families (Minuchin, 1974), or the power relationships between the members of a subsystem. Hierarchy has three aspects:

1. *Power:* relates to who has the power. In a healthy family, the parents have the power.

2. *Order:* relates to the pecking order of wielding power. When the parents are not there and the oldest child, followed by the next-oldest child, and so on, clearly has the power, the family is considered functional. If, however, the youngest rules the roost, this represents a serious hierarchical dysfunction.
3. *Balance:* refers to shared power. When both parents share in decision making, the parental dyad is viewed as balanced and functional. As children grow older, a healthy system includes them in the decision-making process about areas of life that pertain to them, such as where to go on family vacation.

Family Hierarchy

The member or members at the top of the hierarchy have the most relational power within the system. In an adequately functioning family system, parents and children have different levels of authority that are accepted and respected. Likewise, in a school system, the principal has the final authority and accepts ultimate responsibility for making management decisions.

A system may have different levels of hierarchy. Parents may share authority, but at times one or the other parent may be in charge. Parents may delegate authority to a teenage sibling or a grandparent. In these cases, the functioning of the subsystem is affected by order. Sibling subsystems that have children of different ages tend to have a clear sibling hierarchy. Older siblings normally serve the dominant role in interactions with their younger siblings (Dunn & Kendrick, 1982). A dysfunction in hierarchy would exist if that order were not followed in a family unless an obvious factor—such as the oldest sibling having mental retardation—were involved.

School System Hierarchy

School systems, too, have different levels of hierarchy. Teachers are the ultimate authority in their classrooms. Team leaders may be at the top of the hierarchy with regard to decisions made by their team. Counseling departments may designate one person as the director of guidance. Finally, a principal and an assistant principal typically lead the decision-making process (somewhat like a parental subsystem).

Dysfunctional Hierarchy

When the hierarchy in a family or organizational system is unclear, as with a weak parental subsystem, turmoil and chaos reign. In highly stressed families, this lack of management may be evident in many ways. Children may come to school wearing dirty or torn clothing. Messages from school to home may be left unanswered and papers unsigned. Nichols and Schwartz (2004) stated:

> All too often this hierarchy is subverted by a child-centered ethos, which affects helping professionals as well as parents. Parents enmeshed with their children tend to argue with them about who's in charge and to misguidedly share—or shirk—the responsibility for making parental decisions. (p.132)

At times the hierarchy in a family or system is clear but inappropriately reversed, with children having as much or more power than their parents or teachers. In families where one child's demands take priority over the needs of the rest of the family members, a problem in hierarchy is evident. When a child functions in a parental role and assumes an inordinate level of responsibility for his or her age, hierarchy dysfunction is operating in the family system. This type of dysfunction is called *inversion of the hierarchy*.

Cross-Generational Coalition

One type of hierarchy shift is called a *cross-generational coalition* (Nichols & Schwartz, 2004). In the structural family systems model, Minuchin (1974) defined a coalition as an inflexible alignment between two or more family members against another family member. When the alignment occurs between a parent and a child or a grandparent and a child, the alignment is crossing generational boundaries.

Family Coalitions

In families, cross-generational coalitions are seen when a child is drawn into an alliance with one parent against the other. These coalitions typically occur when spouses are disengaged from one another. The child may be expected to assume excessive responsibilities, may be the confidant for a parent, or may be asked to compensate for the absent spouse by providing emotional support (Nichols & Schwartz, 2004).

School Coalitions

In schools, a cross-generational coalition occurs when, for example, a student is in an alliance with his or her parents against a teacher, or a school counselor is allied with a student against the child's parents or teachers. In these case, hierarchical and generational boundaries have been crossed inappropriately.

Detouring

A hierarchy dysfunction often seen in enmeshed systems is called *detouring* (Minuchin, Rosman, & Baker, 1978) or scapegoating (Boszormenyi-Nagy & Spark, 1973).

Family Detouring

Within families, this pattern is seen when parents detour their energy away from potential spousal conflict or distance to focus together on a particular child. Detouring may take the form of parents uniting to protect a vulnerable child, as in the case of a child with intellectual deficits or chronic illness, or uniting to blame a child as the cause of family problems, as with the acting-out adolescent. In either case, the family focus is exclusively on the identified child. This child then has the hierarchically inappropriate power to control family interactions by his or her behavior. Boundaries are blurred, with the ultimate result being the temporary avoidance of marital conflict that might destroy the family.

School Detouring

Detouring may be observed within an organizational system in situations in which multiple staff members are involved with a child. When decision making about a child causes emotions to run high, this may be an indication that conflict between staff is being detoured through the child.

> Mr. Bucci, a teacher, and Ms. Fergason, the assistant principal, disagree about the management of one of Mr. Bucci's students, Vince. Mr. Bucci feels blamed by the assistant principal. He and many of his colleagues think Ms. Fergason does not provide adequate support for them when they intervene in management problems in the classroom.
>
> The next time Vince acts out, Mr. Bucci sends him directly to the assistant principal's office. Ms. Fergason gives Vince 2 days of after-school detention under the teacher's supervision. Mr. Bucci, who disagrees with this consequence and has other commitments after school, fails to enforce the detention. Vince is caught in a detouring of conflict between his teacher and the assistant principal.

Sibling Hierarchy Dysfunction

Daniels-Mohring (1986) conducted an observational study comparing the interactions of pairs of siblings in which the older sibling had been diagnosed with psychiatric problems with the interactions of same-age control sibling pairs in which the older child had not been diagnosed with psychiatric problems. The researcher found that the older siblings who were diagnosed as having emotional disturbance lost some of their relational power within the sibling subsystem. This loss of role disrupted the typical hierarchy organization of sibling interactions in which the older sibling is in a dominant position. Now the youngsters with emotional disturbance had to cope with problems of identity in dealing with their peer networks and also had to adapt to the loss of power within their own family systems.

To diagnose hierarchy dysfunction, the community or school professional might ask the following types of questions:

Do parents defend the child even when the child's behavior is obviously inappropriate?

Are parents inconsistent with discipline—for example, threatening to ground the adolescent and not following through?

Does one parent act more like "one of the kids" than like an authority figure? Does the child talk back to the parents, exhibiting lack of respect?

When parents begin to disagree, does the conversation shift to focus on the child's behavior?

Hierarchy dysfunctions are common in families and systems. Often the people involved are unaware of the hierarchy reversals in their interactions. The professional who observes a hierarchy problem may be able to affect the system simply by offering a neutral comment on the process, such as: "I understand Billy's concerns about serving detention, but

I think it's important that we present a united front to him to avoid confusion" or, "Hey, Leanne, do you always talk to your mom that way? It surprises me because you're usually so respectful during afterschool activities." Observational comments such as these may be sufficient to help the parent reflect on his or her behavior and take action to reestablish the appropriate hierarchy.

Involving School Personnel in Transformation of the Family System

In his book, *Intensive Structural Therapy*, Fishman (1993) devoted a chapter to ways in which therapists can involve school personnel in empowering the family. He presented the following basic principles for school professionals to bring out the family's capabilities (pp. 180–184):

- Ensure that the therapist, not the school, determines the agenda for the therapy.
- Explore the parents' attitudes toward school and school authorities.
- Assume that the child is strong and that the problem is one the family can handle.
- Search for conflicting loyalties and hidden agendas.
- Encourage an attitude of shared responsibility and involvement between family and school.
- Clarify boundaries and roles.
- Establish an alliance between parents and school.

According to Fishman, involving school personnel in therapy is invaluable in aiding the transformation of the total family system. His model of choice is collaboration, with clearly defined roles. He gave a sad example of a student, typical of many in that he had more loyalty to the school than to the family, who ended up killing another student with a knife. Fishman indicated that schoolmates can be closer than other family members to a student, and they can be powerful forces in a therapeutic endeavor, particularly with adolescents. Because poor peer relationships during middle childhood have been found to be predictive of later emotional and social dysfunction, as well as of drug use and antisocial behavior, Fishman advocates that schools play a large role in bringing about transformation.

> Our work with schools is more important than ever, and perhaps more sensitive now, when budgets and, frequently, tempers are already stretched to the limits. As the economy is rapidly changing and there are fewer jobs for the undereducated, success in school becomes all the more essential. (p. 193)

Summary

The three major areas in which observations can be made regarding family transactional patterns are boundaries, subsystems, and hierarchy. *Boundaries* indicate the quality of distance and closeness within a family. The four *subsystems* are the subgroups of the family system that provide the building blocks of family interaction. Diagnosis of family interaction patterns must include some assessment of how well each subsystem sustains its roles and functions. The concept of *hierarchy* describes the distribution of power and decision making within a system.

Once family interaction patterns have been assessed, the child's behavior can be viewed within the context of his or her family structure and transactional style. Armed with an understanding of these contextual variables, the school or community professional can better promote individual academic and emotional development in children and youth. The Appendix includes an ecostructural assessment process.

Case Example

Charles W., a 9-year-old boy, was referred to the evaluation team as a result of his poor school performance during this semester. He had been placed in a third-grade classroom and received resource help in reading and math because of severe learning disabilities. Recently, he had begun acting out by refusing to dress for physical education. Soon after, he began to dawdle during class assignments, frequently commenting that he could not understand the work.

The teacher consulted with the school psychologist and confirmed that the work she was giving Charles was within his capability. After an initial note sent home regarding this problem, Charles's mother, Mrs. W., had phoned the teacher each week to check on Charles's progress. Despite the teacher's sending Charles's assignments home, he was falling farther and farther behind in his studies.

Mrs. W. reported that Charles would get up every morning complaining of a stomachache. She would coax him out of bed, and even though he looked pale and had dark circles under his eyes, she sent him to school. Mrs. W., who did not work outside of the home, picked up Charles from school each day. She reported that ever since the teacher's initial report regarding Charles's missed assignments, she spent every afternoon helping Charles with his homework, even after her two other children, ages 12 and 15, returned from school.

When asked how her husband felt about Charles's performance problems, Mrs. W. replied that he was angry and upset. She said Mr. W. worked long hours and had no idea of how Charles really felt or if he was completing homework. By the time her husband returned home in the evening, Charles usually was preparing for bed.

Mrs. W. volunteered that her husband had never understood Charles's problems. Ever since Charles was diagnosed as having a learning disability, her husband had been negative and withdrawn in his interactions with Charles. According to Mrs. W., her husband had expectations for Charles that were beyond his capabilities, and Mr. W. tended to blame her for Charles's not achieving in school.

Questions and Comments

1. *From the information provided, what is your hypothesis about the structural characteristics of this family (i.e., subsystems, boundaries, hierarchy)? What data support this hypothesis?*

The referral team hypothesized that Charles's mother and father had an unresolved conflict, at least regarding Charles, and probably more extensively. Distance between the father and Charles was indicated by the mother's report that the father was "negative and withdrawn" in his interactions with Charles, and that by the time the father returned from work, Charles usually was preparing for bed. Apparently, Charles and his father had limited interactions.

In general, the father was disengaged from the family system and the mother and Charles were overinvolved in their relationship. Enmeshment was indicated by the mother's "coaxing" Charles out of bed, her overconcern about his physical appearance, her picking him up after school each day, her weekly phone calls to the teacher, and her daily help with his homework.

The parents' marital conflict seemed to be detoured onto Charles in that, despite his mother's extensive help, Charles still was unable to perform at school. Apparently the mother was not willing to make appropriate demands on him. This behavior can be viewed as a reaction to what she considered inappropriate and negative demands by the father. According to the available information, the other two children were functioning adequately and did not seem to be the focus of parental conflict.

2. *If the family dysfunction were to be resolved, what would the family structure probably look like?*

In the ideal structure for this family, the mother and father would be equals in the family hierarchy. They would make joint decisions regarding their child's school problems and support one another in carrying out plans for helping their child. The adolescent child would be higher in the sibling hierarchy than either of the two younger children. All boundaries between subsystems would be appropriate and flexible, as indicated by open communication, the expression of individual identities, and clear roles and functions within the family.

3. *What types of intervention strategies might be appropriate for working with this family?*

To work toward a functional family structure, the referral team would want to make certain that the father would be involved in meetings and other future communication regarding Charles. Both parents might be brought in to review Charles's records and clarify his functioning level, to decrease the possibility of misunderstanding Charles's abilities.

Further, to interrupt the enmeshment between Charles and his mother, the team might suggest that Charles be required to complete his assignments during school hours or stay after school for study hall. As another suggestion, Charles's oldest brother might be enlisted to help him with some homework assignments, which would have the added benefit of building some cohesion in the sibling subsystem. Finally, the team might suggest that Charles be allowed to ride the bus home from school to increase his peer interactions and level of independence.

Extension Activities

Activity #1:

Reflection: Thinking back to your childhood and family of origin, reflect on how you would describe your family in terms of subsystems, boundaries, and hierarchy. Was there a marital subsystem, or did you grow up in a single-parent family during all or part of your childhood? If there was a parental subsystem during all or part of the time, how would you describe it in terms of the structural hypothesis (e.g., enmeshed, disengaged, or semipermeable boundaries; emphasis on balanced or shared decision making)?

Unless you were an only child, describe the sibling subsystem in your family of origin. How did the siblings follow or fail to follow expected behaviors (e.g., oldest being responsible, middle being the glue, and youngest being playful)? Would you describe the boundaries of the sibling subsystem as enmeshed, disengaged, or semipermeable? What behavioral descriptions can you think of to substantiate that belief? Recall the influence of the extrafamilial subsystem and determine its significance and impact on the life of your family of origin.

Journal: From learning about boundaries, hierarchy, and power in your family of origin, what can or will help you in the future with your immediate/nuclear family? How has your mode of operation, learned within family-of-origin structures, been generalized to your school and/or work relationships? What meaning or significance do you attach to the strengths and challenges of your family of origin relative to structural concepts?

Activity #2:

Observation: Watch a few television sitcoms involving families. After each one, reflect on a structural hypothesis in terms of boundaries, subsystems (marital, parental, sibling, extrafamilial), (enmeshed, disengaged, semipermeable), hierarchy (power, order, balance), and alignments/coalitions (positive, negative, neutral).

Journal: Write about what you noted in watching the sitcoms. If you watch sitcoms regularly, do you now see any pattern to programs you watch? If so, what do you find attractive about the types of shows you watch? Can you learn something from these programs that will help you understand your family and other families?

In-Class/Training Discussion: Discuss the sitcoms and the patterns that emerged. How would you describe the human nature you observed? Why do people enjoy watching sitcoms?

Activity #3:

Discussion: Discuss the importance of knowing about the structural concepts described in this chapter in relation to your family of origin. How can knowing about structural concepts help you as a school or community professional? What could you do to share this knowledge with others in a school setting? How might you network with professionals in the community or school external to your work about what you have learned from reading this chapter?

Activity #4:

In-Class/Training Exploration: Consider a family about whom you can provide substantial information. Provide everyone in the group with basic information about the family. Then, as a class, attempt to construct a structural hypothesis using the information provided in the ecostructural assessment section in the Appendix. The family may be from a school or the external community. The important part of this exercise is to practice putting pieces of the puzzle together and to become accustomed to dealing with the concepts; less important is being accurate in the hypothesizing. [An alternative exercise: Have several group members or the leader write up information from a child's life and distribute it to all class members for use as a common base for group hypothesizing.]

Activity #5:

In-Class/Training Discussion: How can knowledge of structural concepts inform professionals and improve their work with at-risk and special-needs children and youth? How can professionals find answers to the more private or difficult questions that allow them to draw actual structural hypotheses? What ethical considerations come into play when school and community professionals become involved with structural concepts as they relate to children/youth and their families and communities?

Historical Factors in Family Systems

$\mathcal{T}$o the same extent that historical information about human growth and development is important to understand the individual, family history plays an important role in understanding family systems. What we are and how we behave today maintains some continuity with a history that extends back several generations. This chapter focuses mainly on the theory of Murray Bowen (1966, 1978, 1985), who emphasized the historical aspects of family systems. Bowen's theory expands the consideration of behavior from the individual to the family system, and also from the present to the past.

Concepts and Terminology

A number of specific concepts from Bowen's work address the notion that personal family history is important in the formation of a person's identity and life choices (Guerin & Guerin, 2002; Walsh & McGraw, 2002). The concept of *differentiation of self* addresses the theme of individuality and self-integration. *Emotional transmission* describes the forces by which family prejudices, rules of behavior, and patterns of relating are relayed through several generations. The concept of *birth order* deals with how factors within the sibling subsystem affect personality development and relational patterns throughout a family's history.

Triangulation refers to the process by which historical patterns of relationships are played out in the present. In addition to covering these topics, this chapter describes and provides examples of *genograms* (McGoldrick, & Gerson, 1999), a technique for mapping family history.

Differentiation of Self

The concept of differentiation of self is the core around which Bowen's theory was built (Guerin & Guerin, 2002; Nichols & Schwartz, 2004; Walsh & McGraw, 2002). Differentiation of self is the process by which a person becomes increasingly less emotionally dependent upon the family and more able to make independent choices and decisions. This process involves the ability to keep intellectual and emotional systems separate (Bowen, 1985).

For example, suppose you were bitten by a dog at a young age, and you now are afraid, almost phobic, of dogs. If you see a dog and you automatically run out into a busy street to avoid being chased by the dog, your emotions are controlling your actions. If, however, you can see a dog and ask yourself, "How dangerous is this dog? Is it a miniature poodle or a Great Dane? Is it housed within a fence or on a chain?" Before you decide whether to run, your emotions are being mediated by your intellectual system. When your emotional system is mediated by your intellectual system, your capacity for making choices increases (Kerr & Bowen, 1988).

In family systems therapy the key to being a healthy person involves a sense of belonging to one's family, as well as a sense of separateness and individuality (Corey & Bitter, cited in Corey, 2005). Differentiation of self in a family of origin is a lifelong process.

Levels of Differentiation

Bowen made it clear that until individuals are "on their own" financially, they cannot be totally differentiated; thus, children cannot be expected to have achieved a high level of differentiation. Nevertheless, Bowen's description of levels of differentiation is helpful when dealing with children and youth, as well as their families and, at times, colleagues.

Higher Levels of Differentiation

People who are well differentiated can make choices about personal behavior based on information as well as feelings (Guerin & Guerin, 2002; Guerin & Chabot, 1992). These individuals are not overly dependent in their relationships. They can cooperate and negotiate with others in patterns that may differ from their family experiences. Their behavior is based on a set of personal values and principles derived from their experience and moral development.

According to Roberto (1992), they have "goal direction, clear values and beliefs, flexibility, security, autonomy, conflict tolerance, and neurotic-level symptoms under stress" (p. 12). Furthermore, they have a more defined *basic self* and less *pseudoself,* or less *fusion,* in close relationships, and they focus more on goal-directed activities. They typically evaluate themselves realistically and can be involved in intimate relationships without anxiety.

Clearly, higher levels of differentiation are not possible until adulthood. Although Bowen (1985) believed that no one living in his or her parents' home can be operating at a high level of differentiation, he also proposed that we tend to achieve a level of differentiation that is the same or lower than that of our parents, unless we attempt some purposeful intervention to change this pattern. Stated more simply, "like begets like" in terms of differentiation. Therefore, a child's or adolescent's predisposition for a general level of differentiation can be viewed in light of his or her parents' emotional patterns.

Midrange Levels of Differentiation

People functioning in the midrange of differentiation have "definite beliefs and values on important life issues but still tend to be overfocused on the opinions of others" (Roberto, 1992, p. 12). Some of their decisions are driven by emotional reactivity. They are concerned that others who are important to them will disapprove of their choices, and they adapt to please the other person. Kerr (1988) noted:

> They are sensitized to emotional disharmony, to the opinions of others, and to creating a good impression. They are apt students of facial expressions, gestures, tone of voice, and actions that may mean approval or disapproval. (p. 43)

They can react wildly to praise or criticism, being elated or dashed depending on whether they've received approval or disapproval. Rather than having self-determined goals, they seek love and approval. At work, their sense of success is driven by their superiors' approval rather than by their own values.

Lower Levels of Differentiation

Among the signs of low levels of differentiation (Roberto, 1992) are clinging or combative behaviors in a child or adolescent (Guerin & Guerin, 2002). People with low levels of differentiation are influenced excessively by others and dependent upon or reactive to their opinions. They have difficulty keeping their emotions in check, and they often deny feelings or outbursts that are out of proportion to external events. Boundaries between self and others are poorly defined. They tend to feel responsible for others or to blame them and have an inability to see themselves clearly in relation to others.

People with low levels of differentiation may feel a need for intense closeness to combat loneliness, or the opposite, a need for much distance to relieve fear of fusing with another. Their principles and values are based on emotional reactions or family prejudices rather than on a well thought-out personal identity (Bowen, 1985).

Relational Patterns and Differentiation of Self

Bowen (1985) wrote that we tend to form relationships with, and marry, persons at our same or a similar level of differentiation (Walsh & McGraw, 2002). Those who have a low level of differentiation show a connection between level of differentiation and co-dependency. As defined by Beattie (1987), a co-dependent individual has allowed another person's behavior to affect him or her to the extent that the co-dependent person is obsessed with controlling the dependent person's behavior. Specifically with regard to the alcoholic family, Kaufman and Kaufmann (1992), stated:

> Proof of the co-dependent's own adequacy becomes based on his or her abilities to keep the alcoholic sober. In other words, alcoholic and co-dependent worldviews are absolutely consistent. Alcoholics think other people make them drink, and co-dependents think they should be able to make the alcoholic not drink. The same unrealistic efforts to gain self-esteem by controlling the uncontrollable are often modeled by both parents in an alcoholic family. (p. 214)

In co-dependent relationships, both partners fit into the low level of differentiation. Highly reactive emotional forces control the relationship. Partners describe feeling tied to the relationship even when it causes them pain. Physical or emotional symptoms in one member of the couple develop when the level of stress is too high for the relationship to manage, given the attending low level of personal differentiation.

Extent of differentiation also impacts individuals' effectiveness in work and organizational settings (Weinberg & Mauksch, 1991). The ability to maintain appropriate concentration on tasks, to adopt suitable organizational roles with peers, superiors, and subordinates, and to sustain productivity may be related closely to level of differentiation. Thus, understanding general levels of differentiation can be helpful in work relationships.

Assessment of Differentiation

The extent of differentiation in a family or work system may be assessed by testing the emotional reactivity in that system. To try this out, take some stance about what you believe or who you are that is different from that of others in the system, and observe the response. If others respond with their own "I" positions, differentiation is high; if you guessed right about the others being different from you then their "I" position will be different. If you were wrong and they are genuine in agreeing with what you said then they will state their agreement from an "I" position and may or may not request that you keep their response confidential. Some people are not open at work about their positions on issues because they do not want to cause friction or fear retribution for disagreeing and remain silent. Silence usually means agreement in people's mind but it is not necessarily true. If they try to engage you in arguments to change your mind, differentiation is presumably lower. The best way to hypothesize about differentiation is noticing whether the other person or people try to get you to change you mind; awareness of the degree of emotional energy the individual(s) invests in trying to convince you that you are wrong about the issue also helps confirm/disconfirm your hypotheses. A terse negation of another's view, with voice tone that sounds rejecting demonstrates emotional reactivity as much as vociferous disagreement. Failure to agree to disagree about an issue generally indicates lower levels of differentiation.

In family interviews, level of differentiation may be assessed by how well individuals can express a feeling or thought without eliciting emotional reactions from other family members. Can one person cry or express anger and be comforted or confronted by the rest of the family without everyone else dissolving into tears or displaying explosive tempers? In the special-needs family, can family members show empathy and understanding for the child with a disability without feeling as if they were responsible for the disability or feeling guilt at not having the disability themselves? In at-risk families, do the family members see themselves as victims and blame others for their situation? Do they turn these feelings inward, displaying the accompanying low self-esteem, and become frozen and unable to act? Do they explode and externalize their feelings?

A convenient way to assess one's own level of differentiation is to determine the extent to which returning to one's parent's home elicits feelings that were familiar and uncomfortable during childhood and adolescence. As an indication of your personal level of differentiation, how quickly do you revert to feeling like a child rather than an adult in your family or revert to old patterns of relating with family members? In a school situation, parents who come to a conference and act like children instead of adults may have slipped back into a familiar relationship pattern learned in childhood.

As mentioned, differentiation represents the core construct (Guerin & Guerin, 2002) in the Bowen model (1985). This process extends throughout the lifespan, with the individual moving from the total dependence of infancy toward increasing independence and self-integration. To a great extent, differentiation represented, for Bowen, the struggle for emotional development in the face of the forces of family history. As such, it is a major determinant of quality of life in relationships. Although differentiation is a concept specific to the Bowen model, it integrates well with other major lines of thought in family systems theory.

Manifestations of Differentiation

For school and community professionals, the concept of differentiation may be meaningful in terms of making sense of both child behavior and organizational dynamics within the community or school. In the earlier grades, children who exhibit clingy behavior, excessive dependence on adult direction, and less well-developed peer relationships are likely to come from families with low levels of differentiation. In adolescence, low levels of family differentiation may be expressed by intolerance for others, personally-loaded rebellious behavior such as name calling, and limited acceptance of changes in schedule, routine, or expectations. Low differentiation also may be expressed through chemical dependency, teen pregnancy, and rigid thinking.

Families of a child with special needs may show a tendency toward lower levels of differentiation. Chronic stress and chronic anxiety are a strain on even a healthy family's adaptive capabilities. When coping with the functional and emotional needs of a child with a disability, personal emotional issues may take precedence over reason and thought. Thus, even when the parents of a child with special needs are receiving the correct information, their capacity to use the information to change their behavior effectively may be limited by their anxiety and lower levels of differentiation of self.

Children who are at risk often come from families who are functioning at lower levels of differentiation. Like families having a child with special needs, these families face chronic stress and anxiety that make constructive coping difficult. The underorganization and disorganization evident in some at-risk families is a sign of stressors that make higher levels of differentiation less frequent.

From a school and community perspective, colleagues and administrators who exhibit a flexible approach to managing children and youth, instructional methods, and system policy are likely to have higher levels of personal differentiation. These professionals are able to understand and relate to a variety of perspectives, to consider multiple factors in decision making, and to engage in healthy and productive collaboration.

Emotional Transmission

In addition to believing that the members of a family tend to have similar levels of differentiation, Bowen contended that each family also has its own set of issues that elicit intense emotional reactions (Fenell & Weinhold, 2003). For some families, the tension centers on gender-role issues, with rules about what women should do or how men should behave. For others, issues of religion, having or not having children, or achievement are deeply rooted in family myths and values. Family myths and secrets are often attached to a specific stage of the family life cycle. Passing these issues from generation to generation and the patterns of relating over generations of family life are known as emotional transmission.

Transmission of Family Issues

Emotional transmission within a family can be seen in how children and youth react to peers from different cultures or backgrounds. Satir and Baldwin (1983) described families as being either open or closed in structure. Open family systems allow for change, depending upon the family's life cycle stage as well as the emotional and relational context. People from open family systems learn values and morals that do not embody extreme prejudices or judgments about others. Acceptance of self and others is the theme transmitted through the life of families characterized as open. The emotional transmission of unconscious and unresolved issues is low in these families.

In contrast, closed family systems are noted by their level of rigidity and negativity. These families are based on control, dominance, and conformity. Children in closed families develop low self-esteem, indicated by their judgmental attitude toward others. Prejudicial values are transmitted in closed systems across many generations. The emotional transmission of unresolved issues, family secrets, and inappropriate myths is common in closed families.

Assessment

To discover which prejudices and family issues have been emotionally transmitted in your family, ask yourself the following questions:

What topics did your parents never talk about?
What don't your children or other children/youth talk to you about?

What things about your life would surprise or shock your parents or colleagues? What is a statement guaranteed to induce guilt or shame in you?
Where did this statement originate?

In terms of group activities in the school or community, values-clarification exercises often will uncover issues or prejudices that have been emotionally transmitted to children and youth. A simple exercise such as the following may help identify family issues:

> How would you complete the following sentences? Women are....
> Men are.... A wife is.... A husband is.... A mother is.... A father
> is.... How would your parents complete these sentences? How are
> the two sets of answers different?

Often the experience of being asked to identify and discuss one's own values will help begin the process of breaking the cycle of transmission.

Family Patterns of Emotional Transmission

According to Bowen's theory, emotional transmission also is responsible for patterns of family relating over generations (Fenell & Weinhold, 2003; Guerin & Guerin, 2002; Jacobson & Gurman, 1995; Roberto, 1992). As he developed his theory, Bowen classified family relational patterns as being either cohesive or explosive in nature (Guerin, 1976).

Cohesive Families

Cohesive family systems have extended families that usually cluster together in a limited geographic area. Communication in these families is characterized by frequent telephone calling, visiting, and shared communication. Immediate and extended family members are taken into account in making various family decisions, such as where the family will live, take vacations, and attend church and school.

At the extreme, cohesive families can be highly intrusive systems that do not allow for personal differentiation or privacy. The pattern observed in dysfunctional cohesive families parallels the enmeshed family pattern described in chapter 3 and the Appendix (structural family therapy). Typically, dysfunctional cohesive families show extensive "leakage," or emotional transmission of anxiety, from the extended family into the immediate family.

I married into a cohesive family—very different from mine. My husband's family didn't shut bathroom doors, they communicated daily even though nothing new or unusual was expected. Nothing happened to one family member without it affecting everyone else in the family. When Jennifer didn't get into her preferred sorority, the matriarch commented, "It is as if there were a death in the family."

I was told regularly to "eat more," as if I were a child, and that I needed to gain weight. I couldn't gain weight, as I had my mom's genetic, underweight structure. Friends called me "tapeworm" because I ate so much without gaining weight. My husband's family could only see that I was different from theirs and they were anxious to make me become like them. Everyone knew everything about others in the family.

The maternal grandmother lived across the street from where my husband grew up. The two of them speculated on how much our wedding gifts cost and whether to keep or exchange them. My husband chose the china pattern. About a month after we were married, his mom came to our home when I was out of town and rearranged our furniture. I always felt an undercurrent of tension about things and seldom relaxed or felt "in my element" around his family.

Looking back many years later, I saw my husband's family differently. They were the opposite of my family of origin—and healthier in some ways.

Explosive Families

Explosive family systems are characterized by extensive fragmentation (Guerin, 1976). From family roots in one geographic location, in fewer than two generations the extended family has scattered over a wide area. This family system is characterized by few ongoing relationships between members. The immediate family is on its own, without much support from the extended family. Family contacts tend to be ritualized and predictable, such as holidays and family reunions. Family members generally do not share their everyday lives with one another or really know one another at an intimate level.

This type of multigenerational pattern may leave the special-needs family without extended family resources for helping with the functional and emotional demands of a child with a disability. Therefore, the stress in the immediate family may be higher. For families that historically are explosive in nature, outside support services are especially important to the family's well-being. This is the topic of chapter 9.

At the most severe level of the explosive family system, the extended family becomes fragmented in response to a dramatic family event that leaves members not speaking to one another over many years or even generations. This type of avoidance is known as an *emotional cutoff*. Explosive families that are dysfunctional parallel disengaged families, as seen in the structural model described in chapter 3 and the Appendix.

Although the level of contact in highly explosive families is minimal, the level of differentiation is extremely low. A couple who has moved to another area to take the "geographic cure" from their family may be as poorly differentiated as a couple who lives next door to their in-laws and sees them every day. In both cases, if the decisions about living arrangements are made in reaction to issues stemming from the family of origin, the level of emotional reactivity to the nuclear family is high. The emotional transmission of family anxiety results in the couple's decisions of where to live being dictated to reduce that anxiety. In one case, anxiety is relieved by closeness; in the other, by avoidance.

Friedman (1986) discussed how emotional transmission can continue through multiple generations. He gave this example related to "individuals who have been catapulted out of their families to achieve."

> The "standard bearer" usually is the oldest male, or the only male, or anyone, male or female, who has replaced a significant progenitor two or even three generations back. Such individuals have great difficulty giving emotion or time to their marriage or their children…. Success has the compelling drive of ghosts behind it. They have too much to do in the short span of a lifetime. In addition, failure is more significant because it is not only themselves or even their own generation that they will have failed. (pp. 420–421)

Manifestations of Emotional Transmission

The process of emotional transmission can be seen in many children and youth. For example, overachievers often feel compelled to make up for some failure or unhappiness in their parents' lives or for the disability of another sibling (Seligman, 1991c). They may be pushed by the expectations of their parents or grandparents beyond their level of ability. The aggressive child may come from a physically abusive or aggressive family. Parents who abuse their children or one another are more likely than nonabusive parents to have grown up in an abusive environment themselves (Ammerman & Hersen, 1990b; Meier & Sloan, 1984; Peled, Jaffe, & Edleson, 1995).

Depression also is a symptom that often is transmitted through many generations of family life. Severe depression—unexpressed anger turned inward— results from a context that does not tolerate the expression of anger. In these families, people believe that displays of anger will precipitate a crisis or that someone will be extremely hurt by the anger. This pattern of fear around anger typically has many generations of unexpressed and unresolved feelings behind it.

My mother told us a story about her revered father, a gentleman farmer whose passion was rarely seen, unless values he held sacred were violated. The story goes that Thomas was on the large porch talking with the "hired hands" on the farm. One of them made a disparaging remark about another hired hand on the porch being an "idiot." Although the man indeed was of low intelligence, it was a hateful comment that stirred my grandfather's ire. Within a second, he knocked the man who made the comment off the porch. Thomas was afraid he had killed the man and vowed never to show his anger again.

From that experience, my grandfather passed down a multigenerational process of not expressing anger. His family had an unspoken proscription against expressing anger, and my mother and siblings passed that down to their children, who continue to pass it down to the next generation. Incidentally, some of the men in the family also suffer from depression.

Realizing the forces of emotional transmission may help the professional to remain nonjudgmental about certain prejudices, values, or ways of relating that are evidenced by children and their families. When these issues are viewed as multigenerational in origin rather than personal, more objectivity and easier problem resolutions are possible. The professional can help reduce reactivity to prejudice and other manifestations of those who have lower levels of differentiation.

Birth Order

Theories of personality related to ordinal sibling position were developed by Freud and Adler in the early 1900s. Family constellation has also been a major topic of Walter Toman (1993). Murray Bowen based much of his theory on Toman's description of family constellation. One of the factors often considered when looking at historical patterns in families is sibling position (see Sulloway, 1996, which brings sibling position into focus). Literature regarding siblings has addressed birth order as well as circumstances within the immediate and extended family at the time each of the siblings is born.

Since the 1970s, the trend has been to focus on birth order while also going beyond where a child is in the family constellation by considering what was happening in the immediate and extended family at the time of each sibling's birth and extended the consideration to the psychological position of the sibling. In defining sibling status, the psychological position includes consideration of family crises, death of a sibling or other member of immediate or extended family, time intervals between siblings, family size, gender of siblings, talent and/or beauty with their impact, special place (e.g., only girl/boy, twins), effects of disabilities, illnesses, trauma, and favoritism. Beyond simple birth order, these other considerations represent how individuals fit into the family system and are predictive of the siblings behavior as well as how they will interact with other family members. "It is the actions and interactions within the family and the interpretations that each person assigns to these that give initial meaning to children's lives and to the family as a whole" (Bitter, Roberts, & Sonstegard, 2002; p. 46).

Personality Factors

Adler and other researchers characterized differences in personality according to whether they are firstborn or laterborn.

Firstborns

On the basis of his observations, Adler (1959) characterized firstborn siblings as dependable, conforming, and believing in rule and responsibility. He further hypothesized that as adults, firstborns tend to have a feeling of natural power. Nichols and Schwartz (2004) characterized firstborns as "having a tendency to identify with power and authority: They employ their size and strength to defend their status and try to minimize the cost of having siblings by dominating them" (p. 124).

Others (Leman, 1989; Somit, Arwine, & Peterson, 1996; Toman, 1993) also have written on birth order. Additional descriptions of firstborns include being "driven," scholarly, ambitious, serious, and critical of their work. Leonardo da Vinci was suggested as an example of a self-critical firstborn. On the down side, firstborns also have been described as inflexible, negative, and selfish. They, too, may reflect more than take action, as well as sticking to a decision without taking into consideration other alternatives.

Examples of firstborn presidents in the United States (Somit, Arwine, & Peterson, 1996) are as follows:

George Washington   Franklin D. Roosevelt
John Adams   Harry S. Truman
James Madison   Lyndon B. Johnson
James K. Polk   Gerald R. Ford
Ulysses S. Grant   Jimmy Carter
Warren G. Harding   Bill Clinton
Calvin Coolidge

The authors also listed the following Supreme Court Justices as firstborns:

Stephen Breyer   Lewis F. Powell, Jr.
Anthony Kennedy   Harry A. Blackmun
John Paul Stevens   Warren E. Burger
William H. Rehnquist

Laterborns

Laterborns, according to Adler, tend to be more active, aggressive, and nonconforming. Youngest children were described as having a tendency toward dependency and passivity. Nichols and Schwartz (2004) characterized them as "underdogs," stating that "laterborns are more inclined to identify with the oppressed and to question the status quo. They're more open to experience because this openness aids them… in finding an unoccupied niche" in the family (p. 124). In their view of Adlerian theory, the family ends up as a collection of niches rather than a "shared" family context. Nichols and Schwartz suggested that, among other good examples of laterborns are Joan of Arc, Marx, Lenin, Jefferson, Rousseau, and Bill Gates.

Adler's Sibling Identification Constructs

Among the theoretical constructs that Adler developed to explain sibling identification are dethronement, enthronement, and deidentification.

Dethronement

Adler (1959) developed a number of different theoretical constructs to explain the process of sibling identification. One is the concept of dethronement, a process affecting firstborns following the birth of a sibling (Schvaneveldt & Ihinger, 1979). The child who has been the sole recipient of parental care in the past loses a certain status within the family and feels rejected. This helps to explain the firstborn's need to conform and excel in an effort to regain the throne, or status in the family.

Enthronement

Another construct that has been derived from Adlerian theory is that of enthronement (Shulman & Mosak, 1977), which describes the relationships of youngest children in the family. Enthronement is the process whereby parental forces operate to favor the final child and tend to be somewhat smothering. Youngest children are never forced to experience dethronement, nor do they need to be competitive to gain a special family role. But they may depend upon the power of the baby role to provide their major sense of identification and esteem, resulting in a passive and dependent personality.

Deidentification

A final construct derived from Adler is that of deidentification (Niels, 1980), which is used primarily to describe the personality development of laterborn children. The premise is that laterborns observe areas in which their older siblings are proficient and avoid competing in those areas. Instead, they choose areas of interest that typically are nonconforming and different from those of their older siblings. Second children often look for vulnerabilities in the oldest child and excel in those areas in order to gain praise from parents and teachers (Corey, 2005).

Toman's Framework for Birth Order and Relationships

Building on the work of Adler (1959), Walter Toman (1993) developed a theoretical framework for the impact of siblings on personal identification and relationship patterns that takes into account temporal birth order as well as the gender of siblings. Toman maintained that siblings are important in the identification process through which children acquire a basic social/sexual sense of themselves and subsequent patterns of relating to others.

Based on clinical observations, Toman predicted relational patterns with same and opposite gender friends, as well as choice of marriage partners and potential for marital success in terms of birth order and gender of siblings.

Duplication Theorem

Toman (1993) proposed the duplication theorem, in which "other things being equal, new social relationships are more enduring and successful the more they resemble the earlier and earliest (intrafamilial) social relationships of the persons involved" (p. 78). According to this theorem, marital relationships are easiest when a partner is chosen whose sibling constellation pattern is complementary rather than conflicting with one's own in terms of sibling rank and gender.

For example, when an oldest brother of sisters marries a youngest sister of brothers, the relationship is complementary. When an oldest brother of brothers marries an oldest sister of sisters, the relationship is conflicting in terms of sibling constellation. In conflicting relationships, the partners both hold the same sibling roles. Thus, they compete with each other rather than having personalities that complement one another or work well together.

Other Sibling Factors

Within the concept of birth order, predictions about sibling personality must take into account other aspects of the family constellation as well as ordinal sibling position. Large families may have several sibling subgroups in which, depending upon the ages and spacing between children, several children function as oldest or only children (Toman, 1993).

For example, in a two-child family with at least a 7-year age difference between siblings, both children will be, functionally, only children.

Psychological effects of sibling status also may be mediated by age spacing between siblings. From a survey of 2,200 boys, Peterson and Kunz (1975) found that younger siblings were perceived most positively by their older brothers when the spacing between them was either less than 12 months or greater than 4 years.

The gender of sibling groups, too, must be taken into account in the concept of birth order. Female-dominated sibling groups tend to be oriented around language, accommodation, caregiving, and prosocial interactions (Abramovitch, Corter, & Lando, 1979; Brody & Stoneman, 1983). Male-dominated sibling groups are more physically active and challenging in nature (Abramovitch et al., 1979; Cicirelli, 1972; Johnson, 1982).

Effect of a Sibling With a Disability

Finally, the presence of a sibling with a disability may change the expected birth-order effects in sibling groups (Gargiulo, 2006, Turnbull & Turnbull, 2001). As discussed in chapter 3, Daniels-Mohring (1986) found that an oldest sibling with emotional disturbance tends to lose some personal power and rank in the expected sibling hierarchy. In families in which the sibling with the disability is the oldest, a younger sibling may behave as the functional eldest child. No matter what the actual sibling position of the child with the disability, other siblings may be required to accept responsibility beyond their years if the child with special needs has extensive physical or emotional demands.

After studying 237 siblings of children with congenital disabilities, Breslau (1982) found that, for males, younger siblings of children with disabilities scored higher on psychological impairment than did older siblings of children with disabilities. This effect was particularly pronounced for siblings who were fewer than 2 years younger than the child with the disability. For females, the effect was opposite, with older siblings evidencing more impairment than younger ones.

Breslau concluded that, for girls, the role of oldest female tends to bring with it an increased sense of responsibility for the child with the disability, which may cause her to have depressive/anxious feelings that are more intense than the general stress of other siblings in the family. For males, the impact of being born into a family with an infant having a disability preceding them by fewer than 2 years tends to put them at risk for psychological impairment later in life.

Bowen's Theory on Sibling Position

Bowen's perspective on sibling position functions as a bridge between the birth-order literature and the conceptualization of the family as an active system. Bowen (1985) proposed that knowledge of birth order offers some guidelines within which to predict an individual's family-role assignment. His framework examines the sibling position of people in past and present generations in an attempt to discover family patterns that may have arisen concerning the emotional value associated with the different sibling positions (Nichols & Schwartz, 2004).

For example, if three generations of women are all oldest daughters, family expectations and roles will be passed on about how an oldest daughter should operate. The family pattern might consist of oldest daughters' taking care of their parents and not marrying or leaving home until they are well into adulthood. This pattern sets up a family script that may be acted out generation after generation outside of the conscious awareness of family members. The third-generation oldest daughter may have to struggle with her own needs, her present social culture, and the unconscious demands of her family pattern. If she breaks out of the script and marries young or moves away from her parents to pursue a career, she may feel unexplained anxiety stemming from her abandoning this standard.

In short, certain patterns of personality tend to go along with certain sibling positions. To discover the significance of sibling factors in the life of a child or adolescent, one must take into account ordinal sibling position and also family size, spacing between siblings, and the gender of siblings. With this information, the professional may be better able to understand the personalities of children and their interactions with peers.

Triangulation

According to Bowen (1985), any two-person emotional system is inherently unstable. When two people become anxious about negotiating closeness and distance in their relationship, the anxiety is resolved most easily by bringing in a third person (Goldenberg & Goldenberg, 2004). This results in lowering anxiety between the twosome and creating an emotional triangle (Walsh & McGraw, 2002).

Usually, the least differentiated person in the family is the one drawn in by the dyad (Guerin & Guerin, 2002). Individuals who have higher levels of differentiation of self are more able to observe and control the patterns of relating within a triangle. Individuals with lower levels of differentiation of self tend to be reactive to tensions within the triangle.

Triangles

Bowen (1985) contended that the most stable relational systems are composed of three-person emotional configurations called triangles. Triangles are the building blocks of all systems, including families, work systems, and peer groups. Any emotional system is made up of a series of interlocking triangles.

For example, the student in Figure 4.1 was involved in three different but overlapping triangles when he was reprimanded for stealing lunch money from a peer. The peer reported the stealing to their teacher, who relayed the information to the student's mother. That evening, the student's mother and father considered the problem and determined the consequences for their son. In Figure 4.1, Triangle 1 involves the student, the teacher, and the peer. Triangle 2 includes both parents and the child. The third triangle consists of the student, the teacher, and the mother.

Bowen used the term *triangulation* to describe the pattern of emotional reactions within a particular triangle. This pattern is fueled by emotional reactivity within the system

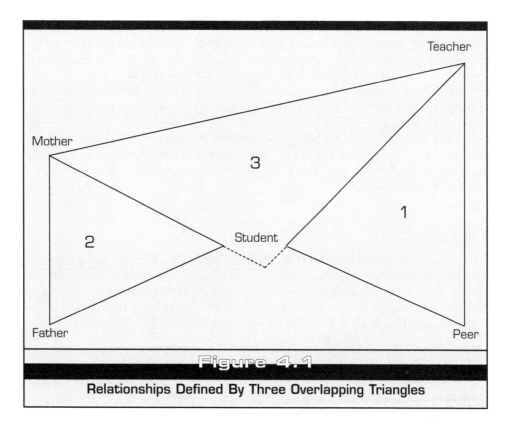

Figure 4.1

Relationships Defined By Three Overlapping Triangles

(Roberto, 1992). The process of triangulation can stabilize anxiety and conflict between two people by the following forces:

> The twosome works to preserve the togetherness, lest one become uncomfortable and form a better togetherness elsewhere. The outsider seeks to form a togetherness with one of the two-some.... The emotional forces within the triangle are constantly in motion from moment to moment. (Bowen, 1976, p. 76)

In dysfunctional families, when emotional forces produce anxiety, patterns of relationships begin to repeat themselves and people eventually have fixed roles in relation to one another.

Parent and Child

In the case of a child or adolescent, the typical triangulation occurs between two parents and one child. Satir called this relationship the primary triad (Satir & Baldwin, 1983). She believed that this triad is the main determinant of the child's identity, self-esteem, and relational patterns. When a family has marital discord, the parent who is feeling most alienated may turn to the child to feel emotional closeness (Nichols & Schwartz, 2004). This child may be favored for involvement with parents in the triangle because of the family's emotional transmission. For example, the child's place in a certain sibling position may be emotionally important to the parent(s), or his or her personality may remind the parents of themselves or one of their siblings, triggering identification issues (Kerr, 1988).

To differentiate a self and develop a fluid sense of self is difficult in a triangled relationship across generational boundaries. In times of anxiety or family stress, the lack of differentiation typically is expressed by the appearance of behavioral or psychiatric symptoms in the most vulnerable member of the triangle—the child. The child who is triangulated is at risk for physical, emotional, or academic problems (Kerr, 1988; Nichols & Schwartz, 2004). In many ways, that is the crux of this book as it relates to children and youth with special needs.

Remarriage

Another example of triangulation is found in second marriages in which the husband and wife initially connect by comparing the breakups of their former marriages and the abusiveness of their ex-spouses. The ability to focus on their former relationships may be the third leg of the triangle that keeps an optimum level of distance in the marital relationship. Chapter 7 in this book addresses the issues of step/blended families.

Families and Community

In times of family distress, the family system may triangulate with an outside force such as the school, social agencies, the courts, or the mental health system. If the emotional tension can be blamed on that outside system or community agency, the family may unite to remain calm.

This form of triangulation often occurs when school or community personnel are faced with evidence of family abuse. Unless steps are taken to avoid triangulation, the family, as soon as it is confronted about the abuse or as soon as Child Protective Services is contacted, the social worker or school professional may become the "bad guy" who is attempting to destroy an otherwise happy family. The family then bonds together and the outside agency serves the role of the third, distant leg of the triangle. To avoid being cast in this position, professionals must maintain their neutrality with these families and focus on keeping open communication among all parties.

Triangles may overlap, and problems in one system, such as the family, may create problems in another system, such as the school (Friedman, 1986) or the community. When dealing with a highly distressed family, if the school personnel find themselves arguing with each other or feeling anxious, overlapping triangles possibly are the cause.

In the example of the student reprimanded for stealing, three triangles were operating. If communication between parties is clear, if levels of differentiation are adequate, and if there are no unresolved or underlying issues among members of the triangles, the problem may be resolved smoothly. If the stealing issue becomes overshadowed by unresolved anxieties between people involved in the triangles, however, the forces of triangulation are operating and the stealing may be exacerbated rather than handled effectively.

For example, if the mother believes that the teacher does not manage her classroom adequately, she may not discipline her son for his behavior. If the father believes that his son is a "mama's boy" and is angry at his wife for giving in to their son, he may explode at the boy or at his wife and reenact his wife's relationship with her abusive father rather than negotiating appropriate discipline. In each of these scenarios, triangulation is in operation.

Professionals in schools and the community can provide a stabilizing force to help children and youth by collaborating with family systems therapists, counselors, or other professionals. Writing about conjoint systemic change in the family and school, Wendt and Ellenwood (1994) clarified a number of means of collaborating, using case studies to demonstrate how the process can work. Community agencies and families can work together effectively to decrease triangulation and its negative impact on children and their families.

Detriangulation

To become disentangled:

1. First, know that the triangle exists.
2. Do not take sides in a conflicting situation.
3. Do not talk to another person in the triangle about a third person and do not listen when someone tries to discuss a third person with you.

For example, if a child comes to you complaining about a professional, a response that would promote detriangulation is, "I'm sorry you feel that way, but I think that things will have a chance to get better only if you talk to that person. I'd be glad to help you set up a meeting with her."

Triangulation also can take place between colleagues in a system. If a co-worker tends to talk to you about other people, the easiest way out of the triangle is to ask that person something about himself or herself or to volunteer something about yourself or your values. These statements are geared toward increasing the connection between you and the colleague, thereby decreasing the need for triangulation to manage the anxiety between the two of you. For further discussion of how community and school professionals can stay out of triangles, see chapter 12.

Triangles or triadic relationships are not dysfunctional in themselves. They actually are the basic building blocks of any system (Jacobson & Gurman, 1995). When the intensity between two people becomes uncomfortable, bringing in a third person will diffuse the tension and allow the system to operate with less anxiety. It is only when the anxiety level within a two-person system cannot be managed that the process of triangulation comes into operation. In this process, relationships are indirect and issues are not resolved openly. The forces of constantly changing alliances keep the tension in the system alive.

Genograms

One technique for studying family history, the social history, typically involves many pages of written material without any standardized format. To use the information presented in a social history, community and school professionals must read the material, organize it in their minds, and assimilate it into their experience of the family.

A more helpful technique maps family history on a chart something like a family tree, called a genogram. The genogram can help the professional and the family view symptoms within a much larger context. The genogram (McGoldrick, 1999a) organizes up to three generations of family data in a one-page visual representation (Nichols & Schwartz, 2004). A genogram can aid the professional in identifying multigenerational patterns, family roles, sibling position, important triangles, and the timeline of significant family events.

Symbols are used, in which squares represent males and circles represent females. The genogram for a two-parent family with two children, a son age 15 and a daughter age 11, is illustrated in Figure 4.2. As much as possible, fathers are drawn on the left side and mothers to the right of them. Siblings are drawn oldest to youngest from left to right. Marriages and generations are connected by a series of horizontal and vertical lines. Figure 4.3 shows these and other commonly used symbols.

The hypothetical genogram in Figure 4.4 conveys the following information: John, age 45, and Elizabeth, age 42, were married for 15 years and had two children, John, Jr., age 13, and Marsha, age 10. In 2004, the couple was separated and subsequently divorced. John remarried immediately and now is expecting a child with his second wife, Selina, age 30. This is Selina's first marriage.

The genogram also conveys that John's parents are both deceased. They died within 2 years of one another, during the period between 2001 and 2003. John's father died of a heart attack and his mother died of "loneliness." At the time of death, they were ages 75 and 70, respectively. John is the youngest of three children, and the only son. His two older sisters, 48 and 50 years old, are both married and have children. Elizabeth's parents are both still living. Her father is 64 years old, and her mother is 62 years old. Elizabeth has a younger sister, age 40, who has been divorced since 1999 but has been involved in a relationship for the past 5 years. Elizabeth's sister has no children.

As indicated in this example, much information can be communicated quickly and concisely through genograms. A good way to begin practicing this technique is to draw your own family genogram. Once you become adept at drawing a basic genogram, you can begin to use the genogram to indicate major triangles, family roles, areas of significant conflict, emotional cutoffs, multigenerational patterns, and family nodal events. For more in-depth study of the use of genograms, see McGoldrick (1999a), as well as McGoldrick, Gerson, and Schellenberger, 1999.

Means of Differentiating

Bowen wrote that when one person in a family becomes free from the reactive emotional process, the lowering of anxiety can filter down throughout the family's relationship system (Guerin & Chabot, 1992; Guerin & Guerin, 2002). By remaining free of the family's reactive emotional process, a therapist can assist in beginning this filtering-down process. Potentially useful to school and community professionals is a description of the process that Bowen recommended for therapists to be more capable of such work, which was described in Guerin and Chabot (1992).

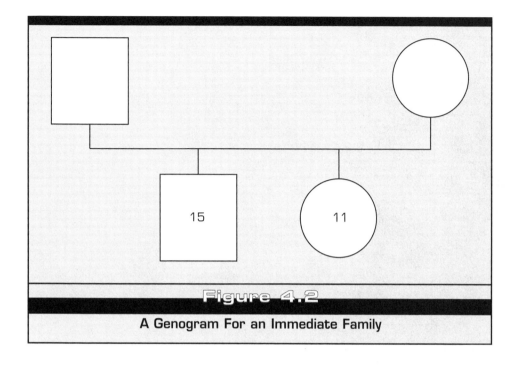

Figure 4.2

A Genogram For an Immediate Family

1. *Know the facts about your family relationship system.* Bowen encouraged his trainees to construct comprehensive family diagrams to document the structural relationships among members of their family and to gather facts about the timing of important events such as deaths, births, and so forth, which he termed *nodal events*. He also taught the importance of including in the family diagram evidence of physical and emotional dysfunction, relationship conflicts, and emotional cut-offs, which he viewed as indicators of a family's level of emotional functioning

2. *Become a better observer of your family, and learn to control your own emotional reactivity to these people.* Bowen charged therapists-in-training with this central task, which was to be accomplished on planned visits with key members from their family of origin.

3. *Detriangling self from emotional situations.* This entails developing an ability to stay *nonreactive* during periods of intense anxiety within one's own family system. To foster the process of *detriangling*, Bowen encouraged therapists-in-training to visit their families of origin at times of predictably high tension, such as the serious illness or imminent death of a key family member. During these visits, the goal was to make contact with family members around an anxiety-ridden issue, to remain less emotionally reactive than other family members, and not to choose sides when competing influences and differences of opinions led to conflict in relationships.

4. *Develop person-to-person relationships with as many family members as possible.* This instruction was aimed at both fostering detriangulation and encouraging

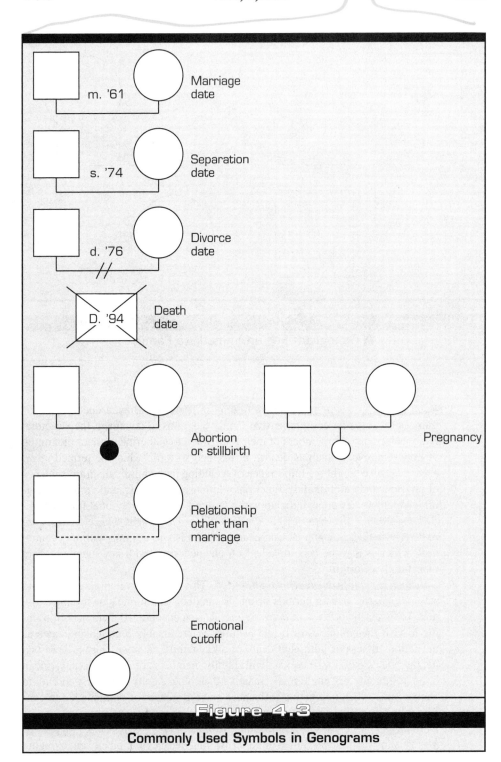

Figure 4.3

Commonly Used Symbols in Genograms

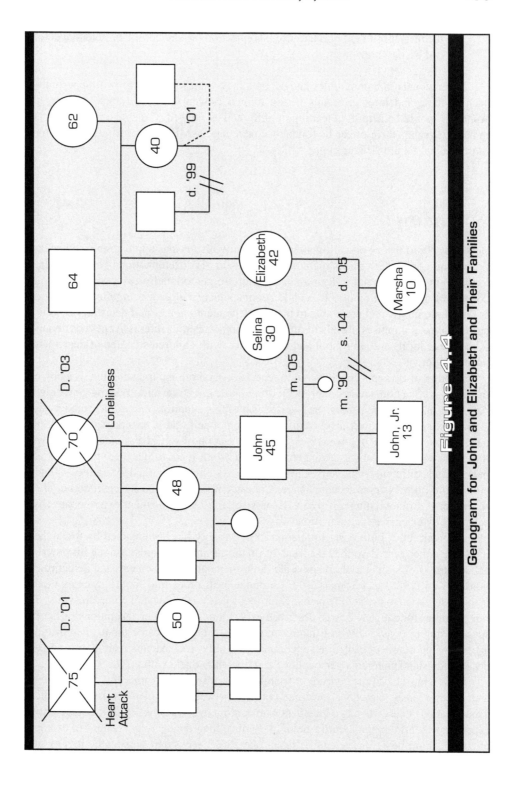

Figure 4.4

Genogram for John and Elizabeth and Their Families

the reestablishment of relationship connections where cutoffs or potential cutoffs had existed previously.

Professionals in communities and schools may want to pursue growth opportunities such as these and meet in groups with a trained Bowen family therapist. Reading the Appendix would be helpful in learning to differentiate the self. Capable therapists trained in family systems theories can be found by contacting AAMFT (American Association for Marriage and Family Therapists).

Summary

Bowen's (1985) theory on multigenerational family history has application to other family systems approaches. The cornerstone of this theory is differentiation of self and relates to the ability to think and reflect when encountering emotional pressures. Based on the concept of differentiation of self, a child becomes increasingly less emotionally dependent upon the family and more able to make independent choices and decisions as well as curb emotional impulses. Levels of differentiation are seen in submissiveness or defiance at the lower levels and, in school and community, with children's degree of dependence or self-initiative.

Another of Bowen's concepts, multigenerational emotional transmission, is a process in which dysfunction such as depression or alcoholism is transmitted across generations. The child on whom the parents are overfocusing their attention, due to their anxiety as a couple, is left with a lower level of differentiation of self that is also passed down to the next generation, again, at lower levels of differentiation of self in a grandchild. One way it may be seen is in the way some children and youth react to peers from cultures and backgrounds different from theirs. Closed family systems are marked by rigidity and negativity, and open systems accept change. Cohesive families, at the extreme, do not allow for personal differentiation or privacy. Explosive families, at the other extreme, are characterized by extensive fragmentation.

The concept of birth order in relation to personality has been studied by researchers including Adler, who described the traits of firstborns and laterborns. Among his theoretical constructs of sibling identification are dethronement, enthronement, and deidentification. Bowen (1985) and Toman (1993) brought birth order into family systems theory using observation to predict life paths. Their focus was on the value of complementary sibling positions for couples. Bowen described expectations that began generations earlier for specific sibling positions with a family (e.g., oldest daughter cares for parents in older age). The importance of birth order encompassed family size, spacing of children, and gender to understand children's personalities and how they relate with peers.

Bowen introduced the concept of triangulation, manifested within the family system, and unconsciously aimed at lowering conflict between two members of the family. Triangulation occurs when two members who conflict over an issue detour the anxiety they experience by bringing in a third person to stabilize their dyadic relationship. An example of triangulation being operational is when one parent seeks and obtains the loyalty and attention of one child by forming an alliance against the spouse. Triangulation can also be seen occurring within a community or school system as well as across systems or subsystems in any human system. Individuals are unwittingly involved in triangulation within the family and may generalize the process of involving a third person in a non-family system to reduce anxiety between two members who disagree at work or in another setting. Finally, family genograms have proven to be a good method for mapping family history as a basis for investigating family relationships. They can be used by social workers and counselors as well as other professionals in community and school contexts to provide a one-page summarization of birth order, nodal events in family life such as marriage, divorce, birth, death, emotional transmission, triangulation, cut-offs, degree of openness, and emotional boundaries.

Case Example

Megan, a 17-year-old high school senior, comes from a family consisting of her parents, both 34 years old, and her two younger brothers, Allen, 12, and Mark, 10. Her parents have been married for 17 years. Her father is employed as a salesman, and her mother is an administrative assistant.

Although Megan always had been an adequate student, her grades began to drop earlier this year, and she since then, she has been absent frequently. When the school counselor met with Megan to discuss these problems, Megan burst into tears and did not return to her classes for the remainder of the day. On more than one occasion, Megan had begun to cry during classes and asked to see her counselor.

Recently, Megan revealed that she and Chuck, her boyfriend of 4 years, were considering breaking up. She reported that Chuck had been spending more and more time with his friends and had told her that he needed his "space." Megan felt that she couldn't stand this rejection and had to end the relationship with Chuck. She also reported feeling that her parents were putting excessive pressure on her about applying for admission to colleges. She was too upset about her problems with Chuck to fill out her applications.

With gentle questioning, Megan admitted that she was fearful about rejection from college. She was not sure that her high school record was adequate in spite of her good grades. Attempting to establish a historical framework for Megan's attitudes, the counselor asked her about her parents' adolescence. Megan revealed the following family history information:

Megan's mother, Anne, is the youngest of two siblings, with a sister 2 years older. When Anne was 4 years old, her parents were divorced, and her father married a much younger woman. Subsequently he had three more children and did not keep in contact with Anne, her sister, or his ex-wife. Megan's grandmother was remarried 5 years later to an alcoholic. When Anne was 17 years old, she became pregnant with Megan. When Anne talked to her parents about her pregnancy, they kicked her out of the house. She then moved in with her boyfriend's (Megan's father's) family and the two of them married.

Megan's father, Albert, Jr., is the oldest of four siblings, all male. His younger brothers are 3, 5, and 7 years younger than he. Albert's father is an attorney, and his mother is a homemaker. They have been married to one another for 40 years. Albert was always an

"A" student and a football star. His family had planned for him to attend college and become an attorney like his father, his namesake. When his high-school girlfriend became pregnant, his parents demanded that Albert "do the right thing" and marry her. They let him know that they were disappointed in him. Albert was forced to go to work after graduation and did not return to pursue his college degree.

Questions and Comments

1. *How would you draw a genogram for this family?* Assume that it is 2006. [The reader can look at Figure 4.5 for feedback after drawing the genogram.]

2. *Using factors from the family history and genogram, how can Megan's behaviors be explained in a historical context?* [A good strategy is to use the chapter subtitles in order to write your speculations.]

   Megan's dependence upon her boyfriend is the result of low levels of differentiation and the emotional transmission of the shame related to her mother's out-of-wedlock pregnancy. Megan is at risk for becoming pregnant herself as part of the family "script" concerning achievement and failure.

   There is a primary triangle between Megan and her parents in which Megan's future is scripted to atone for her parents' failures. Megan has triangulated Chuck in an attempt to defuse the anxiety between her and her parents. By focusing on her relationship with Chuck, she avoids dealing with her anxiety about college and possible failure.

3. *What interventions might be used to help detriangulate Megan?*

   The counselor or social worker could help Megan identify triangulation in her family. She could give Megan information about colleges that are appropriate for her achievement level and assure Megan that her record is adequate for acceptance in college.

   During a meeting between Megan, her counselor, and her parents to discuss Megan's crying spells, Megan could be helped to bring up the issue of her parents' pressure on her. The family history of Megan's birth and the emotional cutoffs in her parents' families of origin are appropriate topics for discussion. Megan then would be liberated from the forces of unresolved loss in her parents' history and would be more likely to develop a higher level of differentiation and self-esteem.

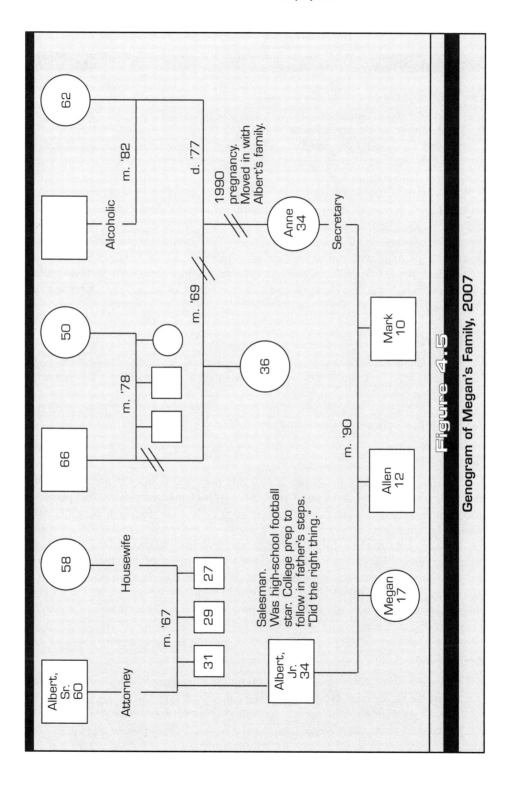

Figure 4.5
Genogram of Megan's Family, 2007

Extension Activities

Activity #1:

Reflection: Reflect on levels of differentiation in your family of origin, as well as your immediate family, if you are part of one.

Journal: How would you describe your family of origin in terms of emotional reactivity? To what extent does emotional reactivity make it difficult for the intellectual system to inform and guide decisions?

Journal: If you are married or in a partnership, how would you describe what you have observed (e.g., during holidays and other family gatherings) about your partner's family and their levels of differentiation? (Remember that those at higher levels of differentiation do not judge others, and they accept differences!) How would you compare and contrast your family of origin with that of your spouse or partner?

Journal: If you have children, consider the levels of differentiation in your immediate family members. What challenges do you and your spouse or partner face in being models for your children?

Activity #2:

Reflection: If you have held a job in the past, reflect on what kinds of experiences you faced at one job site in terms of the levels of differentiation present and how they impacted you.

Journal: What are some examples of higher and lower levels of differentiation that you have observed in a worksite?

Activity #3:

Constructing a genogram: Using information presented in this chapter, map out the genogram of your family of origin. If you cannot go back two generations, find people in your family who will share stories with you so you can develop an accurate picture of your family of origin.

Initially, just focus on filling in the factual information, then let the stories you remember hearing and the ones people repeat to you inform you of the interaction patterns that have been passed down over generations. You might want to audiotape stories if it won't change the frankness and genuineness of those telling the stories. The tapes later could become part of a family gift to other generations. It could be shared with cousins along with the genogram.

Activity #4:

Reflection: Think about your family of origin and immediate family (if you have one) in terms of the family relational patterns being cohesive or explosive.

Journal: Assuming you have or will have children, in what ways would you like to see things change in terms of emotional transmission so that the next generation of your family is healthier?

Activity #5:

In-Class/Training Discussion: The professional literature indicates that relationships are deeply affected by birth order. What examples have you noted related to birth order that support examples provided in this text? These might be from your family, your friends, or other families about whom you have substantial information.

Activity #6:

In-Class/Training Discussion: How have you seen triangles play out in family life or work contexts? In terms of triangulation, have you noticed any repeating patterns in others or yourself?

OR

In-Class/Training Discussion: What triangles of prominence have occurred in your family of origin?

Activity #7:

Constructing a Genogram: If you are part of an immediate family, construct a genogram for your youngest child. Even if you are in a blended family or have grown children, you can still construct the genogram.

Activity #8:

Journal: What human relationship patterns have passed down to your generation from other generations in your family of origin?

PART TWO

At-Risk Children, Resilient Children, and Children With Special Needs

Socioeconomic and Cultural Factors in Families

By being exposed to differing socioeconomic backgrounds and cultural influences, people can enhance their sensitivity to others (Johnson, 2005) and help to dispel stereotypes about families in the various cultural categories. Regardless of cultural background, families have more similarities than differences. They struggle with similar issues and demands throughout the life cycle and strive toward the same ends. Still, some differences place children and youth at increased risk. These factors include socioeconomic status, including poverty and homelessness, and ethnic/cultural values as reflected in the schools and community.

Many of the most common ethnic stereotypes derive more from the environmental influences of socioeconomic status than from ethnic background (Mirowsky & Ross, 2003). For example, a middle-class African American family has a lifestyle more similar to that of a middle-class Caucasian family than to the lifestyle of a poor African American family, regardless of common African heritage. As Wilson (1982), a sociologist, argued, "Class has . . . become more important than race in determining black life chances in the modern industrial period" (p. 389). Sociologists Mirowsky and Ross (2003) stated, "Education is the key to an individual's position in the stratification system. It forms the main link between the socioeconomic status of one generation and the next" (p. 78).

At the same time, ethnic background influences child and adolescent development. It also influences how families cope, express themselves, and interact with external systems such as schools (Shore, 2004). Rather than adhering to a single standard, professionals might ask themselves, "Within this person's experience, is this behavior adaptive, normal, or pathological?" For example, when African American, Latino, or Asian American parents discipline their child, they expect the child to indicate acceptance by lowering his or her eyes. Making eye contact may be interpreted by a parent from these backgrounds as defiance. By contrast, parents from Anglo-Saxon backgrounds expect their children to maintain eye contact to indicate attentiveness when they are being disciplined. Anglo children who lower their eyes may be thought of as being passively resistant.

Socioeconomic Differences

The most powerful cultural determinant of how families interact with society is socioeconomic status (Coleman, 1987). This is particularly evident when comparing middle-income families with families coping with poverty.

Poverty

As a consistent factor across cultures, persistent poverty was found to be strongly correlated with less optimal home environments. Studies recapped by Donovan and Cross (2002) indicate that as much as a half of the gap in achievement in preschool children and a third of the gap in achievement of elementary/secondary students can be attributed to high-income versus low-income families and their home learning environments. Parenting practices of those living in poverty manifest differently. For example, social disadvantage was correlated with harsh discipline by socially disadvantaged parents.

The following statistics represent the first year for which the U.S. Census Bureau took data in which respondents were allowed to list more than one race (Proctor & Dalaker, 2003). This does not allow absolute race comparisons between 2001 and 2002 but does indicate poverty trends.

- The official poverty rate in 2002 was 12.1%—up from 11.7% in 2001. In 2002, people below the official poverty thresholds numbered 34.6 million, a figure 1.7 million higher than the 32.9 million in poverty in 2001.
- At 16.7%, the poverty rate for children did not change between 2001 and 2002 but remained higher than that of 18–64 year-olds and seniors 65 years of age and older. The number of children in poverty increased to 12.1 million in 2002, up from 11.7 million in 2001.
- The poverty rates in 2002 for non-Hispanic whites (8.0% for those who identified with no other race groups) and Asians (10.0% to 10.3%, depending on the definition of race) were not different from the rates for the closest groups available in 2001. Among people who reported being black in 2002, 23.9% to 24.1% were in poverty, again depending on the definition of race. Both figures were higher than the 22.7% for those who reported being black in 2001. For Hispanics (who may be of any race), the

poverty rate was 21.8% in 2002, unchanged from 2001. In 2002, 7.2 million families (9.6%) were in poverty, up from 6.8 million (9.2%) in 2001.

• For married-couple families, the number in poverty and the poverty rate rose between 2001 and 2002 from 2.8 million to 3.1 million, and from 4.9% to 5.3%, respectively. The number of female householder families in poverty with no husband present increased to 3.6 million in 2002 from the 3.5 million in 2001. The poverty rate for these families was unchanged from 2001, at 26.5%. The poverty rate in the Midwest increased from 9.4% in 2001 to 10.3% in 2002. Poverty rates in the Northeast, South, and West were unchanged between 2001 and 2002.

• The number in poverty and the poverty rate for people living in the suburbs rose from 12.1 million and 8.2% in 2001 to 13.3 million and 8.9% in 2002. The number in poverty and poverty rate did not change in central cities or outside metropolitan areas between 2001 and 2002.

The trend is toward an increase in poverty overall in the United States and particularly in the Midwest. This is the second consecutive year in which the poverty rate and number living in poverty both increased over the previous year.

In that socioeconomic status is the most powerful cultural determinant of how families interact with society (Coleman, 1987), professionals in social service contexts, including schools, should learn as much as they can about responding to those living in poverty.

Weissbourd (1996) did indicate that most poor children are poor temporarily. In America, only 8% are poor for more than 6 years, and more than 30% experience poverty some time in their lives. About 17.5% of children who are poor live in ghettos, and about 19% of African American children live in ghettos. These children are at risk for failure in school or life.

School and community professionals are urged to take a strengths-based view in reaching out to all at-risk children/youth and their families (Allison et al, 2003; Maton, Schellenbach. Leadbeater, & Solarz, 2004). Weissbourd suggested that we view at-risk children as vulnerable but not create a self-fulfilling prophecy that dooms them to failure. He reminded us that "over 75 percent of poor children ages 6–11 have never experienced significant developmental delays, or emotional troubles, or a learning disability in childhood" (p. 17). Thus, we should keep in mind that not all children who are poor need extensive intervention.

Poverty, Achievement, and Disability

Professionals have long been clear that environmental factors influence student achievement. Murphy and Forsyth (1999) indicated that the social welfare of children and their families is declining. In looking at extensive literature and existing findings, they stated:

> These data reveal a society populated increasingly by groups of citizens that historically have not fared well in this nation, especially ethnic minorities and citizens for whom English is a second language. Concomitantly, the percentage of youngsters affected by the ills of the world in which they live—for example, poverty, unemployment, illiteracy, crime, drug addiction, malnutrition, and poor physical health—is increasing. (p. 8)

The relationship between poverty and childhood disability risks has been examined over time (Fujiura & Yamaki, 2000), and poverty has been described as a root cause in terms of increasing the odds of a child being born with or acquiring a disability. Birenbaum (2002) reflected on poverty, welfare reform, and the disproportionate rates of children who are poor having disabilities. In its 1999 annual report to Congress, the U.S. Office of Special Education and Rehabilitation Services (OSERS) data showed a 68% rate for students who are in special education living in homes where the income was below $25,000 a year. In the general population of youth, the rate was 39%.

After reviewing literature on poverty as impacting quality of life in families of children with disabilities, Park, Turnbull, and Turnbull (2002) reported that 28% of children aged 3 to 21 who have disabilities live below the poverty level set by the U.S. Census Bureau. They found five dimensions of impact on family: health, productivity, physical environment, emotional well-being, and family interaction.

In terms of the reality in which we in the United States live, the facts speak for themselves regarding the challenge of poverty in relation to both at-risk children/youth and children with disabilities. In this book the latter are referred to as children with special needs. In the following discussion we will consider three factors in relationship to socioeconomic issues: family systems factors, parent factors, and child/youth factors.

Family Systems Factors

One of the first issues that professionals face in working with low-income families is the reality of how a poor environment affects the normal workings of family life. Working with poor families from inner-city Philadelphia, Aponte (1976a, 1994, 1998; Aponte & DiCesare, 2002) found that the structure of these families (see chapter 3) was loose and undefined. He used the term "chaotic" to describe the lack of clear leadership, poorly defined boundaries, and unstable structure in these poor, inner-city families. His perceptions of the relationship between the professional and the family were that "the socioeconomic difference creates a communication gap that complicates the task of mutual understanding" (1976b, p. 432).

Underorganization → *more likely in poor families*

Aponte wrote about the underorganization in the poor family:

> This brings us to a specific phenomenon that is, I believe, central to understanding what it means to do therapy with the poor—underorganization. Social destitution in the absence of a strong sense of self and cohesive familial and social network can injure the fundamental structure of the individual's psychological development, the formation of family, and the vitality of a community. Individuals may fully develop neither their intellectual and emotional capacity, nor the ability to form intimate and committed personal relationships, nor their potential to perform effectively in society. Families may fail to serve as stable, safe, nurturing nests for their members. People may not learn to live in community where they learn to depend upon one another. Life becomes difficult, painful, and even frightening. (Aponte, 1994, p. 15)

In 1994 Aponte wrote: "People certainly suffer deprivation, but I believe that at the core they suffer a poverty of despair. This is a poverty that robs people of their souls—of meaning, purpose, and hope" (p. 1). To be socioeconomically disadvantaged represents an extreme stressor on the integrity of the family system. Because the adjustment of children and youth to the school and community environment is tied to the family's well-being, when poverty threatens family stability, the children will suffer. Children and youth from poor families obviously are at risk, and if a child with special needs is part of the poor family, the stress is multiplied.

Other Studies

Schoon and Parsons (2002) concluded that "the family context clearly plays an important role in enabling young children to fully develop their competencies" (p. 268). With a particular interest in resilience, these researchers contrasted socially disadvantaged families with socially advantaged families in children under 8 years of age. Among many other findings, they indicated that socioeconomically disadvantaged young boys are more at-risk than girls at the same socioeconomic disadvantage. Teenage motherhood was found to increase the risk for educational and behavior problems, and being born to a mother having children after age 30 was detrimental for socioeconomically disadvantaged families.

Large family size also had a detrimental impact on socially disadvantaged children. Early social disadvantage was found to have lifelong consequences related to completion of education, employment, and success. "The fact that young people with above average competences lose out against their more privileged peers suggests a tragic loss of potential" (Schoon & Parsons, 2002, p. 270).

Family involvement was found to make a difference in academic success in urban high school students (Scales et al., 2005). Knowing that families have a powerful effect on the success of their children in school, Lopez, Kreider, and Coffman (2005) looked to intermediary organizations and studied the results of helping to build capacity for family involvement.

Jeynes (2005) did a meta-analysis of 41 studies examining the relationship between parental involvement and the academic achievement of urban elementary school children (p. 237). He found that regardless of race or gender, any group will benefit from the advantages that parental involvement brings. Academic outcomes improve for all children and youth when their parents are involved in their education. Parental expectations and style were found to have strong relationship with academic outcomes.

Delsing, van Aken, Oud, De Bruyn, and Scholte (2005) studied family loyalty and adolescent problem behavior in relation to the family group effect. They found that in adolescents, internalizing and externalizing problem behavior was best predicted at the level of the family, versus the level of the individual adolescent. They also found that families who had less trustworthy/just systems demonstrated more internalization and externalization problem behaviors. In addition, adolescents viewed as less trustworthy/just had more problem behaviors. The researchers concluded that "processes at different levels of family functioning (e.g., individual, whole-family) should be taken into account when investigating associations between family characteristics and children's outcomes" (p. 127).

Parent Factors

The stress of financial instability influences how parents view themselves as providers for and protectors of their children. Parental stress influences their involvement with, and availability to, their children, their discipline style, and the value system that they teach. Chronic poverty is associated with family instability, violence in home or neighborhood, substance abuse, mental illness of parent, sexual abuse, physical abuse, as well as social isolation. School and community programs face a daunting task in providing services.

Economically-related factors influencing parenting include homeless families, single-parent and absent-parent families, and depressed parents.

Homelessness

On any given night in the United States, between 60,000 and 100,000 children are homeless, and children make up 24% of the homeless population (M. Walsh & Buckley, 1994). Of the children who are homeless, 43% do not attend school and 30% are one grade or more behind their peers (Hall & Maza, 1990).

Another study, by the U.S. Conference of Mayors in 2002, found that 41% of the homeless were families with children, and 5% were youth unaccompanied by an adult. The U.S. Bureau of the Census in 2000 estimated that 43,887 children/youth under age 18 were sleeping in emergency or transitional shelters for a single night. The National Network of Runaway and Youth Services estimated 1 million runaways in 1992, of which 300,000 were runaway homeless youth.

In a study by Kidd and Scrimenti (2004), 170 homeless families were composed of mostly African American women and children. The 170 families included 323 children. Typical of problems that homeless children/youth face is inadequate prenatal care. Nearly half of the babies lacking this care are born with a low birthweight. As a result, 50% are likely to die prior to turning 1 year of age. The study found that developmental delays in intellectual, emotional, and social realms were accompanied by hunger/poor nutrition, externalizing and internalizing behaviors, anxiety, and depression. Homelessness results in a major strain on children and youth, including psychological and physical health problems. Kidd and Scrimenti developed a survey to determine service needs, which they administered on the streets in varied settings.

Single, Unemployed, and Absent Parents

Numerous studies have shown that low-income mothers have the highest rate of depression of any demographic group (Eheart & Ciccone, 1982). Further, there is often no consistent, positive father figure in low-income families but, rather, a male "floater" (Fischgrund, Cohen, & Clarkson, 1987) or a father living in the home who is chronically out of work. If an unemployed father is living at home, he often is tyrannical in his authority and discipline. As Montalvo and Guitierrez (1983) wrote, "The more the man fails against competitive barriers of the American society, the more uncompromising and absolute his power must be at home" (p. 29).

Newcomb and Locke (2005) projected adversity factors (e.g., parent alcohol and drug-related problems, childhood maltreatment) in childhood and parenting for the future by looking at the moderating factor of polydrug use by mothers. Mothers with alcohol or substance abuse problems were found to be more likely to have poor parenting skills as a result of drug use.

A study of mothers' levels of differentiation of self (see chapter 4 and the Appendix) was conducted by Skowron (2005). She found that "greater differentiation of self among mothers predicted child competence" (p. 337) in relation to higher achievement in verbal and math areas, and also lower aggression. The mothers' differentiation of self predicted cognitive skills of children after controlling for the parents' level of education.

Depressed Parent

A child growing up in a home with an extremely depressed parent or a parent who is experiencing role loss resulting from joblessness will bring the effects of these concerns with him or her to the classroom.

> A 7-year-old who had been doing well in his first year of school suddenly began to be distracted in the classroom. He was not listening to the teacher's directions and had received numerous negative consequences over a 3-week period. After 3 weeks, when the teacher called home, she discovered that the father had been laid off from his job 1 month before.
>
> When asked, the boy volunteered that his father's job loss was a principal source of anxiety for him. The boy stated that he worried all the time about his family and money problems.
>
> The teacher began to make her school contacts directly with the father, who was at home. She told the father of his son's concerns and asked that the father provide some reassurance for the boy. She met with the father to devise a plan for getting his son's behavior back on track and for reinforcing the boy's behavior when he would begin to pay attention again.
>
> With this plan, the teacher was able to give the father a new identity as a powerful figure for his son, regardless of his temporary joblessness.

Meeting Parental Needs

Parental roles in the home often have an effect on which interventions will work with a student in the classroom and which ones will work in the home environment. When planning family contacts, school and community professionals must take into account parental needs and demands. Looking at parental needs, Eheart and Ciccone (1982) studied 36 low-income mothers whose children were diagnosed with developmental delays. The biggest problem reported by these mothers was the stress of meeting their children's basic needs, such as feeding, cleanliness, and safety. What the mothers wanted most in terms of services was a support group where they could talk to other mothers who were having similar problems.

Luthar and Latendresse (2005) studied parenting significant for preadolescent adjustment. The study group consisted of 614 sixth-grade students from high-income and low-income communities to determine if socioeconomic status (SES) was related to impact of parenting on their preadolescent children. The stereotype related to affluence and poverty was not supported.

> Children's perceptions of seven parenting dimensions were considered here, and the average levels on four of these were found to be similar among low- and high-income students. Closeness to mothers, closeness to fathers, parent values emphasizing integrity, and regularity of eating dinner with parents. (p. 223)

Inner-city children fared worse on parent criticism and insufficient after-school care. Concomitantly, low-income children "did significantly better than wealthy students on the last [dimension], high parent expectations" (p. 223).

Maslow (1970) proposed that love and belonging, as well as self-care needs cannot be addressed before basic physiological and safety needs are met. Within this context, talking with an impoverished mother about showing unconditional positive regard for her child or even about establishing a home behavioral program may be useless when she is trying to make sure she has electricity in the home. The mother may be more inclined to talk with someone who will listen to her feelings and struggles than with someone who is trying to tell her how to handle her child differently. Only after the mother feels heard and supported will she respect suggestions about her discipline style.

Child/Youth Factors

Professionals must be aware of the culture, worldview, experience, values, and self-image of economically disadvantaged children and youth (Arnold, 2002). Most children growing up in a poor environment experience prejudice daily. In addition, poverty has an impact upon where the family will live, because fewer and fewer living options are available when the family income is low or the family is dependent upon welfare programs. These factors all influence the growth and development of children in the family and how they approach the demands of growing up, including demands of the educational system (Garmezy, 1991).

Unmet Needs

Bernheimer, Weisner, and Lowe (2003) examined families living in poverty and having a troubled child or a child with disabilities. Often these children were not receiving help in schools even though they had significant problems in academics. Children with serious behavioral or health issues likewise were not receiving treatment regularly. The researchers found that having a special-needs child did not keep the parents from being employed. Working poor parents dealing with children with troubles "depend less on disease-specific diagnoses and more on the broader problems of sustaining a daily routine for the family and dealing with low-wage, no-benefit, episodic jobs" (p. 415).

Socioeconomically disadvantaged children have experienced so many unmet needs that they see little hope of ever changing their lives or fulfilling their dreams. They become frustrated over the lack of opportunities available to them and, as a consequence, can become aggressive, violent, apathetic, and depressed (Smith, 1978). In addition, they are at risk for school failure (Becker & Luthar, 2005).

The following story, relayed to me by my deceased colleague Chris Mohring, illustrates how one school professional responded to a child-related school problem stemming from parental poverty.

> Charles was a 14-year-old placed in a special education program because he was a slow learner and demonstrated aggressive, out-of-control behavior. In the program for 2 months, he had been experiencing failure and rejection by his peers. After some observation, the director found that Charles had personal hygiene problems. His dirty clothes and body odor led his peers to taunt him, which in turn led to his aggressiveness and withdrawal. Engaging Charles in the classroom was futile. If pushed, he would explode and become verbally or physically abusive.
>
> The director talked to Charles and found that he was aware of his body odor. He had no running water at home and was able to take a bath only about once a week. At an age when he was increasingly sensitive to peer-group social interactions, he also was aware of his lack of academic achievement. Coupled with the inadequacy of his hygiene, he was left with a profound sense of alienation. The director asked the parents' permission to have Charles shower in the gym before school each day. After he began bathing every morning, the teasing diminished. He obviously felt better about himself, and he began to succeed in school.

In this case, the school professional understood the parents' poverty and the dilemma that it created for Charles. The intervention provided for one of Charles's basic needs.

Studies of Delinquency

Minuchin et al. (1967) studied 12 low-income families with delinquent boys between the ages of 8 and 12 who were living in a residential treatment center and 10 low-income families with children who were not delinquent. They found that the delinquent children viewed their home environments as impermanent and unpredictable, and that they had learned to react to the present moment rather than to what might be in the future.

Parental responses in the families with delinquent boys were random and unpredictable, hindering the children's ability to internalize rules and set limits for themselves. The emphasis in the delinquent families was on controlling behavior rather than on guidance. Because the boys had no expectation of predictable rewards for their performance, their motivation was reduced and they did not learn to be proud of themselves for competence or achievement. Instead, these boys learned that gang involvement and hustling were the subsistence and survival strategies that meant competence in their culture (Coates, 1990).

By the time children who grow up in poverty reach adolescence and are able to think abstractly, they realize that the things they see in the media are not available to them and will not be theirs without years of hard work and a great deal of luck. The disillusionment that sets in is a source of stress in itself, and quick sources of gratification become even more appealing. In the study by Minuchin et al. (1967), many of the delinquent boys had been caught stealing or selling drugs as a way of quickly obtaining the money and status they desired.

Predictors for Success

In a prospective study, Ripple and Luthar (2000) examined inner-city high school students in an effort to determine personal predictors for success. Both overage for grade and high rate of absences were found to be predictive of later dropout from school. The researchers found that these easily accessed indices can be used to find students who are overage for grade with high absence records and provide interventions to help instill a value of school achievement before "their academic and personal difficulties become crystallized in the course of their developmental trajectories" (p. 294).

Conclusions

When dealing with socioeconomically disadvantaged families, the school and community professional must consider family systems factors, parent factors, and student factors (Garmezy, 1991). For these families, the process of developing a conceptual style, a world-view, and a motivational style begins long before their children enter the school system. By the time school professionals encounter families who are economically disadvantaged, frustration, apathy, and depression must be included in any realistic picture of the overall family system. These factors typically have immediate impact on families' interactions with the educational system.

Many school and community professionals have experienced the suspicion, mistrust, and reticence common in the reactions of many poor families toward them. Professionals should not take these reactions personally. Instead, they should keep in mind the historical and socioeconomic context that breeds this type of negativity and strive to convince the parents that the common goal is the adjustment of their child or adolescent. Professionals can best serve the child/youth by maintaining their own personal boundaries (as described in chapter 4) and by understanding the parents' initial response to contact by professionals in school and community settings. A good source for exploring these concepts is *Working with Families of the Poor*, P. Minuchin, Colapinto, and S. Minuchin, 1998).

Ethnic Differences

According to McGoldrick, Giordano, and Garcia-Preto (2005b), the United States had the greatest rise in immigration in the 20th century: "More than one million legal and undocumented immigrants came annually, most from Asia and Latin America" (p. 17) in the late 20th century. The 2000 U.S. Bureau of the Census reported 28,000,000 first-generation immigrants, or 10% of the U.S. population. In the unparalleled diversity within the United States, different regions of the country have different ethnic populations. On the West Coast 20% of the population is foreign-born. By comparison, in the Midwest, only 2% are foreign-born. In Los Angeles, 40% are foreign-born; New York has 3% foreign-born.

By the end of the 21st-century, Caucasian Americans will be in the minority. Thus, school and community professionals must consider different cultural realities when serving children/youth and their families. Further, children and youth in the United States must grow up knowing more about different cultures and ethnic backgrounds so they can eventually live within and guide others in a far greater melting pot than once conceived.

Following an overview of ethnic and cultural issues in a broad context, we will examine the traditions, beliefs, and perceptions of life experiences of four ethnic groups most represented in the United States: African Americans, Asian Americans, Latino Americans, and Native Americans.

Understanding Cultural Issues

Reading about cultural issues is inadequate to understanding the richness that tradition brings to a family. School and community professionals also must develop personal sensitivities to and methods of exploring these issues with the families they encounter. Beyond reading excellent resources such as *Ethnicity and Family Therapy* (McGoldrick, Giordano, & Garcia-Preto, 2005a), professionals can be educated in a deeper sense about our differences and similarities through interaction and exchange with the families themselves.

School and community professionals also must keep in mind that not all members of an ethnic group are alike in respect to lifestyles, values, or achievement (Bailey, Skinner, Rodriguez, Gut, & Correa, 1999). In a text on African American families, Willie (1991) indicated that African Americans from different class levels (affluent, working-class, poor) have different and distinct lifestyles related to family composition, childrearing, and community participation. Affluent African American parents in that study were active in their children's schools, the working-class mothers attended some school meetings, and the poor African Americans had little community involvement beyond church attendance.

Just as we have to realize that members of ethnic groups have within-group differences, we must realize that most U.S. citizens are a hodgepodge themselves. For example, I come from Irish, Scottish, and German ancestry. My daughter comes from mostly Irish ancestry, and French and Cherokee Indian also are part of her heritage. I grew up with a third-generation, Irish American mother whose family reared their children with an Irish ethnic identity even though my mom's mother also had German ancestry. Typical of Irish families on a farm, a maiden aunt (sister of my second-generation Irish grandfather) lived in the home where my mother grew up. Aunt Maggie imparted the Irish heritage and was the functional matriarch, except with the nine children who were the responsibility of my Irish and German American grandmother.

When I first read the book *Ethnicity and Family Therapy* (McGoldrick, Pearce, & Giordano (1982), I was surprised to see that the template described for Irish families was the same as I experienced growing up—despite my father being of both Scottish and Irish heritage. In the vernacular of the day, "Irish mothers rule!" I learned that the Irish are matriarchal, so it made sense to me that the dominant part of my hodgepodge that won out in the area of ethnic identity would be the Irish ancestry, likely because of the presence of my Great Aunt Maggie. Ethnicity is complex and one-sided only in the case of immigrants who remain within their small ethnic circles throughout life and marry a person of like ancestry.

The point is that families usually identify more with one ethnic group than another within their ancestry, and when a couple marries and has children, the ethnic ancestry is combined for their children and what is passed down to the next generation in terms of ethnic identity becomes what we see in the children and youth served in schools and communities. At the same time, some people are not aware of their ethnic identity and may have to read and search to find their heritage.

A nun in my school once asked me about my ethnic background. I wore two braids throughout my elementary years, in keeping with the Native American custom, because I liked the stories and lore of the Native Americans living in northern Michigan. For some reason, I identified with them and felt like I was more like them than the children I sat beside in school. I looked at the nun and said, "I don't know, Sister, but I believe I'm Indian." She and the other nuns around us burst out laughing at the green-eyed, blond child's statement.

In reflecting on that memory, I realized that not all elementary-age children are schooled in their ethnic identity even though the values and beliefs of their family history are passed down. Over time, I became aware of my Irish heritage and the ethnic identity was sealed. Without being conscious of it as children, aspects of ethnicity are being transmitted to us about the ethnic group(s) to which we belong.

As a young child, I believe that I was telling the nuns something that I knew at an unconscious level: Some things are as strong as ethnicity.

Ethnicity is a strong part of who we are, but not the whole story. It does demonstrate a basic need to belong and to have historical continuity in our lives. A large part of our identity is tied into our ancestral group(s) and with whom we share values and customs over generations. McGoldrick, Giordano, and Garcia-Preto (2005b) described the meaning of ethnicity.

> Based on a combination of race, religion, and cultural history, ethnicity is retained, whether or not members realize their commonalities with one another. Its values are transmitted over generations by the family and reinforced by the surrounding community. It is a powerful influence in determining identity. It patterns our thinking, feeling, and behavior in both obvious and subtle ways, although generally we are not aware of it. It plays a major role in determining how we eat, work, celebrate, make love, and die. (p. 2)

Life Strategies Related to Psychological Problems

Cultural background affects every person's value system, style of responding to stress, way of defining self, and approach to life. For example, the way members of different cultures respond to emotional problems (their own and those of others in the culture) is based on the overall life strategy of the culture.

Middle-class Americans from an English cultural background tend to be independence-oriented (McGill & Pearce, 2005) and to develop a concept of self based on their potential future. Much inner turmoil may precede any external expression of discomfort in British/Irish families, where emotional experience is taught to be contained within the individual.

Japanese American culture assigns shame to the emotionally distraught individual. Internal conflict is viewed as a lack of centeredness of the individual within society. This view stems from traditional Asian cultures, in which the general emotional strategy is one of role conformity and a balancing of life forces within familial and societal roles (Ho, 1992; Kuo, 1984). Asian Americans tend to keep family members with mental disorders in the home unless they are acting out, and to underutilize mental health resources (Lee & Mock, 2005a; Lin, Inui, Kleinman, & Womack, 1982).

Lee and Mock (2005a) indicated that Asian Americans do not differ from other Americans in prevalence of problems with mental health; however, they have more symptoms of depression, as well as somatic complaints than Caucasian Americans. Six predictors of mental health problems among Asian Americans are: employment/financial security, woman as more vulnerable to mental health symptoms, older age, social isolation, recent immigration, and refugee pre-migration in light of post-migration adjustment.

Jewish American culture tends to attribute emotional problems to external influences. This value stems from an Eastern European and Middle Eastern life strategy that teaches the sharing of life. Life comes with and from people, and problems are solved by sharing. Individual expression is secondary to family and community.

Iranian and Italian Americans tend to project emotional problems onto outside events or forces such as loss and social or religious prejudice rather than attributing them to internal processes. For the most part, however, in these two cultures outsiders are not involved in family business. The family solves its own problems; family loyalty and solidarity are the first priority (Giordano, McGoldrick, & Klages, 2005; Jalali, 2005).

In these cultures, disgracing the family is a cardinal crime. Because of this credo, psychological problems often are ignored, disguised as physical complaints, or contained within the family for a long time before any outside intervention is sought. By the time help is pursued, many difficulties have become physical problems such as ulcers, anorexia, and bulimia.

Native Americans acknowledge culture-specific syndromes that are born out of a belief in spiritualism, harmony with nature, and reincarnation rather than acknowledging traditional forms of mental illness (Glover, 2001). Some of these syndromes include spirit intrusion, in which ghosts of past ancestors return to affect a person's behavior; soul loss, resulting from behavior that is against tribal law; and windigo psychosis, an extreme form of psychotic behavior connected to the seasons (Kelso & Attneave, 1981). To be able to join with the family in defining a problem, community and school professionals who deal with Native American families will have to understand their cultural definitions of illness (Sutton & Broken Nose, 2005).

Cultural Values

Aponte (1994) wrote poignantly about culture and values:

> The poorest in America, either through slavery (African Americans), conquest (Native Americans), or colonization (Puerto Ricans), have lost much of their original cultures. These cultures once told them who they were and gave them values that helped structure their families and communities. With these cultures there also came purpose, whether in mythology or religion. They had reasons for living and loving that were independent of economic achievement.
>
> America's pragmatism and consumerism have since filled the space created by the loss of the original traditions and rituals of these cultures. The result has been tragic for minorities. (p. 2)

Distanced from their heritage, they have attempted to replace their lost cultural values and traditions with American substitutes, such as consumerism. Aponte juxtaposed this situation with that of immigrants from Europe and Asia who, not subjugated, brought their heritage into America.

> Their ghettos, even with poverty and discrimination, became nurseries that fostered identity, social role, and personal values. They contended with American society from a core that affirmed who they were, what they were worth, and why they should strive. (p. 3)

Overrepresentation in Special Education

The Committee on Minority Representation in Special Education (Donovan & Cross, 2002) found that minority children and youth are overrepresented in special education programs. To reflect those data in three different ways, the committee developed a Risk Index, an Odds Ratio, and a Composition Index.

1. The Risk Index provides an approximate percent of students in the racial/ethnic groups who were identified by disability.
2. The Odds Ratio compares index of risk by dividing the risk index of one racial/ethnic group by that of another to yield a comparison.
3. The Composition Index was found by dividing the number of students in one group who were enrolled in a disability area by the total of students in the same disability area.

Using 1998 data from OSERS, this committee found that 14% of all black students, 13% of American Indian/Alaskan Native students, 12% of white students, 11% of Hispanic students, and 5% of Asian/Pacific Islander students were served in special education, in comparison to an overall (across the five racial/ethnic groups) rate of 12%. African American students were most at risk for being assigned to classes for children/youth with mental retardation and emotional disturbance. African American students had the highest Odds Ratio (1.18). The largest discrepancy was with Asian/Pacific Islander students, who had a lower risk index than Caucasians across all disabilities.

The category of Learning Disabilities is the largest and fastest growing disability category. Black, white, and Latino students are placed in that category at roughly the same rate. Asian/Pacific Islander students are represented at a much lower rate, and American Indian/Alaskan Native children at a somewhat higher risk of placement.

Hosp and Reschly (2002) reinforced findings regarding referral rates with a meta-analysis of racial differences, finding significant differences of racial groups. The rate of referral for intervention or assessment was lower for Caucasians than both Latinos and African Americans. Hosp and Reschly (2002) looked into predictors of restrictiveness of placement for black and white students and found similar restrictiveness of placement for the two groups as Donovan and Cross (2002). The same three variables are important for black and white students with learning disabilities:

1. Severity of learning problem
2. Presence of behavior problems
3. Family involvement

These three variables, being the same for black and white students, shed a different light on the disproportionate numbers of minority students receiving special education services.

The Office of Civil Rights (OCR) related gender differences found in disability categories using data from 1998. Males are more represented than females in every category of disability. Males comprise 80% of those served in ED/BD classes. In learning disabilities, 70% of the students served were male. In mental retardation classes, males constituted 60% of the students served. Within each racial/ethnic group, males were highly disproportionately represented in ED services, with black males being the most disproportionately represented. American/Alaskan Native Indians were next highest in discrepancy, and white students third.

Dropout Rates

Dropout rates for BD/ED students and LD students were found to be particularly high. Almost a third of students in those two disability categories do not graduate from high school. According to Hodgkinson (1990), Native Americans have the highest dropout rates (35.5%) of all the ethnic groups in the United States. Scanlon and Mellard (2002) studied dropouts with learning disabilities between ages 16 and 21. They recommended that practitioners evaluate policies and procedures regarding dropouts, review the school system's transition-related practices, address attendance issues, consider graduation as only one acceptable outcome, and help students improve self-understanding so they can become self-advocates. Dropout rates by race/ethnicity (National Center for Education Statistics, 2005) were reported for black, white, and Latino Americans. Dropouts of Latino

Americans were highest at 25.7%, then black Americans at 11.3%, and white Americans at 6.5%.

As a result of language and color barriers, African American, Asian Americans, Latino Americans, and Native Americans are the least well assimilated in our present culture. By virtue of their minority status alone, many of these families feel isolated from institutions such as schools that are meant to serve them. This sense of isolation puts the children at risk for educational and behavioral problems.

The following discussion focuses on the general traditional values of each of the four cultural groups that comprise the largest minority populations in the United States at the beginning of the 21st century: African Americans, Asian Americans, Latino Americans, and Native American Indians. The growing numbers of minorities are significant, and minority populations likely will replace the Caucasian majority within the century.

African Americans

The African American culture encompasses a diverse group, such as Caribbean and African cultures and American southern and urban groups. The discussion here, like that for the Latino culture, should be taken as global rather than specific to a specific heritage. Different from immigrants, most people originally of African heritage were not here by choice but as a result of being captured and brought to America against their will (McAdoo, 2001).

According to U.S. Census Bureau decennial reports in 2000, 12.3% of the U.S. population was black, and that percentage is expected to double by 2050. In 2005 the rate had shifted to 12.1%. In 2000 the U.S. Census for the first time allowed a category for biracial and multiracial selection that brought the number up by 1.8 million people who viewed themselves as black and at least one other race. Referring to Viadero (2000), Bainbridge and Lasley (2002) related that blacks are three times more likely than whites to be from poor families in the United States.

Connectedness and Interdependence

The African principles of human connectedness and interdependence can be seen in present-day African American cultures (Hale-Benson, 1982; Hines & Boyd-Franklin, 2005; Ho, 1992). Most African American families are embedded in a complex kinship and social network. This network may include blood relatives as well as close friends. The concept of an augmented family—one in which extended family or friends live in the home for various periods of time—is an integral part of the African American culture.

The humanistic values of cooperation and "we-ness" inherent in the augmented family arrangement are extensions of an African cultural base (Delaney, 1979; Hines & Boyd-Franklin, 2005). The kinship bonds that developed in this culture also were influenced by shared trauma and remain essential for coping with the oppression experienced in U.S. society (Staples, 1994).

Religion/Spirituality

African Americans turn to one another in the community for support and relief (McAdoo, 2001). They traditionally have placed high value on religion or spirituality. Churches also have provided a refuge from racism and reinforcement of family values and positive racial attitudes. More recently, however, a Gallup poll found that 32% of the African Americans attended church only for holidays, weddings and funerals (Gardyn, 2000, cited by McAdoo, 2001).

Role Flexibility

Another characteristic of the African American culture is role flexibility or adaptability (Black & Jackson, 2005; Hale-Benson, 1982; Hines & Boyd-Franklin, 1996; Mack, 1981). Family members interchange roles and functions without engendering instability in the family system. Thus, older children, grandparents, and neighbors may provide child care, discipline, or household tasks as needed.

Accordingly school professionals may have to expand their definition of "family," or who is responsible for helping a student with problems in this cultural context. For example, the grandmother in African American culture is a central figure in many families, and up to three generations provide support as well as strength (Jones, 2004; White, 2004).

Childbearing and Childrearing

Another consideration in the African American culture is the importance of childbearing and childrearing as validation for women. Prior to the emancipation of slaves, families were frequently separated, so African American men and women were not allowed to legalize their marriages. Procreation was encouraged to increase the labor supply, and fertility in African American females was considered an asset. A woman's identity was tied to her role as a mother (Hines, 1990). The result was a matriarchal society with multiple nurturing figures (Pinkney, 1975).

Childrearing styles became authoritarian to encourage self-sufficiency and toughness in children, because the mothers knew that the children could be taken away from them at any time that they became useful. African American women were viewed as all-sacrificing, and they frequently turned to religion to deal with the grief of constantly losing their children. Upon this basis of physical disconnection the present African American experience was formed. School professionals should increase their awareness of these multigenerational forces before intervening in the relationships among parents and children in this culture.

Interactions With the School

African American cultural values extend to the school experience, with overt manifestations at the high-school level. Counselors and teachers have expressed frustration at the large number of African American girls who become pregnant early in adolescence and drop out of school in favor of taking on a parenting role. The self-esteem that many of these girls gain in being a mother outweighs the motivation to continue their studies and work to achieve a career identity (Hale-Benson, 1982; Hines & Boyd-Franklin, 1996).

Many social welfare programs have reinforced this dynamic. Even for those African American girls whose mothers are working at professional jobs and are career-oriented, the peer culture often perpetuates the sense that motherhood is the primary identity of value. By understanding the multigenerational patterns that contribute to the maternal identity, educators may lead young people to alternative role models through which they can begin building self-esteem around competency early in the educational process.

Families With Special Needs

Nazzaro (1981) identified two primary issues as affecting the diagnosis and treatment of African American children and youth with disabilities. First is the tendency of an Anglicized culture to diagnose African American youth as having conduct disorders or juvenile delinquency when they have behavioral problems. Nazzaro argued that behavior viewed as antisocial in a disadvantaged African American culture—which is often behavior used to achieve status—may go unnoticed when working within "the majority controlled system." Second, African American children and youth with learning disabilities are often misdiagnosed with mental retardation because of test biases and dialectic use of language.

Ford and Harris (1995) found that person–environment transactions and related sociocultural influences were stronger predictors of underachievement among gifted African American students than were intellectual and academic factors. "Such factors as a positive self-concept, an understanding of racism, and the existence of support systems," they wrote, "are more predictive of African-American success than academic ability" (p. 198).

Asian (Pacific) Americans

The general cultural category of Asian American includes Chinese, Filipino, Japanese, Korean, Vietnamese, Cambodian, Indian, and Japanese. This population doubled between 1970 and 1990 (Ho, 1992). As of 2000, almost 12 million Asian Americans were living in the United States (Lee & Mock, 2005a), 5% of the total population in the United States. Asian Americans have the lowest proportion of households headed by women, the lowest divorce rate, and the lowest childbirth rate of all ethnic groups in the United States (Momeni, 1984).

Socialization

The major socialization goals for Asian American children reflect traditional values: a sense of collectivity and identification with the family, dependence on the family, obedience, and a sense of responsibility and obligation to the family (Lee & Mock, 2005a; Serafica, 1990). These strong ties mean that at least one grandparent often is living in the family home. Ho (1992) listed the following important cultural values among Asian Americans:

- Filial piety and unquestioning loyalty toward parents
- Shame as a behavioral influence for reinforcing expectations of the family and for communicating proper behavior

- Self-discipline, modesty, humility, and stoicism in adversity, with an emphasis on the middle-position virtue of feeling neither haughty nor unworthy
- A sense of belonging and togetherness in contrast to the typical American search for perfectionism and individualism
- Awareness of social milieu and sensitivity to the opinions of others
- Fatalism, or detachment with resignation to fate's impact on one's life, bringing equanimity as well as a pragmatic orientation
- Inconspicuousness stemming from fear of being identified as an illegal immigrant or of being ostracized by the racist segment of American society

Values

Differences between Western and Asian family values are dramatic.

> In contrast to Western cultures [in which] the nuclear family stresses independence, autonomy, and self-sufficiency of the individual members, in Asian cultures the family unit is highly valued and emphasized throughout the life cycle. The teachings of Confucianism, Taoism, and Buddhism have a profound, lasting influence as Eastern philosophical approaches to life and family interaction even when they are not specifically articulated. (Lee & Mock, 2005a, p. 271).

Traditional Asian roles identify fathers as educators and disciplinarians, and mothers as protective and nurturing. A wife is expected to be totally obedient to her husband. Loyalty and respect for one's parents and elders is of utmost importance. Behaving well is valued more highly than self-expression (del Carmen, 1990).

Education is highly valued by Asian Americans (Lee and Mock, 2005a). In 2000, certain groups of Asian Americans—Asian Indians, Chinese, and Japanese—were more likely than Caucasian Americans to hold a college degree. At the same time, Laotians and Cambodian Americans were more likely to have below a ninth-grade education. Clearly, the groups that comprise Asian Americans show vast differences.

The most stressful period of development for Asian Americans is adolescence, during which many of the traditional Eastern values are in direct contradiction to the Western American values of independence and self-sufficiency. Whereas creative ideas and questioning of values are encouraged in the U.S. educational system, Asian American cultures stress loyalty and obedience. American society considers self-expression and self-disclosure as desirable; the Asian cultures are more implicit, nonverbal, and intuitive.

Cooklin (2002) indicated that traditional values are shifting in China. Cultures evolve, and this should not be surprising. The notion of obedience was challenged as a value in relation to discussing it with present-day elders who do not see the children being obedient. Cooklin described an intervention with a family made by Salvador Minuchin, in which the "sacrosanct grandmother" value was upturned, and it resulted in progress for the family. Cooklin indicated that those who are part of a culture are least likely to describe what they experience. Outsiders can more easily describe values being lived out by members of a different culture.

Interactions With the School

The Asian American community is accepting more egalitarian views of male and female roles (Lee, 1996). Such a dramatic change in values, however, may cause some role and marital strain in early generations of Asian immigrants. School and community professionals may witness the effects of parental disagreement about gender roles as confusion and anxiety in Asian children and youth, particularly adolescents who are struggling with their identity. Community and school professionals have to be aware of the possibility of this conflict and avoid triangulation into the primary struggle between the parents.

Families With Special Needs

One of the most frequently cited areas of concern regarding Asian Americans is their general underutilization of mental health services (Ho, 1992; Lee & Mock, 2005a; Tashima, 1981). Although foreign-born Asians and Asian women married to American military men are at high risk for adjustment problems, their reliance on mental health services is often limited. When they do receive mental health services, they tend to be diagnosed as schizoid, schizophrenic, or having retardation, as a result of the language barrier and their low emotional expressiveness.

Frequently, the diagnosis is inappropriate. Therefore, children and youth in these populations may grow up in a household with a severely depressed or dysfunctional parent who is not receiving treatment or who is receiving inappropriate treatment. The children may show moodiness, physical and cognitive lethargy, or withdrawal that stems from their modeling the behavior of a parent.

Asian Americans have the lowest rate of using services in mental health, regardless of gender, age, or geographic location. Also, because the culture discourages self-disclosure and strong expressions of feeling, they are more likely to show emotional strain and problems through somatic complaints (Ho, 1992; Lee & Mock, 2005a). In the holistic view of health in Asian American culture, physical complaints stigmatize the individual less than emotional problems do. This internalization of problems makes school phobia more likely.

Chinese parents in particular may not seek help for problems of a child with a disability. As a culture, the Chinese deal with family problems inside the network of the family and extended family to keep guilt, shame, and stigma from being brought on the family (Lee & Mock, 2005b). Chinese parents often blame themselves or their children if the disability is not resolved (Wu, 2001).

In this circumstance, school and community personnel can help the parents know that they can't be responsible for solving the disability. Professionals have to be careful not to implicate Chinese parents for not reaching out for assistance earlier, as the parents, in addition to their reluctance to seek outside help, may be unaware of opportunities for help that are available.

Nazzaro (1981) spoke to the impact of bilingualism on the diagnosis of Asian American children, particularly in the areas of hearing, language arts, and learning disabilities. He reiterated that the passive learning style and self-controlled emotional values of this culture often result in misdiagnosis. These qualities may lead school professionals to view Asian American children as cognitively slow, disinterested, or unmotivated, which calls for understanding on the part of school professionals.

Latino Americans

Like the African American group, Latino Americans encompass many different cultural subgroups including, among others, Brazilian, Central American, Columbian, and Cuban. The discussion in this section centers on the commonalities of cultural values across the subgroups rather than on the specifics of any one subgroup.

According to Ho (1992), the Latino American population was "the fastest growing ethnic group in the country…and…if present trends continue, this group someday will replace blacks as the nation's largest minority group (p. 94). Ho's prediction in 1992 has been reinforced by Roberts (2004) and Gonzalez (2001). It is predicted that by 2100, more than half of the U.S. population will be Latino.

Cultural Values

Traditional Latino values in general place importance on spirituality, dependence, sacrifice, respect, machismo, and personalism. Garcia-Preto (2005) described personalism as

> a form of individualism that values those inner qualities in people that make them unique and give them a sense of self-worth. In contrast, American individualism values achievement. Dignity of the individual and respect for authority are closely linked to personalism. (p. 162)

Latino family members are viewed as interdependent, with no sacrifice too great for the family. Parents sacrifice and give themselves up for their children. Children, in turn, are expected to show gratitude by submitting to the family rules. Although the mothers conduct the everyday running of the family, including discipline, the children are to see the mothers as more passive than the fathers; the mothers' job is to teach respect for the father as the ultimate decision maker. Boys are to be aggressive and macho in the outside world but, in contrast, are to mind their mothers at home. Girls are viewed traditionally as helpless and needing protection (Adkins & Young, 1976; Hines, Garcia-Preto, McGoldrick, Almeida, & Weltman, 1999).

Ho (1992, p. 99) identified the following unifying cultural concepts across the Latino American subgroups:

- *Familism*, the importance of family and family obligations, and putting aside one's own needs for the betterment of the family
- *Personalism*, which relates to self-respect and dignity as well as to respect for others
- *Hierarchy* related to socioeconomic status, for example, the father being the head of the household and the children obeying their parents and older siblings
- *Spiritualism*, seen as more important than material satisfaction and emphasizes linking directly with the spiritual realm
- *Fatalism*, with an emphasis on transcendent qualities such as "justice, loyalty, or love.

Interactions With the School

The preceding cultural values are evidenced in several ways in the classroom. For one, Mexican Americans and Native Americans share the highest school dropout rate of all ethnic groups in this country (Bennett, 1990). In addition, adolescent Latino girls may seem, from a European American perspective, to be overprotected and denied privileges appropriate in the dominant culture. By contrast, when the teacher, from an Anglo point of view, believes a Latino male child is out of control and needs discipline, his parents may consider the behavior as natural and driven by the male's inherent nature to be macho. In these instances, an unspoken conflict can easily arise between cultural value systems.

In a study of Puerto Rican families, Montalvo and Guitierrez (1983) studied a large number of children experiencing elective mutism after they entered preschool. Those authors found that the children came from families who had limited interaction with the outside world. The parents spoke Spanish at home and were shy and fearful of the English-speaking culture—communicating to their children that the outside world was a frightening place.

Soon after these children entered preschool, many were subjected to some type of teasing or they perceived intimidation by an adult. Their parents seemed intimidated by the school personnel. From that point, the children who could speak English did not speak at all at school, though they continued to speak Spanish at home. The teachers backed off and gave the children time to integrate into the English-speaking environment.

Montalvo and Guitierrez noted that school professionals who encouraged the parents to ask the school to make more, rather than fewer, demands upon their children resulted in more assertiveness by the parents. Their confidence in other areas increased, too, resulting in positive changes for the children.

Families With Special Needs

In a study of narratives about the identities of Latino mothers in relation to having a child with special needs, Skinner, Bailey, Correa, and Rodriguez (1999) found positive narratives based on the sacrificing mother and the child being a gift from God.

When facing stress, Puerto Ricans ask their family for help. The expectation is that someone in the family, particularly someone in a stable position, will help others who have a problem or crisis (Garcia-Preto, 2005). Thus, accessing social services becomes a last resort.

A study of Puerto Rican parents with children having learning disabilities or mental retardation (Harry, 1992) found that parents discounted the labels placed on their children because of the different cultural meanings of disability and normalcy. Harry recommended that professionals become sensitive to the values and norms of these children and youth and cautioned that professionals first must "become aware of their own values, and of the fact that most human values are not universal but are generated by the needs of each culture" (p. 36).

Adkins and Young (1976) wrote of their experiences with an early intervention program for Latino children in El Paso, Texas. They identified many factors that interfered with Latino families' being able to obtain appropriate help for their children with disabilities. They noted a culturally based mistrust of medical institutions and a fear of medical procedures and testing that kept many children from obtaining an adequate diagnosis of their difficulties. Even when a diagnosis was made, the families often turned to religion, folklore, or superstition rather than to doctors or educators for advice on how to intervene with their child. The families also felt cultural pressure to take care of their own problems, including those associated with children who were not functioning normally, and a fear of losing face if a family member were to be found to have a disability.

Finally, there was a cultural tendency toward overindulging children found to have a disability. These children generally were treated as dependent and incapable, so everything was done for them. When professionals from outside the culture begin to recommend that families try to teach their child independence or self-help skills, they often were confronted by the force of this cultural stereotype.

Puerto Rican parents define "normalcy" more broadly than educators, and they prefer milder labels than the educational system uses (Zayaz, Canino, & Suarez, 2001). They view the child's disability as being like a family member who is viewed as normal, or to the child's having problems with learning a second language, or attributable to the educational system practices.

Bailey, Skinner, Rodriguez, Gut, and Correa (1999) examined Puerto Rican and Mexican families with children having disabilities who extensively used services from medicine, education, and psychology. Of the parents studied, 37% utilized additional services for their children in conjunction with these standard interventions, including religious rites, herbs, and massage.

In describing parenting in Cuban American families, Bevin (2001) indicated that Cuban American families with a child who has a learning disability would search and use every resource possible to help their child, regardless of financial sacrifice. The mothers tended to be the ones who explored the options and the fathers may or may not be involved.

Native American Indians

In the United States, more than 2.5 million people from 562 recognized tribes (U.S. Department of Interior, 2005) identified themselves as being American Indian (U.S. Bureau of the Census, 2000). In the 2000 Census report form, an additional 1.6 million reported being American Indian plus another race. Even though American Indians, or Native Americans, make up only 1% of the U.S. population, they have been described as having "fifty percent of the diversity" existing in the country (Hodgkinson, 1990). Some have a great-grandparent who is an American Indian, and others were born on a reservation. Others who claim American Indian descent have no identification with their heritage, having always lived in a city and having had no exposure to native customs or language.

Many Native American Indians live in both worlds, balancing their two identities. Thus, speaking of this culture in general is difficult. Too, cultural identification among the tribes varies widely, and each tribe holds a different worldview. Tribes have dissimilar practices and customs, as well as differences in family structure and views of spirituality. Those connected to tribal traditions have "a radically different view of themselves than the one created by the dominant culture. The importance of this should never be underestimated" (Sutton & Broken Nose, 1996, p. 35).

Whereas the dominant culture in the United States identifies siblings as brothers and sisters, in the Native American cultures in general, the extended family of cousins are "brothers" and "sisters," and the grandparents form the primary relationship. A grandaunt or granduncle hold the same position as grandparent in providing training and discipline. Parental roles are filled by the parents as well as by the parents' siblings (aunts and uncles). In-laws are not part of the Native American lexicon; a daughter-in-law in the dominant culture is called a daughter in the Native American culture. Marriage thus erases distinctions between natural and inducted family members. Families become blended rather than joined by marriage (Sutton & Broken Nose, 2005).

Cultural Values

American Indians value the family's solving problems together, and this includes their extended families (Glover, 2001). They think in terms of "we" (Sutton & Broken Nose, 2005) rather than the competitive "I" of the dominant culture. Communal sharing is highly valued, and those who give much to others are held in the highest regard. Native American Indians place great value on hospitality—feeding, housing, clothing, and transporting visitors and travelers (Attneave, 1982).

Cautioning again that the Native American population is not a homogenous group, Garrett (1995) described their values as consisting of

> sharing, cooperation, noninterference, being, the group and extended family, harmony with nature, a time orientation toward living in the present, preference for explanation of natural phenomena according to the supernatural, and a deep respect for elders. (p. 188)

Going on to describe the values of the dominant culture in the United States, Garrett explained that the two worldviews are diametrically opposed to one another:

> Mainstream values emphasize saving, domination, competition and aggression, doing, individualism and the nuclear family, mastery over nature, a time orientation toward living for the future, a preference for scientific explanations of everything, as well as clock-watching, winning as much as possible, and reverence of youth. (p. 188)

Thus, according to Garrett, Native American culture emphasizes self-mastery and inner strength, as well as developing personal abilities in children. Ideals held in high regard include kindness, sharing, autonomy, and noninterference, or allowing individuals to make choices as well as to take responsibility for their choices. Good choices always have the impact on the tribe in mind (Glover, 2001). The elder tribe members communicate values through storytelling, highlighting spiritual and humanistic qualities, as well as modesty.

Humor has also been described as important to the American Indian culture. Herring and Meggert (1994) wrote, "Indians use humor's ability to erase, cleanse, or change what was embarrassing, oppressive, sorrowful, or painful" (p. 68). Those authors discuss specific strategies involving humor that counselors can use when working with Native American children.

Coming from a history of victimization, Native Americans look for authenticity, respect, and concern for others when they meet with professionals (Sutton & Broken Nose, 2005). Respect is paramount for community and school professionals who work with children and youth of American Indian descent.

Interactions With the School

According to Saunders (1987), Native American children come to school ready to learn, yet by the end of fourth grade, their achievement declines rapidly. The explanation is that the changing family life and the pressure to succeed applied by educators conflict with Native American cultural values that place family ties, intrinsic worth, and traditional beliefs first (Garrett, 1995; Glover 2001).

Sexual abuse in Native American families is a thorny issue, as sex is not considered an acceptable topic for discussion. Child-abuse prevention education requires pre-work to build trust (Willis, Dobrec, & Sipes, 1992).

The difficulty of working with Native American adolescents who are attempting to differentiate from the family was highlighted by Topper (1992) in a case study. He viewed development of an independent adult identity as challenging in this culture because of the economic underdevelopment of the reservations, their restricted funds for support services, the culture clash, and fallout in social and medical areas stemming from all of these factors.

Alcohol and drug abuse are high among some Indian tribes (Sutton & Broken Nose, 2005). Trimble (1992) likened the effect to a second "trail of tears," noting that Native American youth in certain tribes have a higher rate of abuse than any other minority. Discussing the difficulty of applying traditional approaches to these problems, Trimble recommended a cognitive-behavioral approach for drug abuse prevention and intervention, geared specifically to youth.

Families With Special Needs

In describing the result of high rates of alcoholism in some American Indian tribes, Glover (2001) referred to the high fetal alcohol syndrome rates in children. Special services are offered as soon as they are identified.

As we mentioned earlier, American Indians share with Latino Americans the highest school dropout rate of all the ethnic groups in the United States, cited as 35.5% (Hodgkinson, in Garrett, 1995). Focusing on cultural discontinuity, the blame is placed on a cultural clash with the dominant culture. Whereas Native American culture stresses family, leadership, and noninterference, the dominant culture emphasizes achievement and monetary gain.

Across-Group Response of Families to Special Needs Children/Youth

Perceptions of having a child with a disability and the resulting caregiving needed of parents vary both within and across different cultural groups (Ferguson, 2001; McCallion, Janicki, & Grant-Griffin, 1997). Researchers report positive feelings concomitant with the challenges they face (Ferguson, 2001; Hastings & Taunt, 2002; Scorgie & Sobsey, 2000). White Americans reported more negative impact than black Americans, who reported experiencing fewer burdens and more gratification as caregivers of children with disabilities (Neely-Barnes & Marcenko, 2004).

Latino families have been found to feel less burdened than Caucasian families. Blacher, Lopez, Shapiro, and Fusco (1997) compared Latina mothers who did and did not have a child with mental retardation. They found that depression in mothers who had a child with mental retardation was predicted by several factors, including low family cohesion, absence of partners, mothers' poor health, as well as less use of passive appraisal as a coping strategy.

Neely-Barnes and Marcenko (2004) examined the 1995 National Health Interview Survey Disability Supplement to explore the impact of a child with a disability on the family. Keying into impact across and within different groups, they found that "family impact of disability varies across racial/ethnic groups" (p. 289). The two predictors of family impact on Caucasian families were greater medical needs and receipt of therapies outside the school setting. The five significant predictors of impact on Latino families related to services included "personal care needs, receipt of special education services, receipt of therapies outside of the school setting, having a person other than the parent who coordinates services, and less frequent participation of the child in organized activities" (p. 289). Medical needs was the only significant predictor of family impact found for non-Latino African Americans. Caucasian and Latino families also reported slightly greater impact of having a child with a disability than reported by African American families.

Cognitive Styles

School professionals also must consider the influence of culture on cognitive style. For more than 35 years, studies have attempted to discern the differences between the thinking of mainstream American cultural groups, such as Anglo Americans, and that of minority groups, such as Latino, African, Asian, and Native Americans (Anderson, 1988; Cohen, 1969; Hale-Benson, 1982).

In general, the research points to two very different cognitive styles manifested in the mainstream and in minority cultural groups. Various researchers have referred to these styles as field-independent versus field-dependent (Anderson, 1988), analytic-cognitive versus relational (Cohen, 1969), and linear versus circular (Hale, 1981). Western European or Anglo thought is characterized as field-independent, analytic-cognitive, and linear in nature, whereas Latino, African, and Native American thought tends to be field-dependent, relational, and circular in nature.

Historically, American public schools have tended to reward Euro-Western cognitive styles. Characteristics of this type of thought are the following:

task-oriented	logical
standardized	scheduled
objective	factual
meaning is absolute	individual mastery
mechanistic	deductive

By contrast, characteristics of minority thought are the following:

process-oriented	affective
creative	flexible
subjective	group cooperation
meaning is contextual	inductive
humanistic	

School professionals must begin to adapt their teaching methods and curriculum to address these contrasting forms of thought (Reed, 1993). The edited book Donovan and Cross (2002) stemming from the Committee on Minority Representation in Special Education, provided features of effective school interventions (e.g., smaller class size, direct instruction, early intervention, awareness of expectations and self-fulfilling prophecy, qualified teachers with children having disabilities and recommended ideas for effective, research-based practices such as reading for fluency and meaning, more intensive instruction than typical students due to impoverished oral language environment. In particular they recommended Rightstart (see pages 188–191) due to research results finding significant differences in preventing achievement problems among minority students from low-SES homes who had been taught using this curriculum. Improved outcomes in learning for LD students was described in Vaughn, Gersten, and Chard's (2000) article on research syntheses on math, reading, comprehension, written expression that also benefit higher-achieving students. Their principles of instruction diverge from earlier underlying process approaches and include: a plan of action to guide learning activities that provide procedural facilitators/strategies; interactive groups or partners to improve reading/writing; students and teachers as well as peers engage interactive dialogue to improve reading/writing; integrating bottom-up and top-down instruction; and reciprocal teaching, peer tutoring and peer-assisted learning. Their article emphasized that the principle of instruction for LD students benefits all students and thus does not detract from teacher preparation. Rodriguez, Parmar, and Signer (2001) studied the use of culturally and linguistically different concepts of a number line by fourth grade children in bi-lingual special education classes. These authors recommended helping represent problems via pictures/symbols by refocusing attention there to help with problem-solving; helping students know which mathematical operation is required by correctly interpreting the language of the problem; number line and other basic concepts being periodically reinforced and refocusing students on proof that their estimates and answers are accurate through concrete representation; and reinforcing the use of all information provided to solve a problem, especially diagrams. The findings and recommendations in these three publications fit with the above-delineated thought process of minority children and youth and are focused on students with disabilities in particular.

> Teachers of CLD students with disabilities need to emphasize the correct representation of narrative information into symbols or diagrams and provide activities that help students understand that there can be a variety of relationships between symbols. (p. 209)

For professionals who wish to study the issue of cultural diversity in more depth, the seminal work on ethnic issues in families is by McGoldrick, Giordano, and Garcia-Preto (2005a). They suggest cultural-specific intervention strategies that professionals may find useful.

Affirming Diversity and Promoting Equity

Increasing understanding of ethnic differences can be approached on two levels:

1. Activities aimed at achieving a greater personal awareness and sensitivity
2. Specific programs that have been used to increase intercultural awareness and connection on the school and community level

Personal Awareness

McGoldrick, Giordano, and Garcia-Preto (2005b) proposed that "the most important part of ethnicity training involves...coming to understand (your)...own ethnic identity" (p. 32). Only by becoming aware of our own prejudices and values can we learn to open our minds to the values of other cultures. In a self-assessment, the following questions are adapted from McGoldrick and Giordano (1996, p. 24):

1. How would you describe yourself ethnically and socioeconomically? Is your present socioeconomic position the same or different from that of your parents and grandparents?
2. Who in your family influenced your sense of ethnic identity? How did they teach you these values?
3. Which ethnic groups other than your own do you think you understand best, and least?
4. Which characteristics of your own ethnic group do you like most, and least?
5. Imagine that your socioeconomic level will decrease drastically over the next year. What would change about your life?

By asking yourself questions such as these and discussing your answers with friends and colleagues, you will increase your awareness of your values, prejudices, and fears.

To increase personal awareness of other ethnic groups, school and community professionals will benefit from developing an attitude of problem solving in alliance with the family. When beginning contact with a family of differing cultural or socioeconomic background, a first step is to take a stance of respectful curiosity and openness to learn. The following techniques, with examples, may prove useful:

1. *Self-disclosure and joining.* Introduce yourself as "Ms./Mr./Dr. _____. I'm your son's _____." Don't use the parents' first names unless they give you permission to do so. Tell the family an interesting story about your cultural background: "I grew up with a house full of kids, and my husband is an only child. What a difference that makes!"

2. *Family self-identification.* How do the family members see themselves? "Your last name is unusual. Is it German or Swedish? Do you know anything about that culture?"

3. *Clarification about questions.* Tell the family why you need to know the information you're asking, how it will be used: "Could you tell me something about the Mormon religion? I'm really not that familiar with it. I wonder if Mark might share some of your traditions with our class."

4. *Cultural heritage.* Ask questions about family rituals: "The holidays are coming up soon. How does your family celebrate?"

By expressing an interest in the family's beliefs and values, the professional begins the relationship with the family in a spirit of openness and acceptance. This will provide the foundation for developing a problem-solving alliance with the parents—vital for helping their children adapt to the school environment. Reading about the ethnicity (McGoldrick, Giordano, Garcia-Preto, 2005) of the populations served in your school and community will help you understand family cultures that are different from yours and will allow you to converse and interact with them more easily about their beliefs and values.

Espousing ethnic pride as important to a healthy self-concept, Ford and Jones (1990) described a method to promote cultural awareness in 9- to 12-year-old African American children with developmental disabilities. The project involved 10 weeks of daily sessions, lasting 30 to 45 minutes, in which the African American students, their teacher, and the teacher educator developed an ethnic-feeling book. This intervention also could be implemented in community settings.

Institutional Sensitivity

As described earlier in this chapter, one of the difficulties with educating minorities in American public schools is that our educational institutions have been formed from a base of Western European thought and values (Trimble, 1992). Hale-Benson (1982) argued that to optimally address the needs of minority children, schools must make changes in their ideology, method, and content (p. 152). Ideologically, education must teach minorities how to struggle and survive. Methods should include cognitive strategies that are more relational and creative than cognitive and structured (Williams, Davis, Cribbs, Saunders, & Williams, 2002).

The content should be ethnocentric in nature—teaching the history, crafts, music, historical and political figures, and important events of various ethnic groups. Wendell and Leoni (1986) developed an ethnocentric curriculum including general information about the cultural values of 19 ethnic groups and provided suggestions for ethnocentric lessons and activities for each cultural group. Some local education departments have developed similar guides.

To respond to the needs of various minorities, Cummins (1989) recommended that schools develop an intercultural orientation based on the values of inclusion, collaboration, interaction, and experiential learning rather than try to force minorities to conform to an Anglo orientation. Some of the ways he and others have proposed to help schools create a climate that is welcoming to minority parents and reinforcing to students' identity are as follows (Cummins, 1989; Lynch & Stein, 1987):

1. Respect the various cultural groups by hanging signs in the main office that welcome people in the different languages of the community.
2. Recruit parents or other people from the community who can tutor students in different languages or provide a liaison between the school system and other parents. In some instances, these parents could be paid with money for teacher's aide positions or grant money allocated for this purpose. This recommendation also can be carried out in the community.
3. Include greetings and information in the various languages in newsletters, parent handouts, and other official school communications. Make materials about school and community services available in the appropriate languages at local churches, community centers, markets, and other businesses frequented by families.
4. Display within the school pictures and objects representing the various cultures and religious groups of the student body.
5. Encourage children to write contributions in their native language or about their family culture for school or community newspapers and magazines.
6. Provide opportunities for students to study their culture in elective subjects and in extracurricular clubs. It is often eye-opening for students to become aware that, for example, Africa and China had extremely advanced cultures at a time when the British (whom we typically study in history classes) were still living in dirty, flea-infested castles.
7. Encourage parents to help in the classroom, library, playground, community, and clubs so all children have the opportunity to interact with people of different cultures.
8. Invite people from ethnic minority communities to act as resources and to speak to children in both formal and informal settings. These individuals also might be asked to provide training to school and community personnel to sensitize staff to the values and beliefs of the families they serve.

Frequently, school professionals report that the services offered for parent involvement are underutilized. In an effort to discover the barriers to parent involvement in a socioeconomically disadvantaged neighborhood, Lynch and Stein (1987) conducted three studies, in which they interviewed 434 families who were receiving special education services. The sample consisted of Latino, African American, and Anglo families from a metropolitan school district in southern California. According to family self-reports, the main barriers to parent participation in school meetings were work, time conflicts, transportation problems, and child-care needs.

When asked what could be changed to encourage parents to attend, the parents who were interviewed suggested that the schools hold bilingual meetings, select times convenient for parents, provide transportation, provide advance notice of meetings, provide child care, inform them of the subjects pertaining to their children, and send personal notes or make calls about the meetings. These same recommendations are useful for professionals in community settings such as after-school and summer camp programs.

This study highlights the importance of being sensitive to parents' needs. The types of services the school offers and the times of school and parent meetings may have to be geared differently based on needs of each unique community. Boyd-Franklin (1989) suggested training African American parents for professional positions in the schools, to serve as role models, and also to make available cultural material.

Gorman and Balter (1997) reviewed the available quantitative research for culturally sensitive parent education programs related to childrearing. They described in detail a number of programs for African American and Latino families. They did not find efficacy studies for Native American and Asian American parents.

Investigating the academic achievement and effects of black and Hispanic 12th-graders living in intact families in terms of level of religiosity, Jeynes (2003a) found that black and Hispanic students with a high level of religiosity scored as high on achievement measures as white students. Black and Hispanic students living in families of high religiosity achieved significantly higher in academics than black and Hispanic students who were not living in highly religious families.

McIntyre (1996) presented guidelines for providing appropriate services to culturally diverse children and youth who have emotional or behavioral problems. These guidelines were developed by a task force on ethnic and multicultural concerns formed by the Council for Children with Behavior Disorders. McIntyre related that the guidelines do not make distinctions between races, cultures, sexual orientation, or generational status, and that educational and therapeutic practices should not be prescribed on those bases. Instead, the guidelines call for multifaceted and complex practices in schools and treatment. He wrote, "We cannot support, condone, or excuse behaviors, even culturally based, if they undermine basic human rights and the more commonly held values of humankind" (p. 142).

The following seven goals were delineated as a result of the task force effort:

1. Removing culturally different students from special programs if their behaviors are culturally based rather than emotional and/or behavioral in nature
2. Providing respectful and culturally appropriate education and treatment to those who do not have emotional and/or behavior disorders but are culturally different
3. Implementing assessment procedures that are culturally and linguistically competent
4. Recruiting professionals who are culturally different
5. Providing training in modifications of practice that focus on characteristics of culturally different students who have emotional and/or behavioral disorders
6. Creating a welcoming atmosphere in which culturally different students with emotional and/or behavioral disorders are valued, respected, and safe
7. Enhancing the cultural knowledge of professionals, students, and the public

All seven of these goals could be applicable in community settings working with children and youth.

Sontag and Schacht (1994) investigated differences among ethnic groups concerning parents' perceptions of their need for information and sources of information, as well as the nature and preference of parental participation in early intervention for children with special needs. In regard to the effective dissemination of information to minority families, the researchers found differences within specific minority groups; elusive local networks for communication, each having different opinion leaders and communication channels; an interest in funding as well as technical assistance to help develop culturally relevant solutions; and suspicion and skepticism within the community toward those who come from the outside to help make changes.

The researchers related that Native American children receive a lower level of service than Caucasian children. Also, minority parents reported a low level of involvement in early intervention activities with their children but wanted to increase their participation. These findings indicate that schools should make a greater effort to include parents from ethnically and culturally diverse backgrounds in decision making.

McGoldrick, Giordano, and Garcia-Preto (2005b) presented information about typical responses of various groups, as well as guidelines for participants of ethnicity training. They indicated that Caucasians have seven typical responses when discussing racism:

1. Distinguishing themselves from the majority who hold power and privilege, they emphasize other oppression they experience, such as being Jewish, poor, abused, having a disability (they say essentially, "Why focus only on racism when we also experience oppression?")
2. Shifting the discussion from oppression by Caucasians to internalized racism of one group (e.g., light- or dark-skinned African Americans) or between groups such as conflicts between Latinos
3. Resisting categories with statements such as "We are all human," "We do not see ourselves are defined by color/culture, but as distinct and individual," or "It's reverse racism to force anyone to identify with a race or culture," along with variations of "Don't blame me for this; my ancestors hadn't come over from Ireland by then"
4. Indicating they feel unsafe with "politically correct" standards, essentially blaming minorities for making them feel uncomfortable
5. Admitting criticism is on track, but then keeping the focus on themselves by expressing shamefulness
6. Disqualifying a point made, with comments such as, "Why bring up ancient history?" or "I can't talk with people when they are so angry; they need to calm down first"
7. Being confused about what to say concerning racism and opting out of speaking

The authors recommended that, in response to discussions by minority members about racism, Caucasians not try to equalize the experience of another's racism by describing similar suffering; not try to shift the focus to their good intentions.

> Resist any response that could negate the experience that is being described. The only reasonable position for people of privilege to take is to "listen and believe." (p. 35)

School and Community Applications

The literature offers a number of strategies that individual school or community personnel can use at the classroom or group level to increase cross-cultural awareness in children and youth. Schniedewind and Davidson's 1998 book, *Open Minds to Equality: A Sourcebook of Learning Activities to Affirm Diversity and Promote Equity* includes activities for upper elementary and middle school students that teachers can use to foster an understanding of cultural and racial differences. Community programs, too, would also find this material effective in group work.

Looking at the relationship between academic functioning and several contextual factors facing African American college students, Williams, Davis, Cribbs, Saunders, and Williams (2002) recommended that counselors and those organizing recreational activities in the community "might consider simultaneously involving their teen participants in neighborhood clean-up efforts or anything that might help them directly confront the negative aspects of their community (p. 426). They also suggested emphasizing the role of community-based youth organizations being linked to school partnership to "help engage young people in activities that support academic skills in alternative learning environments" (p. 426). Linking with Schools of Education at local universities would allow recently graduated and upwardly mobile minority youth to provide a model, as well as coordinate activities for their community.

Four Arrows (2003), a.k.a. Don Trent Jacob, suggested shifting attention from discipline to virtue awareness in Native Americans:

> Teachers need to develop and work from a holistic perspective, weaving virtue awareness continually into all aspects of teaching and curriculum. (p. 2)

He emphasized the importance of students' grasping the larger picture of interconnections so they can realign with virtues versus misguided values. For example, Native American youth may see violence as courage. Four Arrows, a professor at Northern Arizona University, recommends that teachers reveal values through stories, class discussions, role playing, and critical examination of how virtues play out and why harmonious relationship matter. He views this as different from "character education," which may be authoritarian or superficial, as constant integration of virtue awareness in the curriculum is interwoven throughout the school day in its many contexts.

Speaking to disparity in academic achievement between African American males and other groups, Fashola (2003) shows how after-school program services can decrease some disparities in achievement. Fashola has described four programs offered during after-school hours that improved the achievement of minority students. He also provides ideas for improving talents of African American males beyond academics. Fashola recommended that

> Principals, teachers, administrators, and community members intending to address the needs of African American males during the nonschool hours should use this article as a resource to help them to build on existing initiatives or to select the components of

> the program that best fits their needs when designing an after-
> school program. (p. 427)

Hayes (1996) studied storytelling and its influences on first-grade students in a sub-
urb of Chicago, looking at whether stories could increase interest in and positive feeling
for people from different cultural backgrounds. She concluded that rich learning opportunities can be established in this manner. Phillips-Hershey and Ridley (1996) shared a
model for increasing acceptance of diversity by regular education students so that peers
with mental retardation also benefited by subtle association of being different. They recommended that the school counselor collaborate with general and special education teachers to provide "an integrative experience that incorporates the basic understanding of
group processes and group developmental stages with planned neutral activities" (p. 291).

Isaacs and Duffus (1995) described a Scholars' Club to increase achievement by high
school minority students. Primarily an honor society, the club members also took part in
community activities such as fashion shows, public speaking, peer tutoring, and mentoring. The researchers found that self-esteem among the participants was enhanced through
these support experiences.

Moles (1993) reviewed the literature, looking for suggestions for helping parents
strengthen learning for their children. He suggested that low-income and minority families
would benefit from a variety of family interactions including leisure reading; family conversations about current events or life in the family; home life activities that would stimulate language development; and the demonstration of personal interest, as well as intense
involvement by parents in their child's development.

Garrett (1995) reiterated the recommendations by Little Soldier (1985) and Sanders
(1987) for countering the cultural discontinuity in schools that led to dropout by Native
American youth. The suggestions included

- increasing opportunities for visual and oral learning,
- using culturally relevant materials,
- respecting family-related and tribe-related absences,
- using Native American elders as mentors,
- using peer tutoring to amplify the values of sharing and cooperation,
- encouraging intergroup rather than individual competition,
- emphasizing the present with short-term goals, and
- modeling appropriate behavior and skills.

Values clarification exercises also can be useful for dealing with value conflicts. To
help Native American children and youth reach solutions to value conflicts that retain and
strengthen their pride in their heritage and values, Garrett (1995) made the following recommendations to school counselors:

- Encourage the youth to make choices and to take a look at specific choices as examples from everyday life.
- Help the youth discover and examine available alternatives when faced with choices.
- Guide the youth to weigh alternatives thoughtfully and reflect on the consequences of
  each.

- Encourage the youth to consider what they prize and cherish (for example, by making a list or writing a short story together).
- Give the youth opportunities to make public affirmations of the choices they have made (for example, through a role play).
- Encourage the youth to act, behave, and live in accordance with the choices they have made and to be able to justify their choices through appropriate communication.
- Help the youth examine repeated behaviors and life patterns in relation to the choices they have made.

Also from the area of school counseling, Walsh and Buckley (1994) spoke to what homeless children have said they want from the adults who assist them. They do not want to be judged or labeled. They desire a trusting relationship that respects and honors confidentiality. Although they want to talk with others about their lives, they also want to choose when and where they talk. They want reassurance that they are not alone. "Finally, they express a great concern that others know that they, their families, and others in the shelter are 'nice people'" (p. 14).

Gustafson (1997) related how ethnic awareness in her sixth-grade class increased after studying a slain civil rights leader from their community, Edwin T. Pratt. The students learned much about civil rights, public speaking, writing grants, and public art. They created a memorial that was dedicated on the last day of school. As a result, the students' came to appreciate the sacrifices made by those with the courage of their convictions. Activities such as this encourage children and youth to act rather than remain idle.

Gonzalez and Padilla (1997) found that the resiliency of Mexican American high school students could be predicted based on one factor—a sense of belonging to the school. This speaks for itself, and schools can find many ways to encourage belonging through involvement of family and community. They spoke to how resiliency is not a trait but, instead, a capacity that develops over time within a supportive environment.

For teachers to be successful in multicultural schools, they have to relate curriculum content to the cultural background of their students. In an article in *Educational Leadership*, Wlodkowski and Ginsberg (1995) outlined four conditions necessary for culturally responsive teaching and gave examples of norms under each of the four conditions:

1. Establishing inclusion
2. Developing positive attitudes
3. Enhancing meaning
4. Engendering competence

For those who are culturally different, the authors encouraged holistic approaches that engage the students in the learning process.

Another article of particular interest, written by Franklin (1992), describes culturally sensitive instructional practices for African American students. Suggestions include

- using and accepting dialect in specific situations;
- presenting real-world tasks related to the cultural background of the children/youth;
- including a "people focus" through small groups, an instructional approach that meets the preferred learning style of many African American learners;

- using grouping patterns that allow African American children and youth to problem-solve together and be allowed to go off-task on occasion;
- employing cooperative learning for content-related tasks;
- using peer cross-age grouping to allow informal interactions; and
- using peer tutoring to foster relationship building.

Sexton, Lobman, Constans, Snyder, and Ernest (1997) reported on early intervention-ists' perspectives on their multicultural practices with African American families having children with special needs. The professionals were positive about the multicultural aspects of their interactions with families. They also suggested inservice training on issues facing African American families. These same professionals, however, were less positive about administrative support for multicultural practices. They recommended that adminis-trators, as well as interventionists, should attend the inservice training. Sexton, et al. (1997) stated:

> A portion of the training related to the use of positive behavioral supports with young children could consider how cultural values, beliefs, and preferences affect the acceptability of various behav-ioral techniques. (p. 326)

They further recommended that parents from different perspectives speak to other fami-lies, interventionists, and administrators in training sessions.

Promoting Equity

Organizations such as church schools can make a significant positive impact on dropout rates and achievement (Jeynes, 2002). These organizations are cross-generational and thus provide children and youth with access to an adult community, which promotes the devel-opment of social capital. He pointed to the need for the establishment of a new institution, stating:

> It is a demand not for further classroom indoctrination, nor for any particular content, but a demand for child care: all day; from birth to school age; after school, every day, till parents return home from work; and all summer. (p. 38)

He elaborated by noting that the new institutions must "induce the kinds of attitudes, effort, and conception of self that children and youth need to succeed in school and as adults" (p. 38).

Monkman, Ronald, and Theramene (2005) examined social and cultural capital to explain how inequality is reproduced in schools. Knowing that high-status knowledge and cultural practices and access to developing them is crucial, their study analyzed the dynamics of students successfully negotiating social and cultural capital in a Spanish-speaking, low-income, urban school community. The researchers indicated that Latino ties are often stronger than ties in other ethnic groups. Thus, identification of families with their neighborhood is important for accessing capital and for tapping resources. School and community personnel can help build social capital, and the relationship of teachers with families is essential for building both social and cultural capital.

Children/youth and their families need to be clear about what is expected of them and teachers can help lessen the effect of lower income levels and dropout if they know about and share an interest in helping to build social and cultural capital. They can be pivotal in creating social unity and augment the development of cultural capital. In their study, Monkman et al. (2005) describe

> how a teacher assigned more social and educational value to social and cultural knowledge and practices that are sometimes not recognized and acknowledged by teachers. She also helped students develop their abilities to actively engage in learning processes in ways that are more typical of more elite schools than the rote learning one often finds in lower income schools. (p. 29)

The description of this teacher and her teaching is invaluable as a model for elementary schools and as a model to make available for teachers to read.

Teacher and co-chair of the National Coalition of Education Activists, Stan Karp (1997), reflecting on inequality and responding to others' views of educating for a democratic life, stated:

> The core issue is inequality. Schools are being asked to compensate for structural inequities in our society that the economy has magnified in recent years. (p. 41)

Karp went on to say that the structuring of schools leads to inequality from the inside (giving the practice of tracking as an example), and leads to inequality outside the school with schools merely reflecting divisions of race and class in the larger society.

Summary

The most important factor in dealing with families of different ethnic and socioeconomic backgrounds is an openness and willingness on the part of school and community professionals to learn about family values and beliefs. The specific activities and strategies used to accomplish this goal will differ from community to community, from school to school, and from professional to professional. Professionals who appreciate diversity project a model of valuing ethnic differences.

With the most powerful cultural determinant of how families interact with society being socioeconomic status, persistent poverty with its less than optimal home environment stretches some families beyond the breaking point of functional living. Children may be the recipients of harsh disciplinary methods and are at risk for failure in school and/or beyond. Not all children living at or below the poverty level will require time-consuming intervention; and, we do know that poverty affects achievement in schools and is a major risk factor for children who also have a disability.

Family factors contribute to risk in low-income homes in relation to large family size, underorganization, and early social disadvantage that impacts the education of their children as well as when they are eventually employed. Family functioning is cast as the most accurate predictor of adolescent internalization (e.g., depression, anxiety) and externalization (e.g., delinquency, conduct disorder) problems. Beyond family factors, parent factors influence children when parents do not feel adequate as protectors and providers with less time and energy to help their children learn values and appropriate behavior. Violence, substance abuse, mental illness, physical and sexual abuse as well as social isolation occur more frequently with parents who are homeless, single, unemployed, or depressed; all of which negatively impact their children. Child/youth factors in low-income homes include differences in culture, worldview, experiences, values, as well as self-image that develops at a young age. Needs of children with learning and other problems go unmet in those living at or below the poverty level. Delinquency is more frequent in this population and is sometimes reinforced by parents as models of similar behavior. It becomes incumbent on professionals in school and community settings to understand any parental or child behavior indicative of a lack of trust and focus on the common goal of the healthy adjustment and learning of their child.

The United States has often been referred to as a "melting pot;" the reality is that diversity within the mixture can be as noticeable as a whole carrot in a pot of vegetable soup. Ethnic groups have diversity within them in terms of values, achievement orientation, lifestyle, and other factors. Whether aware of commonalities with those sharing their ethnicity, the patterns their ethnicity creates in their thinking, feeling, and behavior are passed down the generations and remain a strong force in their identity. Considerable differences exist between the current majority with Euro-American driven values that include competition, individualism, immediate family, consumerism, winning, reverence for youth and the minority values of Native American Indians (e.g., sharing, tribe and extended family, cooperation, spirituality, harmony with nature, inner strength, elders respected, humor, concern for others) African American (e.g., connectedness/interdependence, tribal families, we-ness, religion, adaptability, child bearing and maternal identify) Asian Americans (e.g., collectivity, identify with family, dependence on family, obedience, responsibility to family, loyalty, modesty, self-discipline, stoicism, education), and Latino Americans (e.g., importance of and obligation to family, interdependence, sacrifice, respect, spiritualism over materialism, machismo, respect for self and others, dignity, hierarchy with father as head).

Case Example

José, a 14-year-old boy, has been diagnosed with attention deficit hyperactivity disorder (ADHD). His mother is a Latino American, and his father, who died in an accident when José was 5 years old, was of Cherokee descent. José's ADHD was diagnosed in the second grade, when he was having difficulty learning to read and paying attention in class. At that point, José's mother took parenting classes to learn strategies for dealing with a child with attention/concentration problems. José had been enrolled in resource instruction for his reading problems.

In addition, his teachers were asked to seat José in the front of the room for increased structure and to provide him with positive reinforcement as often as possible to keep his motivation at a maximum. The boy had been prescribed Ritalin by a local psychiatrist and had received counseling for 6 months to help with the grieving process following his father's death. José took the medication until the sixth grade, when school personnel, his mother, and the psychiatrist all agreed that it should be discontinued. José's reading skills improved, and he was functioning at grade level without the medication until the eighth grade.

During his eighth-grade year, José became increasingly distractible. His teachers tried sending notes home to his mother, keeping a weekly assignment sheet and sending it home on Fridays, and having José attend an after-school study hall. In spite of these efforts, José repeatedly failed to turn in assignments. During the first semester, he failed two classes as a result of receiving zeros from the absence of homework. Most recently, he had become verbally belligerent and threatening when his teachers tried to intervene.

After an episode involving a physical fight with another student, José's mother was asked to attend a meeting with his teachers, the school counselor, and the social worker. José's mother revealed that she, too, was having difficulty with José at home. He was refusing to do basic chores, even though he had willingly helped in the past. He had frequent temper outbursts, hitting walls and throwing books around in his room. She expressed concern about the crowd of friends with whom José was spending time, considering them to be a "rough" group of primarily Latino boys who had a reputation for troublemaking and "machismo."

José's mother said that she felt badly for José because he lacked a father figure in his life. At age 14, José was beginning to identify with the macho image and to believe that self-control and doing the right thing were not necessary. He had no appropriate male role models, as the mother had not remarried and none of her family lived close by. Although José attended a Catholic church with his mother, he did not seem to relate to any of the men in the church.

Questions and Comments

1. *What intervention strategies could be used with this family? How could cultural issues be included in the interventions?* [Prior to reading about the intervention used, consider strategies on your own, then see how they compare to the following remedy.]

The team developed a strategy for dealing with José's problems that included imposing positive and negative consequences for his behavior at school and at home, as well as having the school social worker hold weekly meetings with José and his mother. It was agreed that the natural consequence for José's failure to turn in assignments would be for him to attend summer school or repeat the eighth grade. The team, including as many male staff members as could attend (to impress upon José the power of the message in a way that had meaning in his macho culture), met with José to tell him about the program and remind him of the consequences. He, of course, resisted but began meeting with the social worker.

The social worker began by asking José questions about his family. He refused to answer them and said he didn't want to talk about his family. His mother was present, and the social worker asked her if she would offer some family background information. She was asked specifically about her Latino culture and her husband's Cherokee Indian heritage.

While José listened, his mother described his father's beliefs about spiritualism and harmony with nature. She described his father as a strong man but one who practiced emotional restraint and was noncompetitive. José's mother admitted that she knew very little about her husband's religious beliefs. She said he had talked about "healers" and spiritual healing, but she did not know the details.

Following this meeting, the social worker went to the library and checked out books on Native American culture and beliefs. In subsequent meetings, he read to José and his mother from these books. The mother asked questions about what was being read while José sat by sullenly, seeming not to listen. The social worker also told José and his mother that some universities across the United States pay tuition for individuals of Native American heritage and commented that if José did well in school, he likely would be able to attend one of the universities without charge.

2. *How might things change for José following the interventions described? What are some potential results?* [First, reflect on expected changes and then read what actually occurred.]

The first hint that the program was working came when José chose as his topic for an assigned paper for history class "The Plight of the American Indian." In his paper, he identified how the Indian culture had endured numerous hardships, yet kept its pride and sense of community. He wrote about the cultural values of silence, nonreactivity, and balance with nature. His teacher was so impressed with the paper that she showed the class the video "Dances with Wolves," which depicts the strength, creativity, and harmony of the American Indian culture.

At this point, changes in José's behavior became evident. He became more self-controlled. He began to talk with his social worker about cognitive strategies for relaxing and remaining nonreactive when he was angry or upset. He accepted his social worker's helping him establish a study structure to use at home, to help him become "balanced," as the Indian culture proposes. José began to dress in more of the Native American attire and was heard talking to peers about himself as a Cherokee Indian.

As this example illustrates, the professionals' openness and creativity in dealing with José enabled him to be able to "save face" in his community by forming a new identity of strength born of control and passive resistance. The school used the power of José's ethnic background to help him adapt to classroom demands.

Extension Activities

Activity #1:

Reading: Read children's and young adult literature that depicts the diversity within your school system. Ask the librarian for titles.

Reflection or Journal on Reading: How has reading about diversity affected you? Has it evoked any strong feelings? How could you use this literature with children or youth and their families?

Activity #2:

Guest Speakers/Leader Instruction: Invite minorities from diverse backgrounds to speak to your class/group, either on a panel or individually. Be sure they know what you are looking for before they come. If possible, provide the speakers with questions from class/group members prior to their speaking engagement so they can better judge the interests and knowledge of your group.

Participant Instruction: Divide into small groups and share your reactions, thoughts, and feelings about the speakers' message(s). Have any of your questions remained unanswered? How can you find answers to your remaining questions?

Activity #3:

Readings/Discussions: Read a book or story or view a movie or video about diversity. Possibilities for video include "The Color of Fear" and "Homeboy." The movie "Boys in the Hood" on DVD has been effective, even though it might be better used in conjunction with the content of chapter 9 (on violence). In your class or group, discuss your insights, the ideas you found enlightening, what touched your heart, what surprised you, what you did not like, what you disagreed with, and what questions remain.

Activity #4:

Invited Speaker/Leader Instruction: Invite a diversity trainer to your class/session. Ask that the trainer involve the participants in activities that will allow them to increase their understanding, respect, and empathy for those from diverse backgrounds. Ask the trainer to facilitate rather than lecture. If you do not know a speaker within the community, contact a university or the NAACP for suggestions. Sometimes members of the clergy can provide contact information for speakers. Or you may find someone in the class who knows an excellent speaker on diversity.

Activity #5:

Experiential Activities/Leader Instruction: Check out David Johnson's (2005) ninth edition of *Reaching Out: Interpersonal Effectiveness and Self-Actualization* and use some of his in-class activities to explore diversity.

Activity #6:

Journal Swap/Leader Instruction: Have each person in your group/class read a different professional journal article on diversity. A good periodical to consult is the *Journal of Multicultural Counseling & Development*. You also can retrieve something of interest on the Internet. Most universities have online opportunities for searching national journals under key words such as "multicultural" and "diversity in schools/communities."

Participant Instruction: In groups of four or five, share information from your articles, with each discussion taking about 15 minutes. Then pool your wisdom as a whole group/class by describing at least one of the following:

- Any change you experienced in your heart as a result of what you read or heard
- What information was new to you
- Which data were surprising
- What ideas you think would be useful for schools, homes, and communities
- What you found hard to believe
- What you found disheartening

6

$\mathcal{F}$amilies and $\mathcal{A}$doption

$\mathcal{A}$lthough being adopted does not automatically place a child at risk, it may bring more potency to preexisting risk stemming from factors other than the adoption. Abuse, neglect, or institutionalization prior to adoption increase an adopted child's risk for delayed growth and development, functioning in school, and adjustment in life. Further, misinformation and lack of information can reinforce the stigma of adoption, which introduces another risk factor.

If family members and the preadoption professionals who work with them are unaware of how the societal context affects adoptees, they are less likely to know how to prepare and protect the adopted child from being wounded by adoption stigma, or not know how to help the child face stigmatization. For example, the response of "I'm sorry" after telling someone that a child was adopted conveys a negative societal attitude toward adoption. These "verbally ignorant" (Pertman, 2000) responses in front of an adoptive child can eventually cause the child to feel like a second-class citizen. Thus, the risk does not come from being adopted but, rather, from deep-seated societal attitudes that the child can absorb over time from classmates, adults, books, and other media.

The shifting frequency of adoption and diversity of forms of adoption, along with the burgeoning of international adoption in recent years, require accurate and up-to-date information for families who adopt, as well as people in the school and community who interact with them. The study of adoption is moving gradually toward a strengths-based approach, with an emphasis on resiliency in adoptive families and children.

A History of Adoption

Possibly the earliest written information regarding the regulation of adoption is found in the Code of Hammurabi, 1780 BC. Adoption seemed to be common and well-accepted then, done with the consent of the birth parents via a written contract that essentially relinquished their rights. The adoptive child was an equal heir, and sometimes the adopted son was granted the status of "eldest son," whose role was basically to be the executor of the estate by arranging equal shares among the heirs upon a parent's death (Halsall, 1998). In ancient Rome, Greece, China, and other cultures, adoption was a frequent and acceptable practice, and the adopted child often was cherished or indulged in other cultures. The society of Oceania viewed as selfish the parents who kept all of their children when a relative was childless (Leon, 2002).

Adoption practices in Oceania had some similarities with what North Americans currently refer to as *open adoption* (discussed later in the chapter). In recent times, subcultures within the United States and cultures around the world have viewed adoption as "normal" and without social stigma (Akbar, 1985; Billingsley, 1992; Boyd-Franklin, 2003; Carroll, 1970; Hines & Boyd-Franklin, 2005; Johnson, 2002; Leon, 2002; Linnekin & Poyer, 1990; Modell, 1994; Nobles, 2004; Staples, 1994; Terrell, 2001; Terrell & Modell, 1994; Wegar, 2000).

The Advent of Orphanages

Orphanages, or "foundling homes," came into being in the 13th century in Italy (Boswell, 1998). Johnson (2002) described them as a death sentence for infants until the 1930s in American and European cities. This was because the infant mortality rate in orphanages was extremely high, as a result of respiratory and gastrointestinal diseases exacerbated by malnutrition (Frank, Klass, Earls, & Eisenberg, 1995).

Not until the 1930s, when enough orphans were living beyond infancy, could researchers investigate the effects of living in orphanages (Johnson, 2002). Frank and colleagues (1996) related five risk areas for infants/children in orphanages through time and cultures as

1. infectious morbidity,
2. nutritional deficits with attendant suppression of growth,
3. impaired cognitive development,
4. problems in socioemotional development, and
5. physical/sexual abuse by employees in the orphanages.

Adoption became the prevalent answer to the inadequacies of orphanages. Until the mid-20th century, adoption did not carry the secrecy and stigma that developed thereafter. It was viewed as an answer to the societal issue created in orphanages.

Later Influences on Adoption

By the middle of the 20th century in the United States, many adoptive children were not known by others as having been adopted and were assumed to be biological children—except those close to the family who kept "the secret." Although some adoptive parents openly shared that they had adopted their child, open adoption was rare. Open adoption took hold in the United Kingdom in the 1960s, stemming from adopted children's "genealogical bewilderment," as well as professional concerns that lack of disclosure with the child could cause distrust and other issues. These concerns were voiced at the same time theoretical explanations of relationships were shifting with an emphasis on connections and relationships becoming valued (Silverstein & Demick, 1994; Sykes, 2001).

Beginning later in the 20th century, adoption in the United States was impacted by

1. availability of reliable birth control via "the pill";
2. legalized abortions, eliminating undesired pregnancies; and
3. less criticism attached to having an out-of-wedlock child, which resulted in more young mothers keeping their children.

These three societal shifts decreased the number of infants available for adoption in the United States. At the same time, many women who had chosen to delay motherhood while establishing their careers were having difficulty becoming pregnant. Concurrently, medical science was developing in-vitro fertilization, the use of donor eggs, and other aids, which allowed women to begin motherhood at far later ages than in the past.

Of the women who were treated unsuccessfully for infertility, only 15% attempted adoption (Hollingsworth, 2000). Fisher (2003) suggested that the decisions of women who expended vast financial resources on trying to become pregnant, and clearly wanted to have a child, may have reflected the force with which the stigma of adoption operated in society. Perhaps some were unwilling to adopt domestically because they feared protracted custody disputes like those highly publicized in the news, or they had exhausted the financial resources necessary to adopt internationally.

The scarcity of infants available for adoption in the United States led to new scenarios: looking toward other countries with high availability of infants, considering older children for adoption from public welfare foster programs, as well as children in sibling groups and children/youths with complex needs. Another change came with the Adoption and Safe Families Act of 1997, in which the courts shifted the priority from "the best interest of the family" to "the best interest of the child." This law has led to fewer children being bounced from one foster home to another and intermittently returned to their parents, who repeated the same destructive patterns of behavior (e.g., physical abuse) that led to foster care in the first place, before finally allowing the children to be adopted.

The Multidisciplinary Scope of Adoption

In the 21st century, adoption in North America includes "a surprisingly diverse set of family circumstances. Although each involves the transfer of parenting rights and responsibilities from a child's biological parents to others, these circumstances present very different opportunities and risks for children and families" (Grotevant, 2003, p. 753). Respected researchers and theorists studying adoption have long referred to the "adoption triad" or triangle. This triad consists of

1. the adopted child,
2. the adoptive parents, and
3. the birth parents.

Among the different forms of adoption are

- relative/kinship,
- tribal (Native American),
- public agency (foster home),
- private,
- closed/confidential,
- open (four levels),
- domestic,
- international,
- complex needs/special needs,
- transracial,
- biracial, and
- multiracial.

Within those different forms of adoption are the "surprisingly diverse set of family circumstances" that Grotevant referred to, encompassing each member of the adoption triad.

Diversity of Adoptive Parents

Circumstances relating to the adoptive parent(s) include the following:

- Married couple with/without biological and/or other adopted children
- Married couple with a blended family
- Cohabitating couples with/without biological and/or adopted children
- Single heterosexual male or female with/without children
- Lesbian or gay couple with/without children
- Single lesbian or gay with/without children
- Stepfamily with one parent being a biological parent and the other a stepparent to those children or child without adopting them because the other biological parent is sharing custody
- Parent(s) with a disability
- Parents with a racial or cultural background different from the child/youth to be adopted

Although this list presents quite a diverse sets of circumstances, it does not account for all the diversity in forms of adoption. The two other members of the adoption triad have diverse circumstances as well.

Diversity of Birth Parents

Among the diverse set of circumstances for birth parents are

- death of both or only biological parent (e.g., accident, fire),
- abandonment (leaving child with no identifying information),
- termination of parental rights early or later in the life of the child/youth,
- relinquishment at birth with an adoption plan by birth mother and/or birth father,
- relinquishment by birth mother at birth with birth father denying paternity and/or legally severing rights,
- relinquishment after a short time with infant in the home of the birth parent(s) or foster family,
- early teen pregnancy,
- rape of birth mother, and
- pregnancy resulting from incest.

This list could be expanded.

Diversity of Adopted Child

Adopted children, too, come from a diverse set of circumstances such as the following:

- Loss through death of parent(s)
- Loss of biological family and its cultural and genetic heritage in closed and two levels of open adoption
- Loss through the only living parent having a disabling permanent cognitive/psychological condition
- Foster care in a foreign country
- Institutionalization in a foreign country in orphanages that may have been adequate or inadequate for shorter or longer term
- Public-agency involvement with one or multiple families involved in foster care in the United States
- Short-term or longer-term foster care in the United States accompanied by emotional, behavioral, physical, incest, or abuse issues stemming from treatment by the birth family prior to being placed in foster care
- Child with a disability unrelated to birth circumstances and later adoption (e.g., cerebral palsy)

The list could continue.

Complexity of Circumstances

Clearly, adoptive families are diverse in nature, and many have complex circumstances. Their pathways diverge dramatically based on the three members of the adoption triad and the mix of circumstances, temperament of the child or youth adopted, parenting abilities and experiences, composition of the family, life circumstances (e.g., financial security, education, health), familial and social networks of support, family-of-origin and extended family support, transgenerational transmission of dysfunctional family patterns, and more.

Because of the combination of circumstances that bring an adoptive family together, we cannot generalize research or other information about each part of the adoption triad to all. Yet, credible research offers much information about adoption that can help school and community professionals teach and serve these adoptive children and youth and their adoptive families, as well as the third member of the adoption triangle—the birth parents. The birth father, in particular (Miall & March 2005a), is often left out of support systems, and birth fathers have been marginalized during the adoption process (Clapton, 1997; Daly, 1988; Day, Lewis, O'Brien, & Lamb, 2005; Dienhart & Daly, 1997; Freeark et al., 2005; Grotevant, 2003; Nock, 1998).

To be of maximum support to adoptive children and families, professionals in behavioral sciences—counselors, social workers, and psychologists—must be knowledgeable about, and collaborate with, the complex web of disciplinary areas. This widening scope (Grotevant, 2003) extends to history, anthropology, and sociology (Wegar, 2000); economics (Pertman, 2000; see his chapter 8); biology and genetics (Lebner, 2000); epidemiology in relation to international adoption; and the legal and political sciences.

Primer on Forms of Adoption and Adoption Plans

Until fairly recently, few options beyond kinship and closed adoptions were available in North America. Today, adoption has many variations, including several levels of open adoption, as well as burgeoning international adoption. Tribal adoption is a relatively recent option, with a legal basis in the Indian Child Welfare Act of 1978.

Forms of Adoption

The forms of adoption are described briefly in the following paragraphs.

1. *Kinship adoptions.* As is obvious, in kinship adoptions a relative adopts a child, either at birth or later. Grandparent(s) or a member of the extended family of either the birth mother or father (usually the birth mother) adopts the child. Today, rather than being a consequence of out-of-wedlock circumstances, as in earlier times in North America, kinship adoption usually results from parental neglect, abuse, or addiction, with the courts' terminating parental rights. According to Grotevant, kinship adoptions are "arguably the fastest growing type of adoption in the United States … and are currently being viewed as part of the solution to the large number of children in the foster care system" (2003, p. 753).

Frequently, grandparents, aunts/uncles, or cousins step forward to adopt rather than allow the child to be adopted outside the family. When the adoption takes place past infancy, the courts usually have severed parental rights because of their neglect or abuse of the child or their drug/alcohol dependency. Among other reasons, adoption also results from death of the parent(s) or the parent(s)' relinquishing rights because of advanced age or their inability to properly care for the child.

2. *Closed adoptions.* Closed adoptions maintain confidentiality among members of the adoption triad. Some states have changed their laws to "unseal" adoption records, enabling adopted children to search for their birth parents after some specified age. State laws differ in regard to birth parents' rights to search for their birth child.

3. *Open adoptions.* In contrast to closed adoption, open adoption allows some level of contact between birth parents and adoptive parents prior to adoption and/or beyond. The contact is made either through an intermediary, such as a social worker, or face-to-face between the birth parent(s) and the adoptive family.

4. *International adoptions.* Although international adoption is a complicated process, many North American families travel to another country to adopt a child, siblings, or children from more than one family. These adoptions most often occur in the birth country of the adoptive child. In the United States, internationally adoptive parents are not required to readopt or federally register the child as adopted when they return to the United States, but many internationally adoptive parents choose to file the paperwork in the United States.

5. *Tribal adoptions.* In 1978 the Indian Child Welfare Act was signed into law in the United States. The law requires the tribal court to authorize adoptions of children/youth considered to be a member of their tribe; however, some adoptions by Native American tribes pass through tribal courts, others through the state courts, and some Native American children live with relatives without a legal arrangement (U.S. Department of Health and Human Services, 2004). The definition of eligibility for membership differs across tribes. Communal decision making has always been part of Native American life, with tribal courts/councils collaborating with parents. Parental rights, custody, and adoption are under the scrutiny of tribal courts. The federal law was intended to assist tribes in maintaining their cultural heritage.

Adoption Plan

When birth parents decide to place a child for adoption, those involved in the adoption triad have to determine the form of adoption. Under the best of circumstances, the adoption plan is made prior to the child's birth, with all members of the adoption triad involved and supportive of the form—public or "other" (could be private, independent, kinship, or tribal)—and either closed or open (with open adoption specifying the level of openness in writing).

If the child is born prior to the birth parent(s)' deciding to place the child for adoption or a decision to place the child for adoption is reached without an adoption plan, the newborn usually is placed in a foster home on a temporary basis. This temporary setting permits time to reach a decision on keeping the newborn or placing the newborn for adoption.

A decision to place the child for adoption involves screening records on prospective adoptive parents. If the birth parent(s) choose an open adoption that allows them to meet the adoptive parents, the coordination requires even more time, with the newborn in foster care. In some states, if a private adoption is chosen, regulations require that at least one birth parent and the adoptive parent(s) meet, even if they never see one another again. Because birth parents and adoptive parents are not always well served by meeting one another, the initial meeting should be with the lowest level of contact allowed by state law. In some cases, there is only brief contact between the adoptive and birth parents.

When the newborn is placed in a foster home from birth, the birth parents and extended family have no contact with the baby after leaving the hospital. Thus, they do not form a relationship with the baby, and the level of emotion for birth parents and extended family members alike would be expected to be different than in kinship adoption.

If the extended family has known the child for some time and been in a familial relationship, as in the case of children whose parents' rights are in jeopardy because of neglect, abuse, or drug dependency, the family can be expected to have difficulty losing the established familial relationship as the result of a non-kinship adoption. Regardless of the form of adoption, the birth mother carries a psychological awareness of the adopted son or daughter (Fravel, McRoy, & Grotevant, 2000) and deserves follow-up support over time to grapple with the emotional issues.

Empirical research validates that birth mothers experience the presence of the adoptive child for the remainder of their lives (Fravel et al., 2000) regardless of the form of adoption. Fully disclosed adoption generally has a more positive effect on the birth mother.

Core Areas of Adoption

Six core areas pertinent to specific aspects of adoption are as follows:

1. Data and statistics on adoption, including trends
2. Societal views of adoption, as well as social constructs and values surrounding adoption
3. Effects of adoption on children and families
4. Forms of adoption including open adoption, breaking silence with disclosure, closed adoption, and changes that impact previously sealed records/secrecy
5. General information and research related to international adoption as well as effects of institutionalization
6. Multiple risk factors in adoption with a subsection on complex needs of adoptees such as extreme neglect or physical or emotional abuse, as well as adoptees with a disability; this area also includes foster children adopted domestically on an individual or sibling group basis

Following these six core areas are two additional focal areas that transect the previous six core areas. The first of these two describes adoption adjustment in relation to Erik Erikson's psychosocial tasks from infancy through young adulthood (Erikson, 1963).

These psychosocial tasks pertain to all children, youth, and young adults, and this focal area centers on the psychosocial tasks in relation to adoptees. That discussion emphasizes adolescence, when the psychosocial task of *identity formation* versus *role confusion* necessitates positive integration of the adoption story into the fabric of the adolescent's identity, incorporating the adolescent's dual heritage. The second focal area transecting the six core areas relates to the ongoing support and intervention after adoption that is provided to adoptive children and families.

Data and Statistical Research on Adoption

For the first time in a decennial census, the U.S. Bureau of the Census in 2000 included adopted children as a category of relationship separate from the categories of natural born son/daughter and stepson/stepdaughter. Thus, the 2000 census has become the principal source of nationwide data on adopted children and families (Kreider, 2003). The 2000 census data reported that 2.5% of all children were adopted, 5.2% were stepchildren, and 92.3% were biological children. The number of adopted children in the United States reported by householders in 2000, which collected data from one in six households, was 2.1 million (Kreider, 2003). Based on one in six households, the number of adopted children in the United States from the 2000 figures was 1,586,002 under the age of 18 and 472,911 older than 18 (Kreider, 2003).

In 1992, 5% of adoptions were intercountry, 18% were public, and 77% were private, independent, kinship, or tribal. In 2001, the picture had changed dramatically, with 15% of adoptions being intercountry, 39% public, and 46% private, independent, kinship, or tribal. States show a vast difference in percent of adoptions within these three types (e.g., public, private, intercountry). Intercountry adoptions are undercounted because adoptions finalized in a foreign country are not required to be filed in the United States. Therefore, obtaining a realistic percentage of adoptions that are internationally based is not possible, but it certainly is higher than 15% of all adoptions. Some internationally adoptive parents do file to obtain additional legal recognition in the United States, but others do not. Tribal adoptions, too, are undercounted because there is no legal arrangement when the child is living with relatives. The breakdowns by state show extreme disparities. For example, the highest percent of public agency adoptions was in Illinois (82%), and the lowest percentage of public agency adoptions was in Alabama (10%).

Trends in Foster Care

Trends in foster care in public welfare agencies in the United States from fiscal years 2000 through 2004 show a relatively stable number of children served, just over 800,000 (AFCARS, 2005). This was a dramatic increase from 461,163 children in foster care at the end of the1994 fiscal year (NAIC, 1996). AFCARS "collects case-level information on all children in foster care for whom State welfare agencies have responsibility for placement, care, or supervision and on children who are adopted under the auspices of the State's public child welfare agency" (Child Welfare Information Gateway, 2005, p. 2).

The trends chart from AFCARS (2005) also provided information on the number of foster children waiting to be adopted, which declined from 132,000 in 2000 to 118,000 children in 2004. In a special report from the 2000 census, Lugaila and Overturf (2004) reported that, for all children under age 18, 2% of children in the households were not relatives. Of that 2% who were not relatives, 23% of the children living with the householder were foster children. Note the difference in ages, as AFCARS data were from foster children under 16 whereas the special report on the 2000 census by Lugalia and Overturf pertained to children under age 18. Among all children in households reported in the 2000 census, only 0.4% under age 18 were foster children. Most of the .04% referred to those foster children under 12 years of age.

National Adoption Attitudes Survey

The National Adoption Attitudes Survey (Dave Thomas Foundation for Adoption, 2002) surveyed 1,416 Americans and asked if they wanted to adopt where they would turn for advice or information about adopting a child. From the wide array of options, they considered most important, in order: foster care agencies (57%), local social welfare agency (55%), faith-based community (48%), friends/neighbors (41%), Internet (29%), media (17%), and some other source (5%).

Societal Attitudes and Constructs About Adoption

This second core area on adoption relates to societal attitudes regarding adoption. Society is part of the widest crucible within which adoptions occur, part of the macrosystem within ecological systems theory (Bronfenbrenner, 1988; Bronfenbrenner & Morris, 1998). The four ecological systems pertaining to adoption (Schweiger & O'Brien, 2005, p. 513) are

1. microsystem (adoptive family relationships and goodness of fit);
2. mesosystem (school, peers; biological and/or foster families);
3. exosystem (social services; pre-/postadoption supports in community); and
4. macrosystem (social policy, legislation, court decisions, and cultural and societal perceptions regarding adoption). This is the "jumping-off place" for adoption.

This core area has the following key components: the stigma of adoption, societal attitudes, and the social construct of loss associated with adoption in our culture that is not true in some other past and current societies around the world.

Because the form of adoption is not always clear, many school/community professionals are either uncomfortable with or do not know how to interact with the birth parents. If the adoption is fully open, from birth through the child coming of age, it almost always involves contact with the birth mother and also the maternal side of the birth family (Fravel et al., 2000). Thus, the birth mother or an extended family member may attend a community or school function alongside the adoptive parents. Professionals should acknowledge the presence of a birth parent without identifying him or her as such. An appropriate response to any of the triad could be something like, "It's good to meet such a caring person in Joseph's life. He brings a lot to our class."

Researchers, social scientists, and professionals in the field of adoption and others have reflected on the stigma related to adoption (Leon, 2002; Miall, 1998; Miall & March, 2005a, b, c; O'Brien & Zamostny, 2003; Pertman, 2000; Wegar, 2000). Beginning in the 1960s, social consciousness began to increase, including the effects on all three members of the adoption triad—the child/youth who was adopted, adoptive parents, and birth parents—as well as society as a whole.

In scrutinizing the impact of the dominant ideal of the primacy of "genetic family" on community attitudes regarding adoption, Wegar (2000) went further, using the term "genetic ideal" concerning the stigmatization of social status, or social positioning, of adoptive families She exposed the many contributing factors as

- inadequate theoretical explanations and psychopathological explanations of any negative outcomes;
- lack of resiliency-based perspectives;
- subtle and not-so-subtle judgment by professionals in the field of adoption;
- lack of public knowledge about the realities associated with adoption outcomes and reliance on the media for information;
- prejudice toward illegitimacy and infertility;
- lack of preadoption services that prepare the family to expect, recognize, and counteract stigma; and
- lack of postadoption services that teach adopted children and their families to be aware of the differences in their family rather than deny them, and also aware of the stigma associated with the differences.

In response to the stigmatization, parents can choose to celebrate and enjoy those differences, encouraging the adoptive child as he or she continues to grow and thrive. Does a difference in nonbiological children matter to family, or is family "not necessarily blood kinship …[but] relationships nourished and sustained by the accumulation of thousands of daily acts of support and care" (Washington, 1991, p. 38, on Ernest J. Gaines' writing, as cited by Wegar, 2000, p. 367).

The term *social kinship* speaks volumes and describes well the wisdom that Gaines and others have shared in their writing and research (Akbar, 1985; Billingsley, 1992; Boyd-Franklin, 2003; Hines & Boyd-Franklin, 2005; Modell, 1994; Nobles, 2004; Staples, 1994; Terrell & Modell, 1994). Some cultures and subcultures hold no stigma about nonbiological kinship in adoption. As indicated in Wegar (2000), one of those is a minority subculture within our society: African American families are tribal by nature, and biological kinship is no different from social kinship in this subculture. Much can be learned from this way of living together.

The "verbal ignorance" of schools can have a damaging effect on adopted children (Pertman, 2000). This is particularly true in elementary school, when children are trying to "fit in" with others and shaping their self-perceptions. As a result, many adoptive parents choose to keep the knowledge of the adoption within their family and friendship circle through the elementary years. Pertman pointed to the importance of school professionals' using positive language about adoption and suggested that teachers be open and straightforward concerning the issue of adoption. When openly discussing adoption, educators have the opportunity to normalize it for other students rather than avoiding and perpetuating the stigma. Adoption expert Joyce Maguire Pavao said, "People who have secrets about them think there's something wrong with them" (cited in Pertman, 2000, p. 89).

Pertman (2000) related a story about the tragic death of both parents of a 1-year-old girl. The mother, on her deathbed, had asked her brother if he would adopt and rear their daughter if anything happened to her husband. A few months later, the baby's father was killed in an accident, and the brother of the deceased mother and uncle of the toddler immediately filed to adopt the baby. Just prior to the court hearing, the godparents of the baby intervened, contending that the uncle was not related by blood because he was adopted (as was his deceased sister) and one of the god-parents was a cousin of the uncle applying to adopt his niece—a "blood relative" of the toddler whose parents had died.

In keeping with his sister's request and his promise to adopt her daughter if her husband were to die, the uncle met the judge, who interjected his beliefs/prejudices in the decision by awarding the toddler to the godparents because of the biological connection. Fortunately, this decision was reversed on appeal.

Pertman related a number of stories revealing the dark side of humanity and stigma associated with adoption. He indicated that wills may be contested because adopted relatives are not "true" relatives. His book, *Adoption Nation,* is replete with examples of the stigma attached to families who adopted their children. His book also reports "the good news" of changes that have taken place, as well as hope for the future.

O'Brien and Zamostny's (2003) integrative review of empirical literature pointed to societal assumptions that attachment problems will exist and that adopted children will have multiple problems. Therapists were seen as discounting the role of adoption, and many indicated a need for information on adoption. O'Brien and Zamostny pointed to needs of adoptive families to be supported when they face stigma and bias, as well as cope with responsibilities related to having adopted a child/youth from a low-incidence population. (The U.S. Census 2000 reported that 2.5% of all children are adopted, making it a low-incidence situation.)

Professionals are not always able to separate fact from fiction about adoption (Grotevant, 2003), nor do adoptive parents using the Internet always find accurate reports. Adding to the problem of inaccurate beliefs resulting from inaccurate information is the media's highlighting sensational, highly visible adoption cases gone wrong. These decidedly are not the typical outcomes of adoption.

National Adoption Attitudes Survey

The National Adoption Attitudes Survey by the Dave Thomas Foundation for Adoption (2002) asked respondents for their *main source of information about adoption* in general. The findings? First was "family and friends," and following close behind was "the news."

Because of the kinds of media reports of adoption disruption and dissolution in the United States, many prospective parents have chosen international adoption (Kaslow, 2003). In reality, the incidence of disruption/dissolution is extremely low, and previous empirical research estimated far higher rates than those found in reporting by public agencies in the various states (Evan B. Donaldson Adoption Institute, 2004). The Child Welfare Information Gateway (2004) cited Festinger's (2005) review of 25 reports on adoption disruption, which found both dissolution and disruption to be relatively constant since the 1980s. As well, the report (Child Welfare Information Gateway, 2004) cited findings by Festinger (2002) that dissolution in adoption is extremely rare.

Miall's Sociological Studies

Highly regarded for her research that takes a sociological view of adoption, Miall's (1998) studies included one of involved community assessment of issues related to adoptions that were open, involved birth parent/child reunions, and disclosed confidential information. In 1998, only 29% of the respondents who were surveyed agreed with open adoption, and males were more likely than females to support open adoption. Reasons for disapproval of open adoption were that conflict between birth and adoptive parents would ensue; that the child would be confused; and that adoptive parents did not need help so it was not necessary. But many of those who disapproved of open adoption thought medical information would be helpful, if both sets of parents had anonymity.

In Miall's (1998) study, a large majority of the respondents viewed birth reunions as positive for adoptive adults and birth parents, if both parties agree to the reunion. The few who did not support reunions thought they would bring back unpleasant memories or create difficulties for the families.

In a later study, Miall and March (2005b) assessed support of community members for different types of adoption, posing questions about: confidential/closed adoption; fully disclosed open adoption with contact between birth parents and adoptive parents in face-to-face interaction; and two types of mediated adoption (the first involving an exchange of letters/cards between birth and adoptive parents through a social worker without ever meeting face-to-face; and the second with birth and adoptive parents meeting prior to adoption, then exchanging cards/letters through a social worker).

This study found the most support for the level of openness involving birth and adoptive parents meeting prior to the adoption, with card/letter exchanges mediated by a social worker thereafter. The respondents also desired that the adoptive parents receive biomedical information so they could anticipate possible problems, understand their child better, and help the child in adolescence—when identity versus role confusion is the main psychosocial task (Erikson, 1963). Miall and March (2005b) concluded that

> the larger community is not as conservative in its views toward adoption and openness, nor as enthusiastic about fully disclosed adoption as the professional community might believe. (p. 406)

They also indicated that families should choose the form adoption takes, with the best interest of the adoptive child as the basis for that choice.

Miall and March (2005c) compared their results on attitudes toward open adoption with surveys of attitudes toward open adoption by Rompf (1993), by the Evan B. Donaldson Adoption Institute (2004), and by the Dave Thomas Foundation for Adoption (2002). When looking at the results of Miall and March's Canadian survey and the other three surveys, "the majority offered some form of conditional support for open adoption regardless of the level of openness assessed, either somewhat approving of it or regarding it as a good idea in some cases" (p. 88). In the National Adoption Attitude Survey (Dave Thomas Foundation for Adoption, 2002) the birth child was part of the equation in open adoption. A large majority approved of confidential/closed adoption continuing to be available (Miall & March, 2005c). A vast majority also approved of birth reunions. The unconditional release of confidential information on birth parents to adult adoptees was strongly supported. But unconditional release of identifying information about adult adoptees to birth parents with the adoptive parents' permission was supported by a bare majority. Furthermore, 55% of the respondents did not approve of releasing adult adoptee information to birth parents unless the adopted adult agreed.

In their community attitudes study, Miall and March (2005a) addressed the motives of birth fathers regarding adoption placement and single parenting. Generally speaking, those surveyed or interviewed perceived birth fathers who chose to place their child for adoption as unselfish, caring, and responsible. Men respondents thought the birth father would not be able to be a good provider as a single parent and also viewed birth fathers as at the mercy of the wishes of birth mothers. When the birth mother could not or would not raise the child and the birth father decided to rear the child versus place the child for adoption, the respondents viewed that decision as positive.

The stereotypes of mothers as nurturers and fathers as providers seems to run deep in the societal psyche, marginalizing the role of the birth father in adoption as opposed to the respondents' views of the importance of fatherhood for men. Most respondents considered fatherhood as learned.

A Canada-wide telephone survey by Miall and March (2005c) investigated whether respondents supported changes in the form of adoption. The findings were compared with two major U.S. survey research studies on adoption (National Adoption Attitudes Survey, 2002; Benchmark Adoption Attitudes Survey, 1997), as well as two other studies. In this study Miall and March probed societal attitudes toward gay adoption, open adoption, birth reunions, and the release of confidential information (unsealing records).

Traditional couples who are married were rated as the most acceptable adoptive parents, and common-law couples received "very acceptable" ratings as adoptive parents (Miall & March, 2005c). The majority of male and female respondents assessed single males and females as "very acceptable" or "somewhat acceptable" as adoptive parents. Same-gender partners were rated least favorably as adoptive parents overall. Women were significantly more likely than men to rate gay male couples as "very acceptable" to adopt. The overall findings from the Canadian study were comparable to an ABC News random-sample survey conducted in the United States in the spring of 2002. The 47% acceptability rating for lesbian/gays as same-gender partners to become adoptive parents was a dramatic increase from a Time/CNN poll in 1994 that found overall support in the United States to be 28% supportive of same-gender couples to adopt.

In an intriguing study, college textbooks and readers published between 1998 and 2001 were critiqued regarding their portrayal of adoption in terms of amount of coverage and content, including stigma and anticipated negative outcomes in what was written in the textbooks and readers (Fisher, 2003). The study found little coverage in textbooks on marriage and family, as well as readers used in undergraduate courses. Clearly, the students receive the subliminal message that adoption is peripheral, not central, when studying families. In terms of content analysis, negative findings were reported, versus positive findings.

Social Constructs

Leon (2002) asked the question: Is loss in adoption naturally occurring or socially constructed? In his portrayal of other cultures, he found a total absence of loss and stigma associated with adoption. In these cultures, adoption was viewed as natural and common (Akbar, 1985; Billingsley, 1992; Boyd-Franklin, 2003; Hines & Boyd-Franklin, 2005; Modell, 1994; Nobles, 2004; Staples, 1994; Terrell & Modell, 1994).

In responding to a number of articles on adoption, Friedlander (2003) pointed out the incredulity of some people's opinions about loss always being associated with adoption, because

> the psychosocial experiences of adoptees and their families are as diverse as those of people from any other cultural group, practitioners must understand that adoption is not a formula for traumatic loss any more than being female is a formula for passivity. (p. 745)

She also pointed out the subtle difference and maximal impact of referring to adoption by saying "She was adopted" instead of "She is adopted." This directs the listener (and, more important, the adopted child standing next to the mom/dad making the statement) to view adoption as a personality trait when using "is adopted," rather than viewing adoption as a circumstance or event in "was adopted." In subtle ways, the things adults say influence how the adopted child takes in his or her meaning about adoption.

Pertman (2000) related a story of being in the grocery store with his 5-year-old son when a woman started asking about his son's birth mother, using pejorative terms in a condemning tone of voice. After the exchange in the grocery store, Pertman told his son many stories about his birth parents that showed them in a positive light, knowing that, eventually, part of his son's identity would be formed from what he would hear about and how he takes in the information about his birth parents.

Research indicates that adopted children are just as well off as other children, if not better, in the final analysis (Johnson, 2002). Nothing is inherently inferior in these children, the families who adopted them, or their birth parents. There is a residual stigma associated with the infertility of the man, which led to the adoption (Freeark et al., 2005). And there are issues of out-of-wedlock babies with prejudicial judgment about the birth mother. There is a parallel prejudice against allowing homosexuals to adopt children. And the prejudice of racism can disallow transracial adoption.

A "hundredth-monkey" explanation of behavior might be operating across societies. It goes like this: Long ago, a monkey began to peel bananas before eating them. Other monkeys watched and imitated this action, gradually spreading the practice. It was spreading around the globe until one day there was enough mass of monkeys (thus, the label of hundredth monkey) peeling bananas so all the monkeys around the world began to peel bananas. With the expansion of the global society through the Internet, old beliefs and attitudes might be transformed sooner than in previous times. At one time in the United States, when orphanages were closed because of their dehumanizing and debilitating circumstances, adoption was viewed as a positive solution to a social problem. Perhaps our society can again hold that view and erase the stigma that harms innocent children.

Effects of Adoption on Children and Families

The effect of adoption on children and families has been the main focus of research on adoption over time. Most of the research has been directed to effects on the adoptee and, to a far lesser extent, effects on the adoptive family. In most of the early studies, researchers concentrated on adoptees who exhibited externalizing problems of a behavioral nature such as delinquency, as well as internalizing problems of an emotional nature such as depression. The early studies on the impact of adoption often examined clinical populations rather than sampling the overall population of adoptees. As a result, the effects of adoption appeared far more negative than later studies, which sampled the overall population of adoptees. The early studies also had not parceled out the population of adoptee circumstances, such as being adopted at birth, after multiple foster settings, or having been abused/neglected or drug-exposed. Although the early research helped to identify aspects worthy of later study, it did not provide an accurate overall picture of effects of adoption.

This core area, highlighting more recent research on effects of adoption, is organized in three areas: background on effects of adoption, general areas of study on effects of adoption, and specific areas of study, such as gender differences.

Background on Effects of Adoption

The more recent reviews of the research literature on adoption emphasize resilience and protective factors to a greater extent (Friedlander, 2003) than formerly. O'Brien and Zamostny (2003) recommended that future research on adoption "discuss the magnitude of the differences, the practical significance, and the strength of the relations found among variables" (p. 694). They also suggested that research be grounded in theory, provide information on societal and cultural factors that influence views of families with an adopted child or children, use methodology within acceptable limits of social scientists, and "focus on resiliency and successful outcomes for adoptive families" (p. 679).

Although adoption may carry risk, it also brings possibilities that are enriching for all involved in the process. Johnson (2002) quoted respected adoption researcher Richard Barth:

> Adoption is a time-honored and successful service for children and parents. The outcomes of adoption are more favorable for children than any social program that I know. My own research and that of my colleagues indicates that the modest difficulties experienced by children who are adopted are far outweighed by the significant benefits that they receive from having a permanent family. (p. 51)

Empirical research (Alexander, Hollingsworth, Dore, & Hoopes, 2004; Miall, 1998; Sobol, Daly, & Kelloway, 2000; Sykes, 2001), effect-related research, and integrative reviews of adoption research over the last 10 years (Haugaard, 1998; Johnson, 2002;

Nickman et al., 2005; O'Brien & Zamostny, 2003; Peters, Atkins, & McKay, 1999) demonstrate that some subgroups of adopted children face challenges beyond what can be expected of typical growth and development (e.g., identity formation in adolescence). At the same time, the kinds of adjustment issues seen in adoption usually can be attributed to factors other than adoption, such as deprivation or abuse during institutionalization in orphanages, neglect and violence before parental rights were terminated and the child was adopted, drug exposure in utero and/or thereafter, or multiple placements in foster homes before termination of parental rights resulting in attachment/bonding problems (Friedlander et al., 2000; Johnson, 2002; Pertman, 2000). Another explanation for the finding that more adopted children had problems than their proportional representation in society was suggested as being attributable to the "greater willingness for parents of adopted children to seek help from behavioral specialists" (Johnson, 2002, p. 49).

General Areas of Study

Nickman et al. (2005) summarized 10 years of research related to adoptees under 18 years of age. They reviewed recent literature in relation to developmental influences, outcome of adoption placement, psychological problems, and treatment of adopted children. They identified adoption variables affecting the development of the child—symptoms such as post-traumatic stress disorder, externalizing (e.g., conduct problems, delinquency) and internalizing (e.g., anxiety, depression) behaviors, or attachment problems. They pointed out what other experts in the field of adoption have repeated frequently: Different circumstances result in different severity of risk factors. Among other questions, they brought up a topic for future study that can be answered only over time: "Does open adoption mediate risk factors of adopted children?"

Peters, Atkins, and McKay (1999) conducted an extensive review of adoption literature prior to 1999 and research relating to behavioral, diagnostic, and demographic characteristics to try to explain the higher rates of behavior problems among children who were adopted. They concluded that "it may be time for a new awareness and appreciation for the normative aspects of adoption" (p. 297). They recommended resilience literature when considering adopted children and families:

> An awareness of what is special or unique to families with adopted children can offer support and understanding to children and parents without invoking poorly operationalized pathology models that lack empirical support. (p. 325)

O'Brien and Zamostny (2003) conducted an integrative review of empirical research about adoptive families, covering empirical research conducted between 1985 and 2002. As a result, they suggested building on strengths, education, and normalization of challenges faced by the family or child/youth, and intensive therapy when obviously crucial for healthy outcomes.

Adjustment problems were the topic of review and synthesis by Haugaard (1998). His study was predicated on determining whether there is indeed an increased risk in adoption and, if so, suggesting some preventive measures. He pointed out that if increased risk was found only in subgroups of adoptees (e.g., trauma prior to adoption), it would be harmful for professionals and parents to assume that increased risk was associated with all other types of adoptions. If the findings of subgroups are generalized to all, this could influence parenting styles and practices, as well as parental expectations of the child.

Self-fulfilling prophecies can create negative outcomes that otherwise would not exist. Thus, if the question, "Is adoption a risk factor for the development of adjustment problems in children?" is answered with, "No, it is a risk factor for only certain subgroups of adoptees," parents of adopted children, mental health professionals, and society must be informed so that low expectations do not result in a self-fulfilling prophecy.

Haugaard (1998) further pointed out the heterogeneity among adopted children/youth and the expectation that newborns experience very different circumstances than those adopted when they are school age. If the circumstances of the adopted child influence risk factors, combining different subgroups of adoptees in research will lead to underestimating the risk for some groups and overestimating the risks for other subgroups of adopted children. Haugaard divided the characteristics of heterogeneity into three groups relating to all members of the adoption triad:

1. Adoption by a stepparent married to an adoptee's birth parent, or parent(s) unrelated to the adoptee
2. Age when the adoptee was placed
3. The circumstances that resulted in the child being placed for adoption by the birth parent(s)

Haugaard's review of literature led him to conclude that the risk for adjustment depends on whether the researchers were studying clinically or nonclinically based children. As might be expected, in the nonclinical samples the risk is not prevalent. The clinically based studies found what was considered an overrepresentation of adopted children/youth, and, relatedly, that the adopted children were at greater risk for adjustment problems than nonadopted children/youth.

In a sampling of nationally representative adolescents, Miller, Fan, Christensen, Grotevant, and Van Dulmen (2000) compared adoptive and nonadoptive youth in terms of psychological and behavioral problems. Using a survey that covered a variety of variables, the authors found that adoptive youth were "at higher risk in all of the domains examined, including school achievement and problems of substance abuse, psychological well-being, physical health, fighting, and lying to parents" (p. 1458). They indicated that major drawbacks of the study were lack of information on age at adoption—considered a salient factor because the later the child is adopted, the more family adjustment and problems the youth experiences.

Specific Research Areas

The effect on the development of children who were adopted was broken down by circumstance categories that separated different possibilities of impact on the adopted child/family (Johnson, 2002). Categories of circumstances included

1. post-institutionalized children and impact on cognitive recovery, attachment, behavior problems and social deficits, and physical growth, as well as adoptive families of post-institutionalized children;
2. drug-exposed children; and
3. infant adoption and whether it had a negative effect.

Johnson's (2002) review initially reported studies on children at the time when orphanages in the United States were closing and children were being placed at differing ages in adoptive, foster, or birth-family homes. This provided a population for post-institutionalization and follow-up studies related to reversal of deficits (e.g., bonding, physical and emotional development, severe difficulties in behavior, emotions, and learning) stemming from the early childhood institutionalization. These studies demonstrated that adoption was able to reverse some deficits the children experienced from institutionalization and that adopted children "were generally doing as well if not better than those children restored to their birth families" (p. 42).

The second category of adoptions reviewed by Johnson (2002) related to drug-exposed children during pregnancy or thereafter. He indicated that interpreting data on children whose birth mothers took illicit drugs is complex because the pregnant mothers ingested different types and amounts of illicit drugs, making it impossible to define "drug-exposed" children. Johnson also pointed out the controversy about whether cocaine and some other drugs affect the fetus. A body of research indicates

> catastrophic neurologic damage or premature termination of pregnancy in a limited number of cases and can affect an infant's neurologic status in the immediate newborn period. However, the long-term effects are not as clearly defined. (p. 48)

This research was conducted with preschool and school-aged children. Johnson added that there is a lack of research with this population comparing those who are adopted with those who remain in their birth families.

In spite of the higher risk resulting from illicit drug use during and after gestation, in most areas these children were functioning within the normal range and were almost indistinguishable from the non-drug-exposed children. And 85% of the birth mothers in the studies also had exposed their unborn children to alcohol, which is well established as a tetratogen. Johnson (2002) concluded:

> The fact that outcome was as good as it was speaks not only of the powerful positive effect of an adoptive family on development in children exposed to illicit drugs, but also to this dangerous though legal chemical. (p. 49)

A refrain true of other serious risk factors was reiterated: The adopting family can neither eradicate all deficits nor ameliorate all problems of children exposed to drugs while in utero or afterward.

The third category of studies Johnson (2002) reviewed on adoption investigated whether adoption has a negative effect on children's development when they were adopted under 12 months of age. Adopted and birth children were described as indistinguishable through preschool age. Some differences were found as they aged that depended on preadoption circumstances.

Also reviewed by Johnson (2002) was a study of adopted children (92% adopted before 12 months old). Outcomes were compared to nonadopted children with similar circumstances and the general population at 22 and 33. At age 22, adopted women showed positive adjustment in all domains, often better than the general population, while adopted men were doing as well as nonadopted males. At age 33, nonadopted adults had more employment and social difficulties; "both men and women in the birth comparison group were in less favorable social and material circumstances than the majority of the adopted children at age 33" (p. 50). The subtle differences at age 22 likely related to preadoption experiences, as well as inherent loss.

> With competent, loving, and often socially and economically advantaged families, adopted children generally do better than comparison groups of children who are placed in foster care or who remained or were reunited with their birth mothers." (Johnson, 2002, p. 50)

Outcomes in follow-up studies of infant adoption are almost entirely positive. Mainstream researchers "do not believe that infant adoption constitutes an immediate loss at placement that inevitably disrupts early attachments" (Leon, 2002, p. 653).

Some time ago, LePere (1988) identified successful adoption factors, and even longer ago Raynor (1980) identified factors that tend to interfere with successful postadoption family adjustment. According to these researchers, parents who see adoption as different from biological parenthood are more successful than those who reject the differences. Those who continue to deal with adoption revelation are more successful.

With adoption involving a child of a different race or from another culture, Friedlander et al. (2000) recommended that parents and adopted children explore the culture of the child's birth and also cultivate friendships from that culture. They also recommended that the child's developmental level be taken into consideration so he or she doesn't have an overload of information earlier than can be cognitively processed or emotionally handled.

Parental prejudice and self-fulfilling prophecies tend to diminish the likelihood of successful adoption adjustment. Parents who hold images of the ideal child and attempt to mold their adopted child to their expectations tend to have greater difficulty. When parents have early doubts and do not adequately address them, adjustment is more problematic.

Gender differences were reviewed (Freeark et al., 2005) in relation to shaping the adoption life cycle with an emphasis on the overfeminization of adoption and marginalization of men/fathers and boys/sons. They concluded that women are left to "address emotion, connection, and communication, and family dialogues about adoption may engage daughters more successfully than sons" (p. 86). This article gives consideration to understanding why boys and girls who are adopted have disparity in rates of behavior problems and explores gender differences relating to emotional expressiveness, seeking social support, as well as formation of identity as the inherent cause of the higher rates of problem behavior in boys.

Another issue—infertility—is experienced differently by men and women, primarily because the birth father doesn't carry the child in utero for 9 months. Whether the infertile partner is the man or the woman, the woman tends to bear the most emotional consequences. Furthermore, the adoption itself may be based on gender considerations (Freeark et al., 2005). Thus, gender affects all three parts of the adoption triad (birth parents, parents who adopt, and the adopted child/youth).

Open Adoption

Open adoption basically means that the adoption is revealed to those involved. Communication that is open among the members of the adoption triad has longer roots than most realize. According to Sykes (2001), open communication among the three members of the adoption triad began in the 1960s in England. In the 1960s the problem of "genealogical bewilderment" by children who were adopted became a concern of an English professional (Sants, 1964, cited by Sykes). So, too, the issue of deception of adoptees by adoptive parents became a concern (Kirk, 1964, cited by Sykes) when adoptive parents participated in "pretending" that the family was just like biologically parented families.

Ascendant Theories

Early adoption practices had been based on attachment theory, with consideration for the primacy of bonding with the adoptive parents. Intrusion in the life of the adoptive family by birth family contact or discussion of them was thought to impact the well-being of the child negatively. Over time, attachment theory became descendant and other theories ascendant, as no research evidence emerged that attachments are made before birth or immediately after birth. Rather, attachment is viewed as developing from the repetition of mutual interactions of nurturing by caregiver(s) during the first months of life. Some of the activities between child and caregiver that result in attachment are feeding, comforting, affection, and stimulation. Hill, Fonagy, Safier, and Sargent (2003) wrote about attachment in terms of the family versus between two individuals and described "the ecology of attachment in the family" by portraying processes in attachment on individual, dyad, and family levels. The decline of attachment theory paralleled the movement of open adoption.

Another ascendant theory, family systems theory, took an open approach that encompassed the whole family system, and even the whole social network. And still another ascendant theory was feminist theory (Gilligan, 1982; Miller, 1986), with its emphasis on relationship and connection versus separation. This theory has an underpinning of psychoanalytic theory, holding that healthy development involves a process of separating self from others increasingly over the course of the lifetime, beginning with separation from the mother.

These ascendant theories justifiably provided a challenge to the deficit model. In essence, the deficit model took a view of adoption as second rate.

Self-in-Relation Model

The self-in-relation model was applied to adoption by Silverstein and Demick (1994), who suggested that it points to a process with possibilities for providing each member of the adoption triad with ways to tolerate not only stress and pain but also the complexity of adoptive relationships. It allows for empathy to build over time such that changing needs of the members of the adoption triad can have their needs met through openness. Those authors contend that an adoptive triad that is child-centered will be responsive to the changing needs of the child/youth with honesty, empathy, and energy.

If the adoptee has contact with the birth parent and the birth parent marries and has children, those children, and any children born who were kept by a birth parent before the birth of the adoptive child, are the adopted child's half-siblings. When open adoption contact is face-to-face with a birth parent's entire family, rather than solely with a birth parent, it is crucial to consider the adoptive child's needs in relation to the half-siblings as well as any extended birth-family members with whom there is contact with the adoptive child.

This consideration also applies to the birth father if the birth father and adoptive child have ongoing face-to-face contact. The birth father, however, is usually absent either because he has denied paternity or relinquished his rights. Professional exploration of the birth father's involvement in the decision-making process appears emergent, and over time the "invisibility factor" of birth fathers could change.

Levels of Openness

Various researchers have described the degrees of contact in open adoption in different ways (Demick & Wapner, 1988; Grotevant & McRoy, 1998; Miall & March, 2005b; Sobol et al., 2000; Zamostny et al., 2003). Usually they suggest three or four levels of open adoption. Here we will consider of a model with four levels of openness, loosely based on the levels described by the above experts, ranging from least to most open.

Level I—*restrictive open adoption*: The adoptive parents send to the birth parent(s) periodic (e.g., annual or semi-annual) letters about the adoptive child, which may include pictures, through an intermediary, such as a social worker. There is no exchange of identifying information about the birth parents and adoptive parents. In this least open level, the birth parents and adoptive parents do not meet one another.

Level II—*semi-open adoption*: Prior to adoption, the birth parent(s) and adoptive parents meet face to face without sharing identifying information. Subsequently, letters/pictures are sent once or twice a year via an intermediary.

Level III—*open adoption*: Prior to adoption, the birth parent(s) and adoptive parents meet face to face and exchange identifying information (e.g., names). Once or twice a year, the adoptive parents send a letter updating the birth parent(s) on the adoptee's life, and the triad in addition meets face-to-face on occasion. The birth parent(s) sends a card to the adoptive child twice a year (birthday and other holiday). (Level III could easily turn into either Level IV or II, depending on the nature of the relationship between the adoptive parents and birth parent(s), and a shift in level could be done formally, in writing.).

Level IV—*fully open adoption with continuing contact*: Contacts between the birth parent(s) and adoptive parents occur from birth through the child coming of age, and the child is included in the contacts. Either prior to the child's birth or while the newborn is temporarily in a foster home, the birth parent(s) and adoptive parents meet and agree to the plan for fully open adoption with ongoing face-to-face contact among all three members of the adoption triad. Important at this level is that the child is included in the ongoing contacts. The frequency of contact varies over time and responds to the needs of each member of the adoption triad in terms of the child's emotional needs and the changing circumstances in the lives of the birth parent(s) and/or adoptive parents (such as moving to a different state or how contact with half-siblings affects either/both families and individual members of the adoption triad).

Benefits of Open Adoption

In 1994, the benefits of open adoption for the three members of the adoption triad were delineated by Silverstein and Demick, with an emphasis on development of empathy. Benefits to birth parents include

- assurance that their birth child is well-loved and safe,
- an increased sense of control resulting in reduced feelings of shame/guilt (as contrasted with a closed adoption), and
- affirmation for the legitimacy of feelings toward their birth child.

For adoptive parents, benefits that accrue from open adoption are

- a deeper sense of the vibrancy of the birth parents' love/concern for their birth child,
- the opportunity for adoptive parents to be in a relationship with their adoptive child in which the child is fully aware of the dual heritage from the beginning, and
- lessening of stress resulting from the lack of secrecy and "the intolerably unknown."

For the adoptive child, contact with the birth parent(s) provides

- a deeper and more meaningful connection with the adoptive parents;
- elimination of the disconnection/denial that is present without openness,
- increased empathy for the birth parent(s) over time, resulting in fewer fantasies about a "perfect family" out there; and
- clear and consistent information that results in an inner sense of control when facing issues related to adoption.

The number of open adoptions is increasing dramatically. This form of adoption potentially improves outcomes for adopted children/youth. Johnson (2002) pointed out extensive research that reported improved outcomes for all members of the triad in open adoption (Sobol et al., 2000; Sykes, 2001).

Adoption disclosure in African-American families was studied by Alexander and colleagues, (2004). The researchers found that most of the parents (usually the mother) were sensitive and creative in telling their child the "adoption story." One family said about the decision to adopt: "I felt if we were going to be a family of trust …. It should come from us and not from outside" (p. 453). Interestingly, the description of disclosure did not mention the birth father. Also, almost all the families told the adoption story once and did not bring it up again.

Comparison With Closed Adoption

Closed adoptions evolved when psychoanalytic theory was ascendant and the view of health was one of independence (Silverstein & Demick, 1994; Wegar, 2000; Zamostny et al., 2003). Silverstein and Demick (1994) quoted Demick and Wapner (1988) in stating:

> [C]losed adoption—may be conceptualized as *dedifferentiated* [all family members consciously or unconsciously deny that the child has been adopted], *differentiated and isolated* [adoptive parents shelter the adoptee so that he or she will not learn about the biologic parents from others and/or will not have to deal with the

stigma of being adopted), or *differentiated and in conflict* (the adoptee may fantasize that the biologic parents would treat him or her differently, and/or may threaten to leave the adoptive family to find the "real parents" when of age). (pp. 241–242)

They contrasted this with open adoption, indicating that more open adoption could result in *differentiated and integrated identity*, as well as higher self-esteem on the part of the adoptee. As well, they depicted birth parents as potentially more able to integrate their child's identity and "to avoid blaming 'bad blood in the background' for any of their difficulties" (p. 242).

Searches and Reunions

Johnson (2002) referred to sealed adoption records—which were common practice in the past—giving way to adult adoptees' making contact with birth parents as another way for adopted men and women to resolve the "loss aspect" of adoption. With the changes in attitude toward openness in adoption, as well as legislative changes in unsealing adoption records, connections between adopted individuals and birth families have been facilitated through the Internet and investigators specializing in tracking down birth parents and/or adopted children. Agencies have also provided opportunities for adoptees over age 18 to connect with their birth parents through a process in which the adopted child (currently young adult) and birth parent(s) must participate jointly to make the connection complete.

The connection sometimes is made by the public agency that facilitated the adoption. Additional agencies and organizations provide the same service. Essentially, they enable the birth mother/father to write a letter to the birth child who was adopted and provide contact information such as phone number, email, and/or address. Some of these letters include information about the circumstances of the adoption, and others omit this information if the circumstances would not be advantageous (e.g., rape, death of birth mother/father).

Sally [not her real name], a social worker, has had a letter in the agency file for years, in hopes that her birth daughter will one day try to contact her. She had difficulty writing the letter because she knew her hopes would be dashed if her birth daughter did not request to see the letter. Sally made sure the letter was on file the day of her birth daughter's 18th birthday.

So far, after a year, the birth daughter has not contacted Sally. There are several possible reasons. Maybe the adult daughter would like to contact her birth mother but has no idea where to seek the information. Or possibly the child really does not want to contact her birth mother, for a variety of reasons.

Whatever the case, searches and reunions are difficult to achieve because of ambiguities in the law, a lack of information, and misinformation about the process. For example, most laws do not allow the birth child to contact the birth parent until after age 18, and at that time, the adult child may not realize that this is a possibility.

Friedlander (2003) believes the child who was adopted would breathe a sigh of relief not to be involved in a search or reunion prior to adulthood.

> Searches and reunions are risky business for adoptees at any age, but without compelling medical reason, those who have not been raised with an open adoption from early childhood should be discouraged from searching before they reach adulthood. (p. 748)

This opinion contrasts with the opinion of others that adolescents have unique needs related to identity versus role confusion (Erikson, 1959, 1963).

People and families are different. The form of adoption that is best for one is not necessarily best for another. In the end, the families involved (birth and adoptive) must make a decision in which the child does not participate, always keeping the child's best interest at the forefront.

For instance, what if the child was conceived under a circumstance of rape, incest, mental incompetence, psychoses, murder, death while giving birth, or other complex and disturbing possibilities. In some cases, the best interests of the adoptive child will not be served by revealing the circumstances, at least until the adoptive child is mature enough to integrate the reality without lasting damage to emotional and behavioral health.

The birth mother, too, deserves to be treated with dignity and respect and not to have the circumstances of the conception revealed against her will. Adoptee and adoptive parents would do well to reach out for counsel from professionals who can help them reach a decision, and to come up with a plan if the decision is to move forward with the search.

International Adoption

World War II and the Korean Conflict spawned waves of international adoption, and the number of international adoptions has increased dramatically beginning in the 1990s (Volkman, 2003). In 1992, 5% of adoptions were intercountry.* In 2001, the picture changed dramatically, with 15% of reported adoptions in the United States being intercountry adoptions (U.S. Department of Health and Human Services, 2004). The DHHS statistic is thought to be lower than the true number because when the adoption takes place in another country, there is no requirement that the child be "readopted" in the United States. Thus, the real figure is higher than 15%. Most of the children made available for international adoption during the last decade have been from China and Russia (Fisher, 2003, citing the U.S. Department of State, 2002).

This fifth of the six core areas, international adoption, emphasizes the effects of institutionalization on the international adoptees. Not all internationally adopted children were institutionalized, though. Some countries (e.g., Korea) place children in foster homes prior to their being adopted internationally.

---

*The U.S. Government uses the term "intercountry" instead of "international," so that term will be used when reporting government data here.

Reasons for International Adoption

Some reasons for prospective adoptive parents seeking to adopt internationally are (Kaslow, 2003; Schwartz and Kaslow, 2003)

- the higher availability of babies and older children,
- altruistic prospective parents motivated to adopt children who otherwise might spend childhood and adolescence in orphanages,
- less restrictive requirements to become an adoptive parent than in the United States (e.g., age),
- religiously oriented prospective parents feeling a "call" to adopt abroad, and
- preference for a closed adoption with no opportunity for birth parents to try to reclaim the child or having to face legal complications or expend funds on attorneys to keep their adopted child if a birth parent were to try to reclaim their birth child in the courts.

Unlike past practices in international adoption, in which ties to the birth country were severed in favor of absorption in the new homeland (Volkman, 2004), in today's world international adoptees

- anticipate the exploration of their international identities,
- often have adoptive parents who maintain their birth names or use them as middle names,
- are encouraged to and helped to learn about their birth country, and
- meet Americans who immigrated from the country in which they were born.

In addition, some parents enroll their adoptive child in private classes to learn the language of their birth country. And some journey to the birth country with their adoptive parents when they are old enough to understand and absorb the culture of their birth. All of this is in stark contrast to practices in the middle of the 20th century, when adoptees knew little of their birth country.

Volkman (2003) described exploration of the birth country as particularly intense for those from China. In China, with its restriction of one child per family, the birth mothers often leave their child on the steps of an orphanage with or without a note, because the male child in the family is the one who is designated to care for his parents as they age. Therefore, Chinese adoptees are mostly girls, and usually nothing is known about their birth mother.

Effects of Institutionalization on International Adoptees

Judge (2003) studied the effects of institutionalization on adoptees from Eastern Europe. As a result, she recommended that adopted children who had been in institutions and were not catching up developmentally be referred for special services. She further recommended that, before filing for adoption from Eastern European countries, prospective adoptive parents be informed about the possibility of the children having developmental delays with potential needs for education or other services.

Pomerleau and colleagues (2005) did a comparison study on health status and psychological development of children adopted under 18 months from China, Vietnam, Taiwan, Thailand, South Korea, Cambodia, and Eastern Europe (mostly Russia).

Improvement was observed in adoptees with better nutrition, shorter preadoption experience, and younger age at adoption when also accompanied by an absence of signs of neurological difficulties that led to assuming rapid gains in motor and cognitive development were possible. In addition, important determinant factors of adoptees related to the home environment, higher levels of parental education, strong financial resources, and sound parenting.

Johnson (2002) reported on previously institutionalized Romanian children adopted by families in Canada and the United Kingdom. He found that developmental delay was pervasive in children adopted by families in both countries, but from this bleak beginning, the adopted children made considerable progress over the course of the first years. A longitudinal study that Johnson reviewed found no effect on IQ from early institutionalization, though the same study did find a greater likelihood of the adoptees' having more social/emotional problems than comparison children.

Multiple Risk Factors in Adoption

The sixth core area concerns multiple risk factors and adoption in relation to

1. adopted children/youth with complex needs stemming from extreme neglect, physical or sexual abuse, disability, and adoption after 5 years of age; and
2. foster children adopted domestically on an individual basis or as a sibling group with/without previous multiple foster placements.

Although the term *special needs* is prevalent in the literature, to bring greater clarity to this book and, specifically, multiple risk factors resulting from adoption, the term *complex needs* is used here for the most part. Glidden (1994) defined complex needs in adoption as those of children "who are older, are members of a minority, have disabilities, and/or need to be placed as a sibling group of more than two" (p. 198). The complex needs generally derive from experiences prior to adoption; however, children with a disability may have been born with or developed the disability after birth. Barth and Berry (1988) included in the group of children with complex needs those who are age 6 and older, and Schweiger and O'Brien (2005) emphasized the rising number of older children who have been physically or sexually abused, experienced neglect, have emotional or physical disabilities, are over 1 year old when adopted, and/or are members from one sibling group adopted as a family unit.

The Risks

The risks in adopting children with complex needs and those adopted domestically after foster placements relate to emotional, behavioral, cognitive, or physical issues at home, school, and/or community. Adoptive children with complex needs on whom data can be tracked are from the child welfare system that placed the child in foster homes while trying to find an adoptive family.

Schweiger and O'Brien (2005) distinguished between the increasing disruptions (breakdown of a placement before legal finalization) and dissolutions (breakdown of a placement after legal finalization) in American adoptions. They estimate that between 10% and 15% of all adoptions are disrupted, with the highest number of disruptions being in the category of adoptive children who have complex needs stemming from life experiences previous to their adoption.

According to the Child Welfare Information Gateway (2004) report on numbers and trends, establishing realistic numbers on disruption and dissolution is difficult. The report did indicate that the numbers are not rising for either group, and that most research on disruption and dissolution ranges between 10% and 25%. It is more difficult to obtain an accurate count of disruptions because some records are closed, without names or Social Security numbers, and only public foster care data are available on dissolutions of adoptions.

The reasons given for disruptions related to older age of the child when adopted, number of foster-care placements prior to adoption, and the child's behavioral/emotional needs, as well as turnover of staff in adoption agencies. The number of different staff members involved in providing services to a family is given as a reason for disruptions in adoption. Lower functioning of the family was found to be associated with more support from professionals in school and therapeutic contexts, educators, and extended family.

Adoptive parents in extreme situations who find that they are unable to adjust to the severity of the behavior issues in the child, and therefore choose dissolution of the adoption, are not dysfunctional families. Generally, they are families who were not prepared by the adoption agency to understand the nature and scope of the child's complex needs. Further, these adoptive parents require intensive in-home services and financial relief, which are lacking.

Successful Adoptions

On an upbeat note, Reilly and Platz (2004) stated, "Despite the challenges associated with adopting children with special needs, the majority of adoptive parents in this study reported good adoption outcomes" (p. 64–65). Adoptions of children with some types of complex needs are more successful than average. Glidden (2000) found that, over an 11-year period, adoptive mothers of children with developmental disabilities were positive about the adoption and adjustment of the family. She encouraged families to adopt these children and indicated that having more than one child with a disability in a family did not impact the family adjustment negatively.

Some time ago, Samuels (1990) found that cross-race adoptions and adoptions of children with disabilities had higher than average success rates (about 75% being successful). Simon and Altstein (2002) came to the same conclusions from their study of 100 transracially adopted children. Specifically with regard to mental retardation, Glidden (1989) noted a similar finding of success.

The success rate of adoptions may be prompted by the following factors:

1. Parents adopting children with complex needs may be better informed and more considered than other adoptive parents in their decisions.
2. Caseworkers who deal with adoptions that present challenges usually orient their work toward matching the child with a family that can best provide for his or her needs.
3. The parents may hold more realistic expectations of the adopted child, particularly with regard to potential problems, because, prior to the decision to adopt, they became informed and educated about the challenges the child will face.

For these parents, seeking and using an external support network is often encouraged. Children who have complex needs and foster children have the backing of financial incentives aimed at compensating the adoptive parents for their adoptive children's increased needs.

Foster Children Adopted Domestically

Foster children waiting for adoption include teenagers with previous multiple foster placements that left them scarred and untrusting because they were moved from one foster home to another, children with disabilities, minority children, and transracial children/youth. There is no waiting line of prospective adoptive parents in the United States wanting to adopt these children like there is for international adoption, even though the circumstances those children faced in orphanages are similar in terms of having experienced neglect and worse.

Fortunately, changes in laws governing adoption in more recent times have opened doors for single prospective parents, those with disabilities, and lesbian/gay individuals or partners to adopt foster children. These people are partially responsible for lowering the numbers of children awaiting adoption in the United States. In the 1990s, the legal and social work systems concluded that the "best interests of the child" was a better yardstick than "family preservation" when children were removed from their biological homes or abandoned. As a result of that significant shift, adoption by nonkinship couples and individuals began increasing (Pertman, 2000).

A form of domestic adoption known as "fost-adopt" allows potential adopters to cut through the red tape and length of time required to adopt a child. This program presents a level of risk, acknowledging that the adoption may not work out, but at the same time offers an opportunity for the child to be adopted from birth. The foster parents complete paperwork stating that they will adopt the foster child placed in their home at birth, or shortly thereafter; if the child is not returned to either birth parent, the foster parents move directly into adoption.

Adoption of Sibling Groups

The most difficult foster adoption scenario seems to be with sibling groups. Research by Leung and Erich (2002) found that sibling adoption strained the family system more than any other single factor and resulted in poor family adjustment. When the sibling unit included more than two children, the potential for dissolution increased. These researchers did not recommend sibling unit adoption because of the poor family adjustment.

One of my mother's closest friends and her husband adopted a sibling group with four children. The level of need was evident from the first day of the adoption. She and her husband had the resources to pay for assistance, so that factor made little or no difference on the behavior issues of any of the siblings.

Later, the couple had a biological child, and eventually they divorced, likely precipitated by the strain from the sibling-group adoption. All of the children had dramatic emotional and behavioral issues (for example, head banging). The life of this family was totally consumed by problems stemming from the sibling adoption.

Research evidence demonstrated that children may be better served if they are separated, allowing more attention to one than rather dividing the attention among several children.

Adoption Adjustment

A child's positive adjustment to adoption is a complex process. Brodzinsky and colleagues (Brodzinsky, 1990; Brodzinsky, Schechter, & Henig, 1992) identified several stages in the adjustment process and showed how Erikson's (1959, 1963) psychosocial tasks of development relate to each of these stages in life.

Infancy

If the child was adopted before 1 year of age (infancy), many adoptive parents must resolve their feelings related to the infertility of one of the couple and develop realistic expectations of the child in relation to their expectations for the biological child they were unable to have. Finally, the parent(s) must develop appropriate attachment to the child.

The task for the adoptee in this stage is to resolve Erikson's trust-versus-mistrust stage. Unless the adopted child was brought home from the hospital soon after birth, the infant is adjusting to the new home and developing secure attachments. Difficulty with this task is more evident when placement is delayed or the child has had multiple placements during infancy or a number of different caregivers. Similarly, children in orphanages who later were adopted internationally will not have had the same caregivers to provide security by their daily presence with the infant.

Preschool Years

For children during the preschool years, Erikson's developmental tasks are the resolution of autonomy versus shame and doubt and of initiative versus guilt. As is typical of all children at this age, adoptees are learning about birth and reproduction. In cases of interracial or international adoption, the child will become aware of differences in appearance and therefore may step into the questioning phase earlier than other children do.

Although experts have not always agreed about the best time to disclose the adoption to the children, most indicate that this is preferable during the preschool years (Freeark et al., 2005; Hajal & Rosenberg, 1991). Some adoptive parents are at a loss to know how to respond to their child's questions at this age. Underlying this unease is a fear that talking about the adoption may result in a loss of closeness between the adoptive parents and child (Watkins & Fisher, 1995). Once the discussion begins, however, parents usually become calmer and begin to build a truthful version of the child's life story that matches his or her cognitive and emotional understanding, marking a significant developmental milestone for the adoptive family (Freeark et al., 2005, p. 94).

Because of gender differences, little girls are more involved than boys with information exchanges and expression of emotions, and their faces illustrate how they feel. The parents, in turn, provide more details of the "adoption story" when talking with girls than with boys. By contrast, the boys tend to express themselves physiologically and behaviorally rather than verbally.

This early stage may influence all the later stages in terms of conversations about adoption, reflecting the pattern developed with the son or daughter during the preschool stage. Mothers more often than fathers take the initiative—reading literature, talking with others who adopted a child, and attending presentations about adoption. Mothers, too, typically model an openness that daughters are more likely to pick up on than sons. Fathers typically allow their wives to take the lead while staying more in the background (Freeark et al., 2005).

As a side note, the birth father usually is marginalized in adoption (Day et al., 2005; Dienhart & Daly, 1997; Freeark et al. 2005; Grotevant, 2003; Nock, 1998), and discussions about birth parents are about the birth mother. The adoptive child, then, develops a concept about the birth mother but thinks little about the birth father.

In any case, during the preschool years conversations related to the adoption are crucial to the child's forming a basis for later understanding when cognitive development allows greater depth. In short, the dominant theme during this stage should be to foster an awareness of the child's being "chosen."

Middle Childhood (Elementary School Years)

Erikson's developmental task for children in the middle childhood years is to resolve the issue of industry versus inferiority. For the adoptee, this task may be particularly difficult, because the child's increasing cognitive ability leads to an awareness that being "chosen" by one family implies being relinquished by another (Brodzinsky et al., 1998). This awareness may challenge the child's sense of security and belonging. Unless the adoption is fully open, with both birth parents having ongoing contact that includes the adoptive child, the child may start to ask questions about the family of origin, including why his or her birth parent(s) chose adoption.

During this stage, parents must be sensitive to the child's ambivalence and potential sense of rejection, which is apt to be accompanied by grief and insecurity signifying the loss (Friedlander et al., 2000). Openness to the child's need to explore adoption issues is extremely important. If the adoption has not been disclosed to people outside the family during the preschool years, it sometimes is disclosed now (Hajal & Rosenberg, 1991). As a result, children hear comments about noticeable physical differences between the parents and the children and have to learn how to assimilate some unfortunate comments (Pertman, 2000).

Freeark et al. (2005) suggested two major shifts for children in this stage—social and cognitive. The children are not as protected as they were when they were younger because they are exposed to a wider world in schools. Without the former security and closeness of family to protect them, all children, including those who were adopted, experience a sense of insecurity, some to a greater extent than others.

Unless the adoptive child has had ongoing contact with the birth parent(s) from early childhood, he or she will be trying to integrate the dual family history. Realizing that an adoptive family is different from a biologically created family also becomes clear in the eyes of the adoptive child's peers.

Complicating the picture is that peers begin to assume greater significance in the lives of children, so their opinions have a greater impact on adoptive children. Adoptive children face questions about their adoption from curious peers, and other children use the adoption as a way to exclude a child who needs to feel accepted by others at this time. This dynamic makes adoptive children in the middle years more vulnerable when working on the psychosocial task of industry versus inferiority. Between the ages of 5 and 7, a higher incidence of academic, psychological, and behavioral challenges emerge for children who were adopted at infancy (Brodzinsky et al., 1998). Families bring different strengths to help inoculate their children from the stigma of peers' viewing adoption as an inferior family condition.

Typical of children at this age, boys hang together in larger loose-knit social groups, compared to girls, whose relationships involve fewer girls but deeper levels of intimacy revolving around shared interests. Girls are far more likely than boys to discuss adoption with one another, or to attach significance to that family form. Freeark and colleagues (2005) stated:

> The social norms regarding emotional expression and relatedness are likely to parallel those that most adopted girls have experienced in their families, typically guided by their mother. (p. 96)

Adoptive boys exhibit more externalizing behaviors, such as conduct disorder, attention deficit disorder, and impulsivity, compared to peers of the same age (Miller et al., 2000). For boys, dominance is more important than affiliation; thus, the externalizing of problems makes sense. Freeark and colleagues (2005) posed an interesting question in this regard: "Does the active engagement of an adoptive father in tackling the complexity of how men and boys can acknowledge feelings make a difference in his son's adjustment?" (p. 97).

In the middle years, children wonder whether relinquishment for adoption is related to their gender. They also wonder if their gender mattered to their being chosen by their adoptive parents. Again, professionals in school and community are advised to read and offer age-appropriate books to children in the middle childhood stage and follow up with group discussion. This can help to normalize the adoption processes and dispel stigma. Professionals also can suggest books for families related to the loss their child may feel. Bibliotherapy (Bradley et al., 2004) is a means to help parents respond positively to their child's task resolution of industry versus inferiority.

Adolescence

Erikson's (1959) psychosocial task during adolescence is the resolution of identity versus role confusion. Like all adolescents, the adoptee faces biological issues and the usual adolescent concerns regarding identity. For children ages 10–14, the family is still the primary context for development (Muuss, 1996). In spite of peer relationships rising in importance, children at this age still need and want to be accepted by and feel close to their parents

(Noller, 1994; Richardson, 2004). Contradictory to these identified needs, the family spends less time and expresses less affection with children in early adolescence (Richardson, 2004; Stemmler & Petersen, 1999). As a result, just when identity issues are beginning to emerge, parents and their budding adolescents are finding less close, meaningful communication. Benson, Galbraith, and Espeland (1998) surveyed more than 100,000 adolescents across the United States in which only 26% indicated that their parents were available and approachable to them.

Knowing that all children reaching adolescence are dealing with identity versus role confusion, these identity concerns understandably are magnified for adoptees. Adolescents often connect adoption to their sense of identity, and in international and biracial adoptions they also must deal with racial identity and physical differences from family members (Volkman, 2003).

Closed adoptions, with the confidentiality and secrecy issues, combine the task of developing a separate identity with fear regarding the adolescent's desire to explore his or her personal background. Silverstein and Demick (1994) maintained that opposing forces of this nature do not have to be antagonistic or oppositional in nature. They stated:

> In fact, adopted children *are* related to their birth families, as are the adoptive parents (via adoption). However, the nature and meaning of these relationships are inherently different and, if not addressed in a spirit of mutual empathy, *potentially* antagonistic. Rather than providing an adolescent with a safe psychological space, it would seem that confidentiality is just as likely to exacerbate the struggle between parent and child over who has the privilege or power to define the other's reality. (p. 121, italics in original)

During the stage of adolescence, some adoptive parents assist the teen in learning about the birth parents or at least give their permission for this search to take place at some point (Bergquist, 2003; Friedlander et al., 2000; Hajal & Rosenberg, 1991). Adolescents adopted from other countries are well aware that their identity is different because of the dissimilarity in appearance from their adoptive parents. By adolescence, these adoptees also recognize that their social status and experiences in life would have been markedly different had they remained in their birth countries in orphanages or foster homes (Friedlander et al., 2000).

Unless the form of adoption is fully open with ongoing face-to-face contact including the adoptive adolescent, adoptees at this age often fantasize that their birth family is the perfect family, with unrealistic feelings stemming from such fantasies. Whatever the adoption-related issues, adolescents must deal with them to foster their sense of self and move toward identity rather than role confusion. Parents' openness and comfort in discussing issues about adoption have been found to be closely related to the older adoptees' sense of identity and self-esteem (Hoopes, 1990).

Sobol and colleagues (2000) found that preadolescents who were adopted with full disclosure about birth parents were more satisfied than those who had less open adoptions without full disclosure. This finding was attributed to the clear information that is crucial to identity formation in fully open adoptions from a very young age. In a school survey comparing adopted and nonadopted adolescents, using a large representative sample from the United States, boys who were adopted were found to have more problem behaviors than adopted girls and more problems than same-age nonadopted boys (Miller et al., 2000). Freeark and colleagues (2005) suggested that these findings may be indicative of the pattern established in the preschool years:

> It appears that the suggested protective factors we noted at ear-lier developmental periods (especially mother involvement, open communication between parent and child, understanding of one's own and others' emotions, and peer culture values that support personal expression) may be serving adopted adolescent girls bet-ter than their male counterparts as they work through the identity, differentiation, and autonomy issues of adolescence. (p. 98)

Burrow and Finley (2004) studied transracial and same-race adoptions in terms of adolescent adjustment and identity formation. Overall, the transracial adoptions produced results similar to those of same-race adoptions. Transracial adoptees' grades in school were significantly higher than same-race adoptees. As well, the academic expectations of transracial adoptees were significantly higher but were accompanied by "marginally more distant father relationships and higher levels of psychosomatic symptoms than their same-raced adopted counterparts" (p. 582).

Young Adulthood

Erikson's task for this stage is intimacy versus isolation. During this time, adoptees frequently delve deeper into exploring the adoption. If it was a closed adoption, the adoptee may begin to search for his or her birth parent(s). At this time, the adoptee may be facing issues related to becoming a parent in the future in light of having been adopted. If the genetic history is unknown, issues may involve medicalization and geneticization (Lebner, 2000). Too, loss may be a focus for some adoptees at this stage. Addressing issues of intimacy and the ability to form bonds with others is crucial. Usually, the parent–adoptee bond is reaffirmed during this stage as the young adult "adopts" the parent(s) who raised him or her (Hajal & Rosenberg, 1991).

Factors leading to successful adjustment are acceptance by the birth parents and the adoptive parents' sharing information and assisting with a search (Bergquist, 2003; Friedlander et al., 2000). Overall, the best predictor of the adoptee's social adjustment is his or her perception of belonging and stability in the adoptive family (Hoopes, 1990). Helping a child, adolescent, or young adult successfully resolve one psychosocial task will increase the likelihood of resolving the next psychosocial task. If the previous psychosocial tasks were negotiated successfully, intimacy versus isolation is more likely to develop.

Borders, Penny, and Portnoy (2000) investigated current functioning as well as psychosocial well-being of adult adoptees and their matched group of friends. They found more similarities than differences between the two groups. The similarities related to satisfaction with life, regrets about life, life purpose, and intimacy, as well as substance abuse. Ways in which they differed were related to self-esteem and connectedness, as well as depression. The authors attributed greater variability within the adoptive group than to the friend group to the status of the search for birth parents.

Ongoing Support and Intervention After Adoption

When dealing with adoptive families, any action on the part of school and community professionals that enhances successful adoption and adjustment of the child and family thereafter is desirable. Friedlander (2003) stated:

> A major pitfall in working with children and adolescents is overlooking the need to strengthen the child's emotional bonds with the adoptive family and the community. (p. 747)

Too often, professionals fail to focus on the capacity of individuals and families to be resilient. "To date … few post-adoption service models have been developed, and fewer still have been tested for effectiveness" (Schweiger & O'Brien, 2005, p. 512).

Support and Intervention in the Community and School

Professionals in schools and communities can make a valuable difference in the lives of adoptive children and youth and their families. Support networks, classmates, friends, and neighbors can support the adoptee and family and help counter stigma and become comfortable in communicating with others about adoption. Leung and Erich (2002) stated, "Having available support networks is essential to achieve adoptive family stability" (p. 813). People involved in the adoptees' life can learn to help by normalizing all forms and types of adoption, as well as receiving specific information and recommendations that help them respond to the various issues that emerge at different ages and stages in the lives of adoptive children and youth.

These measures can help to prevent or ameliorate the impact of stigma that too often leads to the adoptee's lower sense of self-worth and self-esteem. Self-worth relates to how adoptees perceive themselves at the core of their being, whether they feel valued by others and incorporate it into their perception of self. Self-esteem is related to feelings of success and mastery in academics, athletics, the arts, and so forth.

Community leaders, teachers, and staff members in the schools have many opportunities to help change attitudes and to normalize adoption. Fisher (2003) found that the textbooks used in marriage and family courses devoted approximately 2½ pages to adoption. This means that school counselors, social workers, and psychologists would benefit from reading journal articles, chapters, and books on adoption.

At a minimum, the support of school psychologists, counselors, and social workers is needed to change attitudes toward adoption and protect adopted children from hurtful actions and comments during the elementary school years. One simple and effective strategy for teachers is to read a book about adoption to entire classrooms of children. This is a normalizing method in which the teacher models acceptance and helps the adoptive child "fit in" with peers.

During adolescence, teachers, school psychologists, social workers, and counselors can be sensitive to the teen's identity formation by integrating the dual heritage through course content and other opportunities that are rich in meaning. Assuming adoptees have their birth parents' information about ethnic background, the professionals can provide books for students to incorporate in reports either about their personal dual background, or, in a more subtle manner, they can be assigned a particular research topic that matches their birth family backgrounds. In community settings, professionals can add racial/ethnic books and magazines that appeal to adolescents to their resource bookshelves. Out-of-school-time (OST) programs can assign books to be read during specialized reading times (e.g., DEAR/drop everything and read, SSR/sustained silent reading) when everyone in the facility picks up a book or magazine to read for 20 to 30 minutes at the same time each day.

Reading material aimed at adolescents from selected ethnic backgrounds can be made available in school and community settings for checking out, reading while waiting for what is scheduled next, and as resources for written and oral reports. Community or group projects that include adoptees of like racial or ethnic background provide opportunity for normalization of differences to occur. If reading materials are supplied that relate to projects engaged by other groups of adolescents (e.g., inner-city tutoring of African American elementary children; clean up of Latino neighborhood), it enhances knowledge of the birth background for an adoptee of interracial birth parents who was adopted by parents of a different race/ethnicity. With this type of project not only does the adoptee learn about birth race/ethnicity but also has an opportunity to build a sense of self-identity based on pride in one's dual heritage.

In terms of the adoptive parents, one of the most beneficial activities that school professionals can pursue is to help them develop realistic expectations for their children. Many adoptees are the only child in the family, and parents may benefit from information about child development and age-appropriate achievement. Potential resources for parents include websites, printed literature and books, a resource library with books to lend to parents, and discussions within groups such as PTA.

Offering parent training is another way to cover this territory. Groups prior to the child's entering middle school can be especially helpful in alerting parents to the stage and should be encouraged to guard against the tendency to make biological or genetic interpretations of their child's behavior or academic achievement. The educator's ability to place observed behavior in an appropriate developmental context can be helpful.

As to adopted children themselves, high-status peers could be paired with new students who are adopted out of multiple foster homes. "Birds of a feather flock together" often casts the same light on those who associate with one another. High-status peers being associated with any new student helps the new student benefit by others seeing the new student with someone they respect and like; this opens doors for others to be interested in an association with the new student (adoptee, foster child, or simply new to the school). This helps set up a positive peer group early in the new student's entry to the school, or for that matter a community program. The peer can ease the student's transition to the new school by familiarizing him or her with the schedule, busing, and cafeteria, and introducing the child or youth to others in the school. Nothing needs to be said by professionals about the adoptive status of the child or past placement. It is best put as helping integrate a new adolescent into an existing group or school.

Young children and adolescents alike are capable of helping new children join them in the new setting. The point is that anyone who works with children and adolescents in groups of any kind should be mindful of new individuals joining an existing group or class and notice when a child seems to feel left out. If aware that a child recently moved from multiple foster homes to permanent adoption, the teacher, social worker, or counselor could match the recent adoptee with a peer who is extroverted and empathic enough to create new opportunities for the child that are more natural than if the adult does all the work of making connections and introductions.

Many examples of *goodness of fit* are among suggestions offered by Schweiger and O'Brien (2005). These ideas could serve to generate opportunities for school and community professionals to adapt so they, too, can support adoptive families who have children with complex needs that manifest as emotional (internalization such as depression), behavioral (externalization such as conduct problems and juvenile delinquency), or are of a physical nature (such as stomachaches).

Children who were adopted as a sibling unit by one set of parents have particular needs for competent help by school personnel. School professionals can learn to know how to be of help to sibling groups adopted as a unit, as well as youth with severe behavioral problems. It is especially challenging to work with children from multiple foster homes who were born into poverty and whose parents had their rights terminated because of drug abuse. Much skill and effort are required on the part of the adoptive parents and school and community professionals to prevent these children from spiraling downward and ending up in jail or drug-dependent themselves.

From a lighter, more hopeful perspective, with more knowledge and heightened awareness of the issues related to children who are adopted, professionals can adjust group activities to better meet the needs of adoptees of all ages. For example, Pertman's (2000) suggestion to draw an orchard (or family tree) may help a child or adolescent. Professionals and others in community and church settings should deal with the child's questions in a relaxed, open manner with attention to the individual's needs. For example:

> If you were adopted, you can represent your family tree in any way that appeals to you. If you know both sides of your birth family, you might portray the tree as an orchard or create another idea to depict it. If you know little about your birth family, you may find it useful to represent yourself as a graft to the tree of your adoptive family.

A teacher, group therapist, leader, camp counselor, or other individual involved in helping a child or youth delve into family roots is well served by remembering the principle of *normalization*. In this capacity, the adult is an excellent role model for all children and adolescents and helps to minimize stigma. Further, professionals in schools, especially social workers, counselors, and psychologists, should become familiar with what is available in formal postadoption services in their locale and refer families to these more formal offerings by an adoption agency or in a community setting. Other external resources to tap into for information include agencies experienced with both pre-/postadoption services, websites on the Internet, and educational materials (chapter 10 is devoted to resourcing).

Community professionals who provide services within the schools, as well as external to the schools, need information and creative ideas for supporting children and youth who were adopted and their families. Much has been written on adoption (Barth, Berrick, Courtney, & Albert, 1994; Brodzinsky, 1990; Brodzinsky et al., 1992; Brodzinsky et al., 1998; Freeark et al., 2005; Friedlander, 2003; Glidden, 2000; Grotevant, 2003; Grotevant et al., 2000; Hoffman-Riem, 1990; Liptak, 1993; Leung & Erich, 2002; McRoy, 1999; Miall, 1998; Miall & Marsh, 2005a, 2005b, 2005c; Miller et al., 2000; Pertman, 2000; Reitz & Watson, 1992; Rosenberg, 1992; Schwartz & Kaslow, 2003; Schweiger & O'Brien, 2005; Simon & Altstein, 2002; Wegar, 2000; Zamostny, O'Brien, Baden, & Wiley, 2003), and community and school professionals can educate themselves to be more comfortable serving or teaching adoptive children. The book *Adoption, Race, and Identity*, by Rita Simon and Howard Altstein (2002), focuses on infancy to young adulthood and is a good starting point for adoptive parents in today's world. The text by Reitz and Watson (1992) also stands out in the literature related to adoption.

Formal Postadoption Services

Formal services on a postadoptive basis are helpful to some families. Overall, adoption is successful as viewed from the perspective of low disruption rates, but some adoptive families need considerable multifaceted and intensive postadoption services. In these cases, it is crucial to keep the same staff members involved with the family to avoid disruptions with children who have major behavior problems (Barth & Miller, 2000).

Barth and Miller categorized postadoptive services as education/information, clinical services, and material services:

1. *Educational services* include "literature, seminars, support groups, or the adoptive agency itself" (p. 452) that inform parents about what is offered.
2. *Clinical services* the adoptive parents want include counseling, even though few would engage the service or use it when available, and respite care, which, when used, was highly praised.
3. *Material services* in which the adoptive parents are interested include subsidies, medical care, and options for special education.

Three adjunct services that could guide the development of postadoption service paradigms are intensive family preservation, family systems therapy, and attachment therapies.

Barth and Miller (2000) described two noteworthy treatment options for those involved in postadoptive services:

1. Multisystemic family therapy (MST)
2. Assertive community treatment (ACT)

Recommendations by Howard and Smith (1997) synthesize postadoption options for strengthening adoptive families.

> Several additional adaptations have been recommended, including: viewing adoptions in a family context; not blaming parents for children's difficulties; understanding how adoption affects children at each developmental stage; and honoring the child's past. (p. 453)

The simpler recommendations for postadoptive services are especially useful when children are adopted past infancy or have disabilities, unless the disability leaves the child medically fragile. The suggestions also can provide important information during adolescence when identity formation incorporating the dual heritage is a task for adoptive youth, as well as during young adulthood if birth parent searches are engaged.

The dramatically more challenging and frustrating family experience is when adoptive family adjustment is poor as a result of the adoptive child's or youth's behavior problems. Many well-trained and experienced intensive, in-home behavior intervention service providers are able to help the adoptive child and parents begin to establish trust and reduce the behavior problems so the adjustment problems do not result in dissolution. No one wants to see one more foster placement in the string of foster placements, which most likely will continue to erode the child's hope and reinforce existing trust issues that are necessary for the relationship building required for behavior change.

Intensive In-Home Interventions

Intensive in-home interventions conducted by well-trained and experienced professionals are necessary for extreme, deeply rooted behavior problems of traumatized or biologically compromised children. These services involve professionals' being in the home helping the parents from the time the child gets up in the morning until the child leaves for school or daycare, and again when the child returns home at the end of the day and on weekends. Intensive in-home services typically involve 20–40 or more hours a week of a professional's time in the home to help the parents establish the kind of relationship necessary for trust to take hold and skills to be learned.

This level of intensity of in-home services can make a huge difference in behavior change *if* it is instituted immediately upon adoption of the foster child with severe behavior issues and carried through as long as necessary for the adoptive parents to be able to keep the behavior interventions in place without the professionals in the home. This type of intensive in-home service should be tapered off slowly and monitored closely (i.e., daily for a period of time, then every other day, and eventually weekly) for 6 months. Monitoring can be done through phone calls or e-mails, followed by detailed parental reports on behavior (both growth and any regression).

If the child exhibits degeneration of behavior, intensive in-home services must be reinstituted immediately. The sooner the behavior is brought back in line, the less likely the child will be to need intensive services over time. The alternative is a child who bounces from one foster home to another until coming of age, and then being on the streets to wreak havoc, often becoming drug-dependent, and finally ending up in jail or prison. The single most important factor in ameliorating problem behaviors in children and youth is to maintain hope.

Prevention

Prevention is the key to heading off a child's or youth's extreme behavior problems. This means reporting abuse and extreme neglect in a timely manner with the earliest legal time frame for severing parental rights, followed by swift movement from a single foster placement to an adoptive home with well-prepared adoptive parents who have realistic expectations, and including the formal postadoption services and support necessary. These steps will result in briefer disequilibrium in family adjustment before a tolerable, then acceptable, level of family adjustment is established.

Being realistic about expectations and providing the required services are essential, as is matching the foster child with a well-prepared and capable family willing to take the steps to achieve successful family adjustment. If both parents work, one of those parents preferably will take a leave of absence from work, if necessary invoking the Family and Medical Leave Act, which requires employers to allow unpaid leave for up to 12 weeks without negative repercussions at work or loss of job. Some companies provide adoptive parents with special benefits, including aid packages with an average of $4,000 in reimbursements to the family per adoption (Pertman, 2000).

Support Networks

External network supports are important for the successful adjustment of adoptive families, and formal postadoption services can provide opportunities for developing these external networks (Leung & Erich, 2002). Adoption agencies and community programs aimed at providing formal postadoption offerings often provide these services through their personnel who work with individual families on a postadoptive basis, in formalized postadoption programs offered for adoptive children aimed at each of Erikson's developmental stages, or in age- and parent-support groups facilitated by a leader from the agency or community setting.

Any service that has a good reputation whose mission is to provide a continuum of postadoption services can become an opportunity for families to investigate. If one service doesn't fit their needs or their sense of comfort, another certainly should be checked out as a possibility. The best fit for one family will be different for another. This depends in part upon need and also upon how comfortable the adoptive parent or child is with any others served in a group context.

The Role of Men

Freeark and colleagues (2005) provided a number of useful recommendations for formal postadoption services professionals. Their conclusions focused heavily on the need to decrease the stigma related to birth fathers and help adoptive fathers and sons connect better, to balance what these authors refer to as "the feminization of adoption." Women possess incredible strength in helping adoptive children, but this can mask the potential of men to contribute to their adoptive child's life. They single out boys in particular because boys are impacted more negatively than girls by the birth father's absence. Drawing men out to discuss the adoption story and practice communicating about it should become part of any group process run by postadoption services.

If couples counseling is offered in postadoption services, the adoptive husband should be encouraged to speak frequently, or the counselor/social worker/other therapeutic professional should draw him out in the discussion so he will become more comfortable and fluent in speaking about his role in the adoptive family. Freeark and colleagues (2005) recommended that

> constructive, creative nonverbal forms of expression and relating (e.g., adventure therapy, art therapy) should be explored as ways to engage the men and boys in the adoption circle in addressing adoption issues through modalities that play to their strengths. (p. 99)

An example of postadoption services is a father–son basketball game followed by a potluck dinner, then discussion in groups after the meal. These discussions could be led by fathers who are professionals in adoption services in the agency providing the postadoption services. Birth fathers might be invited to receive letters about and pictures of their birth child in semi-open adoptions and get to know their birth child in the same way that birth mothers do in fully open adoption, with ongoing face-to-face contact with the adoptive parents and child. Professionals must be ever alert to perpetuating the stigmatization of birth fathers and check their potential biases regularly.

Issues With Adult Adoptees

Borders and colleagues (2000) studied adult adoptees and their friendship groups. They cautioned professionals to make no assumptions about what matters most to these adults or their functioning level. At the same time, they recommended that professionals be attentive to any desire to initiate a birth parent search and assist with that process. The adoptive parents may need the support of a postadoption professional to bolster their sense of connection with their child.

In international adoption, some adoption agencies offer opportunities for guided experiences in the birth country. Volkman (2003) described any form of visiting the birth country by Korean adoptees as complex, with adoptees "wrestling with their own fantasies of origins, articulating new forms of 'cultural citizenship' and understandings of what it might mean to be both Korean or not" (p. 2).

Finally, professionals in community settings should be aware that some adopted children are predisposed to emotional difficulties, particularly in the areas of trust, sensitivity to rejection, feelings of belonging, and stability, self-worth, self-esteem, and identity. Misbehavior in these children may arise from their neediness and identity confusion.

Case Example

This case example, based on my early family history, can be used to integrate family systems theory with its transgenerational influence, interaction patterns, life-cycle variations on a theme relating to adoption, and other pertinent family systems concepts. My father died when I was young, so my mother became my prime influence, though she related many stories about my father that I assimilated into my thinking and values.

In reading this case study, your task is to find concepts about family systems that you have read in chapters 1–4 and the Appendix.

***

I take a broader view of family—the "it takes a village to raise a child" thinking—in my family life. This stems from the influence of my immediate and extended family, as well as the way I was reared, values imparted, and models observed when I was young.

My mother related stories of life on the farm on which she lived during the Great Depression. My grandmother cooked for everyone (the children and the maiden aunt living with them, as well as the multiple hired hands, who all ate in the huge dining room together). The stories about my grandfather were analogous to a leader of a tribe who took responsibility for keeping order and making sure everyone was treated with dignity. The way in which all the people living and working on the farm were spoken of fit the notion of extended family. With the maiden aunt and a great uncle who always seemed to be there to tell us stories, my view of family was enlarged from an early age.

I heard stories of my father before he met and married my mother, of his taking in youngsters who were in trouble when they were in their teens, his "straightening them out," and how grateful they were. He brought in a sister who was addicted to a painkiller and kept her through the withdrawal period and beyond, until she was able to function again.

My father had been mayor of our tiny hamlet before I was born, and at the time of my birth, my parents owned the only grocery store in the village. My father rented movies to project on the side of the grocery store for the community every weekend in the warm weather. It became clear to me that he felt a sense responsibility to others, and that others looked up to him and sought his advice.

My mom was the kind of teacher who made home visits, typical of the 1950s in the United States. When I became a teacher, I made home visits even though it was no longer part of the culture of schools. I knew home visits mattered from my experience of going on many home visits with my mother.

In an incident that had a large influence on me, a community social worker who was trying to get parental rights terminated for a child in my class asked me if I would be the foster parent and eventually adopt the girl. She had the correct impression of my view of the "village as family." The modeling and stories from my extended family fueled my sense of belonging, responsibility, and connectedness and awareness of what John Donne wrote about: "Don't ask for whom the bell tolls; it tolls for thee" and, "We are all a part of the main."

My mother read and talked about Pearl Buck. She took a special interest in this author because my mother's parents were missionaries in China, and my mother heard story after story about the culture that Pearl Buck wrote about. Honoring one's elders is one value of that culture, and my mother honored her father. She was also close to her mother and provided a lovely relationship model for me. She treated her mother with great respect. Her father died before I was born, so I never knew him.

Questions and Comments

1. *Do you see this family as functional or dysfunctional? In what ways and what leads you to those conclusions?*

2. *Describe this family in family systems terms.*

3. *How can family history and background influence later decisions in regard to adoption and types of adoption?*

4. *In relation to adoption, how might the mother's and/or father's values influence the author's values from childhood?*

Extension Activities

Activity #1:

Reflection: In recent years, media attention has highlighted international adoption and the horrors of orphanages. Also, accounts are widespread of adoptive parents who had been the parents of a child for years losing their child in court cases when birth parents fought to regain the child. Consider situations you have known, heard of, or experienced that relate to adoption issues. Recall any families you have known who have an adopted child, domestic or international. Are these successful adoptions?

Journal: How have you increased your knowledge about adoption from reading, class/training sessions, discussions? What remaining questions do you have about adoptive children/youth, and how they and their peers are impacted by stigma?

Activity #2:

In-Class Discussion (Leader Instructions)

If any of your students have personal familiarity with adoption, either as a child who was adopted, an adoptive parent, or placed their child for adoption, ask if they are willing to relate their personal experiences. Alternatively, invite someone with this experience to speak to the class/session. Pass out index cards and have the students jot down questions for the speaker(s).

Activity #3:

In-Class Expert Speakers (Leader Instructions)

Arrange for an expert or a panel of professionals to come to the class/session and address the issues covered in this chapter (e.g., psychosocial tasks at adolescence, support and intervention on a follow-up basis after the adoption, stigmatization, open adoption, international adoption, risk factors and adoption, domestic transracial adoption, tribal adoption, secrecy/closed adoption, breaking silence and its impact).

Afterward, open the group to questions.

Activity #4:

Panel of School Social Workers/Counselors/Psychologists (Leader Instructions):

Have social workers/counselors/psychologists who are familiar with adoption issues from their work in elementary, middle, and high schools speak to your class/session about the impact on schools of the different kinds of adoption covered in this chapter.

Have the students/group members write questions to ask the panel at the end. You may want to obtain permission of panel members and class members to be videotaped so you will have it available for future class/training sessions.

Activity #5:

Invitational Administrative Social Workers or Chief Counselors Panel (Leader Instructions):

Arrange for an administrative social worker/counselor or other mental health director from your local community mental health center to speak to the class/group about the impact on community programs of the types of adoption and core areas covered in this chapter. Follow up with question cards, with a moderator handling the question and answer session.

At-Risk Children From Nontraditional Families

*H*istorically, in the United States the primary model for the family has consisted of a married man and woman and their biological and adoptive children. For some time, this definition has not reflected the increasing diversity in family forms in North America. The traditional, intact, immediate family now lives in the same neighborhood with the *nontraditional* family form, which includes divorced, single-parent, blended, cohabitating, multigenerational, lesbian/gay, and foster configurations of family. A family with an adolescent who is lesbian, gay, or bisexual also can be considered as nontraditional.

Family form is related to the spousal/partner subsystem or lack thereof (e.g., widow, single parent). All family forms are influenced strongly by ethnicity; religion or lack thereof; financial status including no, one, two or more wage earners within the household; level of education; and regional and geographic influences, among other factors. To reiterate an essential dynamic: Those who work with children and families must accept each family's view of its form or configuration rather than adhere to a preconceived definition that differs from how the family describes itself.

Even though the term *nontraditional family* seems out of sync with the current reality that these families are no longer the exception to the former norm of the intact nuclear family, this terminology is used in the professional literature. Even though it bespeaks a deficit-oriented perspective of diverse family forms (Hartman, 2003; Visher, Visher, & Pasley, 2003) rather than the strengths-oriented perspective advocated in this text, the term *nontraditional* is used here to be consistent with the literature and avoid confusion.

Whatever the family form, traditional or nontraditional, any significant change in family form (e.g., death of parent, divorce, remarriage and blended) will affect the children, and they need support and professional intervention or referral for counseling or therapy, especially during the crucial transition period. Divorced and single-parent families have been found to stabilize, generally, after a transitional period of about two and sometimes three years (Hetherington, 2003); in remarriage and stepparenting, the transition period is approximately five years (Visher et al., 2003), punctuated by times of turbulence and eventual stability for those who succeed.

We must acknowledge that conflict between the parents and partners in any family can impinge on healthy development of children in that family and recognize signs that children will benefit from intervention. A *Report of the Task Force on the Family* (Family Pediatrics, 2003) sums it up:

> No particular family constellation makes poor or good outcomes for children inevitable. A stable, well-functioning family that consists of 2 parents and children is potentially the more secure, supportive, and nurturing environment in which children may be raised. That children can be successfully brought to adulthood without this basic functioning unit is a tribute to those involved who have developed the skill and resiliency to overcome a difficult and fundamental challenge. (p. 1545)

The Changing Family

Table 7.1 presents a comparison of family patterns in America. The family constellation clearly has changed dramatically over the past century. Major contributors to this change have been a shift in the marital relationship and the influence of immigrants and their family structure and values.

Shift in the Marital Relationship

The marital relationship has undergone significant changes since the beginning of the 20th century. Cherlin (2004) depicted the deinstitutionalization of marriage in America, describing mid-20th-century marriage as *companionship* versus the *institution of marriage* in the early 20th century. The companion marriage is characterized as having

> a sharp division of labor.... They were supposed to be each other's companions—friends, lovers—to an extent not imagined by the spouses in the institutional marriages of the previous era....
> The emotional satisfaction of the spouses became an important criterion for marital success. (p. 851)

Spouses valuing the marriage-based immediate family assumed roles of provider, homemaker, and parents.

Table 7.1

Comparison of American Family Patterns

First Marriage Families	Step/Blended Families	Single-Parent Families	Lesbian/Gay Families	Foster Families
Typical life changes with shifts of space and people	Loss of relationships (parent–child; grandparents) and loss of dreams for what family life would be	Unless adoption by single parent, everyone experiences loss of important relationships, and dreams	Stigma with loss of status in school, community, and potential for loss of extended family because of homophobia	Children lose family friends, community, environment
Two adults with different family histories	Everyone has a prior family history	Parent and child begin with similar family history	Different family histories for children and one or both parents, if adopted; if formerly married with children, everyone has a prior family history	Family history is different for children joining established family
	Bonds between parent and child longer than those of marital dyad		If stepchild adoption as a result of deceased spouse, parent–child bond is longer than lesbian/gay commitment	
	Biological parent lives elsewhere	Unless status is due to death of a parent, biological parent(s) elsewhere	Biological parent elsewhere if adopted, inseminated, or divorced from prior hetero marriage	Biological parent(s) elsewhere
	Many children live in two homes	Children may belong to two homes	May live in two homes if: stepfamily arises from divorce from previous marriage and in lesbian/gay commitment; or single lesbian/gay parent with broken commitment	Children may belong to two homes
	Lack of legalized relationship of child and stepchild (i.e., not adopted)		Legal relationship with one parent and child due to current laws regarding adoption by homosexual commitment, or lesbian birthparent through donor insemination	No legal relationship between child and foster parent(s)

Source: Adapted from *How to Win as a Stepfamily* (2nd ed., p. 194) by E. B. Visher and J. S. Visher, 1991, New York: Brunner-Routledge.

The second shift, to *individualized marriage,* was related to a changing division of labor (two-income households), less stigma associated with childbearing outside marriage, cohabitation, gay marriage, higher median age of marriage, and rising divorce rates. These changes were accompanied by the transformation of divorce law in the 1970s, in which couples were permitted to develop personalized agreements for divorce within the loosened limits of divorce law.

Cherlin (2004) described the deinstitutionalization of marriage as not having guides/expectations that specify roles and behavior; instead, this form is characterized by choice and alternatives regarding whether to marry, the sequence leading to marriage, childbearing within/outside marriage or cohabitation, same/different gender unions, and flexibility in roles within relationships. With the current goal of intimacy and personal growth through open interaction and honest sharing of feelings between partners, if one partner no longer feels fulfilled, he or she is far less likely to stand by the past value of the *companionship* marriage.

Immigrant Influences

Diversity in the conceptualization of family in the United States arrived early with non-white, non-European immigrants, including slaves from Africa. In the later 20th century and beyond, the influx of families from different parts of the globe has increased substantially, accompanied by definitions of family influenced by their cultural and ethnic heritage (McGoldrick, Giordano, & Garcia-Preto, 2005b) and the associated norms and expectations (Fuligni, Tseng, & Lam, 1999; Phinney & Ong, 2002). The result is a global society within one country. Although this has been true to a lesser extent ever since the European settlers began to colonize North America, the power structure belonged to white settlers and their progeny. Only in more recent years have descendents of non-European immigrants and slaves, as well as North America's indigenous people, begun to share in the power structure within the United States.

The Resiliency Factor

This book is based on family systems theory, concepts, and practices from a strengths-based perspective—with its emphasis on resiliency. Children are naturally resilient. In the past, pathologizing and expecting problems in children from divorced, blended, single-parent, or lesbian/gay families led the profession to focus on weakness rather than embracing resiliency as an expectation for children and youth and their families (Coltrane & Adams, 2003; Kelly & Emery, 2003) while concomitantly working to reduce risk factors (Fraser, 2004b). Professionals should be optimistic about possibilities rather than looking for pathology or assuming that if a child or adolescent faces emotional, behavioral, or learning challenges, this somehow indicates that they are caused by being part of a nontraditional family form, such as single-parent family following divorce (Amato, 2003; Kelly & Emery, 2003).

Some families with significant risk possess or develop resiliency factors. Thus, community and school professionals might not realize the depth, variety, or seriousness of the family life behind the scenes because a child may appear to be well-adjusted, functioning normally, and achieving like children and youth of a similar age. Some children and youth are adept at covering up underlying problems in the family out of fear or shame, and they live in denial and emotional pain from holding their feelings inside. And children may not realize that life could be otherwise because their family life has always been dysfunctional and they are unaware that the circumstances under which they live are not healthy. Many dysfunctional family issues are covered in chapter 8, which addresses dysfunctional behaviors such as addiction, neglect, maltreatment, and incest.

When an observant professional suspects that something is amiss in a child's life and probes the underlying situation, the professional may be surprised by the child's or family's capacity to face adversity with resilience. But discovering hidden worlds that are shattered and fragile can open doors for school and community to connect the child and family with necessary supports and services and find ways to reduce circumstances that place them at risk (Fraser, 2004b).

Still applicable is Weissbourd's (1996) warning not to oversimplify the changes that children face:

> Divorce and other modern trends need to be seen in terms of the kinds of interactions that imperil individual children and in light of the basic needs of every child. How do these trends affect whether children receive continuous, caring attention from a parent or guardian? How do these trends affect whether children are able to draw support from peers and community adults? How do they affect children's opportunities for accomplishment and recognition?
>   Viewing children in terms of these basic needs reveals that most children are not simply better or worse off because of these trends; they are likely to be vulnerable in different ways. Those who make policies and those who work for children need both to understand these differences and to identify the family, school, and community circumstances that will help children stay in one piece when both their parents are working or when their families are torn apart. (pp. 48–49)

Children and youth are not necessarily worse off because of risk factors such as divorce, being illegitimate, member of a blended family, or from a family headed by a single parent, or lesbian/gay parents, and they are vulnerable in different ways. Children and youth from nontraditional families may or may not face more adjustment issues than traditional families with high stress resulting from marital conflict (Zimet & Jacob, 2001). The task of professionals in social services and education is first to ascertain which children are vulnerable, then help them develop resiliency. This can be done through the lens of possibility while working concomitantly to decrease risk factors through a multisystems, transactional perspective (Fraser, 2004b), further detailed in chapter 10, on resiliency. Professionals also should make appropriate referrals when indicated.

Families of Divorce

Almost half of all marriages end in divorce (Teachman, Tedrow, & Crowder, 2000). Divorce rose sharply in the 1970s before leveling off at about half of first marriages ending in divorce since 1980. This figure has not changed significantly since 1980. Once divorced, a higher divorce rate for second marriages continues to be reported on Center for Disease Control (CDC) websites.

Effects on Children

Family Relations devoted a special issue to divorce, including its impact on children (Braver & Cookston, 2003; Pasley, 2003). It revealed marked differences between divorce today, compared to divorce prior to 1970, when considerable stigma was attached to divorce. Only in the last few years have the long-term effects of divorce on children been studied (Braver & Cookston, 2003). At the beginning of the 21st century, long-term studies on divorce's effects on children (Braver & Cookston, 2003) brought a new perspective. A strengths-based perspective has emerged, revealing a more positive portrayal of the impact of divorce on children. We now know that most children from divorced families are emotionally well-adjusted (Amato, 2001; Hetherington, 1999a, 2003). This is mitigated by a period of disequilibrium in the lives of children and parents alike, with an adjustment period that lasts 2 to 3 years (Hetherington, 2003).

Marital conflict may contribute as much or more than divorce to the maladjustment of children, youth, and young adults. Williams, Ayers, Van Dorn, and Arthur (2004) suggested that

> removing the conflict through divorce is preferable to letting the conflict remain. Even though family management problems are a risk factor for conduct disorder and delinquency, family structure is not. ... The children of divorce may be at less risk than those who remain in households experiencing parent conflict. (p. 220)

The biggest problem following divorce often relates to the subsequent economic instability. Poverty is a major risk factor, particularly with mothers who become the major caregivers. This can lead to adjustment problems in children and youth (Bartfeld, 2000).

How parents handle divorce has a large influence on the course of adjustment of their children. Teyber (1994) said:

> Children's long-term reactions vary greatly, depending primarily on how the parents respond to the child during and after the separation. In particular, the amount of parental harmony or disharmony children experience after divorce will be the most important determinant of their long-term adjustment. (p. 10)

Initially and in the short term, children are almost uniformly upset by parental divorce. Adults who as children experienced their parents' divorce pinpoint the initial stage as the most stressful in their lives. Even when conflict between the parents is obvious, children do not want their parents to divorce. Typically, during the first year after divorce, children experience increased fear, depression, anger, and guilt; however, these abate in the second year (Teyber, 1994).

In a study of relationship changes with their fathers 20 years postdivorce, Ahrons and Tanner (2003) reported:

> Custody did not directly affect reported changes in the quality of their relationship with their fathers; however, increased inter-parental conflict, early father remarriage, and low father involvement in the early postdivorce years were associated with worsening relationships over time. Those who reported that their relationships with their fathers got worse also reported poorer quality relationships with their stepmothers, stepsiblings, and paternal grandparents. (p. 340)

Most adult children in the study, however, indicated that over time the quality of the relationship they had with their father had improved or remained stable.

Gender Factors in the Child–Parent Relationship

Past research found that, overall, boys tended to have a more difficult and prolonged adjustment to divorce than girls did (Teyber, 1994; Weissbourd, 1996). Mothers routinely were assigned as the custodial parent (Guidubaldi & Cleminshaw, 1985; Weissbourd, 1996), and the boy's primary male role model then became a part-time parent. Teyber (1994) reported that boys who have experienced parental divorce are more likely to fight with their mothers and be disobedient, whereas the same-aged girls often had no problems getting along with their mothers. The aggressive and uncooperative behavior seen in boys at home extended to schools and was attributed to the fact that almost all of these children were living with their mothers. The girls were living with the parent with whom they have same-sex identification, whereas the boys, in most cases, lost theirs. Thus, divorce was viewed as more problematic for boys than girls.

Teyber (1994) noted that problems in daughters from divorced families are more apt to emerge (1) in adolescence as they begin dating and exploring heterosexual relationships, and (2) when they enter a stepfamily (p. 13). Chase-Lansdale and Hetherington (1990) also found greater behavioral reactivity in sons than daughters; being with parents of the same gender (i.e., father–son, mother–daughter) was reported as more likely to result in the child's greater well-being.

Keith and Finlay (1988) found that daughters of parents who divorce face a higher probability of divorcing later in life. Sons have a lower probability of ever marrying, and if they are from a lower social class background, they are more likely to divorce if they marry. More recent statistical reports by the CDC verify the higher likelihood of adult children being divorced if they did not grow up in an intact, two-parent family (Bramlett & Mosher, 2002).

Kapinus (2004) examined the effects of parental attitudes toward divorce on their young adult children's attitudes in relation to the adult child's gender. The findings show that parental attitudes toward divorce are most influential during the late teen years. Further, "the effect of parental divorce affects offsprings' attitudes independently of parents' attitudes only for daughters" (p. 132) and, "Postdivorce conflict between parents and reduced closeness to father following divorce are associated with prodivorce attitudes among daughters and less positive attitudes toward divorce among sons" (p.132). Clearly, gender differences are found across the life span in terms of response to divorce.

Age Factors in Children

Community and school professionals should be aware of age-related findings for children and youth with adjustment issues. According to Kelly and Emery (2003), preadolescent boys were at greater risk than girls for negative outcomes (see Amato, 2001; Hetherington, 1999b).

Grades in school and behavior of an internalizing and externalizing nature were investigated in relation to age of the child at the time of parental separation/divorce (Lansford et al., 2006). Divorce/separation when the child was younger was more negatively associated with behavior problems than parental separation/divorce later. But later parental separation and divorce was more negatively associated with grades in school. These researchers recommended that, prior to adolescence, interventions for children with adjustment issues would be better placed on preventing the internalizing/externalizing behaviors. For adolescents, they recommended promoting excellence in academics.

The effects of separation/divorce on very young children, birth to age 3, were studied in comparison to intact families (Clarke-Stewart, Vandell, McCartney, Owen, & Booth, 2000). The psychological development of these children was not found to be related to parental separation. Rather, associations were found in level of income and education as well as ethnicity, beliefs about childrearing, and depression. Also, "in very early childhood, parental separation affects girls more strongly than boys emotionally and boys more strongly than girls intellectually" (p. 323). In comparative terms of the child's age during the time of parental separation/divorce, they indicated that the prognosis is best for children birth to age 3.

In an early study of 40 adolescents conducted at the University of Georgia, a high level of parental conflict was found to have a detrimental effect on the academic and behavioral performance of adolescents, regardless of whether their parents were divorced. According to this study, if parents continued to battle after a divorce, the effects on their adolescent children were worse than the effects on children whose parents stayed in a high-conflict marriage (Rich, 1986). Others (Schwartz & Kaslow, 1997; Weissbourd, 1996) agreed with this finding.

Postdivorce Psychological and Adjustment Factors

Bogolub (1995) provided a number of reasons for postdivorce dysfunctional parenting that were related to chronic psychological struggles. Among the factors contributing to dysfunction were "disorganization, fragility, impulse-ridden behavior, or excessive narcissism" (p. 184) on the part of the custodial parent. Bogolub further noted that social isolation can contribute to dysfunctional parenting after divorce. Serious parenting problems often stem from the parent's emotional challenges, poverty, and inadequate social support.

Wallerstein and her colleagues (Wallerstein & Blakeslee, 1989; Wallerstein & Kelly, 1980) conducted a 10-year longitudinal study of 131 children from 60 divorcing families. They found that the custodial parent's functioning and the level of conflict between ex-spouses during the entire postseparation period were the primary determinants of the child's well-being.

Stinson (1991) identified parental factors that have been related to more positive adjustment for children living with divorced parents:

> Positive relationships between the child and both the custodial and the non-custodial parent, particularly with the same-sex parent, as well as a positive relationship between the divorced parents themselves, positively affect child adjustment" (p. 13).

Free access to the noncustodial parent has been shown to have a positive effect on children's adjustment to divorce (Ferreiro, 1990).

Frequent visits by the noncustodial father have a good effect on the relationship (Arditti & Keith, 1992). The National Survey of Families and Households examined non-resident fathers' ties to children and cooperative coparenting (Sobolewski & King, 2005) and concurred with the finding that frequent contact with the noncustodial father is likely to be associated with healthier adjustment in their children.

> The positive association between cooperative coparenting and father–child ties is not limited to certain groups of children. We found no differences in this regard by the child's gender, race, whether the parents were ever married, whether the child has a step-father, or indicators of socioeconomic circumstances, ... household income, mother's education, and father's education. (p. 1209)

Cooperative coparenting is likely to enhance contacts between father and child, resulting in better relationships that may contribute to healthier child adjustment.

Wallerstein (1983) outlined the following six psychological tasks for children in adjusting to divorce, which are as relevant today as they were more than nearly a quarter century ago:

1. Acknowledging that the marital separation is real
2. Staying out of parental conflict and distress and resuming age-appropriate involvements
3. Resolving feelings of loss
4. Resolving feelings of anger and self-blame
5. Accepting the permanence of the divorce and giving up reconciliation fantasies
6. Achieving realistic hopes regarding their own future relationships

Intervention With Children of Divorce

We know that the more stability children have in their lives, the better they will cope with their parents' divorce. These children need continuity, familiarity, and predictability—which professionals in community and school can contribute. Schools and the community can provide structure and routine, as well as consistent discipline, all of which aid children of divorce. Empathy is paramount, and appropriate referrals may be helpful, along with recommendations for resources (see the Appendix).

According to Kelly and Emery (2003):

> Interventions are more likely to benefit children from divorced families if they seek to contain parental conflict, promote authoritative and close relationships between children and both of their parents, enhance economic stability in the postdivorce family, and when appropriate, involve children in effective interventions that help them have a voice in shaping more individualized and helpful access arrangements. (p. 360)

These authors provided a hierarchy of useful interventions for professionals, including

- parent education programs for children and parents;
- enhancement of financial stability postdivorce;
- mediation versus adversarial divorce regarding child custody;
- collaborative "lawyering";
- settlement conferences with a judge;
- for parents in constant litigation, assigning a parenting coordinator of arbitration programs; and
- group and family therapy for parents and children.

Emery, Sbarra, and Grover (2005) singled out mediation as the most important intervention in ameliorating the negative impact of divorce on children. The authors indicated that no other kind of intervention has made a more positive impact in divorce.

In their recommendations for postdivorce intervention, Kelly and Emery (2003) advocated a family systems approach and broader systems interventions encompassing social and legal systems. Like many other leaders in the field, they encouraged efforts to reduce conflict between parents, authoritative parenting with closeness between children and both of their parents, and enhanced financial stability after divorce. They also recommended including children in making access arrangements that fit their situation when appropriate for their maturity level and needs. Although those authors agreed that some children are harmed by divorce, they stated that "the majority of findings show that most children do well." They also reminded educators and practitioners that painful memories related to parents' divorcing are not evidence of pathology.

Professionals can benefit the children they serve by adhering to several basic guidelines:

1. Be aware of the potential impact of divorce upon the child/youth, keeping in mind that children are naturally resilient but will need support from those who know and care for them.
2. Take into account the individual child and his or her coping mechanisms and temperament when trying to help children move through the psychological tasks necessary for healthy adjustment to divorce, and don't try to infuse suggestions for action before the child has the opportunity to share his or her feelings.
3. Encourage authoritative parenting. This means keeping both parents involved with their children as much as possible and sending information via mail to the

noncustodial parent if there is not shared custody. Maintaining the parental subsystem even though the marital subsystem is dissolved is of primary importance in children's adjustment to divorce. This includes encouraging the child not to "take sides" and to stay outside any conflicts between the parents. Repeat the message to the child/youth that he or she is not responsible for the divorce.

4. Have a list of referral sources on file, including: therapists who specialize in divorce issues and child adjustment for children of the various ages; support groups for separating and divorcing parents; books and other resources.

In addition, professionals may

- assign special responsibilities to enhance the child's self-esteem,
- determine what the child's interests are and encourage him or her to share that expertise, and
- invite children to become involved in extracurricular activities that match their interests.

Single-Parent Families

Of children under age 18, U.S. census data indicate that 26.7% live in single-parent households; of these, 20.9% live in a mother-only family and 5.8% live in a father-only family (Lugaila & Overturf, 2004). In 2000, more than 19,000,000 children under age 18 were living with single parents in the United States.

Approximately 1.4 million children were born to unwed mothers in 2003 (Hamilton, Martin, & Sutton, 2004). Although most of these mothers keep their out-of-wedlock children as single parents, some are adopted by relatives and others become part of the foster care system and may be adopted because of the rise in numbers of never-married mothers (Pan & Farrell, 2006). Also, the number of single parents who adopt or become pregnant through insemination outside of a committed relationship has increased dramatically. Black and Hispanic families have the highest levels of female-headed families (Kjos, 2002).

Differences in Single-Parent Family Constellations

A number of different types of families are subsumed under the label single-parent families. Some single mothers conceived the child or children outside of marriage or within a cohabitation that ended; some single parents are widowed; others result from divorce; and some children are adopted by a single mother or father. Many single parents in the United States have a low income or are living at or below the poverty level and others are middle class or affluent; some divorced single parents receive child support, and others do not. Some single-parent families have one child, and others have several children.

All of these differences are accompanied by different stressors and risk factors. If one or more of the children or the parent has a disability or other individual risk factor, the stress is compounded for the single parent. According to Anderson (2003), "financial hardship is frequently noted to be the most significant challenge" (p. 123) for single-parent families.

Time Management

A notable difference between married and divorced families is a lack of time to "do it all." As Anderson (2003) stated:

> Certainly, the basic tasks of everyday survival are likely to take a greater proportion of the single parents' waking energies than those of parents in two-parent families. Many single parents complain that they rarely have periods of respite, and that there is no time in the day, week, or year that they are not performing chores or responsibilities, or worrying about them. They must manage their children, a household, a job, and at least a marginal social life without going under, and without the assistance of a partner to help with minor and major emergencies. (p. 123)

The single parent's responsiveness to his or her children decreases when trying to work and provide for the family's functional needs, such as cooking, shopping, laundry, and cleaning, without the support of a partner (McLanahan & Sandefur, 1994).

Hierarchy Dysfunction and Parentification

One of the most common problems in single-parent families is an imbalance in hierarchy. Children from single-parent homes resulting from divorce often grow up faster than other children their age with two parents. With one parent, there is less supervision of children, and they tend to hold greater sway in decision making.

In single-parent families resulting from divorce, the oldest or highest-functioning child often is cast in the role of substitute parent, a process called parentification (Bogolub, 1995). The parentified child, who usually is the oldest daughter or son, may become the parent's confidant and the recipient of inappropriate information about the divorce, especially negative comments about the other parent.

Koerner, Wallace, Lehman, Lee, and Escalante (2004) investigated the effects on adolescent sons and daughters who heard sensitive disclosures from their mother after divorce (e.g., financial concerns, anger toward ex-husband, personal concerns). Regardless of gender, frequent and continuing maternal disclosure of sensitive information was associated with the child's maladjustment, which consisted predominantly of disobedience toward parents.

Hetherington termed negative disclosures about an ex-spouse *instrumental parentification* (1999b). The parentified child often will begin to exhibit academic or behavioral problems. If the single parent then tries to exert influence as a disciplinarian, the child may respond with oppositional or disrespectful behavior. This reaction is born out of the parent's inappropriate dependency upon the child.

Another potential in single-parent families is *inversion of the hierarchy*, in which the child basically is "calling the shots" and the parent is disempowered. In this scenario, the son or daughter takes overwhelming responsibility for household tasks or caring for other children in the family (Schulman, 1984; Teyber, 1994).

Nichols and Schwartz (2004) recommended that those who work with families recognize these patterns and help the family adjust to the changing circumstances following divorce and a single-parenting. At the same time, parents who remain in an authoritative role and become involved in cooperative coparenting (Sobolewski & King, 2005) can refocus the energy of their children as well as the parental dyad in productive ways.

Authoritative Parenting

Leaders in the field repeatedly echo the need for authoritative parenting (Hetherington, 1999b, 2003; Kelly & Emery, 2003) along with demonstrations of warmth, caring, and support for their children (Hetherington, 1999b). In a longitudinal study of divorce, children of divorce were found to have fathers and mothers alike who were "less authoritative in their parenting—that is, they were less warm and responsive, more irritable and punitive under stress, and less firm and consistent in monitoring and controlling their children's behavior" (Hetherington, 2003, p. 327). The custodial mother leaned toward being coercive, and noncustodial fathers leaned toward permissiveness as well as distancing or being indulgent.

Prevention and Intervention in Single-Parent Families

The most effective buffers against long-term emotional stresses of divorce are adequate social supports for single parents and their children (Benedek & Brown, 1995). Thomlison (2004) described social isolation as "a keystone risk factor for neglect" (p. 116). Single parents who turn to their child for emotional support will benefit greatly by seeking resources outside the home in terms of both social and parenting needs. Strengthening parental and family support networks may reduce stress and isolation and increase control over the environment and provide resources for dealing with children's behavior problems (Bronfenbrenner, 1986).

Single parents who live near supportive family members are fortunate to receive help with childrearing and maintaining a home. Single parents and their children benefit further from the involvement of friends, neighbors, and faith-based communities. Sociologist James Coleman (1987) found that if children from single-parent homes are supported by community, educational, and religious networks, they are no more likely to drop out of school than children from two-parent families. Thus, community and school can be vital in the web of support that promotes children's well-being.

Especially when a single-parent family is new to a neighborhood, it is important to get all family members involved in a network of support as soon as possible. Professionals in community and school settings should facilitate the integration of newcomers, including children new to a school.

When Berman and Turk (1981) interviewed members of Parents without Partners about their adjustment to divorce, the single parents reported that the most important determinant of their overall positive mood after their divorce was the presence of a social support system. Hetherington (1999b) suggested that "the most effective solution for such difficulties in parents is the formation of an intimate caring relationship with a new partner" (p. 114). This may be easier said than done. What community and school professionals can do is to locate resources for social networks and provide this information to single parents.

Preventing adjustment problems in families headed by mothers of children of divorce and advancing prevention of problems in the first place were the foci of research by Haine et al. (2003). Their subsequent recommendations included fostering resilience factors including coping, warmth, and discipline by the custodial mother, as well as encouraging a quality relationship between father and child. From the risk factors related to negative expectations (e.g., abandonment), changes in the environment after divorce (e.g., moving), and interparental relationship (e.g., conflict), the authors developed a "problem-driven theory" for preventing maladjustment in children of divorce.

A study investigating children of divorce and intervention-induced resilience related to New Beginnings, a parenting program for single-parent mothers (Hipke, Wolchik, Sandler, & Braver, 2002), found that when mothers' demoralization was high or children's self-regulatory skills were low, children were not as likely to maintain the gains they developed. As a result, the authors recommended booster sessions for these mothers and their children.

Benedek and Brown (1995) and Guidubaldi and Cleminshaw (1985) stressed the importance of support variables—the availability of helpful relatives, including in-laws, as well as friends and paid child-care assistance, and a positive relationship with the ex-spouse—as important factors in the well-being of single parents.

An inservice education program to sensitize educators to the risks faced by children in single-parent households is highly recommended as an educational strategy. Community professionals can make the presentations or provide brief synopses for teachers, providing pertinent information for the educators in their community. Throughout, professionals should adopt and project an attitude of acceptance toward separating and divorced parents.

In cases of joint custody, schools and community settings must make sure that both parents receive copies of important communications that are sent home, including invitations to parent–teacher conferences and community/school activities. If one parent has been assigned sole custody, his or her written permission is required for the noncustodial parent to be included in these communications. Therefore, the professional must ask the custodial parent for permission to contact the other parent and at the same time give reasons why including the other parent is important to the child's well-being. Professionals should avoid favoring one parent over the other unless there is proven violence or severe abuse of a physical or sexual nature in the background.

Weissbourd (1996) made specific suggestions for involving noncustodial parents, primarily fathers, in their child's education—for example by inviting them to attend parent–teacher conferences and school assemblies, by scheduling activities at night so they will be more able to attend, and by sending them their child's report cards. "Reachable moments" for fathers include the child's entry into school, graduation, and other special occasions, as well as physical illnesses. Noncustodial fathers can form deeper connections with their children, fostered by school and community professionals.

Mentoring is another effective way to involve more adults in the lives of children. Mentors should be instructed in ways to strengthen both the child and the child's family and not undermine any of the child's relationships with family members. Freedman (1993) recommended that children of divorce be surrounded by "mentor-rich" environments with a variety of community adults.

How to Help Your Child Overcome Your Divorce, by Benedek and Brown (1995), offered suggestions for professionals that remain applicable today. Those authors considered security and predictability as essential anchors for children, and school and community settings can help fill this need. Building on the child's strengths in academic areas will bolster the child's self-esteem and self-efficacy. If a child is experiencing academic problems, the teacher can help on a one-to-one basis and supervise homework in concert with the parent. The sooner a positive behavioral intervention is planned and implemented, the more quickly problems can be prevented and functional behavior promoted. School personnel can recommend books written for the children's age levels and possibly make available a lending library.

Remarriage/Blended Families

Some researchers and leaders in the field of stepfamilies (e.g., Visher et al., 2003) use the terms "blended" and "remarriage" to avoid the negative associations with the "step" terminology. Here, the terms stepparent, stepmother, and stepfather are retained for purposes of clarity.

A U.S. Census Report, *Living Arrangement of Children: 2001* (Kreider & Fields, 2005), indicated that 15% (10.6 million) of children under age 18 live in blended (remarriage) families. Close to half of these children (5.1 million) live with one stepparent and their biological or adoptive parent. Some blended families are created when a remarried parent and the new spouse have a child together; thus, existing children are half-siblings of that child. The general consensus among researchers is that the integration, consolidation, and emotional connection in blended families takes longer than the 2- to 3-year adjustment period after divorce—typically from 5 to 6 years (Visher et al., 2003). Leaders in the field of remarriage in families with children, Visher and colleagues indicated that easily half of all Americans can expect to be part of a stepfamily some time in their life.

Premarriage

Regardless of the circumstances of single parenthood, if stemming from divorce or death, the remaining parent should not jump into dating too soon. The parent and the children alike need time to adjust and establish a new family life together. The too-early presence of a new partner tends to heighten children's feelings of loss and anger and prolong their adjustment to the parental loss.

Once a couple has established a new, loving relationship, obstacles arise before an eventual remarriage. How the premarriage stage proceeds for everyone in the family depends in part upon the age of the children at the time of the remarriage. Younger children will still be mourning the loss of their biological parent in the shorter term and may continue to have fantasies about their divorced parents' reconciling (Benedek & Brown, 1995; Bogolub, 1995; Friedman, 1981). If the child has served an institutional parentified role in the single-parent household (Hetherington, 1999b), the remarriage may represent, on the one hand, a relief from responsibility and, on the other hand, a threat to his or her position in the family (Weissbourd, 1996).

Adolescent children may have a particularly difficult time accepting the remarriage because of their own identity and sexuality concerns typical of that age. For adolescents who have just begun dating, watching their parent being "in love" and going through the rituals of courting may be embarrassing and threatening. Adolescents of divorce also may be acutely aware of the reactions of the other biological parent to the remarriage (Framo, 1981). The ex-spouse may reexperience the sense of rejection and depression from the initial divorce, and the adolescent may respond with support and concern for the still-single parent, as well as anger at the parent who plans to remarry. Adolescents who themselves are struggling with the dynamics of heterosexual relationships may become embroiled in a loyalty struggle (Visher & Visher, 1991; Visher et al., 2003).

At any age, the children ideally will have had positive involvement with the fiancé or fiancée and his or her children, if any, prior to remarriage plans. As a couple, the partners should tell the children about their engagement. They should acknowledge the care they took in reaching their decision. They also should tell the children that although they love each other, they do not expect "instant love" between the children and the new mate (Visher & Visher, 1996). From this point on, the parent should be available to the children to listen to their questions and respond to their feelings so the children will feel affirmed and accepted. This is also a good time to provide age-appropriate books and other media on blended families.

Within the boundaries of the family hierarchy, children might be given a role in planning and participating in the wedding ceremony and the new living arrangements. Here is an example of how one couple helped their children feel included in their remarriage:

> A couple was married after three years of dating, following each of their divorces. The woman had three children from her previous marriage, and the man had two children. Their wedding ceremony consisted not only of the traditional wedding vows for the couple, but also of vows to join the two families in a commitment. Each parent initially recited part of the vows with his or her own children. At the end of the ceremony, all of the children and both parents recited a phrase together. For this couple, the symbolism of coming together was expressed through these rituals.

The lifetime parent should remain at the top of the hierarchy, in charge of the children, but the new partner should back him or her up in parenting. If the two disagree about how to handle a situation, it should be discussed in private. Otherwise, the adults leave themselves open to "splitting," with children making one adult the "good guy" and the other the "bad guy." Interactions between the child and the stepparent might begin with minor decisions such as to what movie to rent or see together.

Successful Remarriage

Visher and colleagues (1997; 2003) described the following characteristics of successful remarried families:

1. Members of blended families hold *realistic expectations* about their lives together. The family members know their family is different from their former

two-parent family and do not long for it to become an "ideal" family. They accept the realities of blended family life. They develop flexibility. They do not expect "instant love," realizing that integration takes time.

2. Children are allowed to *mourn the loss.* Unrecognized losses and those not grieved tie up energy and contribute to difficulties in the present situation. Group support with others facing the same kinds of losses is helpful in mourning losses. Also, maintaining bonds and experiences with the extended families (e.g., grandparents, aunts/uncles, cousins) is important. The continuity and stability of established family connections help in the grieving process and letting go and eventually being able to move on.

3. The couple is *strong and unified.* Successful remarriage requires spousal time together to develop and enrich the marital subsystem. This time together is essential for building trust and shared experiences. Children will feel secure in knowing that the marriage is stable and unlikely to end in divorce when the spouses present a unified front, back one another's decisions, and model effective couple relationship skills. The children also will benefit from the functional, semipermeable boundaries, as well as a balanced hierarchy, in which the power and responsibility are in the "right place," without parentification or inversion of the hierarchy with a child ruling the roost.

4. The couple forms *satisfactory blended family relationships.* The stepparent usually has entered the family system slowly, working to develop his or her relationship with the children. A friendly relationship is a necessary prerequisite to becoming responsible for discipline of stepchildren. Older children adjust to a coparenting relationship more slowly than younger children, who more readily accept the authority of the new stepparent based on the authority they ascribe to adults in general. The stepparent may not develop a disciplinary role at all with some adolescents. Regardless of who is viewed as an "authority," successful blended family members treat one another with respect and dignity and accept each other's foibles and idiosyncrasies.

5. The family establishes *satisfying routines and constructive rituals.* Positive shared memories and a sense of belonging engender good relationships, supported by familiar ways of doing things. Successful blended families typically share their prior rituals and ceremonies with one another, then combine, retain, or develop new ways of blending these routines and rituals. Successful blended families are flexible as well as resourceful, and they generalize their flexibility outside the family, which results in greater self-competency in the family. Successful blended families share chores around the house, spreading out responsibilities.

6. The *separate households build a "parenting coalition."* The stepparents become part of the coalition, forming permeable boundaries from which the children come and go with ease. Parents and stepparents are not competitive, and they curtail loyalty conflicts on the part of the children. Successful stepfamilies feel independent of the other household and, at the same time, feel connected through the children. This coalition is especially helpful in relation to holidays, graduations, weddings, births, and funerals.

Initial Struggles

Immediately after the remarriage, the families have to begin the process of "blending." Difficulties during this stage may occur at the individual, subsystem, or family levels.

Individual Level

At the individual level, each person in the blended family has concerns about bonding with other family members. Blended relationships are new and untested, and all members of the family will not necessarily accept one another automatically (Visher & Visher, 1991, 1996; Visher et al., 2003). In addition, each individual has personal issues related to dissolution of the former marriage and family. Repercussions of the previous loss include insecurity, low self-esteem, fear, and grief.

Subsystem Level

Subsystem-level difficulties may be in the marital subsystem, the parental subsystem, or the sibling subsystem. The marital subsystem has to nurture attachment within a different situation than first-married couples, who have no children around to interfere with their time together to establish the marital relationship. Usually each brings a history of failure to the relationship (Visher & Visher, 1996). Some couples have to work through the early-marriage stage at the same time they are dealing with rearing children and/or helping adolescents leave home, both of which require considerable effort for healthy transitions.

The parental subsystem faces issues of hierarchy and role definition of children in both of the reconstituted families. Blended families often involve children brought into the new family from a former marriage. As one mother in a blended family stated:

> We discovered that we had too many actors for the traditional parts of mother and father, and we had to create some new roles for them. My husband has found a spot as an older friend and advisor to one of my sons.... After giving up ... my accustomed role of nurturer, I have learned to be comfortable playing the part of counselor and house manager to my husband's children, leaving the mothering to their mother. (Barney, 1990, p. 146)

Joint custody, with the children living in each home for equal amounts of time, is far more common than it was in the past. Each family with whom the child spends time has its own parental subsystem. Frequently, parents in blended families hear the children say, "He's not my father" or "She's not my mother"—most often in response to disciplining, which can be troublesome in blended families (Visher & Visher, 1996).

Benedek and Brown (1995) suggested that the stepchildren will not regard a stepfather as an authority until he has earned their respect and trust. They recommended that "the mother should remain the children's prime disciplinarian while being clear with the children about the stepfather's authority and backing up his efforts" (p. 243). Parents must establish and maintain a united front so the children do not triangulate a parent. Disagreements between spouses are best discussed in private. If children think they are in charge of making family rules because their desires are more important than those of a spouse, a hierarchy dysfunction will develop.

Finally, the sibling subsystem in blended families is often divided into a number of subgroups, which can result in confusion and difficulties early on. Some siblings live with this family and others with the other parent, and stepsiblings also may live part of the time with their other parent and other stepsiblings. Sibling rivalry thus takes on a new meaning (Framo, 1981; Visher & Visher, 1991).

Family Level

Members of the blended family come together from what may be two very different historical backgrounds. The rules and rituals of one family may be quite different from those in the other family. Adding to the complexity, the children in a blended family often spend time with the family of their noncustodial parent. Behavior that is allowed at dad's house may not be tolerated at mom's house, and vice versa. Schedules, eating habits, religious beliefs, rituals, and bedtimes—all are likely to differ from one family to the other. Flexibility and tolerance for differences are necessary to minimize struggles across families (Visher & Visher, 1991).

Long-Term Struggles

After five years or so, the blended family that remains together usually will have resolved its initial cohesion struggles. Still, blended families experience unique problems and concerns throughout the family life cycle. When children reach adolescence, identity and commitment issues often resurface. Stepparents who felt bonded with and accepted by their stepchildren may suddenly find themselves the "bad guy" once again. When normal adolescent power struggles arise, a parent may, in a flare-up of anger, threaten the child with return to the noncustodial parent if the child doesn't "straighten up." Adolescents, in turn, may threaten to run away to their other parent when they aren't happy with the rules of their current family.

Any changes of custody and living situations must be decided by parental consensus and not during the heat of an emotional battle. When the parents discuss these changes calmly and decide that it is in their adolescent's best interest to change homes, the parental hierarchy remains intact; there is no inversion of the hierarchy and no enmeshed boundaries.

When the new spouses have children of their own, cohesion issues often resurface. Stepchildren who had bonded with their new parent may feel that their place in the family has been usurped by the baby. As one 13-year-old girl stated, "My 'real dad' told me that I would become second best with my mom and stepfather when the baby was born. It turns out that he was right. Why should they care about me when they have this cute little boy who belongs to both of them?"

In terms of school influence, teachers may notice that children who live in blended families go through periods of acceptance and periods of regression. They should continually take into account the long-term nature of adjustment to divorce and remarriage when trying to understand the needs of children who become members of a blended family.

Prevention and Intervention

Along with realistic expectations, prevention is key to the eventual integration and stability of remarriages with children. Prevention through education about the dynamics of parent remarriage is the best way for parents to get off on the best foot possible.

Professionals in school and community settings should take note of children who live in blended families and reinforce the parental subsystem, which in turn will benefit the children. When sending notes home to "parents," for example, professionals might include more than one copy for children in blended families so the children can provide the information to all those who play a "parent" role in their lives—stepparent, other relative, and noncustodial parent, for example.

In interactions with stepparents, professionals should remind them of the child's feelings about remarriage. Loss is associated with more than death; divorce represents a very real loss to children and adolescents. Further, when a parent remarries, the child loses hope that the original parents will reconcile one day. Some children also suffer losses in attention from the parents when another child is born into the family or stepchildren become part of it. It is important to hammer home the message that being supportive of one's ex-partner/spouse will be beneficial to the children. Anyone in the role of parent should be supported rather than minimized or put down, and the relationship between the other parent and child/adolescent should be fostered.

One helpful exercise is to ask children as a group to discuss how their families celebrate certain holidays. Some children will say that Thanksgiving isn't Thanksgiving without a turkey and dressing, and for others a ham and cranberry sauce must be the centerpiece of the Thanksgiving dinner table. When children are exposed to different symbols from different peer families, they may be able to more easily negotiate the rituals and symbols in their new blended family systems.

Barney (1990) suggested that professionals make an effort to normalize the concepts of blended family, foster family, and other nontraditional family constellations. This may be done through small-group discussions in which children from different family forms share their experiences, as well as a curriculum that addresses the changing picture of the family.

The National Stepfamily Association has projected that more than half of all children will be members of a stepfamily at some time in their life. In the 21st century, blended families are common enough that they have become normalized in the eyes of many children in schools. This may be less true for parents of intact families and families in which neither parent has been divorced, as they may not have been exposed to the same diversity as the schools. School and community social workers, counselors, and psychologists can make information available to help all parents better understand blended families.

Lesbian and Gay Families[1]

The two segments considered here are (a) families headed by lesbian/gay parents, and (b) lesbian, gay, and bisexual youth within families.

Families with Gays/Lesbian Parenting

Lesbian/gay families have between 6 and 10 million children in the United States, according to Mercier and Harold (2003). This is not a new family form, as social scientists have been collecting data on this form since 1980 (Mercier & Harold, 2003). Increasing numbers of children reared in lesbian and gay households have been noted over the past several decades, with estimates of "between one and five million lesbian and gay parents in the United States" (Parke, 2004; p. 387). Children from previous heterosexual relationships, donor insemination, and adoption come into these homes. In referring to same-sex partners, Fisher (2003) stated, "Much more common are 'second parent adoptions,' in which the partner of someone who is already a legal parent of a child (by either birth or adoption) officially adopts the child" (p. 340).

Laird (2003) characterized the presumable greater acceptance of gay/lesbians over the course of the last decade—as evidenced by television shows, movies, heterosexual actors playing homosexual roles, homosexual actors coming out publicly, President Clinton's appointment of high-level government officials who were gay/lesbian, as well as other changes. She claimed that this is not necessarily evidence that "political and social meanings … increased visibility for both the heterosexual and gay populations, and noted the contradictions and paradoxes facing what seems to be 'acceptance'" (p. 176). Laird pointed to the "don't ask, don't tell" approach in the military, increased attacks and violence directed at gay people, openly gay men not being allowed to serve as leaders in Boy Scout troops, as well as custody issues and adoption blockages faced by gay/lesbian couples.

Many of these families experience the same stresses as heterosexual and single-parent families in terms of economic sustainability, the development of familial support systems, issues surrounding divorce, issues of stepparenting, and issues of child rearing itself (Casper & Schultz, 1999). Beyond those similarities, three primary issues have been noted in questioning whether gays and lesbians should be allowed to raise or adopt children:

1. Are the children likely to suffer developmentally in a lesbian or gay home environment?
2. Are these children more likely to become gay themselves?
3. Are these children more likely to experience sexual abuse than children raised in traditional or other nontraditional families?

Given that homosexuality was a criminal offense in the United States as late as 1962, was considered a mental disorder until 1972 in the *Diagnostic and Statistical Manual of the American Psychological Association* (DSM), and that a presidential task force discouraged homosexual adoptions in 1987, state laws not surprisingly vary widely in their handling of gay adoption issues. Lesbian/gay-headed families who adopted sibling units as well as older children who had previously experienced abuse reported higher levels of functioning than families adopting younger children with no previous abuse (Erich, Leung, Kindle, & Carter, 2005).

---

[1]This section on lesbian and gay families was written by Dr. Nora Alder, Associate Professor of Teacher Education at Virginia Commonwealth University.

Because schools are microcosms of society at large and because society is still divided on the viability of lesbian and gay relationships as well as lesbians and gays as parents, teachers and principals in schools and professionals in community settings are likely divided, too. Yet the reality of children of lesbian and gay families is evident. As such, those entrusted with the care for and education of these youngsters are morally bound to establish positive working relationships with the children/youth and their families to support their growth and development. Further, schools are legally bound to protect their gay/lesbian students from gay-related attacks (see *Nabozyne v. Podlesny*, 1996).

Research on children growing up in lesbian or gay families has been relatively consistent since the 1970s in finding that these children are as developmentally stable and mentally healthy as children reared in heterosexual homes (Casper & Shultz, 1999). Further, the research found no clear indication that these children are more likely to become gay or lesbian than their heterosexually raised counterparts (James, 2004). Further, sexual abuse, physical abuse, and physical punishments are less likely in lesbian or gay families (Gartrell, Deck, Rodas, & Peyser, 2005; Golombok, Perry, Murray, Mooney-Somers, & Stevens, 2003; Vanfraussen, Ponjaert-Kristoffersen, & Brewaeys, 2003) than other family forms.

Gartrell and colleagues (2005) found that incidents of sexual and physical abuse in lesbian families were below national norms. In fact, only 5% of the girls had been sexually abused (by unrelated men). This is compared to an overall (i.e., within and outside family) 38% of women in the United States who reported being sexually abused as children. None of the boys living in lesbian-headed families had been sexually abused, compared to 5%–10% in reports of childhood sexual abuse by men in the United States.

In their study examining lesbian families created by donor insemination, Vanfraussen and colleagues (2003) compared parental child-rearing behavior of biological lesbian mothers and the social lesbian mothers with heterosexual mother/father couples. The findings revealed that, despite being the primary wage earners, social mothers (lesbian families) were found to interact more than the heterosexual fathers with the children. No differences were found between the lesbian and heterosexual mothers in terms of parent–child interactions. Overall, a more egalitarian situation was found in the lesbian households in terms of child rearing, and the children indicated a strong view of the social mothers as a part of the family. This is important because, with no biological link, the social mother had to construct her role without the benefit of biologically based notions of parenthood.

Golombok and colleagues (2003) explored the concern with gender development issues in children reared by lesbian families. Conflicting theories on gender development are derived primarily from traditional psychoanalytic theorists, genetic theorists, cognitive developmental theory, and social cognitive theorists.

- The *traditionalists* hold that the absence of a father interferes with successful resolution of the Oedipal conflict and, hence, typical gender development. They also believe the parents play a key role in gender development through modeling and differentiated reinforcement of role behavior in sons and daughters.
- The *genetic theorists* support the notion of biological determination and that the parental child-rearing styles are not influential.
- The *cognitive development theorists* also see the role of the parent as having a minor influence on gender development, believing that the child's construction of gender roles is gleaned from the broader world around them.

- The *social cognitive theorists* underscore the interaction between social and cognitive processes in gender development.

Clearly, these divergent theories would predict different outcomes for the children's gender development in lesbian-reared families.

Gender identity and gender role behavior tend to be fixed and important to children's sense of well-being. Attitudes about gender-related issues, however, are more open to parental influence and change (Golombok et al., 2003).

Using multiple measures and responses from lesbian and heterosexual couples, single parents, children, and teachers, Golombok and colleagues found no evidence of gender-identity problems in the children from lesbian-mother families.

> From a theoretical perspective, this contradicts the view that heterosexual parents are essential for children's acquisition of gender-typed behavior. Instead, it lends support to theoretical explanations that emphasize the importance of either prenatal or cognitive processes in children's gender development and to explanations that focus less on the role of parents and more on the role of peers. [p. 31]

Golombok and colleagues (2003) also found no evidence that the lesbian-reared children were less well-adjusted or developmentally challenged. Lesbian and heterosexual single-parent mothers alike reported more negative relationships with their children, and their children had more indications of psychological issues from teachers than their coupled counterparts. Possibly, then, the involvement of a second parent is more central to the well-being of the relationships between mother and child, as well as the child's development, than the involvement of a father in particular.

In a study focusing on lesbian and adoptive family functioning, the children's behavior, and familial support systems, Erich and colleagues (2005) found adequate support systems and healthy family functioning and child behavior. These findings are also in line with findings for donor-insemination families (Vanfraussen et al., 2003).

Mercier and Harold (2003) noted a struggle in lesbian families as to whether to disclose to schools. The lesbian parents who did come out were pleased with the staff's interactions with them and their children. Many of these couples visited their children's schools and looked for signs of celebrating diversity, which they said was a major factor in choosing schools for their children. A recurring issue was whether to appear at school functions as a couple. The lesbian women were concerned that their children would be harassed later. One nonbiological parent discussed staying out of her child's school life because the father was an active participant in that arena. Lesbian biological mothers in this study tended to be involved in their children's academic and extracurricular activities.

Professional organizations in the United States have registered support for lesbian/gay adoption. An American Psychological Association committee report in 1995, cited by Fisher (2003), supported lesbian/gay adoption. In the *Human Rights* magazine of the American Bar Association, Gibson (1999) supported lesbian and gay adoption, indicating that studies have not found children reared in gay/lesbian homes to be disadvantaged.

In 2002, an American Academy of Pediatrics (AAP) committee indicated concern that children born to, or adopted by, a gay/lesbian couple need the security that having two legally recognized parents brings. The AAP committee stated, "[T]he American Academy of Pediatrics supports legislative and legal efforts to provide the possibility of adoption of the child by the second parent or coparent in these families" (p. 339).

The overwhelming evidence from the studies cited here indicates that growing up in a lesbian or gay home does not place children at developmental or psychological risk. The only risk association was from the stress on children who are teased by their peers, especially without the intervention of parents and professionals (e.g., teachers) who are intent on restricting the teasing and helping children learn coping strategies.

Lesbian, Gay, and Bisexual Youth

A different component of family in relation to diversity in sexuality is composed of youth in the family who are lesbian, gay, or bisexual (LGB). In almost all situations, LGB youth are children of heterosexual couples and live in intact, divorced, blended, single-parent, and adoptive families. Thus, they are found in every type of family form in our society.

D'Augelli, Grossman, and Starks (2005) studied parental awareness of the sexual orientation of their adolescent. One-third of the adolescents had not told their parents of their sexual orientation for a variety of reasons—the prospects of emotional/physical harm, hurting their parents, rejection, eviction, relationship deterioration, financial disruption, and other factors (e.g., religious, cultural, privacy, lack of closeness to parents). More feared disclosure to their father than their mother, with boys being three times more likely than girls to indicate that they would never tell their father.

LGB youth with telltale signs of gender differences had parents who were more aware of their orientation than the youth lacking clues and more definitive identity as being gay or lesbian than bisexual. D'Augelli and colleagues (2005) stated, "Youth with more aware parents showed less internalized homophobia, which may reflect the longer period of time they were aware ... as well as greater family support ..." (p. 481). The authors concluded that LGB youth whose parents were aware of their sexual orientation experienced less verbal abuse concerning being gay, lesbian, or bisexual and the youth had come through the bad times with less fear. The third who had not disclosed to their parents were described as "less atypical" during childhood and thus able to cover their sexual orientation. More than half of these youth indicated that they would never disclose to their fathers, and the authors suggested that the adolescents' prediction about the parental response could justify the lack of disclosure.

Those authors underscored the importance of family support in adolescence and highlighted the need for providing support to the adolescents prior to disclosure to parents, as well as after disclosing. Community and school personnel can help students in need during and after disclosure, including referral, in which the professional must be knowledgeable and experienced in supporting LGB youth in the process of disclosing to family members.

Gay and lesbian teenagers are more likely than heterosexual teens to attempt suicide (Anhalt & Morris, 1998; Bagley & Tremblay, 2000; Safren & Heimberg, 1999). Studies of teenage gay suicide survivors indicated that family stress related to their sexuality is the primary factor in their suicide attempts (Goldfried, 2001). Further, LGB youth are at risk for bullying and harassment in school/community (D'Augelli, Pilkington, & Hershberger, 2002).

Murdock and Bolch (2005) noted the lack in assessing the unique characteristics of LGB contexts (e.g., victimization, exclusion in schools) as a result of students' LGB identification. Those authors also pointed to the need for taking resilience into consideration among the LGB population.

Murdock and Bolch (2003) studied social support and its impact on school climate and school adjustment among 101 LGB students in high schools in three areas: exclusion/inclusion, victimization within the school for being LGB and teacher social support, and family/friends social support. The combined effect of a school that is negative toward LGB youth and provides little support resulted in higher vulnerability for the youth. As might be expected, the researchers found that academic success was related to more than school climate and included the youth's personal experiences. A greater sense of belonging was demonstrated in schools in which teachers provided support for LGB youth and there was less exclusion of LGB students. The LGB group facing the most difficulty was found in schools with low teacher support and higher victimization.

> Students who reported a homophobic school climate, but who had support from teachers and did not have high rates of victimization reported a psychological sense of belonging that was just as high as the students in Cluster 2 who did not experience a homophobic climate, but who also reported low social support from teachers. (p. 168)

Among the authors' recommendations for counselors and teachers was that intervention to break the negative cycle is critical for the most vulnerable LGB youth—those who have low family and peer supports and become known by classmates as being victims. Other recommendations included

- supporting and facilitating a positive school climate regarding LGB youth so they experience a sense of belonging;
- posting an LGB sticker or book, openly reprimanding derogatory comments about gay individuals, and/or integrating LGB-specific issues into class curriculum or discussion;
- assisting LGB youth in locating social situations that are supportive;
- helping LGB youth concerning family concerns (e.g., coming out); and
- tuning in to any mental/physical health issues such as addiction or risk for suicide.

Common sense dictates that the earlier the intervention for the most vulnerable youth, the more likely the result will be positive. Professionals from community settings can help school personnel in their efforts to create safe schools where LGB youth know that they belong and are accepted.

As noted by O'Dell (2000), given the general lack of public support for same-sex identity, "the capacity to be psychologically empowered as a lesbian originates with self-validation" (p. 181). Assistance in developing self-validation, early intervention with LGB youth viewed as victims by their peers, accepting peers with a climate allowing LGB youth to feel a sense of belonging in schools, and support by teachers and counselors are the keys to working with self-identified gay, lesbian, and bisexual teens in school and community settings.

With healthy guidance from adult models, the groundwork may be laid for lasting shifts regarding acceptance, if not appreciation, of diversity of all kinds. William James said, "The best use of life is to invest it in something that outlives it."

Conclusion

For educators in the 21st century, the definition of "family" and its characteristics may be complex and confusing. This chapter provides some guidelines for understanding the adjustment process of the child and family in divorced, single-parent, and blended families, as well as lesbian/gay headed family forms. Factors that place children in these family forms at risk include learning, socioemotional, and/or behavioral problems. The risk factors are not a prescription for disaster, and awareness of risk can help professionals prevent or ameliorate any problems that stem from nontraditional family forms and families having LGB teens. Just as families need to remain flexible in adjusting to new family forms, so, too, must school/community professionals maintain flexibility and openness to understanding family dynamics in nontraditional family forms. As always, interest in and emotional connection with each family are the most important tools to understanding and working with families in community and educational contexts and making a difference in the lives of their children and youth.

Summary

The days of the nuclear, intact family as the primary family constellation have faded in the face of a host of other emerging family forms. The changing demographics in the United States, with its influx of immigrants who bring with them varied beliefs and family patterns/configurations and forms, have contributed to changed definitions of family. Children/youth who are growing up in nontraditional families are more the norm than the exception in the 21st century.

The deinstitutionalization of marriage with undefined societal expectations of spousal roles in the mid-20th century and the shift to *individualized marriage* brought less predictability to children's home lives. With parents no longer feeling tied to remain partners "until death do us part," children's awareness of divorce and cohabitation became common. Thus what had once been the bedrock of children's stability—an intact family—was tied to the shifting meaning spouses and society held for marriage.

Important to any form of support or intervention with families challenged by change in family form, function, values, and expectations is recognition of the reality that the capacity for resilience runs deep in most children and youth. Capable of crossing the troubled waters of family life without unalterable harm to their sense of self-worth, learning, behavior, personality, and value system, the now common diversity in family form is seen from a perspective of positive psychology with a realization that those who are vulnerable will need support and intervention in building resilience capacity rather than viewing them from a deficit model.

With the rate of divorce skyrocketing in the 1970s and then leveling off, those studying children of divorce have only recently been able to study effects on children who grew up after societal attitudes shifted to greater acceptance of divorce.

At the same time, parents finding themselves in a markedly lower financial situation as a result of divorce cannot mask harsh reality from their children. Fear, anger, and depression merge and it is crucial to reinforce the expectation that children will gradually adjust to divorce, usually within two to three years. The parents' lead in handling loss of economic and other forms of stability is predictive of better adjustment in children, and most children have a difficult initial adjustment to divorce with gradual improvement over time.

Gender and age differences exist in children's responses to divorce. Girls' adjustment is generally more positive than that of boys, and parental attitude toward divorce is most influential when their children are teenagers. Children zero to three adjust more quickly to divorce than older children. Prevention or early intervention of internalization (e.g., anxiety) and externalization (e.g., conduct problems) is crucial for healthy adjustment for children of divorce.

Initially most children of divorce face disorganization in their home life, as well as inadequate support by the custodial parent, vastly lower income or poverty, and a social support system inadequate to the task of furthering child adjustment. Cooperative coparenting, allowing the noncustodial parent to be involved with the child, and frequent contact with the father are crucial to counteract a negative trajectory. Predictable, familiar routines are important for children of divorce; professionals can aid parents in forming authoritative stances and reinforce the importance of keeping partner/spousal conflict to a minimum, with mediation being the most valuable assistance in establishing healthy child adjustment. With an eye to resilience, parents can be reminded that painful memories are not evidence of pathology.

Single-parent families include diverse types and low income is the greatest challenge; although lack of time to accomplish the tasks of everyday living also creates strain. Single-parent families are rife for both hierarchy problems and parentification of their children. It is easy for the oldest daughter or son to fall into one of these dysfunctional situations, and school/community personnel should advise parents if signs of either are noticeable. Clearly, authoritative parenting is the antidote to an inversion of the hierarchy, with a child overreaching an age-appropriate limit to power. It is essential that single parents become aware of the importance of the warmth and support they provide their children. Professionals also can help by stressing the impact of parental support networks, informing them of available networks, and pointing out the need for extended family being an ongoing part of the life of their children by providing support that adds stability to a strained family system. Professionals also can find ways to become or locate informal mentors, tutors, and special buddies for those children who need additional attention.

Remarriage and blended families present their own set of challenges for adults and children alike. Professionals should openly reinforce the need for parents to stabilize the family before slowly reclaiming one's personal life, eventually dating, and possibly one day remarrying. Adolescent children in particular struggle with parents dating, and children of all ages benefit from being aware of a closer stage evolving with a prospective partner so they are not taken by surprise.

Children do better if they are involved in decision making about how two households will come together through remarriage. It is imperative that parents convey there is no expectation for an easy transition, and the expectations in blended families is that it takes far longer to adjust. In newly blended families, parents must take a strong, unified stance in regard to expectations and daily life. Developing new traditions and rituals can help a blended family move toward more meaningful togetherness.

In remarriage there is a difference between initial and long-term struggles and experiences of individuals as well as subsystems (e.g., siblings, partners/spouses). It is very challenging for a newly remarried couple with children from both previous marriages/partnerships to find the time they need to continue solidifying their spousal/partner relationship. When the ages of children overlap across families, it takes time and energy to realign a hierarchy with the stepsibling subsystem. Everyone needs to know it is typical for this to take time to evolve. Recoupled parents must display tolerance for children and youth's family life struggles. Adjustment in blended families takes 5 to 7 years, and all family members are served by this knowledge to stave off disappointment and frustration. Those in the throes of blending the family benefit from counseling and support groups so that problems can be addressed in a timely manner before they escalate and cause harm to future relationship building.

The last nontraditional family form, lesbian and gay families, covered in this chapter is one with which many professionals have little training and less experience. Although the media has helped shift attitudes toward lesbian and gay individuals, it is not so when it comes to families with gay parents. Research shows that lesbian and gay people were the least preferred choice to adopt children or become foster parents. Prejudice toward gays and lesbians remains high, and stereotypes fuel such concerns. Research is clear that children of lesbian and gay families fare extremely well in terms of life adjustment, there is a lower incidence of sexual abuse within this family form, and there is no higher percent of children of gay and lesbian parents who become homosexual. Gender identity among children is similar regardless.

Lesbian/gay/bisexual youth (LGB) are another way families demonstrate diversity. Most parents are unaware and uninformed about the LGB status of their child. When parents are more aware of their child being LGB, the youth experiences less internalized homophobia, less verbal abuse, and greater support from their families. Sadly, the highest incidence of suicide is among these youth, and family relationships are usually what precipitates the attempt at suicide. LGB youth are the brunt of considerable harassment in schools. Yet, too, we are cautioned to remember that children and youth are resilient when receiving the support they deserve in schools and communities, and school climate makes the biggest difference in their lives.

For the school/community professional, awareness of the issues and dynamics of nontraditional family configurations/forms is imperative. If children from alternative family situations who are at risk for academic as well as emotional and behavioral problems are identified early, many future problems may be prevented. Further, in the interests of children and youth with whom they interact, professionals must accept the realities of modern life and help strengthen vulnerable children. Instead of a deficit view, including stigmatization of children from nontraditional families, a strengths approach is emphasized.

Case Example

Hannah, a 10-year-old girl in the fourth grade, had begun to complain of frequent headaches and being tired much of the time. Her complaints had resulted in her being excused from class almost every day. In addition, her school absences had increased during the previous 2 months, and her grades, which had been average, had deteriorated.

After sending home numerous written notices, the teacher phoned Hannah's mother and requested a meeting with both parents. During this conversation, the mother informed the teacher that she was not sure whether Hannah's father would attend the meeting. She gave the teacher her husband's office number and suggested that she contact him there to inform him of the meeting.

When the teacher contacted Hannah's father at the office, he agreed to a meeting time. He also informed her that he and his wife had decided 3 months ago to divorce but were still living in the same house, awaiting a settlement agreement. He tended to work late to avoid being in the same house with his wife for extended periods.

The parents both arrived for the meeting and listened, sullenly, while Hannah's teacher described her concerns about the girl. The parents stated that they had not told their children about their plans to divorce, but they believed the children were aware of the divorce because they had overheard their parents arguing. The teacher asked them how the stress of the present arrangement might be affecting their children.

The parents then began to blame each other for Hannah's problems. The mother stated that Hannah was upset because her father was never at home. The father opined that Hannah was responding to her mother's lethargy and crying spells.

It became clear to the teacher that the father had initiated the decision to divorce. When she inquired as to why the couple was still living in the same house, she was met with another round of accusations. The father claimed that if he were to leave the home, his wife would "take me to the cleaners" by filing charges of desertion. The wife retorted that her husband was staying in the home to "play a waiting game, hoping I will give up and let him off the hook."

Questions and Comments

1. What interventions could be tried with these parents? [Develop strategies for meeting with the parents, the points you would cover, suggestions you would make, and resources you would recommend. Then read the following description. This exercise can be completed alone or in small or large groups.]

   Initially, the teacher could point out that Hannah's difficulties were most likely a response to the family confusion and her resulting heightened stress. The teacher could ask about any signs or symptoms of stress in the other children, ages 16 and 12.

Once the teacher has elicited the parents' concern about their children, she and/or another professional from the school or the community (e.g., a social worker) could give them information about the effects of parental divorce on children of different ages and about the necessity for providing as much stability and predictability as possible. A follow-up meeting soon after the initial meeting would be recommended. In the meantime, the teacher could gather appropriate information and request the assistance of another professional in planning for the follow-up meeting.

In the second conference, the professional(s) could suggest that the parents together discuss the plans for their divorce openly with the children and explain why the living situation had not changed. Another suggestion might be that the parents each consult their attorneys to get a time frame for resolving the settlement issue so the children would have a general plan of what would be happening. The worst possible outcome for the children, it should be pointed out, would be for the children to become embroiled in the parents' disputes and experience loyalty conflicts. The professional(s) then could share typical concerns about divorce in children of Hannah's age and suggest that each parent sit down with Hannah and reassure her that

- the divorce is not her fault;
- her parents' separation does not mean they don't love her;
- she will continue to have contact with both parents after the divorce;
- she should not feel responsible for her parents' happiness;
- her parents will get the support they need from their friends and other adults in their extended families, rather than putting this pressure on their children;
- both of her parents will be available to Hannah whenever she would like to discuss her feelings about the divorce, and she has permission to talk about it with her friends; and
- it is important for Hannah to attend school, be with her friends, study, and do the things that 10-year-olds do every day.

Finally, the professional(s) could offer the parents resources for learning about the effects of divorce on themselves and their children, as well as books and other media for their children. The professional(s) could offer the parents information about postseparation support groups and a group for children of divorced parents, if available, along with a list of approved private counselors specializing in divorce issues including children and youth. Suggesting mental health community programs in the area would be helpful, along with any brochures offering more specific information. If indicated, other professionals (e.g., school psychologist, community social worker) might be called upon to attend the follow-up conference.

Extension Activities

Reflection: In recent years, media attention has focused more and more on divorce, remarriage, single-parent households, and gay/lesbian-headed families. Consider situations you have known, heard of, or experienced that relate to nontraditional families. Recall these families and your reactions to their situation.

Journal: How has your increased knowledge about the topic of divorce, single-parent, remarriage/blended, and lesbian/gay families impacted you personally and professionally? What remaining questions do you have about children/youth affected by these situations?

In-Class/Training Panel Discussion:

Leader instructions: Ask for students/group members to volunteer to serve on a panel and speak about their personal experiences from being in one of the following categories: (a) their parents divorced while they were still living at home; (b) they were reared by a single parent for part of their childhood; or (c) they are a member of a blended family. Invite each member to prepare a 5-minute talk about his or her background to be used as a springboard for the question-and-answer session.

While the panel members are speaking, the university students or trainees who are not on the panel will write on index cards questions they would like answered. Prior to introducing the question-and-answer session, a moderator (e.g., professor/trainer or community professional) will facilitate the brief sharing of backgrounds. The moderator then will collect all of the question cards and pose the questions to the panel members and serve as a facilitator in the discussion.

AND/OR

In-Class/Training Panel Discussion:

Leader instructions: If you have students/group members who are old enough to have formed immediate families, ask them to volunteer for a panel to speak about their personal experiences related to being in one of the following categories: they are/were a divorced parent, they were/are a single parent for part or all of their children's childhood, or they are a parent in a blended family.

Invite each member of the panel to prepare a 5-minute talk about his or her background to be used as a springboard for the question-and-answer session. In the meantime, while the panel members are speaking, those not on the panel will write on index cards questions they would like to have answered. Prior to introducing the question-and-answer session, a moderator will facilitate the brief sharing of backgrounds. The moderator then will collect all of the question cards and pose the questions to the panel members, as well as facilitate the discussion.

In-Class/Training Expert Speakers:

Leader instructions: In a small group or as a whole-class/group activity, work together to arrange for either one expert or a panel of experts to come to the class/session and address the issues discussed in this chapter—divorce, single-parent, remarriage, and lesbian/gay families. You might want to arrange for a series of speakers, one of whom could talk for a half-hour at each class/session, or you might prefer to have several speakers come to one class/training session to cover diverse topics related to divorce and its impact on children, blended families and their challenges, single-parent households, and lesbian/gay commitments with children.

For help in locating speakers, you might call the American Association for Marriage and Family Therapy (800-374-2638), use an Internet search engine (e.g., Google) to reach a website that will provide names of licensed professionals in your area, or call the local mental health community program in your area for recommendations. Prepare the speaker(s) by discussing audience characteristics, including their range of experiences, what information you would like them to cover, any remuneration, whether other experts will be there, how long the talk should be, and whether a question-and-answer period will follow. This exercise will help you replicate similar activities in the future.

Invitational Principals' Panel Leader

Instructions: In a small or large group, arrange for a panel of principals from elementary, middle, and high schools to speak to your class/session about the impact on schools of the special populations covered in this chapter. If possible, include principals and/or assistant principals who represent urban, suburban, and rural schools. In advance, provide the speakers with similar kinds of information similar to that suggested for the panel on nontraditional families. Use the same format as above, having students/group members write questions and a moderator ask them of the panel. The moderator should allow attendees to submit questions anonymously.

Invitational Administrative Social Workers' or Chief Counselors' Panel Leader

Instructions: In a small or large group, arrange for a panel of administrative social workers/counselors or other mental health directors from your local community mental health center. A combination of those administering services for different populations may be useful (e.g., children, youth, adults) in speaking about the impact on community programs of the special populations covered in this chapter. If possible, include administrative mental health specialists who represent urban, suburban, and rural settings. Beforehand, provide the speakers with information similar to that discussed for the panel on nontraditional families.

At-Risk Children From Challenged Families

*I*n addition to the challenges posed by the norm shifting from traditional to nontraditional families in the United States is the risk posed to children from challenged families. This chapter addresses those families with abuse or dependency on alcohol and other drugs (AOD) and child maltreatment (neglect and abuse). Family therapists and counselors, social workers, social/clinical/counseling psychologists, pediatricians, educators, sociologists studying family life, and other professionals in related fields view the American family as experiencing increasing dysfunctional behaviors since the middle of the 20th century. Three decades ago, Murray Bowen (1976) predicted this decrease in family functioning in relation to societal regression.

At the same time, the human capacity for resilience encourages helping professionals in their efforts to find strategies that will lead to evidence-based practices within multiple contexts (Obama, 2006). We must work together to transform dysfunctional behaviors in families so that children and youth neither live with AOD abuse and dependency nor maltreatment in the home or community.

This chapter first addresses family systems challenged by AOD abuse or dependency. This is followed by a discussion of the various forms of child maltreatment. Professionals who come into contact with these types of dysfunctional behaviors sometimes assign blame to a "problem person" in the family. The underlying principle of this entire book, and particularly this chapter, is that dysfunctional behavior must be viewed as part of a system, not as a problem existing solely within an individual. Rather, people are buffeted by other forces and factors (Deater-Deckard, Petrill, & Wilkerson, 2001; Ploman & Asbury, 2001). Some families manifest multigenerational transmission of dysfunctional patterns that may be supported by protective factors (see chapter 4 and the Appendix, on multigenerational transmission). Among other factors are the time in history when individuals grew up, their country of origin and subculture in juxtaposition to the dominant culture in which they live and learn, and larger systems touching their lives.

Furthermore, life is not static. It is dynamic, with individuals changing through maturation and as a result of life experiences. Protective factors can make a difference for the better. Professionals in community and school settings can help to move children toward higher levels of functioning and end a multigenerational, degenerative pattern that has been passed down from one generation to the next.

Families with Alcohol and Other Drug Abuse and Dependency

AOD dependency is clearly increasing. What are the reasons? What are the solutions?

Facts and Figures on AOD Dependency

According to the National Institute on Alcohol Abuse and Alcoholism (NIAAA, 2004) close to 18 million adults in the United States are alcoholic or abuse alcohol. The NIAAA stated:

> Several million more adults engage in risky drinking that could lead to alcohol problems. These patterns include binge drinking and heavy drinking on a regular basis. In addition, 53 percent of men and women in the United States report that one or more of their close relatives have a drinking problem. (p. 2)

By comparison, in 1994 this same government agency (NIAAA), now within the National Institutes of Health, estimated that 14 million adults in the United States have had problems with drinking.

Estimates of the number of Children of Alcoholics (COA) under 18 in the United States vary widely. One of the more recent estimates (Grant, 2000) reported that more than 28 million children live with one or more adults who have been dependent upon or have abused alcohol, compared to a reported 7 million nearly a decade ago (Natasi & DeZolt, 1994). Using data from the National Longitudinal Alcohol Epidemiologic Survey, Grant (2000) found that about 25% of children in the United States under the age of 18 were exposed to alcohol abuse or alcohol dependency in the family. The National Association for Children of Alcoholics (NACOA) website gives an estimate of 11 million individuals under the age of 18.

For Children of Drug Abusers (CODA), estimates are even more difficult to apprise, because users of illicit drugs are unlikely to respond to surveys honestly, even under guarantees of anonymity. Further complicating realistic CODA estimates is cross-addiction, in which parents are dependent on both alcohol and drugs, and experts believe that this number is considerable.

Background and Approaches to Treating AOD Abuse/Dependency

According to McIntyre (2004), two discernable functions are served by those with AOD dependency:

1. The chemical abuse/dependency may be primary in causing problems and conflict for both the chemically dependent individual and the family as a whole.
2. The symptom of AOD abuse bespeaks "underlying, unmet needs, undeveloped life skills, and unresolved life issues that the substance abuser and her or his family are attempting to take care of through the use of the substance(s)" (p. 238).

Parents who are in recovery for AOD dependency may or may not be taking active steps to maintain recovery. And some parents who are no longer actively using AOD still exhibit characteristics of active AOD dependency (e.g., control issues, anger) and fail to demonstrate positive change in the critical areas for recovery. Others go to meetings and receive treatment but are simply "going through the motions" with little to no observable growth.

Freeman (2001) and Benshoff and Janikowski (2000) have described the use of the rehabilitation model for substance abuse and dependency. This model considers alcohol and chemical dependency as a disability rather than a disease and deals with functional limitations of AOD dependency. Further, it emphasizes multiple systems collectively working on solutions to problems.

Kurtz (2002) detailed the history of the disease concept of alcoholism and how Alcoholics Anonymous developed in relation to it. McGovern (2002) overviewed articles published in *Alcoholism Treatment Quarterly* regarding trends in alcohol treatment between 1980 and 2000. McGovern credited two of the articles published in that issue (Kurtz, 2004; Morgan, 2002) for pointing out the emphasis on spirituality in Alcoholics Anonymous and similar groups in the process of recovery, stating that

> the current acceptance of spirituality as a legitimate component of holistic health can be traced to the influence of the alcoholism/ drug dependency treatment field. The overarching power of spirituality is best reflected in the lives of recovering persons who are the face and voice of recovery and success. (p. 196)

Harry Aponte (1994) has been a leader in integrating the spiritual dimension into family therapy. His conceptualization is of a spiritual and philosophical base that guides the process of structural family therapy. Commenting about the evolution of structural family therapy, Aponte and DiCesare (2002) stated:

> Today's structural therapy acknowledges a soul to the therapeutic process that lies in the human bond between therapist and client. It recognizes the ultimate mystery of the human spirit, and bases its work on the free will of the human being that can, must, and will choose its own path. The therapist's power is powerless in the face of the client's free will. The therapist's knowledge meets the unknowable of the human soul. The therapist who is expert in the professional sphere is quite humbly nonexpert in the human dimension of the therapeutic encounter. (p. 4)

A segment of alcohol-dependent people seek a treatment or support group different from that offered by AA and lean toward options described in Solomon's (2005) book. One example is Project WELL (Finkelstein & Markoff, 2004).

The profession as a whole prefers to use the term *in recovery* for AOD to signify that the person has quit drinking and/or using drugs and continues to seek active ways to maintain sobriety. Another term, used in some drug rehabilitation programs, is *wellbriety*. This terminology is gradually replacing the term *recovered alcoholic*. Most professionals who treat people for AOD dependency do not think it is possible to recover from any form of chemical dependency. Those who attend AA or NA meetings are inculcated in the process of being *in recovery* as a lifetime process, realizing that they will always be vulnerable to AOD.

Most professionals working within the culture of recovery believe that if an individual who has been in recovery consumes alcohol or other drugs, he or she will return to the status of "active chemical dependency" and will not be in recovery again until they have stopped using AOD. Some programs, however, are based on the belief that recovery is possible, and that the person can drink socially again—referred to as "controlled drinking."

Evidence for a trial of controlled drinking comes from Cloud, McKiernan, and Cooper (2003), who critiqued current approaches of controlled drinking as a goal for treatment and stated:

> Empirical evidence suggests that some who are younger, who have less severe history of alcohol use, who have never been treated or diagnosed for alcohol disorders, who possess no family history of addiction, and who believe in self-efficacy over alcohol use could benefit from a single and well conceived controlled drinking trial. (pp. 67–68)

In any case, relapse prevention for AOD dependency (e.g., Gray & Gibson, 2004) is critical so that the family will remain as stable as possible after treatment and the individual will understand the relapse–feelings cycle (Freeman, 2001). Time is truly of the essence in these kinds of situations. The longer the relapse before intervention, the harder it is to restabilize the family.

Characteristics of Families With AOD Dependency

The most agreed-upon characteristics of children and families in which parents are AOD-dependent are

- the AOD-dependent person's denial of the problem ("There's an elephant in the living room but no one notices");
- rigid external boundaries, isolating the family from social supports;
- rigid internal boundaries, manifested by poor interpersonal communication and a lack of expression of feelings; and
- unresolved family history with sudden or traumatic loss of a member.

The impacts on children of parental AOD dependency relate to behavioral, medical and psychiatric, and educational problems in the home, school, and community (Ackerman, 1989; Brooks & Rice, 1997; Brown & Lewis, 2002; Byrne, Edmundson, & Rankin, 2005; Freshman, 2004; Hilarski, 2005; Hogan, Gabrielsen, Luna, & Grothaus, 2003; Kaufman & Kaufmann, 1992; Lopez & Kelly, 2003; McIntyre, 2004; McNeece & DiNitto, 2005; Nastasi & DeZolt, 1994; Saitoh, Steinglass, & Schuckit, 1992; Schlesinger & Horberg, 1988; Treadway, 1987; White & Savage, 2005; Woititz, 2002; Yalisove, 2004). To the above list, Markowitz (2004) would add "impaired empathy."

All except the last of the above-listed characteristics can be observed by trained professionals, although it should be noted that the above characteristics are not universally observed in every family with a parent who is dependent on alcohol or drugs. Each family has its own mix of characteristics and impacts on children in the family. According to Markowitz (2004), far more is known about children of alcoholic parents (COA) than children of parents who abuse or are dependent upon other drugs (CODA).

Professionals in schools and community settings may suspect that the child comes from a family with alcohol or drug dependency. Complicating the matter, though, is that the characteristics are applicable to other forms of dysfunctional behavior in families as well (Markowitz, 2004). For that reason, professionals should not jump to conclusions but simply be aware of the possibility for AOD dependency within the family when they notice the characteristics listed.

Parental Impact of AOD Dependency on Their Children

Professionals working with children in community and school settings must become aware of the impact of parental AOD dependency on the parental subsystem (Markowitz, 2004; Nastasi & DeZolt, 1994), as the ability to parent is effectively diminished severely when the parent is dependent on alcohol or drugs. The affected individual's emotional availability to his or her spouse and children is limited, and depending on the severity of the addiction, many other aspects of the individual's functioning may be impaired. The website of the National Association for Children of Alcoholics (NACOA) states that

> alcohol is a key factor in 68% of manslaughters, 62% of assaults, 54% of murders and attempted murders, 48% of robberies, and 44% of burglaries" [www.nacoa.net/impfacts.htm]. Whenever a

parent is the cause of one of these infractions due to alcohol abuse/dependency, the impact of the parent(s) on their children is a marked sense of shame and, for some children, the result is eventually following in the parent's footsteps.

In most literature the non-dependent spouse has been viewed as an "enabler" who tolerates aberrant behavior to preserve the relationship and family (Brooks & Rice, 1997; Zelvin, 2004). Lacking a functional marital subsystem, the non-dependent spouse often turns to older children for emotional support and assistance in coping with the demands of managing the family (Markowitz, 2004; Zelvin, 2004). This fits the concept of emotional parentification described in chapter 7. The hierarchy in the family is disrupted, and the boundaries between the family and external systems become rigidified to preserve the family secret. Thus, family members are cut off both from external supports and from one another (internal supports).

Typical Role Responses of Children to Parental AOD Dependency

The family of chemically dependent parents is characterized by inconsistency, conflict, and emotional stress (Brooks & Rice, 1997; Dulfano, 1992; Markowitz, 2004). Treadway (1987) quoted a child living in an alcoholic home:

> I could always tell what kind of night it was going to be by how my father came in the door. I would listen for how he put the key in the lock. If he fumbled around and didn't get the key in, I would know it was going to be the kind of night that I would just make myself scarce. (p. 18)

This child describes families in which the addiction organizes the family system. Children in this kind of family feel that the adults they are supposed to trust and depend upon are unpredictable. The children learn to survive by becoming self-sufficient, by blocking out feelings, and by learning not to depend upon others. Even when the parent stops drinking, these family patterns and personality styles remain intact (Brooks & Rice, 1997; Dulfano, 1992; McIntyre, 2004) unless the parents receive help in regaining the reins and changing the existing dysfunctional patterns.

More than two decades ago (1985) Wegscheider-Cruse identified patterns or "adaptive" roles that children assume to survive in an addictive family (1985). The terms she created—Hero, Scapegoat, Lost Child, and Mascot—have become standard in the professional and popular literature about families with AOD dependency. Nastasi and DeZolt (1994) charted the four roles, and Brooks and Rice (1997) gave examples of each. Glover (1994) focused solely on the Hero in the alcoholic family and provided recommendations for school counselors. Others elaborating on these roles include Benshoff and Janikowski (2000), McFarland and Tollerud (2004), and Wolin and Wolin (1993). Finally, Children of Alcoholics Foundation (COAF) is dedicated to breaking the cycle of parental alcohol and other substance abuse and incorporates these roles. The following is a consolidation of descriptions from the references cited in this paragraph:

Family Hero or Super Kid:

- Often the oldest child in the family
- Overachiever, needs to control, can't fail, a perfectionist
- Successful in school, sports, community, clubs
- Brings recognition to family and underneath thinks this will cause the parent(s) to quit abusing alcohol or drugs
- Hides feelings of hurt, inadequacy, confusion, and guilt
- Self-critical, poor self-esteem, sense of inadequacy, lonely
- Overly responsible for caregiving of others
- As an adult, is likely to become a workaholic and marry a dependent person, unless getting effective help

Family Scapegoat:

- Typically delinquent; perpetually in trouble
- Abuses drugs/alcohol
- Defiant
- Weak performance in school
- Acts out to draw attention away from the alcoholic/addict; accepts blame for problems in the family; hides feelings of hurt, abandonment, anger, rejection
- Often the identified patient when parents seek therapy
- Feels lonely, guilty, low self-worth
- Without transformation, as an adult is likely to become an alcoholic or addict

Lost Child:

- Usually the middle child or later in the sibling constellation within the family
- Shy, quiet, aloof, and, because overlooked, often withdrawn, a loner
- Hides feelings of unimportance, abandonment, inadequacy
- Often perceived inaccurately as antisocial
- Extended fantasy life
- Tries not to add to burden of family and appears to be independent
- Teachers/coaches often don't notice this child's needs because of the "invisibility" factor
- As an adult, probably will be indecisive, nonassertive, depressed, isolated, and have physical illnesses, without help

Mascot or Family Clown:

- Often the youngest child
- Clowns around, jokes, is "cutesy"
- Hyperactive and unable to handle stress
- Hides feelings of sadness, anxiety, fear, helplessness, and insecurity; unable to relate in an honest manner
- Confused and fears losing contact with reality
- Vulnerable to alcohol dependency as an adult because of weak mechanisms for self-control and immature means of receiving attention

- Likely to marry a hero and/or fall into repeated cycles of dependent relationships
- Frequently a raconteur as an adult, still seeking attention and keeping others at arms-length by storytelling—unless receiving help

These personality patterns and roles often become so ingrained in the developing child that they are carried long into adulthood. The behavior patterns are evident not only at home and in the community but also in the classroom. Treatment may be through family systems therapy, individual counseling or group work, Alateen, or other forms. The COA or CODA may be an adult before shedding the dysfunctional role, becoming authentic.

With treatment, the Hero can learn to recognize the desire to excel as a personal choice and channel the role into bringing others together as a team, group, or family that functions well collectively. The Scapegoat can transform and let go of knee-jerk reactivity and replace it with responsible leadership that helps others see the value of diversity and creative energy. The Scapegoat also can play the role of devil's advocate when making decisions in a group, so that all sides are considered prior to making a decision. The Lost Child can heal and draw others in by relating from an authentic desire to be of service. The Mascot can recognize that spontaneity is useful for others to enjoy life, and can use his or her personality to bring levity to gatherings.

Emotional, Behavioral, and Learning Risks of COA and CODA

Thomas (2000) referred to effects and risk for children of drug abusers (CODA) including "increased risk for disturbed affect, low educational performance, conduct problems, juvenile offending and substance abuse..." (p. 370). Markowitz (2004) indicated that parents using illegal drugs such as cocaine and heroin are more frequent among minorities and those in poverty, with their "children experiencing or witnessing violence, sexual abuse, neglect, and abandonment" (p. 289). Markowitz further characterized what these families share in common:

> the existence of some significant degree of impairment in empathy on the part of at least one parent (or primary caretaker). The dynamics of COAs can best be understood as a special case of narcissistic injury suffered at the hands of empathically impaired parents. What makes this a special case is the intermittent presence of behaviors induced by mood-altering substances in parents whose non-drug-involved personalities may be dramatically different from what they appear to be while "under the influence." (p. 285)

Without the capacity to understand chemical dependency, the CODA faces a situation in which the parent or parents value the alcohol/drug more than the child, and, thus, the child does not have a secure attachment with the parent. The value placed upon the parent–child relationship is sometimes dependent upon the child's responses to the dependency (e.g., facilitating/interfering with use of AOD). Making things more complex is that the non-dependent parent may be so overwhelmed trying to deal with the dependent spouse that he or she likewise is not able to form the necessary child–parent attachment.

Some time ago, Knight (1994) identified behavioral patterns for CODA (Children of Drug Abusers) that remain relevant today. These patterns are not necessarily found in any one or all CODA. They are typical behaviors observed in different children to different extents, and some are also seen in children from families with other kinds of dysfunction. Knight's behaviors include, in addition to physical symptoms, the following:

- Absenteeism
- Neglected physical appearance
- Fluctuating academic performance
- Fatigue and lack of energy
- Psychological symptoms
- People-pleasing behavior
- Conflict avoidance
- Problems controlling mood and behavior
- Attention problems
- Social isolation

She presented a long list of reasons for educators *not to identify* COA (Children of Alcoholics) but, instead, to ensure that "chemical dependency-related education and prevention efforts [be] directed to all children" (p. 282). This also would be true in community settings where children are served (e.g., after-school, out-of-school-time (OST) programs). She suggested that self-identification could be the best method of identifying these children, as anonymity and safety would be in the individual child's hands. She also views partnerships between school, family, and community as pivotal in providing support and resources necessary for children of alcoholics.

Because of the increased risks for CODA, Vail-Smith, Knight, and White (1995) stressed the importance of training school personnel, including counselors, on how best to help these children. The counselors they interviewed saw elementary counselors as having a key role in providing education, support, and referral for these children.

Prevention, Support, and Intervention in Families With AOD Abuse/Dependency

Professionals in community and school settings have many opportunities to help these children and their families, sometimes by suggesting or being part of a planned intervention with an AOD-dependent parent (Pianta, 2000). When working with children of parents with AOD dependency, professionals in community and school settings can provide support and promote healing through, among other things, curricula focusing on the process of AOD dependency, the expression of feelings, identity formation, and responsiveness to differences in cultural background of families (Bagnall, 1991; Bates & Wigtil, 1994; Hanson, 1996; Marshall, 1992; Markowitz, 2004; Nastasi & DeZolt, 1994; Nastasi, Moore, & Varjas, 2004). School and community professionals can provide information about local chapters of Alateen, Narateen, or local Children of Alcoholics (COA).

Lewis, Dana, and Blevins (2002) emphasize structured group work to help children deal with affect and building effective communication skills. They advised that "children of troubled parents need to know that they are not to blame for family difficulties and that their attempts to meet their own needs are in no way detrimental to other family members" (p. 143).

Straussner (2001b) discussed AOD in relation to different ethnocultural backgrounds, relating to the traditions, cultures, and expectations of various groups. Some come to treatment with little or no understanding or knowledge of treatment for AOD abuse and dependency.

McFarland, Gabriel, Bigelow, and Walker (2006) stated that "American Indians have the highest prevalences of substance abuse and dependence among the racial and ethnic groups...but are served by the country's most complicated behavioral health care system" (p. 1469). Others, too, have written about culturally competent treatment for substance abuse, specifically concerning Native Americans (Evans, Spear, Huang, & Hser, 2006; French, 2004; White, 2004).

Nastasi and DeZolt (1994) viewed prevention as paramount. They wrote of the importance of "creating school cultures that foster the development of social competence and personal efficacy of all children, with particular attention to the needs of COAs" (p. vii). Their ESCAPE model can be embedded within existing curricula.

Markowitz (2004) stated:

> Appropriate treatment can help clients to overcome excessive shame, guilt, boundary confusion, disabling need for control and approval, and the tendency to repeat their traumatic early experiences. The narcissistic injury and damage to the sense of self, sustained as a result of impaired parental empathy, can begin to be worked through with the help of informed, empathic clinicians. (p. 300)

Often the nondependent spouse/partner is aware of, and uncomfortable with, the family situation but feels unable to break out of the family rules and proceed toward change. Community and school professionals can direct the nondependent spouse to resources that can help change the family system. Other suggestions include attending local Al-Anon meetings or support groups and recommending literature on the family dynamics of addiction. As nondependent spouses become healthier, they may be able to provide more support for their children and become more able to engage the addicted spouse in treatment.

Freeman (2001) conceptualized intervention as dynamic rather than as static. She also pointed out the need to consider the barriers presented by immediate family members to rehabilitation, as well as interaction with larger systems such as schools, the legal system, work, and the mental health system. Her emphasis on family systems is important in recognizing the importance of involving the entire family in treatment.

Adolescents Facing AOD Use

In that alcohol and drug abuse in teens has risen in recent years (Luthar & D'Avanzo, 1999), teens and their families require particular attention. For these adolescents and their families, a multisystemic approach has been found necessary (Freshman, 2004). Professionals working with adolescents who have AOD problems are advised *not* to use an adult model of chemical dependency, and to involve school, family, and community partnership for both prevention and intervention.

Luthar and D'Avanzo (1999) studied contextual factors in relation to suburban and inner-city adolescents. Teens in the suburbs reported levels of use of substances that were significantly higher than youth in the inner city. Nichols and Schwartz (2004) reviewed family-based intervention for adolescent substance abuse, highlighting research that focuses treatment within a cultural context and thereby increases effectiveness in high-risk adolescents and families.

Support groups for students who return to school and community programs after in-patient treatment are beneficial. Although most treatment facilities provide these services, individuals in rural areas may find that schools are a better source for providing such groups. Networking with churches, synagogues, and mosques is another possibility, and almost every town in America has chapters of "Anonymous" groups into which teens might fit.

Maltreatment of Children

Maltreatment of children is the overall term for a category that includes neglect, as well as physical, emotional, and sexual abuse. Since the 1950s, U.S. society has gone through considerable change, as the stress accompanying societal changes has surged into family life. These include changes in

- gender roles;
- continuing and increased participation of women in the workforce;
- redefinition of family values;
- skyrocketing divorce rates (which eventually leveled off);
- rising use of drugs for recreational purposes;
- increases in alcoholism and under-age drinking;
- the explosion of the Information Age, requiring more specialized and advanced training for technical jobs;
- more people living longer because of developments in medical science; and
- dramatic demographic shifts with the influx of Latino and Asian immigrants.

Government responses to meet these needs have fallen short.

Other changes include medical advances, which are allowing seniors to live vastly longer. The term *sandwich generation* refers to those who are raising children while also providing care to their aging and sometimes medically fragile parents. Massive changes in almost every arena of life are bound to extract a toll in different ways on families.

At the same time, multigenerational transmission of dysfunctional patterns of behavior can be predicted to affect families in ways that can be traced back through generations in that family. Most patterns of dysfunction are transmitted from one or the other side of the family tree, or both sides if the pattern existed on both sides (e.g., alcoholism, child maltreatment). Learning more about family history, thus, can point to potential patterns in current families.

Maltreatment of children is one form of dysfunctional behavior that seemed to sky-rocket since the 1950s, but could this be attributed, in part, to exposing a former shroud of deception, or to improved reporting of child maltreatment? Perhaps the current statistics are more realistic. As professionals, and then the media, became more aware of the preva-lence and impact of child maltreatment, more opportunities for treatment became possible for children and families. Alternative Response (Loman & Siegel, 2005) is one such oppor-tunity that supports families with suspected child maltreatment in its less extreme forms and yields positive results.

Notwithstanding the propensity for generational transmission, not all individuals who maltreat their children were themselves maltreated as children. Kaufman and Ziegler (1987) found that most children who were abused did not actually transmit it to the next generation by abusing their children.

Many authors have focused on evidence-based treatment (Beers & DeBellis, 2004; Bolger & Patterson, 2003; Cicchetti & Toth, 2005; Henderson, 2000; Corcoran, 2000, 2003; Ernst, 2001; Flores, Cicchetti, & Rogosch, 2005; Giles-Sims, 1997; Lambie, 2005; Lutzger & Bigelow, 2002; Macy, Barry, & Noam, 2003; Moe, King, & Bailly, 2004; Scannapieco & Carrick, 2003; Skowron & Reinemann, 2005; Stevens & Higgins, 2002; Wilkes, 2002b). All forms of child maltreatment put children at risk for failure in school and life. Professionals can help to create the conditions for multisystems change that make a positive difference in the lives of maltreated children as well as their families with AOD.

Facts and Figures on Child Maltreatment

Of the 3,503,000 children investigated or assessed by Child Protective Services in 2004, 872,000 were found to be victims of child neglect or maltreatment (Children's Bureau, 2004). The breakdown was as follows:

   62.4 % experienced neglect
   17.5 % were physically abused
   9.7 % were sexually abused
   7.0 % were psychologically maltreated
   2.1 % were medically neglected

In addition, 14.5% of victims experienced "other" types of maltreatment such as "aban-donment," "threats of harm to the child," and "congenital drug addiction" (p. 24). The per-centages total more than 100% because some children were victims of two or more forms of maltreatment. Almost 84% of the victims were abused by at least one parent. Approximately 39% were maltreated by their mothers acting alone, about 18% by their fathers acting alone, and about 18% by both parents. Nonparental perpetrators accounted for 10.1% of the total number of victims.

The numbers among ethnic/racial groups of child maltreatment victims reported for 2004 were as follows:

   African-American children, 19.9% per 1,000 children of the same race
   Pacific Islander, 17.6% per 1,000 children
   American Indian or Alaska Native, 15.5% per 1,000 children
   Asian, 2.9% per 1,000 children

Caucasian, 10.7% per 1,000 children

Hispanic, 10.4% per 1,000 children

The data also included "likelihood of recurrence," defined by the Children's Bureau, Administration for Children and Families, as a child experiencing a second substantiated or indicated occurrence of maltreatment within a 6-month time period. Of the states that reported those figures, prior victims were 84% more likely to experience maltreatment than children who had not been found to be a victim of maltreatment in the past. Further, the report stated that child victims who were reported with a disability were 61% more likely to experience recurrence than children without a disability (p. 28). Thuppal and Sobsey (2004) estimated that the incidence of child abuse and neglect among children with disabilities overall appears to be about twice as high as it is for the general population.

The oldest children (16–21) were least likely to experience recurrence of maltreatment, and children from birth through age 3 were most frequently found to experience another occurrence of neglect or maltreatment. The rate of children who die of abuse or neglect was about two per 100,000 in the national population in 2004. Many children who are maltreated experience multiple types of maltreatment (Chalk, Gibbons, & Scarupa, 2002; Children's Bureau, 2004; Golden, 2000).

Many incidents of child maltreatment go unrecognized and unreported (Alvarez, Donohue, Kenny, Cavanagh, & Romero, 2005; Alvarez, Kenny, Donohue, & Carpin, 2004), As a result, statistics from the Children's Bureau underestimate the actual prevalence of child maltreatment.

Indicators of Maltreatment of Children by Parents and Caregivers

Neglect and/or abuse are more prevalent in families at or below the poverty level, as well as those with parental AOD issues described earlier in this chapter. In addition, higher levels of child maltreatment are related to parents having been maltreated as children and, for girls in stepfamilies, in relation to sexual abuse. Overall, though, maltreatment crosses age, gender, race, religious, and socioeconomic background and is found in families where neither parent was maltreated (Donohue, Romero, & Hill, 2006; Giles-Sims, 1997; Golden, 2000; Scannapieco & Carrick, 2003; Thuppal & Sobsey, 2004).

Cicchetti and Toth (2005) stated, "Child maltreatment exemplifies a toxic relational environment that poses significant risks for maladaptation across biological and psychological domains of development" (p. 409). This emphasizes that child maltreatment has dire consequences, so strong efforts must be made to prevent as well as provide effective treatment to the children and families who experience its destructive pattern.

Overall signs that could indicate the presence of child maltreatment, according to the Child Welfare Information Gateway (2006b), are as follows:

The child

- shows sudden changes in behavior or school performance;
- has not received help for physical or medical problems brought to the parents' attention;

- has learning problems (or difficulty concentrating) that cannot be attributed to specific physical or psychological causes;
- is always watchful, as though preparing for something bad to happen;
- lacks adult supervision;
- is overly compliant, passive, or withdrawn;
- comes to school or other activities early, stays late, and does not want to go home.

The parent

- shows little concern for the child;
- denies the existence of—or blames the child for—the child's problems in school or at home;
- asks teachers or other caregivers to use harsh physical discipline if the child misbehaves;
- sees the child as bad, worthless, or burdensome;
- demands a level of physical or academic performance that the child cannot achieve;
- looks primarily to the child for care, attention, and satisfaction of emotional needs.

The parent and child

- rarely touch or look at each other,
- speak of their relationship as entirely negative,
- state that they do not like each other.

Ackerman and Graham (1990) offered an older, and still useful, listing of indicators or circumstances that signal potential for child maltreatment. They suggested that not all indicators are necessarily observable, but information in the child's file or through communication with parents or other family members can offer additional signs of possible child maltreatment. They warned that the number of circumstances within a family is not what is indicative of child maltreatment but, rather, how the family copes with situations. Ackerman and Graham's indicators include (pp. 204–205)

- parents who act indifferent, intolerant, or overanxious toward the child;
- existing history of family violence;
- socioeconomic problems such as unemployment;
- a child who was born prematurely or had a low birthweight;
- parents who were themselves abused or neglected as children;
- blended family with a stepparent or a parental cohabitee;
- a single or separated parent;
- a mother younger than 21 at the time the child was born;
- a history of mental illness;
- AOD dependency;
- a child who, as an infant, was separated from the mother for more than 24 hours postdelivery;
- a child with a mental or physical disability;
- children in the family spaced closer than 18 months; and
- a child who was never breast-fed as an infant.

As a cautionary note: When signs of maltreatment are present, no one should conclude automatically that maltreatment is the cause. The signs merely point to the possibility of maltreatment and should alert the professional to continue observing the child closely and consulting with experts in child maltreatment if the concern continues.

Definitions and Forms of Maltreatment

Federal definitions guide the states by providing minimum standards for writing definitions of child maltreatment. The Keeping Children and Families Safe Act of 2003 amended the Federal Child Abuse Prevention and Treatment Act (CAPTA) and is the foundation by which States are guided in writing definitions. The overall definition of child abuse and neglect is defined by the federal government as

> any recent act or failure to act on the part of a parent or care-taker which results in death, serious physical or emotional harm, sexual abuse or exploitation; or an act or failure to act which presents imminent risk of serious harm.

The four types of maltreatment, discussed next, are neglect, physical abuse, emotional maltreatment, and sexual abuse.

Neglect

Neglect has generally been defined as the failure to provide for the basic needs of a child. To that definition, Cicchetti and Toth (2005) would add lack of adequate supervision. Neglect may have physical, medical, educational, and/or emotional aspects. Examples of each follow:

- *Physical neglect*: inadequate or inappropriate food/shelter
- *Medical neglect*: failure to seek repair of a broken bone
- *Educational neglect*: failure to support special education IEP requirements
- *Emotional neglect*: allowing underage drinking

The Child Welfare Information Gateway (2006b) and National Children's Advocacy Center (2006) provided examples signaling the potential for child neglect. The child may be

- frequently absent or tardy from school;
- repeatedly sleepy, tired, listless;
- consistently hungry, begging classmates or stealing money or food, emaciated;
- lacking necessary medical (e.g., immunizations, glasses) and dental care (e.g., cleaning, cavities);
- habitually dirty with noxious body odor;
- lacking appropriate clothing for the weather (e.g., no coat/boots/gloves when snowing);
- abuses alcohol or other drugs;
- states that no one is home providing care;
- self-destructive; or
- extremely lonely with high need for affection.

The adult (parent, guardian, or other caregiver) may show

- indifference to the child,
- apathy or depression,
- irrational or bizarre behavior,
- failure to provide adequate nutrition,
- abandonment, or
- AOD abuse.

The Children's Bureau (2004) reported that 62.9% of perpetrators who were parents maltreated through neglect, and 9.9% who were investigated and found to neglect children were friends or neighbors.

Clearly, neglect is the most prevalent of the four forms of child maltreatment. Although physical and emotional maltreatment and sexual abuse are more obvious forms of child maltreatment than neglect, and they have received more attention from professionals and the media, neglect remains more common and is debilitating to children (Children's Bureau, 2004; Corcoran, 2000; Gil, 1996; Green, 1991; Golden, 2000; Henderson, 2000). Schumacher, Slep, and Heyman (2001) offered that "limited socioeconomic resources are the most consistently documented risk factor for neglect" (p. 231).

Physical Abuse

Physical abuse of a child is considered to be injury of a physical nature that results from shaking, throwing, kicking, punching, choking, burning, as well as hitting, beating, or stabbing a child with one's hand or other object. The term *physical abuse* is descriptive, but it is essential to determine that what is observed on the child's body was not the result of an accident and was the result of an adult actively inflicting bodily injury on the child. (Cicchetti & Toth, 2005). And not all signs are physically observable. The Child Welfare Gateway (2006b) and National Children's Advocacy Center (2006) provide many possible indicators of physical abuse, including

- swollen areas, burns, bites, bruises, broken bones, or black eyes that cannot be explained;
- fading bruises or other marks after an absence from school/child care;
- bizarre explanations for injuries;
- the child appears frightened of the parent/caregiver and protests or cries when it is time to be with the person;
- the child shrinks away at the approach of adults;
- the child tells others about an injury inflicted by a parent or caregiver;
- the adolescent is a chronic runaway.

As well, physical abuse should be considered a possibility when the parent/guardian/ caregiver

- delays in getting treatment for the child's injuries or gets inappropriate treatment;
- provides conflicting, unconvincing, or no explanation when the child has obviously been injured;

- describes the child as "evil" or uses other pejorative terms;
- employs harsh physical discipline; or
- has a personal history of being abused as a child.

Before making a report to CPS, one should be aware of conditions frequently mistaken as physical abuse of a child. Bays (2001a) cautioned that those required to report suspected child abuse take the time necessary to obtain a complete physical examination that would rule out possibilities for conditions unrelated to abuse. Conditions that have been mistaken for child abuse include bruising, infections, coagulation disorders, and dermatologic conditions, among others. Also, cultural differences should be taken into consideration, such as characteristic marks left after acupuncture.

Emotional Abuse

Emotional abuse is a form of abuse that results in emotional impairment and damages the child's sense of self-worth, stemming from criticism, threats, and/or rejection, as well as parental/caregiver withholding of care, support, and guidance. Although it is difficult to prove, it almost always accompanies other forms of maltreatment. Emotional abuse relates to unrelenting, severe obstruction of the child's basic needs (Cicchetti & Toth, 2005).

Characteristics that should be considered as potential signs of emotional abuse in a child are

- showing extremes in behavior such as being exceedingly compliant/demanding or overly submissive/aggressive;
- being either parentified or babyish;
- thumb sucking or rocking;
- compulsive behaviors such as hair pulling, twisting objects, pencil tapping, leg swinging;
- marked delays in physical or emotional development;
- attempted or threatening suicide;
- delinquency;
- physical conditions such as ulcers, asthma, extreme allergy, speech disorder; and
- expressing lack of attachment to parent/guardian/caregiver.

On the part of parents/guardian/caregiver, emotional abuse of a child should be considered a possibility when the adult (Child Welfare Information Gateway, 2006b; National Children's Advocacy Center, 2006)

- consistently belittles, shames, blames, or berates the child;
- ignores and isolates the child;
- insults, puts down, or calls the child names;
- terrorizes or humiliates the child;
- involves the child in corruption;
- lacks concern about the child and won't consider accepting help that is offered to resolve the problems the child is experiencing; and
- overt rejection of the child.

Sexual Abuse

The Federal Child Abuse and Prevention and Treatment Act (CAPTA) has defined sexual abuse as

> the employment, use, persuasion, inducement, enticement, or coercion of any child to engage in, or assist any other person to engage in, any sexually explicit conduct or simulation of such conduct for the purpose of producing a visual depiction of such conduct; or the rape, and in cases of caretaker or inter-familial relationships, statutory rape, molestation, prostitution, or other form of sexual exploitation of children, or incest with children. (Child Welfare Information Gateway, 2006c)

Sexual abuse may involve indecent exposure, fondling genitals, penetration, rape, sodomy, or incest, as well as prostituting a child to collect money or producing child pornography. Incest is sexual abuse perpetrated by a family member. A broad definition of sexual abuse is "sexual contact or attempted contact between a child and a caregiver or other adult for purposes of the caregiver's sexual gratification or financial gain" (Cicchetti & Toth, 2005; p. 410).

Behaviors that could indicate the potential for sexual abuse and should automatically send up a red flag of concern when observed in a child, include

- difficulty walking or sitting;
- suddenly refusing to change for gym or other physical activities;
- talking about nightmares or bedwetting;
- sudden changes in appetite;
- bizarre, sophisticated, or unexpected sexual knowledge or behavior for age;
- seductive behavior;
- substantial weight change;
- pregnancy or venereal disease under age 14;
- recurring urinary/yeast infections;
- swelling/itching in genital area;
- genital bruising or bleeding;
- running away from home;
- talking about sexual abuse by parent/caregiver; and
- overly concerned for sibling's welfare.

Signs that a parent or other adult may be a child sexual abuser include being (Child Welfare Information Gateway, 2006b; National Children's Advocacy Center, 2006)

- overly protective or limiting the child's contact with other children, especially in relation to the opposite gender;
- secretive and isolated; and
- jealous or controlling with members of the family.

The Children's Bureau (2004) reported that 2.6% of parents who were perpetrators of maltreatment engaged in some level of incest.

Bays (2001b) described a number of types of conditions (i.e., behavioral, dermato-logic, congenital, urethral, anal, traumatic, infectious) that may make a parent, caretaker, or child care worker suspect child abuse when there is no child abuse present. When sexual abuse is suspected, the child should be evaluated by a medical professional. To avoid mistaken diagnoses and trauma, clinicians must be aware of conditions that appear to be signs of sexual abuse but are not. In cases of uncertainty, specialists from a variety of specialty areas should be sought (e.g., dermatologist, urologist, geneticist, pathologist).

Roots of Child Maltreatment

In earlier times, many professionals writing about and doing research related to parental child maltreatment viewed it as being a repetition of what the parents had themselves experienced (Ackerman & Graham, 1990; Berger, 1985; Egeland, 1993; Fennell & Weinhold, 2003; Hampton & Gelles, 1991; Vondra, 1990), and that most abusive parents and people who marry abusive spouses were themselves abused or neglected as children (Kaufman & Zigler, 1993). With the rise of systems approaches and social ecology, resilience research, feminist theory, and recognition of culture affecting family views of child maltreatment, the multigenerational transmission of child maltreatment explanation has been supplemented with other insights (Brooks, 1992; Purvis & Ward, 2006; Walsh, 2003a). These include community, social, cultural influences.

Community-level Roots of Child Maltreatment

Ernst (2001) examined community-level factors in relation to child maltreatment in a suburban county (Montgomery County, Maryland). She contrasted findings with a similar study on child maltreatment in Cleveland, Ohio. Using two theoretical frameworks (ecological perspective and community social organization), she found that instability, economic disadvantage, and family characteristics related to levels of child maltreatment. She stated that

> although residential mobility has differential effects in urban areas, variation in rates of child maltreatment remains tied to economic disadvantage and poverty. In suburban areas, the face of poverty and the resources available to address needs may be different. (p. 140)

She also recommended preventive services for families with high risk for child maltreatment, as well as those with previous involvement with CPS or juvenile justice. Clearly, the community in which one lives makes a difference in the stress levels that impact child maltreatment.

Molnar, Buka, Brennan, Holton, and Earls (2003) described neighborhood intervention strategies as holding promise for parent-to-child physical aggression. Schuck (2002) explored abuse in childhood and the risk of developing antisocial behavior in terms of neighborhood structural characteristics and its influence on the later development of criminal and violent behavior in these children. She found intensified criminal and violent proclivities in children who were maltreated and remained in neighborhoods that had negative characteristics (i.e., residential instability, ethnic heterogeneity, low concentrated advantage). As well, a high concentration of disadvantage in a neighborhood was found to increase criminal patterns stemming from maltreatment during earlier childhood.

Social Ecology Roots of Child Maltreatment

The theory of social ecology (Bronfenbrenner, 1979) focuses on interchanges between the environment and the individual nested within multiple systems (i.e., family, extended family, peers, neighborhood, school, community, treatment providers). Each nested system influences the life of the child, and changing the social ecology can reduce child maltreatment (Swenson & Chaffin, 2006).

Culture and Gender Roots of Child Maltreatment

Culture is an important consideration in understanding different views of and responses to child sexual abuse (Purvis & Ward, 2006) and its roots. As it intersects the family, violence is viewed as having a gender and societal foundation in roots of child maltreatment. Brooks (1992) argued that a successful program of antiviolence has to include gender sensitivity, stating,

> Just as young girls deserve the opportunity for socialization into achievement and self-sufficiency, boys deserve to be freed from the extreme emphasis on physical violence and emotional toughness as proof of masculine worth. (p. 31)

Morgan (2000) concurred that a society endorsing patriarchy and male dominance will easily result in battery against women. Modeling of violence in the home easily transfers to a child who learns that violence is a means of resolving disagreements, and it can transfer to child maltreatment in conflicts between father and child. Clearly, to develop an understanding of, response to, and intervention with perpetrators of child maltreatment as well as violence against women in families when battery is witnessed by children, we have to look beyond the family to society.

Family Characteristics as Roots of Child Maltreatment

Loman (2006) provided information on the characteristics of families frequently encountered (FE) by Child Protection Services in relation to chronic child abuse and neglect. He identified *shifts or changes* in FE families that were associated with forms of child maltreatment, which he referred to as the *abuse–neglect shift*, saying that "neglect decreases are related in some measure to the relief of financial stresses" (p. 33).

A second shift in the family was when no teenagers were mentioned at the first report of maltreatment but at least one teen in the home was mentioned at the time of the second report of maltreatment. Loman's primary finding in this shift is that

> as children age in FE families, certain problems of child abuse and neglect, more characteristic of younger children, give way to interactions within the family that would be better described as conflicts, fights, locking children out of homes, rejection, and the like. (p. 35)

Loman (2005) related four combinations that demonstrated that FE families often have several problems as well as needs:

1. Domestic violence and adult AOD in more than half the families
2. Emotional problem or mental illness in a child coexisting *less frequently* with either an AOD adult or domestic violence
3. Distress related to finances and lower self-esteem of caregivers in the family
4. Distress related to finances coexisting with domestic violence in the present or past

In addition to Loman's research, characteristics of families who abuse children have been studied by a number of professionals over time (Ammerman & Hersen, 1991; Berger, 1985; Green, 1995; Hindley, Ramchandani, & Jones, 2006; Martin, 1980; Oates, 1991; Otto & Smith, 1980; Weissbourd, 1996). A summary of factors found to contribute to child maltreatment by parents across these studies is as follows:

• Isolation from social supports
• High levels of environmental stress, such as financial and medical problems
• High levels of parental conflict
• Dominant/submissive pattern in the marital relationship
• Neglect
• Parental mental health problems
• Low levels of physical contact of any sort
• Inconsistent and overly punitive discipline
• Chaotic family structure

Ammerman and Hersen (1990c) suggested that children who present behavioral problems have a higher likelihood of maltreatment but noted that this characteristic alone is not sufficient to result in abuse. Risk for maltreatment also is increased greatly when parents use physical punishment as a way to discipline a child. Finally, Vondra (1990) suggested that attachment can be a factor, saying, "Attachment issues can apparently predispose vulnerable parents to maltreat their own children" (p. 153).

Roots of Maltreatment in Children with Disabilities

The Committee on Child Abuse and Neglect and Committee on Children with Disabilities of the American Academy of Pediatrics (2001) described potential causal factors of maltreatment of children with disabilities as related to the "higher emotional, physical, economic, and social demand on their families" (p. 509). The Committee cited limited social and community support as placing parents of children with disability at higher risk for maltreatment. These families tended to feel overwhelmed and to feel that they did not have the ability to cope with care and supervision of their child with a disability. Also mentioned was a lack of parental breaks or respite from responsibility of caring for their child. Also, children with behavioral challenges were viewed as increasing the possibility of physical abuse of those with disabilities.

The Committee report (American Academy of Pediatrics, 2001) further stated:

> Families who report higher stress levels may actually have greater
> insight into problems associated with caring for a disabled child,
> whereas parents with a history of neglect of a child may not expe-
> rience the level of stress that a more involved parent may experi-
> ence. (p. 509)

Sexual abuse of children with disabilities was described as more likely because of

- less opportunity to establish a trusting relationship with a person to whom the child feels comfortable disclosing abuse;
- higher levels of dependency for meeting physical needs, which accustoms some children to having their bodies touched regularly, appropriately or inappropriately;
- a large number of caregivers, resulting in more possibilities for being abused—countered with the positive aspect that one of the caregivers would be likely to be aware of manifestations of injury or abuse; and
- intellectual limitations, which make them less able to differentiate appropriate from inappropriate adult behaviors.

According to Ammerman, Lubetsky, and Drudy (1991), characteristics of families including children with disabilities that can increase the risk for maltreatment include

> (1) disruption in the formation of infant–caregiver attachment,
> (2) prolonged stress associated with raising some children with dis-
> abilities, and (3) increased vulnerability to maltreatment. (p. 210)

Sobsey (1994) presented an integrated ecological model of abuse in individuals with disabilities and identified factors related to the potential victim and the potential offender, because of learned helplessness and learned compliance. Those with *learned helplessness* have come to believe that fighting back does no good; they do not think anything they can do or say will change the outcome. *Learned compliance*, or over-compliance, is often encouraged as a means of getting help from service providers. As Sobsey wrote:

> Although it is true that many of these individuals exhibit some
> form of unacceptable behavior, that behavior often results from
> desperate attempts to exercise the last remaining bit of control
> that they have over their own lives. The elimination of unaccept-
> able behavior without teaching any positive alternative obliterates
> these last attempts at self-empowerment, leaving them in a state
> of learned helplessness and extremely vulnerable to all forms of
> abuse. (p. 165)

Community and school professionals who provide parent training and behavioral intervention for families can help to lower the incidence of child abuse in families by being aware of the many roots of maltreatment, as well as by working with the nested systems to marshal resources to meet needs of these families.

Risk Factors for Child Maltreatment

Being aware of risk factors for child maltreatment can feed in to support, prevention, and intervention. Bolger and Patterson (2003) gave the examples of internalization of problems during childhood and adolescence becoming associated with adult depression and anxiety disorders. Aggression and antisocial behavior in childhood were predicted to continue across the lifespan. Childhood rejection by peers was associated with higher levels of school failure as well as delinquency and psychopathology.

In their work with at-risk youth, Macy, Barry, and Naom (2003) found that "many of the most destructive youth health-risk behaviors are correlated with a childhood history of stressful and threatening experiences," with the behavior of adolescents resulting in "teen pregnancy and teen paternity, sexually transmitted diseases, substance abuse, violence, suicide, and homicide," and these were correlated with child maltreatment as well as aversive childhood experiences (p. 11).

Hindley, Pamchandani, and Jones (2006) reviewed studies of risk factors for recurrence of maltreatment. They found that neglect (as opposed to the other three forms of maltreatment) was the greatest predictor for recurrence of maltreatment. Although community and school professionals cannot meet the basic needs within the family, when they become aware of neglect, they can network with other systems with the resources to assist the family in meeting its basic needs or with resources for treatment for causative factors (such as AOD) underlying the neglect. As well, they can connect parents with faith-based communities and other nongovernmental resources of support (e.g., free/reduced child care, free infirmary for ill children) that allow parents to continue working. And job training resources are available for individuals without a job.

The child may incur many health risks as a result of the various forms of maltreatment. These can appear as physical manifestations or emotional/psychological problems.

Physical Risks

Foremost as a result of physical abuse is brain injury. Especially when the abuse occurs at age 3 or younger, it poses major risks to the child's growth and development. Sometimes life itself is in the balance from inflicted head injuries. Brain injuries include contusions, intracranial and intraocular hemorrhages, atrophy, and brain changes related to memory and emotion (Chalk, Gibbons, & Scarupa, 2002).

Prior to current brain neuroimaging techniques (Bonnier et al., 2003), most incidents of shaken baby syndrome—a condition of high current interest—would have been diagnosed as "undetermined brain damage," and the high potential for future anomalies of a developmental or neurological nature developing up to two years later would not have been attributed to the situation that resulted in the initial trip to the emergency room (Sobsey, 2002). Russell and Britner (2006) indicated that half of adults in America are not aware of shaken baby syndrome or its devastating effects.

Barlow, Thomson, Johnson, and Minns (2005) described long-term neurologic, behavioral, and cognitive sequelae of inflicted traumatic brain injury, including shaken baby syndrome. In their research they found a wide range of sequelae including blindness, epilepsy, speech/language abnormalities, behavior problems, learning disabilities, mental retardation, attention deficit, memory problems, and more. Because these problems show up in our schools and communities, professionals must be aware of this as possibly related to physical abuse.

Sexually transmitted diseases permeate society at all levels. Therefore, STDs, including HIV, should be considered as a real risk in assessing children for sexual abuse.

Emotional Risks

Psychologically or emotionally, maltreated children are vulnerable to affective disorders, attachment problems, and maladaptive self-system processes (Cicchetti & Toth, 2005). Lawyer, Ruggiero, Resnick, Kilpatrick and Saunders (2006) queried adolescents who had been victimized and found that those who were sexually assaulted by people they knew, including a family member, were at greater risk for post-traumatic stress disorder (PTSD). Golden (2000) referred to major emotional risk for child maltreatment, in particular, post-traumatic stress disorder, major depression, and other psychiatric conditions.

Another way to look at manifestations of child maltreatment is as externalizing versus internalizing behaviors. *Externalizing behaviors* are those that can be seen outwardly, such as aggression, substance abuse, oppositional-defiant disorder, and delinquency (Kolko, 2002). Sexual abuse has been linked with externalization via aggression and risky behavior such as AOD abuse. A serious conduct disorder may result when a child who was sexually abused suffers from but is not treated for post-traumatic stress disorder (PTSD).

Bolger and Patterson (2003) used teacher ratings, peer nomination, and self-reports to examine externalized behaviors. They found that 31% of elementary-age girls who were maltreated and 24% of elementary-age maltreated boys were in the clinical range for externalizing problems.

Maltreated males showed a propensity to be aggressive (Eckenrode, Powers, & Garbarino, 1997). Relatedly, the rate of reported abuse as children was found to be much higher in juvenile delinquents than the general population (Maxwell & Widom, 1996). Adolescents who were sexually assaulted by people they did not know, or who were mere acquaintances, were found to be at greater risk for delinquency (Lawyer et al. 2006). Delinquency, teen pregnancy, and drug abuse were 25% more likely to be found in adolescents who were maltreated than in those who were not (Kelley, Thornberry, & Smith, 1997).

Internalizing behaviors, by contrast, are behaviors that the child does not show overtly. In a study by Bolger and Patterson (2003), the maltreated children had more problems of an internalization nature (i.e., anxiety, withdrawal, depression, somatic complaints) than the comparison group that was not maltreated; 34% of maltreated girls and 24% of boys who were maltreated had internalized problems. Maltreatment of children also involves the risks of suicidal ideation or attempts to commit suicide, somatization, anxiety, and dissociation (Cicchetti & Toth, 2005). Maltreated females, in particular, tend to become self-destructive (Eckenrode, Powers, & Garbarino, 1997). Guterman (2001) reported depression and loneliness, as well as low self-worth and hopelessness in some maltreated children.

Sexual abuse was associated with increases in internalization of problems including emotional problems such as depression (Wise, Zierler, Krieger, & Harlow, 2001) and suicidality. Young children who have been abused exhibited bedwetting, nightmares, and psychosomatic complaints, as well as developmental regression and withdrawal (Thaxton, 1985).

Socialization Risks

Children growing up in violent and abusive homes learn to focus on the needs and moods of their parents rather than on themselves, to avoid punishment. Overall, problems with peer relationships were found for maltreated children (Cicchetti & Toth, 2005).

This may be revealed in the dichotomy between displays of aggression toward their peers but overly fearful responses to teacher reprimands. Children who were maltreated were found to have more problems with peer relationship than classmates who were not maltreated (Bolger & Patterson, 2003). Maltreated children were less popular, were rejected, and were less likely to have a best friend who also considered him/her as a best friend.

Risks for Learning

Sullivan and Knutson (2000) found that abuse was 3.4 times more common in children who were identified with special learning needs as compared to other children (i.e., 9% maltreatment prevalence rate for nondisabled children, 31% rate for children with disabilities); 22% of maltreated children were identified as being in need of special education services. Close to one-third of students placed in special education were found to be maltreated.

Maltreated children often feel extreme anxiety about any sort of failure, so they hold themselves back from attempting new experiences or from struggling with challenging academic material. After conducting a pilot study of maltreated children with post-traumatic stress disorder (PTSD), Beers and DeBellis (2004) found that the group of children who had been maltreated had significant attention deficits as well as deficits in abstract reasoning/executive functions, as compared to the matched comparison group of children who had not been maltreated. Those with PTSD were more distractible and impulsive and made more errors on tasks requiring sustained attention.

Risks to Health Throughout the Lifespan

Gutierres and Van Puymbroeck (2006) found that adult women who were victimized as adults and who abused alcohol and drugs used substances so they could block painful memories or cope with physical pain. Perry (2000) indicated that women who were sexually abused as children have a greater likelihood of difficult childbirth, as well as gastrointestinal and gynecological disorders. Other somatic problems in adulthood associated with child maltreatment include chronic pain, headaches, and fatigue, as well as heart disease, cancer, chronic lung disease, and risky behaviors.

Costs to Society of Child Maltreatment

The financial cost to society resulting from child maltreatment has been suggested as motivation for change regarding maltreatment. Chalk, Gibbons, and Scarupa (2002) indicated that, in 1996, federal and state expenditures on child welfare programs exceeded $14 billion and that more than half these funds were for out-of-home placements, foster care, and adoption. These authors also pointed to lost wages, failure in school, health problems from neglect and abuse, as well as counseling, mental health, law enforcement, and the courts.

About 20% of families receiving CPS services were from FE families (Loman, 2006). Over 5 years, this comprised about half of all expenditures on families. The funds were

expended on foster and group care, residential treatment, day and respite care, and treatment services. These figures did not include administrative and case-management costs.
All of the data point to the need for prevention programs before these problems become
deeply embedded and are much more difficult to dislodge and reverse.

Responding to and Reporting Abuse

The Children's Bureau (2004) reported that

> The three most common sources of reports in 2004 were from
> professionals—educational personnel (16.5%), legal or law
> enforcement personnel (15.6%), and social services personnel
> (10.5%). (p. 8)

Medical personnel made 7.9% of the child maltreatment reports, and mental health personnel made only 3.8% of the reports. This lapse in reporting is being confronted openly in
the professional community (Alvarez, Donohue, Kenny, Cavanagh, & Romero, 2005;
Alvarez, Kenny, Donohue, & Carpin, 2004) as a need that has to be addressed.

Historically, incest has been handled as a legal issue. Offenders typically are separated
from their families, and criminal charges are brought against the individual. Often, even
after a child has disclosed the sexual abuse, he or she will deny the initial report. These
children often are subjected to overwhelming pressure from the family. When the investigation begins, the child is usually blamed for instigating the shame and potential breakup
of the family. The nonoffending parent often rejects the victim, too, accusing the child of
lying, being seductive, or causing trouble. The motive to preserve the family is so strong
that even siblings who have been victimized themselves may reject the child who has told
the truth. The child, then, suffers not only from the abuse but also from abandonment and
isolation from the remainder of the family system.

All of these dynamics are important to consider when reporting cases of physical and
sexual abuse. Through their words and actions, professionals can be helpers to the child
and the family as well as enforcers of state laws. Being a helper to the family does not
mean that the professional should fail to report the abuse but, rather, that he or she should
provide the necessary supports and attitude that will alleviate fallout from reports of suspected abuse.

Each state has the responsibility for determining and informing the groups of people
who are required to report child maltreatment (e.g., teachers, police, mental health professionals). At the same time, anyone who is concerned about possible child maltreatment can
and should report their suspicions. These reports are not considered accusations but,
instead, expressions of concern, requesting that CPS conduct an investigation and, if finding reason, to assess the suspicion. Reporting a suspicion of child maltreatment does not
require evidence or proof, because investigators, not those making a report of suspected
child abuse, make that determination. States typically have laws protecting individuals
who make reports from prosecution or liability.

When professionals or laypeople suspect child maltreatment, they should contact local
child protective services (CPS), their state's child abuse hotline, or law enforcement.

Professionals whose job it is to investigate and assess reports take it from there. Also, there is a national level hotline (1-800-4-A-CHILD). If making a report, the information to convey includes

- name of the child and location,
- name of suspected perpetrator and relationship to the child,
- description of what you saw or heard that made you suspect child maltreatment,
- names of other individuals you believe know about the abuse, and
- your name and phone number.

Although your name is not provided to the family, from the information provided, the family may figure out who made the report. In reporting, you may request anonymity, but CPS will be in a better position to help the child if you do provide your name. Professionals should follow the procedures of the system within which they work. These procedures should be available in writing and read by all professionals in school and community settings prior to beginning a new job. When changing jobs, professionals should seek the reporting requirements for child maltreatment in the hiring agency/system, as these requirements do vary.

If written procedures are not available, the professional should consider taking the following approach to reporting cases of abuse:

1. Talk with the parent/caregiver, and tell him/her about your suspicions and why you hold them (i.e., what you saw/heard).
2. Inform the parents/caregiver that this information must be reported to child protective services. Indeed, many policies require that parents be informed before a report is made.
3. Give the parents the opportunity to make the call to child protective services. If the parents do not call, professionals are legally obligated to do so.
4. If possible, make the initial telephone contact with protective services in the presence of the parents/caregiver. In making parents/caregivers aware of the process, they are given the opportunity to feel somewhat in control. They then will be more likely to feel actively involved in resolving the problem rather than becoming defensive and isolating themselves from helping professionals.

An investigation by James and DeVaney (1994) revealed that although a large majority of school counselor trainees and school counselors indicated they would report sexual abuse by a stepparent to the authorities as required by state law, only 41% of the trainees and 44% of the counselors indicated they would report suspected abuse by a teacher. The researchers suggested that the underreporting might occur because of concern over disrupting staff relations. That concern, the researchers posited, often supersedes counselor and trainee concerns for client welfare or state law. Like families who do not report abuse, school personnel may find that fear of recrimination and loyalties overrides their responsibility. The investigators recommended inservice training so counselors will understand their "duty to report, proper reporting procedures, preplanning, and the necessity of consultation in all suspected child abuse cases" (James & DeVaney, 1994, pp. 261–262).

When contemplating reporting suspected sexual abuse, a quote from Madanes et al. (1995) is useful:

> If I believe in personal responsibility and I also believe that the only reality is in action—that not to act is to act—then I must recognize that in my therapy I need to protect human rights and to prevent violence. To avoid action, to remain neutral, is to be on the side of violence and abuse. (p. 9)

In conclusion, Kesner and Robinson (2002) stated:

> When viewed from an ecological systems perspective, the interaction of the expertise of the school social worker and the teachers will most effectively address the issue of identification of child abuse. In today's society, schools are becoming agents of social change. Rather than ponder the reasons for and propriety of this new role, school personnel should be at the frontline in the battle to address child maltreatment, because no one else is better positioned to ensure the health and safety of children. (p. 229)

Prevention of and Intervention/Support With Child Maltreatment

To reiterate—prevention can be differentiated as primary and secondary prevention of maltreatment. Primary prevention involves planned strategies as well as formal programs to prevent neglect and abuse from occurring. Secondary prevention stops abuse from becoming worse; it also can prevent abuse from occurring to other members in the immediate and/or extended family. As a whole, prevention, of course, is far more effective than intervention (Daro et al., 1990).

Prevention Programs and Services for Child Maltreatment

Prevention for child maltreatment can consist of "public awareness campaigns, skill-based curricula designed to teach children safe practices, parent education programs and support groups, home visitation programs, respite and crisis care programs, and family resource centers" (Cicchetti & Toth, 2005, p. 428). Community and school settings, for example, could invite a local group to present a play on appropriate and inappropriate touch. And movies are available to introduce neglect and abuse. This sometimes "kicks off" the curriculum or module presented by familiar faces in the school/community setting.

Particularly for younger children, a module or curriculum can deal with appropriate and inappropriate touching and what to do if touched inappropriately, privacy issues, asking for help, expressing feelings about maltreatment, and means of self-protection to prevent maltreatment. Skills training teaches children how to respond to inappropriate behavior. The community and/or school social worker and school counselor can help develop a curriculum if one is not available, or adapt and expand an existing curriculum to meet specific needs.

Another purpose in prevention programs and services is to increase reporting by children. Once they are provided with information and find professionals who are compassionate and caring, children can more readily approach one of these professionals and discuss their experiences and concerns.

Public awareness campaigns teach signs of child maltreatment, as well as what to do if a person recognizes that he or she might have been neglected or abused or thinks another child has been maltreated. Public awareness has to convey that even though one sign does not necessarily signify maltreatment, a preponderance of recurring signs should be taken seriously and considered as stronger potential for child maltreatment. And once children who have been neglected or abused are taught the signs of maltreatment, it opens the doors for them to consider talking with someone they trust about their home or other life experiences that they think may be maltreatment.

Specifically relating to preventing maltreatment of individuals with disabilities, Sobsey (1994) identified overlapping curricular areas, including personal safety skills training, individual rights education, assertiveness and self-esteem training, communication skills training, social skills training, sex education, and self-defense training (p. 178). Sobsey offered useful information for all school professionals about building safer environments; recruitment, training, and leadership; and abuse prevention and intervention teams.

Hazzard (1990) provided evaluations of elementary school maltreatment programs and pointed to the lack of prevention programs for children with disabilities despite their increased risk for maltreatment, especially sexual abuse. Following a review of the literature on abuse and neglect, Zuvarin and Starr (1991) recommended differences in prevention strategies by race and suggested that the target population include very low-income white mothers and teens from low-income black families. In particular, black teens would be targeted if they bore a first child prior to age 18, had a history of adverse family life without close attachment to a primary caregiver, had few close interpersonal relationships, and had infrequent contact with their families.

Cicchetti and Toth (2005) indicated that home visitation has met with success in preventing maltreatment of children. They specifically pointed out an exemplary model by David Olds and colleagues. McGuigan and Pratt (2001) suggested that prevention within child treatment programs should serve at-risk families at least until the child is 5 years old. Bentovim (2002) focused on preventing those who have been abused sexually from becoming abusers in the future.

Also in relation to sexual abuse was a study assessing the relation of child maltreatment (abuse, neglect, multiple household dysfunction) to nine categories of adverse experiences in childhood (Dong, Anda, Dube, Giles, & Felitti, 2003). It found a strong relationship between sexual abuse and multiple adverse childhood experiences (ACEs) that increased as the severity of the sexual abuse increased. These researchers concluded,

> This approach should unite what are traditionally considered categorically different health and social disciplines. Specifically, improved coordination of adult and pediatric health care and related social and legal services may lead to earlier recognition, treatment and prevention of CSA and numerous other types of ACEs. (p. 635)

Intervention Programs and Services for Child Maltreatment

For some time, intervention with neglect has been aimed at strengthening families and linking them with resources that can help them meet their basic needs (Hughes & Gottlieb, 2004). Social workers and counselors can help strengthen the family by advising them on how to reduce their stress, providing concrete support, offering therapy and drugs for parents and children when necessary, using a family therapy approach, and presenting parenting education (Green, 1991). Community programs and school settings are in an optimal position to help parents develop the skills necessary for effective parenting.

A pilot study to examine child neglect in relation to managing emotion in child maltreatment was conducted by Shipman, Edwards, Brown, Swisher, and Jennings (2005). They primarily studied emotion in children who experienced neglect and how neglect may interfere with the emotional development of children. And in examining prevalence of child maltreatment, Scher, Forde, McQuaid, and Stein (2004) conducted a telephone survey of adults about their childhood and maltreatment and concluded that it is important to aim interventions at negative sequelae of maltreatment in childhood and tailor the intervention to needs as well as expectations of those who are in the high-risk category for maltreatment.

A longitudinal study by Ethier, Lemelin, and Lacharite (2004) confirmed differences among maltreated children in both emotional and behavior problems. Steel, Sanna, Hammond, Whipple, and Cross (2004) tested a model that predicted abuse-related characteristics and mediating variables (e.g., coping, attributional style). They recommended that future research relate to intervention variables amenable to psychotherapy to lessen the impact of childhood maltreatment. Their work indicates that secondary prevention is important and the most important intervention strategies are to decrease severity and duration of psychological symptoms.

Incest as a Special Case

For many professionals, incest is one of the most emotionally loaded family dysfunctions. Professionals have a strong tendency to blame the offender and protect the victim. Although protection is important, the professional in school and community settings can best adopt a healing attitude toward these families by recognizing that all of the family members are victims and are involved in a family system that is out of control. Only through healing and regaining control in the family system can family members move beyond the initial stages of identification into healthy resolution of the problems.

One suggestion from the mental health field is to refer to those involved in incest as incest *survivors* rather than incest victims. This minor language change promotes an atmosphere of healing instead of one of emotional damage.

Because the courts do not stop offenders within a family from reoffending with another child in the family (Wilson, 2004a), providing training or information to court personnel, largely judges and lawyers, would be useful in dealing with family sexual abuse cases. They must be informed about how abusive families function so court decisions will produce different results. Wilson (2004b) cautioned that offenders should be given the opportunity to "rebut the presumption" that other children are at risk for being abused:

> Without this opportunity, a child who never faced a significant risk of abuse may be removed from his home or unnecessarily lose his ties to a parent.

After taking all factors into account, adoption sometimes is considered to be the best outcome for the child. In the introduction to their training manual promoting adoptive families as a healing resource for children who have been sexually abused, Minshew and Hooper (1990) wrote:

> Sexual abuse is the ultimate violation of childhood. Not only are children violated physically and denied the right of ownership of their own bodies, but they quickly learn that adults, in most cases parents, cannot be trusted. It is generally acknowledged by psychiatrists, psychologists, and child development specialists that the trust relationship between children and parents is absolutely essential to the children's emotional development, for upon this first trust relationship depends their future ability to give and receive love, as well as their view of themselves as persons worthy of being loved. (p. 3)

Maltreatment by People Outside the Family

In lesser numbers, children are victimized by adults in their lives other than family members, and by strangers. Community programs and schools can provide a much needed service. Fontana and Moolman (1991, p. 27) listed 10 rules for lowering the risk of child abduction and molestation that are still useful in the 21st century:

1. Always know where your children are, and be sure they know where you are. Require them to call you when they arrive at their destination.
2. While shopping, never leave your children unattended.
3. Go to public restrooms with your children, or send a trusted person along.
4. Do not leave your children unattended in a car while you are shopping.
5. Be sure your children have adult supervision when they are playing outdoors in secluded places.
6. Provide schools with authorization as to who can pick your children up.
7. Be sure your children know how to make an emergency phone call to the police or operator. Teach them their address and phone number, including the area code.
8. Find responsible baby-sitters with glowing recommendations. After each time, ask your children about the baby-sitter and listen to what they say.
9. Teach your children to run away if someone tries to pick them up or to give them a present when they are away from home.
10. Teach your children to say *no* to adults who ask for assistance, offer gifts or rides, or offer to take their picture. Be sure they know that they should come to you immediately and tell you what happened if any of those situations occur.

A list such as this can be provided to parents in the form of a printed card, a flyer sent home with other school/community information, or a newsletter article. In addition, it can be printed on posters placed strategically in the community.

Other Programs and Services

For professionals, the first step in knowing how to help children from abusive family situations is to understand the dynamics of abuse. Attending workshops or lectures dealing with issues of abuse and neglect may be useful, as is reading about child maltreatment. With this as a start, professionals in school and community settings can prepare training and support materials to meet the needs of their specific settings and the families and children they serve.

Professionals who are aware of the need to reduce stress on families of children with disabilities can organize educational opportunities, as well as support groups. Skills training for parents of children with disabilities can help them organize their lives and thereby reduce problems that create stress. Stress management training, relaxation strategies, and recreation are helpful in this regard.

Garbarino and Eckenrode (1997a) suggested the use of applied behavioral analysis, followed by helping parents to use nonviolent disciplinary techniques. Professionals can provide the necessary parent training, and community and school professionals can collaborate in this effort.

Beyond training, the school and community settings can address the isolation of abusive families by offering parent support groups. Involving parents in positive outlets with their children may decrease negativity in the family system. Community and school professionals who work to build a relationship with these parents then may be in a position to make a referral to a local chapter of Parents Anonymous or to outpatient counseling or psychotherapy.

The National Committee for the Prevention of Child Abuse (1998) provided the timeless list provided in Figure 8.1. This can be distributed to the internal and external community.

Fontana and Moolman (1991) suggested five ways that friends can help stressed-out parents let off steam. These will remain useful as long as we have families!

1. Sympathetically listen to the parents talk about their life situation.
2. Empathize with their struggle, and avoid showing disapproval through words or body language.
3. Offer to help the parents (e.g., shopping for them).
4. Baby-sit for the children so the parent(s) can get away for a while.
5. Learn about neighborhood resources, such as mother's groups, respite centers, and Parents Anonymous, and tell the parents about them (adapted from p. 272).

Gil (1996) contended that no one treatment model is considered most effective. What works with one family/child may not with another. Nothing is hopeless, and perseverance will pay off.

Summary

Children from families with dysfunctional behaviors such as parental AOD abuse/dependency and child maltreatment remain at risk for academic, behavioral, emotional, physical, and medical problems. The earlier the child/adolescent is identified and provided with the support needed to prevent or reduce future problems, the more likely the problem will be halted or the child removed from the abusive conditions. Being at risk means that a child

---

The next time everyday pressures build up to the point where you feel like lashing out—STOP! Try any of these simple alternatives. You'll feel better . . . and so will your child.

1. Take a deep breath . . . and another. Then remember you are the adult.
2. Close your eyes and imagine you're hearing what your child is about to hear.
3. Press your lips together and count to 10 . . . or better yet, to 20.
4. Put your child in a time-out chair. (Remember the rule: one time-out minute for each year of age.)
5. Put yourself in a time-out chair. Think about why you are angry: Is it your child, or is your child simply a convenient target for your anger?
6. Phone a friend.
7. If someone can watch the children, go outside and take a walk.
8. Take a hot bath or splash cold water on your face.
9. Hug a pillow.
10. Turn on some music. Maybe even sing along.
11. Pick up a pencil and write down as many helpful words as you can think of.
12. Save the list.

Source: National Committee for the Prevention of Child Abuse: www.childabuse.org/alterntv.html

Figure 8.1

Twelve Alternatives to Lashing Out at Your Child

---

has one or more significant risk factors the majority of children do not experience in the home or community. Removing risk factors may be impossible but becoming resilient in the face of risk is infinitely possible with proper support.

Families with AOD issues are described as having difficulties that show up in denial of the problem as well as rigid external and internal boundaries, and they often have a history of sudden or traumatic loss of a member of the family. These families are typically inconsistent and experience frequent conflict as well as emotional stress. Children in these families find trust and predictability lacking and may generalize it to other adults. They may survive using denial as a coping mechanism and by being self-sufficient rather than asking for assistance.

The "adaptive" roles in which children in AOD dependent or abusing families have been cast include the family hero, scapegoat, lost child, and mascot. These attempts at coping with chemical dependency in parents eventually become fixed patterns in the personality of the child. All four roles can be transformed with professional help so that children of alcoholics and other drugs can lead functional lives.

Child maltreatment includes physical, medical, educational, and emotional neglect as well as physical, emotional, and sexual abuse. Maltreatment of children continues to rise in the United States and is found in all types of families regardless of education, family form, income level, race, or religion. Neglect and abuse are more prevalent in families at or below the poverty level as well as in families with parents who have AOD dependency. Children with disabilities have a far higher incidence of maltreatment than others. All children who are maltreated are at risk in the biological and psychological domains as well as in learning.

The roots of maltreatment relate to the family within community, social, and cultural contexts that influence its trajectory. The impact of child maltreatment is not only on the child and family but also society. Professionals in school and community settings must report suspected abuse to officials (e.g. Child Protective Services). In doing so it is invaluable for professionals take a collaborative approach to reporting and involve the parents/caretakers in the process.

Professionals in the school and community are in an ideal position to be a voice for children through prevention and intervention programs. Because these professionals see children on a continuing basis, they should be aware of the risk factors, characteristics, and reporting responsibilities in cases of suspected of neglect or maltreatment. In knowing the signs of potential dysfunction described in this chapter, professionals can join forces with family members in helping to intervene so that stabilization and secondary prevention become possible.

Case Example

Bob is a 14-year-old boy whose father abandoned the family when his mother became pregnant with him. Bob's mother, who works as a clerk at the nearby convenience market part-time, drinks and is dating an alcoholic who physically abuses her. Bob has come home from school to find his mother passed out from alcohol. He also has witnessed her fighting with her boyfriend and ending up with a black eye. He has a 15-year-old sister in foster care because one of his mother's boyfriends sexually abused her when she was 13. Bob feels responsible for protecting his mother from her boyfriend and worries about her drinking and driving.

Because Bob has been truant and talks back to authority figures at school, he has been in a class for students with behavioral disorders for more than a year. He does have some physical education and exploratory classes, which involve rotating through subjects, such as art, music, and foreign language, during the 9-week grading periods, with the general education students. Recently he has been talking back to the female teachers at school.

Questions and Comments

1. What family systems concepts described in chapters 1 through 4 are operational in this family? How do these factors in Bob transfer to the school setting? Given the information provided, what hypotheses might you draw?

   Bob is a parentified child, as evidenced from desire to take care of his mother. This is an inversion of the hierarchy, with Bob acting more like the parent than the mother acts. Boundaries are enmeshed, with Bob assuming a spousal role with his mother when he tries to protect her from the boyfriend.

Bob may be acting out against authority figures at school because he is angry that his mother does not take care of him. Because she is obviously dysfunctional, he chooses not to attack her but, instead, to transfer his anger to other women. Female teachers in particular are the brunt of his verbal attacks.

2. How would you describe this family's dysfunction related to the topics of this and the three previous chapters?

Bob has lived in a single-parent home from birth. His family likely falls in the lower socioeconomic status category. His mother abuses alcohol and may be an alcoholic. Bob witnesses violence and abuse of the mother by the boyfriend. Bob also is neglected by the mother. There is, as well, impaired parental empathy with narcissistic injury to Bob.

3. To help Bob in school, what might the teacher in the class for students with behavioral disorders do?

She first might help him identify feelings. Then he would benefit from learning to direct his feelings to the proper person or to let off steam in the gym.

If Bob were to say negative things to the teacher, she could reply, "I don't think I've said anything disrespectful to you. What is going on that makes you seem upset with me?"

The teacher might pair Bob with another teacher whom he likes as a mentor. This would provide Bob with a caregiver to substitute for the lack in his home. Another teacher as mentor would allow the teacher in the class for students with behavioral disorders to serve without role conflicts of mentor/caregiver and provide firm, fair, consistent rules that are enforced.

4. What might the teachers in the general education classes do to help Bob when he is obviously struggling?

If the teachers recognize when Bob is picking a fight, they can send him to the guidance counselor or to the gym to use the punching bag. An alternative strategy would be to send him to the principal's office for up to 10 minutes of quiet time, not as a punishment. He would be required to return to class after the 10 minutes.

5. How might the teacher in the class for students with behavior disorders approach the mother?

She could ask Bob, "Is it okay if I talk to your mom about you being upset that her boyfriend beats her up . . . and that you worry about her drinking?" When meeting with the mother, the teacher could describe the behaviors she has witnessed in Bob at school and ask, "How can we work together to help Bob?" Bob may or may not be included in this conversation, depending upon his preference. Because trust is a major issue, it is important not to violate Bob's request for confidentiality.

Extension Activities

Reflection: In recent years, the media have focused heavily on the violation of children in our society. Consider situations you have known, heard of, seen in a movie, read about, or experienced in which parental AOD dependency, neglect, physical abuse, emotional maltreatment, or sexual abuse directly affected a child. Reflect on your reactions to when you first became aware of these situations.

Journal: How has your new knowledge about COA, CODA, and maltreated children affected your willingness to judge or suspend judgment of parents who are AOD-dependent and perpetrators of maltreatment? What questions do you still have about these types of violations of children and youth?

Excursion: Attend one or more of the following open meetings in your area: Al-Anon, Alcoholics Anonymous (AA), Adult Children of Alcoholics, Adult Children of Dysfunctional Families, Gamblers Anonymous, Overeaters Anonymous, Women for Sobriety, or similar meetings. Your local newspaper likely lists meeting times and places. Note if you may attend only open meetings. Call your local AA phone number, and inquire about attending a meeting.

Journal: Write about your impressions of the Anonymous meeting(s) you attended. What was your greatest challenge? What surprised you the most? How might you share your insights with others?

In-Class/Training Discussion: How can you share your insights with others in your class or training session? What questions have surfaced from attending the Anonymous meeting(s)?

In-Class/Training Panel Discussion Leader Instructions: Ask for students/group members to volunteer to serve on a panel and speak about their personal experiences in one of the following categories: ACOA; observed violence in the home; physical abuse; emotional maltreatment. I suggest omitting sexual abuse because of its uniquely sensitive nature. Impress upon everyone that, before agreeing to be a panel member, they should volunteer only if they are confident of their ability to handle their emotions. It is helpful if they have spoken publicly about the issue previously so they have an idea of how they will handle this discussion in a public setting.

Each member of the panel is to prepare a 5-minute talk about his or her background to be used as a springboard for the question-and-answer session. Before the panel discussion, those who are not on the panel will receive cards to write questions they would like answered while the panel members are speaking. A moderator will facilitate the brief background-sharing session and the question-and-answer session. The moderator will collect all of the question cards and pose the questions to the panel members so that similar questions are not repeated and different types of questions are answered.

AND/OR

In-Class/Panel Discussion Leader Instruction: Ask for students/group members to volunteer to serve on a panel and speak about their personal experiences or the experiences of someone they have known closely who fits into one of the following categories of recovery: AOD-dependent parent, neglectful parent, maltreating parent. Invite members of the panel to each prepare a 5-minute talk about their background to be used as a springboard for the question-and-answer session. While the panel members are speaking, the students/trainees who are not on the panel will write on cards questions they would like answered. Prior to the question-and-answer session, a moderator will facilitate a brief background-sharing time. Afterward, the moderator will collect the question cards, group them, rephrase similar questions, and prioritize them before posing the questions to panel members.

In-Class/Training Discussion: How has your understanding and way of responding to child maltreatment shifted in your life over time, and to what do you attribute any shift(s)? What surprised you the most about what you read in this chapter in relation to child maltreatment? What did you find difficult to read or believe? How do you think you could contribute to improving the lives of children who are experiencing neglect, physical abuse, emotional maltreatment, or sexual abuse? What could you do in the community/school setting to help other professionals understand and work with these families? What questions do you still have about neglectful, physically abusive, emotionally maltreating, or incestuous families?

Leader Instruction for Speaker Panel During Class/Training Session: Ask the whole class/group to work together and invite a variety of people from the external community who are in recovery from AOD dependency to serve on a panel for the class/group. A week prior to the class/training session, have the class/group members write questions they would like the speakers to address, and e-mail or mail questions to the speakers. This allows the speakers to tailor their remarks to the interests and knowledge of the class/group.

This exercise is designed to prepare the students/group members to replicate this type of activity for their community/school settings when they are working as professionals. Thus, the instructor/trainer must not do the legwork for the group. If the students/group members do not know how to locate people in recovery, have them call the local AA phone number and ask for assistance. Or have them call a local inpatient or outpatient provider facility for AOD dependency.

OR

Leader Instructions for Panel of Students to Present During Class/Training Session: Find high school students who are willing, able, and stable enough to attend a class/group session and serve on a panel of teens in recovery from alcohol/substance abuse. A local chapter of Alateen may be able to assist. You may want to focus on speakers who are from family systems with parental AOD dependency, speakers who are in recovery from AOD dependency, or a mix of both. Alternatively, you could invite university undergraduate students who are in recovery from AOD abuse or dependency to sit on the panel. If they are under 18, they will need written parental permission.

In-Class/Training Expert Speakers: In a small group or as a whole class/group activity, work together to arrange for one expert or a panel of experts to come to the class/session to address the dysfunctional areas (AOD dependency, child neglect and maltreatment) covered in this chapter. You might want to arrange for a series of speakers, or you might prefer to have several speakers come at once to serve on a panel covering diverse topics related to AOD dependency, neglect, physical abuse, emotional maltreatment, and sexual abuse.

To find speakers, call the American Association for Marriage and Family Therapy at (703) 838-9808 or check the website at www.aamft.org to request names of licensed professionals in your area. Prepare speakers by discussing the audience characteristics, including their range of experiences, whether remuneration is available, what you would like them to cover and how, whether other experts will be there, what the audience has read concerning the topic, how long the talk should be, and whether questions will be asked.

By taking part in arranging this type of activity, you will learn what is involved so you will be able to replicate such activities in the future. Have the students/trainees write thank-you notes to the expert speakers.

Invitational Principals'/Administrators Panel Leader Instruction: Arrange for a panel of principals from elementary, middle, and high schools (or administrators/supervisors from inpatient AOD treatment centers and a Mental Health Center) to speak to your class/session about the impact on schools/community of the at-risk children and youth covered in this chapter (i.e., parental AOD dependency and child maltreatment). If possible, include principals/mental health supervisors who represent urban, suburban, and rural areas.

Prepare the panel of speakers by discussing the characteristics of your group, including their range of experiences, whether remuneration is available, what you would like the panel members to cover and how, who else will serve on the panel, what your group has read concerning the topic, how long the talk should be, and whether questions will be asked after they all speak or after each panel member speaks. Assign students/trainees to write thank-you notes to each member of the panel.

Bullying and Violence in Schools and Communities

Erik K. Laursen

O ur society is influenced by violence at individual, family, community, national, and international levels. A large portion of the entertainment industry profits from the distribution of violence—movies, DVDs, rap music, video games—and guns are readily available. This culture of violence sends a message to children and youth that violence is an acceptable way to deal with conflict.

This chapter will explore the environments where children and youth experience violence and bullying and the reasons why children display these aggressive behaviors. Most important, violence prevention and intervention measures in schools and communities are suggested.

Dr. Laursen is a Vice President for Learning and Program Development at United Methodist Family Services in Richmond, VA, a human services agency providing a continuum of services to children and families. He has worked with children in educational and residential treatment settings for more than 30 years and has written several articles on strengths-based practice. He has presented workshops and consulted at the local, state, and national levels as well as in Germany focusing on programming for children in trouble, relationship building, crisis intervention, and strengths-based practice. He is a Senior Trainer in Life Space Crisis Intervention, Response Ability Pathways, Resilience in Practice, and Healing Racism. Dr. Laursen is an Affiliate Professor at VCU's School of Education and a Fellow at The Academy for Positive Peer Culture.

Exposure to Violence

Children are exposed to violence in the home, school, and community. It is pervasive in the media. The most common exposure is in the home, most often violence between parents.

Violence at Home

There are few studies that directly report the number of children who witness domestic violence. However conservative estimates (Carter, Weithorn, & Behrman, 1999; Edleson, 1999) suggest that 3.3 to 10 million children and adolescents witness domestic violence each year. Carlson (2000) estimates that 10% to 20% of American children are exposed to adult domestic violence each year. Based on recent U.S. Census data (U.S. Census Bureau, 2005), this would indicate that approximately 7.3 to 14.6 million American children are exposed to adult domestic violence annually.

One-third of American children and youth have witnessed violence between their parents, most on multiple occasions (Child Witness to Violence Project, n.d.). Domestic violence seems to influence children and youth more than the violence to which they are exposed in the community. Although the most common and observable domestic violence is physical assault, violence covers a broad spectrum from verbal and emotional abuse to sexual assaults, and, at the extreme, murder.

Some children and youth who have witnessed violence in the home have to deal with the aftermath of the violence by helping an injured parent, calling the police, and/or witnessing the attacker's arrest. In some instances, the abused parent leaves home with the children and seeks safety in shelters, which adds to the stress.

Edleson (1999) reviewed 84 studies related to children and youth who witnessed domestic violence. He summarized the following types of problems that children and youth may develop after observing violent acts by adults in the home:

1. *Psychological and emotional problems,* such as aggression, hostility, anxiety, social withdrawal, and depression
2. *Cognitive functioning problems,* such as impaired verbal and quantitative skills
3. *Attitudes,* supporting the use of violence
4. *Longer-term development problems,* such as depression, trauma-related symptoms, and low self-esteem among women and trauma-related symptoms among men

In a study by Singer, Miller, Guo, Slovak, and Frieson (1998), recent exposure to domestic violence was significantly predictive of a child's engaging in violent behaviors. Further, children and youth experiencing domestic violence showed higher levels of behavioral, social, and emotional problems (Schechter & Edleson, 1999). These children learn that aggression is part of intimate relationships (Groves, 2003), and, thus, they are more likely themselves to integrate violence as "normal" within their own relationships and newly formed families.

Witnessing family violence or abuse has been associated with higher rates of antisocial behavior (Miller, Wasserman, Neugebauer, Gorman-Smith, & Kamboukos, 1999), delinquency, and adult criminal activity. Further, exposure to domestic violence has been linked to mental health issues and teen pregnancy.

Exposure to Violence in the Media

The media are the most common source of exposure to violence for children and youth in the United States. Media violence can be in the form of television programs, movies, videos, and computer games. Children and youth of color and low income tend to spend more media hours per day than other groups of children and youth and are especially vulnerable to violence and the racial stereotypes communicated by the media (Levin & Carlsson-Paige, 2003). Although causal effects between media violence and engaging in violent behavior have not been established, media violence and aggression in children and youth have been linked. Children and youth viewing or engaging with violent media consider violence more favorably as a conflict-resolution method; tend to be more desensitized to violence; and perceive the world as a frightening place (Robinson, Wilde, Navracruz, Haydel, & Varady, 2001).

Violence in the Community

Children and youth are exposed to community violence most commonly by witnessing fights, and they may be victims of violence or bullying by others. Inner-city children and youth are more likely than those in suburban areas to witness acts of violence by guns or other weapons in their neighborhood or school.

In a sample of 476 university students with a mean age of 20 (Scarpa, 2001)—303 were female, 170 male, and 3 not reported; and 66% were White, 4.2% Black, 4.4% Hispanic, 1.1% Native American, 6.4% Asian, 12.4% other, and 5.3% not reported—95.6% reported having witnessed some form of violence, such as being chased by gangs or individuals, robbed, threatened with serious physical harm, punched or hit by a family member, punched or hit by a nonfamily member, mugged, sexually assaulted, exposed to a weapon, seriously wounded by violence, stabbed, shot, or exposed to a dead body. Of the sample, 90.2% reported having been exposed to violence at least three times in their lives. Up to 5% had witnessed someone being killed, sexually assaulted, or shot, or had known someone who had committed suicide; 10% to 30% had observed the stabbing of a person, the breaking in of another's home, the breaking into their own home, or a dead body (not at funeral). Finally, between 35% and 74% had witnessed one of the following violent acts: someone wounded by gunfire; hitting by a family member; chases by gangs or individuals; someone being beaten, mugged, or threatened with harm; hitting by a non-family member; or a gun or knife being used as a weapon. The study respondents reported that witnessing a violent act was 1.3 to 1.4 times more likely than being a victim. Students who had witnessed violence reported higher rates of depression and aggressive behavior than those who had not witnessed violence.

Martinez and Richters (1993) found more depression, anxiety, intrusive thoughts, and sleep problems in children and youth who had witnessed community violence or had been victims of violence. Isaacs (1992) found that exposure to community or family violence negatively affects children's ability to experience and adjust to high levels of emotional stress, their self-image, their hopes for the future (such as their odds of surviving into adulthood) and their beliefs in a just and kind world, their willingness and ability to form positive relationships, their sense of morality, and their normal/adaptive social, emotional, physical, and educational development.

Violence in Schools

During the 1999–2000 school year, there were 32 school-associated violent deaths in the United States (DeVoe et al., 2004). Of these, 24 were homicides and 8 were suicides. With a student population of 51,360,000 during that school year, this translates to fewer than one homicide or suicide per 1 million students. During the same school year, there were 2,124 homicides and 1,922 suicides of youth ages 5–19 in the larger community. From the beginning of the 1998 school year to the end of the 2002 school year, the number of homicides at school declined from 33 to 14 homicides of youth at school. Overall, violent crime in schools has declined since 1994, when the annual rate of serious violent crime was 13 incidents per 1,000 students. The annual rate of serious violent crime in 2001 was 6 incidents per 1,000 students.

At the same time, another form of violence—bullying—is increasing and is perhaps the most underreported safety problem in U.S. schools. It affects students' sense of safety more than any other problem and contributes to an environment of fear and intimidation in schools (Ericson, 2001). Bullying takes place where adults are not present or when fewer adults are supervising large numbers of children—in the halls, on the playground, in the cafeteria, in the locker room, during recess, on the school bus.

Data from the School Crime Supplement to the National Crime Victimization Survey (DeVoe et al., 2004) indicated that 7% of students ages 12–18 reported being bullied in the past 6 months. They concluded that grade level was inversely related to students' likelihood of being bullied (i.e., 14% of 6th graders, 7% of 9th graders, and 2% of 12th graders reported that they had been bullied at school). Private-school students were less likely than students in public schools to report being bullied (7% versus 5%). Counter to common belief, urban and suburban students were less likely than rural students to report being bullied (7% versus 10%).

Lessons to Be Learned From School Shootings

Following the 1999 Columbine School incident in which Eric Harris and Dylan Klebold killed 12 students before taking their own lives, the nation has increasingly turned its attention to school violence and bullying. Though children and youth are 100,000 times more likely to be killed in an automobile accident than at school, important lessons can be learned from these extreme events.

Newman (2004) reviewed 25 cases of rampage school shootings between 1974 and 2002, all of which involved male aggressors. Most of the shootings, 60%, took place in rural locations; 32% took place in suburban schools; and only 8% took place in urban schools. Newman included two cases from countries other than the United States in her dataset, as controls. Some necessary but not sufficient conditions for school shootings emerged from her analysis; she concluded that had any one of these factors not been present, the shooting would not have happened.

Factor 1: Marginality

Nine in 10 shooters had a few close friendships; they belonged to outcast cliques but were not socially successful. Three-fourths had been bullied, physically threatened, assaulted, or had their personal property damaged or stolen.

Factor 2: Individual Vulnerabilities

The boys involved in school shootings were challenged by mental illnesses that influenced their sense of marginality. More than half had schizophrenia or bipolar disorder at the time of the shooting, and the majority had a history of severe depression. Four in five shooters had suicidal thoughts before they opened fire. Two-thirds of the boys lived in two-parent families, and the majority had a history of family problems.

Factor 3: Cultural Scripts

Cultural scripts are blueprints for problem solving influenced and disseminated by the way a society solves it problems. "The shooter must believe that unleashing an attack on teachers and classmates will resolve his dilemma" (Newman, 2004, p. 230). School shooters reflect on their difficulties, consider many options, and try alternatives, such as clowning or, as Eric Harris and Dylan Klebold did, joining the Trench Coat Mafia. When they realize that these solutions do not work, they carefully plan and rehearse their rampage.

Factor 4: Under the Radar

School shooters do not display the types of behaviors typically associated with troubled school behaviors and, therefore, are not caught before the shooting. Two-thirds had never, or rarely, been in trouble in school, and only one-fourth had been suspended. But two in five shooters had engaged in violent writings in school essays or on the Internet. Although some of the offenders had criminal involvement, those events were not connected to the warning signs. Most of the parents were shocked when they learned that their son had been involved in a school shooting.

Approximately one-third (Schuster, Franke, Bastian, Sor, & Halfon, 2000) of children and youth in the United States live in homes with at least one firearm. In a national survey (Josephson Institute on Ethics, 2001) of more than 15,000 youth, 60% of high school and 31% of middle school boys said they could get a gun if they wanted to.

Violence and Children and Youth With Special Needs

The amended and reauthorized Individuals With Disabilities Education Act (IDEA) includes special provisions related to discipline of students with disabilities. These provisions were designed to assure that students with disabilities are not removed from their parent-approved program unilaterally and arbitrarily if their aggressive and disruptive behavior is related to their disability. Nothing in IDEA, however, prevents schools from disciplining children and youth with disabilities.

Leone, Mayer, Malmgren, and Meisel (2003) reviewed several studies to determine the suspension rates of students with disabilities. They reported that a disproportionately high percentage of students with disabilities had been suspended, particularly students with emotional disturbances and learning disabilities. Most of these suspensions, however, seemed to result from nonviolent behaviors and generally did not cause injury to others. Behaviors triggering suspensions seemed to be fairly similar for children and youth with and without disabilities. Some evidence suggests that suspensions result because school systems lack more proactive, supportive approaches.

Bullying

Media reports of bullying and violence are only the tip of the iceberg. Most bullying goes unnoticed, unreported, or is written off with statements such as, "It's part of growing up." True, bullying is most prevalent in elementary and middle schools and declines in high school. Still, bullying continues into college, workplaces, and the next generation of families, suggesting that bullying is a learned behavior. The earlier we intervene in teaching people caring ways of relating to others, the fewer incidents of bullying there will be.

What Is Bullying?

Bullying is a systematic way of harming others, involving repeated physical, verbal, or psychological attacks, harassment, and intimidation directed against a victim who cannot properly defend himself or herself. This power imbalance can be caused by size or strength, or by the victim being outnumbered or less psychologically resilient.

According to Olweus (1993), "A student is being bullied or victimized when he or she is exposed repeatedly and over time, to negative actions on the part of one or more other students" (p. 9). Bullying includes assault, tripping, intimidation, rumor spreading and isolation, demands for money, destruction of property, theft of valued possessions, destruction of another's work, and name calling. The United States also recognizes, as forms of bullying, sexual harassment, ostracism based on perceived sexual orientation, and hazing (e.g., upper-level high school athletes imposing painfully embarrassing initiation rituals on their new freshmen teammates). Not all taunting, teasing, and fighting among school children and youth constitutes bullying. According to Olweus, two students of approximately the same strength (physical or psychological) who are fighting or quarreling are not engaged in bullying. Rather, bullying entails repeated acts by someone who is perceived as physically or psychologically more powerful.

How Widespread Is Bullying?

According to National Institute of Child Health and Human Development researchers (Nansel et al. 2001), one in seven U.S. students is bullied. The U.S. Department of Health and Human Services, Substance Abuse and Mental Health Services Administration

(SAMHSA), the Center for Mental Health Services (CMHS), and other agencies have acknowledged the gravity of bullying. As a result, SAMHSA/CMHS launched a Bullying Prevention Initiative titled *15+ Make Time To Listen, Take Time To Talk .... About Bullying* (U.S. Department of Health and Human Services, 2004b).

In 2001, Olweus conducted a large-scale study (Olweus, 2003) of 11,000 students in Norway, using the same questions he had used in an earlier study conducted in 1983. The two major findings were as follows:

1. An increase of students being victimized by 50% since 1983
2. A 65% increase of students reporting that they were involved in bullying incidents at least once a week either as bullies, victims, or bully-victims (i.e., a student who is both a bully and a victim of bullying)

In one U.S. study, Nansel et al. (2001) used a nationally representative sample of sixth- through tenth-grade students to examine bullying on and off school grounds. Of the respondents, 13% reported being bullies, 10% reported being victims, and 6% were bully victims. It should be noted that this study excluded elementary-age students, who typically report higher levels of bullying than middle and high school students.

What Do We Know About Bullies?

Bullies, as might be surmised, view violence and the use of violence more positively than nonbullying students (Olweus, 1993). Middle school students with positive attitudes toward aggression hit, kicked, pushed and shoved, threatened, and bullied more frequently than their classmates (McConville & Cornell, 2003). Bullies tend to be more impulsive, have a desire to control others, and have little empathy for the victims.

Consistently, studies indicate that boys are more likely than girls to be bullies. Boy bullies rely on physical aggression and are likely to be physically stronger than most other boys. Verbal bullying, however, is the most common form of bullying, and physical bullying is the least common form (Rigby & Slee, 1999). Girl bullies primarily use teasing, spreading rumors, exclusion, and social isolation as a way to harass, embarrass, or isolate others. These latter forms of bullying are referred to as *indirect bullying*. Some researchers speculate that girls value social relationships more than boys do, so girl bullies set out to disrupt social relationships through gossip, isolation, silent treatment, and exclusion. Girls tend to bully girls, and boys bully both boys and girls.

Although bullying tends to be most widespread in elementary schools, bullying continues in middle and high school. Bullying by boys declines substantially after age 15 (Salmivalli, 1999), and girl bullying declines significantly after age 14 (Ortega & Lera, 2000). Still, interventions in middle and early high school years continue to be important.

Forms of Bullying

For the purposes of the discussion here, bullying is considered in the forms of group bullying, racial bullying, cyber bullying, and gay bullying.

Group Bullying

Often, bullies do not operate alone. Some children and youth who normally do not initiate bullying alone are involved in group bullying. These are called passive bullies, henchmen, or bystanders. Early studies (Smith & Sharp, 1994) conducted in the United Kingdom found that almost half the incidents of bullying were one-on-one and the other half involved group bullying. Children and youth who engage in group bullying often feel less responsibility and guilt for their participation, particularly if other students or adults do not stop the bullying.

Racial Bullying

Racial bullying involves hostile or offensive actions against people because of their skin color, cultural or ethnic background, or religious affiliation. Manifestations are racial slurs, offensive gestures, or joking about a child's cultural traditions, such as their customs, music, dialect, or dress. In a study by Nansel and colleagues (2001), 25% of students victimized by bullying reported that they were teased or harassed about their race or religion, and 8% of them reported frequent racial bullying. DeVoe and colleagues (2004) conducted a study in which 8% of White students and 6% of Hispanic students reported being bullied but found no other differences in the percentage of students who reported that they had been bullied in relation to their race/ethnicity and sex.

Cyber Bullying

Bullying no longer is restricted primarily to the hall, cafeteria, locker room, and school-yard of our public schools. Children and youth now are exposed to online and other electronic humiliation and bashing 24 hours a day, 7 days a week. Cyber bullying involves repeated forwarding and spreading of hurtful images and/or messages by using "information and communication technologies such as e-mail, cell phone and pager text messages, instant messaging (IM), defamatory personal websites, and defamatory online personal polling websites" (Belsey, 2004). Bullies use this technology to harass victims instantaneously around the clock and with the capacity of worldwide dissemination.

Cyber bullying is much more common than most professionals who work with children and youth think it is. Belsey (2004) found that nearly half of sixth graders were subjected to cyber intimidation at least once a week. I-SAFE America, an Internet safety education foundation, conducted a nationwide survey of 1,500 students from grades four through eight to find out their experiences with bullying online (National i-SAFE Survey, 2004). The survey found the following:

- 57% of students said that someone had made hurtful or angry comments to them online, and 13% said it happens "quite often"
- 53% of students admitted saying mean or hurtful things to someone online, and 7% admitted to doing it "quite often"
- 35% of students had been threatened online, and 5% said it happens "quite often"
- 42% had been bullied online, and 7% said it happens "quite often"
- 20% had received mean or threatening e-mail
- 58% had not told their parents or another adult about their online experiences

Gay Bullying

Gay/lesbian/bisexual/transgender (GLBT) youth are harassed and threatened because of their sexual orientation (Chase, 2001). GLBT students are more likely to skip school than their heterosexual classmates because of the fear, threats, and property vandalism directed at them (Garofalo, Wolf, Kessel, & Palfrey, 1998). The Chase (2001) survey revealed that 22% of gay respondents had skipped school in the past month because they felt unsafe.

GLBT youth often feel they have nowhere to turn. In a survey by Stepp (2001), four in five gay and lesbian students disclosed that they did not know one supportive adult at school. Reis (1996) found that 15% of lesbian, gay, and bisexual students had to see a nurse or physician as a result of injuries they had received from a physical attack at school.

What Is Unknown About Bullying?

At present, we do not know whether certain forms of bullying—racial bullying, cyber bullying, or indirect bullying such as rumor spreading or exclusion from peer groups—are more harmful than other types. Clearly, much depends on the victim's vulnerability. Still, certain types of bullying may have a longer-term impact on the victim.

Also unclear is what happens when a bully stops bullying. Does another student take that bully's place? Must the victim change his or her behavior to prevent another student from stepping in? Specific studies on displacement are lacking, but, it seems that the more comprehensive the school approach to tackling bullying, the less opportunity there is for another bully to rise up.

What Do We Know About the Victims of Bullying?

Olweus (1993) identified two types of victims: (a) passive or submissive victims, and (b) provocative victims. Research related to the first type of victim (Bernstein & Watson, 1997; Olweus, 1993) provides a list of characteristics associated with victims of bullying. Most victims have at least one, but typically more, of these characteristics.

- Most victims are more anxious and have lower self-esteem than students in general.
- They often do not like themselves, seeing themselves as failures and unattractive.
- They tend to be quiet, be sensitive, and cry easily.
- They often are loners and have few friends at school, but this does not hold true for their relationships outside of school.

Junger-Tas and Van Kesteren (1999) found that having friends at school reduces the risks of being bullied. More than half (51%) of the victims in their study (in the Netherlands) said they had no friends at school, while only 11% of those who reported they had more than five friends were bullied. Victims are often excluded from peer groups, and they do not like recess and lunch time. They typically disapprove of violence, are not aggressive, and do not tease others. Through this behavior, they may signal that they are unlikely to retaliate if attacked.

Olweus's second type of victim—the provocative victims—makes up only 10% to 20% of victims. This group presents very different behaviors and may themselves try to bully weaker students. These victims often are considered difficult because they have a hard time concentrating and typically are restless and socially and developmentally immature. In addition, they tend to be clumsy and quick-tempered and regularly attempt to retaliate when attacked.

According to Farrington (1993), most bullies victimize students of the same age as the bully. In that study, 10% of victims reported that a student younger than themselves bullied them, and 30% of victims reported that the bully was older.

Any student who is different or stands out in some way can become a victim of bullying. When children and youth are asked who gets bullied, the list of characteristics includes physical, mental, or speech difficulties, eyeglasses, skin color, hair color, language, height, weight, hygiene, posture, clothing, gays, lesbians, bisexuals, transgender, children and youth of color, smart kids, "dumb" kids, and kids who are bad in sports (Farrington, 1993). Bernstein and Watson (1997) found that the only constant variable linked to victimization was that the victims tended to be smaller and weaker than their peers.

The literature on the risks associated with witnessing or being a victim of violence is summarized in Table 9.1. The verdict is clear: Children and youth exposed to hostile and violent environments are battered psychologically and physically. They struggle to survive using the methods they have observed in adults. When relationships are broken within the family, school, peer group, and community, they swim in "rivers of pain" (Davis, 1987).

> *Rivers of Pain*
> Hurt people hurt people.
> —Native American Proverb

Raychaba (1993) described the inner pain and the sense of powerlessness of youth who are victims of traumatic life events. They rarely believe that professional helpers understand their pain, and most of them desperately want love and a better future. While Columbine shooters Eric Harris and Dylan Klebold often have been portrayed as brutal murderers, they may have expressed their unbearable emotional pain when they were heard to say, just before they began shooting their schoolmates, "This is for all the people who made fun of us all these years" (Dube, 1999).

Protective Factors

Osofsky (1999) studied the ability of children and youth to bounce back in the face of community violence and war. She found that the most critical protective factor for a child is a strong, positive relationship between the child and a competent, caring adult. Not surprisingly, this is congruent with results of Werner and Smith's (1992) longitudinal study of the children of Kauai. Over a forty-year period, Werner and Smith followed into adulthood a cohort of children born into poverty. Initially, one third was considered at particular risk because they were also burdened by multiple stresses such as family alcoholism, violence,

Table 9.1

Summary of Risks

Family	Lack of bonding/belonging
	Watching family violence
	Poor supervision
	Availability of guns
	Poor communication
	Authoritarian parenting style
	Parent who was a teen mother
	Single-parent home
Community	Community violence
	High mobility
	Availability of guns
	Gang activity
	Crime
	Low socioeconomic status
School	Poor supervision
	Negative school climate
	Low expectations
	Teacher who models violence
	Teacher who models bullying
	Lack of schoolwide understanding
Peers	Gangs
	Negative peer culture
	Cyber bullies
Individual Risks	Impulsivity
	Attachment
	Lack of empathy
	Poor social skills
	Use of cigarettes, alcohol, marijuana
	High rates of school suspensions

divorce, or mental illness. This study documented the tug-of-war struggle between stressors and protective factors; stressful life events were often balanced with protective factors within their care-giving environments. The great majority of children initially designated as "vulnerable" developed personal strengths, self-reliance, and protective buffers which enabled them to overcome the negative odds. Werner and Smith made a simple but profound observation about these survivors: "The resilient youngsters in our study all had at least one person in their lives who accepted them unconditionally regardless of temperamental idiosyncrasies, physical attractiveness, or intelligence" (p. 205). Most resilient children established this close bond early in life, if not with parents, then with grandparents, aunts, uncles, neighbors, youth leaders, or church members. Later in life, girlfriends or boyfriends and their families often took on the role of surrogate parents. During adolescence, a teacher often filled the caring role for both girls and boys who succeeded despite the odds against them. The teacher was the catalyst for helping them academically and also served as their confidante and role model.

Carter, Weithorn, and Behrman (1999) expressed the importance of caring adults in this way:

> Children and youth exposed to violence need to be able to speak openly with a sympathetic adult about their fears and concerns, and also, ideally, have someone intervene to improve the situation. Most children and youth rely on one or both parents to provide nurturing support in the face of crises and emotionally challenging situations, but ongoing exposure to violence can sometimes hamper the parents' abilities to meet these needs. Parents living with chronic violence may feel emotionally numb, depressed, irritable, or uncommunicative, and thus may be less emotionally available to their children and youth. (p. 6)

Aspy and colleagues (2004) interviewed 1,098 randomly selected parent–teen pairs in two Midwest inner-cities to investigate the relationship between youth assets and risky behaviors while controlling for demographic factors (youth grade, youth race, youth gender, parental income, family structure, and parent education). The youth assets were nonparental adult role models, peer role models, family communication, use of time (groups/sports/religion), good health practices (exercise/nutrition), community involvement, future aspirations, and responsible choices. The behavioral risk factors that were investigated in the study were physical fighting and carrying a weapon to school. The authors found that grade level, gender, parental income, and family structure were significantly associated with not fighting, and only gender and race were significantly associated with not carrying a weapon. Further, nonparental role models, peer role models, family communication, religion, and responsible choices were significantly associated with not fighting. Four assets—nonparental role model, peer role model, community involvement, and future aspirations—were significantly associated with not carrying a weapon in the past 30 days.

Kliewer and colleagues (2004) explored the influence of emotional regulation skills, the quality of caregiver–child relationships, caregivers' skill in emotion regulation, and neighborhood cohesion as mediating protective factors on the adjustment of 101 African-American, 9–13-year-olds after being exposed to violence. All factors except neighborhood cohesion were found to be protective factors for the children and youth in the study.

Parental monitoring and family support were found to be protective factors for rural adolescents who began to use cigarettes, beer, wine, and liquor after witnessing violence (Sullivan, Kung, & Farrell, 2004). Gorman-Smith, Henry, and Tolan (2004) examined the risks of 263 African-American and Latino inner-city male youth who had witnessed community violence and its relation to the perpetration of violence. Further, the study examined the moderating effects of family functioning. Youth with good parenting and higher levels of emotional cohesion were found to be less likely to be exposed to community violence and subsequently to engage in violence themselves.

In a study of 349 middle school boys and girls from 9 urban schools, Ozer and Weinstein (2004) investigated protective factors and psychological functioning following recent exposure to violence. They concluded that support from specific individuals, including parents, siblings, and teachers, perceived school safety, and easy access to discuss violent events with others showed protective effects between exposure to violence and psychological functioning. Hodges, Malone, and Perry (1997) found that having friends, especially friends who will help protect against bullying, seems to reduce the chances of victimization.

The above protective factors are summarized in Table 9.2. Even after careful analysis, though, we still do not have answers to these two questions: Why do some of those with numerous assets turn out violent? Why do some of those with few assets turn out without any major scars? Brooks Brown (Brown & Merritt, 2002), who had a 10-year friendship with Dylan Klebold and an on-and-off association with Eric Harris for a few years, wrote:

> People ask all the time why Eric Harris and Dylan Klebold did what they did on April 20, 1999. I believe it was hopelessness. They saw no real future for themselves, and no acceptance from those

Table 9.2

Summary of Protective Factors	
Family	Parenting practices Family relationships and support Parental involvement/monitoring of child's activities Acceptance Caring relationships Two-parent (adult) household SES
Community	Caring adult relationships SES
School	Strong school culture High expectations (behavior and academics) Caring teachers
Peers	Confidantes Caring peers Peers who help protect against bullying Positive peers
Individual	Humor Creativity Independence Emotional self-regulation Female Attendance in school Participation in groups/sports

around them. They became self-hating. Then they started to hate those around them. Then they became angry, and then they became violent. Finally, in one insane, twisted moment, they believed they had power of a world that had kept them down....

I knew Dylan long enough to know how he didn't start out as a monster. He became one. That's what makes his fate so scary.

The next day, Dylan could be your son. Your neighbor. Your best friend. Not some faceless, anonymous killer who comes out of the dark and snatches your loved ones. A regular person who faces the cruelty of the real world just like the rest of us—and in whom something erodes away over time.

It's too late to stop Eric and Dylan. But maybe if we realize what we're doing to one another and take action now, we can save the kids who would otherwise go down the same path. (pp. 251–252)

The challenge before us is tremendous. We must strengthen our work to claim children and youth who have lost or are losing the grip with their families and communities. There are no disposable kids.

Caring Relationships

Over the past 10 to 15 years, the fields of education, mental health, and social work have been at the center of the resiliency revolution (Mangham, McGrath, Reid, & Stewart, 1995; Rutter, 1987; Werner & Smith, 1992), which has shifted from "fixing" kids to promoting positive youth development (Benard, 1995; Benson, 1996). The literature on resiliency has demonstrated that unfortunate beginnings do not inevitably lead to poor adjustment. This challenges professionals to change their views regarding the needs of children and youth burdened by trauma, to become firmly anchored in the belief that all children and youth, families, and communities have strengths or assets.

Families, communities, schools, and peer groups can be powerful environments or niches where kids can thrive both socially and academically. These social entities can answer the basic human need for belonging and connectedness (Baumeister & Leary, 1995; McNeely, Nonnemaker, & Blum, 2002). Children and youth who feel connected with teachers and prosocial peers are more likely to resist negative peers and gangs (Goldstein & Soriano, 1994). Caring relationships, high expectations, and opportunities for participation can serve as a protective shield for those from troubled and impoverished homes (Benard, 1995). Even though the importance of caring relationships is widely touted as the route to successful intervention, little has been said about the specific nature of successful helping relationships.

In-depth interviews with youth in residential care in Virginia and Michigan (Laursen, 2002; Laursen & Birmingham, 2003) concentrated on understanding, from the youths' perceptions, the behaviors of caring adults. The seven behaviors that emerged from analysis of the interviews were respecting, empathizing, credibility, listening, affirming, instilling values, and making time. These behaviors and their underlying beliefs about youth are displayed in Table 9.3.

Table 9.3

Seven Habits of Caring Relationships

	Behaviors	Beliefs
Respecting	Giving young people a say in decisions that affect them	Their feelings are valid and they are the best expert on themselves
Empathizing	Seeing the world through the young person's eyes	The same story has many versions
Credibility	Doing what you say you are going to do	Adults are accountable to the young persons they serve
Listening	Putting the young person at the center of concern	Young people are valuable and worthy
Affirming	Saying positive things to and about a young person and meaning it	Even troubled youth have positive qualities and constructive behaviors that can be acknowledged
Instilling Values	Being a role model and holding young persons accountable without blaming	Children must learn self-discipline, and those who teach them must practice what they teach
Making Time	Making time for children and youth a top priority	Young people are important and worth an investment in time and energy

The young people in this study affirmed the importance of cultivating caring relationships, facilitating high expectations, and supporting participation in activities that afford opportunities for success. They repeatedly stressed the impact of having a caring adult who was more than just available to them. These adults being accepting, supportive, understanding, and interested made all the difference.

Identifying the elements of caring relationships is the first step in helping teachers and other school personnel understand and develop their relationship-building skills. The seven habits of caring relationships can serve as a springboard for developing a competency-based training program for relationship building.

Caring School and Community Cultures

Rather than trying to "fix" children and youth who engage in violence and bullying, we must transform ourselves and the environments we offer children and youth. This requires courage and creativity and a willingness to take a hard look at what is required to make schools and communities safe and free of harm for all children and youth. Safe and caring schools must be based on universal developmental needs, including belonging, independence, mastery, and generosity (Brendtro, Brokenleg, & Van Bockern, 2002). All children and youth have the same basic needs: a protective environment where they can grow and mature.

According to world-renowned psychologist Urie Bronfenbrenner (1986), children and youth need social communities that nurture their physical, emotional, intellectual, and spiritual needs. An absolute minimum of connection for each child is at least one adult who deeply cares about him or her. Many children and youth are deprived of even this slim diet of human nurturance.

Wellness means embracing and celebrating life in its physical, social, psychological, and spiritual dimensions. This is the basis for leading productive and fulfilling lives, learning to manage pain in ways that do not cause harm to self or others. Four gifts essential to a caring school culture are: the gift of safety, the gift of hope, the gift of giving, and the gift of cheering children and youth on (Laursen, 2002).

The Gift of Safety

Many children and youth are subjected to violence at the hands of those who should be protecting them. Therefore, they often have to make their own decisions without the guidance of elders, and they have learned from experience that they cannot count on anybody else. They come to believe they have no one else to trust. As a result, many become narcissistic and self-centered and resort to aggression and violence as their first line of defense. The first gift we can give children and youth, then, is safety—both emotionally and physically.

Although all children and youth need to feel safe, children and youth who have witnessed violence in the family and in the community have an even greater need for a safe school and community environment. "When the environment is unsafe and uncaring, energy that the growing child should direct into developing human competency may be expended on defenses in order to survive" (Ryan, 1997, p. 132). We must create a school culture characterized by clear expectations, clear boundaries, and consistent adult intervention when boundaries are broken. Creating a physically and psychologically safe environment is achieved through adult supervision. This means deploying adults to the halls, the playground, the cafeteria, the locker room, the school buses, and other places that have been identified as unsafe or vulnerable places.

Depending on the setting, the need for awareness of the whereabouts of children and youth will vary. In some schools it may be sufficient for adults to be seen in the hall, and in other schools, they may have to be in sight-and-sound distance of children and youth at all times. In schools and communities with high levels of violence, safety can be guaranteed only by close supervision. David Prescott (personal communication, December 11, 2003) suggests that adults supervise the area that fits between 10 and 2 on the clock face, as shown in Figure 9.1. If we attempt to scan a larger area—for example, the area between 9 and 3 on the clock face—we will miss too much of what is going on with safety issues.

School administrators, teachers, and community resource personnel should develop clear descriptions of supervisory responsibilities to include acknowledging

- the whereabouts of all children and youth at all times;
- the whereabouts of other adults;

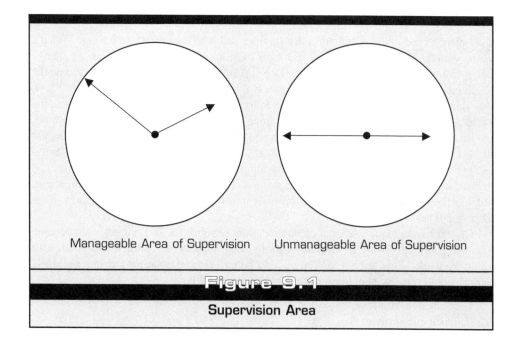

Manageable Area of Supervision   Unmanageable Area of Supervision

Figure 9.1

Supervision Area

- the mood of individual children and youth;
- the mood of the group as a whole;
- the combination of children and youth who may be interacting and the relationships between them;
- which children and youth have had a challenging day and what events made it challenging;
- who is soon approaching the need for medication;
- what kind of conversations are taking place;
- children's and youths' reactions to current situations, conversations, or internal activities, which we may not even know is taking place (i.e., we need to be watching their faces and body postures so we can be assessing their feelings).

When supervisors invite children and youth to take responsibility for their actions, to learn to respect others, and to develop integrity in their lives, the supervision should include acknowledging when the children and youth make good decisions, not just catching them doing something wrong.

There is no clear recipe for supervision. The level of supervision has to fit the developmental and safety needs of each setting. When supervision is too lax, children and youth are not given the opportunity to grow and change, because the environment is unsafe. When supervision is too strict, children and youth may conform to the environment but do not learn to take responsibility for their own behavior, and they do not have the opportunity to make "safe mistakes" from which they can learn. Supervision must be vigilant but not intrusive, and it must fit the age and ability of the children and youth.

The Gift of Hope

If we plant a seed in the middle of a dry summer and it fails to grow, do we ask, "What's wrong with the seed?" No. Likewise, we must look around and ask, "How can we change the environment so the seed can grow?" (Deegan, 1996). Our challenge is to overcome the hopelessness that Columbine student Brooks Brown talked about.

Many children and youth have nothing to look forward to, and they do not expect the world to treat them fairly. Because of lost hope—physical, emotional, spiritual, cultural, and financial—some follow a path into violence and drugs. Their presenting behaviors are all too familiar—disillusionment, narcissism, rage, violence, self-abusive behaviors, bullying. For those who have experienced severe trauma, losing or giving up hope is a defense mechanism, a way to protect themselves against continuing oppression, rejection, abuse, and injustice. When the environment is properly nurtured, however, hope emerges from the deepest darkness.

Crystal Kuykendahl (personal communication, October 15, 2001) urges us to become "merchants of hope" with the responsibility to bring hope to the children and youth with whom we work—hope for success, hope for a better life, and hope for a better world. As merchants of hope, we should give children and youth CPR:

Care, change, courtesy
Patience, persistence
Resilience

Even in the midst of despair, good teachers and community professionals will find a ray of hope to nurture the hearts and minds of their students. Brendtro and Shabazian (2003) wrote that children and youth

> need adults who believe in their absolute worth and potential in spite of behavioral difficulties. Adults who listen, enjoy children and youth, and provide them with opportunities to help and serve others give these young people proof of their value. (p. 121)

Children and youth who feel that they are "in good hands" and trust the adults around them are likely to increase their hope for change. Bertolino (2003) suggests the acronym HOPE as a fundamental philosophy in working with children and youth:

> **H** — Humanism: Connect with adolescents through respect and genuineness.
> **O** — Optimism: Be on the lookout for positive change; it is always possible.
> **P** — Possibilities: Search for possibilities and use creativity to facilitate positive change.
> **E** — Expectancy: Expect positive change. (p. 47)

The Gift of Giving

Many children and youth, in their short lives, have had vast experiences of loss. These losses may involve the loss of caring adults, beliefs or values, nurturance, attachment, safety, and more. Children and youth with a disrupted or an unsupportive upbringing often lack a sense of belonging. They have low self-esteem and are reluctant to, or refuse to, try to master new things because they are afraid of failure. They give up easily, are dependent on others, and often devalue education. Because they have not had an opportunity to develop their independence, they are easily swayed or misled by others, and they blame circumstances or others for their own actions. They have not been given the opportunity to be generous and, therefore, have little concern for others and tend to be heartless in their interactions with others. Not surprisingly, they end up taking rather than giving. To create a caring school and community culture, adults must make *giving* the norm—giving children and youth the chance to develop a sense of belonging, mastery, independence, and generosity.

If we are sincere about the gift of giving, we must reexamine many of our institutional practices carefully to determine how often we *give* children and youth opportunities and how often we *take* opportunities from them. All too often, in our effort to hold children and youth accountable, we end up taking from children and youth and thereby re-create the dynamics of trauma we were supposed to alleviate.

As an example: 15-year-old Martha was expelled from school because she brought a bread knife to school. Upon her arrival at school on the day of the incident, she told her first-period teacher that she had brought a knife and placed it in her locker. The teacher called the school security officer, who found the knife and handcuffed Martha until the police came to pick her up. During the expulsion hearing, Martha explained that her mother, who suffered from depression, had attempted to commit suicide with the knife the previous night. Martha thought she could keep her mother safe by bringing the knife to school. The school, however, adhered to its zero-tolerance policy and expelled Martha. In doing so, the system lost an opportunity for caring. Martha needed a counselor or teacher to talk to her. Martha was internally screaming for help when she told her homeroom teacher about the knife, and the teacher should have asked, "Why did you bring the knife?" Martha needed a strong-shouldered, caring adult who could support her emotionally and find help for her mother.

Institutional punishments—or consequences, as we like to call them—are often rigid rules to apply uniformly to a violation. The unique circumstances of the children and youth are not considered when meting out the consequences. When we practice the spirit of giving, we see problems as opportunities for learning. Our goal is to *teach* children and youth accountability rather than assigning accountability. Benevolent and generous natural consequences show children and youth that we want them to belong and that we want them to have the opportunity to develop independence.

The Gift of Cheering Children and Youth On

The fourth gift in a caring culture is to cheer children and youth on their way. In cheering children and youth on, we must be authentic and genuine and act from the heart. Children and youth are quick to detect if we are merely going through the motions. Courtney Mills (personal communication) says we must notice every "mouse step" that children and youth take in the right direction: "They don't have to be exactly right before you cheer them on." The point is progress. Doing something better should constantly be noticed, acknowledged, and praised. From a management perspective, Ken Blanchard (Blanchard, Lacinak, Thompkins, & Ballard, 2002) stated that praising must be TRUE:

Timely
Responsive
Unconditional
Enthusiastic

We cannot praise too much as long as it is TRUE. Being genuine in offering praise and recognition is essential for change. Adults must watch for desired behaviors, attitudes, and values, and then be sure to mention these when they see them. Acknowledgment, however, makes little difference if children and youth are not excited about their work and sense that they do not have some control over it. These two components must be in place before implementing the others. We need to create sparks before we fan the flames with the power of catching children and youth doing things right.

Preventing and Intervening in Bullying and Violence in Schools and Communities

Bullying and violence are pervasive issues that require multisystemic prevention and intervention efforts. Because of the multiple interactions of risks and protective factors, effective interventions must be comprehensive, multifaceted, rich in services, culturally appropriate, family supported, individualized, coordinated, and monitored. Further, interventions are more effective when they are designed and implemented consistently over time with input from the child, the family, and appropriate professionals (Goldstein & Conoley, 1997; Vickers & Minke, 1997). Programs based on punishment, control, and containment have not been effective in preventing violence or bullying. Instead, these programs have been found to escalate problems in schools (Mayer & Leone, 1999).

Communities and schools also can draw upon their resources to strengthen and enhance intervention planning. Leone, Mayer, Malmgren, and Meisel (2003) recommend three guidelines for schools to follow when they plan violence prevention interventions:

1. Interventions must be schoolwide and based on a public health model.
2. Evidence shows that punishment, control, and containment are ineffective in preventing or intervening in existing violence.
3. Interventions must be comprehensive with several components, must involve a broad range of services, and must be supported over a sufficient period of time.

Prevention Strategies

Schools and communities should plan their prevention programs based on a public health approach conceptualized as a three-tiered effort using universal, selective, and indicated prevention strategies (Tolan, Guerra, & Kendall, 1995).

1. *Primary prevention strategies* attempt to reach everyone in the school—students, teachers, parents, and other community stakeholders. These universal strategies

are designed to support 80%–90% of the students and include education programs, clearly articulated expectations related to caring behaviors, belonging, classroom-management strategies, and consistent use of incentives and consequences.

2. *Secondary intervention strategies* are used with 10%–15% of the students in each school. Examples are anger management, social-skills instruction, mentoring, and behavior contracting.

3. *Tertiary strategies* are employed with 1%–5% of the students in school. These students are challenged behaviorally and academically and require individualized services including wrap-around and mental health services.

Primary Prevention Strategies

Of the many schoolwide programs, the most noted is the multilevel, multicomponent, school-based Bullying Prevention Program developed in Norway by Dr. Dan Olweus. The program is designed to prevent or reduce bullying for students 6 to 15 years of age in elementary, middle, and junior high schools. The program attempts to restructure the existing school environment to reduce opportunities and rewards for bullying. The school staff is largely responsible for introducing and implementing the program, with efforts directed toward improving peer relations and making the school a safe and positive place for students to learn and develop.

Although intervention against bullying is particularly important to reduce the suffering of the victims, it also is highly desirable to counteract these tendencies for the sake of the aggressive student, as bullies are much more likely than other students to expand their antisocial behaviors. Research (Olweus, Limber, & Mihalic, 1999) shows that reducing aggressive, antisocial behavior also may reduce substance use and abuse. Several best practices have been identified (Virginia Best Practices in School-based Violence Prevention, 2005).

Young children are extremely motivated to help others, and when their contribution is being acknowledged and appreciated, they beam with pride. Because the life experiences of many children and youth have taught them that they can count only on themselves, however, they often present themselves as self-centered, placing their own needs before anything else. Thus, many children and teenagers appear to be reluctant to reach out to others even though they do have an innate desire to help and make a difference in the lives of others. The predisposition to be helpful must be nurtured, and adults must provide opportunities for children to develop this sense of responsibility, compassion, and social conscience (Brooks & Goldstein, 2001). When children and youth are presented opportunities to be of assistance to others, they are ready to put their own needs aside and go to work.

For individuals to feel positive about themselves, they must feel accepted by others and feel that they deserve this acceptance. In most student–professional relationships, the first condition for engendering a positive sense of self-worth is present: Most helping professionals are accepting of and empathetic toward the people with whom they work. Helping professionals go to great lengths to let troubled students know that they really are not as bad as they think they are, that they are worthy as individuals, that they have many fine qualities, and that they are accepted for who they are. But just telling someone that he or she is a fine person and treating him or her empathetically is not sufficient to develop a positive self-concept. Students may think we are being nice to them only because we feel sorry for them or perhaps even because we are getting paid to be nice (Vorrath & Brendtro, 1985).

When a child or youth is a member of a caring peer group, he or she is expected to, and has the opportunity to, help others. Thus, the peer-group approach provides the natural ingredients for an improved self-concept. Many children and youth know that much of their behavior is irresponsible and damaging to self or others, and they do not believe they are making worthwhile contributions to life. To change this, they must start making positive contributions to others and stop harmful behavior. Therefore, adults must cultivate caring environments where youth stop their hurtful behaviors and have ample opportunities to help others. These are the precursors for a positive self-concept.

Secondary Prevention Approaches

A multitude of small-group interventions has been shown to play an important role in improving school safety. Most secondary programs are in the form of aggression management, conflict resolution, social-skills training, and values clarification. These interventions are taught in group sessions and are aimed primarily at teaching children and youth to identify events that trigger stress and anger. The programs teach children and youth more prosocial ways of dealing with conflict situations and social relationships. They typically are time limited, even though they vary a great deal in length. Many programs use role playing and modeling as alternative ways of dealing with anger.

Tertiary Prevention Approaches

Children and youth who show dangerous patterns and a potential for more serious violence require more intensive interventions that may involve multiple agencies, as well as family support. By working with families and community services, schools can intervene comprehensively and effectively. Children and youth in this category may need specialized mental health services.

Life Space Crisis Intervention (LSCI)

Nicolas Long developed *Life Space Crisis Intervention* (Long, Wood, & Fecser, 2001), a therapeutic approach to talking with kids in crisis. Life Space Crisis Intervention (LSCI) skills empower school staffs to intervene effectively when confronted with the repetitive patterns of self-defeating behavior that are common in troubled and troubling students. LSCI is an advanced, interactive therapeutic strategy for turning crisis situations into learning opportunities for children and youth with chronic patterns of self-defeating behavior. LSCI views problems or stressful incidents as opportunities for learning, growth, insight, and change. This strengths-based intervention uses a cognitive-behavioral approach to behavior management and problem solving.

LSCI provides a roadmap to navigate conflict to desired outcomes using crisis as an opportunity to teach and create positive relationships with youth. The 40-hour LSCI training is based on 27 specific skills needed to respond successfully to a student's crisis. These concepts are anchored in supporting, caring relationships between the student and the staff. LSCI teaches staff therapeutic talking strategies to help children and youth during stressful moments, as well as the awareness and skills to understand and manage their own feelings and counter-aggressive tendencies when intervening with aggressive or out-of-control behaviors.

The foundational belief of LSCI is that the process of helping involves having the ability to listen deeply to the personal stories of children and youth and to recognize that their messages often are not in their words but, rather, in their underlying thoughts and feelings. The real strength of the LSCI program is its emphasis on teaching, and practicing specific interviewing techniques to help staff and students debrief a problem situation or critical event. Research (Dawson, 2003; Grskovic & Goetze, 2005) has demonstrated the effectiveness of LSCI in reducing crisis in schools, including violence and bullying.

Summary

The environments where our nation's children and youth face violence are complex and interrelated. This chapter provided a framework for understanding children's exposure to violence in the home, in the media, in the community, and in schools. School shootings are an extreme form of violence from which important lessons can be learned. School shooters as a group tend to have few close friends and suffer from mental illnesses. Further, they believe that their extreme acts will solve their problems. Finally, they have not shown overt problems in school and in the community, and if and when they have, they tend not to get caught.

Bullying is most prevalent in elementary and middle schools, but continues through high school, college, and into the workplace. While bullying is widespread, it often goes undetected and unreported. More boys than girls are bullies, and bullying is most common in elementary schools. Bullying takes many different forms, such as group, racial, cyber, and gay bullying. However, it is unknown if any type of bullying is more harmful than another. Research suggests that the impact is related to the victim's vulnerability.

Children's ability to bounce back from violence is related to their individual protective factors and those available in their environment—in their family, in the community, in school, and from their peers. A strong, positive relationship with a caring adult has been shown to be the strongest protective factor against violence. Adults can enhance their ability to form reclaiming relationships by respecting, empathizing, being credible, listening, affirming, and instilling values in the interactions they have with children and youth.

Adults can work to transform the cultures, especially in schools, in which they interact with children and youth by offering four gifts essential to a caring school culture: the gift of safety, the gift of hope, the gift of giving, and the gift of cheering children and youth on.

Strategies to reclaim children and youth and their environments must be based on caring, must be systemwide and comprehensive, and must be based on a public health model which includes three strategic interventions. Primary strategies are preventive and attempt to reach everyone; secondary strategies are used with 10%–15% of the children and youth who need additional support; and tertiary strategies are individualized and targeted at the 1%–5% of children and youth who demonstrate the greatest challenges.

Case Example

James is 15-year-old high school student who has had a tough life. His mother has a history of heroin abuse and has been involved in multiple abusive relationships. James has witnessed several incidents of violence in the home. He particularly remembers when an ex-boyfriend set his mom on fire and James put it out. The mother's boyfriend currently is under investigation for sexually abusing one of James's half-sisters.

The boy has lived on and off with his mother but has lived mostly with his maternal grandmother, who has custody of him. He attends ninth grade in a public school, where he receives special education services for students with emotional disturbance. Over the past two years he has had several episodes of suicidal ideations and attempts, four of which resulted in hospitalization. James says he becomes suicidal when he gets angry. His anger, however, is not directed at other people. He has frequent nightmares about his mother dying. He reports that he often hears a deep voice telling him to kill himself, and he reports thoughts about being killed by jumping into the street.

James has trouble sleeping and worries a lot. He appears much younger than his age and often is teased at school. He prefers to stay in the classroom during lunch and rarely interacts with other students.

Questions and Comments

1. What services and supports would you put in place for James? What strategies would you suggest that the teacher and the school put in place?

   [Before reading further in this text about what was done to support James, reflect on your initial idea for intervention. Consult this and previous chapters for suggestions.]

   The treatment team involved with James and his family developed a plan that would place him in a residential treatment program. The team, which included James and his grandmother, agreed that James needed support in medication management, anger management, social skills, and conflict resolution. In addition, James would receive intensive mental health services to help him cope with the trauma and losses throughout his childhood. The grandmother and James also were involved in weekly family counseling to keep a strong family involvement and connection.

   It also was agreed that James would attend the 10-week EQUIP program (Gibbs, Potter, & Goldstein, 1995) offered at the residential treatment program. This program is designed to help students develop anger-management skills, social skills, and values. Upon completing the program, James and his grandmother received intensive in-home services to help the transition back to the community.

   Teachers at James's school agreed to attend a bullying workshop to learn how to address teasing and how to create a caring school and classroom culture. James's teacher involved the students in his room in developing expectations for classroom behaviors. The teacher also held daily class meetings designed to strengthen the relationships among the students in the class.

Extension Activities

Reflection: Reflect on your elementary, middle/junior high, and high school years. Recall examples of bullying that you witnessed and/or experienced in the school or community. Think about how these were handled. What was done that helped the healing process? Hindered it?

Journal: What did you learn form the experience(s) that could become "pearls of wisdom" to offer others when they have similar experiences?

Invite a Speaker: Invite a LSCI Senior Trainer (can be located at www.lsci.org) to your class session. Ask the trainer to role-play a Symptom Estrangement Reclaiming Intervention. Discuss the role-play.

Training Activity: Assign students to watch the movie *Bang Bang You're Dead* (available at video stores).

In-Class/Training Discussion Starters: What were some of the incidents of bullying and violence? How did these incidents impact the youth in the movie? How did the incidents impact the adults in the movie? How did you feel when you saw the movie/video? Describe what you could do to prevent harassment and bullying where you work or plan to work.

In-Class Activity: Set up a production of the play *Bang Bang You're Dead*. The play is free and available at www.bangbangyouredead.com, for students to perform. The same site provides other resources, too, including follow-up discussion questions.

Community Factors
in Resilience

*I*n the 1970s, social scientists began to ask the question, "What accounts for why some people stay healthy and do well in the face of risk and adversity while others do not?" (Patterson, 2002). What was found in trying to answer this question became known by different terms, and *resilience* is the term used by multiple disciplines that have a strengths-based perspective. Resilience in children and youth from high-risk settings became a topic of interest for social workers, psychologists, counselors, educators and other disciplines in the early 1980s.

From a strengths-based perspective, studying resilience in relation to children and youth who otherwise would be expected to fail in school or life provides us with clues for helping those who are living in high-risk contexts at home, school, in the neighborhood, or community. Children who live in high-risk contexts and those with special needs are the main focus of this chapter.

The shift from a disease-model of asking, "What caused this problem?" to emphasizing the positive has resulted in a burgeoning field devoted to exploring and using what has been learned about resilience, as well as continuing to expand our knowledge with evolutionary research about resilience. Brown, D'Emidio-Caston, and Benard (2001) exposed flaws in using a disease model in education and proposed resilience education as the specific means to empower teachers and students.

Resilience

What is resilience? Over time we have learned that resilience is not as simply put as once perceived by those studying risk and resilience (Fraser, 2004b; Luthar & Zelazo, 2003)— at one time it was described as "overcoming or beating the odds" (Haggerty, Sherrod, Garmezy, & Rutter, 1994; Masten, Best, & Garmezy, 1990; Wang & Haertel, 1995; Werner, & Smith, 1992). Researchers and practitioners in the field of resilience know the value of a multisystemic (Fraser, 2004a) or multidimensional perspective on resilience (Becker & Luthar, 2002; Luthar & Zelazo, 2003), which interweaves the "hard sciences" with the "soft sciences" (Luthar, 2003).

Earlier contributions by Urie Bronfenbrenner (1979, 1986), with his description of nested systems and social ecology, and the genius of Gregory Bateson (1972), with his systems thinking and erasing the boundaries around "inner and outer space," are foundational. As a result of this marriage of yin/soft and yang/hard sciences, the pubescent field of resilience is combining biological, chemical, and other knowledge bases (Luthar, 2003). As a result, resilience is no longer viewed as an attribute within an individual. Solutions are now seen as requiring multisystemic, multidimensional investigation and interventions. Resilience and risk are "both/and" propositions. This shift from individual to contextual has enriched all disciplines that focus on protective and/or risk factors in relation to resilience.

Luthar and Zelazo (2003) stated that "the very term *resilience* is construed by many to represent a personal trait that allows some at-risk youth to succeed in life, with the corollary, of course, that those who do poorly are personally responsible for their problems" (p. 511). What has become clear is that resilience is about a lot more than inner traits. Resilience must be studied in relation to family and community. It is a multidimensional construct that requires the casting of a wide net to "identify the predictors of problems" (Fraser, 2004b, p. 5), as well as to recognize the significant impact of context (e.g., family, school, peer relations, neighborhood, community) on risk and protective factors that bear on resilience.

Resilience is associated with the family systems models that this text covers (Hawley & DeHaan, 1996; McCubbin, McCubbin, Thompson, & Thompson, 1995; McCubbin, Thompson, Thompson, & Fromer, 1998; McCubbin, Thompson, Thompson, & Futrell, 1998, 1999a, 1999b; Nichols & Schwartz, 2004; Patterson, 1997, 2002; Richardson & Hawks, 1995; Walsh, 1996, 2002, 2003a, 2003b, 2003c, 2003d). Resilience emphasizes the positive that can accompany challenging life circumstances of children who live in high-risk settings or have conditions that place them at risk for failure in school or life (Barone, 1999; Cowan, Cowan, & Schulz, 1996; Fraser, 2004a; Kaplan, Turner, Norman, & Stillson, 1996; King, Brown, & Smith, 2003). The field considers risk reduction in terms of "what lies upstream that is 'throwing them in the rapids,'" rather than viewing it from a trait or one-dimensional paradigm. Werner and Smith (2001) stated that

> ...a number of potent protective factors, such as the mother's caregiving competence, the child's autonomy, social maturity, scholastic competence, and self-efficacy, and emotional support from members of the extended family and friends, have a more

generalized effect on the life course of vulnerable children and
youth than do specific risk factors or stressful life events. (p. 164)

You might ask, "Why?" Their answer is that protective factors foster *hope!*

Richardson (2002) stated that "life progression is the function of repeated resilient reintegrations" (p. 313) rather than viewing resilience as simply bouncing back or recovering. Richardson harkened back to Waddington's (1957) roots in embryology and genetics in referring to a "self-righting" mechanism inherent in humans. Others, too, have spoken of the "self-righting" mechanism and tendencies (Brown, D'Emidio-Caston, & Benard, 2001).

Parental modeling of community connections with others influences the feeling of security and belongingness of children. Resilience grows from caring people, and a pervasive sense of belonging provides a safety net of support that allows children to absorb, be part of, and later emulate the small and larger ways in which the community intertwines its roots and flourishes.

Risk Factors

Perhaps, as Henderson and Milstein (1996) indicated, all who succeed despite adversity are resilient and have something to offer in their stories of resilience. The stories are of growing up with significant, chronic and cumulative risk factors while being supported by protective factors within oneself, the family, peers, neighborhood, school, and community (e.g., Barone, 1999; King, Brown, Smith, 2003) leading to stress-resistance, especially when there is a concomitant emphasis on risk reduction.

There is a difference between families who meet typical stressors in life and families who face "significant risk emerging from (a) high-risk status by virtue of continuous, chronic exposure to adverse social conditions such as poverty; (b) exposure to a traumatic event or severe adversity such as war; or (c) a combination of high-risk status and traumatic exposure" (Patterson, 2002, p. 237). Examples of significant risk include living in poverty; diagnosis of chronic illness or severe disability in a child; biological factors such as perinatal risk and significant health issues; ineffectual disposition related to temperament and cognitive processing; impaired parental functioning.

Significant risks create an overload to which some families respond with enhanced functioning and resilience, whereas other families do not develop resilience. That is where the space opens up for social services, educators, coaches, peers, neighbors, community members, spiritual leaders and others to be part of the fabric that supports and helps them remove or reduce risk and rebalance so they become resilient families. In particular, Gilligan (2000) highlighted positive school and spare time experiences in the areas of "cultural pursuits, the care of animals, sport, healing and volunteering, and part-time work" (p. 42).

We know that most children and adolescents who were maltreated in childhood or adolescence demonstrate resilience. Shields and Cicchetti (2001) found that 68% of maltreated children in their study were neither bullies nor victims. Edmond, Auslander, Elize, and Bowland (2006) found that sexually abused adolescent girls living in congregate circumstances or family/foster care homes through the foster care system included both resilient and symptomatic girls. The variable in which resilient adolescent girls were found to be significantly different was that they were "more certain of their educational plans and optimistic about their future and had more positive peer influences" (p. 1) than those who were symptomatic.

Community and neighborhood contexts can promote resilience. As well, and equally important, contextual factors reduce risk with support, primary and/or secondary prevention, and intervention directed at malleable risk factors that have a greater likelihood of making a positive impact on the functioning of children and youth. The contextual opportunities are formal as well as informal in nature and include influential adults in families, schools, and communities, as well as offerings in recreation and parks, faith-based sponsored programs, after-school programs and activities, out-of-school time (OST) programs, and many other formal means of engendering healthy development of children and youth.

One risk factor, such as poverty, may or may not tip the balance toward failure in life or school. Not all children who live under poverty conditions fail at school. Another risk factor is exposure to violence (Kliewer et al. 2004), yet not all children who live in violent neighborhoods and witness it regularly become aggressive or identify with delinquency. Important counter-balancing factors are at work within individuals, families, communities, and society that contribute to resiliency. The more risks that accrue, however, the more difficult it is for the child or adolescent to stay on track and succeed in school and life.

Professionals who have risen above adversity themselves make excellent models because they speak from experience. They have chosen to take a path of compassion and caring (Kornfield, 1993; Noddings, 2002, 2005b; Shepard, 1995).

Earlier research looked at resilient qualities in individuals who recovered from or adapted to stress and problems in life (McMillan & Reed, 1994; Rhodes & Brown, 1991; Werner, 1986, 1989, 1993, 1994, 1995). More recent literature has been cast as helping individuals discern forces that move them toward Maslow's level of self-actualization and to "resiliently reintegrate from disruptions" (Richardson, 2002). This process considers contextual factors (i.e., family, school, neighborhood, community) from a strengths-based perspective (Benard, 2004; Garmezy, 1991; Krovetz, 1999; Werner & Smith, 2001) *while concomitantly focusing on* reducing risk factors (Fraser, 2004a; Peterson & Seligman, 2004; Richman, Bowen, & Woolley, 2004; Williams, Ayers, Van Dorn, & Arthur, 2004).

Tapping into the innate resilience, or a self-righting mechanism, of children and youth who are from high-risk settings or conditions, and enabling them to receive "special" education, can aid them, their families, schools, and communities. As a cautionary note: Those who work in disciplines serving these children and youth must remain resilient themselves, as the field can lead to burn-out (Friedman, 2004; Skovholt, 2001).

In sum, increasing resilience in children and youth and decreasing risk factors is a community responsibility, not the family's or even the school's responsibility alone (Bryan, 2005; Bosworth & Earthman, 2002; Garmezy, 1991; Gilligan, 2000; Waddock, 1995). Families (Patterson, 2002), schools (Bosworth & Earthman, 2002), and communities (Bryan, 2005) must collaborate if risk factors are to be decreased and protective factors expanded.

Protective Factors

Fraser (2004b) defined protective factors as

> those internal and external resources that promote positive devel-
> opmental outcomes and help children prevail over adversity. Like
> risk factors, protective factors include dispositional, familial, and
> extrafamilial characteristics. In aggregate, they are the positive
> forces that contribute to adaptive outcomes in the presence of
> risk. (Garmezy, 1993, as quoted in Fraser, 2004b, p. 5)

We have known for some time that protective factors, or buffers, are associated with resilience in populations from high-risk settings (Garmezy, 1991; Oddone, 2002; Werner & Smith, 1992, 1998, 2001). More recent research has demonstrated that, as Fraser (2004a) and others point out, *both* risk reduction and promotion of the protective factors have to be considered at the same time (Pollard, Hawkins, & Arthur, 1999).

Social workers are in a unique position because they traverse all of these contexts and are pivotal in working within and linking these contexts in a manner that builds connections and caring through the interwoven supportive contexts of the child's life.

Noddings (1995, 2005a) is in the forefront of those who emphasize the importance of developing caring communities (Alder, 2002). Researchers and practitioners using a multidimensional or multisystemic lens for viewing resilience are in accord about the three domains by which to consider resilience in relation to risk and protective factors (Benard, 2004; Cicchetti, 2003; Fraser, 2004b; Luthar, 2003; Werner & Smith, 2001):

1. The individual child/youth with psychosocial and biological characteristics
2. Contextual factors related to the child's family
3. Contextual aspects that relate to factors in peer networks, schools, neighborhoods, and communities

The latter category includes schools as one of the contexts influencing protective factors. From the school perspective, Comer (2001) focused on the need of educators to learn more about what they can do that leads to normal child development rather than abnormal development. Benard (2004), too, takes a positive tack, directing us away from terms such as "at-risk youth" (to describe people) to "high-risk settings/contexts" to guide the terminology consistent with the tenets.

We will follow the essence of the three categories (Schoon & Parsons, 2002) in discussing each:

1. Attributes within the child
2. Family characteristics
3. Aspects within the broader social context of the child

Protective Factors in Children and Youth Facing Adversity

Resilient individuals typically have a temperament and a personality, manifested in early childhood, that elicit a positive response from others (Schoon & Parsons, 2002). They are socially competent and "comfortable in their own skin." They value relationships and help peers and others feel valued. "Observers described a higher proportion of these youngsters as 'agreeable,' 'cheerful,' 'friendly,' 'responsive,' 'self-confident,' and 'sociable'..." (Werner & Smith, 2001; p. 151). Resilient children and youth also are described as social, optimistic, energetic, cooperative, inquisitive, attentive, helpful, punctual, and on task (Sagor, 1996). They laugh at their own mistakes (Young-Eisendrath, 1996) and possess good-natured humor in response to life—not the sarcastic, biting form that humor sometimes takes (Peterson & Seligman, 2004). Resilient children are described as affectionate, good-natured, cuddly, and easy to get along with (McMillan & Reed, 1994), and they actively seek out relationships (Wolin & Wolin, 1996). As resilient children grow older, they play alone and with others comfortably, and as they seek challenging experiences, they appear to be self-reliant and have little fear. They use art, play, and humor as creative outlets that help them escape painful circumstances (Peterson & Seligman, 2004; Wolin & Wolin, 1996).

Over time, the research related to protective factors in children and youth has looked at concepts that are deeper in nature, including self-efficacy and self-esteem. Fraser, Kirby, and Smokowski (2004) defined self-efficacy, as a belief in one's personal effectiveness. Confidence in one's competence serves as an individual protective factor for children because success is related to self-efficacy. The more that a child achieves success in school and other settings, the more it enhances his or her motivation to perform positively elsewhere (Bandura, 1997). Self-control improves self-efficacy, enhancing coping, achievement, and adaptation across contexts.

Bandura, Barbaranelli, Caprara, and Pastorelli (2001) tested a structural model of sociocognitive influences that shape career aspirations and trajectories of children. They found that perceived efficacy, not academic achievement, was the key determinant of children's perceived occupational self-efficacy. Bandura (1997) and Bandura and colleagues (2001) indicated links between academic efficacy (ability to master subject matter through management of the learning process), social efficacy (competence in relating to peers and effectively handling peer interactions), and regulatory efficacy (being able to resist peer pressure and making the "right" choices); these all lead to social acceptance and minimal peer rejection as well as psychological well-being, academic goals, and achievement. Self-efficacy, social competence, social efficacy, and self-regulatory efficacy are all individual protective factors that serve to protect children from abuse of alcohol and other drugs, delinquency, and similar problems.

Gilligan (2000) suggested that professionals can promote self-efficacy and coping skills in children and youth by involving them in making plans related to their lives and learning. Cultivating a sense of where one's life is going and making decisions related to direction are important for those in high-risk settings.

Studies of resilient individuals have revealed the following:

- Resilient individuals typically request and receive help from adults when required (Grotberg, 2003; Werner, 1984, 1994, 1995; Werner & Smith, 1992, 2001).
- Positive reciprocity emerges at an early age. Resilient children and youth reach out to others, assuming they can receive help. Thus, their affirming attitude results in responsiveness from others. In spite of challenging circumstances, resilient individuals view

the world as positive, respect self and others, and are empathic as well as caring (Peterson & Seligman, 2004; Grotberg, 2003b).

- Resilient at-risk children have an internal locus of control and are highly motivated to succeed (Benard, 2004; Henderson & Milstein, 1996; Werner & Smith, 2001).

- Resilient individuals feel personally responsible for their success, which they view as their own (Wolin & Wolin, 1996). They do not blame others or their environments (external locus of control) for their failures or their situations unless in relation to a factor that is indeed externally controlled (e.g., child maltreatment), which is resiliency-in-action when the individual assigns the blame elsewhere (i.e., on the perpetrator).

- In the Kauai cohort longitudinal study reported over the years by Werner and Smith (1977, 1982, 1992, 2001), resilient individuals scored high in self-acceptance, which had the highest correlation with quality of adaptability. Those who were resilient at midlife (2001) were found to score better in relation to anger and distress than those with coping problems. As well, Werner and Smith stated: "A potent protective factor among the high-risk individuals who grew into a successful adulthood was a faith that life made sense…" (p. 151). Adults who provide self-fulfilling activities for children also reinforce an internal locus of control.

- Resilient children have clearly defined goals that are articulated in a mature manner, and they recognize the importance of goal-setting as a method by which they can improve their situations (Masten & Coatsworth, 1998). Thus, mastery of new experiences is important for all children and youth, especially those facing adversity.

- Academic achievement as a freshman in high school was associated with competence as seniors; succeeding at school at an early age is a sign of resilience (Ripple and Luthar, 2000).

- Resilient individuals held higher and more realistic expectations for their future in terms of education and vocations (Werner & Smith, 2001).

- Resilient individuals have the potential for creative development (Gilligan, 2000; Young-Eisendrath, 1996).

- Resilient students often seek refuge from their troubled environments by getting involved in extracurricular activities (Brown & Evans, 2002). These activities may keep them away from potentially detrimental activities such as drug abuse.

- Resilient youth welcome alternative positive experiences such as sports and academic clubs (McMillan & Reed, 1994). Working successfully in groups with peers and emerging as a leader within the peer group can be rewarding for resilient children or youth. The recognition associated with extracurricular activities can motivate them to participate. These activities also provide the opportunity for development of social skills and an expanded social circle, as well as increase Maslow's sense of belonging and give meaning and purpose to life (Gilligan, 2000).

- Choosing to volunteer is related to resiliency in children and youth (Gilligan, 2000; Henderson & Milstein, 1996). Volunteer opportunities include tutoring and visiting nursing homes.

- Werner (1994, 1995, 1997) and Werner and Smith (1992, 2001) spoke of the importance of required helpfulness at home.

- Having a purpose that aids others is associated with resiliency (Keith, 1997; Werner & Smith, 1992, 1998, 2001).

- Young-Eisendrath (1996) wrote of the desire as well as the ability to "feel and understand the needs of others" and "the ability to compromise and to delay meeting one's own desires in order to meet the needs of others" (pp. 71–72).

Equally important is exposure to a positive adult who leads or facilitates the activities and serves as a role model for resilient behavior.

The personal protective factors of resilient children and youth help them find success in the face of adversity. They achieve a wisdom that allows them to grasp life's meaning (Young-Eisendrath, 1996). Resilient children who have been maltreated at home have the capacity to develop insights about their circumstances and don't blame themselves for their family's troubles (Wilcox, Richards, & O'Keefe, 2004). They seek safety for themselves by creating physical and emotional distance from their unpredictable home life and find productive activities to fill their time (Wolin & Wolin, 1996).

Most resilient children have a secure attachment (Byng-Hall, 1995; Bowlby, 1988), which is not always a parent (Gilligan, 2000). This person provides a secure base that allows the child to explore with the knowledge that he or she can return to the security of one stable connection. A child with two parents may find an intact attachment to both, one, or neither. When neither parent serves that need, a grandparent, aunt or uncle, older sibling, teacher, neighbor, or other individual can be the stable rock amidst the troubled waters at home. Although they were studying college students, Trinke and Bartholomew (1997) found a hierarchy of attachment relationships that may operate in adolescents as well. Attachment figures are safe havens during turmoil, and they provide strong emotional ties and a secure base for exploration.

Some children from families with a parent who has a psychological disorder or other problem maintain a sense of separateness from their parents but eventually make peace with them and assume a resilient life (Rak & Patterson, 1996; Werner, 1994, 1995; Werner & Smith, 1992). Werner and Smith (2001) described a range of responses from their middle-aged Kauai cohort in the longitudinal study, with some having detached and withdrawn rather than being enmeshed with their aging parents who had perpetual problems. Others in the Kauai cohort were negative, and some were ambivalent. Physical health issues of their parents (e.g., cancer) in some cases brought about a rapprochement with forgiveness.

Benard's (2004) book, *Resiliency: What We Have Learned*, provides a matrix of personal strengths. The categories of specific strengths include social competence, problem solving, autonomy, and purpose/future. While some peers struggle in school, home, neighborhood, and community settings, the resilient child emerges from a stressful, high-risk environment or condition with positive adaptations and effective coping skills. Resilient children survive and thrive despite adversity.

Protective Factors Stemming From Family Contexts

As the field evolved from viewing resilience as residing within the individual and being about inner aspects such as biological, psychological, and disposition/temperament, the family began to be considered in relation to risk and protective factors. During the early stages of this shift, families tended to be the focus of the perceived problem (i.e., risk factor), and eventually resilience also became attributed to the family (i.e., protective factor) rather than solely to the individual child.

Over time, a new perspective ushered forth one of the more dramatic transformations in the field of resilience. Family strengths and potential for personal and relational change became the foundation of the forward movement related to resilience in the context of family (Walsh, 2002). Fostering family resilience has focused on nurturing strengths and functional behaviors as well as concomitantly preventing or ameliorating dysfunction in families to enable them to meet adversity with the strength and capacity for enhanced resilience.

This view of family resilience was not new to family systems theory and practices. The foundation of family systems always considered family systems within broader contexts. The family life cycle was viewed as interrelating with other systems as well as across generations (see multigenerational family therapy, in the Appendix).

Strengthening the family leads to greater capacity to meet future challenges. A family-resilience perspective leads to generativity through the kinds of relationships that family members build through clarity of communication, open emotional sharing, and collaborative problem solving. They infuse transcendence or spirituality with its cherished values and underlying purpose, as well as aspirations for the future, faith-based living, creative visioning, and capacity for outgrowing their limits like the chrysalis (Walsh, 2002, 2003c, 2003d).

Interestingly, family demographic factors are not predictive of resilience. Children in intact families have been found to be no more resilient as a whole than single-parent families (Amato, 2001; Hetherington, 1999a, 2003). What influences resilience is at least one strong parent–child relationship and support (Hetherington & Blechman, 1996). This commitment promotes a sense of coherence and cohesiveness (Patterson, 2002). Out of their family experience, life makes sense to resilient children, and they learn that they can have control over their lives. The sense of meaning is basic to their motivation. As well, an internal locus of control is derived from knowing they have control over how they respond to life situations even though they may not have control over their conditions (e.g., a high-risk neighborhood).

Overall family functioning and parental behaviors have a positive influence on adolescents' well-being (Grotevant, 1998). The more positive the relationship of parent and adolescent, the greater the adolescent's well-being.

The strengths of single-parent households were described by Anderson (2003). Adequate income was the most essential strength, and employed mothers were cast as having more satisfying networks and being less punitive with children. The children of working mothers who were able to meet the basic needs of the family had better developmental outcomes.

Other factors influencing success in single-parent homes were adequate attention to personal needs and supportive networks. A strong self-esteem of single parents was described as influencing the well-being of children.

Parental involvement in education of their children is credited with higher academic achievement in a number of studies (e.g., Becker & Luthar, 2002). In investigating the impact of parental involvement in education and achievement of minority children, Jeynes (2003b) found an overall positive impact on achievement that was significant for every minority group included in the meta-analysis regardless of racial heritage. Children who were achieving at higher levels benefited from parental involvement in their education.

Low-Income Families

Orthner, Jones-Sanpei, and Williamson (2004) studied a random sample of low-income families using the Family Strength Index. Factors assessed included economic, problem-solving, communication, family cohesion, and social support assets. More than half of their sample consisted of single-parents, with many receiving public assistance. One-third had no health insurance and health problems were frequent.

According to those authors, personal and family safety was a moderate concern for some of the families in the sample, but even more problematic was the poor condition of the homes in which many of them lived (p. 165). Their overall conclusion from their research was that "relationship assets such as communication, problem solving, and social support predict positive outcomes for low-income families" (p. 159), but they pointed to the importance that those working with low-income families be aware of the interconnection between economically and relationally strengthening families: "The data also point to a substantial benefit in family problem solving and children's development when the internal family strengths are strong" (p. 166).

Adolescents

Perceptions of adolescents within the overall functioning of the family system and parental behaviors were examined by Henry, Robinson, Neal, and Huey (2006). In particular, the authors found that parental support and monitoring of adolescents were determinants of overall family functioning. Adolescents who perceived their families as balanced or moderately balanced in overall functioning reported greater parental support. Henry and colleagues stated, "Families may need guidance in finding healthy ways of maintaining their connection to one another as they realign their family boundaries to afford a greater level of independence for adolescents" (p. 328). As well, adolescents and parents were viewed as needing guidance on negotiating of boundaries related to monitoring by parents.

A qualitative study by Ungar (2004) examined the importance of parents/caregivers to the resilience of high-risk adolescents. Ungar indicated that adolescents want parental attachment and benign control with an adult to assist in structuring their world. When parents or caregivers do not fulfill these roles, adolescents will search for contact with an adult by which to "author an identity." Ungar recommended that teens have family sessions to engage youth and their families in attaining a healthy identity.

Girls

Girls from impoverished backgrounds have high rates of risk-taking behaviors such as alcohol and other drug abuse and delinquency. Arnowitz and Morrison-Beedy (2004) explored the relationship of three factors in African American girls between the ages of 11 and 15: connectedness to mother, time perspective, and resilience to risk. Of these, the future time perspective was found to be the key mediator between connectedness and resilience. As a result, they recommended that mothers be helped to make a connection with their daughters that would engender a future time viewpoint so they would not be living in the present with no thought for tomorrow.

In sum, family support is an important protective family factor that can promote resiliency in children (Liontos, 1991). Parents of resilient children often have higher educational expectations for their children, which in turn influence their children's achievement orientation. Resilient children have more of the necessary tools and materials for learning at home and are taken more frequently to community educational activities than children who are not resilient (Henderson & Milstein, 1996).

Under-education of parents relates to lack of resiliency. Werner and Smith (1992, 1998) reported that the mother's educational level impacted the child's resilience at age 2. Peng, Wang, and Walberg (1992) found that fewer than 11% of children were resilient in families in which the parents had not earned a high school diploma. Of students whose parents had at least a high school diploma, 23% were considered resilient. These findings alone point to the need for parent training in low-income and high dropout areas.

Protective Factors Stemming From Community Contexts

Foremost in community contexts are the schools. Schools can provide protective factors for students in many ways, regardless of the presence of high-risk contexts/conditions from which they emanate (Brown, D'Emidio-Caston, & Benard, 2001). The community context also encompasses neighborhoods and other community contexts, which are equally important and powerful in terms of providing protective factors for children and youth.

A hallmark of resilient children is that, at an early age, they seek out and access adults whom they can trust (Fraser, Kirby, & Smokowski, 2004; Hetherington & Blechman, 1996; Rak & Patterson, 1996; Werner & Smith, 2001). Trust is established in the early years in the home. It forms the building blocks for later adjustment at school, translating to reciprocal relationships with teachers and other role models. Especially for children from families with problems, it is difficult to "exaggerate the importance of anchors in their lives—children and adults outside their families who are caring and attentive over time" (Weissbourd, 1996, p. 63).

Parents, though important, are not the only ones who generate trust. Other adults may become as influential as family, if not more so for some children/youth (Sale & Springer, 2001, as cited in Benard, 2004). Many resilient adults recount stories of a special coach or teacher who took an interest in them (Wolin & Wolin, 1993), and this connection made them feel confident in their ability to build other strong relationships. This informal network represents people they can access for help in academic and other areas as well as in crises.

Becker and Luthar (2002) pointed to the need for an ecological approach for middle-school students to meet their needs regarding social–emotional development. The single most commonly reported protective factor was a supportive relationship with an adult. Thus, teachers and other school personnel who are positive and accepting and provide supportive feedback will enhance students' social–emotional growth, including those in high-risk contexts.

Nash and Bowen (1999) wrote about adolescents' perceptions of peers' behavior and the importance they attach to what peers think of them. Resilient children often are involved in extracurricular activities and find these to be supportive, providing a sense of belonging and increased self-esteem (Werner, 1984).

Service learning has become a major thrust in secondary and undergraduate education in colleges and universities (Lerner, 2002, 2004; Toews & Cerny, 2005). In defining service learning, Toews and Cerny stated, "It is a form of experiential education where students learn the course content while applying their knowledge in the community..." (p. 80). Students learn tolerance, empathy, and a sense of civic responsibility during service learning activities. Taking advantage of the opportunities it presents will help build resiliency (Henderson & Milstein, 1996; Keith, 1997). Resilient students often mention that teachers and other school staff members have taken a personal interest in them (Geary, 1988; Coburn & Nelson, 1989), which motivates them to succeed. The interpersonal relationships and competence of these adults are important (Geary, 1988). Teachers should demonstrate caring, respect students for who they are, listen without being intrusive, take them seriously, be available and understanding, provide encouragement, and share humor. Resilient students want the teacher to foster group goals, listen beneath the surface before disciplining, be fair in grading and instruction, encourage their success, and know them academically and personally (McMillan & Reed, 1994). Thus, schools have the opportunity to increase protective factors in many ways.

Brown, D'Emidio-Caston, and Benard (2001) presented a model called PORT (Participation, Observation, Reflection, Transformation), which provides a framework for creating a learning community for resilience education within the school. Amatea, Smith-Adcock, and Villares (2006) emphasized family strengths, highlighting the shift in schools from deficits to strengths, with an eye toward increasing students' academic performance. They honored the reality that families vary in terms of their resources to enhance their children's learning and advised:

> Rather than burden the school counselor with a host of additional responsibilities, we believe that the counselor's main goal should be to develop a working alliance with other school staff around creating an atmosphere that joins the school with families in the critical process of educating their children. Part of the effort to infuse a family resilience approach into school counseling programs is (a) to believe in and articulate its value to all constituents of the school system, and (b) to make it seem simple. (p. 188)

When describing the factors that produce positive outcomes in school, Minnard (2002) suggested redesigning rather than replacing curricula, with protective factors as the foundation. Setting high expectations is essential for schools to engender protective factors leading to high-achieving students.

Protective factors should be promoted in the context of neighborhoods. Nash and Bowen (1999) used a risk and resilience paradigm in studying adolescents relative to their neighborhoods in regard to perceived crime (a risk factor) and prosocial behavior (a protective factor) as the context for adolescent behavior. They presented numerous examples of ways in which social workers could make a positive difference in the lives of adolescents living in high-risk neighborhoods. For example, adults might develop structured, supervised activities during the hours of 3:00 p.m. through 7:00 p.m. (when the most problems occur for adolescents in crime-ridden neighborhoods), midnight basketball, and recreation centers.

Within neighborhoods, social support is a protective factor that lowers stress levels. Neighborhoods with higher social cohesion and informal social control were associated with lower crime and fewer low birthweight babies (Sampson, 2001, cited in Fraser, Kirby, & Smokowski, 2004).

Mentors constitute an invaluable community protective factor. The child/youth learns from an adult model and practices social skills within the relationship that evolves between the two.

Creating Community

Systems theory holds that behavior is affected by many interrelated nested systems one within the other (Bronfenbrenner, 1977, 1986). Thus, change in one subsystem—for example, the community—will reverberate throughout other interrelated systems. Contending that resilience "provides a conceptual base for an intervention that calls for responsive classroom, school, and community environments," Wang and Haertel (1995, p. 159) made clear the importance of community joining with schools to build resilience in youth.

School counselors are "naturals" to serve a coordinating function (Amatea, Smith-Adcock, & Villares, 2006; Keys, Bemak, Carpenter, & King-Sears, 1998) in creating a community that positively impacts children from high-risk contexts (Bemak, 2005; Lambie, 2005; Webb, Brigman, & Campbell, 2005). Community social workers can collaborate with the school counselor in building community through resources that enhance resilience in individuals, families, and communities.

One of the most successful means of encouraging resiliency is to create a positive school–community partnership that fosters a sense of belonging in the students (Smith, Boutte, Zigler, & Finn-Stevenson, 2004; Wang, Haertel, & Walberg, 1994). Through collaboration with external resources (e.g., businesses, volunteers, retirees, YMCAs/YWCAs, faith-based communities, and social-service agencies), schools can be the hub of a community that links and provides services to promote healthy and whole children (Fowler & Corley, 1996).

The school can fulfill an important role by linking families and students to professional service providers and, perhaps more important, by creating a supportive and nurturing community in which students and families are connected in a caring manner (Alder, 2002; Lewis, Schaps, & Watson, 1995; Noddings, 1995, 2002, 2005b; Wynne & Walberg, 1995). These opportunities increase the protective factors, the buffers that augment resilience in children (Werner, 1993b, 1994, 1997; Werner & Smith, 1992, 2001).

Rationale for Creating Community

Families are changing demographically, and technology has revolutionized both home and work. Yet, poverty, crime, sexual promiscuity, drugs, and depression have made it difficult for families, schools, and communities to support and care for the nation's youth the way they once did. Zill and Nord (1994) and Waddock (1993) concluded that families today are less able to provide nurturing, supportive, safe, and secure environments where children can develop and learn. Communities must take stock and rearrange resources to help children grow up as responsible and productive members of this new world (Dryfoos, 1994). With the intention of building better learners, school personnel have an opportunity to lead the way as family and child advocates.

With a vision of social transformation, school and community professionals can become partners in the development of children and in the preservation and development of the larger community (Booth & Dunn, 1996; Dryfoos, 1994). For schools to achieve this partnership, Haas (1993) suggested that schools must move away from the factory model of production with raw materials and move into a new era in which they adopt the metaphor of family resource schools—where schools, as extensions of a child's family, provide the scaffolding for the child's growth that once was provided solely by relatives and neighbors. This will require a shift of attitudes about the roles of the school and of school personnel, who must expand and evolve to meet the needs of the at-risk population.

Comer (1996) provides a model for holism that involves all aspects of children's lives. School counselors are challenged to become advocates for school and community partnerships and to coordinate networks of resources for children and youth from high-risk environments (Hart & Jacobi, 1992). Schools must go beyond the traditional "three Rs" and include the teaching and nurturing that parents have traditionally been expected to provide. Counselors and other school personnel must also reach out to parents through parent education, training, and support groups.

As an outgrowth of the work of the National Commission on Children, Nicholas Hobbs (1975) wrote the now classic *The Futures of Children*, in which he indicated that by not acting in the present, generations to come will suffer from our neglect. Hobbs saw investing in children as a national imperative. This point is as appropriate as it was in 1975, and the evidence of Hobbs' grave warning echoes through our cities and our people.

Relationships are best formed through interpersonal contact (Alder, 2002; Beck, 1994; Noddings, 1995, 2002, 2005b). Communities and schools must keep in mind that relationships are what build resiliency (Noddings, 1995, 2002). Mentoring, lunch buddies, Big Sisters/Brothers, tutoring by retirees, e-mail pen pals linking students with professors, and similar experiences provide opportunities for the relationship building that fosters resilience (Rak & Patterson, 1996).

In other examples of relationship building, adolescent students might provide tutoring to kindergarten children from at-risk environments. These same adolescents may be visited by senior citizens from a nearby community for retirees to share their gardening expertise (Werner, 1994, 1995). The underlying belief here is reflected by the poet Kahlil Gibran (1923) in *The Prophet*:

> No man can reveal to you aught but that which already lies half
> asleep in the dawning of your knowledge. . . .
> If he is indeed wise he does not bid you enter the house of his wis-
> dom, but rather leads you to the threshold of your own mind. . . .
> For the vision of one man lends not its wings to another man. . . .
> (pp. 56–57)

A resource model of family functioning assumes that families continually create their own norms as they interact with history, culture, ethnicity, social class, politics, interpersonal relationships, individual quirks, and so forth. Professionals can frame their views of the family with this in mind and recognize the impact of context. Seeing context as significant, the professional is better able to make sense of family observations instead of seeing the family as abnormal. This strengths-based perspective focuses on the assets of the family while recognizing but not emphasizing its deficits.

Sharing Information With Families

Although helping individuals and family members not to be overly dependent upon outside resources is certainly good, being independent does not mean having to meet all needs alone or within one's own family. The emphasis here is on sharing information that allows family members to learn more about family life and healthy communication and to know how to link with beneficial resources.

Most families of children from high-risk contexts/conditions welcome help from community professionals (Campbell, 1993). Some parents, however, consider this as an invasion of privacy or indicative of their perceived failure or inadequacy. For example, one family may consider a suggestion that the child join a Little League team as a positive intervention that fits the child's developmental level and offers a social outlet. Another family may see the same suggestion as squelching the boy's natural creativity by requiring him to take part in an organized sport rather than allowing exploration of the child's unique physical and social needs. The professional who is aware of the differences between these two families might recommend to the second family that its members explore each individual's creativity and interests through some form of family interaction, such as nurturing a musical interest or playing challenging board games.

Resourcing

Not all families from high-risk neighborhoods or those with children eligible for special education exhibit dysfunctional behaviors, but most can benefit from being able to call upon resources at times of increased stress. The forms of support discussed here are family resourcing, social systems resourcing, school-community resourcing, and external resourcing.

Family Resourcing

Family resourcing encourages school and community professionals to identify family strengths (Hawley & DeHaan, 1996; Patterson, 1997, 2002; Richardson & Hawks, 1995; Walsh, 1996, 2003a, 2003b, 2003c) and builds on Weissbourd's (1996) principles of collaboration, highlighting the interdependence of systems.

Definition of family resources   Several types of family resources have been identified in the literature (Attneave & Verhulst, 1986; Dunst, Trivette, & Deal, 1994c; Epstein, Ryan, Bishop, Miller, & Keitner, 2003; Hansen & Falicov, 1983; Hansen & Coppersmith,

1984; Karpel, 1986a; Patterson, 1997; Walsh & Pryce, 2003). Karpel (1986b) defined family resources as "those individual and systemic characteristics among family members that promote coping and survival, limit destructive patterns, and enrich daily life" (p. 176). He was not referring to finances or other material trappings, nor was he including social service resources within the community. Karpel (1986a, 1986b) suggested three elements of family resources:

1. The family's ability to access coping and survival techniques.
2. The family's ability to limit possible destructive patterns; this ability relates to both external stressors and internal patterns, such as attacking, demeaning, neglecting, or diminishing another. Some families resist destructive patterns, such as a wife's resisting her husband's invitation for a co-alcoholic marriage, or parents exercising a clear hierarchy over an acting-out teenager.
3. The ability to enrich and enjoy life. This element goes beyond dealing with problems and fosters life's more rewarding aspects—caring and sharing, satisfaction, and pleasure, as well as the ability to bounce back.

Karpel (1986a) expanded upon this three-element definition and offered examples of personal resources including self-respect, protectiveness, hope, tolerance, and affection. Relational resources include respect, reciprocity, reliability, repair, flexibility, family pride, and loops of interaction. Personal and relational resources within families are affected by three characteristics: capacity, rules, and active efforts.

Imber-Black (1986) described four family resource areas that direct professionals' attention to the family's strengths rather than their deficits:

1. *The family's religious, cultural, and racial identity.* Avoiding stereotypical thinking about people from other backgrounds is beneficial to healthy family–professional interactions. Professionals should observe family interactions with an eye toward recognizing supports offered through religious groups. Carter (1995, 2005) focused on racial identity as another resource to tap. These linkages are important as school and community professionals reach out to community resources and form partnerships for mentoring and other resiliency-building programs.

2. *The family's inner language, which identifies the family to family members and to others.* The professional should look for myths, metaphors, jokes, humor, and words or phrases with special meaning to the family members, note any examples, and use them at appropriate times.

3. *Individual and family commitments, loyalties, or a sense of connections.* An example is a grandmother who takes over the custody and rearing of her unmarried teenage daughter's child.

4. *The capacity of the family to interact with the outside world in a way that preserves and enhances its integrity as a family.* The outside world is defined as everything beyond the family. School professionals are members of that outside world.

Strategies   Professionals can assess, monitor, and reinforce all four areas of family resources. Again, when collaborating with any family, it is best to look for resources versus deficits (Amatea, Smith-Adcock, & Villares, 2006; Malatchi, 1997; Patterson, 1997, 2002). Setting up a file on each student (cataloging) is valuable, to which information on family resources can be added. Fraenkel (2006) encouraged professionals to "adopt a stance of respectful learner" so family members will provide input about what is valuable for them in programs being developed.

Family members should be a part of meetings intended to investigate their resources (Patterson, 1997, 2002; Richardson & Hawks, 1995). When family members attend meetings, professionals can observe the family's use of inner language, as well as how they interact with the outside world. Existing family resources should be reinforced.

When professionals meet with family members in a meeting and in one-to-one interactions, they should take every opportunity to validate family resources related to resiliency. For example, a teacher might say to a mother, "I can see that Timmy takes after the rest of your family when it comes to being gentle. I wish you had seen him with the new student from Iran!"

The healthy functioning of the spousal system, too, should be supported by professionals in community and school settings. When spouses are planning to take a vacation together, professionals should verbally reinforce their having time to themselves and pledging to work with those who will be caring for the children in their absence, reassuring the parents that "we can handle whatever might come up here."

The sibling subsystem also should be validated as a source of support and a valuable family resource. Professionals need to help frame existing or potential sibling relationships positively (Meyer & Vadasy, 1994; Powell & Gallagher, 1993). Dysfunctional family interaction patterns or roles, such as scapegoating (Satir, 1988), can be addressed. School professionals might suggest extracurricular activities to provide support outside the family, thereby fostering resiliency. Another potential resource lies in the extended family (Walton, Roby, Frandsen, & Davidson, 2003). We can learn from African-American families, in particular, in which extended family members often help to rear the children (Hines & Boyd-Franklin, 2005). Extended family members can serve as important role models for coping with stress and for increasing resiliency in children and youth. Family retreats, family play-group counseling, and parent education groups can be implemented using flexible scheduling and providing babysitting for infants and toddlers. There are many possibilities, and creative professionals can help to make these possibilities real.

Social Systems Resourcing

Cameron and Vanderwoerd (1997) defined social networks as "the actual, reoccurring linkages between a focal person and significant others in her or his environment" (p. 27). Social support comes from the "instrumental, educational, social, and psychological assistance actually received by the focal person" (p. 27).

Social support helps some individuals and families to cope better with stressful events, improving health (Hobfoll & Stephens, 1990), life expectancy (Kennedy, Kiecolt-Glaser, & Glaser, 1990), and success on exams and other academic tasks (Goldsmith & Albrecht,

1993). Advocating for continued social support, Burleson, Albrecht, and Sarason (1994) stated that

> in short, supportive communication can contribute (positively and
> negatively) to how well people recover from illness, cope
> with loss or transition, manage chronic health conditions, deal
> with everyday upsets and disruptions, perform on a variety of
> tasks, and generally feel about themselves and their quality of
> life. (p. xiii)

School and community settings can facilitate social support by connecting people with others who face similar challenges or with people in their community who could serve as positive role models (Comer, 2001; Comer & Haynes, 1991). School professionals, for example, could designate a room for families to meet with other families who share the same needs or with parents who have overcome similar obstacles. The room should be inviting, and the leaders to facilitate the meetings should be selected with care. Group co-leadership by a helping professional and a "veteran" successful parent can facilitate interaction. A number of professionals who are interested in at-risk families and those having children with special needs have written about social network interventions and the value of social support (M. Berger, 1984a; Coppersmith, 1983; Dunst, Trivette, & Cross, 1986; Dunst, Trivette, & Deal, 1994b; Friedrich & Friedrich, 1981; Intagliata & Doyle, 1984; Kazak, 1987; Kazak & Marvin, 1984; Rueveni, 1979).

Background   Systems theorists propose that social networks, with their attendant support, directly and indirectly influence attitudes, expectations, behavior, and knowledge of family members as well as other members of the network. Bronfenbrenner (1979, 1986) described ecological units or social networks topologically, seeing them as a nesting of concentric structures, one embedded within the other. The child and family are at the center, and broader ecological systems—relatives, friends, neighbors, and acquaintances—move out in concentric circles. Beyond that are larger social units including the neighborhood, faith-based settings, as well as social organizations, the workplace, play areas, and schools.

Waddock (1993), too, described ecological units or social networks topologically. She saw them as spider webs of influence moving outward from the center occupied by the child. Moving outward, the broader ecological systems include family and school, then the larger community where services are provided, then state policies. At the outer edge of the web lies the nation and federal government. Counselors and social workers can serve as web weavers to develop linkages that promote resiliency building for families and students between and among these systems.

Social systems theorists contend that these ecological units do not function in isolation but, rather, interact within and between levels. Thus, changes in one unit or subsystem will reverberate and impact upon other units or subsystems. When professionals understand this dynamic, reciprocal, systemic relationship, they will be more likely to plan appropriate interventions that promote resiliency by considering both input from the family, school, and community, and the impact of the interventions on children with high-risk conditions or from high-risk settings.

Definition of social support systems   Social support networks are links between individuals and groups related to size, satisfaction, density, connectedness, and frequency of contacts. As Dunst, Trivette, and Cross (1986) indicated:

> Social support is a multidimensional construct that includes physical and instrumental assistance, attitude transmission, resource and information sharing, and emotional and psychological support. There is general consensus among social systems theorists that social support networks function to nurture and sustain linkages among persons that are supportive on both a day-to-day basis and in times of need and crises. (p. 403)

After tracing research on social support, Turner (1981) concluded that social support is most important in stressful circumstances. In his study, he adopted Cobb's (1976) view that social support consists of

> information belonging to one or more of three classes: (1) information leading the subject to believe that he or she is cared for and loved; (2) information leading the subject to believe that he or she is esteemed and valued; and (3) information leading the subject to believe that he or she belongs to a network of communication and mutual obligation in which others can be counted on should the need arise. (pp. 358–359)

Findings and strategies for social systems resourcing   Social networks, with their attendant support, directly and indirectly influence the attitudes, expectations, behavior, and knowledge of family members and other members of the network, as alluded to by Gerstein (2006). In this web of influence, professionals have the distinct opportunity, through "collective anchoring of the individual life" (Haas, 1993, p. 215), to develop children/youth by providing the tools that allow them to forge a tranquil, thriving, and equitable society.

A variety of findings presented in the literature on social network systems indicates the value of considering social systems as essential assets in reducing stress on family members. Some of these are described briefly below.

- Dunst, Trivette, and Cross (1986) examined effects of social support on parents of children with mental retardation and physical impairment, as well as developmentally at-risk children. These researchers were concerned with the impact of social support on "personal well-being, parental attitudes toward their child, family integrity, parental perceptions of child functioning, parent-child play opportunities and child behavior and development" (p. 403). Their findings supported the positive impact of social support systems on families with children with disabilities.
- Kazak and Marvin (1984) studied stress and characteristics of social support networks of families with and without a child with a disability. They found that mothers are particularly subject to personal stress. Specifically, they found both the overinvolvement of the mother and child and the peripheral role of the father in parenting to be appropriate and to be respected by professionals, "unless there is ample evidence that the marital relationship is impaired" (p. 75).

- Kazak (1987) examined mothers and fathers of children with disabilities or chronic illnesses and compared them to matched parents of children without disabilities, considering personal stress, marital satisfaction, and social network size and density. She found that the mothers of the children with disabilities had higher stress levels. She also found that mothers of children with disabilities had higher-density social networks than the comparison mothers.
- Intagliata and Doyle (1984) examined the effect of training in interpersonal problem-solving skills on enhancing social support for parents of children with developmental disabilities. From this pilot study, they concluded that enhancing problem-solving skills of these parents could be a helpful intervention.
- Friedrich and Friedrich (1981) compared parents of children with a disability with a control group of parents of children without disabilities. One of the many measures they investigated was social support. They concluded that "an appropriate avenue of intervention might increase the availability of social support for these parents to help them cope with this additional stress" (p. 553).
- Minuchin and Fishman (1981) described the technique of enactment, in which the problem is acted out, as contrasted with simply talking about the problem in the family. For example, if a child is disobedient to the parents during a social systems networking session, the professional might ask the parents to act out what they plan to do. This allows the professional to see the problem as it evolves naturally. It may also present an opportunity for the professional to intervene while serving as a model for the social systems network.
- Berger (1984a) recommended the use of enactments in network interventions, creating a context in which those in attendance act differently toward one another. This is helpful when attempting to look at the family and social network as valuable resources. He described network interventions as "especially powerful contexts for the use of enactments that alter network members' definition of the handicapping condition or of what needs to be done about that condition (p. 134)."

School–Community Resourcing

Characteristics of effective school and community programs with some suggestions for establishing effective services follow.

Schools as a source of support   Outside the informal support that families receive from friends, relatives, and one another, the teacher often is the main source of family support (Burke & Cigno, 1996). Quite often, the schools are the first to recognize a problem and to contact the parent when a problem arises (Comer, 2001; Comer & Haynes, 1991).

School counselors, social workers, and psychologists—who are usually trained in providing support—can support families who need assistance.

Just a few of the challenges that students may bring with them when they enter school are poverty, drug abuse, gangs, learning problems, health problems, child neglect and abuse, teen pregnancy, single-parent families, alcohol and other drug abuse problems, and even homelessness. Thus, schools have become a place where education alone is not enough. Families, schools, and external agencies must collaborate to provide education and other services so troubled children do not fall through the cracks (Greenawalt, 1994b; Kupersmidt, Coie, & Howell, 2004; Nastasi, Moore, Varjas, 2004; Smith, Boutte, Zigler, & Finn-Stevenson, 2004).

Slavin and colleagues (1996) described a scenario of a child from the Baltimore slums who had completed kindergarten the year before. His teachers already saw him as being in serious trouble, as his anger and disruptiveness precluded his learning much in school. He was frequently absent and usually 2 hours late. His teenage mother loved her son but felt helpless as she reexperienced her own childhood school history through him. When the child was angry, he was aggressive just like his mother.

After the school contacted the mother the first week of school, she stomped into school, cursing and threatening to take her son out of the school. The social worker made an effort to make the mother feel valued and accepted. Soon the mother began to collaborate with the teachers, the facilitator, a family support team, and the attendance monitor. As a result, the boy's attendance, performance, and behavior improved.

This scenario, in one variation or another, plays out in many forms across the nation. All too often, though, a student's problems are left to the teacher or the building principal and are eventually passed on from elementary to middle school or junior high and to high school, where a once preventable problem has grown to crisis proportions.

When to offer support   The kinds of support services provided should depend on the family's desires and needs, the community, and the specific challenges encountered. In today's complex society, families cannot meet all of their needs themselves. Sooner or later, all families will need and benefit from different kinds and levels of support. Walsh (2003) spoke directly to this reality.

Although one might expect that two-parent, nonminority homes have low stress and are able to cope, communicate, and parent effectively, this is not necessarily the case (Allen, Brown, & Finlay, 1992). Middle-income families are less likely to need financial help to pay for child care or health services, but they can benefit from peer support or parenting classes, as well as a number of other services matched to their needs.

Supportive school programs   At any given time, an observer can find an example of almost any variety of human services located in or facilitated by the school (Comer, 2001; Nastasi, Moore, & Varjas, 2004). According to Dryfoos (1994), these include

- school health teams;
- school-based dental health and general health clinics;
- mental health services;
- psychosocial counseling programs for substance abuse, teen pregnancy, and school failure;
- social skills training;
- family or parenting skills training;
- assistance with selecting an occupation;
- mentoring programs;
- recreation and cultural enrichment classes; and
- after-school centers for academic tutoring or job training with links with businesses, universities, and nonprofit organizations.

Programs show up in all shapes and sizes and reflect the needs of the communities that they serve. Some examples that have stood the test of time and been adopted elsewhere are the following:

- Prior to the opening of Saltonstall Elementary School to students, linkages with city officials, college faculty, and teachers were in place. One feature was the Friday Club, in which every Friday, community partners taught elementary students how to do a variety of things. One volunteer taught students how to build doll houses and then to paint, wallpaper, and decorate the interior. Another volunteer taught students how to play soccer. The Friday Club took place between 8:00 and 10:00 while teachers spent those 2 hours planning lessons (Fowler & Corby, 1996).
- In Monticello, Arkansas, schools worked with HIPPY (Home Instruction Program for Pre-school Youngsters) coordinators to help parents develop social and interpersonal skills that could reduce their feelings of isolation. In one meeting with the school counselor, parents of children entering kindergarten shared their feelings of inadequacy. One mother told the group that she had never hugged any of her five children or told them that she loved them. Through the help of a HIPPY coordinator who followed up on the case, and with the mother's own desire to show more affection, the mother began to hug her children every day. Clearly, the family had begun to change fundamentally when the youngest child said to the mother, "I love you, Mommy. You're special to me." (Greenawalt, 1994b; Harvard Family Research Project, 1995).
- Schools in Indianapolis, Indiana, indicated that they wanted more contact with parents and more parent participation in the schools. Working with Parents in Touch (PIT), schools there set aside 20 minutes a day for parent–teacher conferences, created activity calendars to inform and offer suggestions to parents, and set up homework contracts, homework hotlines, call-in services, parent workshops, and even medical and dental services. (Harvard Family Research Project, 1995).
- In Oakland, California, the Unified School District was facing big problems with its students. Two of the schools in the district—the Health Academy and the Media Academy—sought solutions. Based on a concept first employed successfully in Philadelphia, the schools linked with community resources to offer students academic and career-oriented services in a school-within-a-school setting. Subsequent findings revealed that the students in these schools had improved attitudes toward school, were less disruptive, and were better able to work in cooperative groups. Several students and teachers indicated that Academy students were better mannered and often more "driven" to success than their non-academy peers (Guthrie & Guthrie, 1993).

External Resourcing

External resource networking has to do with helping families form supportive links with resources outside their family, school, social network, and in their community or beyond (city, state, and national, federal). External networking might include tapping into volunteer groups, social service agencies, support groups, counseling services, and a host of diverse other possibilities. As part of their services to families and children, professionals should be in tune with the resources and how they can be offered specifically to those who can benefit from them.

Principles for Effectively Serving Children and Youth

Professionals must find ways of intervening in community and school settings that lower the risk factors for failure and increase the possibility that children and youth become resilient. Weissbourd's (1996) principles for "schools that work" are summarized below:

1. Staff emphasize academics and pay careful attention to results, to academic achievements.
2. Staff have the capacity to respond to the emotional and social troubles and material needs of children.
3. Staff create a safe and orderly but not severe school environment.
4. Staff imbue high expectations for children in every aspect of school functioning.
5. Staff work with parents and children respectfully and collaboratively. When a child has a problem, staff examine the child's role, the family's role, the community's role, and the school's role.
6. Staff need to identify root problems and to turn negative interactions into cycles of success.
7. Staff give parents authority and a sense of belonging; they reach out to all parents and provide a variety of opportunities for parents to become involved in school.
8. Staff work to engage noncustodial parents and other adults of great importance to the child.
9. Administrators mine teachers' wisdom, seek to provide teachers the time, support, and resources they need to work with struggling students and continually promote teachers' learning and professional development.
10. Guidance counselors, school nurses, and other school staff are similarly supported, and school staff [members] are enabled to support and strengthen one another.
11. Staff form effective partnerships with community services, businesses, and other community resources. These partnerships are designed to achieve specific goals that further children's academic achievements. (p. 181)

Weissbourd also set forth principles for effective teachers applicable to OST programs, coaches, camp counselors, and professionals who work with vulnerable children in school or community settings. These include the following:

1. Effective teachers operationalize high expectations for every child and focus on academic results.
2. Effective teachers attribute failure to aspects of a child or classroom that can be positively influenced, rather than to intractable aspects of a child, family, or community.

3. Effective teachers provide every student with the elements from which real and durable self-esteem is built, including specific, tangible skills and achievements, progressively increased responsibilities, and opportunities to give to others.

4. Effective teachers view children as having complex constellations of strengths and weaknesses and communicate this understanding to parents.

5. Effective teachers work to develop children's adaptive capacities, their ability to manage disappointment and conflict.

6. Effective teachers pick up on the quiet troubles that undermine children in school, such as mild hunger or wearing the same clothes day after day and respond aggressively to these problems.

7. Effective teachers view the classroom and school as a complex culture and system and seek to understand the difficulties of a child in terms of the interactions between a particular child and a particular culture and system.

8. Effective teachers engage parents proactively and have the skills to work with parents when a child is in crisis.

9. Effective teachers are self-observing and are responsive to feedback and ideas from both other school staff and children. They see children as active partners in their education.

10. Effective teachers know when to respond to a child's problem themselves and when a child needs to see another professional who has specialized training.

11. Effective teachers innovate, take risks, and reshape their activities based on close attention to results. (p. 183)

Summary

The professional in community or school settings is essential in helping family members receive the support they need for their children, thereby increasing resilience in children from high-risk settings/conditions. Viewing resilience from a multidimensional, multisystemic lens is crucial in building the collaborative efforts from many disciplines involved in serving at-risk and special-needs children and youth. Through interdisciplinary research, the view of resilience has shifted from characteristics inherent to an individual to the complexity involved and wider nature of resilience-building domains. Now realized as contextual in nature, the study and development of resilience relates to three dimensions: the child, family characteristics, and the broader social context of the child. The field is currently concentrating on reducing risk while enhancing protective factors, with this shift viewed as a "second generation of voices" related to resilience research (Wilkes, 2002).

Protective factors or buffers affect the overall life trajectory of vulnerable children and are stronger influences on the lives of these children than any particular risk factor (e.g., impoverishment) or stressful events (e.g., death of a parent). Examples of protective factors include competent parenting; self-efficacy, maturity, and achievement of the child; and support by extended family members as well as social and spiritual networks.

Resilience-oriented interventions engender the necessary experience of hope that nullifies resignation to unacceptable circumstances of life.

Most children who experience significant risk factors are resilient. We now know that a child's self-efficacy (i.e., belief in personal effectiveness) is the most influential factor in promoting resilience, rather than the previously assumed level of academic achievement. Self-efficacy feeds off success by enhancing motivation to achieve while being augmented by the child's self-control. Social-efficacy in competent peer relationships as well as regulatory-efficacy in being able to make mature choices when pressured by less mature peers combine to enhance resilience in children from at-risk home and neighborhood conditions or experiences. Also operational in resilient individuals are: requesting assistance and anticipating that others want to help, an "internal locus of control," self-acceptance despite flaws, clear goals, achievement as freshmen in high school, realistic expectations related to education and careers, creativity, involvement in extracurricular activities that keep them out of harm's way as well as place them in a social network that provides belonging and reinforces meaning/purpose in their lives, volunteering and helping others, and compassion, combined with deferring personal gratification so that others' needs are met.

Emphasis on protective factors within the family context replaced the view of families as being causative factors in terms of risk in children. The underlying theory of this book, family systems, provided the foundation for the interdisciplinary fields converging to transform and expand resiliency research. Professionals using a family systems framework—emphasizing family strengths and potential in relation to the child's development—also supported families in helping shift dysfunctional family patterns.

Demographic differences in family forms (e.g., stepfamilies, single-parent) are not predictive of resilience in children; the main family influence predictive of resilience was identified as the child having at least one strong, supportive parental relationship. Highly positive relationships between adolescents and parent(s) were associated with higher levels of adolescent well-being. Single-parent households were not contributors to risk; the parent's adequate income in satisfying careers as well as supportive friendships and high self-esteem coupled with involvement in his or her child's education serve as protective factors.

Lower income families fare poorly in terms of providing protective factors for their children, yet effective communication and problem solving as well as adequate social support within low-income families were found to contribute to buffering their children from risk factors. Lack of income to meet basic needs hampers parental opportunity to be available to and supportive of their children, as Maslow's hierarchy of needs spells out.

Adolescence is a time when parents must provide strong support as well as monitor the activities of their children. At the same time, adolescents who view their families as balanced in overall functioning reported higher levels of parental support.

Girls living in poverty exhibit more risk-related behaviors (e.g., AOD) than peers living at higher SES levels. Mothers living in poverty need to help their daughters assume a goal-oriented perspective so they do not become mired in decisions in the present without concern for their future.

Community context provides protective factors for at-risk and special-needs children and youth. The school, neighborhood, and community in which children face increased risk can and should be instrumental in providing protective factors. There are many trust-worthy, caring, and approachable adults in these contexts serving as models of resilience as well as mentors. A one-to-one relationship with such an adult can make the substantive difference in the life of a child facing risk.

Service learning provides buffering from risk, and high expectations for students gen-erate higher academic achievement. In neighborhoods, adults should be expected to take responsibility for their children as well as peers living in the neighborhood by providing structure to after-school hours. Adults responsive to the need for social cohesion and social support outside the family make a positive impact on resilience.

The process of creating community is crucial to success in reducing risk while increasing protective factors. By fostering belonging, schools can become a "hub" of serv-ices provided by social services and other offerings. Similar to interdisciplinary research yielding a richer understanding of resilience and risk, practitioners from various disci-plines collaborating to create supportive community opportunities are crucial links in the chain of protective factors serving the whole child and the whole family. School coun-selors, social workers, and psychologists can help engender interest in and links between such diverse resources as businesses, retirees, faith-based communities, and social serv-ices. Relationship building is the connective tissue that allows the community to transform both adults and children, as they form reciprocal relationships and experience greater meaning and purpose in their lives.

Resourcing involves increasing support in four arenas. They include family, social systems, school–community, and external resourcing. Family resourcing centers on identifying individual and systemic strengths within the family that engender coping, improve day-to-day life, and reduce dysfunction. Social systems resourcing involves links between an individual or family in need and others within the context who provide support for education, socialization, psychological functioning, as well as concrete means of meeting basic needs. These systems influence attitudes, behavior, and expec-tations of family members and their other support systems. Social networks are described as moving outward from a center (the child) with family, school, neighbor-hood, community, and increasingly wider realms of networks (e.g., federal) in concen-tric circles around the center. These different levels can be interconnected through a counselor, social worker, or psychologist who brings together available offerings that converge to meet the needs of the child. Social network systems reduce family stress and increase protective factors.

Excluding family, friends, and relatives, school–community resourcing typically entails the teacher being the major support for the family around such issues as physical health challenges, child maltreatment, teen pregnancy, AOD, and gangs. As well, the school counselor, social worker, and psychologist may also be called upon to be part of the support system orchestrated by the teacher. Clearly, needs of families cross all variations of socioeconomic, race, religion, education, and family forms.

Last among the four types of resourcing, external resourcing helps families make links beyond typical types of resources available. Examples include social services, sup-port groups, psychological services (e.g. family therapy) external to school-community, volunteer organizations (e.g., Big Brothers/Big Sisters), as well as others available in the locale.

Case Example Related to Adult Child of an Alcoholic

The oldest of two boys, Harry is the child of an alcoholic father who was verbally abusive, uninvolved, and frequently inebriated on weekends. Most of the father's abuse, at times physical, was directed toward the mother. Harry often disappeared as the battles between his parents raged. When the noise quieted, he reappeared to comfort his mother, whose only source of emotional support came from Harry.

Harry's mother, in turn, spent all her energies on her children, reading to them when they were very young, taking them to the library weekly, and supporting them in their various interests. Harry's father interpreted any expression of anger, sadness, or disappointment as a sign of ingratitude.

As Harry grew up, he became involved in school, supported by teachers who encouraged him in his interests and in attending college. He also became involved in extracurricular activities in high school. Though he began "partying" at the age of 13, he didn't get into any real trouble. He was popular but also suffered from occasional bouts with despair and anger.

During college, Harry began to experiment with drugs and was close to being addicted by the time he was 20. At age 24 he entered therapy for his growing despair and depression. He did not quit using drugs until he was 26.

After graduating from college, Harry entered the field of business and met with success. Eventually he realized that he had other interests and pursued a different career path. At age 27 he began to work with adolescents from troubled families. For a number of years, he served as a youth counselor, then accepted a position teaching adolescents in a residential facility. As a resilient person, he can relate to his students and knows the pitfalls of low self-esteem and an external locus of control.

Questions

1. What are the dysfunctional structural characteristics of Harry's family of origin? How did you arrive at your hypotheses?

2. What behaviors demonstrate Harry's resilience? To what do you attribute these resilient behaviors in terms of personal, family, and school–community contexts?

3. From the standpoint of the job you hold or hope to hold in the future: If you had known Harry when he was young, what strategy would you have used, and what other people and other resources would combine in your work with him?

4. What might school personnel have done for Harry to avoid the cycle of despair initiated in college?

Case Example Related to Female With Diabetes

Nora, the younger of two children, is 11 and in sixth grade. At the age of 8, she was diagnosed with insulin-dependent diabetes. Her older brother, a senior in high school, was described as a model child. He played on the school football team, was an A student, and participated in student government. His plans for the future included attending college, and he already had received early acceptance notices from two colleges. In contrast, his 11-year-old sister Nora was viewed as a difficult child. Her grades were in the low-C range, with occasional Ds and Fs, despite testing that indicated an above-average IQ. Nora had few friends and was somewhat overweight.

During the current school year, Nora had been absent from school because of what she called "low blood sugars." At those times, the school nurse gave her orange juice or a protein snack after calling Nora's mother, a former nurse, to receive instructions.

Recently, Nora had been going to the clinic an average of three times per day. Needless to say, this time out of the classroom was contributing to her poor grades. When one of Nora's teachers contacted her mother about her missed work, the mother became indignant that the teacher would not agree to require less work of Nora because of her health problems and absences. The mother then called the school principal about the "unfair treatment" her daughter was receiving.

In response to the mother's phone call, the principal called a meeting of Nora's teachers. Based on information they received over the year, the team of Nora's five teachers and the principal observed the following about the family structure.

Dysfunctional Family Boundaries

The father, who owned his own business, worked long hours and was essentially unavailable for family time. He seemed to have a better relationship with his son than with Nora and regularly attended his son's football games. The mother had always been the backbone of this family's life. Prior to Nora's diagnosis of diabetes, she had been involved in both of her children's school lives and worked part-time as a tutor. At one time she was president of the booster club at her son's high school and led her daughter's Girl Scout troop.

After the diagnosis, Nora became this mother's mission in life. Nora no longer attended Girl Scouts. She said the other girls made fun of her because of her weight. The mother began to cook specific meals in an attempt to keep Nora's blood sugar in check. The mother quit her job to be available for monitoring her daughter's blood sugar.

Nora began to have tantrums at home when she did not get her way. The mother identified these outbursts as "high-blood-sugar attacks" and tried to calm Nora by giving her what she wanted.

While the mother became more involved with Nora, the father became more distant. He thought that the mother's approach to his daughter was "spoiling her" and "making her weak." The mother believed that her husband did not understand the medical implications of diabetes and thus could not provide sound judgments about managing Nora's behavior.

Overprotection

Prior to the diagnosis, Nora played on a soccer team along with her participation in Girl Scouts. Following her diagnosis, she quit both of these activities and began to spend more time at home. Her mother often allowed her to stay home from school at the slightest physical complaint. During the past 2 years Nora became less functional with peers and more dependent on her mother in all areas of her life. The mother's request to be called by the school nurse each time Nora's blood sugar was monitored exemplifies overprotection. The school nurse was highly trained in diabetes management, and Nora's blood sugar level often was found to be normal despite her complaints. The mother's attention to these "spells" reinforced Nora's dependence.

Lack of Conflict Resolution

Rather than Nora's parents' openly discussing their differing opinions, the mother had become more involved with protecting Nora and the father had become more involved with his business and ignored his daughter's complaints. Although the son may have resented the changes in his family related to their handling of his sister's illness, he had not expressed his feelings to either parent. He had adapted by becoming more involved in his own activities and life outside the home.

When Nora reported that her Girl Scout peers were "making fun of me," her mother allowed her to quit going to Scouts rather than help her reach some resolution in those relationships. The mother was reactive to any perceived mistreatment of her daughter by peers, teachers, bus drivers, or extended family members. Her way of managing her anger was to keep Nora out of school as often as possible, to drive Nora to school so she would not have to deal with the driver or students on the bus, to instruct Nora to avoid peer interactions, and to withdraw from extended family relationships. All of these choices indicated conflict avoidance rather than an attempt to resolve conflicts.

Parental Asymmetry

The mother had taken over sole management of Nora's life, while her father had withdrawn from interaction. The mother made all the significant decisions regarding the family's physical and emotional functioning. No one within the school system had spoken with or met the father. Although he was a respected businessman in the community, he had little influence over the day-to-day workings of his family.

Marital Relationship Subordinate to Parental Roles

Although the school personnel had little information about Nora's parents' relationship, they could hypothesize that it was not going well. The parents had not been out of the home together since Nora's diagnosis of diabetes, because Nora said she was too old for baby-sitters and her mother would not allow her to stay home alone out of fear of a blood-sugar crisis. The father's anger toward his wife may have stemmed from her unavailability to him resulting from overattention to their daughter, and the wife's anger was directed toward her husband because of his withdrawing from family life—contributing to significant tension and distance between the couple.

Questions and Comments

1. What are the dysfunctional characteristics of this girl's family? What information did you use to identify these dysfunctional components?

   This family displayed enmeshed boundaries between the mother and Nora and disengaged boundaries between the father and Nora. [Cite evidence.] The family also showed problems in conflict resolution, both within the family and in dealings with the outside world. [Cite evidence.]

   Nora's mother was extremely overprotective of her daughter following her diagnosis with diabetes. [Cite evidence.]

   Within the family, the parents avoided dealing with their basic differences in how to manage Nora. [Cite evidence.]

   Clearly, the balance of power of this couple was one-sided. [Cite evidence.]

2. What intervention strategies could the school and community use to help change this family's dysfunctional structure? If you perceive a possibility for referral, what might be mentioned to help reclaim overall family functioning? Develop your own ideas before reading the possibilities below.

   The team of Nora's teachers and the principal could request a meeting of both of Nora's parents with all of the school personnel involved with Nora. At this meeting, they might ask the mother, because of her nursing experience, to provide inservice education to all of them regarding diabetes, its management, and its complications. The teachers could ask specific questions about symptoms of low and high blood sugar to become comfortable in dealing with Nora in the classroom. [*Note the focus on family strengths.*]

   In addition, the teachers and school nurse could present an intervention plan to the parents to deal with Nora's frequent trips to the school clinic. Each time Nora would go to the clinic, her blood sugar could be monitored and the level recorded in a log to be sent home at the end of the day. Nora would carry the log with her at all times so when she would ask to leave a classroom, the teacher could check the log for the time of her most recent blood-sugar monitoring and the intervention.

   The parents would be asked to agree that monitoring Nora's blood sugar more often than once every 2 hours would not be necessary unless Nora were exhibiting severe physical symptoms. If Nora had asked to leave the classroom and she had been checked within the past 2 hours, her request could be refused. If Nora insisted that she was experiencing a "low," she could be given a container of orange juice, which each of her teachers would keep in the classroom.

   In addition, each time that Nora did visit the clinic, both parents would be called with a report on her blood-sugar monitoring. The father could be asked to carry a beeper so he could be reached at his office or while on outside calls.

The parents could be asked to agree that each night before Nora would go to bed, they would look over her blood-sugar log with her and discuss any questions. [*Note the effort to bring the parental dyad together to function as a team. Also note that this strategy places the hierarchy on equal footing so one parent does not have more power over the other.*]

The teachers could send home a weekly progress report for Nora in each subject. If Nora has a weekly average of B or above in any class, she would receive reinforcement from the teacher of each class in which she earned the B grade, as well as her parents. [*Note the emphasis on the positive rather than the negative for Nora to receive attention.*]

2. *How could the school involve the community in bringing greater balance and functioning within the family and normalizing Nora's health status? How could the brother's peripheral status be shifted and also help create better functioning within the overall family unit? Think about normalization and family functioning within the context of community and as a family unit.*

The father could contact the Girl Scout leader who replaced Nora's mother in the troop to which Nora had belonged and discuss the possibility of Nora's reentering the troop or, if no space was open, finding another Girl Scout troop for Nora to join. He would be the parent responsible for explaining the blood-sugar situation to the leader, along with the possibility of Nora's attention-seeking around having a "low." If his schedule could be open, he might be the one to pick up Nora after the weekly Girl Scout session. [*Note the use of the community resource of Girl Scouts and also the emphasis on reinvolving the father in an activity he would feel comfortable supporting, and at the same time "peeling the mother off" Nora. Also note that this reunites the split parental dyad to work as a unit.*]

Nora's brother and father could be assigned to engage in a fun activity one night a week, when just the two of them could be together. The son would pick the activity each week, and the father would find time in his schedule to be with his son. The father also would be given the community's Recreation and Parks schedule, with the suggestion that he might consider volunteering as an assistant coach for his son's team. [*Note the use of community resources, as well as the son's picking the activity, which gives him choices in family decision-making.*]

If the family is involved in a faith-based community, a recommendation could consider this resource—for example, in the popular retreats aimed at helping spouses rekindle their relationship.

Because Nora's brother is a good model for his sister in terms of functional behavior, he might be included in resolving his sister's situation. He might be asked to speak with his sister alone about how to meet challenges. And he might benefit from information about diabetes that would help in his interactions with his sister.

Extension Activities

Reading: Read children's and young adult literature depicting resilient at-risk and special-needs children and youth. Your librarian will be able to recommend online searches and library offerings.

Reflection/Journal on Reading: What has your reading shown you about children and youth who are resilient in spite of severe life circumstances and/or individual disposition, temperament, and ability? How could you use this literature with at-risk students?

In-Class/Training Discussion Based on Children's and Young Adult Literature: In the context of family life, can you glean anything from these stories about risk or resilience? In what ways do the stories point out environmental (socioeconomic and cultural) factors as causative factors for risk? Did any specific children in your experience come to mind? If so, what brought them to your attention?

Movies: Use the same structure described in the preceding activity with movies on DVD or video.

Adult Literature: Ask your librarian to recommend some adult books that demonstrate underlying resilience.

Reflection/Journal on Reading Adult Literature: What did you find the most surprising in the books you read? In what ways could you identify with the emotions of characters in the book? What lessons did you learn? Reflect on people you have known who impact others in similar ways. What about them might you wish to emulate to make a positive influence on children and youth facing risk factors?

In-Class/Training Discussion Based on Adult Literature, Professor/Trainer Instructions: If you assign the same book to every student/trainee, hold a whole-class/group discussion on the book. If you assign different books to different participants, divide them into smaller groups of five or six at the most, instruct them to have one person at a time briefly describe the book he or she read and pose questions such as, "How did protective factors in the major characters lead to resilience rather than hopelessness and dysfunction?

Guest Speaker(s), Professor/Trainer Instructions: Invite to a class or training session(s) an individual or individuals who have shown resiliency. Choose risk factors with which your group has the least experience (e.g., poverty). Beforehand, ask members of your group/class what they would like to learn from the speaker(s). Provide speakers with this information so they can reflect on the questions before they arrive to speak or serve on a panel. Also provide speakers with information about the class/group in terms of age, work experience, maturity level, gender composition, goals, and any other pertinent factors.

In-Class/Training Discussion: Reminisce about novels you have read that portray resilient individuals. Discuss factors that contributed to their resilience. Guide the group in considering resilience as a multidimensional characteristic rather than viewing it simplistically. When considering resilience, remind participants to look for contributions of the individual, the family, and the community.

Journal for those with prior professional experience: Reflect on past experiences you have had with families of students labeled for special education purposes. Using hindsight, view these families through a family systems lens. Then write about the kinds of dysfunction you now see these families having experienced. How do you think your new understanding will make a difference in your professional role in the future with similar family situations?

Journal for those with no prior professional experience: You may have read novels or biographies about individuals with disabilities. Consider one that presented enough information about families for you to use the family system lens to determine the types of dysfunction present. You may not find dysfunction, but at least look into and write about the areas described in chapters 2-4.

In-Class/Training Discussion for those without prior professional experience: Describe hypothetical examples of children identified for special education in relation to family boundary dysfunction, overprotection, lack of conflict resolution, and parental asymmetry and marital subsystem dysfunction (see chapters 2-4). It helps if examples include chronic illnesses, behavior disorders/social maladjustment, learning disabilities, and mental retardation.

In-Class/Training Discussion: How can school principals, counselors, social workers, and psychologists benefit from an understanding of family boundary dysfunction, overprotection, lack of conflict resolution, and parental asymmetry and marital subsystem dysfunction described in chapters 2-4?

PART THREE

Applications of Family Systems

Team Functioning and Family Involvement

What is a team? Briggs (1997) defined a team as "a group of individuals who are committed to a shared purpose, to each other, and to working together to achieve common goals" (p. 14). In considering the elements inherent in this definition, Briggs examined five aspects: individuals, shared purpose, commitment, goals, and uniqueness. Having diverse individuals on a team relating to school needs leads to an enriched experience for the student served. Each team member's experiences, personality, biases, and contributions become part of the rich mix that allows for greater gains by students and their families. A shared purpose promotes interdependence and is based on trust. Commitment leads to ownership, so the necessary investment of energy by team members will follow (Walther-Thomas, Korinek, & McLaughlin, 2005).

A team must have a goal or purpose, and that goal or purpose brings meaning to the group. Though goals change, the underlying mission or purpose must be what drives the team (Lawson & Sailor, 2005). A unique identity evolves within a team as the members work together. They form their own subculture within the organization with operating norms and shared values evolving over time.

Team Approaches

Three different team approaches for working with students with special needs are commonly referred to in the literature: multidisciplinary, interdisciplinary, and transdisciplinary teams (Cloninger, 2004; Friend, 2005; Gargiulo, 2006). Because most school programs for students with special needs use one of these three models, or a variation, it is helpful to have an overview of all three. When working with more than one program, two or perhaps all three of the descriptions may be applicable.

A Multidisciplinary Team Approach

In the multidisciplinary model, professionals from various disciplines, such as education, psychology, occupational therapy, and art therapy, each work individually with the child/youth or family. That is, the professionals work in isolation from one another as they evaluate children/youth and provide services. The multidisciplinary model was originally developed to serve patients with medical problems that could be relegated to one discipline, and it is still used in this way today (Cloninger, 2004). In this approach, the different professionals working with the same patient often do not even regard themselves as part of a team. The professionals from the various disciplines share reports, but the lack of coordination across disciplines results in conflicting and inconsistent information that is difficult to implement.

In the multidisciplinary approach, coordinating services to an individual student can be difficult. A major disadvantage of this model is its potential for failing to consider the whole child. Another disadvantage is that two or more professionals can make conflicting recommendations. For example, a therapist may encourage parents who are overly involved in their child's education to back off, while the school counselor might be involving parents in a home–school behavior management program. When the professionals from the different disciplines meet, sorting through their recommendations can be complicated. In some schools, multidisciplinary team members provide their different recommendations and then leave the teacher to sort through their ideas and implement suggestions. Gargiulo (2006) considers the multidisciplinary model for teams to be the least collaborative, least cooperative, least coordinated, and least integrative of the three models.

Interdisciplinary Team Approach

The interdisciplinary team approach is considered more sophisticated and interdependent than the multidisciplinary model (Briggs, 1997; Cloninger, 2004; Friend, 2005; Morsink, Thomas, & Correa, 1991). The interdisciplinary model provides a formal structure that allows interaction and communication among team members. In this approach, each professional does his or her own assessment and implementation, but the group makes programming decisions. With interdisciplinary teams, the outcome is accomplished only through an interactive effort with all disciplines involved in the contributions (Fordyce, 1981). According to Gargiulo (2006), planning is more collaborative in the interdisciplinary team than the multidisciplinary team, but implementation is isolated. He provides the example of physical therapy and other direct services being provided in isolation under the interdisciplinary team approach.

Gargiulo (2006) considers the interdisciplinary model to be more collaborative, cooperative, coordinated, and integrative than the multidisciplinary team model. Nevertheless, it is subject to a number of the same disadvantages. Decisions are affected by the orientation of each professional and, therefore, may result in disjointed outcomes for students. The difficulties inherent in group interaction also can cause problems.

Bennett (1982) stated that "parents may become confused, rather than enlightened, by the interdisciplinary process if sufficient care is not taken to coordinate and synthesize the numerous professional evaluations" (p. 313). He suggested several other problems, too, such as turf issues, differences in assessment approaches and management strategies, and the discouragement of strong, effective leadership if one discipline views leadership attempts as arrogant. .

Transdisciplinary Team Approach

In discussing early intervention teams for children with special needs, Briggs (1997, p. 94) described four key components of the transdisciplinary model:

1. Many disciplines are involved in the delivery of services.
2. Collaborating to reach a consensus for a decision is standard practice. All members help to plan and monitor intervention even if they are not involved directly in the service delivery. Each member of the team is committed to learning from the others, as well as teaching others.
3. Family members are essential to the team. They choose how involved they wish to be in assessment, planning, implementation, and evaluation. Training of family members varies, based on need and over time. The ultimate authority to make decisions resides with family members.
4. A designated team member is in charge of the child so families are not intruded upon too frequently. The role of the coordinator of care is to incorporate team decisions and integrate the goals of other disciplines into a treatment program. A family member may choose to serve in this role, or one member of the team may be assigned this task.

Others have included these key components in essentially the same way (Cloninger, 2004; O'Toole & Switlick, 1997).

The transdisciplinary team model presents challenges in coordinating services. For example, some professionals have trouble with the notion of training other team members to implement procedures that they consider to be their own areas of expertise. Referred to as *role release* (Cloninger, 2004), it can result in interpersonal challenges for professionals serving children/youth. For example, if a counselor is required to train a parent to implement a program, the counselor might feel demeaned when the parent is seen as capable of implementing a program that the counselor had to earn a master's degree to learn.

The transdisciplinary model has a feature called integrated therapy, wherein therapy services become integrated within education. For students under alternative assessment and standards, therapy goals are integrated within educational goals on individualized education programs (IEPs). This feature is based on the assumption that therapists and teachers work together in program assessment, planning, and delivery (Rainforth, York, & Macdonald, 1992). The integrated therapy model generally focuses on students with severe disabilities but is meaningful for all professionals. Gargiulo (2006) views the transdisciplinary team model as the most collaborative, cooperative, coordinated, and integrative of the three team models.

Benefits to parents abound (Orelove, 1995). Foremost is that family members are treated with respect and decide for themselves how much they want to be involved in the decision making. Further, the family can turn to a single professional on the team, usually a special educator, who serves as a synthesizer of information, for answers to their questions. Thus, parents do not have to contact each team member to understand something about their child's education. In addition, the new information and skills the family members gain as part of the team help them better understand their child's behavior and learning.

Orelove (1995) also noted that students benefit from more appropriate solutions and support, which draw from the diverse backgrounds of the team members; the team's holistic view of the learner, which results in a more cohesive approach to working with the student; more humanistic means of dealing with challenging behaviors; and an integrated therapy that preserves the continuity of learning, focuses on naturally occurring activities, and yields more effective results.

Familiarity with the three models described here is useful for all professionals working within or collaborating with the schools in relation to at-risk and special-needs children/youth. Some professionals work with different school systems operating under different models, and others move to new jobs that use a different team model than that of their previous school. Others work with a student who has transferred into the school from a system that used a different model. Understanding how decisions were made and implemented in the previous system is vital to working effectively with the student and his or her family, so they can understand the differences and know what to expect in the new school system.

Educational Team Members

Various people contribute to the educational team process. Frequently, the members work together for the benefit of a student receiving special education in the general classroom or a special education setting (e.g., resource room, self-contained class). Team members exchange their theories, philosophies, beliefs, experiences, and skills. At-risk students are often the focus of the child study team described later in this chapter. Differences of opinion among team members are expected and are beneficial when viewed as contributing to a whole picture rather than as competing with other members' perspectives. The following discussion is about the people who serve on various educational teams. To best meet the needs of children, each team member must gain an understanding of the other members' roles, beliefs, knowledge, and skills.

Family Members

Referring to the 1997 amendments to IDEA, Turnbull and Turnbull (2000) stated that a major reason for these amendments to IDEA was to expand the opportunities for partnerships between parents and agency staff. When the team did not reach agreement, the public agency made the decision, but the agency "must consider parents' concerns and the information parents have provided in making any decisions" (p. 306). Schools were required to provide parents with their child's records, and the public agency was required to keep these records confidential. As well, parents would be allowed to challenge the contents of their child's records.

Since then, IDEA 2004 acquired a new name but not a new acronym. IDEA is now known officially as the Individuals with Disabilities Education Improvement Act and includes changes regarding family involvement. IDEA 2004, aligned with the No Child Left Behind Act (NCLB) of 2001, is a civil rights law that emphasizes *rights as well as responsibilities*. Turnbull (2005) stated, "By imposing new or strengthened accountability expectations on students with disabilities and their parents, the reauthorized IDEA conveys a message about personal responsibilities" (p. 320). He went on to say that shared responsibility for the education of students with disabilities now means that the student and parents "must take more responsibility for their own behavior and for their relationships with the SEAs and LEAs" (p. 320).

Gargiulo (2006) indicated that, over time, the field has evolved and professionals now refer to *family members* rather than simply *parents* because other relatives often are deeply involved in the growth and development of a child/youth. IDEA, however, continues to refer only to parents. Beyond parents' legal rights to participate in assessment and planning, schools should invite parents *and* other family members to participate, and schools should view family members as competent to provide information and suggestions (Chen & Miles, 2004; Friend, 2005).

Some parents do not choose to attend team meetings even when invited. School personnel should keep in mind that parents vary in how much they would like to, or are able to, participate. Recognizing and responding to the differing preferences shows respect for parents and other family members.

The Student

In earlier times school systems overlooked the student as a potential contributor to the team (Brendtro & Bacon, 1994). With the emphasis on personal involvement in growth processes (Field, 1996), students became members of teams more frequently. In 1991, the U.S. Department of Education funded a project on self-determination by individuals with disabilities. This was followed in 1993 with funds for research on self-determination. Walther-Thomas, Korinek, and McLaughlin (2005) offer ways to provide support structures for students to be successful and contribute to their education. Turnbull and Turnbull (2000) stated that parents and students have a right "to be included in the decision-making process.... This means the schools must structure the statewide and local decision-making process in such a way that parents and students have opportunities to meaningfully affect the education they are receiving" (p. 342).

Test and colleagues (2004) reviewed the literature relating to increasing involvement of students in IEPs and concluded that students with disabilities can be active in the IEP process. Generally, elementary school students do not attend team meetings. Secondary-level students are more likely to provide useful input about their educational programs and realistic and accurate information about family considerations. In a heart-rending commentary, Greer (1989) described his mistake of not including a secondary student as a team member or asking for her input about the service delivery model used. Years later the student told him how much she wished he had left her in a special education classroom rather than placing her in general education. Turnbull and Turnbull (2001) encouraged involvement by students and referred to person-centered planning to enhance the quality of life of those with developmental disabilities. Chapters 12 and 13 offer further discussion of students' involvement during meetings and conferences.

The Teacher

The general education teacher has the primary responsibility for the education of at-risk and special-needs children and youth (Turnbull, Turnbull, Shank, Smith, & Leal, 2002). As Turnbull and colleagues pointed out, many people mistakenly think special education necessarily requires instruction by a special education teacher in a special education classroom. To the contrary, the implications of IDEA are that almost all teachers will collaborate with others when working with students who have special needs.

From their observations of students within and outside the classroom, general educators can develop concrete descriptions on which the team can build a realistic picture and base its recommendations. Team members' suggestions are filtered through the general education teacher's lens for practicality. If a student is determined to be eligible for special education, the general educator can provide critical information on the student's strengths and needs that then can be used to develop a realistic IEP (Gargiulo, 2006). As Levine (2002) recommended, teachers can learn about and contribute to descriptions of a student's neurodevelopmental functions with the strengths and challenges made clear.

The Special Educator

The special education teacher is responsible for teaching students with special needs who have been found eligible for special education or related services. The special educator also serves as a liaison between the student's family and the school system. Serving as a member or coordinator of a team of professionals working with the student, the special educator has a unique role in the education of students with special needs. The special educator is an advocate for the student and provides expertise in a specialized field or fields of education. The special educator also offers recommendations for modifying the curriculum or testing and makes suggestions for individual strategies for teaching the student (Friend, 2005).

This team member is helpful during prereferral meetings when educators are investigating the challenges faced by at-risk students and the strategies that work best for each. Special educators can offer suggestions for general education teachers that allow students at risk for failure to succeed in the general classroom.

The Paraprofessional/Paraeducator

The paraprofessional/paraeducator, or teacher's aide, can play an important role in the education of students with special needs. Too often, school professionals do not recognize the wisdom of paraprofessionals. Some paraprofessionals are in classes to support behavioral intervention programs that are too complex or time consuming for the general teacher to employ. Paraprofessionals may serve temporarily until the intervention program is stepped down in terms of requirements on the teacher's time. Giangreco and Doyle (2005) argue that paraprofessionals in special education have more responsibility than their training and pay warrants, but their presence on the team remains valuable.

Chopra and colleagues (2004) used the focus group format to interview 49 paraprofessionals and determine the perception of their roles. Because paraprofessionals often live in the community of the school in which they serve, they are able to provide cultural and linguistic context. These paraprofessionals saw themselves as *connectors* between teacher and parent, student and teacher, student and peers, student and parents, families and community services, as well as students and curriculum.

Werts, Harris, Tillery and Roark (2004) investigated parents' perception of the role of "paraeducator." They found that parents were pleased with the role of the paraeducator in the life of their child with special needs and hoped that they would receive further training, be treated as valued members of the educational team, and be present at IEP and parent meetings. The authors predicted that as a result of the No Child Left Behind legislation, which came into effect after they had concluded their research, the "highly qualified" requirement will impact the role of paraeducators in the future.

Katsiyannis, Hodge, and Lanford (2000) looked at legal issues relating to the use of paraeducators in special education and called for the Departments of Education in each state to develop qualifications for the training of paraeducators. French (2001) found that few teachers were prepared to supervise paraprofessionals. The teachers seldom were involved in selecting the paraprofessional but were in charge of evaluating the paraprofessional and relied heavily on oral versus written instruction. Wallace, Shin, Bartholomay, and Stahl (2001) identified competencies that teachers should have to supervise paraprofessionals. Giangreco, Edelman, and Broer (2003) studied paraeducators' use of a planning process and found that the process helped teams in assessing, prioritizing, and developing and implementing action plans. Clearly, the impact of the requirement of "qualified" staff (IDEA 2004) when working with children in special education will impact the hiring and training of paraprofessionals/paraeducators in the future.

The School Psychologist

In most schools, the psychologist functions as an evaluator of students' intellectual and emotional abilities. During the assessment, psychologists measure the student's cognitive and affective functioning level to determine whether the student meets eligibility requirements for certain services in special education. They also present findings to family members (Friend, 2005).

In addition to these responsibilities, school psychologists may be called upon to assess the student's strengths, learning style, or problem-solving approaches (Sheridan, Warnes,

Cowan, Schemm, & Clarke, 2004). Some researchers have suggested that testing of this nature should be requested only if the teacher cannot make educational program decisions without it. In such cases, the teacher should provide the psychologist with a statement of the presenting problem in the form of a question whose answer will lead to effective instruction of the student being referred (Moran, 1978). Suzuki and Kugler (1995) focused on cultural bias, stressing the importance of knowing the background of the student being assessed.

Many school psychologists have assumed the role of helping to develop behavioral strategies to use in the school or at home. Some psychologists also are trained to work with families regarding issues of grief and loss. Increasingly, psychologists are receiving training in family systems models so they can assist in interventions that consider the whole family system rather than just the individual student. Christenson (2004, p. 83) recommended that school psychologists make the family–school partnership a priority for children's academic, social, and emotional learning. That fits well with a family systems approach in schools. As well, professionals in community settings interact with the school psychologist on teams or, less formally, with professionals in schools as well as in private contexts (e.g., clinical psychologist, adolescent psychologist).

The School Counselor

School counselors provide some of the same services as school psychologists, depending upon their training and the needs of the school system. Some school districts have counselors in every elementary building and more than one counselor in each secondary school. Different from most of the team members, school counselors work with all students, not just those presenting challenges. They provide lessons to whole classes and are the "problem solvers of the school" (Friend, 2005).

As part of the educational team, school counselors often provide input on family matters or diagnostic information gleaned from being in classrooms with students or from one-to-one interactions. Counselors are being trained increasingly in family systems concepts and thus are able to provide interventions reflecting the family unit (Bryan, 2005; Milsom, 2002; Mullis & Edwards, 2001). They also may provide input on current group process opportunities in the school. For example, the counselor may lead a group for students who need follow through after in-patient substance abuse treatment or a group for students whose parents are divorcing.

The Educational Diagnostician

Some school systems employ educational diagnosticians—usually experienced special educators who have received additional training, some licensed by their state. They assess students' academic abilities and achievement and provide essential information on which team members rely. Diagnosticians administer formal, standardized measures as well as informal tests of academic functioning. They often engage in trial teaching to determine the method by which the student learns best. Educational diagnosticians work one-to-one with students who have learning challenges, attempting to determine areas of strengths on which the teacher can depend for sound instruction, as well as areas of dysfunction to avoid in designing the individual program of education. In addition, they may work directly on weaknesses in need of remediation.

The School Social Worker

The school social worker frequently is the person on the team who is most familiar with family matters (Newsome, 2005). He or she serves as a family advocate with extensive training in the realm of family functioning. The social worker is also most familiar with community resources that might benefit at-risk students and students with special needs and their families. The school counselor may become aware of an issue with a student that requires family intervention and choose to involve the school social worker. At times, the school social worker and counselor collaborate on a student/family situation. Although well trained in family concerns, social workers may have little training with the family systems concepts presented in this book.

Under IDEA, social work is considered to be a related service. The social worker often is appointed to coordinate services among the community, school, and home. Minnard (2002) highlighted the importance of protective factors in schools and of the

> redesign of existing resources for an integrated effort to improve youth outcomes. Schools built on a foundation of protective factors provide students with the highest security and greatest chance for success. (p. 233)

Evidence-based practice in social work within schools is seen as essential to provide the highest quality of services (Raines, 2004).

Because social workers intersect the domains of community and school, they are the logical professionals to delve into school–community violence and bullying (covered in chapter 9). Professionals espousing positive behavior support (PBS) have advocated for the use of systemwide, or schoolwide, interventions that deter violence in schools and provide a systemic schoolwide approach to prevent or ameliorate behavioral challenges such as bullying and violence (McCurdy, Mannella, & Eldridge, 2003; Scott, 2001; Warren et al., 2003). Social workers can collaborate with those trained in PBS to create positive schools and communities in which children and youth develop self-discipline and responsibility for self and others.

The Administrator

The administrator is responsible for policy and decision making, as well as implementation in matters of placement, transportation, related services, equipment, and scheduling. Educational administrators are responsible for ensuring compliance with regulations. In some school systems, administrators head prereferral and eligibility teams. Lawson and Sailor (2005) stated, "The principal helps other educators and service providers appreciate the need for parents and families to be supported." (p. 557). Administrators who sit on teams include principals, program directors or specialists, and special education coordinators (Cloninger, 2004).

Administrators can free up material, time, personnel, and financial resources, thereby facilitating the implementation of programs and related services for students with special needs. To facilitate effective family interventions, administrators must have some background in family systems concepts. Administrators have unilateral action around many disciplinary situations for students who receive special education. When writing a behavior intervention plan, in conducting a manifestation determination, or in situations involving long-term suspension or expulsion, however, administrators cannot act unilaterally (Yell & Shriner, 2005, p. 56). In the case of a child in special education, the IEP team assumes ultimate responsibility.

The School Nurse

The school nurse frequently is the team member with the most realistic information on the physical health of students with health impairments. DePaepe, Garrison-Kane, and Doelling (2005) stated, "The increase in percentage of students who have health problems that adversely affect their educational performance has been greater than any other eligibility category since 1990. During 1999–2000, 26% of children in early childhood special education received medication" (p. 432).

Among other areas, nurses are trained to deal with first aid, emergencies, seizures, medication, allergies, asthma, diabetes, HIV/AIDS, sickle cell anemia, and cystic fibrosis, as well as to provide information on hygiene and diet. With an emphasis on schools as a hub of the community (Guthrie & Guthrie, 1993) and on the development of full-service schools (Dryfoos, 1994) that provide wrap-around services (Fowler & Corley, 1996; Scott & Eber, 2003), school nurses are critical players in the education of children and youth. The community–school emphasis stems from children not receiving the medical services they need (Allen, Brown, & Finlay, 1992; Harvard Family Research Project, 1995) and professionals in human services looking for creative means to meet their needs.

Other Specialists

A variety of other specialists may be included on teams for students with special needs. For example, physicians can provide input on health and medication (Cloninger, 2004) and screen for common medical problems. Although few physicians attend team meetings, they often provide valuable input by phone or written communication. Physicians vary widely in their ability to deal with school-related problems (Levine, 1982, 2002). As early as 1982, Bennett underscored an increasing involvement of physicians on interdisciplinary teams. Morsink, Thomas, and Correa (1991) saw the role of the physician as primarily a consultant to the team.

Most beneficial is ongoing communication between the physician and the staff at the school, whether the physician attends meetings or provides input to be used in team meetings. DePaepe, Garrison-Kane, and Doelling (2005) consider input from the personal physician important so the school nurse can most effectively coordinate services for the student. They related the American Academy of Pediatrics (1990) emphasis on collaboration for student health services.

Depending on the need, occupational or physical therapists are included on the team for a student with special needs. Occupational therapists work with fine-motor skill development, including skills such as buttoning, zipping, writing, and typing. They also work with students with severe physical impairments on daily living skills such as eating with utensils.

Physical therapists assist students who have more severe physical disabilities. Physical therapists work with gross-motor skill development, including walking, balancing, skipping, playing ball, relaxing, and general coordination. Certainly when consideration of related services is part of the discussion, a professional providing the service being considered should be present at the team meeting.

Team Functioning During Educational Touchpoints

T. Berry Brazelton (1992), a well-known American pediatrician, discussed specific situations that offer parents and children opportunities to deepen their relationships. Likewise, meeting the educational needs of at-risk and special-needs learners involves several touchpoints, though most students will not go through all of them. Touchpoints are times for strengthening parent and child relationships as well as parent–professional relationships. Educational touchpoints, discussed below, include screening, prereferral, referral and assessment, eligibility and individualized educational programs.

Screening

Screening involves routine tests such as group achievement or intelligence tests, as well as screening tests for vision and hearing. Turnbull, Turnbull, Shank, Smith, and Leal (2002) explained that

> screening helps school staff identify whether a student is having difficulties because of some mild or "invisible" impairments, whether a student so identified may benefit from still further evaluation, and whether there may be other causes for the student's difficulties. (p. 45)

Screening can result in selecting students at risk for difficulty in school and is the domain of the general education classroom teacher with assistance from the nurse (i.e., hearing, vision) or school system personnel assigned to conduct screening tests. When a student has a problem in school, whether the problem is academic, organizational, or behavioral, the teacher should be concerned. Although solutions will vary according to the nature of the problem, understanding the cause of the problem is crucial to the resolution of all problems. Understanding the cause requires careful and systematic exploration of the student's performance, behavior, prior school experiences, developmental age, disability, and family life.

Because the classroom teacher has the responsibility for the student's education, he or she is the appropriate person to begin exploring most problems (Friend, 2005). Classroom teachers also have the most knowledge of, and experience with, the students in their classrooms. The teacher has the opportunity to observe the student in a variety of situations and thus is able to make decisions that are more sound than those based on a brief observation under nonclassroom conditions. The teacher also has the opportunity to observe the child across the whole day and week, which is particularly helpful for tracking and understanding underlying family problems. For example, the teacher might observe that Mondays are particularly stressful for a student and wonder what occurs on the weekend at home.

Wise teachers involve the family in determining the cause of a problem they observe. Family members often have observed the problem that is showing up in school and should be consulted when their child's learning suffers. The teacher can approach parents in a way that does not alarm them but, instead, invites them to help wrestle with the challenge they are facing together. The involvement of parents is particularly helpful to the achievement of at-risk children (Slavin, Madden, Dolan, & Wasik, 1996). Kenneth Leithwood (1997) corroborated the relationship between achievement and parental involvement in their child's education.

Perhaps most important, the teacher is responsible for creating positive change by applying the information gathered during the screening process. The teacher analyzes problems and attempts interventions based on the analysis. He or she carefully documents these interventions for future use if the need arises. When changes or interventions attempted by a teacher do not produce results, or if the teacher runs out of solutions, it is time to ask for assistance from a team of other professionals and continue to involve the family.

Prereferral—Teacher and Student Assistance Teams

In most school systems, committees or teams operate more or less formally to help teachers who need assistance with at-risk or special-needs students. This is called teacher collaboration or consultation, and the prereferral team has been termed Teacher Assistance Team, Student Assistance Team, Instructional Support Team, and Schoolwide Assistance Team (Buck, Polloway, Smith-Thomas, & Cook, 2003). Another term is instructional assistance team, or IAT. Gargiulo (2006) stated that these teams

> call for collaboration between general educators and other professionals for the express purpose of developing creative, alternative instructional and/or management strategies designed to accommodate the particular needs of the learner. (p. 60)

The prereferral step is *not* the beginning of the special education process. The purpose of the teacher and student assistance team is to help the teacher and student solve specific problems that led to the request for assistance. This team assists the teacher and student by analyzing information and suggesting possible modifications (Buck, Polloway, Smith-Thomas, & Cook, 2003; Carter & Sugai, 1989; Switlick, 1997). Modifications may include involving family members or providing family members with training. Chapter 12 includes more extensive information about teams that assist teachers early in the process of identifying challenges and discusses family involvement in those teams.

At one time professionals viewed all problems as deficits within the student. Today, most professionals recognize the importance of context. In the classroom the student is influenced by variables such as teaching style and organizational arrangement. But it is difficult for teachers to judge the effects of these variables on the achievement and behavior of a given student. Also, different students respond differently to the same teaching techniques and behavior management strategies. When academic troubles or inappropriate student behaviors arise, adaptations in instruction, different management strategies, or fresh strategies in the home may reduce the problem. Members of the teacher/student assistance team are viewed as consultants whose aim is to help the classroom teacher and student devise strategies for overcoming learning or behavior problems.

Effective communication is critical. Professionals will not take family members by surprise if they have kept the family continually informed or involved as team members. In addition, family members are a valuable source of information about their child. When a student's performance varies noticeably between contexts such as home and school, the teacher should examine potential causes of that discrepancy. Also, family members sometimes suggest the very intervention that the teacher successfully adopts, which precludes the need to refer and assess a student.

Sometimes prereferral does not result in improved learning or behavior on the part of the child/youth. If the problem is substantive, the next stage may be referral and assessment for special education and related services. It should be noted that not all students who are referred have received the service of a teacher and student assistance team.

Referral and Assessment

Students and their families may enter special education by the process of referral and assessment. The potential for a positive experience increases if all professionals handle this process in a sensitive and efficient manner, respectful of family members' contributions as well as their fears and apprehensions. Professionals must keep in mind that families likely will feel vulnerable at this touchpoint.

The classroom teacher develops the referral for special education. He or she communicates the student's status, reports prior interventions, specifies the referral question, and prepares the student for referral. The referral question (Suzuki & Kugler, 1995) asks what the teacher would like to determine from the assessment process that will follow. An example of a referral question is: "Would Harry benefit from remedial instruction in reading?"

After the referral is made, the building administrator ensures that parents are informed of their rights and that they consent, in writing, to the assessment. Consent to the evaluation does not constitute consent for placement in special education or related services (Turnbull, 2005). Parental consent for placement and/or related services must be taken up at a different time than consent to evaluate (Turnbull & Turnbull, 2000). Reevaluation also requires parental consent, unless, after reasonable attempts to obtain parental consent, the parents have failed to respond to the request to reevaluate. The building administrator also must ensure that appropriate assessment is conducted by qualified professionals and that the instruments used are free from cultural bias.

School districts must provide written information, called procedural safeguards, to parents regarding their legal rights. Professionals should review that information to ensure that it is clear enough for the parents to understand. All parents must receive such information before giving consent for assessment. School professionals should obtain and read a copy of the procedural safeguards and find out who has the responsibility for providing this information to parents, as that responsibility varies from one school system to another.

Further, parents must be provided with a description of any action to be taken with their child, the rationale for that action, and alternatives proposed by the school. At this point in the referral and assessment process, the proposed action is to determine whether a disability exists and, if so, what types of individual programming would be most appropriate. Next, parents must be informed about assessment procedures, data, and other information that will be used to decide whether to continue the assessment. Names and purposes of tests that will most likely be used are helpful for parents.

The team conducting the assessment includes

- parents of the student being considered for special education;
- one or more general education teachers of the student being considered for special education, if the student is or may be in general education;
- one or more teachers of special education;
- a qualified representative of the school system who provides or supervises instruction to special-needs students, and who knows about availability of resources in the school system;
- if no member can interpret the instructional implications of the assessment process, someone capable of doing so;
- any other individuals with special expertise, such as those who provide related services; and
- when appropriate, the student.

Following the assessment, parents must be provided with the information that the committee used to reach a decision to refer their child. The information must include the "student's involvement and progress in the general curriculum, or for preschoolers, in appropriate activities" (Yell & Shriner, 2005, p. 31). As well, behavior in the school context, peer relationships, and health status are usually described.

Eligibility Questions and IEPs for Special Education

After the formal assessment of the student is completed and the evaluation reports that interpret the assessment results are written, the team makes three decisions (Friend, 2005). They must answer three questions:

1. Does the student have a disability?
2. Does the disability adversely affect the education performance of the child/youth?
3. Can the needs of the student be met through special education?

Team Membership

The team answering these questions must include the parents of the child with a disability and, when appropriate, the student. Parents "must be afforded an opportunity to participate in any group meeting where decisions may be made with respect to the identification, evaluation, placement, or provision of FAPE [free appropriate public education] to the child" (Turnbull & Turnbull, 2000, p. 142).

Guidelines regarding student membership on teams vary across states and localities. Guterman (1995) investigated high school students receiving learning disabilities services in separate classrooms and found that, although the students did not view the special education classroom as efficacious, they valued it because of the unresponsive system in general education. Student involvement in making decisions about their education can be helpful.

According to IDEA (2004), if the child is or may be participating in general education, no fewer than one general education teacher of the student is required to be on the team, thereby assuring general education involvement in developing the IEP. No fewer than one teacher of special education or, where appropriate, no fewer than one special education provider of the child must be a member of the IEP team. A representative of the school system also must be a member of the team, along with a professional capable of interpreting instructional implications of results from the assessment. Related services personnel serve at the discretion of the school system or parent. Other individuals with special knowledge and expertise about the student also may be team members. For example, nurses are valuable on the team when the student has education-related health needs.

Determination of Eligibility for Special Education and Related Services

In examining the results and interpretations of the various professionals who have evaluated the student, the team must answer the three questions that Friend (2005) proposed—whether the student has a disability, whether a disability adversely affects the educational performance of the child/youth, and whether the student's needs can be met through special education.

Consideration of whether the student has a disability must be discerned based on state and local education specifications in line with federal law. Reviewing the assessment and evaluation data, the team makes a collective judgment about whether the student has a disability as specified by IDEA. More than test scores must be taken into consideration in determining eligibility. Also, if the learning problem exists because of lack of instruction or lack of proficiency in English usage, the student is not eligible for special education. These aspects were added to the amendments because of the large number of students identified as having a learning disability. With the reauthorization of IDEA, these requirements remain intact, and in an effort to reduce overidentification of students with learning disabilities, IDEA 2004 removes the former identification process of showing a discrepancy between achievement and ability as reason for classification as LD.

The second question—whether the disability adversely affects the student's education performance—must also be answered. If a student has a disability but has treatment (e.g., medication) that controls the disability, the student's disability does not adversely affect his or her educational performance. The school nurse and the general education teacher, however, will have to be sure that the student receives the required medication if it has to be administered during the school day. IDEA 2004 added that the student's response to the intervention could be part of the eligibility process and positive results from the intervention would result in the student's not being eligible for special education under IDEA.

The third question—whether the student's needs can be met through special education and related services—allows the final decisions to be made. Typically, students who go through prereferral and move into the referral/assessment/eligibility and IEP phases of the process can have their special needs met. IDEA 2004 allows a maximum of 15% of funds to be used for prereferral interventions, and they may in fact demonstrate that special education is not necessary.

If the team decides that a student has a disability that requires special education, the committee must identify the disability and recommend what, if any, services are required. These recommendations relate to the educational and other related services that the student needs if he or she is to receive an education appropriate to his or her learning needs and abilities. Parents should be invited to all meetings involving these questions and decisions. Placement decisions are made by the IEP committee, and consideration must be given with parental input, as well as within the least restrictive environment with "documentation of the extent to which a student's educational program matches that provided to nondisabled students and addresses the goals and standards of the district and state" (Yell & Shriner, 2005; p. 37).

Individualized Education Program

The individualized education program (IEP) is the cornerstone of educational programming for students with disabilities. It is the vehicle used to develop programs that provide free and appropriate educational experiences for each of these students. The 1997 amendment emphasizes the participation of general education teachers and "reflects the emphasis on general curricular involvement found throughout IDEA" (Yell & Shriner, 2005; p. 33). Since the 1997 amendment, a psychologist has not been required to be a member of the team, and an individual who can interpret the instructional implications of the assessment process is required and may be a teacher or other member of the committee.

The IEP team is considered to be the proper place for considering placement decisions (Turnbull & Turnbull, 2000). Only when the student's participation in the general curriculum with supplemental support and services will not benefit the student can removal to a different setting or curriculum be considered. Thus, those involved in planning the IEP must begin their deliberations with the general curriculum as the preferred course of study for all students.

In terms of present level of performance, IDEA 2004 changed the terminology from "educational performance" to "academic achievement and functional performance." This change clarifies and expands what is a more narrowly designed focus of the program. The term "general curriculum," previously used, became "general education curriculum" with the same focus on academics as in NCLB.

In the past, IEPs included "specific, measurable annual goals and accompanying short-term objectives or benchmarks...developed for each area of need" (Gartin & Murdick, 2005, p. 327). IDEA 2004 removed the short-term objectives/benchmarks for each of the annual goals and replaced them with academic and functional goals. The purpose of this change was to reduce paperwork and underscore academics by aligning with NCLB. Also to reduce paperwork, schools are now required to include in their progress reports "progress the child is making toward meeting the annual goals." The term "sufficient" was removed as a descriptor of progress. At the same time, students who have alternative assessment procedures must have IEPs that include short-term objectives aligned with alternative achievement standards (Smith, Polloway, Patton, & Dowdy, 2006). Chapter 13 includes more information on IEPs, with a focus on families.

In sum, providing the best educational opportunities for the student requires careful planning and implementation of the team process. Without such consideration, the team would not be able to function effectively and student needs would not be met. The prereferral process relates to both at-risk and special-needs students, whereas the referral and assessment, placement, and IEP processes pertain to special-needs students.

Planning and Implementing the Team Process

Four primary factors are important to effective planning and implementation of team process:

1. Clarity of purpose and vision are critical to productive team functioning.
2. Smoothly functioning teams must employ effective task behaviors (e.g., giving information, summarizing) and maintenance behaviors (e.g., encouraging, harmonizing).
3. Leadership is best when it is shared, and the chairperson is most effective when assuming a democratic style.
4. The involvement of all team members is critical to effective team functioning.

Clarity and Unity of Purpose and Shared Vision

Groups that work together effectively perform as a collection of individuals with clarity of purpose and goals (Larson & LaFasto, 1989). A shared vision (Senge, 1990) is described as one of five requirements in successful organizational life. When a school team knows why inclusive education is important and uses collaborative processes to achieve this goal, they are sharing a vision that its members clearly understand and embrace (Walther-Thomas, Korinek, & McLaughlin, 2005). Lawson and Sailor (2005) focused on unity of purpose as being "grounded in an understanding of interdependent relationships, and it is a unique feature of collaboration" (p. 541). They see professionals who are interdependent as sharing concern and expertise in a holistic way that systemically focuses on the child and family.

Teams to help learners with special needs usually meet to plan or review educational or behavioral programs. For the at-risk student, the team meetings are usually oriented toward problem solving. The following are typical activities in planning meetings that require clarity and unity of purpose and shared vision:

- Meeting in a collaborative setting to problem-solve
- Meeting before a referral to review information and provide suggestions

- Reviewing referrals for special education services
- Deciding whether a student is eligible for special education
- Determining placement options
- Considering related services
- Developing an IEP
- Annually reviewing a student's educational program
- Reevaluating

Awareness of the activity to be conducted allows team members to know their purpose from the beginning, and clarity of purpose improves team functioning (Garner, 1994).

Task and Maintenance Behaviors

Any behavior of a team member that supports the team's purpose can be classified according to its basic function. Team members speak either with the intent to get the group task accomplished, known as *task behavior*, or to improve relationships among members, known as *maintenance behavior*. Benne and Sheats (1948) provided the classic and time-honored work in this area.

The following are types of task behaviors correlated to task functions, with examples of each related to teams in schools:

1. *Initiating.* For effective team functioning, someone must take the initiative. Examples of initiating are proposing tasks, actions, or goals, suggesting a procedure, and defining group problems. Someone might say, for example, "Let's build an agenda" or, "Let's write the suggestions on the chart so we don't forget them."
2. *Giving or seeking or information.* For a task to be accomplished, there must be a clear and efficient flow of information, facts, and opinions. An example of giving information is, "I have some research data that might help in reaching a decision." This sharing of information ensures that decisions are based on as much information as possible. Like information-giving, information-seeking helps the entire group, not just the one asking the questions or providing the information. An example of information-seeking is, "How did Charlie perform during resource activities?"
3. *Clarifying and elaborating.* This task behavior involves interpreting ideas or suggestions, as well as clarifying issues before the team. These statements communicate a collaborative stance. Examples are: "Let me elaborate and build upon that idea"; "I think what Mr. Jones means is that he doesn't know whether his son has the self-confidence to return to the general education classroom full-time. I agree and . . ."
4. *Summarizing.* This task behavior involves pulling together related ideas and suggestions or offering a decision or conclusion for team consideration. Summarizing allows all the team members to reflect on where they have been, where they are, and where they must go. Summarizing statements are interjected at various times during a team meeting, not just in concluding the meeting. An example is, "It seems as though we have made these points so far...."

5. *Consensus testing*. Although not all decisions can or should be made by consensus, much teamwork is a result of consensus decisions. Consensus testing involves making statements that check with team members to determine the extent of agreement. For example: "Have we made a decision about his speech therapy?" This statement reminds team members that they must commit to a decision sooner or later.

Not all team processes are about task functions. Maintenance functions are critical for the team to function smoothly within a supportive climate that maximizes the contribution of each team member. Team maintenance functions are outlined as follows:

1. *Gatekeeping*. Gatekeeping statements attempt to keep the channels of communication open, facilitate participation by team members, and invite sharing. Without gatekeeping, information is lost, multiple conversations develop, and quieter team members can be cut off and withdraw. Examples of gatekeeping are: "Mary never had the opportunity to explain her suggestion" and "If we would all speak one at a time, we could hear everyone's ideas."

2. *Encouraging*. This maintenance behavior allows relevant information to be shared, heard, and considered. It involves being respectful, warm, and friendly toward others. An example is, "Mrs. Guissepe, is there something you would like to add before we move on?"

3. *Harmonizing and compromising*. The aims of harmonizing are to reconcile disagreement, reduce tensions, and allow team members to explore differences. An example is: "It would be beneficial if each of you would specify your objections to the other rather than name-call." An example of compromising is: "It looks as if Dan and I both have viable suggestions. Also, the team looks evenly divided about these two suggestions. To move forward, I would like to focus on Dan's suggestion and retract mine." These types of statements should not be overused. In addition, it is easy to use them inappropriately and thereby reduce the team's effectiveness. You do not want to harmonize or compromise if it results in masking important issues or discounting creative solutions.

4. *Standard setting and testing*. This maintenance behavior focuses on the effectiveness of the task and maintenance behaviors of the team members at a specific point in time. It is a matter of watching to see how the group is operating and then sharing your perceptions with the other team members. Examples are: "Are we off task?" "I can't keep up. Could someone summarize this discussion for me?"

Together, task and maintenance behaviors allow team members to get the job done smoothly and efficiently. Each team member is responsible for these behaviors. It is helpful to observe these behaviors in others, as well as to note their absence.

Shared Leadership

Leadership is the shared responsibility of all team members, including student members (Walther-Thomas, Korinek, & McLaughlin, 2005). The chair of the team cannot be responsible for all of the task and maintenance behaviors, nor would that be desirable. Shared responsibility makes for more effective team functioning, and applying team skills is essential to team effectiveness (Cloninger, 2004; Garner, 1994).

Beyond each team member's responsibility for assuming a role in leadership, the role of the chair of the team is important (Briggs, 1997). In particular, the chair should empower all team members to assume leadership. Pfeiffer (1980) examined studies on the effects of leadership styles on the special education team. He found that when the chair is too directive in resolving problems, his or her ideas often are seen as unacceptable and may lead to hostility by other team members. The team members in the study considered it important to be given a voice in decision making and in sharing ideas and suggestions. Pfeiffer also found that team members do not want problems handed to one discipline or individual to solve. He maintained that at least two team members from different disciplines should be involved in all aspects of the problem-solving process.

Sharing responsibility for team process does not simply happen, and team members can benefit from training to help them become contributing members (Mainzer, Deshler, Coleman, Kozleski, & Rodriguez-Walling, 2005; Losen & Losen, 1994). Effective sharing of responsibility must be nurtured and reinforced by the chair as well as by other team members. Losen and Losen (1985) recommended that the chair offer guiding suggestions, provide information timed to be of value, stimulate self-direction, appreciate others' values and views, and respect differences in opinions. They also recommended that the chair *not* provide direct orders, interrupt proceedings with personal suggestions, ignore team members' suggestions, withhold praise or encouragement, make general critical or nonobjective comments, or demand respect or allegiance.

Lawson and Sailor (2005) have advocated a new style of leadership that is collaborative and develops empowerment, relying less on rules and compliance and more on connections. Orelove and Sobsey (1996) and Sobsey (1994) suggested steps that administrators can take to facilitate a transdisciplinary approach for individuals with severe disabilities. The following are ideas that encourage the team process:

1. Encourage individual team members to see themselves as responsible to the team.
2. Encourage the team to see itself as responsible to the student and family and to see the learner from a family systems perspective.
3. Encourage family members to become involved at the level they choose.
4. Encourage the team to develop a mission statement.
5. Arrange school schedules to allow for regular team meetings, with coverage of classrooms when necessary.
6. Demonstrate effective communication skills during team meetings.
7. Encourage teachers and related services personnel to work together with family members to assess students and to develop goals and objectives.
8. During meetings, encourage the use of clear, simple language that parents, paraprofessionals, and other professionals can understand.
9. Do not prevent conflict; help to resolve it when it occurs.
10. Promote respect for team members' diversity and differences.
11. Reaffirm who has been assigned each task/objective and who has primary responsibility.

Involvement of Team Members

Involvement of all members of the team, including parents, must be encouraged. After conducting a qualitative study, Park and Turnbull (2002) reported three quality indicators of professionals that parents of children with behavioral challenges found important in team members—respect for their child, possessing the skills necessary to meet their child's needs, and commitment.

Support for the involvement of paraprofessionals was highlighted (French, 2001; Katsiyannis, Hodge, & Lanford, 2000; Giangreco, Edelman, & Broer, 2003; Giangreco & Doyle, 2005; Wallace, Shin, Bartholomay, & Stahl, 2001). Involving all team members, especially parents, is critical to effective team functioning (Carney & Gamel-McCormick, 1996). A beginning point is to listen to parents' concerns and experiences of having a child with a disability (Blue-Banning, Summers, Frankland, Nelson, & Beegle, 2004).

Pfeiffer (1980) recommended that a general education teacher serve as a constant team member to represent general education. A standing team member is more likely to help the occasional member feel more comfortable and be more involved in the team process. Also, role clarification positively affects participation during team meetings. Losen and Losen (1994) urged careful pre-meeting preparation, stating that without preparation, team members' contributions "may, at best, prove meaningless, and, at worst, disruptive" (p. 121).

Factors Affecting Team Effectiveness

Fisher (1980) identified three factors that influence team effectiveness: intrapersonal factors, interpersonal factors, and group-identity factors. Each of these has implications for the involvement of team members.

Intrapersonal Factors and Teamwork

Team members should be open-minded about potential outcomes and sensitive to the feelings and beliefs of other team members. Each must be committed to the team and its process and be willing to commit time and energy for that purpose (Blue-Banning et al., 2004; Garner, 1995a). Everyone working with the same people and communities has to stop working at cross-purposes—and to be "on the same page" (Lawson and Sailor, 2005, pp. 540–541).

Each team member must actively share responsibility for the team's decisions (Garner, 1995). Team members should also share their honest feelings and ideas. Along the same lines, they should express their views even when they realize they may be criticized. They must also find ways to criticize constructively, especially during team meetings.

Effective team members are competent. Larson and LaFasto (1989) found that technical competence is important, along with personal skill in collaboration. Problem-solving teams need individuals with integrity—people who can be trusted and who trust others. Creative teams thrive with independent thinkers who are confident, tenacious, and have initiative. Continuing to search for new knowledge and resources is important, to keep up-to-date on skills for working with children having problem behaviors (Park & Turnbull, 2002).

Interpersonal Factors and Teamwork

Collaboration is necessary to effective team functioning (Blue-Banning et al., 2004; Harry, Rueda, & Kalyanpur, 1999; Hunt, Soto, Maier, & Doering, 2003; Lake & Billingsley, 2000; Minke & Anderson, 2005; Osher & Osher, 2002). For group decision making to be productive, all team members must participate and encourage the participation of the other members. Clear roles, responsibilities, and lines of communication are essential to collaborative efforts.

The importance of trust cannot be overlooked. Trust promotes the open expression of personal interests, as well as strengths and weaknesses, and communication based on trust leads to a more realistic division of tasks. Along with trust, Gargiulo (2006) places high value on honesty, empathy, and genuineness in working with families.

Blue-Banning and colleagues (2004) found the following six effective interpersonal team indicators: communication, commitment, equality, skills, trust, and respect. Team effectiveness increases when members are skilled communicators, so team members should make it a point to learn effective communication skills, including listening. Under communication, the indicators included sharing resources, being clear and honest, and being positive. Other indicators of communication were being tactful and open, listening, making frequent communication as well as coordinating information.

Members should evaluate problems and issues, not other members. A climate of mutual trust evolves from this sort of communication. To be effective, team members must clarify communications that are unclear, check others' reactions, and describe ideas in detail so others can respond accurately. If members disagree with an idea, they should objectively state their reservations rather than react in a judgmental manner.

Groups and Teamwork

Focusing on the group goal is vital to effective team functioning (Friend, 2005), and all members must share in resolving the goals. Having a clear purpose allows the team members to direct their energy and effectively and efficiently conduct their important, rewarding, and necessary work.

Emphasizing results is also important to the group. Professionals should employ research-based teaching practices, and team members must be familiar with the practices that research demonstrates are effective with special-needs students (Friend, 2005).

Patience with group process is necessary, too, especially during the early stages when the team is being established. Members must have ample opportunity to think through ideas, allowing for more creativity and, as a result, more effective decisions. The team should avoid unrealistic "formula answers" to difficult problems.

Martin, Marshall, and Sale (2004) found that attendance of the student and a general educator during IEP meetings "produced value-added benefits for IEP team members, especially parents" (p. 285). And Friend (2005) stated that "team effectiveness depends as much on the extent to which each member helps the team accomplish its business as it does on the expertise members bring to the teaming situation" (p. 140).

A unified commitment is critical to highly effective teams, in which an esprit de corps is palpable and team members are loyal and dedicated to the team. Effective team members identify with being part of something larger than the self.

Other Factors Related to Teamwork

Garnering external support as needed is essential to highly effective teams (Larson & LaFasto, 1989). Without the necessary human and nonhuman resources, a team will not operate to its fullest potential. Team members must seek and find the expertise of those outside their group if that need becomes apparent.

Finally, teams must develop standards of excellence that convey team values. The standards may stem from internal needs or outside pressures, such as funding and legislation. Whatever the case, the team's purpose should be exemplified in its high standards.

Team Development and Functioning

Different models of the stages of team development have been conceptualized, two of which are related here. The first has been applied universally in analyzing team process. The second was used originally for teamwork in hospital settings. Both are directly transferable to the discipline of education. Beyond stages, Bailey's triaxial model considers the developmental task of organizing effective teams.

Tuckman's Five Stages of Team Development

Professionals in the field of education have described stages of team development that are meaningful to schools (Briggs, 1997; Garner, 1995). Cloninger (2004) suggested that "being part of a team is a dynamic, ever-changing process, with most teams going through stages of learning and implementation and then recycling through those stages" (p. 19). Based on the longstanding work of Tuckman (1965), the typical stages of any team are forming, storming, norming, performing, and transforming.

Writing about early intervention teams, Briggs (1997) provided a lengthy description of each stage with functions of members and leaders and suggested ways to improve the group process within each stage. This has evolved and been augmented by others.

Stage 1: Forming

When a team first forms, it is characterized by confusion, uncertainty, anxiety, and ambiguity, as well as excitement and enthusiasm. Team members are figuring out what their mission and purpose are and whether they have the resources necessary to be a member of the team. Because members are hesitant to speak openly, interactions may be superficial. In this phase of development, the team needs a strong leader who is capable of navigating uncharted waters. This phase also involves identifying resources and establishing norms.

Stage 2: Storming

As the team moves from observing to participating, relationships among team members become more contentious and fractious. The leader often becomes the "whipping boy or girl," and hostility and disagreement are likely. Underlying this friction is movement toward reconciliation of two common fears—isolation and absorption. Resolution of the disagreements leads to affiliation. Although uncomfortable, this chaos is a necessary step in the right direction. The leader at this stage must be comfortable with disagreements and be able to apply conflict-management skills to help resolve them. As well, the leader must acknowledge differences and move the team toward agreeing to disagree in some situations and in other situations attaining definition of the territory and a sense of direction.

Stage 3: Norming

Over time, harmony develops, and team members become more aware of their similarities, downplaying their differences. The team's work moves along well. Members work together creatively in reaching goals. The team members know what is expected of them and each other. Ways to come together and be apart are well established. At the end of this stage, the leader begins to pull back and encourages others to develop effective processes that bring about continued growth and development.

Stage 4: Performing

This stage is characterized by balance and stability, in which cohesion and collaboration among team members are obvious. Team members are more comfortable working as a team, and they have a sense of pride in their teamwork. An esprit de corps has evolved. The leader reinforces and encourages, as well as points to ways to network with outsiders to accomplish the team's work. Effective leaders also "cheer on" team members.

Stage 5: Transforming

As its work comes to a conclusion, the team seeks new challenges or disbands. Not dependent on one person or a leader, the team functions as a whole. Personal mastery is evident, and members feel fulfilled. For a school team, the end of a school year brings the opportunity to review the past year and team process, as well as evaluate it and plant seeds for change for the next school year.

Lowe and Herranen's Six Phases of Team Development

In their classic model, Lowe and Herranen (1981) identified six phases in team development. They described patterns of interactions, common emotions, and team productivity for each phase, as well as functions of members and leaders. Although this model analyzed teamwork in hospital settings, it relates well to the field of education.

Phase 1: Becoming Acquainted

Team members bring different perspectives to the team. Some members are mandated to be on the team, and others enter by choice and in recognition of the team's value. While team members are becoming acquainted, the leadership style might be autocratic, democratic, or absent. Most often, the highest-ranking professional has the leadership role by default. Interaction patterns are polite, impersonal, and social in nature. There is no group consensus regarding team goals; each professional on the team sees his or her goals as most important. Emotions are held in check, with few conflicts. Phase 1 is characterized by high individual productivity and low team productivity.

Phase 2: Trial and Error

This phase begins once professionals recognize the need to collaborate on common goals. The typical interaction pattern that emerges is to pair with an ally. This pairing, however, increases individual productivity but not group productivity. Role conflict, role ambiguity, and role overload stem from team members' testing the waters. Members continue to be concerned about turf issues.

Phase 3: Collective Indecision

In this phase, members attempt to avoid conflict and achieve equilibrium. Boundaries begin to form. Team members become aware of the appeal of groups as well as their disadvantages. Little is accomplished, however, because accountability and leadership are lacking and conformity is expected. Because the team does not deal with role conflict, morale is low and there is covert anger. Both team and individual productivity suffer. Team members do not feel heard by other team members.

Phase 4: Crisis

Stemming from a crisis resulting from collective indecision, roles and responsibilities are defined and boundaries are drawn. An informal and a formal leader emerge, and group process becomes a focus of attention. Members now feel free to express their emotions, including negative emotions, because they sense the group can now handle them. Team members begin to value one another for their unique expertise and potential assistance in achieving the team's goal. Team productivity, however, continues to be low.

Phase 5: Resolution

Teamwork finally emerges when the team members commit to working as a unit. Open communication leads to shared leadership, decision making, and responsibility. Individual and group accountability are apparent, and team productivity is high. This phase is fragile, however, and the team has to maintain these gains.

Phase 6: Team Maintenance

Sharing by team members allows the team to focus on its goals. In the school setting, team members see the student from a holistic view and value other members' expertise. Effectiveness depends upon internal group processes and how conflicts are handled. Expectations are clarified continuously, norms evolve, team members respect self and others, accountability is important, and a common language develops. This is the critical phase in team development.

Every team does not go through all of these phases, nor will teams go through each stage in a fixed sequence. "It does seem clear, however, that virtually every team experiences growing pains as a normal part of the process of evolving into a smoothly operating unit" (Orelove & Sobsey, 1996, p. 21).

The Triaxial Model

Bailey (1984) proposed a triaxial model for understanding processes within teams that focus on individuals who are at risk or have special needs. The model highlights the complex and difficult task of organizing effective teams and provides insight into avoiding, recognizing, and ameliorating problems of team members. This timeless model, based on the work of Tseng and McDermott (1979), sheds a different light on teamwork and is worthwhile for teams operating in schools. Bailey's model has three premises, called "axes":

1. Team growth is a developmental process. Some problems in team functioning can be attributed to the stage of development at which the team is functioning.
2. Teams are composed of individuals. Thus, some problems may result from interpersonal problems or subsystems within the team.
3. The team is a functioning unit. Some problems, therefore, can be expected to stem from whole-team dysfunction.

An understanding of these axes can help team members pinpoint intervention for problems that arise.

Axis I

Team growth is a developmental process. Problems related to the developmental stage of a team can arise during a given team meeting. The six typical steps in IEP meetings are as follows:

1. Review assessments
2. Discuss present status
3. Develop a long-range plan
4. Make placement decision
5. Determine instructional objectives
6. Design an implementation plan

Team members should analyze their interactions within meetings to determine whether a pattern of dysfunction emerges. One or more steps might show up as problematic. In other cases, the actual sequencing of steps might have to be changed.

Axis II

Teams are composed of individuals, and the ideal team has a leader who performed previously as a member of the team. Each member has equal power and influence. On the ideal team, conflicts and disagreements are based on substantive issues rather than personality conflicts. The following are potential problems relating to individuals:

1. A dominant leader may emerge who is resented by others, cuts down on discussion, or fosters dependency. The team should be based on collaboration, not domination.
2. Dominant team member(s) may emerge, stemming from personalities, hierarchies, or perceived power. Dominant behavior is counterproductive when the person with power will not respect or listen to others' opinions. Not all domination is obvious; it may be subtle.
3. "Inferior" team member(s) may emerge. The opinions of anyone on the team, but most often teachers and parents, may be perceived by some professionals on the

team as inferior, less worthy. Members who are viewed as inferior will eventually stop contributing, and that withdrawal reinforces other team members' view of them as inferior. All contributions should be valued.

4. A conflict may arise between two members, resulting in team dysfunction. Conflict is a natural and expected part of team functioning, but when it pervades meetings and interferes with planning, it is dysfunctional.

5. One member may continually be in conflict with all others, which is highly disruptive to team functioning and is even more dysfunctional when the person is highly vocal. Eventually the person is rejected, regardless of the quality of the input.

6. The team may develop factions in which subsystems compete with one another. Winning should not take precedence over the task of the team—which is to meet the student's needs.

7. A member may feel isolated from the group and not appear to belong to the team socially. A feeling of being in the "out crowd" is not conducive to healthy team functioning.

Axis III

The whole team is a functioning unit. In Axis III the structure or organization of the whole team is the subject of scrutiny. Ideal teams are well organized, have clear roles, and are structured, yet flexible. Four types of dysfunction of teams follow:

1. *The underperforming team:* Team members are unskilled or not invested in the team process. The task is not completed because the entire team is dysfunctional. Team tasks are perfunctory. Often the underperforming team has an ineffective leader, and members are unable or unwilling to take responsibility for seeing that the team accomplishes its goals.

2. *The overstructured team:* Members' roles are rigidly defined. Meetings are inflexible, and substance takes a back seat to structure and the agenda. Rigidity in roles and routines restricts interactions and prevents the discussion of social and emotional content.

3. *The team with ambiguous roles:* Members are unclear about who does what. Planning is not integrated, because of territoriality or confusion and withdrawal. No one takes responsibility for team process, and the result is inadequate planning for the student.

4. *The disorganized team:* Leadership, direction, and structure are lacking. Meetings are chaotic. This problem stems from either poor leadership or confusion about roles and purpose. Members sometimes become overly involved in discussing their social lives. At other times, members enter and leave the meetings as a result of arriving late, leaving early, and going out to make phone calls.

In sum, this three-dimensional model allows the determination of the level of dysfunction: team development, team subsystems, or whole-team functioning. This breakdown allows for a considered diagnosis of team dysfunction and improves the likelihood of teams being functional in the school context.

Challenges to Team Functioning

The variety of challenges to team functioning can be divided into four categories: philosophical and theoretical differences, isolation of family members, interpersonal challenges, and resistance to change. In any group, challenges should be framed as potentially resolvable.

Differences in Philosophical and Theoretical Orientations

Team members often confront differences in training as well as theoretical and philosophical orientations (Cloninger, 2004; Courtnage & Smith-Davis, 1987). Therapists are typically trained in a medical model, which emphasizes determining the underlying cause of the behavior and then focuses therapy on that cause. Family systems therapists, in comparison, are trained in theoretical models that view challenging situations less linearly (Nichols & Schwartz, 2005; Walsh & Williams, 1997). The emphasis on individual versus systemic thinking may lead to misunderstandings among team members. Further, it is likely to result in fundamental differences in approaches to students and family members.

This difficulty is intensified by the isolated preparation of professionals such as teachers, counselors, therapists, nurses, and occupational therapists. Professionals frequently use their own jargon when meeting in teams, and other team members, especially parents, may not be familiar with this terminology. Briggs (1997) pointed to the importance of recognizing and identifying the differences in team members' philosophies and theoretical orientations. With proper communication, these differences can strengthen team functioning.

Philosophical and theoretical challenges to team functioning can be intensified or reduced by the team model employed. A multidisciplinary approach (discussed earlier in the chapter) has a greater likelihood of facing philosophical and theoretical problems. The nature of this approach lends itself to such misunderstandings. In comparison, because of its interactive nature, the interdisciplinary team model is more conducive to team collaboration, with fewer theoretical and philosophical challenges.

Isolation of Family Members

Another challenge to effective team functioning is the isolation of family members, or professionals not taking into consideration the family's zone of proximal development, desires, needs, abilities, resources, and time constraints (Harry, Rueda, & Kalyanpur, 1999; Osher & Osher, 2002). Parents may be apprised of their rights, but they may not understand those rights (Armstrong, 1995) and deserve an explanation.

Gargiulo (2006) emphasized the shift over time to value family as important in meeting the needs of children/youth with special needs. This view goes beyond involving only parents in their education. Some children and youth are more influenced by grandparents, uncles and aunts, or siblings than their parents, and some live with family members who are not their parents.

Family members may be confused by the educational processes. If they are involved only in developing the IEP, their isolation is exacerbated. It is important to solicit family members' involvement throughout the process—from prereferral with student assistance teams to planning the educational program. Long-term involvement will reduce the sense of isolation of any family members who choose to be involved in the educational life of the student with special needs.

Interpersonal Challenges

Professionals trained in a medical model may feel threatened by the egalitarian nature of teams that include parents and paraprofessionals. But trusting others to provide helpful information is imperative to the effective functioning of such teams (Gargiulo, 2006). Another interpersonal challenge is a lack of clarity regarding team members' responsibilities. Each person's role, therefore, must be clarified continuously. If team members are unsure of their functions, role conflict will ensue.

Resistance to Change

People resist change for a variety of reasons. Although resistance should be viewed as normal and expected in any change process, it can be destructive. Team members may resist change because they (a) feel inadequate, (b) fear the unknown, (c) lack trust, or (d) are unable to see the larger picture. Generally speaking, when team members become more familiar with team functioning, they overcome their feelings of inadequacy and resistance.

Fear of the unknown, which may surface when professionals are faced with working collaboratively on an egalitarian team, can be reduced through effective communication.

As changes are being planned, all members should be involved in planning and decision making. When team members are not part of the change process from the beginning, they are unable to see the larger picture and will have difficulty understanding the goals and the need for change. Once they understand the benefits to the total team functioning, they are likely to be more supportive.

Involving Families in Teams

Whenever family members are involved in team meetings, professionals must make them feel comfortable and wanted, and they must view them as capable of contributing meaningful input (Blue-Banning et al., 2004). Parents should never be pressured into accepting a delivery model or program if they believe another option is more appropriate. Schools should let parents know that their participation is desired and that they have an important contribution to make in the planning process. More specifically, involving families in reviewing test data and options for service delivery models, as well as in decision making and goal setting, is important to the team process.

Reviewing Test Data

During the team meeting, when the student's eligibility for special education and related services is being determined, parents' reactions to the test data shared at the preteam meeting should be solicited. For example:

> Mrs. Smith probably remembers that, during the preteam meeting, I suggested that her daughter Kristie could be experiencing

greater anxiety than we originally anticipated. When we reviewed the results of the tests, I was able to demonstrate the level on which Kristie is functioning compared to other students in kindergarten. As a result, I think Mrs. Smith understands why Kristie needs special help. Short-term placement in a resource classroom for children with learning challenges is meaningful in particular so Kristie will regain her self-esteem and confidence in her ability to function successfully at school tasks. Mrs. Smith, do you have anything further to add?

Falik (1995) has written about family reactions to having a child with a learning disability. Imagine hearing at a team meeting for the first time that your own child is labeled with retardation or a learning disability. You likely would be shocked and unable to participate further in providing input or suggestions. This points out the need for sensitivity and empathy on the part of school professionals when dealing with families (Gargiulo, 2006).

Information provided during IEP team meetings should summarize assessment results, as going point-by-point through test data takes too much time. Providing summaries, charts, outlines, or descriptions of tests may be helpful. Some family members will find data provided in this way easier to follow. Brief written descriptions of each of the subtests used may be helpful, too, but it is critical that those descriptions be written in lay terms and at the reader's level. If the family representative speaks another language, written translations of the documents and descriptions should be provided.

Professionals are responsible for making family members feel comfortable by communicating at their level of understanding. Professionals can help family members feel free to ask questions and clarify what they do not understand.

Consideration of the Service Delivery Model

For schools in which inclusion is preferred (Fisher & Frey, 2003), discussing the value of inclusion with parents is important. Parents will benefit from hearing about the training that has been and will continue to be provided to teachers. Parents are more likely to become advocates for inclusive schools if they know what support will be made available for their child to succeed in an inclusive setting.

Because parents are involved in considering service delivery options for their child, they must be familiar with the variety of alternative service delivery models and the choices within each model (Bradley & Switlick, 1997), such as co-teaching with its complementary instruction, supportive learning activities, and team teaching (Friend, 2005), as well as indirect services, including problem solving, group problem solving, and peer coaching.

Parents should learn about the options for service delivery at the earliest possible stage, which usually results in more acceptance and fewer complaints later. It is also a good check-and-balance for other team members so they do not recommend a particular delivery model for a student too quickly. When parents are involved in listening to the deliberations, they are more likely to be deliberative.

As the team considers a student's placement, the parents will benefit from a review of advantages and disadvantages of different delivery models. With this knowledge, parents can better contribute to the decision making.

When considering general education classroom activities in which a given student might engage, team members can indicate how the time spent in the general education program may benefit the student more than special classroom involvement. Switlick (1997b) provided various scenarios of flowing in and out of general education and special classrooms in a flexible manner and indicated that success depends on

- teacher attitude toward the disability (especially emotional disabilities),
- team teaching and collaboration between the general educator and the special educator,
- student-centered (not content-centered) instruction in the general education setting,
- integration of specialized curricular objectives in the general education setting. (p. 255)

Orelove and Malatchi (1996) recommended that the IEP team develop a matrix of the goals for the student and the time/activity blocks of the school day.

Decision Making

Once test results and service delivery model options have been reviewed, a decision must be made about the student's placement and program. If parents are involved in the steps prior to this point, and prior to the meeting when the decision will be made, they will more likely support professional recommendations.

When team members do not agree on the program, they must discuss the reasons for their disagreement and try to resolve them through consensus. When team members do not agree about the program placement, the decision can be deferred for further research. When there is no consensus on a decision, however, Gamel-McCormick (1995) recommended listening to the parents and taking their thoughts into consideration.

Goal Setting

After making a recommendation for placement, related services and the student's IEP must be considered. Parents are involved in these determinations, too. Students receiving special education must have written goals if the child is subject to alternative assessment and standards. Some school systems go beyond the minimum requirement of IDEA 2004 and require that all students receiving special education have written objectives. Objectives should be written in simple, clear language that the family members and the student can understand. When written, family members must be involved in the development of both the goals and the objectives.

In addition, the family members and student should be informed about how long a student generally takes to achieve a given goal or objective. Family members benefit, too, from knowing that the IEP is not a binding contract but a working agreement with stated goals for their child as well as related services. Finally, family members need to know the responsibilities that come with their rights to involvement in their child's education.

General Guidelines for Family Involvement

Blue-Banning and colleagues (2004) conducted a qualitative study using focus groups with family members of students with and without a disability as well as service providers and administrators. They developed indicators of behavior by professionals who were considered to be effective when collaborating with others and described six themes: communication, commitment, equality, skills, trust, and respect. They stated, "The results of this study underscore the point that common sense and ordinary human decency are at the heart of positive partnerships between families and professionals serving children with disabilities" (p. 181).

Carney and Gamel-McCormick (1996) summarized the school professional's responsibility with regard to family involvement on interdisciplinary teams as follows:

1. Appreciating and valuing parents' involvement in the team at the level they desire to be involved
2. Remembering that the family is in the midst of a typical process of change and adjustment and at the same time are experiencing an event that is very different from other families
3. Recognizing that the child's fit within the family might be a priority concern
4. Respecting the family's cultural patterns and beliefs and the impact they will have on whether and how the family participates on a program planning team
5. Communicating accurately and honestly with parents (p. 464)

Summary

The first of three models of team approaches is *multidisciplinary* in nature with professionals from diverse disciplines (e. g., social work, education, PT) separately evaluating and providing services. They do not typically view themselves as being members of a team but as lone professionals providing input through their discipline's lens. The inherent lack of collaboration and coordination often leads to contradictory recommendations that may confuse both professionals with the main responsibility for the child's education and development as well as family members.

The *interdisciplinary* model has greater interdependence because of the formalized structure: all disciplines share recommendations from their respective evaluations. Because this model involves isolated intervention, it has similar disadvantages to above.

The *transdisciplinary* model for teams moves beyond the other two models and involves delivery of therapeutic services integrated within educational settings; thus, it facilitates integration of noneducational goals (e.g., PT, counseling) for students under alternative assessment and standards. Furthermore, services take place within the educational contexts, allowing the teacher and paraprofessional to benefit from observing methods of working with the student so they may help the child by implementing what was modeled (e.g., lifting). It is a collaborative, cooperative, coordinated model with family members able to probe the teacher rather than having to consult professionals from several disciplines, thus they grasp elements of their child's development and learning more easily.

Membership on educational teams varies based on needs related to the particular student. Members learn from professionals representing diverse disciplines and generalize their learning to other individuals they serve. Since 2001 and the passage of NCLB, parents are required to assume greater responsibility for the learning and behavior of their child. In addition to the parents, professionals consider other family members to be potential contributors in a child's education and development. Professionals should expect and respect variation in the degree of involvement family members may wish or are able to provide. A student being a team member furthers the individual's self-determination.

The teacher is a stable member of the team with general educators maintaining responsibility for the education of students. The teacher is able to provide descriptive information about the child's performance in class, thus making it easier for all team members to make effective decisions and realistic recommendations. Special educators often serve as liaisons between professionals and family members, advocate for the child, recommend adaptations leading to increased time in regular classrooms, and suggest modifications that help at-risk students learn effectively in the regular classroom.

With the emphasis on inclusion, paraprofessionals increased as a support for interventions in student learning/behavior. They too serve as team members and, because they often live in the school zone where they work, can be effective connectors between family and professionals. There is need for stronger training of paraprofessionals and those who supervise them.

The school psychologist serves on teams to evaluate intellectual/emotional status and cognitive/affective functioning in relation to eligibility for special education and related services. He or she may also assess learning style, strengths, and problem-solving strategies. Some school psychologists have been trained in family systems concepts and refocus the team on the family, and some have become part of behavioral intervention programs designed and carried out in school, home, and/or neighborhood.

School counselors have increasingly been exposed to family systems concepts. Many meet with whole classes and can incorporate stories or lessons that help a group of students more easily understand or relate to challenges faced by particular peers. They may lead a student group aimed at a particular population (e.g., divorce, death of a parent), or they may be part of follow-through for youth discharged from an in-patient setting.

The educational diagnostician establishes achievement levels and abilities as well as administers formal or standardized testing to present to other team members. He or she may also engage in trial teaching to determine learning strengths for teacher use.

The school social worker is generally the team member most familiar with family matters and often advocates linking resources across settings. Trained in family studies and/or therapy, they typically have little background in family systems concepts. Social work is considered a related service under IDEA (2004), and social workers help integrate the provisions of services via evidence-based practices. Able to influence school-wide programs, social workers may provide guidance for programs to prevent community violence and bullying or link with professionals involved with positive behavior support.

Administrators are relied upon to make materials, time, personnel, and tangible resources available to children; they are also responsible for federal compliance of employees. They can make unilateral decisions except for special education's behavioral intervention plan, manifestation, suspension/expulsion, which are all the domain of the IEP team.

The school nurse can provide team members information on physical health status of a student. They are familiar with first-aid, emergencies, seizure, medication, allergies, asthma, diabetes, HIV/AIDS, sickle cell anemia, cystic fibrosis, hygiene, diet, and more.

Educational *touchpoints* provide opportunity for deepening relationships between professionals and student or family member(s). These opportunities are evident during screening, prereferral, referral and eligibility, and IEP meetings. The first touchpoint, screening, involves all students being screened in relation to achievement, intelligence, vision, and hearing. Some students are found to be at risk for learning, behavior, or other challenges.

As a touchpoint, prereferral involves a team meeting to consider alternatives that meet the needs of the student; consideration is given to all contexts in which the student interacts (i.e., home, school, neighborhood, community). Recommended adaptations may relate to instruction or behavior, and family members sometimes provide ideas that work at home or help professionals understand the cause of the problem.

A potentially sensitive touchpoint arises in referral and assessment because it may lead to special education or related services that parents, the child, or family members find difficult to understand or accept. There are federal requirements concerning parental rights and responsibilities in the referral process.

Professionals are responsible for determining whether the student has a disability and if it affects the child's educational performance. As well, the team is charged with determining whether the needs of the student can be met through special education. In answering these questions, parents must be included in the team process, and the student may be a team member. Development of the Individualized Educational Program (IEP) remains a team process and is reviewed annually.

Regardless of the type of team involved, clarity of purpose and vision, shared leadership, and involvement of all team members forms a foundation for planning and implementation. Training in communication skills is constructive for team members, including family member(s) and the student. Task behaviors important for team members to master include initiating, giving or seeking information, clarifying and elaborating, summarizing, and consensus testing. Coexisting with task behaviors are maintenance behaviors that include gatekeeping, encouraging, harmonizing and compromising, and standard setting and testing.

Team effectiveness involves intrapersonal, interpersonal, and group-identity factors. Intrapersonal factors relate to open-mindedness, integrity, trust, creativity, commitment to the team process, sharing responsibility, courage to express unpopular views, use of constructive criticism, and competence borne from continuing education. Interpersonal vitality is seen when team members listen openly to one another, are involved in frequent communication, coordinate information shared, and use effective task and maintenance behaviors. Group identity is fostered through a clear purpose and shared goals as well as believing that the team process is more important than individual opinions or desires.

A team goes through stages of development over time. One description includes five stages, including forming, storming, norming, performing, and transforming. Development of teams has also been cast in six phases that include becoming acquainted, trial and error, collective indecision, crisis, resolution, and team maintenance. The triaxial model, specific to special-needs students, considers team processes in relation to the team as a developmental process (what stage the team is in), interpersonal membership, and team as functioning unit. Recognition of these three axes helps prevent team problems from developing and identify when and where to intervene with team process problems.

The functioning level of teams varies across time and may be negatively impacted by differences in philosophical/theoretical orientation among team members, with failure of members to agree to disagree and move forward with the team's solidarity intact; isolation of family members from the team process; challenges of an interpersonal nature, such as unclear or ill defined roles of team members with role conflict ensuing; and destructive, rather than constructive resistance stemming from different sources (e.g., fear, trust issues).

Family members become involved in team meetings when they review test data, serve as members of an IEP team; provide input regarding service delivery model for their child; set goals for the child in terms of learning, development, or behavior; and when the child receives related services. It is during these meetings that opportunities can be found for touchpoints that deepen relationships between professionals and family member(s)/child.

Extension Activities

In-Class/Training Role Play: Select a case study from one of the chapters in the first two parts of this text or locate or develop one of your own. Role-play a team meeting for a pre-referral or another situation, using the case study as the springboard. Provide "stances" for each person playing a team member. For example, a parent may play a shrinking violet, a special educator play a role in which he or she is overly outspoken, an administrator may be writing notes about something else and not paying attention (i.e., disengaged), and so forth.

The professor/trainer can take the role of leader of the team meeting and assign someone to take the role of recorder, assign another as timekeeper, and make another responsible for drawing quieter members into the discussion. Give group members who are not in the role play some definite things to observe (e.g., task and/or maintenance functions found in the listings in this chapter).

After the role play, ask those who were involved to discuss the meeting. Then have those observing the role play discuss what they saw and noticed about the different stances (e.g., shrinking violet) and how their behavior, or lack thereof, affected the process. Have the participants list questions of interest that they could ask experienced team members in schools.

In-Class/Training Speaker or Panel: Invite one or more speakers from a local school system to speak with your group. In addition, you might ask one member of several different school systems to speak so you will show ways that school systems do things differently.

In-Class/Training Activity: Use the "fishbowl" activity, place experienced team members in the center circle and inexperienced team members in the outer circle. Prior to the class/training time, provide questions so they will come prepared. After discussing the questions, have those in the outer circle pose questions first. Then have those in the outer circle share what they observed while listening.

Read, Then Make Journal Entries on Indicators in Article: Go online to locate and read the article by Blue-Banning and colleagues (2004), originally published in *Exceptional*

Children (2002), Volume 20, Issue 2, pages 167–184. After reading the entire article, study the listing of indicators in this chapter and reflect on what matters to family members of children with disabilities. Use these indicators matched with the six themes with the next extension activity.

Observation of a Team Meeting: Find a school system that will allow you to attend a team meeting. Be sure you have the necessary signed permission regarding confidentiality that is required in the system where you observe. Prior to the meeting, let the team leader know why you will be there and what you hope to gain from observing team process. Take notes if that will help you focus on the task and maintenance functions listed in this chapter. Be sure to thank the team members for allowing you to attend the meeting and assure them of your confidentiality.

Bridge With Observation Assignment From Class/Training Above: Students may share their experiences with the proviso that they do not tell which system they observed or the names of any children, family members, or professionals involved in the team meeting. This protects everyone and likely will result in more opportunities for observing in the future. List the remaining questions of students on a chart or board.

Reflection: Reread the task and maintenance indicators while reflecting on the task and maintenance behaviors you observed during meetings you have attended in the past (e.g., gatekeeping, encouraging, harmonizing, clarifying, summarizing). Was anything in particular missing that would have helped? If so, how could you develop your personal communication to enhance this type of task or maintenance function for use in the future?

Interview Assignment: Locate a variety of members of an educational team at three different levels (elementary, middle, and high school) and request an interview with at least three different types of professionals (e.g., nurse, teacher, administrator, parent). Set up 15–30 minute interview slots at the schools. Prior to the interviews, develop questions about the process of teamwork that interest you. If your group did the role-play of a team, use the questions generated to help develop your questions.

Look to the topics in this chapter to guide your development of questions. It is interesting to ask a number of the same questions of different team members in the same school to see if their views are similar or different. Assure those you interview that what they share will be confidential and that you will not reveal names or school systems where the interviews were conducted.

In-Class/Training Bridge With Interviews Above: Highlight confidentiality as essential professional behavior, and require that no one identify the school system or school where interview(s) took place. Pair group members with contrasting backgrounds, interests, and experience. For example, pair someone with no experience in team meetings and someone with professional experience, or someone with elementary experience or interest with someone having secondary interest or experience. If several members of the group are family members of a special-needs or at-risk individual, pair them with group members who do not have that background.

Assign your discussion topics or allow the pairs to develop their own with their interviews as a basis. Have one or both members of each pair share highlights of their discussion. At the end, ask group members what kinds of things they think they still need to learn to be effective team members in the future—whether inside a school system or in the external community (e.g., social worker, professional counselor).

Family Conferences and Teacher–Student Support Teams

$\mathcal{S}$chool and community professionals have the opportunity to help family members foster the development, socialization, and academic achievement of their children. Even though family linkages are crucial to the development of children and youth, quantitative and qualitative research by Dunst (2002) found that families become less involved with their child's education over time. The positive relationship of parents involved with their child's education holds for achievement of Caucasian and minority students alike (Jeynes, 2005). Luthar and Latendresse (2005) examined preadolescents' perceptions of parenting in low-income as well as high-income communities and found that closeness to parents was important in both communities and that an educational emphasis made a difference in both communities. The influence of the extended family was also found to be valuable (Walton, Roby, Frandsen, & Davidson, 2003).

The family conference is a crucial component in school/community–family interaction, and an important mechanism for identifying unmet needs of at-risk and special-needs students who are in the general education classroom. The earlier the family involvement, the better (Buck, Polloway, Smith-Thomas, & Cook, 2003; Turnbull & Turnbull, 2001). For more than 15 years we have known that, if school professionals include the family when a student's challenges are noticed early, the chances of being referred for special education decreases (Burns & Symington, 2002; Fuchs, Fuchs, & Bahr, 1990; Fuchs, Fuchs, Bahr, Fernstrom, & Steker, 1990).

Embedding family systems concepts and practices in professional communications (Mullis & Edwards, 2001), such as teacher–student support teams and family conferences, is likely to have an even larger impact on the behavioral and socioemotional challenges of children and youth. Earlier interventions of this kind are more likely to result in success by children and youth, thereby lowering the possibilities for failure in the school and community.

Basic Considerations for Home and School/Community Interactions

Classroom teachers, as well as principals, are in a unique position for relating to families of at-risk and special-needs students, as family members do not interact routinely with school counselors, social workers, psychologists, and other helping professionals. Their contact with these specialists typically is irregular and in response to problems. The teacher, however, has frequent opportunities for routine contact with family members.

This contact provides a basis for establishing and maintaining a trusting relationship. Whereas the family member may view the school psychologist as intimidating and judgmental, the teacher more often is seen as understanding and nonthreatening. Parents view teachers in the most positive light of all of the school professionals. The various contexts in which teachers and family members relate to the student enrich the information and idea exchange between family members and the school and provide the teacher with opportunities to build upon the parents' trust.

In community settings, the social worker tends to be the most trusted professional. In either school or community, someone from the same ethnic (e.g., African American, Latino) background or who speaks the native language of the family member more easily bridges the cultural gap and builds trust.

Three considerations are central to the family systems perspective and fundamental to all human interactions between home and school/community: sensitivity/caring, trust, and shared locus of influence.

Sensitivity/Caring

Successful interactions with others stem from a genuine interest in and a sensitivity toward people (Gargiulo, 2006; Simpson, 1996). Those who serve children/youth and their families must have an authentic interest in others, as well as a desire to invest time and energy in joint problem solving.

The success of family–professional interactions hinges on the professional's attitudes, values, and sensitivity. Fortunately, professionals can learn the human interaction skills that are beneficial to building relationships (Johnson, 2005). Acquiring these skills is not sufficient, however. Professionals must also be committed to meeting families' needs. Although professionals and family members alike must assume the responsibility for sound working relations, professionals have the primary obligation to convey the attitude and motivation essential to helpful interactions. Developing these skills is basic to professionalism. Nel Noddings (1984, 1995; 2002, 2003, 2005b) has been in the forefront of information on this topic.

Trust

The most important characteristic of a successful family–professional interaction is trust. Trust emerges if people feel safe enough to take interpersonal risks. The risk-taking then can lead to successful, productive relationships. For trust to take hold, boundaries between professional and family must not be violated (Nelson, Summers, & Turnbull, 2004).

Several interactive elements are essential for the development of trust in the family–professional relationship. First, both the family member and the professional must be willing to invest time and energy in a shared commitment to the child or youth, to advocate assertively for the child, to be sensitive to each other's needs, to confront as well as reinforce one another, and to maintain a positive, honest outlook.

In their interactions, family members and professionals must be honest and direct, even though this may involve significant interpersonal risk. In his text, *Conferencing Parents of Exceptional Children,* Simpson (1990) provided a questionnaire listing 20 risk-taking situations that professionals often face in relation to parents (see Figure 12.1).

As a useful exercise, educators might complete the questionnaire in Figure 12.1 and then answer the following five questions:

1. What items were you surprised to see on the questionnaire?
2. Do you note any items that you believe are inappropriate to interactions with families?
3. Did you learn anything new about yourself? If so, what? If not, why?
4. Which items are more difficult for you personally?
5. Would you add any items to the questionnaire? If so, what are they?

Also beneficial is to discuss your answers to these questions with others who completed the questionnaire. This can provide insight into the different ways of managing risk-taking situations.

Shared Locus of Influence

Effective human interaction is a mutual, shared activity. Regardless of the specific purpose of the interaction, all interchanges provide opportunities to trade information and views, share feelings, and make joint decisions. Establishing trust and a sound working relationship requires a shared locus of influence. This means that the professional, the child or youth, and family members mutually share influence in decision making (Gamel-McCormick, 1995).

Shared decision-making by family and professionals is particularly important in relation to children and youth with special needs. As is seen with IDEA (2004), with rights come responsibilities. Turnbull (2005) stated, "The parent participation principle reflects

How comfortable are you in . . .	Very Comfortable	Somewhat Comfortable	Neutral	Somewhat Uncomfortable	Very Uncomfortable
1. Telling parents you don't know	____	____	____	____	____
2. Telling parents that you made a mistake	____	____	____	____	____
3. Suggesting to parents that another professional made an error	____	____	____	____	____
4. Suggesting to parents that they should consider therapy for themselves	____	____	____	____	____
5. Telling parents that there are behaviors displayed by their children that you dislike	____	____	____	____	____
6. Displaying your emotions in parent–educator conference	____	____	____	____	____
7. Confronting parents with their failure to follow through on agreed-upon plans	____	____	____	____	____
8. Talking about your own problems in a parent–educator conference	____	____	____	____	____
9. Praising parents for things they do well	____	____	____	____	____
10. Having parents take notes during conferences	____	____	____	____	____
11. Allowing parents to observe in your class while you are teaching	____	____	____	____	____
12. Allowing parents to tutor their child at home	____	____	____	____	____
13. Allowing parents to use behavior modification procedures with their child at home	____	____	____	____	____
14. Telling parents their "rights" under PL 94-142	____	____	____	____	____
15. Having parents assume an active role during individualized education program conferences	____	____	____	____	____
16. Having parents ask you to defend your teaching strategies	____	____	____	____	____
17. Having parents bring a friend to individualized education program conferences	____	____	____	____	____
18. Having parents call you at home about a problem their child is having at school	____	____	____	____	____
19. Having parents recommend specific curriculum	____	____	____	____	____
20. Having parents review school records	____	____	____	____	____

Source: From *Conferencing Parents of Exceptional Children* (2nd ed.) by R. Simpson, 1990, Austin, TX: Pro-Ed. Reprinted by permission of Pro-Ed.

Figure 12.1

Risk-Taking Questionnaire

the core concept of *empowerment and participatory decision making*" (p. 323, italics in original) and summarized that "the reauthorized IDEA (2004) imposes many new duties on students and their parents, giving them the message that they are personally responsible for their conduct" (p. 322).

If family members think that professionals are interfering with their ability to influence decisions affecting their child, they may become anxious, frustrated, and angry. Professionals must make sure that parents know they will not only have the opportunity but will be expected to influence decisions concerning their child.

The student is included in the shared locus of influence. Test and colleagues (2004) reviewed literature concerning student involvement in the IEP process. Instruction, verbal rehearsal, role playing, as well as prompting aided high school students during IEP meetings. (The IEP process is covered in chapter 13.) Empowering students (Bailey & Guskey, 2000; Benson & Barnett, 2005; Brendtro & Bacon, 1994; Syverson, 2005) and family (Blue-Banning et al., 2004; Dunst, Trivette, & Deal, 1994a; Mullis & Edwards, 2001) is critical to effective family–professional interactions.

Shared influence and joint decisions usually are more difficult to achieve than unilateral decisions. Sharing the influence, however, maximizes the investment of all of the involved parties in the outcome.

The basic considerations of sensitivity/caring, trust, and shared locus of influence are relevant to all forms of interactions with families, whether they involve family conferences, obtaining assistance for a child or youth, or other professionally initiated interactions. These basic considerations are essential to effective human interactions, and, though they are not linked directly to family systems concepts, they maximize the use of family systems concepts by professionals who work within schools and communities.

General Applications of Family Systems Concepts

Three classic models have application to family systems concepts in family–professional interactions on behalf of students: Satir's family rules and five freedoms of communication, as well as Bowen's concept of detriangling. These theories and concepts are explicated in the Appendix.

Satir's Family Rules

Satir (1983a) studied the dysfunctional family rules with which individuals grew up and how to transform them. Transformation allows the rules, in a new form, to guide the individual while also providing protection (Schwab, 1990). An example of a rigid rule is, "I should never be angry." Adhering to this rule is not always possible, nor is it healthy. Expressing anger may lead to positive change in a situation, as well as discharge pent-up energy that otherwise might explode in unproductive ways or result in health problems such as ulcers. Satir suggested a series of transformative steps, how to evaluate family rules, and how to implement new rules.

Transformation Steps

Satir would have begun by evaluating the first-order transformation, "I can always be angry," with the person. Most people would say, "No, not always." This would be followed by discussion of the second-order transformation, and the response, "I can be angry sometimes." Under the guidance of a professional who is aware of what constitutes healthy family rules, most people who have grown up with the "I can never be angry" rule would respond, "Well, maybe." The third-order transformation would be, "I can be angry when [list three occasions]." Examples might be when (a) "it will make me feel better," (b) "there would be a possibility for change," and (c) "I eventually might feel closer to the person with whom I am upset." These transformative steps allow the individual to use a family rule in a way that can guide him or her for life.

Questions for Evaluating Family Rules

Satir and Baldwin (1983) developed a list of questions for evaluating family rules. School/community professionals and family members can use these questions to determine whether family rules are in need of transformation, and professionals can use the questions when attempting to identify the family rules that guide a given family. The first two questions can help the professional determine potential rules for transformation. The next three questions can help the professional probe areas of human interaction that might reveal a rule in need of transformation. Most ineffective family rules stem from aspects of information sharing, being different from others in the family, as well as expression of feelings, thoughts, or opinions within the context of the family (pp. 202–205).

1. Are the rules humanly possible?
2. Are the rules up to date and relevant to a changing situation?
3. What are the rules governing differentness?
4. What rules surround the sharing of information?
5. What rules govern what family members can say about what they are feeling, seeing, and hearing?

A review of these questions can help family members gain insight into the rules that govern their lives, examine other possibilities, and transform the rules that interrupt their lives. Improved communication and higher self-esteem generally follow such revisions of dysfunctional family rules.

Implementation

Although family members are not always ready or willing to transform their obsolete, rigid, or ineffective rules, professionals can be of assistance on some occasions. An opportunity to discuss family rules might arise during a training or support group for parents or when meeting with a family member who has met a thorny challenge with the child. One way to introduce a family to the concept is to relate the following story:

> A newlywed couple argued profusely for their first two Thanks-
> givings about how to cook the turkey. The husband insisted that
> the legs had to be cut off and placed beside the turkey in the pan.
> The wife was equally adamant that the legs not be removed. One

day, when they were visiting the husband's parents, the wife asked her mother-in-law why she had always cooked the turkey with the legs removed. The mother-in-law replied, "We didn't have a big enough pan to cook the turkey in, so we had to cut off its legs."

The professional then can apply Satir's technique to help transform a family rule. Consider the case of a father and his 16-year-old son who came to counseling because they argued frequently and, on occasion, came close to exchanging blows. During counseling, the counselor learned that the parents had imposed the rigid family rule that "children never question rules established by a parent." Although this rule may have been appropriate for the father's 4-year-old son, it did not fit the adolescent. By its very nature, it could instigate authority problems with any adolescent.

In counseling, the father and son were led through the steps of transforming that rule. The father recognized that his 16-year-old son had become old enough to think about which of the family's rules did and did not fit him at this age. The father came to realize that respect for elders is not automatic but is earned by flexible and supportive rules that fit the age of the children and the specific situation.

Parents need to adapt family rules to the child's developmental level. The following is an example is what the counselor (C) might say to the parent (P).

C: Mr. Emmerson, I'm glad we have this opportunity to continue discussing the situation involving your son, Tim. I've thought about the early curfew Tim has on weekends. Tell me how that came about.

P: Tim has the same rule as our other son, Mike. It would be too late for Mike to come home after 9 o'clock, so my wife and I decided that Tim would have to come in at 9 o'clock, too. We can't see how we could allow Tim to come in later, when Mike has to be home by 9 o'clock.

C: How old is Mike?

P: 12.

C: So Tim is 4 years older than Mike, and he still has to live by the same rules. Is that the way it was in your house when you grew up?

P: No, my older brother got away with murder. He was always coming in late and waking me up. My parents let him come in whenever he wanted, and he got in a lot of trouble. Then, later, they cracked down on me and made me come in earlier than he did at my age.

C: I can see how that could affect the kind of rules you came up with for your two children. Mr. Emmerson, could you imagine Tim always having a 2 o'clock a.m. curfew?

P: No. That's not in the realm of possibility.

C: Then could you just imagine that on some occasion Tim might be allowed to have a later curfew?

P: I suppose so—like for the junior prom.

C: What might be some other times that Tim could have a later curfew?

P: I guess when he's going to a movie that won't be over in time for him to get home by the curfew. . . . And maybe when another parent has offered to go bowling with the kids, he could come in later.

C: Do you think there are enough differences in a 12-year-old and a 16-year-old that they might need different rules?

P: I don't want Mike to think we're favoring Tim!

C: It might be a good idea to talk with Mike and explain why his rule for curfew is different from Tim's. Most kids even look forward to the time when they are old enough for their curfew times to change. I think that when we're most comfortable with our rule differences, our children test us less regarding those inequities. What we're talking about is the recognition, as well as acceptance, of the reality that age makes a difference in all kinds of things.

P: I suppose so. I could even give Mike the example of Tim being old enough to drive.

C: Right. I think that your willingness to agree to change his curfew will make a real difference for Tim. I appreciate your openness to these thoughts. By the way, I have a good article I think you might like to read about age differences in children.

Sometimes, of course, family members are not open to suggestions of how to transform family rules; on other occasions, the mix of people may not be appropriate. Also, when discussing family rules with parents, it is important to keep in mind that although a family rule may not fit you and your family, it may work with another family. Ask yourself: Would a rule change, advance, or restrict the growth of the individual and other family members? Satir's questions posed earlier may help in reaching that decision.

Further Exploration

Before helping family members transform their rules, professionals can benefit by practicing on themselves. The exercise in Figure 12.2 provides you with that opportunity. Also, professionals, parents, the child/youth, siblings, and extended family members involved in the family life of the child/youth would all benefit from reading Satir's classic works, *The New Peoplemaking* (1988) and *Your Many Faces* (1978).

Origin of Family Rules

Most family rules have been passed down for generations and, thus, are affected strongly by family history. McGoldrick, Giordano, and Garcia-Preto (2005b) have addressed cultural considerations. Children from some ethnic backgrounds, for example, are taught not to look adults in the eyes when they are being reprimanded; other ethnic backgrounds have the opposite rule. Sensitivity to cultural differences regarding family rules is important before diagnosing and considering transforming rules.

Satir's Five Freedoms

Satir set forth the following five freedoms as the cornerstone of effective human communication (Satir & Baldwin, 1983, pp. 168–169):

1. To see and hear what is here instead of what should be, was, or will be
2. To say what one feels and thinks instead of what one should

State a family rule that was not healthy. Usually these are dogmatic statements such as, "You can never _____ " or "You should/ought to _____."

Your family rule: _____

_____

Transform your family rule in the following three steps:

1. I can always _____
2. I can sometimes _____
3. I can _____when:
  a. _____
  b. _____
  c. _____

Complete another family rule transformation if it suits you!

Figure 12.2

Transforming a Family Rule

3. To feel what one feels, instead of what one ought
4. To ask for what one wants, instead of always waiting for permission
5. To take risks in one's own behalf, instead of choosing to be only "secure" and not rocking the boat

Flexible family rules that are based in reality provide these five freedoms. The mother–father–child triad is the source of the most powerful rules for behavior. Parents who provide realistic and flexible rules are usually the children of parents who did the same for them. Other parents can be guided in learning how to be more flexible in setting family rules.

As Satir said, people need to "give themselves permission" to see what is there, to say what they think, or to take a risk. Old family rules can be tenacious, as well as destructive. Professionals clearly face formidable odds when encouraging the five freedoms. Nevertheless, they should promote these five freedoms.

First and foremost, professionals should model healthy communication. Ways to encourage healthy communication include

- talking about the five freedoms and what they mean (initially, all school and community professionals would benefit from training in the five freedoms);
- talking about the five freedoms in classes and/or groups, when appropriate;

- making posters of the five freedoms for display in the school/community;
- establishing groups for children/youth that focus on the five freedoms;
- encouraging families to be free by helping them understand and relate to the five freedoms;
- devoting organization (e.g., PTA) meetings to the five freedoms;
- arranging for mental health professionals on the staff of the school or community setting or for an outsider to deliver large-group information sessions on the five freedoms; and
- implementing follow-up sessions in which school/community professionals lead the small-group interactions.

Knowing what the five freedoms mean and actually living them are two different things. Some autocratic leaders will not understand how to implement the five freedoms because they do not allow others to think their own thoughts and feel their own feelings. They see others' freedom as a threat.

Reality is subjective. Individuals react based on their personal backgrounds and view their experiences through personalized filters. Thus, professionals should be careful not to encourage others, subtly or obviously, to adopt their views of any situation. That is the beginning point of living Satir's five freedoms.

This does not preclude the professionals' helping others consider another view or transform ineffective family rules. For example, if a child or youth becomes manipulative, the professional could tell the parent how he or she sees the child manipulating the situation. In this scenario, the professional is exercising the freedom to see and hear what is happening and is exercising the freedom to say what he or she feels and thinks. Using the five freedoms as a guide, the professional is remaining true to himself or herself while serving as a model for the child/youth.

Of course, an individual's interpretation of a situation can be off the mark or in direct opposition to someone else's. Consider the case of a person who loves and values an argument and another person who despises any conflict. The professional is challenged to convince either person of the legitimacy of the other's view of reality. In instances like this, the professional must guide the individuals in testing their realities without violating their freedom to view those realities as they do. For example, the professional might propose a drama that allows the two individuals, the "debater" and the "pacifist" who have different styles of approaching life, to learn something about the other. First, the professional might say to the more confrontational person, the "debater":

> "Will you set aside your personal value for a minute? I'd like you to try a new tactic. I want you to ask your opposite (the "pacifist") a question that will help you understand something about your different perspectives. If you can imagine that possibility, I challenge you to step back and reflect on one or more questions that might pique your interest about how your "opposite" arrived at such a different approach.
>
> "While you're working on your questions, please remember the Five Freedoms—they're posted up front—and think about a metanoia, a shift of heart/mind, that's possible when learning

> what makes those who are unlike you 'tick.' I will be working with the pacifist one-on-one to go through a similar process. Then you two can flip a coin to see who poses the question first—the detective in learning about the other."
>
> With the other person (the pacifist), sit down nearby and discuss with her potential questions that she could pose to find out more about what people and processes in the debater's life led him to choose that approach in engaging others. Guide the pacifist to pose questions that will explore models from childhood, awareness of when the debater's approach became entrenched as the dominant style, who the debater's heroes are, and how he views confrontation as a way to join others, if that is the objective, or, the opposite, to push others away, which might stem from assuming that others won't accept him so he is making sure that he controls the rejection rather than facing the prospect of being rejected by others.
>
> As you coach the pacifist, suggest that she request being the first to pose questions. That immediately forces the issue of taking a different role than would be typical of an individual with a pacifist style. Listen for any family rules or stories that might be a clue to the pacifist style. For example, if the individual's father or mother was a revered model of deference to others, you may gain some information that may be useful later.

A scenario like this one presents an opportunity for people with different styles to consider differences between individuals and reflect on what kinds of life experiences, models, beliefs, and values lead people to their preferred styles of human interaction. When looking at styles of interaction, or stances, the five freedoms should be prominent in your thinking.

Generally, people do not have only one style. We may have two or three. But one style tends to predominate. In times of stress, most of us rely on our dominant style for dealing with conflict. If withdrawal is our dominant modality, it will be the default in times of conflict. If our dominant style is to confront directly, we will automatically assume that style under high stress.

If someone has an ingrained style that he or she wishes to change, this is the kind of situation that may be dealt with either in group or individual situations. This change should be sought only if the individuals are willing participants. In conflicting situations, we want to help ourselves and others live the five freedoms and offer them to others. That means being in reality as it is, saying the truth of one's experience, feeling what one feels without burying it to conform to rules, asking for what one wants, and taking risks rather than remaining secure in stressful situations.

Bowen's Detriangling

A third family systems concept that professionals can use to improve family–professional communication is detriangling (see discussion of Bowen's theory in the Appendix). When the intensity between two people becomes uncomfortable, bringing in a third person will diffuse the tension and allow the system to operate with less anxiety. Disentangling (see chapter 4) involves removing oneself from the anxiety two other people are experiencing. Like other forms of human interactions, detriangling is a complex process. One must be able to identify subtle and obvious means of being triangled as well as triangling others. Words are not the only means to communicate a triangling message. Facial expression, tone of voice, eye contact, and other nonverbal cues help to communicate a conscious or unconscious intent to triangle. For example, raising one's eyebrows and looking upward as though to say, "That's off-base," is a subtle form of triangling the recipient of the "look." As was suggested in chapter 4, detriangling requires knowing that the triangle exists, not taking sides in a conflicting situation, not talking to another person in the triangle about a third person, and not listening when someone tries to discuss a third person with you.

According to Kerr (1988), detriangling is "probably the most important technique in family systems therapy" (p. 56), and being emotionally neutral fosters detriangling:

> Emotional neutrality does not mean a refusal to approve or disap-
> prove of particular aspects of human behavior, and it does not
> mean making rules for oneself about not passing judgment on peo-
> ple's actions. A person who adheres to rules usually appears to be
> more neutral than he actually is. Nor does neutrality mean strad-
> dling fences or being wishy-washy. One can have a very clear posi-
> tion with respect to what occurs in a family and in society and still
> be emotionally neutral. Dogmatic positions, a lack of position, and
> efforts to change others all betray the absence of emotional neu-
> trality. In essence, neutrality is reflected in the ability to define self
> without being emotionally invested in one's own viewpoint or in
> changing the viewpoints of others. (p. 57)

Thus, *detachment* is of value when detriangling. Being able to remain emotionally neutral when two other people are attempting to triangle you is critical. If you can see both sides of an argument, you will know that you are on the right track. Judging other people's process is being intolerant and indicates that you are being triangled (Kerr, 1988).

Seeing both sides of a relationship problem can be tricky, because one person may appear to be the cause of the other person's problem. One person appears to be a victim and the other, the victimizer. Nevertheless, seeing both sides of a problem or argument is essential to understanding the detriangling process.

Implementation of Detriangling

To detriangle, professionals first must see the triangling process accurately. Second, they must censor their personal emotions and detach from judgments or resentments. Recognizing how feelings affect behavior will allow the professional to gain control over automatic responses stemming from those feelings. Then the professional can interact with family members by making statements indicating that he or she is not embroiled within the triangle and can be neutral.

Telling family members about the observed triangulation most likely will not have the desired impact of eliminating or even reducing it because they will have their own view of the situation and probably will not recognize triangulation. Also, teaching anything in a straightforward manner violates the Bowen premise that direct attempts to influence others run counter to differentiating self and, in fact, nullify that process.

Differentiating self is important to detriangling. Kerr (1988) best stated it this way: "Maintaining one's differentiation and detriangling is not an attempt to manipulate or control others but a way of dealing with others' attempts to manipulate and control oneself" (p. 58). Further, when professionals are able to detriangle, they are far more likely to improve the relationship of the other two people in the triangle. According to Bowen's theory, when a detached third person sustains a higher level of differentiation than the other two, the other two will raise their functional levels of differentiation.

Further Exploration

Professionals who are involved with families can learn much from investigating the triangling in their own families of origin. This is best accomplished with the assistance of a family systems therapist. Not all professionals trained in family work are trained in family systems approaches or the concept of triangulation. Professionals might find some local members of the American Association of Marriage and Family Therapists who are familiar with Bowen's concepts.

Bowen's training model, intended for family therapists who would be involved continually in triangling situations, included lifelong work dealing with families-of-origin. School or community professionals may not need a lifelong investigation of personal family process, but at least a minimum of a year of family investigation would be beneficial, to help the professional see the natural triangle that forms in schools and community between the child/youth, parent, and professional.

Family Conferences

The family conference is an integral part of family–professional interactions. The purposes of the conferences include, but are not limited to

- getting to know one another,
- enlisting and providing support,
- reporting progress of the child/youth, and
- problem solving.

For further discussion of family conferences for families of special-needs children/youth, professionals may find useful the texts by Bauer and Shea (2003), Kroth and Edge (1997), Seligman (2000), and Turnbull and Turnbull (2001).

Children/youth, as we have said, may be included in planning for, implementing, and evaluating conferences (Bailey & Guskey, 2000; Benson & Barnett, 2005; Syverson, 2005). Austin (1994) was an early proponent of student-led parent conferences.

Planning

As with so many other activities, good preparation for family conferences is rewarded by participants' feeling comfortable and relaxed. Prepared professionals are more confident professionals. The following are ways to achieve the aims of the conference.

Prepare the Setting in Advance

The physical setting itself can enhance or detract from effective family conferences. First, the seating must be comfortable. No adult wants to sit for up to an hour in a chair designed for a 6-year-old! Beyond the physical discomfort, uncomfortable chairs might signal to family members that the professional is not concerned enough about them to ensure the proper seating. Too, the professional's sitting in an adult chair while the adult family members are sitting in short chairs signals a hierarchy that should be avoided.

Another consideration in planning the setting is to allow for privacy. The professional is responsible for ensuring privacy. A closed door, as opposed to open space, signals privacy and sensitivity to the families' needs. In addition, a room appropriate for the number of people at the conference conveys a sense of confidentiality. It would be uncomfortable for three people to meet in a room that can hold 100 people. Providing an appropriate space indicates the professional's concern for the family members.

Freedom from interruptions is another major consideration in planning the setting. Cell phone interruptions and people walking in and out of the conference space are intrusive. Further, interruptions signal to the family that they are not uppermost in the professional's mind. Family members may also conclude that the professional does not have time for them and their child.

Issues of control and turf may arise when family members meet in the professional's room. When family members are invited into a classroom, as is often the case for conferences, they are in the teacher's territory. This automatically puts the family members and teacher on unequal ground, setting the stage for a hierarchy dysfunction. Family conferences with sensitive content may best be held in a room designated specifically for conferences.

The seating arrangement must be considered. The best arrangement is to sit in a circle at a round table or in comfortable chairs without a barrier between family members and professionals. Professionals should not sit behind a desk during the conferences, as that would erect an automatic barrier between the professional and the family. Parents' sitting on the other side of the principal's desk might call to mind times when they were students sitting in the same position.

Know Your Purpose

The purpose of the conference should be the focal point throughout the stages of planning and implementation. It is easy to become sidetracked when interacting with family members, and a stated purpose, known to all parties including the professional, the child or youth, and family members, will help to keep everyone on track.

Knowing the purpose of the conference, the professional is able to direct all of his or her energy to achieving that goal, whether it is to solve a problem or simply to get to know one another. Beyond that clearly framed goal or purpose are other purposes that should pervade all conferences. Foremost of these are building rapport and trust, as well as gleaning additional family information. A caring interaction process will promote these goals.

Develop the Plan

Formulating a plan is essential to the success of family–professional interactions. Clearly, the plan should be concerned with the stated purpose, such as reporting the student's academic progress or behavior. The professional can easily plan for that purpose by thinking about how to open the conference, the order for sharing content, and how to close the conference. This plan should allow the professional to achieve the stated purpose while also building rapport and getting to know more about the family unit.

To include family members in planning for conferences, professionals might call the family to state the purpose and ask whether a parent or another family member would like to contribute to the plan. This action signals an egalitarian approach to conferences from early in the process.

In planning an opening to a meeting, the professional should use whatever information he or she already knows about the family. At the onset, greetings should match the family's style of interaction. If the family members are formal and proper, the greeting might be in the form of a handshake, for example. Other families may be uncomfortable with formality but open to a warm, welcoming smile. Generally, the professional should act in the way that is natural for him or her, with variances depending on the family member and the situation.

The structural family therapy model (Goldenberg & Goldenberg, 2004), matching family styles of interacting, is referred to as *mimesis*, from the Greek word meaning *copy*.

Satir was a master at matching, or copying, clients. She was, in fact, the subject of research regarding her style (Bandler & Grinder, 1979). For example, when a client would refer to something using a visual metaphor such as, "It really looks good to me," Satir would reply with a visual response such as, "I get the picture."

In neurolinguistic programming (NLP), professionals are initially taught to match the individuals' level and speech patterns, and then gradually alter their own speech pattern with the expectation that the other will follow suit. For example, if a parent asks a question in a clipped and anxious tone, the professional would deliver his or her first sentence in the same clipped style, then gradually flow into his or her natural style to dispel the parent's anxiety, recognizing that parents are able to benefit more from the professional's more relaxed and receptive manner.

Deciding the order or sequence of the meeting is just as important as planning the opening to the meeting. Negatives should be buried in the middle of positives. Thus, reporting of progress of the child or youth should begin and end on a positive note. Because families of children and youth with special needs expect a focus on weaknesses, the professional should, when possible and appropriate, describe weaknesses in terms of challenges, thereby helping to reshape family members' view of the situation. For example, the professional might refer to Joe's "hard-fought battle for inclusion in English class" instead of Joe's "failure to adjust to inclusion."

A strengths-based approach rather than a deficit view of functioning (Allison, Stacey, Dadds, Roeger, Wood, & Martin, 2003; Comer, 2001; Malatchi, 1997; Noddings, 2005a) is supported throughout this book. At the same time, if family members whitewash and minimize serious situations, professionals should present a dose of reality that gets their attention. In those situations, focusing on the positive will not produce the necessary results.

Prepare the Family in Advance

Well before the conference, family members should be informed about its purpose and, as mentioned earlier, be given the opportunity to provide input into the agenda for the meeting. If professionals call parents to a meeting to get to know one another better but don't inform them of that purpose in advance, the parents may assume that their child has done something wrong or is having major problems. Not knowing the purpose of the conference may put them "on pins and needles" needlessly.

The professional should also let the family know whether anyone besides the family member(s) and the professional will be attending the conference and, if so, why those others will attend. For example, if a family member doesn't know that a psychologist will be at a conference, the parent may arrive and be taken aback, jumping to the conclusion that things are worse than anticipated. Surprises of that nature are damaging to trust and to the working relationship between professional and family. Informing parents about everyone who will attend meetings/conferences and the reasons, and inviting the parents to ask any questions will reduce potential anxiety.

Other elements involved in preparing family members include giving them clear instructions about where and when the meeting will be held and advising them what materials they should bring or what preparations they can make for the conference.

Implementing Family Conferences

Traditional recommendations for how to conduct family conferences are the subject of other texts and articles (Berger, 2003; Kaltman, 2006; Kroth & Edge, 1997; Lawler, 1991; Lawrence-Lightfoot, 2003; Olsen & Fuller, 2003). Here, we focus on applying family systems concepts during family conferences. For example, a conference may present an ideal opportunity to help family members transform an ineffective family rule into a guideline that works for them. The professional will want to model Satir's five freedoms by respecting, encouraging, and validating family members' opinions and feelings. Remaining objective and noting triangling also will be beneficial, as will detriangling when possible.

Maintain Self

When meeting with family members, professionals must always stand for who and what they are. This is important in all family–professional interactions but especially during conferences. Think of a time when you first met someone and automatically disliked her or him. Later you may have realized that the person reminded you of someone who had treated you poorly in the past, which colored your view. If the professional acts naturally, the family usually will come to recognize the professional for who he or she is.

Satir used to say to people who appeared to have confused her with someone else, "I think you've put a hat on me." Recognizing this phenomenon, accepting it as human, and being yourself is the best approach for professionals to take. Any preconceived notions by family members will be dispelled as the professional shows consistency over time.

Another way to convey a sense of self in a response is to say something along the following lines: "I wonder if Todd's former principal did things the way we do. Here at Crestwood High, the students and teachers mutually write rules of conduct at the beginning of the year. My role has been to help enforce rules developed by the students."

Catalog Family Patterns

Cataloging family patterns is an effective way to further understanding of a family over time. Just as professionals keep an academic file on each child, keeping a family file on family process—cataloging—is helpful. Sections in such a file include information on the family life cycle, family interaction patterns, historical factors, environmental factors, family configuration and genogram, and the nature of any special needs.

When the professional first meets with family members, he or she begins the cataloging process. As more is learned about the family during subsequent interactions, information is added. Of particular interest are any dysfunctional patterns that could be transformed—for example, a family rule that has hampered growth and development over the generations or the negative result of a triangle between grandmother and daughter transmitted through generations.

The purpose of cataloging current life circumstances and dysfunctional patterns is not to emphasize or dwell on the negative, though. It is to provide professionals with information they can use to help family members change patterns that stunt the growth of the family unit as well as the child or youth. Of course, school/community professionals cannot replace the services of family systems therapists. Educational and community professionals catalog family process to better understand a family and, therefore, to plan more effective interventions. They should not make suggestions that are beyond the family's capability to implement, nor should they elicit negative reactions by proposing what family members perceive as impossible demands and unrealistic expectations. Understanding family process and circumstances will help the professional avoid those situations.

Some observations can be cataloged as facts, and others should be cataloged as hypotheses. Family configuration, cultural factors, and socioeconomic status are facts at the time they are catalogued, but facts do change. For example, the stage in the family life cycle changes over time, and socioeconomic status changes with job shifts and retirement or disability. Although these factors are not always cataloged by school or community professionals, they are important considerations in recommendations to the family.

Some observations about interaction patterns and historical factors are not factual, such as triangulation or level of differentiation, as well as dysfunctional patterns related to the child or youth. Observations of this nature are maintained as hypotheses until several professionals confirm the opinions.

Once patterns or facts about the family have been cataloged and discussed confidentially with other professionals, that information should be used during future conferences. For example, if the professional has corroborated a hypothesis that the oldest daughter is a parentified child, that observation can be discussed with the family during a conference. The professional might find out that this also was true in the mother's family, and that it has become a transgenerational pattern.

Use Mutual Processes, When Appropriate

If Satir's seed model (Goldenberg & Goldenberg, 2004; Schwab, 1990) has one underlying theme, it is working with people as equals. Using mutual processes means that the family members and professionals jointly engage in planning, problem solving, and reporting the student's progress. The professional should be as interested in hearing about the child's progress on the homefront as in sharing the child's progress in the school or community setting. Reporting progress of a child or youth is a two-way street. When family members realize that professionals are as interested in hearing about the student's accomplishments and challenges at home as in telling about the student's progress in school or in the community, they will begin to make the shift from bystander to collaborator.

Some family members will not be interested in mutual processes. The needs of families should be determined on a family-by-family basis (Gamel-McCormick, 1995). Knowledge of the family's life, such as socioeconomic and cultural factors and family life cycle stage, may help to explain parents' desires and needs. Some family members may not want to be involved in the problem-solving process, and others may be overwhelmed or under-organized (Green, 1995) rather than uninvolved.

Evaluating

Professionals should evaluate their use of family systems concepts in planning and conducting conferences, as well as after completing the cycle of family conferences. The following evaluation steps will point you in the direction of using more of what works for you and help you determine ways to make your practices more workable.

Evaluate Your Planning

The purpose of evaluating your planning efforts is to determine what to change or to keep in the future. Did your planning produce the results you wanted? To answer this question, professionals should look back on the setting, primary and secondary purposes, planning process and product, as well as how well the family was prepared for the conference. Answering the questions below can help professionals evaluate their planning efforts. Question 7 concerns how the family members viewed the conference.

1. Did the setting facilitate open, honest, and confidential communication?
2. Was the seating arrangement comfortable?
3. Did your focal point remain the central theme of the conference?
4. Was your opening effective?
5. Did you close on a mutually supportive note?
6. Did the sequence of the conference facilitate open, helpful communication?
7. Was the family member(s) prepared so he or she was comfortable participating in the conference? How do you know?
8. Did the family member(s) indicate anything else you could consider in the future?

Professionals might design a checklist for family members to complete after each conference. The checklist would provide feedback and remove part of the burden of evaluation from the professional's shoulders.

Evaluate Your Implementation

Just as planning must be evaluated, so, too, must implementation. The professional should ask himself or herself about each of the implementation guidelines covered in this chapter. For example, did he or she employ family systems principles? If not, what blocked that process? Once the professional understands what caused the block, he or she can develop a strategy so the next occasion will not yield the same results. Perhaps there simply was no opportunity to transform a family rule; however, the professional could always model the five freedoms. If the professional did not recognize any triangling, he or she might decide to tape-record a future conference for further analysis.

Another good question for the professional to review is whether he or she was able to maintain self. If not, what factors contributed to the lapse? Can the professional point to any behavior patterns across families that might suggest instances when he or she gets pulled into the family's web and does not maintain a sense of self? Does one type of family resonate with any struggle in the professional's own life and, therefore, contribute to less effective strategies?

Other questions to ask include the following:

- Was I able to learn new information about family process or facts related to the family life cycle, environmental concerns, or family configuration?
- If so, can any of the information help me confirm or deny hypotheses I've established? How will I use that information in the future?
- If I met a dead-end in cataloging family process, what contributed to the lack of information? How might I obtain more information in the future?
- Am I possibly colluding with the family in any way by helping the family deny a reality that is difficult to confront?
- Was I able to use mutual processes that fit the situation? If so, how might I use those strategies again in the future? If not, what could I change in the future to enhance mutual processes?
- What factors about this family might make it difficult for me to facilitate mutual processes during family conferences?

These questions can help professionals modify their ways of conducting future conferences with families. Evaluation should be a learning process that affords insights as well as direction. Furthermore, it should make conducting future conferences easier with new and different families.

More information is available in family conferencing with students having special needs. See Diffily (2004), Kroth and Edge (1997), Olsen and Fuller (2003), and Seligman (2000).

Teacher-Student Support Teams

Research and experience have shown that general education classroom interventions are appropriate for at-risk and special-needs students. Although not all students can be educated full-time in general education classrooms, at-risk students and most students with special needs can succeed in these classes (Blue-Banning et al., 2004; Fisher & Frey, 2003; Friend, 2005; Friend & Cook, 2003, 2004; Orelove, Sobsey, & Silberman, 2004; Pugach & Johnson, 2002; Turnbull, Turnbull, Shank, Smith, & Leal, 2002).

With integrated models, professionals can help meet the needs of most students with disabilities while they remain in general education classrooms. Before referring children for special education assessment, general education classroom teachers should consider multiple educational interventions as well as intervention assistance teams (IATS) (Buck, Polloway, Smith-Thomas, & Cook, 2003; Burns & Symington, 2002; Truscott et al., 2005; Turnbull, Turnbull, Shank, Smith, & Leal, 2002). The approach to teacher–student teams described here illustrates a way of implementing Satir's organic/seed model on school teams (Goldenberg & Goldenberg, 2004; Satir & Baldwin, 1983; Schwab, 1990), described in the Appendix. Alignment with Satir's systemically oriented, organic model is seen in the egalitarian nature of this team model that values uniqueness while searching for alternatives.

Preferral Intervention

The term *prereferral intervention* was initially used by Graden, Casey, and Christenson in 1985 (Graden, 1989). A term that is often favored today, Instructional Assistance Team (IAT), focuses on teacher–student support (Truscott et al., 2005). At-risk students are often considered for these interventions, which are characterized by collaborative consultation (Friend, 2005; Friend & Cook, 2003, 2004; Pugach & Johnson, 2002; Walther-Thomas, Korinek, & McLaughlin, 2005). The interventions utilize problem-solving teams, such as teacher assistance teams and intervention assistance teams (Algozzine & Ysseldyke, 1992; Buck, Polloway, Smith-Thomas, & Cook, 2003; Knotek, 2003; Truscott et al., 2005; Turnbull, Turnbull, Shank, Smith, & Leal, 2002).

Soon after Carter and Sugai (1989) called the attention of the field of special education to prereferral interventions, many articles and chapters were written on its value (Fuchs, Fuchs, & Bahr, 1990; Fuchs, Fuchs, Bahr, Fernstrom, & Stecker, 1990; Phillips & McCullough, 1990; Tindal, Shinn, & Rodden-Nord, 1990). Fuchs, Fuchs, Bahr, Fernstrom, and Stecker (1990) defined prereferral intervention for children with special needs as modifications to instruction or classroom management aimed at accommodating a student without disabilities before making a referral. They saw this definition as incorporating a preventive intent—preventing inappropriate referrals and lessening future problems for students by helping the teacher learn to deal more effectively with a diversity of students. Others concurred that intervening before problems become compounded can reduce the need for referral to special education (Burns & Symington, 2002; Fuchs, Fuchs, & Bahr, 1990; Fuchs, Fuchs, Bahr, Fernstrom, & Stecker, 1990; Turnbull & Turnbull, 2001).

More recently, the literature on the prereferral process has included meta-analyses, issue specific studies, and statewide studies (Buck, Polloway, Smith-Thomas, & Cook, 2003; Burns & Symington, 2002; Knotek, 2003; Truscott et al., 2005). Drame (2002) indicated that "teachers [whose] perceived ability to manage their classrooms at schools without a clearly defined prereferral model were more likely to be affected by the presence of negative academic or temperament (e.g., attention-related) behaviors than were teachers at schools that implemented either a multidisciplinary or consultative prereferral model" (p. 47). In a survey of state practices using prereferral interventions, Buck and colleagaues (2003) related several benefits, one of which led them to conclude that, "when prereferral intervention procedures are most effective, the number of inappropriate referrals to special education is reduced and consequently potential cost-savings due to fewer inappropriate placements may occur" (p. 358).

The typical prereferral intervention, like other forms of intervention to early signs of challenging situations, usually consists of the collaboration of professionals rather than the involvement of families and students in problem solving. Idol, Nevin, and Paolucci-Whitcomb (1994) noted the need for parents to be included, stating,

> If a child is having sufficient difficulties in the general classroom to warrant either (a) referral to any collaborative problem-solving group such as child study teams or (b) consideration of using the Collaborative Consultation Model as a means of providing an appropriate education, then parents should be informed and included in decision making. (p. 80)

Besides being involved as partners on teams, a simple way by which families can help is to assist with homework. More than a decade ago, Ysseldyke, Christenson, and Kovaleski (1994) discussed five components of home support for learning:

1. Expectations and attributions
2. Discipline orientation
3. Effective environment at home
4. Parent participation
5. Structure for learning

These components remain crucial for increasing student success today.

Membership on Teams

Members of the various teams that provide assistance to teachers differ from one school system to another and across states (Buck, Polloway, Smith-Thomas, & Cook, 2003; Truscott et al., 2005). Student–teacher support teams typically include the principal or assistant principal, the referring person, the consulting teacher, and other specialists, such as a counselor, school psychologist, or special educator, as considered appropriate by the school or state requirement. Some teams involve fewer people, perhaps three professionals working together to develop viable solutions. Usually the composition of the team is based on the chairperson's selection of relevant members, given the nature of the need.

Bahr and colleagues (2006) refer to three roles of members of general education intervention teams:

1. The *referring teacher*, having made many attempts to resolve the challenge, is looking for new strategies.
2. The *facilitator* conducts and monitors the process of these meetings.
3. The *resource group* helps the referring teacher.

Truscott and colleagues (2005) suggested that professionals in special education are overrepresented on prereferral intervention teams and recommended including parents on the team with general classroom teachers.

Phases of Support

Prereferral intervention can be explained in terms of phases, each of which has several steps.

First Phase

The process of gaining assistance begins with the classroom teacher and the student requesting help for a specific challenge. The teacher, and sometimes the student, describes the academic, social, or motor behavior of concern. The teacher shares the information that has been gathered and explains past efforts to solve the problem. Different schools specify different procedures for these requests. Some are informal, and others require a more formal, written request for assistance.

Whether formal or informal, the next step is to consult with the referring teacher and, if appropriate, the student. One or more members of the team meet with the referring teacher and student. With an eye to solving the problem by emphasizing the student's strengths, the discussion begins with a description of the student's abilities and skills mastered.

An assessment may be made based on what is considered to be a discrepancy between the student's current level of performance and the level of performance expected or desired by the teacher and the student. Relevant classroom variables are analyzed for their influence on this discrepancy between actual and desired performance. Together, the referring teacher and members of the team—which could include the student and a family member—develop an intervention. Then the intervention is implemented and evaluated. If it is successful, the process ends. If it is unsuccessful, the process moves to the next phase. Again, the focus in this book is on family involvement using family systems concepts and strategies.

Second Phase

The next phase involves observations of the child or youth by additional professionals and possibly a family member. The purpose of these observations is usually to collect information on important variables in the classroom setting. Observation also allows comparison of the student to other class members.

Classroom observations are not the only type of observation considered. A social worker, visiting teacher, classroom teacher, other professional, or family member might observe the student in the home or in a community setting. These observations corroborate the student's functioning and point to possible reasons for the lack of the student's anticipated progress.

When observing in the classroom, the observers note the curriculum, the tasks and demands of the academic program, and the student's response to these variables. Also noted, in relation to the student in question and the class or situation in general, are the actions and language of the teacher, family members, siblings, and other relevant individuals. In addition, observers look at the way the work and space are organized in the classroom, including seating arrangements, grouping patterns, and interaction patterns. Then they attempt to describe the causes and consequences of the student's behaviors.

Third Phase

Following the observations, the members of the teacher–student support team meet to collaborate and design interventions based on the observations. Interventions might be changes in instruction in the classroom, changes in the way work and space are organized, implementation of behavioral procedures in the home or school, or the use of other resources available in the school, such as tutoring, sessions with the guidance counselor, or help from a remedial specialist. A family–school intervention might also be planned, or an intervention in the community. If a parent does not attend this meeting, a subsequent meeting should be scheduled with the student or family to discuss the proposed instructional or behavioral changes.

Family Involvement

Family involvement includes training, attending to requests for assistance, and guidelines for solutions.

Training for Professionals

Training on how to obtain needed assistance (Truscott et al., 2005) is crucial to success. The training should communicate the belief that families and the child or youth are important to the process. Actual cases from the school can be described to highlight the value of families being involved from an early juncture.

The training also might involve an introduction to relevant family systems concepts. The school social worker or counselor can provide inservice training for incoming teachers (Mullis & Edwards, 2001). Alternatively, teachers and other new staff members could be required to read information about family systems theory and practices so they are embedded in the processes engaged by team members.

Request for Assistance

In schools with a formal process for requesting assistance, the teacher composes a written request for intervention. Students who are old enough to be involved in making the request might be asked to contribute to its formulation. Preferably, teachers should be required to consult with parents before filing a request for assistance. When this contact is a requirement, the request for assistance should include a description of any involvement by a family member in the past. The description should also include the responses of the family members and their suggestions. If their suggestions have received attention in the classroom, or if combined school–home interventions have been attempted, the results should be reported.

Reporting results of past efforts is necessary so others do not waste time thinking about ideas that have already been shown to be ineffective. Reporting results also determines what works at home that might transfer effectively to the school or community setting.

Family process information is helpful, too. Relevant information the teacher has about the family should be presented in the written request, including information on demographics, family life cycle, special family configurations, historical and environmental factors, and family interaction patterns related to subsystems, boundaries, hierarchy, and power.

Guidelines for Intervention

The teacher should not alarm family members unduly before or after making a request for assistance. At the same time, if it might nip a problem in the bud, this is an ideal opportunity to encourage the family's participation. In some cases, families are reluctant to apply necessary consequences at home. As a result, students arrive at school thinking they can get away with unacceptable behaviors. The teacher might have exhorted the parents to apply appropriate consequences for the child's inappropriate behaviors with no results. If the parents are apprised that their child may be one step from being referred for special educational services, they may begin to do what they can to effect change in their child's behavior and/or learning.

In other cases, the parents may not have followed through with the kind of help their child needed. The teacher may have asked the parents to provide a quiet space along with paper and pencil for the student to complete homework assignments. When they come to realize that their lack of attention to these suggestions will soon result in a more formal request for assistance, it may elicit the results desired. Parental inattention to suggestions may stem from what Aponte (1994) called "underorganization," another factor called "pile up" (McCubbin & Patterson, 1982), or a dysfunctional family.

The first guideline—not to alarm family members unduly but to apply pressure when appropriate—might seem like arm-twisting, and in a way it is. It is a systemic concept referred to as gaining leverage (Senge, 1990).

When other professionals are involved, it is equally important to involve the family and the student in the problem-solving process. Imagine clarifying a problem without the family present only to find out much later, when the child is receiving special education services, that the situation could have been resolved quite easily. A home–school intervention requiring just one inexpensive resource—such as a tutor one night each week—might have taken care of the problem!

Finally, family members should be prepared to contribute to the intervention process, through information presented at school meetings and in newsletters. Once the parents have been approached about the specific situation with their child and have assisted the teacher in clarifying the problem, planning ideas, and implementing the plan, they should receive a written description of the purpose, nature, and process of requesting assistance and intervening. A school or community professional should be available to answer questions and provide any other assistance necessary.

Case Example

A first-grade student, Raheem, was rambunctious and disturbing other students in the classroom to a point at which they had trouble concentrating and completing their seatwork. The teacher tried several strategies. Finally, discouraged at the lack of progress, she called Raheem's parents and explained the situation and the interventions she had attempted.

The parents indicated that their older son, too, had been rambunctious in school. They told the teacher that Raheem had an IQ score of 140 and believed that, like his brother, Raheem might be bored and frustrated with having little to do once he completed his seatwork.

The teacher had not seen Raheem's test scores because the family had just moved from the Middle East, and the children's school reports did not follow them. She enlisted the parents' support in a home–school intervention in which the teacher sent a note home each day, reporting whether Raheem was disturbing others who were working. When he had a day with no disturbances, his parents praised him and spent time reading to him about his favorite subject, outer space.

After Raheem completed each assignment, the teacher presented two options to him. Both were enrichment activities that would allow him to pursue his intellectual curiosity about outer space, and he was given the choice.

This intervention was effective. Raheem settled down and became a model student. The intervention was tried only because the teacher knew that prior to a request for assistance, she was required to bring the parents into the process and provide input into how to solve the problem. Had that not been required, she would have gone straight to the Teacher Assistance Team.

Summary

Sensitivity/caring, trust, and shared locus of control are important elements for professionals working with families and their children who are at risk or have special needs. Parental and family collaboration and participation in the child's education have a positive influence on both development and achievement of children and youth, as does demonstration of value placed on learning. The use of effective communication is basic to all interactions, and this chapter applies this to conferences and teacher–student support teams, in which a school or community social worker may be included if their knowledge, skills, or networking capacity are relevant. Family systems applications are relevant to conferences with families and may be useful during teacher–student support team meetings also.

Family rules that have been dysfunctional in the past can be transformed with the guidance of professionals so that family members live with realistic rules that support all family members. Family members may need support in holding different rules for siblings of different ages, abilities, characteristics, or behavior. One twin may have demonstrated mature behavior and the other not only is irresponsible but provocative by repeatedly breaking established, clear rules. The parents and extended family members may need encouragement not to penalize the mature sibling but to enforce different rules based on behavior. This too can help the less mature child reach for a goal of more leniency by improving behavior.

The Five Freedoms of Virginia Satir form a base for healthy human interaction. These freedoms allow us to be free to experience life by seeing and hearing reality without contorting it to fit another's model; express what is felt and thought rather than holding it inside; feel our own feelings rather that what is expected by others; express wants rather than hope to have them noticed; and risk by trying new ways of communicating that allow the individual to be honest and whole.

Murray Bowen's detriangling is invaluable in not getting caught in the middle of other people's anxiety about their relationship issues. It is crucial that professionals sidestep disagreements within families or members working on a team. Redirecting someone who talks with you about another person's perceived problems is the best way not to become ensnared by their issues. The redirection is making a simple statement such as, "I think this is an important issue for you and your partner/parent/teacher to discuss with one another. If it would help, I will be there when you bring it up, and if you can 'go it alone' that is even better."

Preparation for conferences with family members and children/youth demonstrates respect and consideration to those attending the conference and includes having the room arrangement convey openness and egalitarianism as well as appreciation for privacy needs. The child and family members should know the purpose of a conference or meeting prior to attending. Stating your purpose and inviting the family members to add to that helps begin the conference with clarity and limits sidetracking.

Awareness of family members' interaction styles and interests can help professionals use similes or metaphors that have greater meaning render points made during the conference more memorable. If a parent loves baseball, a story can be told to illustrate a point using that sport. Crucial to all conferences is asking about strengths possessed by the child/youth and family members and keeping them clearly stated and relied upon. Simple reframing is also useful for parents who might be hard on their child who has made significant efforts but fallen short of expectations (e.g., "Gene's determination brought him closer to the goal").

All opportunities to meet with family members and/or children and youth should lead to establishing greater trust through sensitivity and caring as well as sharing in decision making. These interactions also provide considerable information about family process and history that can be catalogued for future reference; although notes should generally be written after the conference unless specific facts are provided that may be helpful in the future and easily forgotten given the amount of information being exchanged. Over time, professionals collaborating about what has been observed in a family may provide the information necessary to exchange with family members so they can begin to understand any dysfunctional patterns that may exist. As well, it allows them to receive help in making changes such as differential rules for siblings or lowering expectations of a parentified oldest daughter.

During conferences and meetings professionals "maintain a self" by accepting diversity and understanding that poor communication on the part of others may stem from past interactions with professionals being anticipated in the present. If experiences were negative in the past, professionals may find family members or the child/youth assuming defensive, aggressive, withdrawn or other equally difficult stances. When you "maintain a self," you do not allow their projections to change who you are or how you communicate. Professionals maintain neutrality as well as positive expectations about the eventual outcomes regardless of initial stances by the child or family.

In hindsight, professionals can use their family systems lens to evaluate their behavior and demeanor and consider their strengths and challenges in communicating with family and children or youth after a conference. Planning as well as implementation are important reflections when considering how family systems concepts and strategies can aide in meeting goals and improving the individual's development, behavior, and education.

Prereferral intervention also allows professionals to make use of family systems concepts, and the most basic is to include family members and child in the early stages of considering the behavioral, social, or educational challenge the child faces. Parents should expect to be involved in their child's learning and development and demonstrate it through their high expectations and value of learning; provision of space and materials necessary for completing school assignments and pursuing personal interests in learning; providing structure, when necessary guiding completion of homework that is not understood; and holding the child responsible for school requirements and rules.

The phases of student–teacher support teams begin when a teacher first contemplates a concern about a student's learning, development, and/or behavior then looks for clues that might explain the challenge. Some teachers look on the internet or consult textbooks for information that might help them understand the situation faced by the child. Typically, the teacher discusses it with others in the setting, trying to get ideas for how to work with the particular challenge. It is always important that professionals not only notice strengths possessed by the child or family members but also use them in planning ways to resolve or mitigate the challenge. Equally important is contact with the family in this early phase, as they can provide insights as well as suggestions that could make a big difference in school success. This is also a time when the catalog of family process can be added to by writing notes of what has been learned or observed about the child and/or family members. A child with a family history of dyslexia, depression, substance abuse, or heredity-linked explanation may not be known without family involvement. Siblings may provide important clues to understanding challenge.

Observations by other professionals are often made in the situation(s) where the challenging learning or behavior occurs (e.g., classroom, cafeteria). This allows for comparison with peers and for an opportunity to discriminate whether the challenge occurs across settings (e.g., home, classroom, recess, community). Eventually, all the information gleaned is used to collaboratively design an intervention that includes input from family members and the child, when appropriate.

Professionals unfamiliar with the process of gaining assistance about an atypical learning or behavior challenge need training in making use of teacher–student support processes. Family systems concepts and strategies can be taught as part of the training, and they benefit the professional in this as well as all other formal and informal endeavors to assist the learning and development of children who are at risk or who have special needs. Interventions make use of all that is written about functional communication in this book, with its foundation in family systems theory and concepts. When parents or caregivers do not enforce rules at home, the child expects the same from professionals in school and community. Likewise, if the child is accustomed to harsh discipline, he or she may take any chance to press the limits of authority in other settings in an effort to assert independence. When professionals learn about home situations, they may understand the reason a child is not always attending to hygiene or other important factors that most children and youth automatically have ingrained in their lives. If family members do not respond to requests for input and assistance or collaboration, a means of gaining leverage can help get past the presenting problem.

Extension Activities

Reflection on Sensitivity/Caring: Think of people whose presence made you feel secure and safe when you were a child, then think of people who make you feel cared for and safe in your adult life. What did these people have in common? How do you see yourself as being like them? In what ways would you like to emulate them? Imagine making changes in yourself so you embody more of the qualities you have valued in others. What challenges might you face in making those changes?

Activity on Risk-Taking: If you did not already take the Risk-Taking Questionnaire (Figure 12.1) and respond to the questions on trust at the beginning of the chapter, do this now.

In-group Pair/Share: Pair with a peer with whom you are comfortable, and share your reflections.

In-group Wrap-up: In the group, suggest items to add to or delete from Figure 12.1. Discuss any questions or thoughts the questionnaire brought up in group members.

Reflection/Journal on Locus of Influence: Reflect on a time you felt disempowered/ disenfranchised when an important decision was in the works. It could be as simple as where to go on a field trip or where the family was going for vacation, or with whom. What impact did those feelings of disempowerment have on you then, and what do you reexperience in reflecting on the situation? How did you respond then? How might you respond now? If there is a difference, what made the difference between how you did respond and how you might respond differently now?

Activity on Family Rules: Use Figure 12.2 to transform an unhealthy family rule from childhood. If you are a member of an immediate family (as a partner with or without children), consider an unhealthy family rule that you would like to see change. Discuss your work on the childhood rule with a sibling if you have one. Discuss your adult rule-change process with your partner or child, if appropriate. This will make it easier to help family members of children/youth who are at risk or who have special needs. Going through the process yourself will lend authenticity in guiding someone else in the process.

Activity on Triangling: Reflect on examples of triangling from your past or current family life. How has this made life difficult for you and/or others? Imagine being in a situation you just reflected on and "relive" it by thinking the ending in a new way—where you detraingle successfully. Be sure to keep emotionally neutral as you imagine yourself staying outside the triangling process.

In-Class/Training Activity for Family Conference: Plan, then role-play a family conference by selecting a case from Part One or Part Two. Go through the planning process with the group. Think through what the professionals might see in terms of family process, and be prepared with effective ways to improve the conference.

Assign members of the class/training group to play roles in front of the whole group. Ask the members who observe to provide feedback about what they observe—what went well, what might have been done differently, what might have been challenging for one that wasn't for another. Ask those who did the role play to evaluate the conference.

Family-Focused Interventions and Individualized Education Programs

*T*wo processes that involve families are family-focused interventions (FFIs) and individualized education programs (IEPs). FFIs go beyond the school to community settings and include positive behavior support (PBS) interventions with families. The IEP is a mandated intervention for children with disabilities in schools, with involvement by the family and any professionals from the community who might collaborate to offer some form of enrichment. The premise of any school-based intervention is that something in the student's school life is not functioning as well as it might be and can be improved.

Before the 1990s, family involvement in schools was unusual. In the early 1990s, when a major federal emphasis·shifted to early intervention, family-focused interventions became part of the landscape (Garland, 1994). Family–focused interventions is a broader term than the IFSP (Individualized Family Service Plan), the latter of which specifies minimum requirements for services to be provided to infants and toddlers birth to age 3 and their families. FFIs are interventions beyond the toddler years but are more intensive than the prereferral interventions covered in chapter 12. In this chapter, family systems concepts are interwoven throughout the descriptions of the FFI and the IEP, with school-related examples.

Rationale for Family Involvement

Children and youth who are at risk or who have special needs benefit from family and school/community partnerships because they offer more resources and greater consistency between home and school/community expectations and approaches (Bauer & Shea, 2003; Epstein, 1995; Sussell, Carr, & Hartman, 1996). Higher levels of differentiation of self (see chapter 4 and the Appendix, under Bowen's theory) and greater ability to regulate emotion are associated with a child's academic achievement and prosocial behavior. In a study of low-income urban families, Skowron (2005) found a link: "Mothers who were better at modulating emotion and capable of both intimacy and autonomy had children who demonstrated higher verbal and math achievement scores and were less aggressive" (p. 11).

Parents who receive needed support are better able to transfer the support to their children, and child functioning improves in all areas. Leithwood (1997) found that parental involvement in children's education accounted for 50% of the variance in children's school achievement. Researchers substantiate and practitioners experience that children's progress in school is related to family involvement with their education (Christenson, 2004; Henderson & Mapp, 2002; Jimerson, Egeland, & Teo, 1999; Miedel & Reynolds, 1999; Simon, 2004; Spinelli, 1999; Tittler, Friedman, Blotcky, & Stedrak, 1982).

Research corroborates the value of school/community involvement with families (Epstein, 2001). The onus is on the schools in how they reach out to families and collaborate with communities to improve the education of children and youth. At the same time, families should not be forced into involvement beyond their capacity. While families of children and youth with disabilities should be invited to participate, school/community professionals need to hear and respond to the parents' perception of how involved they can be (Turnbull & Turnbull, 2001).

An obvious and traditional form of family–student–school involvement is homework. From their research, Kay, Fitzgerald, Paradee, and Mellencamp (1994) found that students with learning disabilities responded more favorably when assignments were made "in the context of a strong support system of teachers, parents, and peers" (p. 551). Emerging from their data were five themes:

> (a) Parents felt ill-prepared to help their children with homework;
> (b) parents needed more information about the classroom teach-
> ers' expectations of their child and of their own roles in helping
> with homework; (c) parents wanted their children to be given
> homework assignments that were appropriate for them as individ-
> ual learners; (d) parents valued and even enjoyed hands-on home-
> work and projects in which the whole family could participate; (e)
> parents wanted an extensive, two-way communication system that
> would allow them to become partners on their child's instructional
> team. (p. 554)

Family involvement pertains to much more than homework, of course. Beyond research supporting the rationale for involving families in their children's education, parental involvement in the education of children with special needs is required by law. As well, the value and requirement of involving parents in school practices is clear in the No Child Left Behind Act of 2001.

Family-focused Interventions

For many years, the field of early intervention has been at the forefront in promoting extensive family involvement in education (Garland, 1994; King-Sears, 1997), with its family-centered programming (Bauer & Shea, 2003). All children enrolled in early intervention programs must have an individual family service plan (IFSP) (Turnbull, Huerta, & Stowe, 2006). The field of early intervention did not make individualized education programs the focus of intervention. Instead, IFSPs were paramount and required parental membership on the assessment team (Garland, 1995).

With the reauthorization of IDEA in 2004, Turnbull, Huerta, and Stowe (2006) described the requirements and significance of written IFSPs. The family and the child are co-beneficiaries with related services such as school social work and counseling benefiting the family as a whole. The trend toward service integration required services to be family-centered and culturally responsive. As well, the law highlighted the significance of family as decision-maker. Families are encouraged by professionals to learn collaborative and advocacy skills that they can rely on when their child comes of school age (kindergarten). Gargiulo (2006) delineates the differences between the IEP and the IFSP that are instructive to families when children with IFSPs enter kindergarten and the IFSP is replaced with IEPs.

The underlying belief of proponents of family-focused interventions is that educators must *individualize* services for families with children who have special needs (Chen & Miles, 2004; Malatchi, 1997; McWilliam, 1996; Turnbull & Turnbull, 2001). As R. Miller (1996) indicated, this should be true for the families of all students, not just those with special needs. Nevertheless, the involvement of families is particularly important for at-risk students, and intervention services must be tailored to their unique characteristics. These characteristics relate to differences in family structure, family interaction patterns, and family life cycle (Gamel-McCormick, 1995). Professionals employing PBS offer a specific family-focused intervention, covered later in the chapter.

Family-focused intervention consists of a sequence of specific activities related to planning, implementing, and evaluating family services (Dunst et al., 1994c). Broader than the IFSP, which relates specifically to early intervention in special education, the FFI is not prescribed by legislation. This section covers the underlying features of family-focused interventions, processes of intervening, types of assistance provided, and positive behavior intervention examples.

Underlying Features

The three underlying features that must be considered when planning family-focused interventions are family uniqueness, goodness of fit, and networking. Family systems concepts fit into these features in interesting ways.

Family Uniqueness

As discussed earlier in the book, families differ in a number of important dimensions (McWilliam, 1996), including stage in the family life cycle and family interaction patterns related to boundaries, hierarchy, and power. For special-needs children and youth, the disability is only a small part of who the child is as a person and family member (Friend, 2005). Also relevant to family uniqueness are cultural (Harry, Rueda, & Kalyanpur, 1999; Obiakor, Utley, Smith, & Harris-Obiakor, 2002) and socioeconomic background (see chapter 5); historical factors within the family, such as triangulation and sibling position (see chapter 4 and the Appendix); family configuration, such as blended families (see chapter 7); and the type and severity of the child's risk or special needs, and the impact upon the family.

All students, including those who are typical, at risk, or have special needs, possess a unique mixture of strengths and weaknesses, skills, feelings, behaviors, values, and potentials (Gargiulo, 2006; Winton, 1996). Thus, plans and interventions involving family members must be individualized to meet the child's uniqueness and personal needs (McWilliam, 1996). Likewise, to be most supportive to families, the plans and programs must respond to the intricacy that each family presents (Jordan, Reyes-Blanes, Peel, Peel, & Lane, 1998). Like snowflakes, families come in infinite varieties.

To elaborate on this theme, the abbreviated case studies of Bobby and Chris on the next 2 pages describe two families. First read about Bobby and his family, then complete the outline given under the case information. Your notes should concern family life cycle; family structure, including subsystems, boundaries, and hierarchy; historical information; cultural and socioeconomic factors; special needs; and family configuration.

Next read the case study of Chris. After you have read the case study, write notes as before, using the outline provided.

Goodness of Fit

When planning a family-focused intervention, the second underlying feature of which professionals should be aware is *goodness of fit* (Bailey, Simeonsson, et al., 1988). *Fit* means a comfortable, beneficial meshing of the unique family needs with the intervention. If family-focused interventions are to help children with special needs and their families, goodness of fit is essential.

Networking

Networking is valuable because sharing resources requires a systems view "in which development of resilience is seen as occurring in the transactions between and among multiple systems and contexts" (Minnard, 2002, p. 241). Systemic approaches reach out to include more resources and avoid narrow interventions.

When making family-focused interventions, teachers must maintain role perspective. They cannot be everything to everybody and balance their career and personal life (Miller, 2002). They need to view themselves, first and foremost, as being responsible for their primary role—teaching—when communicating with others. Various other professionals within and outside of schools are important in meeting the needs of the whole child/youth and must be relied on to maintain a healthy balance and avoid teacher burn-out. Teachers networking with peers also is helpful (Miller, 2002).

Teachers are in a distinctive position in relation to parents of at-risk and special-needs students. They share with the students' families the mutual responsibility for educating the child. As such, teachers have the opportunity to establish a close working relationship with

Case Study: Bobby

Bobby, an 8-year-old, has been in a self-contained classroom for children with emotional disturbance since kindergarten. A shy, withdrawn child, he did not speak to anyone other than the teacher during his first year of school. Recently he is being included in general classes for most of the school day.

The oldest child in his family, Bobby has a sister who is 4 years younger and is not aware that her brother has any problems. Bobby's parents are overprotective and continually hover around him. They pick him up from school each day, even though he could take the school bus home. They appear to be happily married and to support each other, though they spend an inordinate amount of time with Bobby. It is hard to tell if he is Mommy's or Daddy's little boy.

Bobby's mother is originally from Puerto Rico and makes most of the decisions regarding childrearing. The parents together, however, make the rules in the house. This family is deeply spiritual and often speaks of a "grand design." They interact with many friends and relatives, from whom they regularly seek assistance. But they have seen few professionals regarding Bobby, saying that "Bobby will grow out of his shyness." The father mentioned that he, too, is painfully shy and spoke of an uncle of Bobby's who was much like Bobby when he was young. The parents do not want to accept the possibility of their only son's having serious emotional problems, although they are currently accepting help to locate resources that can tell them more about Bobby's problem.

NOTES

Demographics: 8 years old; part-time general education classroom

Family life cycle:

Structure:
        Subsystems
        Boundaries
        Hierarchy

Historical factors:

Cultural and socioeconomic factors:

Bobby's special needs:

Family configuration:

Case Study: Chris

Chris, a 12-year-old student, has been in a classroom for children with emotional problems for 3½ years. He is a "motor-driven." hyperactive youth who talks to anyone who will listen. His mouth and feet are in constant motion. Currently, Chris is in a general classroom for a portion of the school day.

He has close relationship with an older half-brother, 16-year-old Leroy. Leroy protects Chris in the neighborhood and probably fights too many of Chris's battles for him. On occasion, Leroy does feel embarrassed by Chris, especially when Leroy's adolescent friends are visiting and Chris gets rambunctious.

Chris's mother is a single parent. She and Chris's father, a carpenter, are divorced. Chris continues to be upset about that loss and hangs around many of the adult males in the school building. He has developed a close friendship with a custodian and speaks with the assistant principal regularly. Further, Chris has made a special friend of the floating substitute, who is also male. Chris's mother realizes that she may be involved in a lifelong struggle with her son. She has few social supports in friends or family; however, as a social worker, she knows many professionals in the predominately black neighborhood where she works. The mother's main feelings seem to be frustration and isolation. She feels alone in shouldering the responsibilities of the family and has little time to herself.

NOTES

Demographics: 12 years old; part-time general education classes

Family life cycle:

Structure:
  Subsystems
  Boundaries
  Hierarchy

Cultural and socioeconomic factors:

Chris's special needs:

Family configuration:

Case Study Analysis

Refer to the case of Chris in this chapter, then evaluate each of the following three suggestions for possible violations of the three features that underlie effective family-focused interventions.

Suggestion 1: Chris is referred to the medical center for further evaluation of his hyperactivity.

Suggestion 2: Because Chris's mother is a social worker, she is asked to chair a parent group for parents of students in Chris's middle school. The meetings will be held in the morning. The teacher assumes the responsibility of interviewing and finding a "big brother" for Chris.

Suggestion 3: Leroy, Chris's brother, is to be seen by Chris's teacher weekly for counseling sessions.

Your Analysis of Violations of the Three Underlying Features

Uniqueness:

Goodness of Fit:

Networking:

families. Teachers frequently become confidants to parents, trusted professionals on whom the family can rely.

The teacher, however, functions best not as an isolated intervener but as a "hub" through which a network of resources can positively affect families. When social workers or counselors are available to share the "hub" of the network, general and special education teacher are not overburdened. Realistically, the teacher cannot maintain, on his or her own, both the parent–teacher relationship and the primary role of teaching while trying to satisfy the diverse needs of these families. The teacher should see it as his or her responsibility to serve as a facilitator and collaborator with other school/community professionals in helping parents access the variety of resources available in the social-systems.

Families of children with multiple disabilities often need the multiple services of several providers. Overloading them with too many resources may deplete a family system that is overwhelmed already. They may need coaching from the teacher or other professionals within or outside the school to ease up on themselves. The family typically has an identified professional who serves either as the program manager for the child or as a service coordinator (Chen & Miles, 2004).

Another form of networking called CIRCLES (covered later in this chapter) is used when developing an action plan or MAP in person-centered planning. It creates a network, a "circle of friends," for the child or youth to implement plans, relieving the family, and sometimes the teacher, of too much responsibility.

Processes of Intervening

Like most types of interventions, family-focused interventions involve the four processes of assessment, planning, implementation, and evaluation. Organization is a key factor in effective family intervention and requires teamwork. Counselors are recommended as liaisons to establish and maintain cooperation and clarity of shared understanding on teams serving students with disabilities (Dunn & Baker, 2002). Interventions should be based on the best available data, carefully planned, implemented responsibly, and, after intervention, evaluated critically.

Dunst and Deal (1994) listed the following elements to consider in developing and implementing family plans that empower and strengthen families, which are still most relevant in the 21st century:

1. Family concerns
2. Family needs
3. Outcome statement
4. Resources and supports
5. Courses of action
6. Family strengths
7. Partnership
8. Evaluation

These elements are incorporated into the following discussion of family-focused intervention.

Assessment

Sound assessment is the foundation upon which effective intervention rests. Can you imagine a physician prescribing a drug before he or she diagnoses what is wrong? Or, worse, imagine being operated on before the need for an operation had been established!

Assessment for family-focused interventions has two complementary parts related to the family systems theory, concepts, and practices that make this book unique. The first is to determine the status of the family on dimensions including family life cycle, interaction patterns, historical factors such as sibling position and triangulation, cultural or socioeconomic factors, family configuration, needs of the child or youth, and desires of the child and family.

The second component of assessment in family-focused interventions is to elicit the family's needs and determining the family's strengths and resources. Strengths-based assessment requires looking at family and child accomplishments and abilities (Epstein & Sharma, 1998; Epstein, Rudolph, & Epstein, 2000). Relationships characterized by trust and mutual commitment allow family members to feel comfortable enough to provide information to professionals about those needs (Gargiulo, 2006). The professional then can use that information to develop hypotheses about the family's life cycle, interaction patterns, and other aspects of family systems.

Once hypotheses are developed, the professional reflects the information back to the family. For example, the professional might say, "Mr. and Mrs. Estevas, it sounds to me as if Miguel's older sister, Maria, is really feeling the pinch of your spending so much time helping Miguel with his homework. It also seems that the two of you are overloaded with your 2-year-old twins."

Once the professional reflects the information with the family, together they confirm the conclusions and the professional can begin to create a database that is held jointly with the parents. The jointly developed conclusions and data should be explicit. Consider the scenario of a family with an adolescent child and a younger child with a physical disability. The family has asked the adolescent to help the younger child find friends. The parents expect the adolescent to come home after school, wait for the sibling to arrive, take care of the child, and take the child around the neighborhood to meet other children. With this information, the professional might hypothesize, "This looks like a family that is enmeshed, with a parentified older sibling."

To reflect this hypothesis back to the family, the professional would not want to say, "Maybe you're expecting too much from your adolescent." Neither would he or she use professional terminology and say to the parent, "Your family seems to be enmeshed." Instead, the professional's comments would be geared to helping the parents realize that adolescents have needs of their own. Providing information about the family life cycle and differing demands at each stage of development would help the parents view the needs of their adolescent realistically.

As conclusions are developed and agreed upon, the problems and needs are prioritized in terms of the immediacy and seriousness the family perceives. It often helps to make a list of the needs as they surface in the conversation. For example, for the Estevas family, the list might include time for the couple to be together, help with Miguel's homework, time for Maria to do her own homework, time for the mother to be by herself, and the siblings' need for information on genetics and possible impact on their own future families.

Later, the professional would share the list with the family members, and they would prioritize their needs together. The family members would decide that some things are more serious than others and that some things require immediate attention. This prioritization process reflects both seriousness and immediacy. During planning, the list can be used when discussing solutions.

When assessing the functioning of the family, relevant child variables should be assessed along with the adult variables. It is important to establish how family members view their own needs for support, information, or training. Observations of parent–child interactions are another rich source of assessment data. From the information gleaned and the observations made, teachers, social workers, other professionals, and family members develop tentative hypotheses about family needs.

Once the functioning and characteristics of the family are known—including all the dimensions of family systems as well as what the family sees itself as offering and needing—it is time to move into the planning process. This must not be done unless professionals have invested considerable time with family members and come to understand their unique strengths, characteristics, resources, needs, and desires.

Planning

In person-centered planning, information has been gathered during the above-described assessment process "from the child, family, and others supporting the child, considering strengths, interests, needs, and dreams for the future" (Malatchi, 1997, p. 92). Team planning allows professionals to validate the needs and interests of the family and the child/youth, reprioritize those needs when indicated, and elicit the child/youth's and family members' suggestions about what solutions might fit them (Friend, 2005).

From the family systems database, goals can be generated. A goal can be thought of as a vision—a vision best shared by the child/youth and family involved in developing it. A goal essentially is a description of what will occur when the development or challenge is met. Goals should be outcome-oriented, time-limited, and stated so that all involved will be able to recognize when they are achieved.

Goals are not objectives. Goals should be stated in relative rather than absolute terms. For example, reducing temper tantrums to no more than one per evening, as opposed to eliminating tantrums entirely, is a realistic, functional goal. Another example is for an adolescent to complete homework three of the four nights it has been assigned each week, as opposed to completing homework all four nights of the week. Note the difference in these two examples. Reducing temper tantrums is decreasing an undesirable behavior whereas increasing completion of homework is a positive goal. This is another part of strengths-based approach—an eye toward the positive.

Goals are critical to the planning process. They serve as a map to reach the destination. Once educational, social, and behavioral goals have been established, professionals can work with the child or youth and family to generate plans for achieving those goals. Plans are best established according to the three W's: *What* action is to be taken toward achieving a particular goal? *Who* will be responsible for that action? *When* will the action be completed? In family-focused interventions, planning must involve the parents, the student, and professionals.

Examples of plans that might be developed during a conversation with the Estevas family include having the grandmother tutor Miguel, allowing his parents to have time alone with each other at least every other evening, and having an aunt babysit, allowing the mother to go out three mornings each week. Any plans that are developed should be based on family input and the family's prioritization of their needs.

Forest and Pearpoint (1992) described a process for strategic planning and problem solving in education that involves making action plans and tracing the path that will lead to successful implementation (Pearpoint, O'Brien, & Forest, 1995). The beauty of their work is involving a host of people who are committed to the student in helping him or her generate ideas and plans and implement solutions.

The necessity of joint planning involving professionals, the child or youth, and parents cannot be emphasized strongly enough. The probability of success is highest when all parties have had the opportunity to examine alternatives, express concerns, and influence decisions. Family-centered positive approaches that are strengths-based and involve family members in identifying needs make a difference (Sheridan, Warnes, Cowan, Schemm, & Clarke, 2004).

Implementation

No decision has really been made until action has been taken. Likewise, the best of plans are only good intentions until they are implemented. If any party to a plan is reluctant to proceed to implementation, reexamination of the data and the planning process may be warranted. A critical question to ask in such a case is: "What has prevented free expression of concerns during the planning part of the process?" Possibly, Satir's five freedoms were violated, or the individual was generalizing to the planning process a prior experience in which one or more of the five freedoms were restricted.

Lack of freedom to express concerns, perceived or real, is not the only explanation for lack of implementation. Barriers to implementation may be unforeseen. For example, perhaps the grandparent who was going to help the child with his homework had to be hospitalized and could no longer offer assistance. The professional should model flexibility in initiating conversation about the new circumstances and other possible solutions. Flexible rules are a sign of healthy functioning, and some parents need encouragement in this regard. Families with rigid boundaries are less likely to adapt easily to changing circumstances.

If implementation is rocky, the process may be revisited to see if it involved family-centered positive psychology (FCPP), building on strengths. Sheridan, Warnes, Cowan, Schemm, and Clarke (2004) explained the belief underlying FCPP that "the child and family outcomes will be enhanced if members participate in identifying needs, establishing social supports and partnerships, and acquiring new skills and competencies, rather than simply receiving services from professionals" (p. 7).

Low-income, single caregivers involved in quality interactions during interventions learn more about productive caregiving of their child. At the same time, because of the complex and extreme circumstances under which they live, they first must be helped with their mental health needs (Unger, Tessell, Jones, & Park, 2004). If this was not clear in the assessment process, it will have to be revisited during implementation because the situation will block implementation.

Still pertinent are the three types of direct professional support that Bailey and colleagues (1988) listed:

1. Informational support
2. Instrumental support that helps families achieve tasks or functions
3. Socioemotional support such as listening

They also discussed indirect support such as facilitating services and case management, and they cautioned professionals against attempting to provide services in which they were not skilled. For example, in good faith and with the best intent, a teacher might attempt to provide counseling for bereaved parents. Although a caring and supportive teacher can, and actually should, talk with the parents about the death of a child in the family, the teacher should not assume the role of counselor in those interactions.

Building on strengths leads to resilience and the development of protective factors that will matter throughout the child's life (Amatea, Smith-Adcock, & Villares, 2006). An implementation process built on the strengths determined during the assessment process will have a greater likelihood of succeeding.

Evaluation

Once a plan is implemented, the final component in the process is evaluation. Good plans contain built-in evaluation in terms of measurable, time-limited goals. Evaluation also might include retaking the inventory/survey or repeating the process/dialogue used earlier to assess family need.

Too frequently, evaluation looks only to outcomes. Evaluation of family-focused interventions should assess more than simply the degree to which the desired outcome was achieved. Each family member's level of satisfaction with the process should also be determined. It is helpful to ascertain what worked well and what was ineffective or overburdening. This evaluation, combined with the results of a family inventory, checklist, or assessment procedure, can become the basis of an updated assessment to use in developing a new intervention cycle.

With a focus on early intervention, Bailey and colleagues (1998) recommended using eight questions that could serve as a framework for determining the extent to which early intervention has accomplished the goals inherent in a family-centered approach (p. 313). The first three questions are related to family perceptions, asking families whether they view the intervention as having made a difference for the child and in the family and whether the family holds a positive perspective of the services and professionals providing them. The other five questions relate to different domains and impacts on the family.

The four steps of assessment, planning, implementation, and evaluation result in a dynamic interrelated process for change—not a start-and-stop model. It is a cyclical process in which each new round builds on the successes of the last, leading to increased impact and effectiveness. The following are questions to answer about the four processes of intervening:

1. What are some reasons that trust is so important in the assessment process?
2. To what do you attribute the importance of the assessment step in family-focused intervention?
3. Why do goals seem to be the time manager's answer?
4. What is an example of a well-stated goal for a family-focused intervention? Why?
5. Why is mutuality in planning a "sacred cow" (i.e., something extremely important)?
6. How do you see evaluation fitting into the process of family-focused intervention?

Types of Assistance for Family-focused Intervention

Specific types of assistance provided by professionals include emotional support, identification of resources, referral, normalization, reframing, and contextualization. Each of these will be covered briefly.

Emotional Support

Families will not necessarily identify the emotional support of professionals as something they need. Professionals can assume, however, that all families will benefit from emotional support. This is especially true of families with children who are at risk or who have special needs. Professionals should ask parents and their children what forms of emotional support they want and are comfortable receiving. When providing emotional support, cultural differences, too, should be taken into consideration.

Families with children who have special needs are likely to feel grief, isolation, anxiety, or frustration to some extent. Therefore, professionals must provide an atmosphere of trust and safety (Gargiulo, 2006; Miller, 1996) when relating to these families. Conveying a sense of understanding and caring is a basic and powerful way to assist a family (Morsink et al., 1991). Comforting is important to the health and well-being of all people (Burleson (1994). Noddings (1984, 1995, 2002, 2003, 2005b) extends her considerable writing and research to include the importance of caring in community settings.

The best way for school professionals to provide emotional support may be found in reflecting feelings (Pugach & Johnson, 2002). Showing family members that they are understood is a powerful way to provide assistance. Client-centered therapy, developed by Carl Rogers, evolved around the concept of active listening, and particularly the importance of listening to someone who is in emotional pain. Active listening can lead to reality-based feedback (compliments) that helps build confidence.

Because professionals have time limitations and other demands and responsibilities, they may respond with solutions rather than react to the family member at his or her level of emotional response. A professional should take care not to suggest solutions hastily.

Support groups offer another way for children and youth and their families to receive the emotional support they need. Some support groups are arranged by school and community professionals with a trained facilitator. Others consist of parents supporting parents or children and youth supporting one another around specific issues, such as Al-Anon.

Resource Identification

Being able to locate the most beneficial resources is particularly important for at-risk students and their families (Booth & Dunn, 1996; Dryfoos, 1994; Harvard Family Research Project, 2006; Maton, Schellenbach, Leadbeater, & Solarz, 2004; Slavin, Madden, Dolan, & Wasik, 1996). Weiss and colleagues (2005) provide a resource guide with Internet links for families. School personnel can help to achieve goodness of fit in linking people with resources. For example, helping family members use the Internet as a resource may be useful with some families. Information on specialized personnel within the school and community should be provided as available resources. Personal recommendations can be reassuring.

According to Turnbull and Turnbull, one of the most valuable resources for parents of children with special needs and those at risk for failure in school or life is information about parent groups, of which there are three basic types (2001):

1. Parent support groups that come together to share emotional support and assist one another in coping with having a child/youth with special needs or at risk (e.g., addiction).

2. Parent education oriented toward providing information about specific conditions such as learning disabilities. These groups also may train parents in management techniques or other topics such as time management.
3. Parent advocacy groups that teach and encourage parents to become strong advocates for their children. One such organization is the Association for Children with Learning Disabilities.

Murray and Malmgren (2005) implemented a program in a high-poverty urban school that partnered teams of one teacher and one student who had significant behavioral/emotional problems. Pre–post ratings of teachers showed that students who had been matched with a teacher on a one-to-one basis to increase positive involvement had higher grade-point averages after 5 months.

Extended family members have also been used as resources for at-risk families. Walton, Roby, Frandsen, and Davidson (2003) used family group conferences with extended family members to solve problems in a solution-focused, strengths-based approach with adjudicated youth. The participating families found the process to be empowering; the professionals were highly satisfied with the involvement of extended family members; and the judges recognized its potential as a model for others.

Identification of resources may involve helping parents locate and gain access to another parent with compatible needs and interests or helping them find ways to gain needed experiences, such as by sitting in on IEP meetings or visiting alternative programs (Friend, 2005; Turnbull & Turnbull, 2001). Further information concerning resource identification is provided in chapter 10.

Referral

Referrals are indicated when the specialized needs of children and families go beyond what the school/community is required to provide or can reasonably be expected to provide. Teachers should be cautious about stepping out of their roles and beyond their expertise.

Family therapy is a prominent option for referral when the professional can identify structural or interactional patterns in the family that warrant such an intervention. Sibling groups are another option for referral, either when problems arise among siblings, or simply for mutual support (Meyer & Vadasy, 1994).

Referral recommendation should be handled with respect and care, as well as sensitivity to cultural differences. When making a referral for individual or family therapy or counseling, confidentiality is essential.

Normalization

Parents and school/community professionals alike face a challenge in maintaining a balanced and positive perspective that avoids overemphasis on the child's deficits (Malatchi, 1997). The first child in a family sets the stage for what parents expect from future siblings, but parents soon find that what one child was able to do at a certain age is different with the next child. Parents who have a child with a disability may see the child through a "disability filter." They may not realize that most actions of atypical children may be age-appropriate and normal at times. For instance, "normal" students have bad days at school or in the community every now and then, but the same behaviors in a child with special needs tend to be thought of as symptomatic.

Teachers and other school professionals can help the family develop a normalizing perspective. Some professionals in the school/community must check their personal disability filter to be sure it is not set on "deficit-mode."

Reframing

Reframing involves offering alternative interpretations of a behavior or an event that essentially change the meaning of a behavior (Bardill, 1997; Bradley, Gould, & Hendricks, 2004; Nardone & Watzlawick, 1993). The objective is to alter the pattern of the interaction and perspective. For example, many children with attention deficit hyperactivity disorder have difficulty following complex directions and therefore do not comply with directions. A parent may label the child's lack of compliance as defiance. If the professional can help the parent relabel the behavior as "confused," the emotional loading and sequence of parent–child interactions might be changed. Similarly, a parent who complains of a child's pestering may respond differently if the professional emphasizes the child's need for affection and reassurance.

In an example by Bradley, Gould, and Hendricks (2004), an adolescent complained about his curfew time. The counselor used reframing to point out the parents' reality-based safety concern. In the follow-up the counselor selected a song to play that described feelings identified in the reframe around the curfew.

The Appendix describes Virginia Satir's communication process model, including reframing, which can be an effective intervention by school and community professionals. Satir (1983a) referred to helping families see situations with "new eyes" She characteristically said, for example, "Yes, that's how you saw your son yesterday. Now you've learned so much about yourself, your parents, and their parents. How do you see your son now?" The concept of reframing is discussed further in chapter 14.

Contextualization

Contextualization shares some similarities with normalization and reframing. It is a process of helping family members interpret behavior in and through the context in which it occurs. For example, a child may develop physical complaints when confronted with demands on his or her performance that the child feels inadequate to meet. Consider a kindergarten child, Emma, who was the only child in her class who was unable to recognize the letters of the alphabet. She began to complain about headaches and asked to go to the infirmary every time the teacher taught letter recognition in class. Or consider John, an adolescent who became withdrawn and rejecting toward his siblings after a difficult social encounter with peers at school. Or a child who is afraid of a classmate can become aggressive or threatening toward that classmate. Shawn provides an example. He was afraid of a peer's size and threatening manner. Shawn told the peer that he had a black belt in karate and invited him to fight—but Shawn had never even attended a karate class.

School and community professionals can assist family members to respond effectively to a child's behavior by helping them tune in to significant contextual factors. Once the family members notice and understand the context from which the behavior springs, they will accept and respond to the child or youth more readily.

How the family members respond once they understand the context depends on the situation. In the example of Emma, the family members could be coached to support her by commenting on the way they would feel if they were in a class for which they were unprepared. In the second example, John's siblings might be coached not to bother him until he has time to come to terms with the situation at school. This advice is relevant especially for enmeshed families, who tend to get in the middle of the special-needs student's own problems. Or if Shawn's family (in the third example) were disengaged, the professional, after attuning the family to the context, could coach the family to reach out to him by commenting on how threatened they might feel themselves in similar situations. This intervention may lead to stronger positive alignments between the needs of the adolescent and the family members, as well as healthier cohesion in family interactions.

Positive Behavior Support (PBS)

Positive behavior support (PBS) is an approach to family-focused intervention that takes place in the home, school, community, or work setting and frequently cuts across two or more of these contexts. PBS also can be an outgrowth of observations made, hypotheses tested, and conclusions drawn by professionals and families working together in the assessment stage.

Although the best collaborations between family members and professionals tend to preserve their respective roles—that is, teachers teach and parents parent—much of what works in one setting can be applied to the other. The exchange of what works between parents and professionals frequently enhances the effectiveness in both settings.

Family-focused PBS Interventions

PBS is a type of focused intervention with families to ameliorate a child's or youth's challenging behavior and improve the lives of family members and those with whom the child or adolescent comes into contact at school, community, or work. PBS interventions cross contexts (home, school, community, work), and some are more family-specific than others. At the same time, *family uniqueness* may require a change from traditional PBS interventions.

In an intervention discussed by Vaughn, White, Johnston, and Dunlap (2005), a grandmother adopted her grandson because he had been maltreated by his parents. The child's challenging behavior occurred in school but created a work-related issue for the grandmother when the school called her about her grandson several times a week. The PBS intervention (giving the child points for positive behavior every 10 minutes, which he could trade later for tangible items he wanted) was successful. The grandson changed by self-monitoring at school, and the grandmother described his developing a more positive attitude, improving his self-control, doing his homework without cajoling, willingly doing chores, and listening/responding to his grandmother.

In another PBS study, Smith-Bird and Turnbull (2005) pursued quality-of-life issues for a student with challenging behaviors. When they broadened the scope to include quality of life of the family rather than just the individual, the interventions made a direct and positive impact on the entire family's quality of life. The authors attribute this success to the use of the Quality-of-Life Survey when developing the functional behavior assessment

(FBA). Boettcher, Koegel, McNerney, and Koegel (2003) described a family-focused prevention approach using PBS for an anticipated crisis (i.e., an autistic child's challenging behaviors and the mother's being scheduled for major surgery followed by months of recuperation). A PBS family intervention was engaged prior to surgery. The results were even better than expected in terms of working with all family members and mitigating the impact of the autistic child's behavior on the family as a whole. The adolescent son became more self-reliant and assumed responsibility for family matters in a new and appropriate way (e.g., helping with dinner, caring for pets). His preschool siblings, having been primed ahead of time for what to expect each day and using art to demonstrate what life would be like (e.g., when mommy comes home), were good playmates and followed the established rules and directions.

Park and Turnbull (2002) described quality indicators for professionals working with children who have challenging behaviors. The three domains of quality that emerged from an elaborate data analysis were respect for children, skills to meet special needs, and commitment.

System-wide PBS Across Contexts

A family may have semipermeable and functional boundaries, or it may have dysfunctional boundaries that are either enmeshed or disengaged. A family also has a hierarchy of power, balance, and order. Families, too, have positive and negative coalitions. The same is true with schools and community settings. There is a parallel between the inversion of the hierarchy in a family in which a child is ruling the roost and in a school in which parents wield the power.

Often, this example of the inversion of hierarchy is seen in combination with enmeshed boundaries in work-related settings. In a business with enmeshed boundaries, upper management dips into the domain of middle management. Between the subsystem dysfunction of upper and middle management would be several middle managers. In a school system, for example, several middle-managers—school principals—might form a coalition (alignment dysfunction) against the upper management—superintendent—about an issue such as prayer in the schoolyard. The superintendent with enmeshed boundaries takes over functions that principals must have to function effectively.

McCurdy, Mannella, and Eldridge (2003) described PBS as used in an inner-city elementary school with escalating antisocial behaviors. The school was both racially and ethnically diverse, and the intervention brought professionals in the school together with outside behavioral consultants. A leadership team met biweekly over two school years. They reported, as a result, diminished referrals to the office for discipline problems and fewer serious offenses, such as assaults.

Scott (2001) described a PBS intervention on a schoolwide basis, involving a team process including planning, implementation, and outcomes. First they selected the most needy student group—students most at risk for failure—with an overarching aim at prevention for all students. Identifying the location of problems (cafeteria, hall, stairs, gym), the context and problem was juxtaposed with the solutions. The impressive results contrasted the year before and after the change process for number of hours in SAFE (essentially, an in-school suspension room) as well as suspension, broken out by number of students and days suspended. Also broken out was the suspension of minority (African

American) students as a separate group with a caveat about equality being achieved only when the "representation of all students in disciplinary procedures is in accordance with their representation in the population" (p. 92).

Providing a framework for systemic school procedures using functional assessment and wraparound as part of PBS, and using these to create schools that are safe, Scott and Eber (2003) provided a new direction for the field. They gave case examples and linked FBA and wraparound integrated with PBS.

Warren and colleagues (2003) described the use of PBS in an urban setting with positive results. They also took a long-range approach and found support for funding from a variety of sources. Service integration, family support, and youth and community development were highlighted with specific recommendations for each area.

Again, family-focused interventions can be used with at-risk and special-needs students but are not mandated by law. IEPs, discussed next, are required by law for school-age students found to be eligible for special education.

Individualized Education Programs (IEPs)

The individualized education program (IEP) is the cornerstone of educational programming for individuals with disabilities. The IEP is the vehicle used to develop programs that provide free and appropriate educational experiences for students determined to be eligible for special education (Gargiulo, 2006). Two additional components involved in providing special education are *related services* and *supplementary aids and services*.

Because the local school system may go beyond the requirements of federal or state legislation, school and community professionals must find out the requirements of their school system. Some school systems write IEPs for at-risk students, and school systems providing IEPs for students who are not determined to be eligible for special education do not have to follow federal or state regulations regarding content, process, or parental involvement. They may select the elements of IEPs that best fit their system and the type of student served.

Requirements

A written individualized education program for a student must be developed by a committee and must include the parents in the process. The IEP has to be completed before the student can be placed in a special education program, and the parents must agree to the program before it is implemented. These conditions are intended to ensure that the program the student receives meets his or her unique learning need rather than having the individual student meet the requirements of a given program.

The IEP outlines the educational program for a student found eligible for special education. This is followed by annual evaluations as well as reevaluations every 3 years. With the 2004 reauthorization of IDEA, 15 states are piloting programs to offer parents and schools the alternative of using a 3-year IEP instead of a 1-year IEP (Smith, 2005). The annual review is still required but includes current level of progress and status regarding meeting annual goals, with the proviso that the IEP be amended as appropriate (Gartin &

Murdick, 2005). The IEP sets learning goals for the student and specifies the related services (e.g., counseling, social work services, speech/language, occupational therapy) that will be required to help the student meet those goals.

Components

The first component of an IEP was referred to previously as a description of the child's current level of "educational performance." With IDEA 2004, the term was changed to "academic achievement and functional performance," which both expands and clarifies this component of the IEP (Gartin & Murdick, 2005). IDEA 2004 focuses on curriculum that is inherent in No Child Left Behind (NCLB).

The statement about achievement/performance includes strengths as well as weaknesses. Just as family resources must be taken into account when assessing families, a statement of the student's strengths is valuable in the IEP. This information is gleaned from the assessment process.

Annual goals follow the statement of the student's current level of functioning. New with IDEA 2004 is that short-term objectives or benchmarks are no longer required for each annual goal, except for students assessed by alternative assessment procedures aligned with standards of alternate achievement (T.E.C. Smith, 2005). Now, annual goals mean *academic and functional goals* designed to

> (aa) meet the child's needs that result from the child's disability
> to enable the child to be involved in and make progress in
> the general education curriculum; and
> (bb) meet each of the child's other educational needs that result
> from the child's disability. (Gartin & Murdick, 2005, p. 328)

Family involvement in determining goals is crucial, although the language of the law uses the term *parents*, not families. Peers of students with disabilities also contribute information and ideas for the IEP, and IDEA refers to student membership on the IEP team as "whenever appropriate, the child with a disability" (King-Sears, 1997).

A statement of the specific special education and related services required is provided, along with a statement of the extent to which the student will participate in general education programs. IDEA 2004 specifies that the special education and services be "based on peer-reviewed research to the extent practicable" (Gartin & Murdick, 2005, p. 328). Parents should be involved in decision making about the delivery model (see chapter 12) as well as related services. According to Turnbull (2005), IDEA 2004 maintains the principle of parental participation and choice, and the amendment clarifies that parents have *responsibilities* as well. An IDEA violation alleged by any party "may not have occurred more than two years before the party files the complaint" (Turnbull, Huerta, & Stowe, 2006, p. 77). When making a complaint, parents must notify the school about the nature of the child's problem and the parents' proposed resolution.

IDEA 2004 also restricts the right of the parent to amend a due process complaint. The parents must convey their complaint correctly the first time they make it rather than amending the same complaint, which Turnbull indicated would keep the school "on-guard" all the time. In IDEA 2004, the parent, the Department of Education in each state, local school systems, and other public agencies can also make complaints. If parents do not permit their child to be placed in special education, they lose their right to make a complaint concerning the education of their child (Turnbull, Huerta, & Stowe, 2006).

In essence, IDEA 2004 maintained parents' rights

- to a nondiscriminatory evaluation,
- to membership on their child's IEP team,
- to be able to maintain control concerning the release of their child's records and have access to them, and
- to eligibility as a member on advisory boards of the state or school system.

"The family systems approach follows the theory that whatever benefits the child will benefit the child's family (and visa versa)" (Turnbull, Huerta, & Stowe, 2006, p. 104).

Parents should be the ultimate decision makers for their child's education (Winton, 1996). An early childhood special education leader in that field, Bailey (1987), too, viewed families as the primary decision makers for their children with disabilities when developing priorities and goals.

When students remain in less restrictive environments (this includes some self-contained classrooms for children with emotional disturbance) and continue their challenging behaviors over a long time, they have far more difficulty catching up in academics. As well, their challenging behaviors become ingrained so they either remain extreme or take far longer to transform.

Cultural Sensitivity in IEPs

The U.S. Department of Education (2001) collected data from family members across racial and ethnic groups about the extent of their participation in the IEP process during the 1999–2000 school year. They found little difference in participation across the five groups (Caucasian, African American, Hispanic, Asian/Pacific Islander, and Native American). About 80% of the parents indicated that they had attended an IEP meeting, and all the groups agreed that goals for the IEP had been created jointly by members from the family and school. They saw the goals as individualized for their child, as well as appropriate and challenging. Minority parents, however, were less satisfied with their participation than majority white parents were, and the minority parents wanted more involvement.

Friend (2005) suggested that professionals may hold a stereotype that minority parents are less concerned than middle- and upper-class Americans about their child's education. As a result, some professionals might create a self-fulfilling prophecy in which the professionals get what they expect.

Harry (2002) cautioned that when professionals work with families from different cultures on behalf of their child, the family may not understand the professionals' communication. This may lead to less involvement by family members.

Dennis and Giangreco (1996) interviewed 14 special education professionals who were members of minority groups and were involved with IEPs. Six keys to being culturally sensitive emerged and remain relevant today:

1. Appreciation for the unique nature of each family
2. Awareness of how influential the professional is

3. Recognition of personal cultural biases
4. Actively expanding knowledge of different cultures
5. Developing awareness of cultural norms
6. Learning with the families

Those authors presented numerous suggestions to help professionals become more culturally sensitive, including

- seeking assistance from "cultural interpreters" prior to the IEP meeting,
- determining the literacy and language status of family members,
- involving families in planning for the meetings,
- previewing the meeting with families,
- being flexible and responding to the interaction style of the family,
- adapting the timeframe so family needs are met, and
- examining the questions they pose.

Students' Involvement in IEPs

Grigal, Test, Beattie, and Wood (1997) studied the transition component of IEPs for high-school students. They examined the format, compliance with mandates, consideration of best practices, and differences in these aspects across disability categories. They found that the letter of the law was met but that the transition components did not reflect best practices. With the No Child Left Behind (NCLB) requirement for *evidence-based practices* in the education of all children and with IDEA 2004 requiring that special education, related services, and supplementary aids/services be based on *peer-reviewed research to the extent possible* (Gartin & Murdick, 2005), that situation should change—although "should change" and "will change" will be known only in the future.

Mason, Field, and Sawilowsky (2004) used an online web survey to research educators' instructional practices and attitudes relating to students' involvement and self-determination in their IEPs. The survey respondents indicated that these factors were important. Of the respondents, 34% found participation of students in IEP meetings to be satisfactory, but only 8% were satisfied with the approach they were using to teach self-determinations (p. 441).

Direct observation of IEP meetings conducted by teachers revealed that special education teachers talked during 51% of the coded observations, family members 15%, administrators and general educators only 9% of the time, support staff 6%, and students a mere 3% (Martin et al., 2006b). Students did not assume more than minimal leadership, and their knowledge of IEP meetings compared to the other team members was significantly lower. Clearly, students would benefit from training in participation skills. Others on the team would benefit from training as well. Teacher-directed meetings did not seem to provide encouragement for students to be involved in their IEPs.

Martin and colleagues (2006a) studied the effectiveness of teaching students self-directed skills. The result was a strong increase in the amount of time students talked, led, or started IEP meetings. Surveys conducted after the meetings corroborated this finding. Thus, the self-directed IEP has been found to increase students' involvement in their IEPs.

Test and colleagues (2004) reviewed literature on interventions to increase the involvement of students in their IEPs. Students from various disability categories were involved in their IEPs. Expanding student involvement in IEPs by teaching participation skills prior to IEP meetings along with person-centered planning did result in increasing student participation.

Martin, Marshall, and Sale (2004) researched perceptions of participants in secondary-level IEP meetings across 3 consecutive years. Special education teachers were found to spend more time talking than other members of the IEP team. As might be expected, students had the least understanding of reasons for IEP meetings as well as of their role and how to carry it out. When students, as well as general educators, attended meetings, it benefited others on the team, especially their parents.

Advantages and Disadvantages of IEPs

IEPs form a working guide that gives parents the opportunity to reinforce skills at home that are being covered in school. The IEP process also requires parents to interact with teachers in a constructive manner. The emphasis in IEP meetings is on possibilities rather than problems. Another advantage is that families receive a written document (the IEP) to take home so they are able to refer to it as often as they wish. Collaboration between schools and families improves relationships when the process is mutual, demonstrating respect, trust, and cooperation in developing shared goals (Friend & Cook, 2003).

Among the disadvantages of IEPs are that considerable time is required to develop and monitor these plans, as well as to coordinate meeting times for all involved. With IDEA 2004, the reduction of paper requirements has lessened this problem. Parents may have their own struggles with the IEP process, such as a lack of understanding or acceptance of the IEP, transportation problems, or difficulty accepting their child's disability and level of functioning. The parents may have unrealistic expectations of their child or of the professionals who implement the IEP. Although no process or document is perfect, the outcome of the IEP makes it worth the trouble.

Barriers to Family Involvement in IEPs

From both the teachers' and the parents' points of view, involving family members in collaboration with school/community presents some barriers. Ways to avoid and remove these barriers are proposed next.

Avoiding and Removing Barriers Experienced by Family Members

Family members are challenged in their collaboration with schools in various arenas. Among the possible barriers are logistical problems, communication problems, lack of understanding of the school/community system, and feelings of inferiority.

Logistical problems   Examples of logistical problems are difficulty with transportation, child-care problems, lack of involvement of fathers, and time constraints. Some families who are disengaged and do not want to be involved use logistical problems as excuses.

Others are overwhelmed and have few available resources. Still others are what Aponte (1994) called "underorganized," observed most frequently in schools with a preponderance of poor families.

Professionals should find ways to reduce these barriers so parents can participate in the development of IEPs. Solutions may include networking to assist with transportation and babysitting, as well as arranging meeting times that are most convenient for parents. Although parents may be reluctant to ask the extended family for help, extended family members may be useful in solving logistical problems. Also, neighbors, parents of other students, and college students studying special education are all good sources to resolve logistical problems.

Communication problems   A common communication problem relates to language and cultural barriers. Professionals must find ways to connect with the cultural and language diversity in their settings, especially with IEPs. Home visits, translators, written texts, and outreach can be used to counteract these barriers. Repetition of the information is also important (Turnbull & Turnbull, 2001).

Whoever chairs the IEP conference should be able to relate effectively to the family's cultural and socioeconomic background and overcome any language barriers. If that is not likely, a professional with a similar background might be "imported" for the IEP meeting so the family will feel more comfortable and, thus, benefit more from the meeting. Secondary students, too, may enable communication when the adult family members have a language barrier, as these students will be more likely to understand innuendo, humor, and terminology.

Lack of understanding of the school system   Family members may need help from professionals in understanding the school system and their parental rights and responsibilities, or in learning ways by which they can call upon their rights. In explaining parental rights to parents, professionals should be straightforward, provide in writing what IDEA 2004 requires, and discuss it with them. And family members of children/youth with disabilities who have been involved with the schools for a while can help newer parents learn the ropes. Or family members might bring along a trusted friend or extended family member to the IEP meeting so they will have someone with whom they can discuss it in the future outside the school.

Brooks-McNamara & Pedersen (2006) recommended that school counselors assume the roles of gathering, analyzing, and using data as members of leadership teams. They may also be the best suited to help family members understand testing and data collection used in schools.

Feelings of inferiority   Family members easily feel overwhelmed by formal committee meetings, so special efforts should be aimed at helping them feel valued by conveying the role and importance of the home–school partnership. Again, employing an IEP chair who has some link to the family can be helpful. For example, a Puerto Rican family likely would be more accepting of an IEP chair who is Latino. Information also helps build confidence, and family members can be given videos/DVDs, print material, and information on resources available in the community that will help them build their knowledge base about their child and the processes in which they will be involved.

Avoiding and Removing Barriers Experienced by Teachers

Teachers have identified other barriers to involving families in the IEP process. Among them are apathy and time constraints.

Apathy of family member(s)   The teacher will encounter parental apathy from time to time and should not personalize it. Professionals are not responsible for motivating everyone! The teacher should consider each family as unique and recognize the possible reasons for apathy. A busy parent, for example, simply may not have the stamina or time and may consider involvement with the IEP as "the last straw." Professionals need to recognize situations over which they can exert no influence and, instead of trying to improve the situation, conserve their own energy.

Other parents may appear at first to be apathetic, but this attitude may stem from prior experiences with schools/community that were demeaning or negative. With these family members, professionals should reach out to demonstrate that they are not like those encountered in the past. A home visit may help to remove this barrier, or at least shed light on what appears to be lack of concern.

Time constraints   Time is a major factor in developing IEPs. Turnbull and Turnbull (2001) reaffirmed time constraints as a potential problem. Professionals must allow sufficient time to prepare for IEP meetings, even if they have to lean on others to do some tasks. Dictating reports, using volunteers for scheduling, and receiving inservice training in time management are all helpful.

Time barriers can work against effective and clear communication with family members. The path of least resistance for professionals is simply not to inform parents about their rights or encourage their participation. The results are predictable: Parents will become adversaries rather than advocates. Time well spent early in the IEP process will save time in the long term, especially as related to parental involvement.

The IEP Meeting

Turnbull and Turnbull (2001, p. 269) listed components of the IFSP/IEP meeting that provide opportunities for collaboration, including

- advance preparation for IEP meetings;
- initial conference proceedings with "connecting and getting started";
- students, family members, and professionals sharing their visions, expectations, and strengths;
- review of formal evaluation and current academic achievement and functional performance;
- collaborative sharing about resources, priorities, and concerns;
- the development of goals and objectives (for those with alternative assessment);
- determining placement, supplementary aides/services, and related services; and
- summarization and conclusion of conference.

Advance Preparation

During the assessment process, much information concerning the family's unique characteristics and process was accumulated. Those on the team who know the most about family systems approaches should meet with the professionals who will be involved in the IEP conference to explain or review family functioning so their ideas will be taken into consideration. The knowledge they provide about the family's process will aid the professionals' input to fit the given family. For example, professionals would not want to encourage more parent–child involvement for field trips if the parents were determined to be overly involved with their child already. As they begin mutual program planning, professionals will want to keep family characteristics foremost in their mind.

The chair chosen for the IEP conference should be the person who is the best fit for the specific family. Some professionals work better with enmeshed families; others are more effective with disengaged families. A member of a minority group might offer to chair the conference of a minority family. A single parent might be the best chair for a single parent of a student with special needs.

The chairperson's responsibilities are to coordinate the advance planning, chair the actual IEP meeting(s), and provide follow-up support. It is easy to see why some type of matching of family to chairperson is important. In student-led IEP meetings, the professional chairperson might work with the student before the meeting so the student will know the prescribed sequence and role.

Getting Started and Making Connections

The beginning of any meeting sets the tone for what is to come. Keynote speakers at conferences motivate the audience to look forward to the remainder of the conference. Equally important is to get off to a good start in a small meeting that deals with only one student.

In effective human interactions, other concerns or unresolved problems must recede from the mind. Counselors and therapists routinely focus their energies and thoughts, but other professionals may not be as adept at this. Prior to walking into the meeting, professionals should take a minute to clear other concerns from their mind. Thirty seconds of deep breathing followed by a quick review of the child's records and unique family characteristics will help the professional focus. In addition, the professional may want to use a silent affirmation such as, "This student and family [name and family] are my only concern at this time. I give them my full attention."

While everyone is arriving, the chairperson must speak with each family member, including the student. People who are unfamiliar with one another are introduced, and everyone should have a chance to interact informally before the meeting is formalized.

Professionals must keep distinctive family characteristics foremost in their mind during this and other stages of the IEP process. Some family members, for example, respond coolly to a professional's greeting. A student in this family may be disengaged within the family and generalizing this type of functioning outside of the family. Most people operate in similar ways within and outside of the family. And again, cultural background should be considered. Someone from a northern European background, for example, might have a more reserved style than a southern European, who might be more extraverted.

Sharing Visions and Expectations

The student, family members, friends, and professionals should share their visions and expectations for the student. All involved should be encouraged to use imagery to go beyond the edge of possibilities in the child's or youth's experiences with family and friends. If family members who are disengaged have trouble becoming involved, the rest of the team will have to lead the way and set a good example.

If the family and/or friends previously have been engaged in a MAP (Making an Action Plan) (Gee, 2004; Thousand, Villa, & Nevin, 2003), they review that plan with the professionals in the IEP meeting. Pearpoint, Forest, and O'Brien, (1996) and Forest and Pearpoint (1992) reported that they generate enthusiasm and energy by training personnel around the country to use MAP and CIRCLES (a group of supportive friends organized to help achieve the inclusion goals established during the MAP process) to plan and problem solve so the children and youth can be educated in general education classes or participate in typical community settings for children and youth their age.

Review of Formal Evaluation and Current Levels of Performance

If the professionals on the team have done their homework, the chairperson will have received the information on test results and covered that information with the family members. Chapter 11 recommended the use of a pre-meeting conference with families to present test results prior to determining eligibility. Having absorbed this information already, families can join the group of professionals in planning the educational program at the IEP conference. Still, it is helpful to review the test results at the IEP meeting so everyone is reminded of the student's strengths and weaknesses and current level of functioning. During IEP conferences that are held after the initial conference, the teacher(s) should present information on progress to date for goals and/or objectives set at earlier IEP conferences.

Collaboration in Sharing Resources, Priorities, and Concerns

Everyone involved in the IEP process should contribute to educating the child or youth. Family members, including siblings and extended family members, can speak about the ways in which they can be involved in the child's education. Their contributions, plus the sharing of unique resources by other team members, allows for a complete picture of what the child or youth can count on from the team.

Observing the interactive collaboration of general education teachers and special educators can help families and those who provide related services. More than one professional working intensely with the child may engender trust in the processes involved.

A team member can encourage family and friends by making comments such as, "When I was a child, my dad helped me study my spelling words. This may seem like a small thing, but it is really important to your child." Beyond that, sharing resources represents a statement of commitment from all involved. Thus, the child or youth will feel a sense of connection as well as support.

At this stage, the team members discuss their priorities, which are linked to the expectations expressed earlier in the meeting. Examining priorities early in the process can lead to a more productive meeting and help the team members know each other better.

During this component and throughout the meeting, it is important to share any concerns or worries about the child's education. Without voicing concerns, the needs of the child or youth and the family will not be realized. This sharing also helps team members feel heard and supported. Concerns and questions that arise after the meeting must also be addressed.

Development of Goals and Objectives
(for those with alternative assessments/standards)

Among the IEP components discussed earlier in the chapter are goals. IDEA 2004 now requires objectives only for students who have alternative assessment governed by alternate standards from the general curriculum. Family members, including the student when possible, can contribute to developing the goals as well as writing the objectives. They also should feel comfortable responding to the goals and/or objectives presented by the professionals.

When family members are aware of the goals and/or objectives for their child or youth, they are able to follow up more easily at home. Certainly parents want their child's learning to generalize to other situations. Their involvement can focus the rest of the family on common purposes and tasks. Siblings and extended family, as well as babysitters or nannies, may also be able to reinforce learning goals. Family members can be encouraged to reinforce a drill (e.g., multiplication facts) in the car, for example, and to use the natural environment to reinforce learning (e.g., grocery-store math, reading signs and street names).

As with other components of the IEP process, professionals must keep family considerations in mind during the discussion of goals and/or objectives. Other suggestions are follow-up personal contacts, use of print/e-mail to reinforce the goals, involvement in parent groups in the school/community, and pairing families that would benefit from continuing IEP involvement.

Family functioning in the IEP meeting should be considered from a family systems perspective. For example, if a student is presenting his or her ideas strongly and the parents are acquiescent, the professional might hypothesize that the family is demonstrating an inversion of hierarchy. A simple intervention might be to simply say, "Ken, I've heard your point of view, and now I'd like to hear from your dad and mom." As with any intervention, professional discretion is advised. At the least, the professional should note the problematic situation and convey it to the appropriate professionals. The social worker, counselor, and psychologist might find the information helpful in future meetings with parents or other family members.

As a reminder: Educators must not volunteer information of this nature outside the school system without a signed release from the custodial parent or caregiver. With that said, healthy family interactions should be supported whenever possible. As always, professional modeling of effective human interactions is beneficial.

Professional observations should be a beginning point for cataloguing family processes. They should also note possible family dysfunction to consider for referral for other services (e.g., social work, counseling) in the future.

Determination of Placement and Related Services

Turnbull and Turnbull (2001) speak to the gravity of decision making regarding placement and consideration for related services. Parents should receive information that allows them to comprehend the different delivery models. The respective advantages and disadvantages of these models are best presented prior to a formal IEP meeting.

In the past, many professionals assumed that parents would automatically accept whatever the professional recommended. In today's world, professionals should not make any recommendation until the parents have expressed their thoughts and opinions. With effective human interaction skills, the professionals and family members can reach a decision together on placement and related services.

Summarizing and Concluding the Conference

In the final phase of the IEP process, the chairperson summarizes the meeting, lists follow-up tasks, and assigns responsibility for those tasks. Before concluding the meeting, the chairperson makes explicit a timeline for review and establishes means of regular communication between the family and school. Disengaged families, in particular, will likely benefit from more frequent family–school interactions, even if this is in the form of notes home or e-mail. Enmeshed families, conversely, might benefit from less frequent communication about minor changes in the student's progress. Plans for continued follow-up activities should fit the unique family characteristics and needs. Recognizing the reality of the family situation will guide the plans.

Concluding remarks reiterate the value of shared decision making and expressions of appreciation for the family–professional collaboration. To provide meaningful input and involvement, parents and professionals must reaffirm their commitment to the IEP process.

Summary

With its emphasis on family-focused interventions and individualized education programs, this chapter provides useful information mostly for professionals working within school contexts; however, it also helps professionals in community contexts, mainly in relation to PBS (positive behavior support) when they are working with a variety of other professionals across contexts in which the child/youth has needs.

It is clear that parental involvement in a child's education has a major impact on progress of the child in school; as well, it has been demonstrated that school/community involvement impacts children's achievement. Schools must initiate collaboration with families and community to reach the goals of education. In doing so professionals should determine parental and community perceptions about the degree and type of involvement desired. All parents should work with their child(ren) on homework, and those with children determined to be eligible for special education are required to be involved in the education of their children in different ways and are also assured of rights in that regard. Over the last 40 years the federal law regarding rights of the parents have become less emphasized and responsibilities of parents transcendent with the 2004 reauthorization of IDEA.

It is essential that the unique characteristics of families with at-risk and/or special-needs children be taken into consideration when providing family-focused interventions, which were the domain of early childhood special education for many years through their IFSPs (individual family service plans). This book promotes family-focused interventions across age levels/grades. The term is used in a broader sense than IFSPs and highlights collaboration among school and family with community professionals for networking as well as involvement in aspects of assessment, planning, implementation, and/or evaluation of interventions. Consideration of family concerns and needs is essential and other relevant elements include outcome statement, resources and supports, courses of action, family strengths, partnership and evaluation.

Family-focused intervention may include a spectrum of assistance that professionals deem useful or necessary for a particular child/youth. These include emotional support, identification of resources helpful for the child/youth or family members, referral for external services such as family counseling when indicated, normalization so that the child and family understand that even with challenges there are more things about the child that are typical of all children, reframing the situation so that both child and family members are given a different perspective that provides opportunity to understand and accept the special needs in a positive light, and contextualization that aids in a new interpretation of behavior that considers the context and aspects of the precursors within which the challenging behavior occurs. Similar to reframing, this shifts the understanding the underlying factors, thus allowing greater acceptance and empathy.

Described in greater detail in another chapter, Positive Behavior Support (PBS) was a fourth element under Family-Focused Intervention and takes place in the home, school, community, or work place while crossing two or more contexts in which the child/youth demonstrates a need for intervention. Family-focused PBS may be part of assessment with family members contributing information about the different contexts in which the challenging behavior has been observed. Professionals should be respectful of the child/youth, provide skills to meet the special needs of the individual, and be committed to the individual. System-wide PBS is carried out within a particular domain, such as a school. The goal of creating a more consistent approach across the setting, with the aim of reducing overall problems, creates a context that supports those with particularly challenging behavior. The pervasive positive stance and extension across the domains in which all children/youth with challenging behaviors are involved yields safer and more effective school and community settings with fewer referrals to administrators and improved social relationships.

The second major segment in this chapter, Individualized Education Programs (IEPs), covered a wide variety of topics of which those working in schools need to demonstrate knowledge. Professionals must be sensitive to cultural differences and must consider including the student in the development and evaluation of the IEP. Increased student participation results in greater ownership of their learning process and allows professionals to know what matters most to the student, so that it is taken into consideration with placement, goals, and more. Self-directed skills, taught by teachers, help students speak more frequently during IEP meetings, and student-directed IEP meetings result in higher levels of involvement. Teaching students participation skills prior to being part of IEP meetings was found to empower them to provide increased input.

Centered on possibilities, IEPs provide parents with a map of skills their child needs to learn that they can reinforce at home. As well, they increase constructive interactions with teachers and provide opportunities for a greater acceptance of their child's level of functioning, leading to a more realistic expectation of their child.

Barriers to involvement of family members in the IEP relate to logistics, communication, lack of understanding about the school system, and some family members' sense of inferiority. Logistical problems such as transportation, child care, both parents being involved, and time constraints exist to varied degrees across families. Professionals can encourage parents to ask for assistance from extended family members with logistics, include professionals with a similar background/language in IEP meetings as well as make home visits and/or use translators. For apathetic family members, the professional needs to consider each family as having unique characteristics and to try to understand the underlying cause of apathy so they can help establish a trusting relationship with greater family involvement. Educators have limited time to do their work, and it becomes incumbent upon them to find ways to reduce their input (e.g., dictating reports that the secretary then types, asking for help in scheduling meeting times with family members and others attending the IEP meeting).

Advance preparation for the IEP meeting allows professionals to have more effective meetings with more clarity of thought and human connections that build trust among those attending. Reviewing notes describing the family process that has surfaced in the past prior to an IEP meeting helps the professional remain centered throughout the meeting as well as allows for confirmation or shifting of hypotheses in relation to a particular family system.

Eliciting the sharing of one another's visions and expectation is a helpful way to encourage involvement that is positive and may serve to gather more energy toward possibilities for the student. So too does it provide an opportunity for including family members in the implementation of IEP goals that make it more likely that the student will succeed in life and generalize skills to real-life situations. Reviewing test results early in the meeting directs everyone to current levels of performance so that realistic goals are more likely to evolve. Collaborating about potential resources, priorities, and concerns by including family members in the process leads to greater connectivity and support for the child/youth.

The development of goals applies to all students with IEPs. Objectives will be guided for students with alternate standards who had alternative assessment. Both goals and objectives are best when including family members and the student in their development. It is always crucial to consider variations in family systems with an eye toward helping balance any areas with dysfunction (e.g., hierarchy problem with lack of shared power between parents, father in peripheral status).

Family members need information that helps them provide input regarding the determination of placement and/or related services the student may be assigned. Collaboration in this decision making is essential to further the relationship building as well as to serve the best interest of the child, because it is more likely that family members will have a sense of ownership regarding these decisions and convey their affirmation to their child so that he or she cannot engage in splitting behaviors that pit the family members against the school and community members involved in writing the IEP.

A good ending to an IEP meeting will more likely result in effective IEP implementation. A summary of who will do what after the meeting, including the family members' tasks, helps each person attending the meeting to realign the final decisions in their minds and establishes a clear plan of action. Attention to family characteristics and potential for dysfunction (e.g., enmeshment) helps the professionals steer the realistic assignment of tasks, thus reducing dysfunction and emphasizing strengths of the family members. This can end the IEP meeting with shared commitment to implementation.

Extension Activities

Reflection/Journal: Observation of IEP and/or FFI: Contact a local school to see if you can obtain permission to observe during an IEP process and/or a family-focused intervention conducted for a child or youth of the age which you are interested in working with in the future. Let the contact person know that you are interested only in a meeting in which parents or other involved family members are present. Be sure that family members grant permission for you to attend.

In advance, write down the kinds of family observations you want to notice so you don't become absorbed in that task during the intervention or IEP meeting. Be sure your list includes the interaction patterns covered in chapter 3 and the Appendix (boundaries, hierarchy, alignments); family life-cycle stages, and stressors such as pile-up from chapter 2; levels of differentiation, triangling, and birth-order dynamics from chapter 4; and stances, family rules, and the five freedoms in chapter 12.

During the meeting, jot down questions you want to ask a professional. After the meeting, ask if someone has the time to discuss the process with you now, or set up a time to discuss the meeting later.

Write a thank-you letter to those who allowed you to observe, indicating how helpful it was in your learning. Finally, jot down questions to ask during a future class/training session.

Keep absolute confidentiality about what you hear and observe. Do not use the real names of people involved or the names of school/community settings in which your observations took place. Write "Confidential" on the top of any paper you write and be sure it is shredded after it no longer is needed.

In-Class/Training Activity: If students are assigned to observe FFIs, IEPs, or both, provide time in class for sharing in pairs (e.g., pair one who observed only an FFI with another who observed only an IEP process). After sharing, allow time for comments and questions with the whole class/group. Instructors may want to keep an ongoing list over time about the kinds of questions that students repeatedly ask. The instructor can then provide information in class or via handouts that answers these typical questions.

Bridging With Supervision (for Students Reading IEPs During Student Teaching/ Internships): When university students are placed formally for internships in which they are eventually to take responsibility for the teaching, they are legally viewed as being part of the system and allowed to view and observe as well as participate in the IEP process. The intern/student teacher is responsible for signing anything required that indicates that he or she viewed a record on a student.

In university classes with group meetings interspersed during internship/student teaching, the students can discuss requirements and processes as well as paperwork involved in the IEP process. A group meeting of interns with a university supervisor in attendance is a good time for discussing the differences across systems as well as a frank discussion of any observations of what may appear to be a violation. Again, confidentiality is critical.

Classroom and Group Extension of Family Systems Concepts

*F*amily systems concepts can be incorporated in the classroom, as well as in educational, support, and counseling groups in schools for family members and in out-of-school time (OST) learning programs. Family systems concepts and methods can be used to pursue goals in both the cognitive/academic and the affective/social domains. Satir's communication stances can be applied to the academic curriculum, as can the metaphor and reframing techniques described in this chapter. Finally, a socialization method called Temperature Reading can be used in groups or classes in school and community settings, as well as with parent groups.

Satir's Communication Stances

Satir's (1988) five communication stances, described in the Appendix, are as follows:

1. Placating
2. Blaming
3. Superreasonable (the computer)

4. Irrelevant (the distractor)
5. Congruent

The first four stances are dysfunctional, and the goal is to reach the functional congruent stance. School and community professionals should be familiar with the stances and how this knowledge can help them when interacting with at-risk and special-needs children and youth and their families. Professionals also can use knowledge about the stances to identify dysfunctional communication in the schools or community and then to intervene to help others recognize their incongruent communication and begin to use congruent communication. Satir (1983b, 1988) provided many examples of ways in which trained professionals can help others recognize and change their communication stances so they are congruent most of the time.

Like any classic works, Satir's model is as valuable today as when she developed it. Professionals in The Virginia Satir Global Network [www.avanta.net], an international education network founded by Satir, continue to expand on her model.

Background

In two of her books, *Peoplemaking* (1972) and *The New Peoplemaking* (1988), Satir described the four dysfunctional communication stances she had found in families throughout the world: placating, blaming, superreasonable, and irrelevant. Satir and Baldwin (1983) described these stances as "different ways to hide the reality of one's feelings from oneself and from others" (p. 199). Underneath these patterns of inauthentic communication is low self-esteem. In describing Satir's view of dysfunctional communication, Nichols and Schwartz (2004) stated, "If people feel badly about themselves, it's hard to tell the truth about their feelings—and threatening to let others tell them honestly how they feel" (p. 209). Satir presented the functional stance of being congruent as a healthy way of expressing oneself.

All four dysfunctional stances begin during infancy within the primary triad of mother–father–child, yet they all have potential for renovation through what Satir referred to as a process of transformation and atrophy (Satir & Baldwin, 1983). All of these stances are systemic in nature; none is able to persist without the support of another. Thus, a family might present a teaming up of two "supportive," or reciprocal, stances—for example, the placater and the blamer. Only individuals who are congruent are able to maintain their self-esteem when facing stressful situations (Satir & Bitter, 2000). The aspects of communication—*self*, *other*, and *context*, including purpose, time, and place of communication—that are violated or discounted with each type of dysfunctional communication are delineated below (McLendon & Davis, 2002; Satir, 1988).

Placating

A person who assumes a placating stance is trying to conceal personal vulnerability by striving to please others. The placater will go along with something out of the need for emotional survival rather than because of personal commitment and interest. A placater rejects or discounts *self* when doing what others expect; his or her actions derive from fear of being rejected by others. The placater seems like a nice person who avoids conflict and will not turn others down for fear of rejection. Although protective of others, this person really is quite dependent and fragile. This stance might be represented by saying, "Whatever you want is okay, I'm just here to make you happy" (Goldenberg & Goldenberg, 2004, p. 173). Thus, the placater appears to be grateful but in truth is obsequious and feels worthless.

Through a transformative process and letting go of past dysfunction, the placater makes choices that affirm the *self* rather than seeing the self as worthless unless approved of by others. The placater who has gained a sense of personal worth has the capacity for being tender and compassionate. When transformed and congruent, the placater genuinely cares for *others*. The placater becomes authentic in service to others.

Blaming

The person who takes a blaming stance is attempting to mask personal vulnerability by trying to control *others*, as well as by indiscriminately disagreeing with them. This stance allows the blamer to feel a greater sense of personal importance to compensate for loneliness and a personal sense of failure. This person will complain, bully others, and find fault with them. One who assumes a blaming stance discounts the other person or people. An example of blaming typically comes in a loud, angry, finger-pointing manner: "You never do anything right. What is the matter with you?" (Goldenberg & Goldenberg, 2004, p. 173).

Blaming can be transformed into being assertive and taking a stand for oneself. When standing up for oneself, the blamer learns to assert the *self* realistically, as opposed to having a knee-jerk reaction to *others*. The blamer learns to handle power in a positive manner.

Superreasonable (the Computer)

An individual assuming the stance of superreasonable seeks to disguise vulnerability with a detached control that focuses on intellectual experience. This allows the person to skirt emotions and thereby anesthetize feelings. Superreasonable people seem cool, aloof, reasonable, and intellectual, but their stance should not be confused with congruent communication. An example of a superreasonable, stiff, monotone expression, given by Goldenberg and Goldenberg (2004) is, "If one were to observe carefully, one might notice the workworn hands of someone present here" (p. 173). This type of communication discounts both *self* and *other*.

A person who is superreasonable can learn to use his or her intelligence creatively, rather than using intelligence to protect the *self*. The professional will sense the connection with emotions in the transformed superreasonable and be aware of this person's wisdom. When transformed, the superreasonable person uses his or her intellect in effective ways.

Irrelevant (the Distractor)

The individual who takes on the irrelevant stance is pretending that the stressor is non-existent. The irrelevant person diverts the focus from the present, feeling-laden situation to something else. To others, that diversion may seem off-the-wall. Non sequiturs and scatterbrained comments are frequently observed. As Goldenberg and Goldenberg (2004) wrote, "Words are unrelated to what others are saying. For example, in the midst of a family dispute: 'What are we having for dinner?'" (p. 173). This type of communication discounts *self*, *others*, and *context*. Talking incessantly, the distractor appears hyperactive. Distractors feel that others do not care for them, so they take up all the space in a conversation.

Transformed, the formerly irrelevant person has the ability to be spontaneous and have fun. This person becomes a creative individual capable of congruent interactions, having no need to discount *self*, *others*, or *context*. The transformed irrelevant becomes a delightfully spontaneous person who is able to bring others together for merriment.

Congruent

According to Satir (1988), a congruent person provides leveling responses in which the outward expression, actions, and tone of voice fit the spoken word. Central to Satir's beliefs is that self-esteem determines the quality of the individual's relationships, health, and performance. As McLendon and Davis (2002) explained, "There was an integrity or alignment between the inside and the outside, balance and harmony between and among the components, and choice for when, how, and what could be expressed" (p. 171). Not feeling a need to hide or conceal personal feelings, a person with high self-esteem loves and values the *self*. But *others* and *context* do not have to be discounted. This person is balanced. He or she is centered in the truth of his or her own feelings and beliefs. Not afraid to challenge the status quo, congruent individuals take risks to grow and change. They also assume responsibility for personal thoughts, feelings, and actions.

Satir's Stances as a Curricular Area

At-risk and special-needs students can benefit from a curriculum that teaches them about the five communication stances. This might be part of an existing health curriculum or separate, with its own particular designation. The school might expand it to teach students about many of the family systems concepts. This content fits well with OST learning programs.

A well-versed teacher certainly could teach this content, as could the school counselor, social worker, or psychologist. The school might choose to teach the designated content to all students, just at-risk students, those with special needs, or another target group. Different circumstances warrant different decisions. Professionals in community programs likely would teach the stances to all youth in attendance.

Satir's books are written at the fifth-grade level—an age by which children certainly have experienced dysfunctional and congruent stances—so this curricular content is generally more appropriate in middle and high school, when students have the maturity and cognitive capacity to comprehend the concepts (Piaget & Inhelder, 1958). The concepts can be taught to elementary-aged children as well, though this may not be part of a formal curriculum. Rather, the professional could discuss the stances at the age group's level of understanding.

Preparing to Implement Curricula on Stances

Prior to implementing a curriculum on stances, the professional should become familiar with his or her own stances and with ways to respond to the dysfunctional stances of others.

Exploring Personal Stances

Professionals who explore their own stances and their impact on communication will be more likely to give congruent messages and will be better able to recognize and respond congruently to the stances of others. Because stances that are dysfunctional indicate low self-esteem, transformation to a more functional stance involves improving personal feelings of self-worth.

Satir believed that all of us are capable of assuming all four dysfunctional stances but that we rely on some more than others. As she stated, "What is so sad is that these four ways have become the most frequently used among people and are viewed by many as the most possible ways of achieving communication" (1972, p. 78). Satir (1988) estimated that within a typical group of people, 50% will be primarily placaters, 30% will be blamers, 15% will be superreasonable computers, 0.5% will be irrelevant distractors, and only 4.5% will be congruent.

Satir was not saying that people use dysfunctional communication almost 96% of the time during which they are interacting with others. She believed that people fall back on those incongruent stances, learned as children, when they are in stressful situations. Thus, some children and family members relate in a congruent fashion most of the time and slip into incongruent stances when they are under duress.

To better understand yourself and the family in which you grew up, it helps to recall some significant interactions from your early, middle, and later childhood. Examining these interactions in terms of the five communication stances can potentially produce growth. Considering the stances you favored will be helpful, and recognizing the favored stances of each member of your family will lead to even further understanding. Particularly helpful is to note family members in reciprocal stances, such as a placating father and a blaming mother.

After examining the stances from your youth, consider your current life at home and work or school. Examining your communication stances in a variety of recent interactions will reveal the extent to which you have continued to follow the patterns you established during your childhood. Determining the people with whom you assume different stances may reveal how relating to different people in your current life resonates with your past circumstances. Do your childhood patterns and current life have any parallels? When is it easy for you to be congruent? What types of situations call forth the different stances?

After reminiscing about your childhood and comparing patterns established in your younger years with the present, think about a recent situation in which you felt threatened and you relied upon one of the four dysfunctional communication stances. Try to recall the sequence of events and determine the dysfunctional stances assumed by each principal character. Then re-create the scene in your mind but imagine yourself assuming a congruent stance rather than a dysfunctional stance. This exercise will help you to be more congruent in the future. While creating the new scene in your imagination, think about how the other person would react, given a new and congruent response, and then imagine responding with another congruent message. Following the imagery to a new conclusion and using congruent responses throughout the interactions will provide a mental rehearsal for new situations.

Although this exploration and opportunity for rehearsal occurs solely in the mind, it is a powerful means of changing patterns in current life circumstances. The last technique described, which required you to conceive a new possibility, is called *covert rehearsal*. Many mental health professionals believe that to the extent one can visualize or imagine a new behavior, one can execute that behavior. Thus, employing this technique can lead to positive change in the use of functional, leveling, congruent messages.

Another challenge is to look for a new situation in which to employ a congruent stance when you normally might employ one of the dysfunctional stances. Later analysis of your communication, as well as that of the other person, will allow a determination of the communication stances used. If you were not congruent, you could use covert rehearsal to imagine a different scenario.

Another helpful technique is to observe the use of congruent communication by other people or by characters on television or in movies, videos, or plays. These observations can further your own expression of congruent messages.

Dysfunctional stances stem from low self-worth (Nichols & Schwartz, 2005), and mimicking others with dysfunctional stances is not the answer to higher self-esteem. People who have not dealt with many others who are congruent will be helped by finding models that help them expand and grow. If only 4.5% of the population is congruent in communication all of the time, the search for models of functional communication who can be emulated will be worthwhile.

As might be imagined, an individual who understands his or her personal stances will be better able to be congruent when interacting with others. Communicating congruently is especially important when relating to family members of at-risk children or youth and those with special needs, and also is important when interacting with other school and community professionals. Remembering Satir's (1988) estimate that only 4.5% of the population communicates congruently all of the time should help professionals be patient with themselves, children and youth, and their families. No one can be expected to communicate congruently all the time. But professionals should assume major personal responsibility for communicating congruently and realize that others will at least have one congruent communicator as a model.

Responding to Stances

Responding to dysfunctional communication is a challenge. The school and community professional first must identify the stance assumed by the other person. Next, the professional should think about the root causes of the stance—for example, low self-esteem. Then the professional can recall information catalogued about the family background of the person speaking. These steps will help the professional remain centered and balanced and keep the professional from moving in the direction of a dysfunctional stance.

Professionals who are centered and balanced can then communicate with single-level, congruent messages. They must not placate, blame, distract, or become superreasonable in the face of any of those types of communication. The professional's sole responsibility is to communicate in a congruent manner.

Consider the responses a principal might make when faced with a parent who, taking a blaming stance, remarked, "Why don't the teachers ever listen to us? I can't believe Jon is that much of a problem in school. Everything is fine at home."

The principal might be inclined to counter-blame or placate. Or he or she might become superreasonable, providing facts or quoting experts. The best option, however, is to be congruent with a statement such as, "Mrs. Wickham, I realize it's frustrating to keep getting reports about Jonathan being aggressive. The fact remains that he threatened his teacher twice in the last week. If this occurs again, the teacher will file a formal complaint. As before, we recommend family counseling."

As another example, consider this remark by a parent: "I know I've done a terrible job of raising Henry. I'm a miserable parent." The professional might choose to point out the placating stance to her. Another professional might back off from a parent's placating stance, not wanting to kick someone who is already down.

A better course than either of these is to remain congruent with a comment such as, "Mrs. Lathrop, all of us struggle in bringing up our children. I, too, have had many learning experiences. I agree that you can change some things to better respond to your son's needs. To that end, we're recommending a parent effectiveness training group...." With this response, the professional has shared information regarding the problem and has also responded to the mother's discounting of *self* by normalizing her child-rearing struggles.

When communicating with a person who is superreasonable, who discounts both *self* and *others*, any response should emphasize both *self* and *others*. Consider the following example, in which a parent is interacting with the counselor about home issues between two of his children that spill over into both school and the after-school program they attend. The father explains: "I read several child psychology books in my undergraduate years. When you ignore the child's behavior, you don't feed the situation by giving the child attention for inappropriate behavior. Dr. Spock said not to be hard on your children."

To an onslaught like this, the counselor, well aware of the superreasonable nature of the communication, might say, "Mr. Mafigliano, when I'm in the halls and see your two sons changing classes and getting into it with one another, I have a hunch about what I see. I get the feeling that they're not really looking for attention from adults. My hunch is that Joe is a bit embarrassed by Rich's antics and tries to disown him and then Rich feels abandoned and hurt by Joe's embarrassment. You might consider a sibling support group for Joe. There's no fee at the one offered at the county mental health center...."

In this situation, the counselor simply responded that what one sees may be more important than any textbook offering. And the counselor validated the *self* by relying on personal intuition.

The most difficult dysfunctional communication to respond to is the irrelevant stance. This type of communication discounts *self*, *other*, and *context*. School and community professionals must recognize the nature of the communication and not pre-judge the person as not caring about the situation. Consider the following situation, in which a teacher is speaking to a parent about her daughter's inappropriate dress at school: "Mrs. Jones," the teacher says, "I'm sure Shironda doesn't leave home looking like she does in school. She turns over the waistband in her skirts so they are much shorter. She has served in-school suspension for breaking the dress code five times this month, and I'm concerned about her grades and what she has learned this grading period."

Mrs. Jones replies, "Did I tell you that my husband has a case of the flu? It seems like everybody in our neighborhood has the flu these days."

The teacher might be tempted to respond in a number of ways, but the best option is a congruent response such as, "I realize that it's hard to connect with low grades, in-school suspension, and a daughter who's defying school rules. These are critical matters, and I assume you feel the struggle of dealing with them. I have also been concerned that the in-school suspension hasn't worked. I'd like to meet with you and Shironda about this situation. Before we do that, though, I'd like to map out a strategy about how we can approach her blatant violation of the school dress code. . . ." With such a response, the teacher initially refocused on the very real situation or *context* and then on the parental concern, tying it to her personal concern for Shironda. Further, the teacher offered to form a joint plan for dealing with the situation, thereby focusing again on *self* and *other*.

With practice, professionals will become more fluent while interacting with family members and at-risk and special-needs children and youth who engage in incongruent communication. The examples above represent congruent responses by professionals to dysfunctional communication by a parent.

Parental Concerns

When professionals are considering any new academic curriculum, but especially when the curriculum involves new and controversial ideas, parental concerns may surface. With grounding in family systems concepts (Mullis & Edwards, 2001), professionals are in a better position to predict such concerns and interact with parents to alleviate them. An understanding of family systems concepts will help professionals plan curriculum strategies and provide a foundation for meeting parents who are unhappy with curricular change.

In curricular matters, professionals need to recognize that, for some families, the boundary issue is a major concern (Nelson, Summers, & Turnbull, 2004). Issues such as sex education, evolution/creationism are examples. For some of those families, the concern can be alleviated easily with basic information. Other families are enmeshed and overinvolved, becoming agitated about what their children may be learning. Children from disengaged families often act out their parents' concerns, yet professionals will not be told the nature of the parents' concern.

Professionals who have cataloged the family systems processes for families of their at-risk and special-needs children/youth will more readily predict the concerns of those families when curricular change is planned. These professionals will also know how to approach the families to prevent problems from developing. Further, they will be able to use their knowledge of family processes during all of their interactions. As has been noted many times throughout this text, few families of children/youth with special needs are dysfunctional. The same is true of the at-risk and general population. If a professional is aware, however, that a family has boundary problems or a hierarchy dysfunction, this information can be used as a basic framework in any interaction with the family.

Academic Instruction

Concerns about academic instruction can be divided into two areas: (a) the family systems curriculum, and (b) curricular topics other than the family systems curriculum. Professionals in schools benefit from collaboration to promote functional schools. Simcox, Nuijens, and Lee (2006) reflected on school counselors and school psychologists becoming partners to facilitate more culturally competent schools. They highlight family empowerment and use of community resources, with student-centered interventions. They point out the challenge of stakeholders resisting change because of limitations in resources and time.

Of concern in a study by Koh and Robertson (2003) was the importance of making modifications and slowing the pace for student with disabilities. In social skills training, Gresham, Sugai, and Horner (2001) recommended that more frequent, intense training would be helpful for students with high-incidence disabilities. They also suggested directly linking the skills to the students' deficits. As well, they pointed out that "practice should program for functional generalization, which decreases the efficiency and reliability of competing problem behaviors and increases the efficiency and reliability of socially skilled alternative behaviors" (p. 341).

Non–Family Systems Curricula

A non–family systems curriculum has at least three areas of potential struggle with regard to instructional practice and families.

1. Parents may have concerns about the instructional approaches used in the school or in OST programs.
2. Professionals may have concerns about a parent's knowledge of an instructional practice and the need for the practice to remain consistent in all settings.
3. Parents and professionals alike may have concerns about homework.

The following discussion elaborates on each of these concerns. Regardless of the nature of the challenge, professionals are urged "to apply principles from systems-ecological theory to children's learning" (Christenson, 2004, p. 83).

Instructional Practice Concerns

Because professionals use more unique instructional approaches with children and youth who have special needs than with most other students, parental concerns are more likely to surface. To prevent such concerns, professionals should inform parents upfront about the nature of any unusual instruction and its estimated duration.

For example, cooperative learning activities are common in schools. Jenkins, Antil, Wayne, and Vadasy (2003) interviewed general education teachers about using this approach with remedial students who have special needs. Parents who are unfamiliar with cooperative learning can be told that general education teachers have found that it improves self-esteem and results in better academic outcomes for their children.

A demonstration or videotape of the instructional practice may be helpful. Some practices, such as the neurological impress method (NIM), may seem particularly time-consuming and confusing to parents. Using the NIM to teach reading is highly intensive, with a trained professional working one-on-one with a child. Professionals often prefer that children not read on their own or to their parents while receiving instruction in this method. Once the parents see the intensity of the method, they frequently understand why the professional requires a different approach at home, for the time being, than what they had been using.

When concerns about NIM or any other instructional practice arise, professionals should try to lower the anxiety. For example, if a father is concerned that his daughter is learning Touch Math—not realizing that the title refers to the child touching points on paper rather than humans interacting through touch—the professional could easily provide a demonstration or information. If, however, the father's concern is that Touch Math might make his child dependent on an external crutch, the situation is entirely different. All of the family systems concepts and techniques will be helpful when working with parents who have this type of concern. The professional should reexamine the catalog of family process to be better prepared to join the family in resolving their concerns.

Coordinating Home/School/Community Instruction

Again, providing information is the best means to prevent parental concerns about home–school instructional practices. For example, a student with a reading problem might learn to spell best by practicing with a tactile instructional technique. The educator should talk with the parents about this method, explaining how it was chosen (e.g., as a result of trial teaching) and providing information on the instructional practice.

Also, parents can be trained, when appropriate, to help their child practice his or her spelling words according to the tactile method. Some families do not have time for the added responsibility, and others will only make things worse for a child who already needs some distance from an overly involved parent. Examining the catalog of family process, characteristics, and other relevant information will be helpful in approaching parents or other family members involved with the child.

Informing the parents about special approaches also can prevent conflict between the home and school/community program. To extend the example above, if the parents do not know about the instructional practice and are trying to get their child to practice spelling with a look-and-say method that served them well, the child might become confused. Further, the child's spelling test scores might become lower as a result. Wanting to please both the parents and the teacher, the child might not mention his or her confusion in practice techniques. If, however, the parents see the child using a tactile practice method at home and ask the teacher about it, the teacher can provide the necessary information and work to improve the parents' trust level.

Communicating with personnel from OST learning programs is also important to ensure consistency. Some after-school or weekend programs that help students with homework also benefit from communication about special teaching approaches. Again, knowledge of the family's process, life cycle, and characteristics will be valuable when meeting with family members under such circumstances.

Homework

A number of professionals have written about the potentially thorny problem of homework. Some families are overly involved in the child's homework. Others do not provide the needed supplies or study space. Still others do not help their child because they are unavailable, lack knowledge, or are unconcerned.

Of great assistance in determining how to handle homework challenges are family characteristics, life cycle, interaction patterns, and environmental factors. When dealing with overly involved parents, the professional's objective should be to decrease involvement with their child. How that can best be done will be dictated on a case-by-case basis. The same is true in dealing with families that do not provide the necessary supplies or study space or who are unable to help their child. Disorganization of some single parents and the underorganization of some poor parents were addressed in chapters 7 and 5, respectively. Both of those circumstances require an empathic, patient response from school and community personnel. Although school/community programs can support the successful completion of homework in creative ways, discovering the root of the problem is necessary before forces can be marshaled.

Family Systems Curricula

A well-versed teacher can provide the curricular content on stances to middle-school and high-school students. The challenge, however, is in finding time in the schedule of secondary students in particular. OST programs are one answer. School counselors, social workers, and psychologists are excellent resources for providing that information to the parents and siblings.

The actual instruction or teaching techniques to be used are not that different from those used with any other type of instruction. The instructor would prepare an overall unit plan with daily lessons detailing objectives, methodology, materials, and evaluation. Satir's book *The New Peoplemaking* (1988) would be a good text to use with fifth-grade readers and above.

The most important aspect of instruction is the enactment of the communication stances. After describing the four stances, Satir had people pose in the stances. Then she had them work in groups and practice employing each stance one at a time, alternating the stances. Typically, a group of four or five people would reenact the basic family structure. The participants recognized familiar and unfamiliar stances from their own childhood experiences.

A similar experience is valuable today for children and youth and their family members. Participants benefit from demonstrations of the four stances and feedback on their interpretation of those stances. For example, with the superreasonable/computer stance, a participant may benefit from feedback on how to stand straighter. The realization that the physical body registers the deleterious impact of assuming various positions helps the participants recognize the impact of incongruent communication upon themselves and others. Satir (1983b, 1988) provided many suggestions for activities that allow individuals to explore the communication stances.

Techniques Used in Family Systems Approaches

Marshall McLuhan (1967) is credited with saying, "The medium is the message." His words are highly applicable to the manner in which a professional delivers a message. The medium is indeed the message in two techniques used in family systems approaches— metaphor and reframing.

Metaphor

A metaphor is a figure of speech that links a term or phrase to something to which it cannot be applied literally. It suggests a common characteristic between the two. Metaphor allows people to develop a new awareness by connecting two characteristics, events, ideas, or meanings. This technique is helpful in teaching, counseling, and therapy.

An example of a metaphor that might be used when a child or youth is taking on too much is, "It seems as if Joey might be too big for his britches." Another metaphor could be, "Is it possible that Kentu is tied to his mother's apron strings?"

Bradley, Gould, and Hendricks (2004) recommend the use of metaphor in counseling children and youth. They suggest using metaphors for individuals as well as groups when describing particular characteristics, products, and processes. And they recommend the use of children's/young adult literature, movies, television programs, and fairy tales that speak to situations that fit the age of the child or youth. In *The Wizard of Oz*, the Tin Man can be a metaphor for serenity, the Lion a metaphor for courage, and the Scarecrow a metaphor for having "wisdom to know the difference." Metaphors allow people to access information in a nonthreatening way and can reinforce learning.

Walsh and McGraw (2002) described "symptom as metaphor" using the example of an asthmatic daughter to symbolize the mother's feelings of being suffocated in the marriage. The dominant story is that metaphor, like the filter in a camera lens, dramatically affects the meaning that people bring to bear on their lives.

Kottman (2004) stated that in using metaphor in play therapy, "the counselor tracks, restates content, reflects feelings, and returns responsibility through the child's story without imposing his or her own interpretation of the meaning of the story" (p. 122). Kottman warns those using metaphor not to "break" it by pushing the child into the "real world."

Corey (2005) described a gestalt therapy use of metaphor as tuning into the individual's descriptions that provide clues to their inner struggles. Corey indicated that the counselor or social worker picks up on the metaphor to ask questions that help establish underlying meaning of experience. Corey provided the example: "I feel like I've been through a meat grinder," followed up with questions such as, "Who is doing the grinding?"

In an early classic on the subject, *Therapeutic Metaphors for Children and the Child Within,* Mills and Crowley (1986) described the use of metaphor in general, and specifically its use with children. They indicated that metaphor, a style of symbolic language used throughout the ages, can be found in parables in the Bible, the Kabbalah, Zen Buddhist koans, allegorical literature, poetry, and fairy tales. In all of these, metaphor conveys the central message.

Metaphor can be used effectively with children and youth and their families alike. This technique is not easily taught, however, because it is as much artistic as it is technical.

Reframing

Reframing, introduced briefly in chapter 13, is used widely in family systems approaches (Fenell & Weinhold, 2003; Goldenberg & Goldenberg, 2004; Nichols & Schwartz, 2004, 2005; Walsh & McGraw, 2002), as well as in other approaches to counseling and psychotherapy. Underlying reframing is the desire to help others bring a larger and different perspective to a life situation. Reframing shifts the focus to problem solving (Mullis & Edwards, 2001). Certainly, solution-focused interventions are important in school and community settings. Reframing represents an effort to improve a person's situation by altering his or her view to encompass a new way of seeing.

Reframing steps away from blame and replaces it with good intentions and intrigue about life events (Walsh & McGraw, 2002). The use of goals early in a therapeutic process can also be a form of reframing. Family therapists who employ narrative therapy, notably co-founders Michael White and David Epston (1990), help families re-label life circumstances and events so they have a more constructive view. The stories that people tell themselves about their family and lives are brought into a new, more positive light through reinterpretation, thereby changing the meaning that people make of their lives and how they feel about life.

Structural family therapists frequently use reframing to help families realize that the symptom bearer (e.g., a defiant child) is not the problem. The family shares the problem by retaining the status quo by considering the symptom bearer (e.g., juvenile delinquent) rather than the family structure as the problem.

The following story from the Taoist tradition serves as a good introduction to reframing:

> There once was a farmer who had a wonderful horse that the farmer's family depended upon for their livelihood. His horse ran away one day and all his neighbors said how awful was his fate. To this, the farmer replied, "Maybe." A couple of days later the horse returned with a herd of wild horses. The neighbors told him how lucky he was. The farmer said, "Maybe." Soon the farmer's oldest son tried to break in one of the wild horses and was thrown and broke his leg. Again the neighbors said "how awful" and the farmer replied, "Maybe." The next day the people in charge of drafting soldiers rejected his oldest son because of his injury. The neighbors again thought he was very fortunate, and he thought, "Maybe." (J. Daniel, personal communication)

Reframing means transforming the view a person holds of events so a different meaning can be attached. With the change in meaning come changes in responses and behaviors. As Watzlawick, Weakland, and Fisch (1974) summarized:

> To reframe, then, means to change the conceptual and/or emotional setting or viewpoint in relation to which a situation is experienced and to place it in another frame which fits the "facts" of the same concrete situation equally well or even better, and thereby changes its entire meaning. (p. 95)

Like metaphor, reframing can be used with children and youth as well as adults. In the field of family systems, the professional usually redefines the treatment unit to be the whole family rather than the symptom bearer or problematic child, which is the framework seen so often in school and community programs. Reframing is intended to affect the interrelated cognitive, emotional, and behavioral spheres and generally results in a change in how people think, feel, and act.

Forms of Reframing

In all of the many uses of reframing, the process of bringing a different context into play brings deeper meaning to the experience. Karpel (1986b) stated:

> Reframing may be used to accomplish different ends. Like psycho-analytic interpretation, which it resembles, it may be intended to foster insight. In other cases it may be used to make alternative patterns of interaction easier to enact or to make it much more difficult to persist in problematic patterns. From a resource per-spective, it is probably most often used to identify resources that are inherent in the presenting problem itself, as in the use of statements that throw light on patterns of loyalty, concern, and protectiveness in what would otherwise look like destructive or self-destructive behavior. (p. 200)

Reframing can be used to maintain or increase a person's self-worth. Satir and Baldwin (1983) reported the value of helping people focus on observing what occurred in an incident instead of blaming another person for the situation. Satir referred to this as using an "observing ego" to help a client reduce blame and increase trust.

Further, reframing can be used to diffuse negative feelings. An example would be when one family member is angry and her temper is flaring, and the others are upset because she has broken the family rule that no one should express angry feelings. The pro-fessional might reframe the temper to be seen as a "way of bringing out her thoughts."

Another example is to reframe blame as searching for information. Nichols and Schwartz (2004) gave the example of a son becoming disruptive when his baby sister was born. The father reacted in a punitive manner. In therapy, the father was able to shift his focus and realize that his son was feeling the loss of being the center of attention rather than viewing him as "bad." This reinterpretation introduces a new possibility in the rela-tionship between father and son in which the father could carve out time for just the two of them each day. As well, the father could see the importance his son placed on being with his father—his desire for closeness.

In many ways, a clarifying technique can be used to reframe liabilities and perceived weaknesses as strengths. In so doing, the professional may be able to transform meaning attached to the frame. For example, a single mother taking her teenage daughter for ther-apy could be clarified as "caring enough about your daughter to find the resources she needs." Mullis and Edwards (2001) gave the example of an adolescent daughter being dis-respectful and sneaky about going to family therapy. The therapist suggested that maybe the teen was expressing a need for more self-control and recommended finding ways that she could be a decision maker in matters important to her. Underneath the reframing to bring out the positive and new ways of making meaning of life events is an emphasis on resilience—the capacity of the human spirit to grow and develop in positive ways despite difficult circumstances. Resilience is the focus of chapter 10.

Questions to Pose Before Offering a Reframe

Bitter and Corey (in Corey, 2005) recommended consideration of five types of questions the counselor would answer prior to using reframing. Aimed at a therapeutic process, the questions included the following:

> What purpose does this symptom, interaction, or process serve?
>
> How does the individual's behavior protect the self?
>
> What are the social consequences of an action or interaction?
>
> How are the goals of family members at cross-purposes with each others?
>
> Are the goals of the family at odds with the goals of therapy?"
> (p. 435)

Although these are questions to guide counselors, social workers, and psychologists prior to using reframing, they are useful for other professionals, too, to reflect on when hearing reframing by team members who have more depth and experience with clinical practice. More experienced educators with advanced training and expertise who work with families also may use these questions prior to reframing.

Reframing With Children and Youth

When using reframing with children, their cognitive level is an important factor. For example, children who are 7 years and younger overgeneralize how they see their strengths and weaknesses (Piaget & Inhelder, 1969). It may not be effective, then, for an adult to speak about only one aspect of what the child does as a problem. The child may not have the cognitive capacity to understand that difference, and, therefore, reframing will not be possible. For example, a teacher trying to reframe the fighting of two 5-year-olds as a sign of actually liking one another may find that the attempt falls on deaf ears.

Even though young children may not be able to follow a reframe cognitively, they may be able to follow a shift related to emotions. For example, a child who is sensitive to nonverbal changes in the emotional climate, such as making a joke and laughing about the child's irritability, will be able to benefit from this nonverbal reframing. This type of reframing is at an experiential level rather than a cognitive one.

Once children reach approximately age 7, they will be able to understand reframing that relates to concrete as opposed to abstract thinking. At approximately age 12, the child is able to respond to higher-order thinking when a reframe is presented. For example, at this cognitive level, children could understand a reframing statement such as, "You don't argue with those you don't care about."

Timing

The timing of reframing cannot be guided externally. The professional must intuitively sense it to be appropriate, given the readiness of the family member or child/youth. If used at the wrong time or at too abstract a level, reframing can result in a misconnection as well as anger at the professional for having misperceived the situation.

One timing guideline is to wait until highly intense feelings of grief or anger have been diffused. For example, if parents have learned recently that their child has Down syndrome, the timing is not right to share an example of a parent who is in the acceptance stage of grieving. In time, the professional may sense that the family is moving out of shock, denial, or anger. Then the timing would be appropriate to use reframing.

Over time, siblings of children with disabilities may realize the "gifts" brought to them by having a sibling with a disability (Hodapp, Glidden, & Kaiser, 2005). Eventually the siblings may describe themselves "feeling more open, more tolerant of differences, and focused on life's larger meaning as a result of growing up with a sibling who has disabilities" (p. 337). Timing in leading family members to see the positive is critical to having a sense of trust in relationships with those who are guiding them, whether they be school counselors, community social workers, or private psychotherapists.

Using the Language of the Family

In reframing, professionals should use language that speaks to the family. For example, with a visually artistic family, a reframe regarding drawing or other visual imagery might be effective. Likewise, a musical family would appreciate a reframe that is auditory in nature. For a Christian family highly involved in their church school, a Bible story might be used to reframe something. Those who are interested in athletics would value a reframe relating to their interest in a sport of their choice, and someone who is intrigued by vehicles would respond well to reframing of a mechanical nature.

Case Example

A 7-year-old boy whose father had recently committed suicide began to act out by talking back to his mother and resisting instructions. The mother interpreted the behavior as oppositional/defiant and reacted by intensifying her discipline. When the mother mentioned this problem to the boy's teacher, the teacher commented that the behavior seemed to be designed to keep the mother intensely involved with the boy and could be interpreted as the equivalent of anxious, clingy behavior.

In the context of the recent loss, the mother found that the idea of her son being anxious and clingy was much more acceptable than her previous interpretation of his being defiant and angry. Her response, then, was to become more nurturing, which resulted in a reduction of the boy's anxiety and acting-out behavior.

The teacher's ability to reframe the child's behavior resulted in a positive shift in the family system. This shift allowed the mother and son to help each other through their mutual grief and avoided prolonging a painful symptom.

A Socialization Method: Temperature Reading

Socialization is exemplified in this chapter by the family systems strategy of Temperature Reading (Schwab, 1990). Adapted from Satir (1983a), it is a method to clear the air in group interactions (Azpeitia & Zahnd, 1991) and can be used readily in school or community classes, as well as during regularly scheduled meetings of ongoing groups.

Temperature Reading also can be used with families once parents learn the procedure. If the parents do not attend meetings where this technique is used, they need training in the method to carry it forward in the home.

The basic purposes of Temperature Reading are for group members to share their feelings and to detoxify negativity on the part of group members. It could be used in a class session or homeroom, as well as during educational, support, or counseling groups. It also can be used in OST learning opportunities such as after-school and weekend programs.

Features

Satir (1983a) included five types of expressions in a Temperature Reading: appreciations, complaints with recommendations, puzzles, new information, and hopes and wishes (Azpeitia & Zahnd, 1991). A Temperature Reading does not have to include all five features. The needs of those in the group or class determine which of these are useful in that situation. In addition, the amount of time available affects how many are included within and across the five types of expressions.

Appreciations

Appreciations are shared directly with the person being appreciated. In the classroom, a teacher might say, "Tim, you're doing a great job of helping Maria with the transition to a whole new set of instructional materials. I appreciate your help." In another example, a counselor or social worker might tell a parent, "Mr. Juval, I'm so glad you told me about the support group you've attended. Later in the meeting I hope you will tell other parents about it. Thanks."

In a parent training session in which a family demonstrated the parent not directly appreciating her son, the professional could say, "Mrs. Jones, let me play you in a scenario":

> Joey, come on over here and look me in the eye. I'm going to role-play being your Mom: "You know, Joey, I'm so glad you raked the yard this weekend without being asked. It meant a lot to me and gave us time to watch that video together. Thanks, son."

Following this modeling, the professional could ask the mother if she would be willing to try again and ask for feedback. If the mother and son succeed in engaging in authentic sending and receiving of appreciation, the professional might ask each one how the interaction felt. If they respond that they felt a little stiff about it, the professional might compare the situation to putting on a new shoe that could benefit from some wear before it becomes comfortable. If they feel closer or even misty-eyed, that expression would be reinforced by simply saying, "Take that feeling in and remember how it feels and what brought it about."

The appreciative communication focuses on the positive and provides examples for others of directly sharing an experience of appreciation. Eye contact and tone of voice are important in sharing an appreciation. Appreciations honor humanness and lead to authentic human connection. As models for children, parents and teachers can increase the sharing of appreciations in our children and youth.

Complaints With Recommendations

Complaints are a major reason for conducting Temperature Readings. These concerns can provide the opportunity to detoxify negativity as well as provide a structure that allows an individual to voice a complaint in a safe environment where others accept and expect them to be part of the process. As Azpeitia and Zahnd (1991) defined it, "A complaint with a recommendation is the reporting of a discrepancy between what is and an idea or awareness of how things could be better" (p. 86).

Sharing brings validation. When unexpressed, complaints can lead to negative interactions and restrict the openness necessary to bring vitality, commitment, and flexibility, and thereby allows more room for closeness.

Satir (1983a) advised that any complaint be accompanied by a recommendation for change. The recommendation for solving the problem does not have to be carried out. The strategy is intended to help the person look toward solutions rather than merely voice a complaint. But even registering a complaint and being heard are important to healthy communication and release of inner tension—unless this becomes a regular mode of interacting.

In a classroom example of a complaint expressed during a Temperature Reading, a student says, "I'm having a hard time catching up with all the new algebra since I was in the hospital for a week. I hate slowing the class down and wonder if someone might have the time to help me during study hall in the afternoons."

Another example of a complaint during a support group meeting is a father saying to the social worker, "I have a problem with the time of these meetings. I can't get from work to home and feed my son before coming here at 6 o'clock. I find the group beneficial and would like to have the time moved to no earlier than 6:30."

Puzzles

The third feature of a Temperature Reading is to present a puzzle, confusion, question, rumor, or piece of gossip. This feature is used when the person presenting the puzzle has heard something but does not understand fully what he or she heard. Expressing the puzzle allows rumors to be affirmed or denied. The rumor might be about something others could look forward to, something the individual feared, or something the individual was worried about. In any event, the puzzle has not been addressed adequately. Surfacing the puzzle lessens uncertainty and confusion.

An example of a puzzle expressed during a Temperature Reading exercise in the classroom is: "I'm wondering if it's true that anyone who earns two thousand points will be able to attend the Harry Potter movie next Friday afternoon?" Another example of presenting a puzzle is a parent querying a social worker: "I overheard a parent at the basketball game telling someone else that there's a support group called Compassionate Friends. I wonder if you know how I can get in touch with them in this county. My wife and I are still grieving over the loss of our daughter."

New Information

New information allows individuals to let others know about an upcoming event, activity, or other opportunity quickly and simply. It involves forecasting a possibility so others might avail themselves of the occasion. It also helps to prevent rumors from spreading and prevents anyone from being left out or being the last to find out about something with which others are familiar.

A classroom example of providing new information is a teacher saying:

> We have a great speaker who will be at our assembly during third period on Tuesday. Her name is Carol Scearce. She's president of Enlightening Enterprises in Texas. She'll be teaching you how to make mind maps. That's a special and creative form of taking notes developed by Tony Buzan, from England. I hope no one misses school on Tuesday.

Another example of providing new information is a school psychologist telling a parent group:

> I have an announcement I know all of you will be interested in hearing. We now have an easier referral process to the county mental health center. Some of you will remember that the center's waiting list for family counseling was several months long. The center has hired two new family systems therapists, and the waiting period is nonexistent. Be sure to thank Dr. Wojinski when you see her. She was responsible for finding the funds for these new additions.

In an OST program, an example is:

> Next week Mr. Sampson will be here each day to provide individual and group coaching to those who want to improve their basketball maneuvers. Before you leave today, please sign up for the day and time that work best for you to have individual coaching and to be part of a group coaching.

Hopes and Wishes

Hopes and wishes are statements about something that is desired. If a desire remains unarticulated, it has little chance of being fulfilled. Satir (1983a) was concerned that all members of a family or group be able to voice their hopes and wishes. She found that many people will reserve their wishes when they do not have a structure for voicing them.

An example of the expression of a hope or wish is a student saying:

> Mrs. Anthony, I'm wondering if we could have a popcorn party this Friday afternoon during the after-school program. My brother will be home from the service, and he said he wants to visit my school. He'll be here this Friday afternoon, and I wish everyone could meet him and visit with him.

Another example of expressing a hope or wish is a parent commenting before the start of a parent effectiveness training session: "I wish somebody would develop a list of child-care opportunities for our younger children so it would be easier to attend these parent training workshops."

Guidelines

Satir recommended that the Temperature Reading be conducted in families, in groups, and as part of any work group. The guidelines for Temperature Reading involve frequency, leadership, structure, and the training of professionals and parents.

Frequency

Satir (1983a) recommended that Temperature Reading be conducted daily whenever a new group is formed. She noted that once the group stabilizes, the frequency of Temperature Reading can be lessened gradually. For maximum benefit, Satir recommended that Temperature Reading be conducted at least weekly. The more struggles within a group or family, the more frequently Temperature Reading should be conducted. Groups that meet weekly should conduct Temperature Reading before the beginning of each meeting.

In a newly formed classroom, Temperature Reading is best conducted daily for the first week and then gradually reduced to meet the needs of the class. In no case should meetings be held less often than weekly. Homeroom is a good time to conduct Temperature Reading in secondary schools. When teachers have a totally different group of students each period, they cannot invest the time in Temperature Reading at the expense of academic time. In elementary school, Temperature Reading can be conducted the first thing in the morning, when all students have arrived in the classroom but before the start of the academic day. In OST learning programs, a weekly schedule with Temperature Reading as a feature works well.

Family members who are part of a Temperature Reading process in the school will find it easier to implement a similar process at home. Thus, the Temperature Reading conducted during school activities serves as a model for the children/youth. Then, when parents institute Temperature Reading in the home, it will work more smoothly. When parents are involved in Temperature Readings (e.g., in a parent group), the tougher the situation, the better their opportunity to learn from experience. It offers them the modeling they need to conduct Temperature Readings in the home.

Leadership

Temperature Readings are generally most effective when one professional is in charge of conducting them. In the classroom, that person is the teacher. In a counseling group, the counselor should be in charge. In OST programs, the staff member who has the authority and expertise would provide the model of leading Temperature Reading during group meetings with the children/youth.

This is not a situation that should become shared leadership on a rotating basis. Preferably, a professional who is comfortable in providing congruent messages, and in helping others to do the same, should lead the Temperature Reading in groups outside the school.

Structure

While introducing a Temperature Reading, the professional who conducts it initially states the purposes and then describes the five features. Next the leader shares personal experiences with Temperature Reading. Following that, a brief role-play of a Temperature

Reading is conducted. Concluding with a question-and-answer session helps to eliminate concerns about the process and content.

Temperature Reading is valuable for all ongoing groups that operate in school and community settings. Teams that meet regularly would also benefit from conducting Temperature Reading at each meeting, as would all ongoing parent groups, support groups, parenting training sessions, or less structured, yet regularly held, meetings. The Temperature Reading does not take much time, though those that include complaints and puzzles will likely be longer. Temperature Reading should be conducted at the beginning of meetings, to clear the air prior to engaging in new business, thereby increasing the effectiveness of the actual meeting. It also can avoid intrusive, off-track questions (e.g., puzzles) during the middle of a meeting by providing an opportunity to receive answers early in a meeting.

To help parents understand the possibilities of this process, the leader should connect the value of Temperature Reading with family life situations. The leader can recommend that the parents conduct this process at home and share personal and others' experiences with Temperature Reading in family situations. The leader, too, can recommend that families wait to conduct Temperature Reading at home until they are more familiar with how they work in the school or community groups using the procedure.

Training/Preparation

Probably the most effective training for professionals in conducting Temperature Reading is to conduct them regularly in their own work groups. This emphasizes learning by doing, recognizing the adage, "Experience is the best teacher." In conducting real (not practice) Temperature Reading, professionals will face many touchy or confusing situations. Having real-life experience with this activity in their work groups will allow them to plan better how they will respond to sensitive or difficult situations. These situations occur naturally in a spontaneous and open sharing of feelings and thoughts in a group context. Difficult situations should be expected and should not take a professional by surprise.

Preparing parents to be involved in Temperature Reading is important. Parents may not have experienced such an open exchange of thoughts and feelings. Furthermore, they might not believe that professionals value their thoughts and feelings. A few sessions may be necessary to establish trust in the process. Therefore, professionals should not be surprised if, the first several times, a Temperature Reading focuses largely on appreciations, hopes and wishes, and new information—which are less threatening than sharing a puzzle or expressing complaints. When a child or parent shares his or her first complaint or puzzle, his or her concerns should be validated before moving on with the elaboration.

Summary

This chapter demonstrates ways that family systems concepts can be infused into school and community settings for instruction, support, and counseling. Encouraging family members to extend some strategies learned within school or community contexts into family life will help reinforce functional communication in the home. Creative profession-als can design and implement family systems concepts by weaving them within their exist-ing practices whether of an academic, behavioral, or social-emotional nature.

After observing human interactions during speaking engagements around the world, Satir described communication stances common to all cultures and taught these in her human validation process model. She divided the forms of communication into dysfunc-tional and functional stances and labeled them with straightforward terms. The dysfunc-tional stances included placating, blaming, superreasonable, and irrelevant. She referred to functional communication as congruent. Those using communication that is not congruent during stressful life events were viewed as having low self-worth, whereas those using congruent communication under similarly stressful situation were described as possessing high self-worth. The dysfunctional stances, learned in the home at a young age, were described as the default mode into which a person automatically falls when under duress. The stances that are not congruent are systemic with none able to be in place unless sup-ported by another person's dysfunctional stance (e.g., placater–blamer). Each dysfunc-tional stance discounts one, two, or three communication aspects (i.e., *self, other, context*). Transforming stances is helped by learning how the stances played out in one's family-of-origin, observing congruent models, internally replaying past experiences substituting congruent responses, mentally rehearsing for situations evoking stress and/or role playing congruent communication, then, reflecting on stressful communication soon after it occurs to evaluate personal growth and what needs further work.

Placaters discount *self*, fear rejection, and appear to be "nice," but are avoiding con-flict because they fear disapproval by others; they are fragile and typically have strong feelings of low self-worth. Transformed, the placater feels and expresses sincere compas-sion for *others* and serves them with authenticity.

Blamers cover their vulnerable feeling with attempts to control *others,* thus providing a false sense of importance that masks loneliness and feelings of inferiority. It is possible to transform discounting *others* and relate in an assertive manner by taking an "I" position and stating personal beliefs or feelings through *self* assertion that is realistic and doesn't reject the opinions, attitudes, or beliefs of *others* by agreeing to disagree.

Those who assume a superreasonable stance feel vulnerable and hide behind an intel-lectual façade that covers the vulnerable feelings while attempting to protect the *self*. Often appearing aloof, cold, or overly reasonable, others may perceive them as congruent when they really are discounting both *self* and *other* by not being in relationship with those around them. Those more aware of dysfunctional communication may view them as a bit "robotic" in their interactions. As their superreasonable stance transforms, their natural intellectual bent is used in service of others when sharing wisdom they have gained from their depth of study in different areas.

Those assuming an irrelevant stance are the "great pretenders" who divert attention from situations that make them feel uncomfortable. By this diversion they discount all three aspects: *self, other,* and *context*. This is the most difficult type of stance to counter or transform. Their comments are interjected during tense communication and are totally off the subject; some talk non-stop, disallowing others from surfacing stresses that they expe-rience. When transformed, the irrelevant stance is replaced by spontaneous, appropriate humor that connects people in convivial relationships.

The congruent stance described by Satir is responsive to *self, other*, and *context*. Those who maintain a congruent stance under duress have a high level of self-worth, are balanced in their acceptance of differences, and have the courage to take risks. They assume personal responsibility for their thoughts, feelings, and actions.

These stances can be taught as a curricular area in schools or OST programs. Before helping others transform dysfunctional stances, professionals learn about and transform their typical default stance(s) when under duress. Teachers, counselors, social workers, and psychologists have potential for teaching the five stances once they have been trained to understand, recognize, and assist others in transforming them. At that stage they serve as congruent models for others to emulate and can provide examples of the process they used in transforming stances.

A second element in the chapter highlights instruction in relation to non-family systems and family systems arenas that may challenge some professionals. Prevention is the key, and familiarizing parents with instructional variations matters to those whose child's instruction is varied based on individual need. Likewise, it is crucial to provide advance written information on variations that impact all children/youth if parents lack awareness because of a new initiative or when moving from one level/phase to another (e.g., elementary to middle). Technology was experienced differently when parents were in school than in the world of today's children/youth. This will continue to be the case, and other curricular areas will affect instruction and could result in parental concern for a minority of parents (e.g., family-life curricula teaching about safe sex, responding to the multiple intelligences of children with varied modes of learning).

Regardless of content, professionals want to prevent parental concern by providing basic information prior to any new instruction or curricular areas being put into place. The more information provided to family members, the less likely professionals are to receive questions, concerns, or for groups of concerned parents to band together with a negative response. It also helps to bring parents on board who are receptive to change and use them as leaders in sharing information with other parents.

If parents are concerned about a curricular area, a negative reaction can be prevented or ameliorated by informing them of the rationale, process, and value it holds for their children. Regardless of acceptance, it is important that professionals assure parents and caregivers that they will not negate the parents' authority and also that all students must comply with policy and rules unless a written waiver is extended.

Metaphors lead others to a new understanding when linking two characteristics, events, ideas, or meanings. The example in the chapter was using the book/movie *The Wizard of Oz* as a metaphor linking serenity with the Tin Man, courage with the Lion, and wisdom to know the difference with the Scarecrow per the Serenity Prayer. Most important is to offer an alternative understanding and allow the child/youth to make the linkage so that it becomes internalized with the individual owning the central message.

The technique of reframing assists professionals working with individuals or groups. Chapter 13 described reframing and the Appendix clarifies that it is crucial to define the problem in a way that a solution is possible, because the definition of the problem determines how it will be approached. Posing questions can lead to consideration of alternative views of the symptom that expand its definition and is a form of reframing (e.g., the family structure with its inversion of the hierarchy is the problem, not the defiant child).

Viewing the problem differently allows professionals to suggest different ways for the child and/or family members to respond in new ways; this leads to action or strategy to help resolve challenging behaviors and circumstances. Additionally, when shifting one's view of a situation, person, or event, it is possible to bring a new meaning to it, further empowering family members to change.

Reframing may be used to foster insight, in order to create alternative forms of human interactions that may be easier to engage or, in an opposite manner, to make it so difficult that the dysfunctional behavior drops out. Frequently, reframing provides clarity on behavior that belies loyalty, concern, or over protectiveness. As a result, typically it becomes easier to perceive how destructive the behavior has been and to make changes. As well, reframing can assist with allowing the "observing ego" to perceive situations differently by moving outside of blame and toward trust. Diffusing negative feelings is another way reframing is used as well as providing a new frame for blaming as an individual "looking for information," which may kindle resilience in children/youth.

Reframing has timing issues to keep in mind, and these are more art than strategy in that it takes intuition to select the best time to interject a reframe. Certainly it is easier for older children/youth to grasp reframes because they are further from the literal cognitive stage of development, yet younger children can be given simple reframes that may help them make a shift in their understanding of an experience.

Timing matters in relation to most strategies used with children/youth as well as family members; and with reframing, timing is like "location" in real estate (i.e., ¾s of the response). Intuition guides those aware of what they sense in a situation with different people under similar and different circumstances. It helps to hold reframes for later during times of strong emotional experiences. Appropriate timing in using reframing helps deepen trust.

It is always wise to use reframes that speak to the family's life experience. Use artistic reframes for creative children or families, sports reframes for enthusiasts, or spiritual reframes for those who have a strong connection to faith-based life.

The third element in the chapter relates to socialization, referred to as Temperature Reading, as developed by Virginia Satir. It can be used in home, school, or community contexts. The five features of the method include: appreciations, complaints with recommendations, puzzles, new information, and hopes and wishes. Temperature Reading should be a regular communication practice for group members that meet regularly and can be used across a variety of contexts on a weekly basis (e.g., weekly family meetings, school or community classes, weekly/monthly committee meetings, homeroom, opening exercises). Temperature Reading can be less frequent after the group has coalesced as the need declines. When there is a high need for increased communication, Temperature Reading may be daily and slowly stepped down.

Temperature Readings begin the gathering rather than end it, and a time limit must be enforced. Leadership is invaluable to set the stage for an appropriate flow, not getting hung up too long in one area, and modeling congruent behavior. Teachers, counselors, social workers, psychologists, parents, heads of committees or other authority figures have strong potential to lead the process. Whoever leads the process must be able to demonstrate congruent communication in situations they find stressful.

Extension Activities

Pair/Share during Class/Training: Using the self-reflection from the guidance under the heading, "Exploring Personal Stances," pair group members. Direct the pairs to share what they learned about their past use of each of the stances. As well, they should share the stances of other family members and how the stances played out among their family members from childhood.

Class/Training Whole Group Discussion: After the pairs share their reflections on family-of-origin stances, conduct a whole-group discussion by posing questions such as the following:

What is an example of something that surprised you in your reflection on stances?

What about your reflections touched your heart or set off a sense of closeness?

What good ideas did you find from listening to your partners' sharing his/her reflections?

Has anyone noticed a replication of stances from family-of-origin to life today in your immediate family, and what do you think/feel about that replication?

What is an example of a dysfunctional stance you have noticed that is no longer present in your immediate family? To what do you attribute its lack?

Temperature Reading During Class/Training: For training purposes, after reading the content on Temperature Reading in this book, the instructor/trainer leads Temperature Reading with the group each time it meets for five sessions. After that, rotate the individual responsible for conducting the exercise and provide notes to each student that they can read for feedback after their turn in conducting the Temperature Reading. If a student wishes to lead another Temperature Reading later in the term, allow him/her to sign up for a particular day.

Reflection and Journaling on Metaphor and Reframing: At the end of each day, sit down and think of situations you were in when a metaphor or reframe may have helped. Write examples of what you could say as a metaphor or reframe if you were in the same situation in the future.

And/or

Reflection and Log on Metaphor and Reframing: Reflect on any examples of metaphor or reframing you heard in your class/training session each time you meet. Keep an ongoing log of these over 3 weeks.

In-Class/Training Bridge With Log: After 3 weeks of logging metaphors and reframing observed during class/training, have a whole-group discussion of examples observed, how they responded to these internally (feelings), and whether they found themselves making more use of metaphor and/or reframing since they began keeping the log of examples.

Strengthening the Possibilities for a Systems Paradigm

"A competent system is driven by systems thinking" (Zmuda, Kuklis, & Kline, 2004). People in schools and communities, however, have not been trained to think systemically. To help professionals in school and community settings adopt a systems paradigm, a systems change model developed by Virginia Satir will facilitate integration of family systems concepts into school and community contexts.

Communication skills are basic to the systems paradigm. Also, psychological issues that can result in barriers to implementing family systems ideas in school and community contexts include demanding and angry parents and psychiatric difficulties. This chapter presents a five-step problem-solving process, followed by a discussion of interaction between families and school/community. Family systems concepts in school/community contexts do have potential limitations, stemming from lack of training; prevailing norms and established school/community procedures; resistance to change; and the reality constraints of time, money, and availability of trained personnel. The chapter identifies the stages of response to change and addresses the concerns about change using Satir's model for change as a basis.

Communication Skills

Parents' communication skills vary widely. Some parents and other adult family members involved in the lives of children and youth are quite articulate, and others struggle, sometimes as a result of language differences. In some cases, members do not even try to communicate because they are afraid that they will sound foolish or inadequate. Beyond family members' communications skills, everyone else involved in family/school/community interactions—professionals, others in the child's life, and the child or youth—require good communication skills.

People communicate at many different levels, which Satir (1983a) referred to as "the ingredients of an interaction." Understanding these ingredients will help prevent miscommunication and is consistent with the focus of this book—to present family systems theory, concepts, and practices to improve the learning and development of at-risk and special-needs children/youth in school and community settings.

Parent/Family Communication

Helping parents and other family members involved with the child can learn the communication skills needed so they will not feel overwhelmed by their interactions with professionals in school/community contexts and on teams (Turnbull & Turnbull, 2001). Blue-Banning et al. (2004) provided indicators for communication including

- sharing resources,
- being clear,
- being honest,
- communicating positively,
- being tactful,
- being open,
- listening,
- communicating frequently, and
- coordinating information.

Parents and family members help one another by sharing their experiences. Parents are connected with one another in school or community programs through parent groups (Bauer & Shea, 2003), which may include support, information, or training. Olsen and Fuller (2003) particularly advocate support for fathers through their website Parents Helping Parents [www.php.com].

Some professionals endorse the idea of parents as teachers of their child. Family members should help children reinforce what they learn in school. Examples include drilling on multiplication facts, geography lessons when planning a family vacation, and requiring thank-you notes written in cursive once it is taught in school. Some teachers maintain a section on the school website listing homework so parents can check on the student's progress and completion of assigned work. In another example, early in the year, Standards of Learning are sent home so family members will know what the children are learning. These can be obtained from websites with the state Department of Education.

The Harvard Family Research Project (HFRP), which has been in existence almost 25 years,

> strives to promote more effective educational practices, pro-
> grams, and policies for disadvantaged children and youth by gener-
> ating, publishing, and dissemination of our and others' research.
> [www.gse.harvard.edu/hfrp]

Resources the HFRP overviews relate to training parents to work with their children and youth and provide examples of how parents can be trainers of other parents. Family communication in community settings is important as well. Kakli, Kreider, Little, Buck, and Coffey (2006) provide useful information for family-centered practices in after-school programs, which can be accessed on the HFRP website.

Problem areas and research on communication are discussed below. Research and practice indicate how to turn these problems into successes.

Inadequate Processing of Information

Communication problems can arise because parents are unfamiliar with team procedures or because they have not mastered effective communication skills. Unfamiliarity with procedures and processes is remedied relatively easily. Suggestions for helping family members become aware of processes on how to access help abound (Bauer & Shea, 2003; Chen & Miles, 2004; Friend, 2005; Olsen & Fuller, 2003; Turnbull & Turnbull, 2001).

It should be noted that some parents are less articulate because of a personal disability (Bauer & Shea, 2003). If a case worker is assigned to the family, that person is a logical possibility to accompany parents to IEP and other meetings because he or she has formed a trusting relationship with the parents. With the advent of IDEA 2004, parental responsibilities have become more central for children/youth with special needs, so additional support may be necessary. School professionals must help parents understand their rights as well as responsibilities for their child.

Parent Training

A number of professionals have written about involvement of family members of at-risk and special-needs children and youth (e.g., Bauer & Shea, 2003; Friend, 2005; Kyle, McIntyre, Miller, & Moore, 2002; Turnbull & Turnbull, 2001; Turnbull, Turnbull, Shank, Smith, & Leal, 2002). This literature has focused on parental involvement, parents as teachers, parents as partners, homework, teamwork, and attitudes toward the delivery of services. One resource that is helpful to families and special needs children/youth is a University of Kansas website [www.beachcenter.org].

Early on, McLoughlin (1981) introduced a parent/teacher education model for the joint training of teachers and parents of children with disabilities that is still relevant. The model involves competency-based, skills-oriented training with an emphasis on "training together to work together," with the outcome being enhanced cooperation and interaction. The project demonstrated that joint training can be effective in gaining the involvement and support of these parents.

Turnbull and Turnbull (2001) reported that 70 Parent Training and Information Centers (PTIs) are funded by the U.S. Department of Special Education, Office of Education and

Rehabilitation Services. Each state has at least one PTI, as do Palau and Puerto Rico. The PTIs help parents understand the needs of their child or youth, as well as the disability; provide follow-up support for education; encourage better communication with professionals who provide services; foster involvement in decisions about the child or youth and IEP activity; and help them access information from other programs to better understand education provisions for the education of children and youth with special needs, including infants and toddlers.

Ingredients of an Interaction

Satir (1983a) compared communication to a recipe with many different ingredients. A person's interactions with others can be as enjoyable and as complex as that new recipe for the evening meal. It is easy to misread communication if one is not aware of all of the ingredients. Just as leaving out the baking powder in a recipe can result in flattened cookies, failing to understand, recognize, or respond to an ingredient of an interaction can result in flattened communication. Satir described the ingredients in communication. Figure 15.1 shows the ingredients for a two-person interaction involving spoken communication. Point 1 is the initiating point, and point 8 is the responding point of the communication.

Person A, Adam, initiates a message to Person B, Betty. The other six ingredients of the interaction (points 2–7) are part of Betty's internal process before she responds at point 8.

Point 2 represents Betty's internal process of figuring out what she sees and hears, using her eyes, ears, skin, and nose. If she cannot see because she is on the phone, she will not have all the ingredients available to her. Assuming that she can see Adam, Betty will

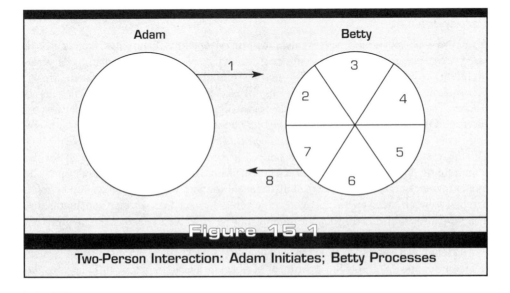

Figure 15.1

Two-Person Interaction: Adam Initiates; Betty Processes

take in his facial expression, body position, muscle tone, skin color, scent, breathing, voice tone, and pace, as well as movement. These factors, called *paralinguistics*, provide well over half of the meaning of the message. Adam's spoken words are only part of the message. How he delivers the words conveys much meaning. Betty will select what she hears and sees from all the possibilities.

Next, point 3 represents Betty's connecting with past experiences and learning, which will determine the meaning she will make of what she sees and hears. Betty might well ask herself, while forming the meaning of the message, how aware of the past and present she is as they relate to self, other, and context. (Those three dimensions were described in chapter 14 in the discussion of the five communication stances.) Betty also could ask herself whether she was aware of any past experiences that could contaminate the meaning she makes of the message from Adam.

Point 4 in the diagram represents the feelings triggered within Betty about the meaning she made of the message conveyed by Adam. She might ask herself, "What feelings do I have about the meaning I've made of the communication?" Note that Satir (1983a), like many people in the mental health field, believed that feeling stems from the meaning or belief a person holds about an event, situation, or communication.

The feelings activate point 5, which is related to feelings about the feelings. Satir (1983a) asked, "What are my feelings about the feelings about the meaning?" At first this may seem roundabout. Consider, however, that Betty may feel angry about the meaning and feel guilty about feeling angry. The feelings associated with the feelings about the meaning have to be sorted out. It is one thing if Betty feels that her feeling of anger is fine and another thing if she feels guilty about feeling angry. Both communication stances (chapter 14) and family rules (chapter 12) come into play here. The feelings about the feelings activate survival rules. Thus, coping stances will come into play if the person discounts self, other, context, or any combination of these elements. The person is easily caught in an old web of feelings.

Point 6 stems from point 5 and relates to Betty's defenses. These may include defense mechanisms such as denying, projecting, and distorting. If she is using defenses, Betty could look to see whether she would cope by a stance of blaming, placating, being super-reasonable, or being irrelevant. If, however, she owns and accepts her feelings, she does not have to defend herself and can decide how she chooses to respond.

Point 7 represents rules for commenting. The five freedoms, described in chapter 12, come into play here. Must Betty see what she "should," say what is expected, feel what she "ought," and wait for permission, choosing to be secure and not rock the boat? Or can Betty exercise the five freedoms? In owning and accepting her feelings, she creates internal safety and does not have to defend herself. She is free to take risks and make choices in what and how she would like to respond to Adam.

At point 8 Betty responds with a message. Ideally, she will have made a meaning that matches the meaning Adam intended. By accepting and owning her feelings, acknowledging and valuing Adam's feelings, as well as considering the context, Betty can take responsibility for her response and express herself in a congruent mode.

The communication, however, is not over yet. Now Adam must go through the same process that Betty just did. Figure 15.2 represents points 9 through 15, as Adam goes through the same steps in the process that Betty went through in points 2 through 8.

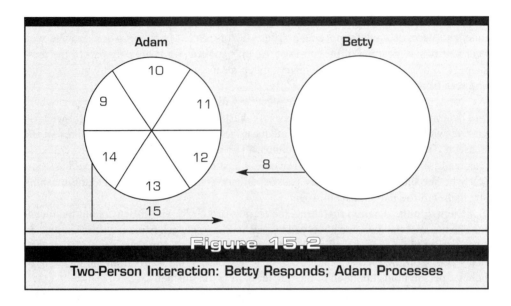

Figure 15.2

Two-Person Interaction: Betty Responds; Adam Processes

As indicated by this discussion, communication is more complex than is immediately obvious. Problems or snags might be encountered at many places. Understanding one's own process is necessary, however, before one can understand that of others.

Effect of Communication Stances on the Ingredients of an Interaction

The complex communication process becomes even more complex when one or both people are not communicating in a congruent manner (see chapter 14). Several variations are possible. Both partners could communicate congruently, or both could communicate incongruently. Person A might be congruent and person B incongruent. Person B might be congruent and person A incongruent. Imagine the possibilities within a family!

Each person in an interaction must consider the internal process of the other. There are many possible ways of misinterpreting others. Miscommunication is understandable in light of the variations in stances. Being aware of the possible stances is essential when communicating with others. To be unaware of the possibility that one's partner might be incongruent or congruent, and that you also might also be either one, would lead to even more communication problems. Recognizing how easily miscommunication can occur underscores the need to clarify any communication that seems unclear or that you are unable to read accurately.

When trying to clarify what another person means by a message, you can look to the ingredients of the interaction for potential assistance. You will have to think about how the person made meaning from your original message, how he or she felt about that meaning, and about the feeling about the meaning. Then you will have to try to decipher the defenses or stances used, as well as determine any freedoms violated by the person's rules for commenting. Before trying to understand another person's process, again, it helps to have examined your own.

Examining Personal Process

The first step in being able to use your knowledge about the ingredients of an interaction is to understand your own. Beginning your investigation with a current interaction is laudable; however, it might be easier to start by recalling a recent, simple, meaningful interaction. It is valuable to recall, as well as memory allows, each of the components in that interaction. You should think back to the first comment the other person made during the interaction and then determine the meaning you attached to it, as well as your feelings about that meaning.

You should then determine your feelings about these feelings, even if you were not aware of them at the time. To determine whether you violated any of the five freedoms (see chapter 12), look to the defenses you used, as well as what rules were operating. This analysis can help you better understand your response. You cannot know the internal process of another person without engaging in "mind rape," but you might try to infer each of the components that form the other person's internal process. This is merely inference and good practice.

After analyzing a past interaction, you can benefit from analyzing several other past interactions to see if any patterns emerge. Do certain types of meaning become apparent from a particular type of message? Are feelings attached to meanings that provide a better picture of yourself? Can you determine defenses or rules operating under your different feelings about feelings? By answering these questions, you can analyze your personal communication style. This type of analysis serves professionals well when they attempt to transform family rules that would perform better as guidelines, as described in chapter 12.

The next task is to analyze the ingredients while an interaction is under way. For one day, during interactions, analyze the interactions that present a low level of threat. Once you have successfully finished that task, analyze the ingredients of a current interaction that is potentially emotionally laden. Do not make too large a leap from a low-threat interaction to a high-threat interaction or your internal process may be too difficult to follow. Amazing as it may seem, everyone goes through this internal process unconsciously and continually throughout each day.

Application Process

An awareness of these ingredients is helpful in overcoming barriers to working with families as well as in gaining access to support groups, networking, and referring to counseling. For example, miscommunication can occur when a professional conveys to parents their need for additional assistance. Parents may mistake that comment as a judgment about their adequacy. Most of us are uncomfortable if we sense that others judge us to be inadequate. Knowing that parents might interpret any recommendation as a judgment of inadequacy can help professionals prepare their communications so they are more likely to be understood as intended. The professional might say, for example, "All of us could use some outside assistance at times of stress and transition."

Psychological Issues

School and community professionals, unlike professionals in mental health centers and child guidance clinics, often do not have the luxury of working with parents who recognize that they may be contributing to their child's problems. What is often found in school and community settings is that parents are unaware that they somehow have played into their child's difficulties.

Losen and Losen (1994) stated that no matter how experienced the team members are in family dynamics, "parents may not be willing to accept even the hint of a suggestion during a team meeting that they are in any way responsible for their child's problems" (p. 113). These parents should not be confronted in team meetings. Instead, parental cooperation should be ensured before including parents in team meetings during which decisions about their child will be made. Lawson and Sailor (2005) suggested that the most appropriate professional is the person who should be working with these parents. Expertise, experience, and superior communication skills are critical in gaining parental cooperation, especially when risk issues are involved.

Although infrequent, problems involving parents who are defensive or belligerent do occur and can create a crisis (Olsen & Fuller, 2003). Among other possibilities, these problems may stem from alcoholism, divorce, and psychiatric difficulties. We will briefly discuss these problems and suggest means for dealing with them. Chapters 7 and 8 of this text covered these kinds of problems in a more comprehensive manner.

Demanding Parents

Most legalistic and demanding parents have experienced prior incidents that led them to mistrust authority. For example, in school settings parents may easily misread efforts to provide procedural due process as trying to "pull a fast one on us." They may have grown up in a family with a hierarchy dysfunction, as described in chapter 3 under the structural family therapy approach and, because of previous power imbalances when facing authority (their parents), they become demanding. Another possibility is that the legalistic parent is assuming a superreasonable stance (see chapter 14) when feeling disempowered and vulnerable. When working with demanding parents, being empathic and understanding rather than judgmental is helpful. Above all else, do not take personally any "projections" of their previous experiences onto you or your colleagues.

A trusted family friend or a professional may be willing to act as a go-between with the school/community. At all times, the focus should be on the best interest of the child or youth. If the parent or family member threatens legal action, an outside evaluation conducted by an impartial evaluator may alleviate the concern. If parents consider such an option, evaluators should be independent and not vanguards of the social system being challenged. The following case example from a school setting illustrates why independent evaluations can be useful.

The parents of a student with a chronic physical illness had a history of demanding special treatment for their son. Frequently, if their demands were not met, they would call the superintendent of schools and threaten a lawsuit. School personnel became so numb to parental complaints that they failed to take note when the boy continued to get poor grades through the fifth grade.

Only after independent evaluations were suggested and completed was the boy's severe learning disability in reading discovered. In this case, parental symptomatic behavior had obscured the focus on the student's best interest.

Some rules of thumb (Losen & Losen, 1994) will help professionals in dealing with demanding and legalistic parents. As suggested earlier, parents should not be confronted during team meetings. If a conflict erupts unexpectedly during a team meeting, decisions should be tabled until the conflict has been resolved. Any hostility or mistrust should be validated, and, obviously, strong feelings should not be denied or ignored. Although remaining congruent is not easy when you or your colleagues are being blamed, it is important to remember what you learned about stances in chapter 14. Ultimately, the professional should communicate in congruent ways even during intense situations. Professionals can better understand the parent(s) by discussing with them the origin of their concerns, as well as their underlying fears. Some will feel vulnerable to discuss their fears, and others will welcome being understood.

Team members should also let the parents know when they are on target in making an intelligible and defensible point of view. A good comment is: "If I were in your place, I'd probably feel the same way" or, "I don't see it that way, but I do understand your feelings about this situation."

When parents become flexible, professionals must not remain rigid in response. A good beginning toward what is best for the child/youth is much better than the prospect of a legal battle that more likely would make things worse.

Psychiatric Difficulties

Parents with emotional problems may be unsupportive and unresponsive, needy and seeking continual input and reassurance, emotionally unstable and disruptive, or irresponsible. These families may have disengaged boundaries. The children may act out, bringing the problem into the open. Sometimes parents present in an irrelevant/distractor stance, and at other times they communicate out of a placating or superreasonable stance, as described in chapter 14. Recall that those who appear irrelevant do not think others care about them. Making eye contact demonstrates care, and active listening, along with empathic expressions, will help family members realize that you are concerned for them and their child or youth.

Placaters feel worthless and do better when asked for their opinions and ideas for solving problems. *Superreasonable* people use intellect, but their inner feelings are extreme vulnerability. Reinforcing and showing appreciation for their depth of knowledge helps them with self-esteem issues and may lead to a closer connection. Working with family members who have psychological issues may leave any professional feeling challenged. Listening to these parents and writing down their complaints helps professionals stay focused and avoid becoming part of dysfunctional communication (Olsen & Fuller, 2003).

Regardless of the type of disruption, the professional must reassure the parents of his or her commitment to their child. Again, remaining congruent is vital to regain balance and reduce stress. Rationale and procedures may have to be clarified and explained during team meetings. Professionals should work with irrational parents prior to the meeting. Parents can meet individually with the professional with whom they have the best rapport. Some parents would benefit from referral for family systems therapy, and the social worker could make this recommendation while meeting with them. Parents will likely provide more meaningful and honest input with one open and supportive professional than at a team meeting.

Actively alcoholic parents should not be invited to a private conference, because their behavior is unpredictable. If they insist on attending and are obviously under the influence of alcohol or other drugs, the meeting should be terminated immediately. Professionals must be careful, however, that these parents do not feel put down by this action and should help them in any way possible to reclaim their self-esteem.

Following the meeting, it might be helpful to share information with the nonalcoholic parent about local Alcoholics Anonymous or Al-Anon chapters. It should be pointed out here that a family member who is in recovery for alcohol or drug addiction is unlikely to present problems, and school/community professionals are unlikely to have difficulty communicating with them.

Professionals (Losen & Losen, 1985, 1994; McEwan, 2004; Turnbull & Turnbull, 2001; Whitaker & Fiore, 2001) have suggested many effective strategies for working with unstable parents. Some recommendations are to

- attempt to clarify the parents' understanding of their child's or youth's problem,
- provide more reassurance than usually is needed,
- establish a strong relationship between one team member and the parents during individual conferences as a precursor to group/team meetings, and
- direct comments made by school/community professionals to the most stable or rational parent.

When working with unstable parents, professionals must refrain from exchanging angry words but should not hesitate to call upon external resources such as police or a minister when needed. Chapter 8 elaborates on families with a serious dysfunction and offers recommendations for professionals about working with them.

Angry Parents

Various professionals working in social systems (e.g., McEwan, 2004; Turnbull & Turnbull, 2001; Whitaker & Fiore, 2001) have addressed how to deal with angry or aggressive people. Although dealing with angry and aggressive parents is unavoidable, maintaining composure under direct attack and confrontation is not an easily developed skill. When a blaming stance is taken to an extreme, it rocks one's ability to remain congruent. Even more difficult is to empathize with these parental fears and frustrations. When under attack, we often fail to remember that what is lurking under anger is frequently fear.

Even sane, rational parents have become angry and let their anger show. Sometimes this is related to life experiences over which they have no power/control. The feelings of powerlessness may seep into interactions. Validating family members' feelings makes a difference. Simply saying, "I understand" can help.

School/community professionals must recognize that parents may have valid complaints, or that a mistake may have been made. Working with the parents to help them vent their feelings and share their understanding of the problem is important.

The following are some rules of thumb for dealing with angry parents:

- Make eye contact.
- Be courteous.
- Do not interject your own opinions.
- Actively listen to the parents.
- Request clarification if needed.
- Reflect parents' beliefs and feelings.
- Nod your head to convey that you understand.
- Summarize the parents' points.

Most important in dealing with angry parents, do not try to solve the situation but, instead, work to build trust by demonstrating caring and concern. That is best done by listening genuinely and remaining open to understanding, even with the angry outer manifestation of anger. Most likely, underneath the anger is a lonely individual who feels out on a limb that is being cut off.

Professionals should also try to distinguish true issues from pseudo concerns by asking appropriate, open-ended questions, such as, "How did this come about?" Avoid questions that begin with "why" because they may lead to defensiveness in the parents. Once everything is out in the open, summarize the points of agreement as well as disagreement. Then determine if the parents have anything to add that would further clarify understanding.

All of these guidelines provide for exploration and understanding of the problem from the parent's point of view. As noted earlier, the initial emphasis is on connecting and building trust. The next step is problem solving.

Problem Solving

Problem solving is a multistep process aimed at resolving conflict. Ellen O'Keefe (2004) wrote about conflict resolution in schools, based on the systemic writing of Peter Senge. Edwards and Mullis (2003) encourage cooperation in teaching problem solving skills to children. The five steps presented next focus on group problem solving. Teams are involved in continual problem solving, and these steps can help them resolve challenges.

Step 1: Define the Problem

Although team members may expect defining the problem to be easy, in reality it is a necessary but challenging step. Hoy and Miskel (2005) underscored the value of recognizing and defining the problem and indicated that this step doesn't receive the attention it deserves.

The focus should be on the underlying cause of the problem, not on the symptoms. People often become wrapped up in symptoms and fail to see the forest for the trees. If, for example, a child or youth is having trouble concentrating and staying in his or her seat in school or in out-of-school time (OST) programs, many professionals attend to the surface manifestations of the problem—the child's behavioral excesses. By examining the problem more thoroughly, however, the team might find that no parent is available to supervise the child or youth before and after school. Lacking supervision, the child might be getting hyped up by eating junk food and watching overstimulating videos or playing video games when the parents are not home. Thus, the problem could be defined accurately as originating at home rather than in the classroom or after-school program.

Step 2: Collect Facts and Opinions

Once the problem has been defined, the team members gather the facts and opinions needed to thoroughly understand the situation. It is important to move forward and not allow the situation to become a crisis—to find out what the situation is, what happened, who is involved, and what policies and procedures are involved. All of these factors will help team members come up with realistic solutions.

Step 3: Generate Solutions

This step involves brainstorming possible solutions. At this point all suggestions are taken (Pugach & Johnson, 2002). If team members were to criticize or evaluate ideas at this stage, they would shut off the generation of creative solutions. Thus, this step should be freewheeling and fast-moving, with everyone on the team providing potential solutions.

Step 4: Select the Solution

The field of family systems has a branch known as solution-focused therapy (Goldenberg & Goldenberg, 2004; Nichols & Schwartz, 2004). In many ways, problem solving shares similar tenets; both emphasize solution-talk. This fourth step has two parts:

1. The team clearly specifies the goals, or end results, expected from the solution.
2. The team evaluates each of the solutions generated in the previous step in light of the agreed-upon goals.

It helps to predict what would happen in each of the solutions that rise to the top (Pugach & Johnson, 2002). These should be put to the tests of potential feasibility and maximization of resources. Based on those tests, the best solution is selected.

Step 5: Implement the Solution

Team members establish timetables to carry out the solution. Further, the team specifies the evaluation techniques to be used and plans for follow-through. Solution-focused interventions with parental involvement result in partnership with families (Christenson, 2004), with "parents as essential partners and a philosophy of shared responsibility permeates school policies and practices" (p. 84).

Interaction Between Families and School/Community

Four aspects of working with families are as follows:

1. Consider the need, desire, and availability of family members to be involved in the care, education, and development of the at-risk or special-needs learner.
2. Address a family systems perspective on team issues.
3. Consider reasons for nonparticipation.
4. Cover ways to overcome unwanted nonparticipation and means of involving families who want to participate.

Need, Desire, and Availability of Family Members

To be family-centered, team members must consider the desires and availability of family members for involvement on the team (Chen & Miles, 2004; Dunst, 2002; Turnbull & Turnbull, 2001). Some families want to be more involved than their schedules and responsibilities allow. Other families are not interested in involvement, regardless of other responsibilities, and educational professionals should respect the parents' wishes. Bjorck-Akesson and Granlund (1995) reconfirmed earlier findings that parents want to be involved in schools by giving and receiving information. Parents were also found to be interested in being involved with decisions about the "kinds of information kept on their children; medical services for their children; and transfer of their children to other schools" (p. 257).

Solomon (1991) reported on California's policy relating to parental involvement in schools, which recommended six ways to design programs to involve parents:

1. Help parents develop parenting skills and foster conditions at home that support learning.
2. Provide parents with the knowledge of techniques designed to assist children in learning at home.
3. Provide access to and coordinate community support services for children and families.
4. Promote clear two-way communication between the school and the family as to the school programs and children's progress.
5. Involve parents, after appropriate training, in instructional and support roles at school.
6. Support parents as decision-makers and develop their leadership in governance, advisory, and advocacy roles. (p. 361)

These guidelines are as pertinent to at-risk and special-needs families as they are to all other families. Christenson (2004) recommended several ways by which school psychologists can be systems consultants to improve family–school partnerships that result in improved learning for all children. Briefly, these included the following:

- Family–school focus within existing structures, including pre-referral, assessment, interventions, and conferences with families
- Describing and giving reasons for a school/home partnership fostering learning
- Reaching out to parents at home, work, and community to support and involve them in the schools
- Early involvement, including after hospital births, so parents know the importance of language, and supporting the parental role in developing school readiness
- Individualizing support based on family need

Her final recommendation was that school psychologists recognize the circumstances when the connection of family and school is not time-effective and let go of continued efforts to involve the family.

A Family Systems Perspective

Mullis and Edwards (2001) emphasize using family systems approaches when consulting with parents. They see an opportunity for helping other professionals learn about family systems, thereby increasing their sensitivity and tolerance to children and youth. Boyd-Franklin and Bry (2000) also recommend a systemic approach for home, school, and community interventions.

Peeks (1997) suggested that the revolution in counseling related to the theory and practice of family therapy should provide the basis for a revolution in public education. She proposed that

> one of the important elements of educational reform be focused on the relationship among parents, students and school professionals. Students should be helped by their parents and school working as a cooperative problem solving team. (pp. 5–6).

Children and youth who are problem-free were described as able to achieve to their potential, thereby improving their collective achievement in the school. It also was suggested that children/youth would benefit by observing their parents' involvement in their education. According to Peeks, as problems of children and youth are resolved by parental input, higher quality education will follow. It makes sense that this would be true in community settings also.

Malatchi (1997) framed the educational paradigmatic shift in relation to the education of children with special needs. She saw the shift as a movement from a system-centered approach to one that is family/person-centered. Focusing on family systems as a base for early intervention, Briggs (1997) stated, "Professionals can learn to move their focus away from treating the child with special needs as the identified patient. With a broader focus, the family system is no longer a problem but part of the solution" (p. 107).

As early as 1983, Pfeiffer and Tittler described how eligibility teams could benefit by adopting a family systems orientation. Their approach recognized that families and schools are intimately interrelated and linked through the child or youth. By shifting to a family focus (Mullis & Edwards, 2001), the referred child or youth is no longer viewed in isolation but, instead, within the context of his or her family. By observing the family, team members can better understand and predict the child's behavior in school and OST programs, as well as social functioning in the family. Also, if other family members can be helped to redirect some stress from the child or youth, the individual's dysfunction should lessen, with an increase in the possibility for remediation in school and community.

Reasons for Nonparticipation

Although professionals should respect the right of parents to choose not to participate in their child's educational program, professionals should determine whether the nonparticipation is based on informed choice (Carney & Gamel-McCormick, 1996; Morsink et al., 1991). Lack of parental participation might be related to specific child and family characteristics rather than choice. McMillan and Turnbull (1983) previously reached the same conclusion, as did Suelzle and Keenan (1981), whose findings indicated that families with lower incomes, older children, and children with more severe disabilities were less likely to be involved in their child's education.

Weber and Stoneman (1986) investigated the differences in family characteristics, maternal knowledge about the IEP process, and the mother's knowledge about the IEP itself for parents who did and did not attend IEP meetings. They found that poor families with limited parental education who were nonwhite and who were headed by single parents were overrepresented in the group of parents who did not attend the meetings. Mothers who viewed teachers and other professionals as responsible for their child's education frequently were nonparticipants.

The above authors emphasized the importance of reaching out to families, to provide programs responsive to their needs, to be sensitive to the demands they face, to empower them, and to provide them with a sense of control. They indicated that parents are able to make informed choices about participation in their child's education when they fully understand both the rights and the opportunities available from the schools. They concluded that many parents lack basic information they need to make informed choices.

Parental anxiety contributes to lack of participation. According to Losen and Losen (1994) and others, parents may be anxious for a variety of reasons. First, they may be concerned about what is happening to the child and feel that they don't have the answers. Especially early in the process, parents tend to depend on team members to identify their child's difficulties and to provide remedial services. Thus, they may feel somewhat at the mercy of the professionals, especially if the parents are not knowledgeable about their child's problem. Second, parents may be worried that they will appear stupid, confused, or indecisive. Thus, they may restrict their input and be passive during the team meetings they do attend.

Third, parents may think they have failed their child. A sense of guilt is common among parents of children with special needs. These parents may be concerned that professionals are judging or evaluating their parenting skills negatively, and that they have made mistakes resulting in their child's disability. These thoughts could lead to passivity by parents. They might think the professionals involved would have better solutions.

Fourth, parents may mistrust the school staff. They may believe that the professionals had misdiagnosed their child or that the professionals are not competent to deal with the child's special needs. Some parents resign themselves to professional input. Others, feeling a sense of helplessness, resist any efforts to reassure them.

Concern and doubt about professionals' competence could also reflect the parents' own personal doubts about how to deal with their child's needs. School professionals must realize that trust is not automatic, that it grows over time and with positive experience. By requesting information from the family and making them part of the team, professionals can help parents realize that their concerns and issues will be addressed and that they are respected.

Fifth, parents may be concerned that their involvement in special education will cause their child to be seen negatively by other teachers as well as peers. Parents with this fear generally have had difficulty accepting their child's level of need and, thus, remain doubtful about the differences between their child and other classmates. They may allow the schools to plan programs for their child, yet not be supportive of those programs in the home.

Sixth, parental guilt feelings may involve fear of criticism (Miller, 1996). Believing that they have failed their children with special needs and others in the process, parents may fear that friends and relatives will learn about their perceived poor parenting skills unless they comply with the school's recommendations. This is true particularly of parents of children who are belligerent and act out.

An additional reason for parental passivity and lack of involvement with their child's educational program can stem from prior negative experiences with schools. For example, a previous teacher, principal, or other professional may have led the parents to conclude that to obtain the best for their child, they should remain silent. Parents also may fear that their child will be mistreated, or that a more restrictive environment will be recommended if they contribute their own personal opinions to the process.

Even though these negative expectations may be unrealistic, it is important to get them out on the table. For example, a parent may have heard through the grapevine that the principal is a strict disciplinarian, or that a social worker might be more negative while interacting alone with parents than during a team meeting. These concerns should be aired and dealt with if parental involvement is to be achieved.

Overcoming Nonparticipation

Again, information should be presented to parents—and all team participants—prior to team meetings. When all participants have received information prior to the meeting, more of the meeting time can be devoted to discussion, which increases the likelihood of participation. And a pre-team meeting between the parents and one professional can alleviate sources of nonparticipation and anxiety. A professional with good communication skills is the best one to meet with the parents to discuss procedures and their child's test results. This professional should answer questions the parents might have and maintain an egalitarian attitude.

This pre-team meeting allows the professional to explain the test results in lay terms and offers parents the opportunity to raise issues and questions about the process. In addition, parents can be made aware of the purposes of the upcoming full team meeting.

By helping the parents to understand its procedures and purposes, the pre-team meeting should reduce their passivity, defensiveness, and resistance to the team meeting. The pre-team meeting also provides an opportunity to deal with parental doubts, guilt, and sense of inadequacy. Dealing with these issues in an intimate conference is far easier than in a full team meeting. The pre-meeting, too, prevents parents' from first learning about significant assessment results for their child during the full team meeting. No professional would want parents to first hear in a team meeting, for example, that their child has been assessed as having mental retardation. To involve parents meaningfully in the team process, services such as baby-sitters and transportation may have to be provided.

Limitations to the Family Systems Approach

Family systems concepts and approaches do have limitations. Many of these shortcomings stem from lack of training, current norms in the schools, and traditional procedures.

Lack of Training

Traditional university training in general education and special education, counseling, or occupational/physical/recreational therapy does not require a course in communication between home and school/community. Some school administrators, however, are required to take a course in school and community relations, and families are typically one of many topics covered in such a course. Realizing that universities generally do not require a separate course on working with families, the family systems approach obviously is considered infrequently in training professionals for work in social systems that serve at-risk and special-needs children/youth.

Social workers, by contrast, are trained to work with families. Actually, that is their major responsibility in most schools and many community programs. Few universities, however, train prospective social workers in family systems approaches. Experts are beginning to recognize that schools interact with students only 9% of their lives and, therefore, are increasing their curricular focus to include a holistic view (Boyd-Franklin & Bry, 2000; Walsh & Williams, 1997).

The development of OST programs (President & Fellows of Harvard College, 2002, 2003a, 2003b, 2004a, 2004b) to engage children/youth in development and learning for families who work beyond school hours has burgeoned over time. In particular, those working in community programs will find varied activities that engage families in OST (2004a) to be of value.

University systems are slow to change their program requirements. Although higher education has been in the process of restructuring, institutions of higher education are not likely to spontaneously provide coursework on family systems. Thus, those who recognize the value of family systems will have to assume responsibility for generating interest in such a course.

Inservice training is another matter, in which change is slow and staff development activities seldom focus on family systems training for school professionals. The state of Virginia did develop a training module on family systems. A trainer-of-trainers model was used with the statewide training. A social worker or counselor from the school or community setting who is knowledgeable in family systems approaches would be a wise choice to serve as developer and trainer. Another good choice is a professional in private practice (e.g., psychotherapist, social worker, or counselor) who is versed in family systems.

Finally, coaching or training in effective communication skills is helpful to school and community personnel. And effective communicators are more effective team members.

Changing Norms

Until recently, with the exception of Project Head Start, family involvement was considered the responsibility of agencies external to the schools. At the same time, professionals in the school were not likely to recommend these services for children with special needs because of the cost of these related services. For at-risk and special-needs children/youth, the norm is beginning to shift to viewing the whole family rather than the child as the unit of intervention (Boyd-Franklin & Bry, 2000; Mullis & Edwards, 2001; Walsh & Williams, 1997), whether in school, community, or home. This norm would likely shift more rapidly if training in family systems concepts were to begin to make an impression on school/community professionals.

School/Community Procedures

Social workers who are familiar with family systems concepts may have such large caseloads that they do not have the time to help other professionals learn about family systems approaches. The past emphasis on placing school counselors in each elementary school was a hopeful sign that family systems approaches would be applied. Whether this continues will be known only over time.

Adding to the challenge, school counselors and social workers may be unfamiliar with family systems concepts or may not have the time to implement the knowledge and skills they have learned about family systems. Many elementary school counselors work only with children rather than entire families. They often work with a group of children for a short time, then move on to another group to be able to serve more students. In these sessions or in school or grade-level events and programs, the emphasis seems to be on education, prevention of bullying, and careers.

Secondary school counselors are almost always in charge of scheduling, which leaves little, if any, time for counseling adolescents, let alone families. Therefore, secondary schools seem to be oriented toward noninterference with families. Secondary students are viewed as old enough to be self-responsible and to accept the natural consequences of behavior. Professionals may view trying to elicit family support as enabling students to remain immature and dependent.

Reality Constraints

A number of reality constraints limit the use of family systems concepts and approaches in school and community settings. The three reality constraints of time, money, and availability of trained personnel are seen most frequently.

Time

The constraint of insufficient time is a concern of all school and community professionals (Zmuda, Kuklis, & Kline, 2004). Once staff members have been trained and are competent in implementing family systems concepts, however, their knowledge will save them time. Over the long term, they will spend less time mired in an individual perspective when a family systems perspective will resolve the problem or facilitate the communication more readily.

Money

Finding money for staff training and for releasing personnel to attend training sessions is a real concern. With diminished funding at federal to local levels, staff development funds may be among the earliest to be decreased or cut. Over the long term, however, full implementation of family systems concepts can save dollars. Consider the example of children and youth with emotional and behavioral disorders. If the whole family were seen as the unit of treatment, many of the problems could be resolved and the child or youth would remain in settings that allow lower staff/child ratios.

Training

Another reality constraint is the lack of trained personnel. Arends (1990) pointed to the slow response of universities to criticism, suggesting that "teacher preparation of the future could be under the auspices of inspired and well-funded district-based human resource development units or state-based special academies for teachers" (p. 117–143). Christenson (2004) focused on accountability in the No Child Left Behind legislation as support for schools to form family partnerships that apply principles from systems-ecological theory. Zmuda et al. (2004) emphasized the importance of change processes including time for colleagues to share their experiences and discuss ways they have implemented changes.

The expenditure of initial funds for staff development in school and community systems would be invaluable. A trainer-of-trainers model that allows more people to be reached with fewer funds is useful. Furthermore, schools of social work and psychology at universities and colleges might design modules and train trainers.

Attitudes, Resistance, and Change

Attitudes are defined as strong beliefs or feelings toward people and situations. We acquire attitudes, both favorable and unfavorable, throughout our lives. A poster seen in a setting serving children/youth bears the slogan, "Attitudes are contagious—are yours worth catching?" Individuals with positive attitudes toward change will bring about positive results.

M. Scott Peck (1978), author of *The Road Less Traveled*, stated:

> It is only through a vast amount of experience and a lengthy and
> successful maturation that we gain the capacity to see the world

and our place in it realistically, and thus are enabled to realistically assess our responsibility for ourselves and the world. (p. 37)

Negative Attitudes

Negative attitudes and resistance to change can greatly limit the incorporation of family systems concepts into the school/community system. A model for change is helpful in understanding, expecting, and validating concerns of employees about the change process.

The most prevalent attitude that limits the use of family systems concepts in schools is: "It's someone else's responsibility to work with those families. I don't have enough time. What do they expect from us anyway? It's not in our job description. Our local education association or federation will support us on that."

Another negative attitude toward change stems from fear of failure and associated repercussions. Teachers and principals, in particular, might be concerned about employing strategies that usually are reserved for counselors, social workers, and psychologists. A natural concern relates to how the use of change strategies might result in a setback, as opposed to the growth and development of the family. Without extensive training and well-understood boundaries regarding who applies these strategies, these fears would be well grounded. Obviously, this is a fear that has to be addressed by anyone implementing change.

A third attitude problem, negative contagion, may arise in some schools where teachers have banded together to block anything new and different. They denounce new endeavors as "old wine in new bottles." As a group, they form a prodigious force that is hard to convert.

Resistance

Resistance to change is normal human behavior. Duke (2004) cited reasons for resistance to change, including the following:

1. Commitment to the status quo
2. Lack of awareness
3. Heightened anxiety
4. Potential disruption and discomfort
5. Risk of failure
6. Potential impact on personal life
7. Increased work
8. Threat to job security
9. Work-related alienation (p. 126)

Among other reasons, Roy (1995) saw resistance to change including: finding new goals unimportant or unacceptable as well as liking how things are functioning; fearing the unknown, fearing failure, and fearing loss of privileges and status; trust issues with change agents; and lack of clarity about reasons for change. Orelove and Sobsey (1996) advised that school professionals expect resistance to change, confront it, and focus on the common goals of the team that benefit children.

Kanter (1995, p. 679) suggested tactics for working with resistance and identified the following ways to build commitment to change:

- Allow participation in planning the change.
- Leave choices within the overall decision to change.
- Provide a clear picture of the change, a "vision" with details about the new state.
- Share information about change plans to the fullest extent possible.
- Divide a big change into more manageable and familiar steps; let people take a small step first.
- Minimize surprises; give people advance warning about new requirements.
- Allow for the digestion of change requests—a chance to become accustomed to the idea of change before making a commitment.
- Repeatedly demonstrate your own commitment to the change.
- Make standards and requirements clear; tell exactly what is expected of people in the change.
- Offer positive reinforcement for competence; let people know they can do it.
- Look for and reward pioneers, innovators, and early successes to serve as models.
- Help people find or feel compensated for the extra time and energy that change requires.
- Avoid creating obvious "losers" from the change. (If there are some, though, be honest with them—early on).
- Allow expressions of nostalgia and grief for the past—then create excitement about the future. (p. 679)

Everyone can take to heart some lessons when participating in a school/community renewal or other change processes.

Feelings of Inadequacy

When people learn new skills, they generally accept additional responsibility. That, in turn, may stretch their abilities, making them feel less confident. For example, most school and community professionals felt uncomfortable with computers until they became computer-literate. The same will be true with family systems concepts. Therefore, professionals who are learning these new skills must be supported. Professionals should be given permission to make mistakes, as people do learn from mistakes. Sharing stories with others and exchanging ideas for problem solving also can be helpful. Those who are newly implementing family systems concepts and strategies will learn quickly that they are not the only ones who feel inadequate. Groups are ideal vehicles for mirroring and learning more about oneself.

Issues of Security

As Maslow (1970) made clear in his classic hierarchy of needs, personal security, both physical and psychological, is a basic need. When the expectations for school/community professionals change and they are faced with making major changes in their work, some worry that if they are unable to keep abreast of the changes, they may be phased out or seen as less worthy. Therefore, professionals must know that the individuals in charge of the change process will prepare them adequately for implementing family systems strategies.

Issues of Trust

Lack of trust is another reason people resist change. When the implementation of family systems concepts is concerned, mistrust is aimed at those responsible for directing and implementing change. When professionals are apprised of upcoming changes only after all of the decisions and planning are complete, they are more likely to resist even the most appealing change. The change-makers, therefore, should solicit input from school/community professionals. Furthermore, these representatives should be professionals who are trusted by their peers.

Narrow Focus

Some school and community professionals will be unable to see the larger picture and will not understand that learning family systems concepts and practices will pay off in the long run, in terms of both time and money. Further, they may not see the most important benefit—that the needs of at-risk and special-needs children/youth will be met. It is imperative to explain the overall picture and reasons for the change, including family systems concepts and strategies.

Change: Response Stages, Concerns About Change, and Stages of Growth

Effecting lasting and meaningful change is a complex and challenging process. The literature on change is filled with advice about initiating change within social systems serving children/youth (e.g., Bolman & Deal, 2003; Boyd-Franklin & Bry, 2000; Briggs, 1997; Brooks-McNamara, & Pedersen, 2006; Caine & Caine, 1997; Christenson, 2004; Duke, 2004; Dunst, 2002; Hall & Hord, 2001; Holcomb-McCoy, 2005; Hoy & Miskel, 2005; Keyton, 2005; Kottler, 2001; Lee, 2005; Mullis & Edwards, 2001; Pugach, 2001; Shepard, 2001; Simcox, Nuijens, & Lee, 2006; Walsh & Galassi, 2002; Zmuda, Kuklis, & Kline, 2004).

Some of these writers recommend policy change or change in practices. Political climates influence social systems that serve children/youth. Some change is driven by legislation (e.g., IDEA, NCLB). Reform movements bring about possibilities of different types of change within social systems. Changes relate to structure, norms, processes, policy, procedure, and more.

Duke (2004) reviewed six models of the change process and reiterated a frequent caution: Change processes are not as linear as implied, and some stages may be skipped. Any model includes a time of discovering the need for change, a period of design to respond to the need, development of a process to make the change, and implementation of the process.

The reason for intentional change is to improve functioning. First- and second-order changes were described early by Watzlawick, Weakland, and Fisch (1974) and relate to the reason or purpose of a change process. *First-order change* is aimed at improving the current system and involves either returning to a prior more functional state *or* making improvements that don't change the basic functioning of the organizational system. *Second- order changes* go deeper and change the system by requiring the social system to consider the system's goals, assumptions undergirding the system, and the existing patterns of human relationships.

Stages of Response to Change

Haimes (1995) cited Moor and Gergen as having identified four stages that staff members go through in response to change: shock, defensive retreat, acknowledgment, and adaptation. Change involves loss, and these stages are similar to those proposed by Kübler-Ross in her book *On Death and Dying*. Initially, people feel threatened by change, and their ability to relate to the change is impaired by their feelings. They must be given the necessary time to adjust to the changes and to discover what their roles in the change process will be. They have to be able to express their concerns, fears, and frustrations before even broaching planning.

In the next stage, defensive retreat, people try to return to the "old way" of doing things. People do not want to move out of their comfort zone. During the time of defensive retreat, leaders should let staff members know what will *not* change, as well as what areas likely will be uncomfortable. A clear expectation about roles is important during this stage of reaction to change.

The acknowledgment stage involves recognition that something good may result from the change, for them and for the child or youth. The sense of loss is replaced by excitement, anticipation, and interest in being personally involved. Planning commences, and people look to the future. Risk taking should be reinforced.

The adaptation stage relates to the assumption of new roles, routines, and methods. During this implementation phase, people who are not on board will become evident. They simply may be stuck in an earlier phase longer than the rest and not really resistant to change. Some of them will eventually move into the adaptation stage. Others, however, may not make the adaptation.

Concerns-Based Adoption Model

The Concerns-Based Adoption Model (CBAM) is highlighted because of its concerns with school professionals and its ability to affect attitudes toward change. It is equally applicable to other social systems that serve children/youth. The model focuses on personal aspects of change, and change is seen as a process rather than an event (Hall & Hord, 2001). Further, it emphasizes the need to understand the point of view of participants involved in the change process and is invaluable in the early part of the change process.

Idol et al. (1994) used CBAM in implementing Collaborative Consultation, as did Erb (1995) in relation to teamwork in middle school education. This model continues to be a viable aid (Zmuda, Kuklis, & Kline, 2004).

The CBAM model has three dimensions: stages of concern, levels of use, and innovation configurations. The discussion here addresses only the stages of concern. Discussion of the other dimensions can be found in Hall and Hord (2001).

Hall, Wallace, and Dossett (1973), and later Hall and Hord (1987, 2001), delineated seven levels of concern about change that relate to what professionals think about an innovation:

1. *Awareness.* In this first stage professionals have little concern about or interest in the innovation. This is the level of concern that people have toward something about which they know little or nothing.
2. *Informational.* At this stage professionals are interested in learning more about the innovation or change. They are not concerned about how the change will affect them but, rather, about its characteristics, requirements for use, and general effects.
3. *Personal concern.* Here, the professional is uncertain about the professional demands of the innovation, as well as his or her personal adequacy to meet those demands. The professional might analyze his or her role in relation to decision-making processes. Potential conflicts with current commitments could also be of concern. Financial and status implications are additional potential personal concerns.
4. *Management.* Professionals direct their attention to the processes and tasks involved in using the innovation, as well as the best use of information and resources. Of prime concern are issues related to organizing, managing, and scheduling the innovation, as well as efficiency and time considerations.
5. *Consequence.* At this stage professionals are concerned with the impact of the innovation on the children they serve. Relevance to the lives of children and youth is of interest, as are outcomes and changes needed to increase the outcomes for the children and youth.
6. *Collaboration.* This stage has to do with coordination with others. Professionals will want to know about ways to cooperate with peers in using the innovation.
7. *Refocusing.* Professionals are concerned here with how the innovation might benefit others. Some professionals are worried about alternative innovations. They will have definite ideas and opinions about proposed or existing forms of the innovation.

With knowledge of this model, professionals can anticipate what will happen during a change process. A basic premise of the model is that anyone can be a change facilitator. The facilitator would know about individual concerns and respond to them so others can be more effective in applying innovations. Understanding the CBAM model can help the professional in any change effort he or she might initiate.

Stages of Growth and the Process of Change

Virginia Satir spoke and wrote about the stages of growth we go through in life as individuals, couples, families, and organizations. McLendon and Davis (2002) stated that

> Satir recognized that awareness did not equal behavior. It could
> open the door for choice; however, healthy choosing requires

practice and support. Her theory of change reveals the emotional processes associated with interrupting a system's status quo. (p. 172)

Satir identified the stages of growth as

1. status quo,
2. introduction of the foreign element and resistance,
3. chaos,
4. new integration and practice, and
5. the new status quo.

Satir's change model is highlighted here because of its family systems perspective and ease of adaptation to school and community contexts. Satir was well aware that change is not permanent and people need a process to help them cycle through the stages of growth many times over the course of a lifetime.

Dodson (1991) wrote that "concepts behind Virginia's model for change were systems theory, life as a process, the inner healer in everyone and the need for education to aid change" (p. 122). Satir saw her model for growth and change as applicable to all domains. Her view of change stemmed from seeing the world through what she called the systemic organic/seed model (see the Appendix). This model is influenced by holistic concepts that hold that human beings have an inner drive to grow and develop. In awakening the healer(s) within, individuals and groups can engage in conscious choices to individuate and contribute to an expanding world.

Essential to the growth process that Satir spoke of is self-esteem, and essential to the development of high self-esteem is an environment rich in nurturance and the freedom to explore and to know, as well as comment on, what is experienced. Satir applied her model for change to "education, prevention, individual, couple, family therapy and world healing" (Dodson, p. 122).

In social-systems contexts, becoming conscious of change is critical for individuals, families, schools, and communities. Otherwise, change is random and haphazard, and professionals, children/youth, and their families will not own the change process or outcome. A description of each of Satir's five stages follows.

Status Quo

We are all familiar with the status quo. Things operate as usual, and we know what to expect. Even though problems pop up daily and the status quo may be painful, it is known and feels safe. We may recognize that change is needed but are fearful because we do not know what will happen if we move out of our comfort zone, even if the status quo is unhealthy and unreasonable.

When an individual, family, or group, such as a school or a community program, consciously chooses to reach out toward something different, the motivation to do so generally stems from one of three stimuli.

1. An individual, family, or group will want to change because the way things are operating is intolerable.

2. An individual, family, or group sees a possibility for something more enriching. Here, the vision of one person or group can provide the necessary motivation for change to begin.

3. The individual, family, or group is experiencing so much pain that it propels toward change.

Obviously, the three motivations go against the homeostasis described in the Appendix. The problem that initiates a change process often relates to coping mechanisms that once served a useful purpose but no longer meet the needs of the individual or group. Whatever the motivation, in this first conscious stage of change, people must become aware of what no longer functions to serve them. Because people fear change, they will resist (see preceding discussion of resistance) coming into awareness about their current function/dysfunction.

When people are in this phase of resisting, yet obviously needing to grow, the change-master* serves the growth process best by instilling visions for new possibilities. Imagery exercises are useful for this purpose and were a hallmark of Satir's work (Goldenberg & Goldenberg, 2004). Imagery speaks to the deeper self, and that part of the self that has hope can speak to the part of the self that is fearful. In a group, the change-master might ask one person to take the hopeless and fearful side with regard to a proposed change and another person to respond from the hopeful or visionary side. Fear must be validated and not squashed before moving forward. Once the fear is validated, people can dream of new possibilities. American tribes have "dream catchers" (Malatchi, 1997). The process of dreaming must take place for change to move forward.

Dodson (1991) suggested questions for the change-master to pose to facilitate the process of dreaming:

1. "If I visited you and the change that you want had happened, what would I see?"
2. "If you had a magic wand and could make one thing different in your life (in your family [team/school]), what would you most want to make different? If that were different, how would that help you?" (p. 124)

The body language of the person who is responding to these questions is important. Then we can see fear and gauge our next response accordingly. Again, fear must be validated or it will control the process of change. Empathy and patience are also important. When they display this level of sensitivity, individuals within groups will begin to trust the leader and the relationship will deepen—a necessary ingredient for later stages in the process. The leader serves as a partner in exploring the new possibilities by encouraging the people involved to see, hear, feel, know, and share their experiences as well as their desires.

With the group having moved this far, the next step is to explore more deeply the nature of the status quo. What has been implied can be made explicit. What has been done

---

*This is the term used by Rosabeth Moss Kanter and is applied here because it seems appropriate, though Kübler-Ross did not use this term.

unconsciously can be brought into awareness. Then a conscious choice can be made for growth and change. The change-master will find the techniques of reframing and metaphor (discussed in chapter 14) useful at this stage.

Satir offered a few examples for this phase (Dodson, 1991). In demonstrating the status quo, she spoke about a mobile hanging over a baby's crib, how all the figures in their place keep it in balance. Removing one would affect all the others, disrupting the status quo. She likened this to what happens when change affects members within a family or teams within a school.

A second image that Satir used was that of a teeter-totter with a heavy person on one side and a light person on the other. The heavier person, sitting close to the center for balance, is not having much fun. The lighter person, having to lean far back, is on the edge. Neither person is in a comfortable position, although the two are keeping things balanced. She used this imagery to help others recognize the price paid for balance.

Satir's third image was that of an individual (and I would add group, team, school, or community program) standing in concrete. The individual may be upright, but he or she cannot move. This very real imagery conjures up feelings of entrapment, of being frozen or stifled.

Generally, a change-master offers an image, then invites those involved to bring their own images to the table, making the exercise more meaningful. The images offered by the group members speak to the deeper self and, therefore, have more power to catalyze energy for change.

During this stage, as well as all the others, the leader must accept the experiences shared and not judge, criticize, or put down anyone either verbally or nonverbally. Satir believed that all human beings have the capacity for change and can be rehabilitated. The more successful change-masters are able to accept and forgive as well as nurture and support.

Introduction of the Foreign Element and Resistance

In the next stage in Satir's model of growth and change, a foreign element is introduced, followed by resistance to that element. Foreign elements include new as well as inner desires to make changes. Resistance to change, described earlier in this chapter, is an expected and normal part of the change process (McLendon & Davis, 2002). Satir (1988) referred to this stage as "reshaping the status quo."

Change is said to be a form of loss or death of a part of the self or loss of typical patterns for functioning in a group. In the same way that the body rejects a transplanted organ, we resist and reject changes in our typical patterns. We are not comfortable wearing "a tight, new pair of shoes." When we resist change, we are trying to maintain balance or homeostasis.

Change-masters have to be attuned to the natural tendency of people to direct their discomfort with change toward the agent of change. People may criticize or express anger toward the leader of change. Change-masters may feel inadequate or think they are not doing things the right way. Alternatively, they view the individual, family, group, or team as impossible. These are all signals that the group is in the stage of resistance. In this stage, the change-master has to be in a place of nonattachment to the results of the change process.

During this stage change-masters must draw on their personal sense of satisfaction and appreciation. They must be self-supporting rather than dependent on others for recognition. Aligning with the momentum of positive energetic change is critical, whether it is with an individual or a group/team. Almost paradoxically, the leader also must be aware of and honor the fear that others have about change. Change is a both/and proposition—both hopeful and anxiety-provoking.

A graphic way of depicting the pull on individuals at this stage is to have one person stand up, have a second person (representing the force for hope) pull that person from the front, and have a third person (representing the force of fear and speaking in "shoulds and oughts") pull the person from behind. The change-master has to focus all three on how they feel in their respective positions. Satir also was known to have a fourth person play the observing ego or evolved self. This part would speak with the other parts and offer advice in a stalemate as well as at other opportune times.

The change-master also must help the individual or group/team focus on the courageous aspect of the self that has chosen to be involved in the change process. The person or group/team could be asked to get in touch with the courageous aspect of the self and speak with that part of the self, moving back and forth from fear to courage.

Also, the change-master might find an opportunity to address the fear and hopelessness that runs deep in some people and groups. If a person were to say, "I don't know what makes you think anything will be any different," the change-master could respond with a more direct statement such as, "It sounds as if you think I may fail you as others have, and then you will be in a worse place because you will have made another commitment and be disappointed again."

Satir proposed that such interaction allows the leader to make contact with the person. It allows the leader to go beyond the resistance stage and be in a deeper place with the person's fears and losses, rather than with the anger often stirred up in resistance. It also allows for contact with the person's higher self/potential, that which the person is capable of becoming.

Chaos

In contrast to the predictable and comfortable status quo, Satir's third stage, chaos, is anything but that. Individuals, families, teams, schools, and community programs commonly ask for help with change when they are in crisis. Often, what they are really seeking is help to return to the homeostasis that preceded the crisis. Yet, the crisis may be the very thing that will allow for a shift in a healthier direction that will move the individual or group past where things were before the crisis and into an improved pattern of being. Thus, crisis brings both danger and opportunity.

Crises signal a need for people to listen more deeply, whether to the deeper self or to others. A responsibility of the change-master at this stage is to help people listen more deeply, moving them toward new possibilities. As in the previous stage, imagery is helpful because it speaks to the deeper self. The change-master should also know and communicate to others that chaos is a positive and necessary step in the right direction (McLendon & Davis, 2002).

Feeling vulnerable is part and parcel of this stage. Thus, another task of the change-master is to help people feel safe. If the change-master can protect people from being harmed by others, through reframing and other means, he or she will be more successful in charting these turbulent waters. If people open up to their vulnerabilities, they will be more likely to discover their inner truths.

When people feel vulnerable, they may get upset and sound off. When someone overreacts in this way, the leader has to do some detective work to determine what set off the person. Perhaps a situation reopened an earlier wound and the outburst was really related to the past. The person may not even realize that he or she was overreacting. The change-master may help by directing the person who is upset to look within, to be still so he or she can see what is underneath the expression of feelings in the outburst. Most people will need time to reflect before they will be able to move forward in their growth process.

Because individuals and teams may perceive this stage as a backward movement, the change-master must frame the chaos as necessary. It is helpful to have mentioned beforehand, during Stages 1 and 2, that chaos is predictable and painful and necessary for growth. When people experience what was expected, it usually is easier to frame the experience in a more positive manner.

The change-master must remain rock solid during this stage. Serving as a model, the leader helps people move into and through fear-based views of the world. Being congruent (see chapter 14) is a necessity. While remaining neutral and nonjudgmental, the leader can point out the dysfunctional stances described in previous chapters.

Satir (1983a) maintained that "the problem is not the problem." The problem is the way of coping with the concern. To help people change unhealthy coping mechanisms, the change-master can encourage them to honor the five freedoms, remain congruent, and help them get in touch with their inner experiences as well as their feelings about these experiences. As discussed, the feeling about the feeling is important. It is one thing to feel angry and another to feel guilty about feeling angry. Once these feelings are discovered, coping mechanisms used in the past can be changed.

Chaos theory is a current interpretation of disorder with a systems perspective. Professionals from many different fields of science theorize to make sense of the world. For a long time, scientists theorized about the world as predictable. In chaos theory, scientists look at nature as complex and dynamic, and they see it as whole. Chaos theory holds that underneath disorder and unpredictability is pattern. One must wade through the disorder to find the pattern. Similarly, where change is concerned, disorder is part and parcel of the movement forward, and those involved must learn to flow with the disarray or at least to tolerate it as a necessary step in the right direction.

New Integration and Practice

This stage is a time of growing comfort with the new. The old, automatic responses and ways of interacting and doing things have gone, replaced by new possibilities. Hope is rekindled. Once the individual, family, team, or group has moved out of chaos, it is time to integrate and practice the new patterns. Practice is necessary to validate, confirm, and reconnect to oneself and others. It is a time of being conscious of one's actions and not doing things automatically.

In this phase change-masters have to remove themselves from a directive role and turn power over to the individuals, group, or team. As part of the shift in power, change-masters have to restrict themselves to asking questions rather than answering them. The change-master's role is to cheer and validate the new growth by pointing it out and focusing on it in concrete ways. Equally important is to support people in authentic ways when they stray off target or revert to old patterns. Without support, the person or group may, out of fear, revert to the old ways. The role of the change-master is to be totally present, aware, and supportive.

The New Status Quo

The adage "Good better best, never let it rest, until the good is better and the better best" fits in this final stage of Satir's growth model. The practice has paid off, and people are no longer in danger of regressing to their old patterns. They feel more creative, energetic, vital, and connected. And, as they have achieved another status quo, they will eventually move into another period of growth and change.

Renewal is important and cannot be overemphasized in the context of the ever-changing universe to which we all must respond. It is infinitely possible to grow while maintaining a form of status quo. Staying in touch with one's experiences—what one sees, hears, thinks, feels, wants—and commenting on them is critical to healthy living.

For anyone wishing to implement systems models, perspectives, and approaches in their work lives, Lao Tzu's philosophy of leadership, dating back to the sixth century, will serve you well:

> Of the best leaders, the people only know that they exist.
> The next best they love and praise,
> And the next they fear and revile.
> When they do not command the people's faith
> Others will lose faith in them and resort to recriminations
> But of the best, when their work is done
> The people will all remark, "We have done it ourselves."

Summary

Change is a way of life, and challenges associated with change in work settings are predictable. Successful infusion of family systems concepts in school and community settings, to aid professionals working with at-risk and special-needs children/youth, requires knowledge regarding aspects of change and their implications.

Thinking systemically about organizational changes is as essential to success in work settings as using family systems theory, concepts, and practices with families. As in family systems, thinking systemically takes all the parts of the organizational system into consideration so that professionals not only can predict what to expect in the process of change but also learn new ways of communicating and problem solving. Thinking systemically helps them deal effectively with difficult situations and challenges of working with both individuals and groups who are internal or peripheral to the work context.

The aim of this final chapter is to provide the understanding and skills necessary to strengthen the organization before and during systemic change so that the goals for change have a higher likelihood of being met. The "ingredients of an interaction" break down human communication into its nonverbal (i.e., paralinguistic) and verbal aspects so that professionals are tuned in to the nuances of communication and prepared to respond to other professionals as well as children/youth and family members in a manner that takes each of the "ingredients" into consideration. As well, knowing the components of interactions allows professionals to reflect on their interpersonal communication in ways that lead to functional interactions and, therefore, closer relationships with others.

A variety of challenging situations occurs in community and school settings when interacting with parents with psychological issues, which may lead to dysfunctional communication. The types covered in this chapter included: demanding parents, psychiatric difficulties, and angry parents. It is crucial to be empathic and nonjudgmental with parents who are demanding, although it also is vital that these parents learn who is in charge so that hierarchy (see chapter 3 and the Appendix) problems are less likely to develop. Demanding parents should not be called down during a team meeting, and conflict signals a need for decision making to be put off until the conflict is resolved. It is helpful to frame needs for assistance as normal at different junctures in everyone's life.

Parents with psychiatric difficulties may have any combination of dysfunctional communication described throughout this book. Professionals who know how to respond to the four types of dysfunctional stances (i.e., placating, blaming, superreasonable, distracting) described in chapter 14 will assist these parents in communicating more effectively. Reassuring these parents of the professional's commitment to the best interest of their child and maintaining congruent communication is essential. Some parents with psychiatric difficulties will benefit from a referral for individual, family, or group counseling or psychotherapy. A parent who is clearly under the influence of alcohol or other drugs needs to be gently reminded that it is not possible to discuss their child under those circumstances and their spouse/partner can be given written material about accessing help from resources designed specifically for their needs. One professional developing a strong relationship with any parent with psychiatric difficulties forms a useful bridge between that parent and other professionals serving their child(ren) and professionals need to direct interactions toward the most stable parent/caregiver.

Parents who are angry usually use a *blaming stance* and easily throw off even the most seasoned and functionally communicative professional. Remaining congruent when facing verbal attacks, and recognizing that underneath the parent's anger often lies fear, help professionals stay on track as well as use communication effectively. Parental venting may be encouraged when it helps get the concern out so they can settle down and engage in functional interactions. Maintaining eye contact, being courteous, listening to parental/caregiver concerns rather than interjecting personal opinions, and asking for further clarification when needed help the professional begin to establish trust so that he or she and the parent/caregiver displaying anger are able to work together in the best interest of the child.

Problem solving is a process of working with others, including parents/caregivers to understand and develop strategies for handling the challenge together. The steps described in this chapter included: defining the problem, collecting facts and opinions, generating solutions, selecting the solution, and implementing the solution.

Professionals must consider the needs, desires, and availability of family and other caregivers regarding level and type of involvement in their child's education or community-sponsored program(s). Many parents of at-risk and special-needs children/youth only want information transfer between them and professionals about placement considerations. Professionals should provide opportunities to develop functional parenting skills, to learn what works with their child and how to use the strategies at home, to obtain support services, to interact effectively with professionals, and to become part of the decision-making process while learning to be involved in leadership roles (e.g., governance, advisory, and advocacy). Being "family-focused" leads to improved results for children and youth in both school and community settings.

Nonparticipation by parents/caregivers occurs for a variety of reasons, and this chapter offers strategies to encourage participation when possible or wanted by the parent/caregiver. Lower levels of participation in their child's education and community programs is more common in lower income families, those with older children, as well as families with children who have more severe disabilities. Limited education, little knowledge of the processes used in special education, minority or single parent status, anxiety related to feelings of inadequacy being confirmed by professionals, guilt about mistakes they have made in parenting, mistrust of professionals and doubt about their competence, and denial of the severity of their child's challenges all affect participation levels in school and community settings. Empowerment of these parents and caregivers helps them claim a sense of control and involvement as well as fulfill legal responsibilities of those with special-needs children. It is helpful to meet with parents prior to attendance at team meetings, especially in relation to test scores and placement. Professionals can prepare parents and caregivers by providing an overview of what to expect in team meetings, answering questions, allaying concerns and alleviating any sense of inadequacy on the part of parents/caregivers.

Limitations to the use of family systems approaches in schools and community settings were described in this chapter in relation to lack of training for professionals, norms within the school or community setting, and traditional procedures. Few teachers trained in the United States have received training in or are required to read a textbook about family systems concepts, practices, and theory. It is far more likely that professionals working in community settings will have received training in family systems while in their university preparation programs. On the job training in family systems is lacking or limited in both educational and community settings. Although it has slowly and marginally increased in the professional literature for education for decades, it has been explored extensively in journals read by social workers, counselors, psychologists, and in other journals read by those in behavioral health professions. There are, however, ways to find well-trained and experienced professionals who can help with on-the-job training related to family systems by contacting the American Association of Marriage and Family Therapists or by looking in particular for therapists in your area who list family systems as one of their specialties; their numbers are limited even though all are trained in family therapy because family systems therapy is one branch within the field of family studies. The second limitation described was related to existing norms within school and community settings. Seldom would an employee in schools recommend family systems therapy for a family because of the cost associated with this related service in special education. At the same time, there is a gradual recognition of the need for working with the entire family when intervening with children in school as well as community settings. Training in family systems would result in an expansion of its impact in both settings. A third limitation discussed was that caseloads of many professionals are extraordinarily high with little likelihood that those with the knowledge and training in family systems have the time to train others in the field.

Reality constraints in implementing family systems include availability of time, money, and training in school and community settings. Some professionals would perceive it as impossible to add to an already heavy work load; others may be concerned that there would not be enough time to implement new approaches once learned due to the learning curve absorbing extra time in the early stages of implementation; yet another constraint described was not enough personnel trained in family systems and lack of preparation in programs that prepare professionals for a career in education or community programs. There are ways to circumvent this constraint by using a trainer of trainers' model or personnel enrolling in modules taken through internet centers that count toward renewal of licensure.

Attitude, resistance, and change were touched on in this chapter, and modeling a positive attitude toward change is essential for professionals to project not only an openness for change but an enthusiasm that renews the interest of peers and family members about the change. Also affecting change are fears of inadequacy, security issues, trust, and a narrow focus that doesn't encompass a wider scope that enables professionals and family members to see the larger picture.

The Concerns-Based Adoption Model (CBAM) was described in relation to how people change over time in relation to concerns about an innovation. In the earlier stages, the concerns are very personal and in relation to how it affects oneself whereas toward the end of the adoption of an innovation the concerns normally progress toward how the professional can help others in adopting the innovation.

The Stages of Growth and Process of Change developed by Virginia Satir moves through the stages: status quo, introduction of the foreign element and resistance, chaos, new integration and practice, and the new status quo. Each of these stages has particular aspects to which those in the helping profession can appeal in assisting others as they move through the process without the extreme difficulty and angst that accompanies many innovations.

Extension Activities

Observe, Journal, Discuss Ingredients of an Interaction: While reading about the *ingredients of an interaction,* you were guided to recall a recent interaction and reflect on the ingredients each step of the way. As well, you were guided to analyze low-threat interactions for a day. This extension activity involves using your "inner observer" during an interaction with another person in which that person is aware of what you are trying to accomplish. You could ask a member of your class/group to do this with you outside class OR inform a family member or friend that you will be observing interactions with them at the time they are occurring. You may stop the interaction to comment on each "ingredient" or jot down a note.

Choose a topical area for the interaction that isn't too complex for your first attempt. If answering the questions earlier in the text was helpful when you were reading about the ingredients, use one or all three of what follows to help you analyze your interactions: Do certain types of meaning result from a particular type of message? Are certain feelings attached to meanings that provide a better picture of you? Can you determine defenses or rules operating under different feelings about feelings? After doing a few of these inner observations, write in your journal about any pattern you find, as well as questions you have.

Bridge with in-class/training: During the next class/training activities, share your experiences and journal with the class or a partner. Be sure to have your questions answered during the session/class.

Visit websites given in this chapter: Before recommending websites to others in a work setting, visit them yourself. Check the websites every now and then to see what has been added and whether they are still available. Begin a notebook with personal comments on each site visited.

Analyze one or more change processes you experienced: Reflect on a change process you have experienced at work or in a community setting (e.g., faith-based institution, recreation center) or as a high school student. Use Satir's stages of growth and process of change model described in this chapter to analyze at least one previous experience. Before reflecting on each of the stages, reread the corresponding section in this chapter. Then, before going to the next stage, reflect on how that occurred in the process you chose to recall for analysis and deeper learning.

After going through each stage in your memory, consider what you might have done differently to improve the change process. What went well in each stage, and to what do you attribute the success of the different stages when things were as anticipated? What was your experience during the chaos stage, and what can you learn about how to remain calm and stable amidst the stage of chaos? Write down some tips or things you want to remember when you face a change process in the future.

Know, Want to Know, Learned (KWL): Revisit the KWL list you composed at the end of chapter 1, and then discuss or reflect on what you have learned. Musing about what more you now want to know may help you focus on your continuing education.

APPENDIX

Conceptual Frameworks of Family Systems Models

Introduction

This appendix provides a closer look at the conceptual frameworks of four family systems models in greater depth. For over a decade, the influences of multiculturalism, feminism, and postmodern social constructionism have influenced the evolution of family systems therapy (Aponte & DiCesare, 2002; Cory, 2005; Nichols & Schwartz, 2005). Quite naturally, but not without consternation, the course of development of the theories, models, and approaches has changed in the field of family systems. This appendix focuses on the four models from the perspective of their unique characteristics, the history of their founders as well as initial development, their conceptual foundation, their views of family dysfunction, and their approach to working with families. I do not bring in all the changes in their approaches over time, rather, I provide more depth about the differences in the ways they approach the profession and the model/theory that guides them. For that reason, you will find the citations are mostly from the early development in the field when the approach was being defined. I have found it easier to understand the different schools of family systems therapy by reading what the developers of the four models defined as their model or theory. Bowen always considered his work as development of theory, so he viewed it as it never having "arrived," but always in the process of evolution. Nevertheless, this appendix provides the "North Stars" of each school of family systems to guide you as you read in greater depth.

Because the audience for reading this textbook is school and community personnel involved with at-risk and special-needs children and youth, rather than family systems therapists in training, I highly recommend that those interested in an overview that encompasses additional threads not covered here read the family systems chapter written by Jim Bitter and Gerald Cory (Corey, 2005). They provide an overview of six family systems approaches. More important, they present eight lenses in family systems therapy that include

- the individual's internal family system,
- sequencing—-tracking patterns of interaction,
- the developmental lens,
- the gender lens,
- the teleological lens,
- the organization lens,
- the multicultural lens, and
- the process lens.

Their eight lenses were built on the work of Breunlin, Schwartz, and MacKine-Karrer (1997). The chapter by Bitter and Corey (Corey, 2005) relates an

> enlarged integration of ideas from multiple models of family therapy. Similar to a piece of classical music, the process of family therapy, it seems to us, has movements. These movements can be described as separate experiences embedded in the larger flow of therapy. (p. 442)

Their four movements included different tasks in the therapeutic context:

- Forming a relationship
- Conducting an assessment
- Hypothesizing and sharing meaning
- Facilitating change

The chapter includes a clear and helpful chart that compares the six systemic viewpoints they describe, a brief example of a family systems session, a genogram of the client, helpful recommendations for future reading, and key words that can be entered online at InfoTrac to locate more information about family systems.

This appendix describes the conceptual frameworks of the four major family systems models:

- Satir's human validation process model
- Bowen's multigenerational theory
- Structural family therapy
- Strategic family therapy

The frameworks presented can assist in better understanding families. The explanation of each of these four models includes a brief historical account of the development of the theory as well as specific theoretical concepts and principles from each perspective. Following those descriptions is a brief section on family assessment. Although not targeted by theoretical perspectives, this information may be helpful to some professionals (e.g., psychologists, social workers, counselors) working in schools and communities. The information in this appendix can enrich your understanding of family systems concepts and will form an important base for understanding Part One of this text, which undergirds Parts Two and Three.

Satir's Process Model

This section overviews the Satir human validation process model. A brief historical account of its development is followed by a description of Satir's philosophical view of humanity, systems approach, and homeostasis. This is followed by a description of six concepts central to Satir's work. Her model contrasts with the theoretical concepts of Murray Bowen's theory, which are presented next. Satir did not spend time propounding theory. Her approach was more conceptually and intuitively based than theoretically grounded. She used the force of her warm, affirming personality to join with family members and collaborate with them in a change process.

Historical Information

Virginia Satir, like Murray Bowen, was one of the earliest pioneers in the field of family systems. She popularized the family therapy movement with her engaging presence and her exciting and practical approach. Bitter and Corey (Corey, 2005) described Satir's approach as an experiential one

> that emphasizes communication and emotional experiencing. Like Bowen, she used an intergenerational model, but she worked to bring family patterns to life in the present through sculpting and family reconstructions. Claiming that techniques were secondary to relationship, she concentrated on the personal relationship between therapist and family to achieve change. (p. 421)

Her method was described by Guerin and Chabot (1992) as "highly personalized, experiential, and immensely popular" (p. 250).

Satir was a teacher from 1936 to 1941. She became interested in families while teaching children and making home visits. She later received a master's degree in social work from the University of Chicago. From 1955 to 1958, she was an instructor in the Family Dynamics Residency Program at the Illinois State Psychiatric Institute in Chicago. In 1959, Satir moved to California and joined the staff at the Mental Research Institute in Palo Alto, where she developed a formal training program in family systems therapy. She left Palo Alto to join the staff at the Esalen Institute in Big Sur, California. She was director of residential training at the Esalen Institute from 1963 to 1965.

According to Guerin and Chabot (1992),

> Satir speaks of the family as a "balanced" system and, in her assessment, seeks to determine the price individual family members pay to maintain this balance. She views symptoms as blockages to growth which help to maintain the family status quo. She is more important as a skilled clinician and teacher than as an original theorist. However, her impact on the practices of family therapists was far from minor. Indeed, she may be the most influential of all the people mentioned in this chapter. (p. 250)

In 1964 Satir published the first of many books, *Conjoint Family Therapy*, which is currently in its third edition (1983b). In 1972 she published *Peoplemaking*, which was intended for the general public and written at a fifth-grade level, so children could also benefit from the book. Satir continued to write a variety of professional and popular books, updating her concepts and methodology. *Peoplemaking* was republished in an expanded version in 1988 as *The New Peoplemaking*.

Satir founded the AVANTA Network, an organization devoted to promoting her process model throughout the world, and the network continues her work today. She held month-long training seminars for professionals in the summers of 1981 through 1987 in Crested Butte, Colorado. It was one of many different training opportunities in the human validation process model. Satir conducted a variety of other training seminars and held speaking engagements around the world until she became ill in the summer of 1988. Virginia Satir died in October of 1988. The January/February 1989 issue of the *Networker*, a professional journal devoted to family systems approaches, contained a tribute to Satir entitled "The Legacy of Virginia Satir." It is excellent reading for those who would like more of a flavor of her life and being.

Satir received many awards for her work. In 1982 Satir received one of the most notable awards when she was among 10 living people that Germany recognizes as having made a positive difference in the world by producing a documentary about their lives. Satir is remembered for her respect for individuals and family members, charisma, emphasis on positive intentions, solution-oriented focus on the present and future, accent on equality, action orientation, and her willingness to join and collaborate with families.

Background Information

Satir was assured of, and convinced about, the potential for goodness and wholeness of people and the world. She believed in human potential and the individual's ability to transform his or her own life.

A description of Satir's "ways of viewing the world" is helpful as a basis for understanding her work. According to Satir, there are two ways of viewing the world. One, which is hierarchical in nature, is known as the threat and reward model and is familiar to Americans. She referred to the other by several different terms, including the "organic and seed" model. Satir and Baldwin (1983) described these two ways of viewing the world in the book *Satir, Step by Step*, which was also presented as a chart by Schwab (1990).

The threat and reward model regards people as inherently bad and weak by nature. Thus, a hierarchy is necessary to determine and maintain standards of behavior. People at the top of the hierarchy believe that they are acting for the good of all. They use rewards and punishments to enforce their standards. From this practice, dominance and submission evolve. People are viewed in terms of their degree of conformity to the standards. Those at the top of the hierarchy do not take kindly to difference. In turn, they do not see themselves as individuals. Instead, they obtain their identity from their prescribed roles. For those beneath them on the hierarchy, the consequences of these ways of defining people and their relationships include stagnation, fear, despair, hopelessness, and rebellion. Those at the top may appear happier with their jobs.

In the threat and reward model, events are seen as linear. Any lack of conformity is interpreted as the hierarchy failing to maintain conformity. This cause-and-effect view of the world results in blame and fault finding. Change is not welcome because it is a threat to the status quo.

In families that operate by this model, parents are dictatorial and accept little input from their children. Family members frequently blame others; there is little acceptance of responsibility for personal behavior. Threats are common, and rules are enforced with punishments. The parents set the standards for behavior and hold to those standards even when they no longer fit the situation. For example, if parents dictate that that men do not cry, they would consider it inappropriate behavior for a son, even when a situation would legitimately warrant crying.

Most school and community professionals have seen children who come from families that operate within this model. The children may find environments like schools and communities in which rules and standards are not carved in stone and punishments are few and far between confusing. It then becomes the task of the school and community professionals to work with them to help them understand expectations and disciplinary procedures that are not consistent between the home and school/community.

There are, however, some school and community contexts that function from a threat and reward model as well as professionals within schools and community organizations who operate from such a position. Satir and Baldwin (1983) provided an example: "The student must follow directions and look at his teacher to prove that he is paying attention, regardless of whether he actually concentrates better by attending in a different way" (p. 162). Schools can expect resentment and hostility under these circumstances.

The seed model contrasts with the threat and reward model. In the seed model, people are seen as having an innate potential for goodness and wholeness. That which is unique within individuals is cause for celebration and support. People are defined in terms of their uniqueness and encouraged to know and value themselves. Relationships are based on mutual appreciation of the uniqueness of self and others and are egalitarian in nature. Change is a by-product of this way of being in the world. A growth orientation is the outcome.

The seed model is a systemic paradigm, with relationships existing among all components. Events are viewed as a result of many variables rather than being linear, as with the threat and reward model. Events within people's lives are understood as a result of complex, interrelated variables, rather than in terms of cause and effect or blame.

School and community professionals will find children and youth whose families ascribe to the seed view of the world to be vastly different from those who grow up in families ascribing to the threat and reward model. Interestingly, a school or community system may operate from a threat and reward model and have children/youth who grew up within a seed model family life. Confusion will arise for students who face dramatically different sets of expectations in the two different contexts.

In reality, the contrast between these two models may not be so obvious. There are more shades of gray than there are actual extreme opposites. It is possible, however, to determine whether a person, family, school, or community ascribes to a threat and reward model or a seed model.

By understanding the two models and determining the model from which the child comes, the professional becomes better able to work with families and children. Rather than blaming a child for not complying with the system in place, the professional can step back and recognize that the family's view has shaped the child's behavior. In ways that are constructive, professionals can work together to help the child be successfully educated within a system that may be quite different than that of the home in which the child has been raised.

In addition to becoming knowledgeable about these two views of humanity, it is helpful to understand Satir's perspective on systems. Satir and Baldwin (1983) stated that in a family, "every part is related to the other parts in a way such that a change in one brings about a change in all the others. Indeed, in the family, everyone and everything impacts and is impacted by every other person, event, and thing" (p. 191).

They further described two types of systems, open and closed. Closed systems operate on the rigid application of rules, regardless of their appropriateness. They described the closed system as "dominated by power, obedience, deprivation, conformity, and guilt. It cannot allow any changes, for changes will upset the balance" (Satir & Baldwin, 1983, p. 192). The family members are ruled by fear, punishment, guilt, and dominance. Self-worth is quite low in these families. Symptoms develop when someone from such a system reaches the end of his or her coping abilities.

An open system is just that—open to change with changing contexts. These systems accept all expression and feelings, including hope, love, anger, frustration, sadness, joy, and compassion. As would be expected, members from such systems have higher levels of self-worth.

Satir also ascribed to the systems perspective of homeostasis (Guerin & Chabot, 1992). Homeostasis involves the innate tendency to establish a dynamic balance amidst changing conditions and relationships. Within families, one will find that family members exhibit complementary and predictable patterns of communication. Family members operate to maintain the survival of the family and achieve balance within the family system. Satir believed that families attempt to preserve homeostasis by finding different means of adapting and adjusting to change. In particular, they establish rules for behavior as well as communication styles. From the efforts to preserve homeostasis stem behaviors that, rather than restoring homeostasis in times of transition, may actually result in symptoms. Satir frequently used the delinquency on the part of a youth as an example of a symptom indicating imbalance in the family system.

Finally, Satir continually emphasized the process versus the content of human interactions. Her focus for intervention was the way in which family members dealt with a problem rather than the content of the problem. She was famous for saying, "The problem is not the problem; the problem is the process." She also contended that once a new process for resolving one situation was learned, then other situations could be resolved with the newly learned process.

Conceptual Understandings

Satir's two models of the world provide a background from which her family systems concepts can be appreciated. As stated earlier, Satir was pragmatically oriented rather than theoretically governed. Even so, Bernhard (1991) wrote a chapter titled "Theory and Practice of the Satir System." This section provides a framework that will allow the professional to better understand family systems and thus better profit from information contained in the remainder of this textbook.

Satir's work is based on six key concepts: triangles and the development of self-identity and personhood, the aspects of the self, learning and change, self-worth, rules, and communication patterns used as coping mechanisms.

Triangles and the Development of Self-Identify and Personhood

Most children have parents who provide them with the basics for human survival. Those parents also provide their initial schooling about the world. The child perceives the world through his or her senses, and anything that is not understood is fabricated. Thus, memories from the early childhood years are a combination of truth and fabrication. The child unwittingly misinterprets information while trying to make sense of what occurs in the family. The more dysfunctional the family, the more misinterpretation occurs. Frequently this misinterpretation follows the child in later life and affects his or her coping abilities. Thus, the family has the initial impact upon coping with difficulties later in life. Satir saw the

> experience of the primary triad (father, mother, and child) as the essential source of identity of the "self." On the basis of his learning experience in the primary triad, the child determines how he fits into the world and how much trust he can put in his relationships with other people. (Satir & Baldwin, 1983, p. 170)

Lifelong patterns of responding to stress develop when the child is very young, according to Satir (Baldwin, 1991).

The child also learns about contradictions in communication—-inconsistencies between what is seen and what is said or between what is felt and heard. An example of such an incongruent message would be a little boy noticing that his mother looked angry and wondering what was wrong. The nonverbal aspects of the communication would affect the child, who attends to voice tone, touch, and looks. The mother, whose parents had taught her that family members must never be angry, would respond by denying feeling angry and indicating that everything was fine. The child would then have to decipher that discrepancy. Further, the child probably would consider himself to be a possible cause of the anger. Such mixed messages damage the child.

In the mother–father–child triad, it is usual for one individual to feel excluded at times. If the child interprets communications between the parents as a rejection of him or her, the child will develop a low sense of self-worth. The child learns about being included and excluded from the primary triad. These experiences help shape the personality of the child.

The child's sense of personal power also develops from the primary triad. There are many possible points children can learn about personal power. They might learn that they have the power to generate negative feelings between their parents, that they have no power, or that they can have a positive impact on their parents.

As was typical of her outlook, Satir saw the possibilities of the triad as supportive, powerful, and resourceful. She emphasized that functional families with high levels of self-worth are cooperative and suggested cooperation as a possible goal for everyone interested in transformation. Summarizing Satir's view of the primary triad, Baldwin (1991) wrote,

> The reason Virginia Satir puts so much emphasis on the primary triad of father, mother and child is that the triad is the place where the individual begins the formation of his personhood and his self-concept. On the basis of his experience in the primary triad, the child determines his place in the world and how much he can trust his relationships with other people. (p. 29)

The Aspects of the Self

Satir used the Eastern concept of the mandala to illustrate her holistic view of the eight aspects of the self. The mandala is a symbol with concentric circles that represent parts of the whole. When taken together, the whole is more than the sum of the parts (Schwab, 1990). Bitter and Corey (Corey, 2005) credit Satir with the development of the self-mandala.

As shown in Figure A.1, Satir's conceptualization of the self has eight aspects: physical, emotional, intellectual, sensual, nutritional, interactional, contextual, and spiritual. The eight aspects interact with one another and influence the individual's health. At the center of the mandala is the core of the human being that Satir referred to as the "I Am" or the "Self." Together the eight aspects of the self and the "I am" core create a system.

Learning and Change

Becoming more fully human was Satir's theme. She hung banners with this theme in her training rooms and devoted her life to enabling people to become more fully human by learning and changing.

Some people change because they are in pain; others because they want to mature and grow (Dodson, 1991). The process of change Satir promoted was similar for both types of people. To change, individuals need to be willing to take risks and learn to feel their life force. Ability and willingness to learn at both the cognitive and emotional levels are essential.

According to Satir, we have all learned how to be human, and we can all learn to be more fully human. As ingrained as some experiences from a stressful childhood might be, we have the capacity to replace our old learning with new and more beneficial learning. Satir focused on learning as opposed to unlearning. She believed that old, obsolete, or unwanted learning will atrophy or fade away when replaced with new and more beneficial learning.

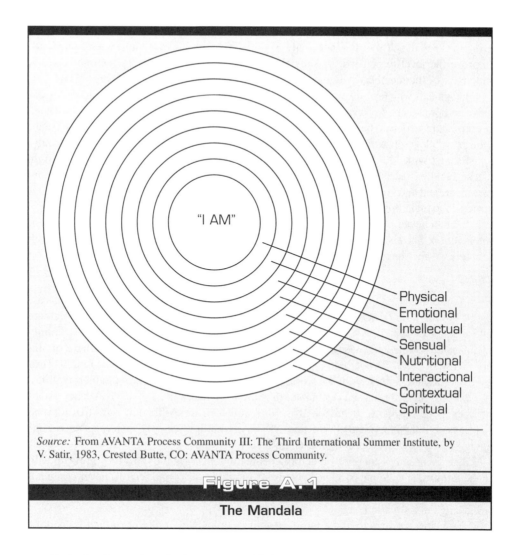

"I AM"

Physical
Emotional
Intellectual
Sensual
Nutritional
Interactional
Contextual
Spiritual

Source: From AVANTA Process Community III: The Third International Summer Institute, by V. Satir, 1983, Crested Butte, CO: AVANTA Process Community.

Figure A.1

The Mandala

Satir also focused on the importance of being supported when taking risks to change, although she did not negate the need for helpers to use tough love when appropriate. The importance of the help of others is a natural evolution from the seed model.

Satir recommended that helpers enable individuals to find their own answers, as opposed to providing ready-made answers and static rules for communication. Further, she believed that we all have within us answers that can be rediscovered. The helper thus assumes the role of a guide.

Self-Worth

Central to Virginia Satir's work and teaching was the concept of self-worth (Goldenberg & Goldenberg, 2004). The value an individual assigns to himself or herself, the self-love and respect that are distinct from anyone else's view of the individual, constitute the person's self-worth. Satir viewed the first 5 years of a child's life as critical when considering the level of self-worth. Later in life, significant others and a positive environment can improve the level of self-worth. Satir also believed that how a family communicates is indicative of the members' feelings of self-worth (Goldenberg & Goldenberg, 2004).

Individuals with low self-worth are anxious and unsure of themselves. They are hypersensitive to how others see them. They may interpret exclusion from a dyad as rejection and become more anxious. The eight aspects of the self are not well integrated or developed in individuals with low self-worth. These people oppose change and prefer the safety of conformity.

Parents with low levels of self-worth beget children with low levels of self-worth. These families ascribe to the threat and reward model. Submission and dominance are prevalent, and incongruent messages are common. Although Bowen used different constructs to explain this, his beliefs were similar to Satir's.

Satir believed that raising the self-worth of individuals was an essential focus for intervention. She also contended that most problems seen in therapy were associated with low self-worth. She explored this topic in depth in *The New Peoplemaking* (1988).

Rules

Each family has a unique set of expectations and standards. Rules include those that are overt, such as who does what chores, and those that are covert, such as "no complaining allowed" (Satir, Bitter, & Krestensen, 1988). The rules of the system dictate how family members are defined and behave. The rules affect the expectations individuals have of others (Schwab, 1990). People assume that others have the same rules as their family. They expect to observe in the rest of the world the same situations that occurred in their families.

Indeed, rules are not only valuable; they are truly necessary for survival. They establish beneficial norms for behavior. It is when rules are inflexible and rigid that they no longer benefit the individuals in the family. Those who rigidly apply such rules have damaging "shoulds," "oughts," and "musts" in their repertoire.

Satir focused her energies on helping people to transform the rules they grew up with in the family. An example of a rigid rule is, "I should never complain." To never complain is not always possible or healthy. Complaining may be a significant way to lead to positive change in a situation.

The helper's role is to assist family members in knowing more about and transforming the rules that impact their lives (Schwab, 1990). With a change in the rules comes improved communication and self-worth. Part III of this text presents information on how to help families work to change ineffective or rigidly held rules.

Communication Patterns

Discussing Satir's beliefs, Goldenberg and Goldenberg (2004) related that, "Dysfunctional communication (indirect, unclear, incomplete, unclarified, inaccurate, distorted, inappropriate) characterizes a dysfunctional family system" (p.172). In the book *Peoplemaking* and *The New Peoplemaking*, Satir (1972, 1988) described four dysfunctional communication styles she found in use around the world. Established out of low self-worth, these patterns are those of

- the placator,
- the blamer,

- the superreasonable, and
- the irrelevant.

These communication patterns are described here as they function in the family; chapter 14 includes information on dealing with these patterns, or stances, in schools and community contexts.

These communication styles, or coping mechanisms, begin in the primary triad as a means of dealing with family stresses. To better understand the four dysfunctional stances, it is important to know about the dimensions of an interaction. Schwab (1990), as well as Satir, Stachowiak, and Taschman (1975), delineated three dimensions of all interactions: self, other, and context. The self is the communicator, the other is the person to whom the interaction is being sent, and the context is the situation in which the communication occurs. Healthy communication contains a balance of all three dimensions.

The placator, with feelings of low self-worth, will try to please others at the expense of self. Incongruent communication results when the self is denied. Placating conceals feelings of inferiority.

The blamer, also feeling low self-worth, tries to control others or is disagreeable. This person is seen by others as hostile and tyrannical. Blamers disregard the other in favor of self and context. Underneath, blamers feel vulnerable and like failures.

Superreasonables also feel diminished self-worth. They deny feelings and intellectualize. Those with whom they work might describe them as rigid, intellectual, or manipulative. The context becomes the whole focus of the superreasonable. When self and other are restrained, incongruency occurs. Superreasonable people feel very vulnerable.

The irrelevant individual, too, experiences low self-worth. Self, other, and context are all discounted in communications. This person appears erratic and inappropriate and feels anxious and lonely.

Nevertheless, congruent communication does exist. It emanates from people with high self-worth. They do not distort communication and clarify as well as improve interactions. There is a balance of self, other, and context in their communications.

All people have patterns on which they rely most heavily. In times of great stress, normally congruent people usually fall back on one of the four dysfunctional patterns. The dysfunctional patterns are complementary and systemic in nature. For example, the blamer and placator need one another to function. Satir emphasized the capacity of all people to relearn what was originally a learned communication style. She believed that individuals can learn to be congruent in their interactions and cease to rely on the four dysfunctional stances.

Although they have been quite briefly described here, Satir's concepts are highly pertinent to this text. This information is a foundation on which to build further concepts as well as methodology. Other chapters focus on how to use this foundation when working with families of at-risk and special needs children and youth.

The Bowen Theory

This section provides an overview of a multigenerational process, the Bowen Theory. A brief historical account of the development of this theory is followed by an explanation of two variables important to understanding the Bowen Theory: togetherness–separateness and intellectual–emotional functioning. This discussion is then followed by a description of Bowen's eight key concepts of human functioning. An understanding of these theoretical concepts is beneficial to education professionals who are working with students who are at risk or have special needs.

Historical Information

Murray Bowen was a pioneer in the field of family systems therapy. He developed the Bowen theory between 1957 and 1966 from observations he made while examining families with a schizophrenic family member. A physician and psychiatrist, Bowen worked at the Menninger Clinic in Topeka, Kansas, and then moved to the National Institute for Mental Health (NIMH) in Washington, DC. Under Bowen's direction, whole families with schizophrenic members were hospitalized while he was working at NIMH. He was later affiliated with the Medical College of Virginia in Richmond, and finally with the Georgetown Family Center, a part of Georgetown University in Washington, DC. Bowen died in October 1990. The March/April (1991) issue of the *Family Therapy Networker*, a journal devoted to family systems approaches, contains a special feature on Bowen's life and work.

Early in the development of his theory on family systems, Bowen decided that a new language, with a systems viewpoint, would be critical to accurately describe families. He was influenced by systemic concepts of biology, which furnished him with a framework for defining the basic concepts of his theory. Kerr and Bowen (1988) clearly stated that general systems theory is "not a satisfactory integrative theory. It is a kind of 'umbrella' theory that has been imposed on a variety of natural systems" (p. x). They further wrote that people and families are "driven and guided by processes that are 'written in nature.' In this sense, the human family is a natural system. It is a particular kind of natural system called an emotional system" (p. 26).

In the Bowen theory, the connection between theory and practice is paramount. Theory and therapy are seen as too intertwined to separate. There is essentially no therapy without theory; theory dictates what will be accomplished in therapy. Between 1959 and 1975, Bowen developed eight concepts that constitute the core of his theory. These were described in a collection of Bowen's works, *Family Therapy in Clinical Practice*, first published in 1978.

Background Information

According to Bowen, biological processes account for a person's affinity for individuality and togetherness. Individuals function differently, however, based upon learning. The more emotionally reactive the person, the more the biological process has the upper hand. The more neutrality and choice the individual demonstrates, the more cognitive and feeling resources prevail.

Individuality (or separateness) and closeness (or togetherness) are two counterbalancing processes within human relationships. Rooted in instinctive drives for autonomy and connection, these forces are by nature fluid and variable. When a person experiences too much separateness, he or she feels the desire for togetherness, and vice versa. Bowen saw the movement to seek equilibrium between these forces as characteristic of all human relationships (Nichols & Schwartz, 2004).

The opposing functions of intellect and emotion similarly seek a balance. The use of logic and reason to describe the world and behave rationally are characteristic of the intellectual system. The automatic functions of the autonomic nervous system, the instinctive states that derive from basic life processes, and the subjective, feeling states are characteristic of the emotional system. The balance of these two systems results in a continual interplay between the functions. In Bowen theory, the balance between the two is achieved when their characters are maintained as separate, interacting entities (Guerin & Chabot, 1992). An imbalance results in the loss of distinction, or fusion, of the intellectual and emotional systems. The intellectual function is abandoned, with resulting reliance on the emotional function.

Choice is limited when a person is overreliant on the emotional system. A person capable of achieving a balance between the emotional and intellectual systems is able to make choices about separateness and closeness (Walsh & McGraw, 2002). Imbalances result in a reactive individual with little initiative for separateness. Boundaries between self and others are affected, and emotions dominate relationships. These people live in conflict, withdrawal, and dependence. Differentiated people are those who are less responsive to their emotional reactivity. That neutrality allows for choice in handling separateness and closeness. It stems from combining both feeling and cognitive resources.

Balancing the force for togetherness with the force for separateness and balancing intellectual functioning with emotional functioning are important principles to understand. Balancing or maintaining equilibrium between these two principles determines the degree of integration of a self and thus the health of the individual (Nichols & Schwartz, 2004). Different degrees of balance between togetherness–separateness and emotional–intellectual functioning are required of different relationships (Kerr, 1988). For example, in marriage, one expects to see more togetherness than in friendships.

Varying movement along the continuum of togetherness and separateness and along the continuum of intellectual and emotional functioning results from the naturally occurring changing circumstances within relationships. Two main variables, the degree of anxiety and the degree of integration of self, govern the equilibrium between the intellectual and emotional systems and the forces toward togetherness and separateness. When anxiety is high or chronic, the tension results in a fusion of the intellectual and emotional systems, with a concomitant increase in the togetherness force. Physical, emotional, or social symptoms are seen as a result of this fusion.

The integration of self is the ability to differentiate one's self from others. Bowen posited that the degree to which one can use intellect to monitor and control emotions while surrounded by the emotional intensity of family relationships determines one's level of integration or differentiation. Also indicative of integration of self is the ability to remain in relationships with others while maintaining a sense of self apart from others during a time of emotional intensity.

Physical, emotional, or social symptoms occur when an individual does not adapt to tension. Chronic anxiety stresses the person, and symptoms develop (Goldenberg & Goldenberg, 2004; Jacobson & Gurman, 1995). Substance abuse, emotional disturbances of children or their parents, and physical symptoms, such as asthma and diabetes, can have manifestations in school and/or community that appear to be related to stress in the home.

Theoretical Concepts

Bowen's observation of the togetherness–separateness forces, the intellectual–emotional systems, and their relationship to the integration of self, the impact of anxiety, and the emergence of symptoms led him to develop eight key concepts of human functioning (Goldenberg & Goldenberg, 2004; Guerin & Guerin, 2002): differentiation of self, triangles, nuclear family emotional system, family projection process, emotional cutoff, sibling position, multigenerational transmission process, and societal regression. The concepts that more directly affect children will be elaborated in greater depth than the others in the following sections. To read the original work, see Bowen (1966, 1976, 1985) and Kerr and Bowen (1988).

Differentiation of Self

Pivotal to understanding Bowen's theory is the concept of differentiation of self (Roberto, 1992), which describes people in terms of their ability to keep their intellectual and emotional systems from becoming fused. People whose systems are fused are dominated by the emotional system and the force for togetherness. People who are able to balance their intellectual and emotional systems are able to make choices about how they will deal with life experiences. Although differentiation describes a capacity to make a choice, Kerr and Bowen (1988) made it clear that this capacity does not determine the correct or best choice.

According to Bowen, differentiation of self and chronic anxiety are the two main variables that explain level of functioning. The level of differentiation within one's family-of-origin affects one's own level of differentiation (Guerin & Chabot, 1992, Guerin & Guerin, 2002).

Anxiety also affects one's level of differentiation of self. As Kerr (1988) stated, "Acute anxiety is fed by fear of what is; chronic anxiety is fed by fear of what might be" (p. 47). Higher levels of chronic anxiety place a greater strain on people's adaptive capabilities. Individuals who are better at differentiating between their own intellectual and emotional systems have more functional means for and choices about adapting to anxiety. They will have fewer symptoms in their lives.

In terms of understanding levels of differentiation of self, Bowen (1978) described the solid self and the pseudoself. He viewed the solid self as the part of a person that is resistant to fusion of the intellectual and emotional systems. It is able to maintain a healthy balance between the forces for togetherness and separateness. The solid self embodies the individual's beliefs, principles, attitudes, and opinions that are nonnegotiable under any circumstance.

The pseudoself is quite different (Roberto, 1992). A fusion of the processes of the emotional and intellectual system results from anxiety and stress. Bowen (1978) referred to the pseudoself as the "pretend" self. It has soft beliefs and principles; thus, it takes its beliefs and principles from someone else. The expected return for this action is belonging to the other and a sense of togetherness.

The levels of solid self and pseudoself are different among individuals and in an individual over time, depending upon life circumstances. When experiencing few stresses, an individual with a low level of solid self may appear to have a strong solid self. However, when a stressful situation results in anxiety, the actual level of the pseudoself will emerge. Having a child with a disability is an example of a stress on parents that can bring out their pseudoselves.

When the intellectual and emotional systems are fused, couples will be at lower levels of differentiation because the emotional system will have the upper hand in the relationship. One member of the marital dyad may adapt for a long time and may even lose parts of the solid self he or she once possessed. Chronic physical illness and psychoses are examples of this situation in its most extreme form.

In the Bowen model, differentiation is separate from being an individual. Sometimes people reactively function on a pseudoself level. They claim their individuality and manifest emotional reactivity to the desires of another. Instead of being closer to the other person, they become further apart.

Triangles

Bowen saw the triangle or three-person unit as the smallest stable relationship system. In families and groups, the triangle is the basic building block of relationships; creating this type of system is part of a human's instinctive nature (Kerr & Bowen, 1988).

Bowen (1978) maintained that when anxiety is low, a triangle will consist of a comfortable twosome and a less comfortable outsider. The twosome will strive to maintain togetherness. A third person is drawn in by the twosome when the anxiety level increases, which results in a lowering of anxiety within the twosome and creates a triangle. When high levels of anxiety affect the members of the triangle, the outsider position may be more attractive because the outsider can escape the intensity of anxiety.

Kerr (1988) described a typical example of how a triangle operates.

> A husband, on the outside (in fact or fantasy) of the relationship between his wife and his oldest daughter, becomes sullen. The wife predictably reacts to his sullenness by focusing more on him and attempting to cheer him up. The daughter, in reaction to being on the outside in relation to her two parents, becomes overly solicitous toward her father. The mother, reacting to being on the outside in relation to her husband and her daughter, criticizes the daughter's physical appearance. The daughter responds defensively, and she and her mother have a long discussion to resolve their differences. (p. 53)

The emotional system, with its force toward togetherness, drives triangles. Individuals who have higher levels of differentiation of self are more able to observe and handle the relationships within the triangle. Individuals with lower levels of differentiation of self, who fall back on the emotional system and need for togetherness, are reactive to any tensions within the triangle (Guerin & Guerin, 2002).

Kerr (1988) noted that anxiety created by family systems often spreads to outside systems. Under stress, anxiety may be spread to the schools, the community, the workplace, or some other agency. Kerr also explained that

> parents never want such an outcome [impaired functioning] for any of their children. For the most part, they dedicate themselves to preventing it. However, their anxiety that things go well may obscure their ability to see that they are acting in ways that foster the very outcome they most want to prevent. (p. 55)

Kerr (1988) perceived triangles in families as lasting forever. He viewed the "emotional circuitry" of a triangle as outliving the people who are its members. When one family member in the triangle dies, another person generally replaces that individual. Through the generations, the family members may be involved in acting out a conflict that was never resolved between grandparents or great-grandparents. As Kerr (1988) stated, "So a particular triangle was not necessarily created by its present participants; nor do triangles form anew or completely dissolve with the ebb and flow of anxiety" (p. 53).

School and community professionals would do well to consider Kerr's (1988) statement that "intolerance of aspects of the human process is a manifestation of being triangled into it" (p. 57). It is critical for professionals to understand human process and their own vulnerabilities and to detriangle from families. Frustrations and intolerance experienced by professionals are signs of a need for them to become better informed about human processes, in particular systemic processes, as well as to develop new ways of working with families or family members.

Nuclear Family Emotional System

This system includes processes and patterns of emotional functioning within a single generation of a family, which replicate those of past generations and will be repeated in future generations. Bowen contended that individuals with similar levels of differentiation marry one another. Spouses with higher levels of differentiation balance their emotional and intellectual systems with little fusion. They generally have few problems in their marriage. Spouses with lower levels of differentiation, with fusion of the emotional and intellectual systems, have more pseudoself than solid self. For them, each process or pattern of symptoms is magnified by anxiety.

The patterns or processes of symptoms fall into three categories of dysfunction within the nuclear family: marital conflict, illness in a spouse, and impairment of one or more children. The symptoms are physical illness, emotional illness, or social illness. All of these are viewed through the family systems lens as being linked to the same basic patterns of emotional functioning within the nuclear family. In other words, the patterns that contribute to the development of an emotional illness are the same as those that contribute to a physical or social illness. Kerr and Bowen (1988) made it clear, however, that "this does not mean that patterns of emotional functioning in a family cause physical, emotional, or social illness; the creation of a specific illness depends on the combination of many factors" (p. 164). More on the impairment of children is found in chapter 4.

Family Projection Process

This process was first described by Bowen in 1966. In later writings, Kerr and Bowen (1988) subsumed this concept under the concepts of nuclear family emotional system and differentiation of self.

The family projection process begins with anxiety in the mother regarding some aspect of her child's functioning, which the child responds to with anxiety. The mother might become anxious about something her child said or did, something she feared her child might say or do, or something she imagined her child to have said or done. The child's anxious response is interpreted by the mother as a problem with the child. The mother might become overprotective in response to the child. Her view of the child stems more from her own anxiety than from the child. However, the mother begins to act as though her view of the child is truth. Eventually the child acts like the mother's image, and the mother begins to calm down. With the mother's greater calm comes the child's greater calm. Finally the child internalizes the mother's perception and behaves like the mother's picture of the child.

Bowen contended that the family projection process is part of every family, varying in content and degree. The content within the same family even varies from child to child. Parents may become anxious about a particular trait or behavior in one child and about a different trait or behavior in another child. Kerr and Bowen (1988) stated that "the mother is not malicious; she is just anxious. She is as much a prisoner of the situation as the child" (p. 201). This realization can help school and community professionals to be nonjudgmental and more patient while working with parents.

Emotional Cutoff

This theoretical concept, which Bowen added to his theory in the 1970s, describes a way of gaining distance from fusion in the family-of-origin. Cutoffs range from minor to major significance. The person who institutes the cutoff is trying to reduce anxiety. The cutoff may in fact reduce anxiety; however, that is not always the case. Not dealing with a difficult situation is relatively easy for most people, but it can also result in losing potentially positive relationships and support as well as opportunities for learning about oneself within the context of the family.

Emotional cutoff describes the manner in which people deal with emotional reactivity between the generations. The greater the emotional reactivity, or fusion, the higher the probability that the two generations will cut off. Cutoffs occur in the forms of both physical distance and emotional withdrawal.

As Kerr (1981) indicated, emotional cutoff reflects a problem of fusion, solves a problem with distance, and creates another problem. Cutoffs are only temporary solutions; the unresolved emotional attachment to the parent continues despite the child's determination to distance from it. In the future, the unresolved emotional attachments are carried over into the child's own marriage or parenting, and the fusion continues. When people use cutoff as a means of dealing with the past, they are using emotional distance in the present. The lower the level of differentiation, the more one can be expected to see cutoff used as an attempt to gain distance.

Adolescence is a time of particular emotional vulnerability. Choosing friends of which their parents disapprove, getting into trouble with the law, and abusing substances are ways adolescents try to cut off from parents. This declaration of independence from family is not the same as differentiation of self. It in no way resolves the emotional fusion with the parent.

Sibling Position

Bowen based his understanding of sibling position on the original work of Walter Toman (1969), in which Toman delineated 10 important categories of sibling position that affect future relationships. The latest edition of Toman's text was published in 1993. Bowen (1978) stated that there was no single piece of information more important to understanding family systems functioning than the sibling position of family members in present and past generations.

Bowen theory stresses the importance of understanding functional sibling position when diagnosing emotional reactivity. A child might function as an oldest child in terms of responsibility or as a youngest child in terms of impulsivity, risk-taking, and dependency. Bowen saw shifts in the functional nature of sibling positions as resulting from the family projection process within the family-of-origin. When siblings function as would be expected by their sibling position, there is likely a low incidence of projection and higher level of differentiation within the family.If an oldest child acted more like a youngest child, the hypothesis would be that the oldest child was the focus of the family projection process. An exaggeration of the characteristics, such as a youngest child being extremely impulsive, leads to the observation that there was a high level of fusion in the family-of-origin and present marriage.

Multigenerational Transmission Process

This concept describes the family projection process through multiple generations. Children who are the object of the family projection process will have a lower degree of differentiation than their parents. Then, as adults, they will project emotional reactivity and lower levels of differentiation onto their own children, which will be passed down to the next generation (Nichols & Schwartz, 2005). Bowen believed that as lower and lower levels of differentiation emerged, a schizophrenic child would develop. He indicated that it would take 8 to 10 generations to produce a schizophrenic individual.

The concept of multigenerational transmission centers on a gradual regression to lower levels of differentiation and emotional reactivity, with the fusion of the intellectual and emotional systems being passed through successive generations. Bowen contended that individuals marry individuals with an equivalent degree of differentiation. Thus, their children would be expected to develop the same or a lower level of differentiation than the parents.

In accordance with Bowen theory, professionals in the school and community need to realize that what is observed in the setting is the result of many generations of this transmission process. This perspective makes it easier to be patient with and understand families and their children.

Societal Regression

The last of Bowen's eight theoretical concepts, societal regression, is based upon the degree of anxiety in society. Bowen hypothesized that the same process of gradual regression to lower functioning that occurs in families is also occurring in society. When there is increasing chronic societal anxiety, society reacts with decisions based on emotion rather than intellect. This process parallels the fusion of the emotional and intellectual systems that leads to lower levels of differentiation and inability to define a self (Nichols & Schwartz, 2005; Walsh & McGraw, 2002).

In 1978, Bowen published a text with a chapter titled "Societal Regression as Viewed Through Family Systems Therapy." In this chapter, he outlined the reasons for his belief that society is regressing. In particular, he pointed to the environmental crisis people have created, the increase in crime and the use of drugs, and new sexual norms. He predicted a series of crises before a major final crisis prior to the middle of the 21st century. Those who survive will, he predicted, be the ones "who can live in better harmony with nature" (p. 281).

The concept of societal regression may not be relevant to understanding families with children having special needs; however, it does demonstrate the value of understanding systems theory. It is easier to understand any system, such as cultures, institutions, businesses, or schools, when one understands theory from the perspective of the smallest relationship system, the family. The concepts of family systems enable professionals to better understand other systems in which they live and work as well as the people participating in those systems, including themselves.

Many influential students of Bowen continue using Bowen theory after his death in 1990. Some of them collaborated with him until he died, and others branched off on their own over time and trained others. Those interested in reading the current literature that uses Bowen theory as a base are directed to the works of David Chabot, Thomas Fogarty, James Framo, Edwin Friedman, Philip Guerin, and Michael Kerr.

Structural Family Therapy

This section provides an overview of the conceptual framework that undergirds structural family therapy. It begins with a brief historical account of the development of this model, followed by three general concepts basic to understanding families in structural terms. These concepts are subsystems, boundaries, and hierarchy. Eco-structural assessment is also described. It ends with a brief commentary on postmodern life, social constructionism, and structural family therapy.

Historical Information

In the 1960s, Salvador Minuchin, a pediatrician turned psychiatrist, and his co-workers at the Wiltwyck School for Boys near New York City began developing a model of family therapy designed to deal with delinquent youngsters from low socioeconomic backgrounds. Their book, *Families of the Slums: An Exploration of Their Structure and Treatment* (Minuchin et al., 1967), was the result of 3 years of research funded by a grant from the National Institute for Mental Health. The approach they developed, which they called structural family therapy, focused on helping chaotic, multiproblem families change those patterns of behavior that had led to the placement of one of their members at the School for Boys. Structural family therapy involves a focus on the present rather than the past, on changing behaviors rather than gaining intellectual insight, and on short-term rather than extensive treatment.

In 1965, Minuchin and Braulio Montalvo, a colleague from the Wiltwyck School, moved to the Philadelphia Child Guidance Clinic, where they began to develop a family-oriented treatment team. This inner-city, traditional child guidance clinic was to become the Mecca of structural family therapy. Many clinicians who eventually became well known as family therapists, including Jay Haley (Haley & Hoffman, 1967), M. Duncan Stanton and Tom Todd (Stanton et al., 1982), Lynn Hoffman (1981), Harry Aponte (1976b), and Marianne Walters (1972), originally worked with families from a structural perspective at the Philadelphia Child Guidance Clinic.

Minuchin's next book, *Families and Family Therapy* (1974), delineated a model of effective family functioning that included the qualities of openness, flexibility, and organization. These three basic traits and the language that Minuchin developed to describe them are discussed in greater detail later in this section. Minuchin also introduced in this book the technique of structurally mapping families to help the therapist develop specific goals for treatment. Further, he discussed the need for the therapist to join in the family's process and language in order to effect change. In Minuchin's approach, it is only after listening to the family and joining with them to bring about change that the therapist can begin to restructure patterns in communication and behavior.

Minuchin's writing not only introduced his theory to the psychological community but also included transcripts from actual sessions in which a structural family therapy approach had been used. Minuchin's therapy style was unique in that he was directive with his patients and very active during the sessions, frequently walking around the room and asking family members to change seats. Considered bold and controversial, he was one of the first trainers in the field to videotape family therapy sessions and show the videotapes to provide examples of principles of structural family therapy. This format later became a strategy of choice in training for all approaches to family systems therapy.

Although Minuchin's original therapy approach was based on the nuclear family as the unit of treatment, in the epilogue to *Families and Family Therapy* (1974) he opened the door for including extended family and other social networks in the concept of "family." He wrote, "To include the entire family as a factor ... enlarges the perspective from the traditional concentration on the individual. ... Yet even this focus distorts the view ... for it ignores the linkages between family and society" (p. 255). In the 1980s, structural family therapy began to include an emphasis upon extended systems that interact with the nuclear family and generational patterns that influence the family.

Although structural family therapy was originally developed from applications to families of lower socioeconomic status, the approach was generalized in the 1970s and 1980s to include all families. This extension came about as a result of 10 years of research Minuchin and his colleagues conducted at the Philadelphia Child Guidance Clinic funded by a grant for work with children having psychosomatic illness. The research involved children who were suffering from diabetes, asthma, and anorexia nervosa. Both the children with diabetes and those with asthma had numerous hospitalizations resulting from episodes of ketoacidosis or breathing difficulties that did not respond to conventional medical treatment.

As part of this research, the identified patients were videotaped with their parents and at least two siblings engaging in a series of interactive family tasks. The videotapes were then coded on dimensions of family structure by blind observers. This videotaped interview included phases during which the identified patient witnessed parental conflict from behind a one-way mirror and sat in the room during a conflict between his or her parents.

Comparison of the results of these interactions with interviews conducted with "normal" children and their parents revealed that the identified patients were much more involved in their parents' conflict than typical children. The patients tended to serve as mediators of parental conflict and to become involved in alliances with one parent against the other. In addition, there was evidence that the children with diabetes had an exaggerated response to parental conflict that resulted in an increase of free fatty acids in the bloodstream.

This research also involved a therapy component in which the principles and techniques of structural family therapy were applied in working with the families. Minuchin, Rosman, and Baker (1978) stated, "Our findings clearly indicate that, when significant family interactional patterns are changed, significant changes in the symptoms of psychosomatic illness also occur" (p. 21).

Minuchin continued his work at the Philadelphia Child Guidance Clinic until 1982, when he went into private practice. During his time at the clinic, he and his colleagues expanded the principles of structural family therapy to working with families coming together as a result of a remarriage, families with a schizophrenic child, families of adolescent drug abusers, as well as numerous other types of families. Minuchin retired in 1996 and is currently writing in the field of family systems (Nichols & Schwartz, 2005).

Background Information

The theory underlying structural family therapy is descriptive in nature. Based on specific values that deal with how the family should function, the therapy is practical and directive. This section describes some of the underlying premises and values that resulted in development of the approach known as structural family therapy.

Minuchin (1974) clearly identified a necessary balance between the general systems principles of homeostasis and adaptability when he wrote,

> The continued existence of the family as a system depends on a sufficient range of (transactional) patterns ... and the flexibility to mobilize them when necessary. The family must ... be able to transform itself in ways that meet new circumstances without losing the continuity that provides a frame of reference for its members. (p. 52)

The concepts of structural family therapy stem from the premise that family members interact with one another in predictable patterns that can be observed and that are repeated over time. Therapy is aimed at changing these patterns by changing the organization or structure of the family. Structure should not, however, be seen as fixed. A given structure may exist only for a brief period and should be seen as dynamic (Goldenberg & Goldenberg, 2004). Minuchin and his colleagues believed that as the behavior of family members changed, the basic patterns and structure of the family would change. As the structure was transformed, the experience of the individuals in the family would be different (Fishman, 1993).

Minuchin (1974) wrote that the primary job of the family was to "enhance the psychosocial growth of each member" (p. 51). To accomplish this task, the family must operate with some predictability and stability. For instance, children should be able to forecast that each time they misbehave they will receive a similar response from their parents. A classic example of the effects of lack of predictability comes from families in which there is an alcoholic parent. Children in these families learn early in life that they cannot depend on the alcoholic parent's reaction to their behavior. Only when they become older are they able to understand that the source of the instability is the parent's drinking behavior.

In addition to creating and maintaining stability, the family must also be able to respond to changing circumstances with some degree of flexibility. Stress upon the family such as moving, financial problems, the illness or death of an extended family member, or the identification of a child with physical or learning problems can overload the general functioning of the family system. If the family is not capable of responding to these demands by changing roles and communication patterns, family conflict and dysfunctional behavior will result.

The role of the therapist is to help families adapt to changing circumstances with changes in the structure of the family. Once the family experiences the changes and the adaptation that goes with the new structure, the homeostatic mechanism of the family should operate to continue the new structural pattern (Fishman, 1993). In families where restructuring changes do not continue or where conflicts are not resolved, what began as a problem of a family in transition may continue as dysfunctional patterns. Eventually, according to Minuchin's theory, these dysfunctional family patterns will result in the identification of a family member (usually a child) with behavioral, emotional, or physical symptoms.

Theoretical Concepts

Minuchin's view of the family as a relational context with predictable structural patterns led to the development of three theoretical constructs regarding family functioning: subsystems, boundaries, and hierarchy.

Subsystems

A two-parent nuclear family is composed of four major subsystems, each with its own interaction patterns and functions. These subsystems include the spousal or marital subsystem, composed of the husband and wife; the parental subsystem, which includes the parents as executives or decision makers for the family; the sibling subsystem; and the extrafamilial subsystem, including extended family, friends, and social supports.

The individuals included in each subsystem differ from family to family. For example, in single-parent families there is no spousal subsystem, and the parental subsystem often includes a grandparent or an older sibling who has parental permission to make decisions regarding younger siblings. The extrafamilial subsystem may include aunts, uncles, and cousins who live nearby or may be composed mostly of family friends or colleagues.

Each member of a family may belong to several subsystems. For example, a teenage child may be allowed periodic entrance into the parental subsystem in the form of babysitting. This same child will also be a member of the sibling subsystem. In addition, the teenager will be an integral member of the extrafamilial subsystem in school or community activities.

Membership in each subsystem will demand different interaction skills and ways of functioning in relationships. When interacting with parents, a teenager must know about respect and authority. When acting in a parental role, the adolescent must know about leadership and responsibility. Interacting with siblings or peers, this same child must learn about sharing, cooperation, and empathy. Furthermore, each subsystem has particular functions for the family system.

The spousal subsystem promotes interdependence of the marital couple, conflict resolution between the pair, and sexual and emotional satisfaction. Although information about this area is not readily available to school and community professionals, some general observations can give them a sense of the patterns of interaction between a couple.

The parental subsystem is responsible for the emotional and physical support of children, the establishment of family rules, the dispensing of appropriate discipline, and the socialization of children. Community and school professionals will find dysfunction in the parental subsystem in the form of abusive, unpredictable, or absent authority. Further discussion of the effects of imbalance in the parental subsystem is contained in chapter 3.

The sibling subsystem provides recreation, companionship, and role modeling for its members. Interaction with siblings provides a social laboratory for learning negotiation, cooperation, and competition with peers of different ages. The child's identity is formed, in large part, from positive and negative experiences within his or her sibling group (Bank & Kahn, 1975).

The extrafamilial subsystem provides a social network with which the family can socialize and compare ways of interacting and family rules. The network offers emotional and instrumental support, such as through the sharing of family celebrations and values and training in general life skills. Often families with a child with special needs become isolated from social supports, resulting in increased tension within the nuclear family.

Boundaries

According to Minuchin, the boundaries of a subsystem are defined by rules that govern who functions within that subsystem and how each person carries out his or her function. An example of a rule that defines a boundary would be, "The children in the family do not make decisions about how bills are paid." This rule places a boundary between the sibling subsystem and the parental subsystem (Walsh & McGraw, 2002).

For subsystems to function appropriately, boundaries must be clear enough to allow subsystem members to carry out their functions without interference from those outside the subsystem. For example, young couples quite often have marital difficulties if there is frequent involvement with and input from in-laws in their early marriage negotiations. If the couple purposefully goes to their in-laws for advice on specific issues, such as money management, there need not be a blurring of boundaries.

In healthy family interactions, boundaries are clear and permeable. When boundaries are blurred, subsystems have problems functioning. In families with blurred boundaries, parents tend to be overprotective and have difficulty with their children's attempts to become appropriately independent. There is little individual privacy (Goldenberg & Goldenberg, 2004). Aponte and Van Deusen (1981) stated that in these types of families, members function as if they were part of one another. Minuchin (1974) coined the term enmeshed to describe families with blurred, unclear, or undifferentiated boundaries.

At the other end of the continuum are families in which boundaries are inappropriately rigid and impermeable. Family members have little to do with one another; there is very little emotional support or closeness in these families. Only a severe crisis or a high level of stress can activate parental involvement. These types of families are called disengaged by Minuchin and his colleagues (Nichols & Schwartz, 2005).

Hierarchy

Minuchin used the term "hierarchy" to describe the distribution of power in families. The member at the top of the hierarchy is the one who has the most relational power within the family. Families operate best when there is a clear hierarchy, with parents occupying the upper levels, adolescents or older children next in line, and younger children at the lower levels.

There are many different ways in which hierarchy problems occur in families. One type of problem occurs in families with weak or ineffective parents. In these families, children tend to not listen to their parents' directions, and there is often much sibling conflict. In many low income or highly stressed families with multiple problems, the weak parental subsystem may be exacerbated by a general disorganization at all levels. Bills are left unpaid, phone calls go unanswered, and there is a general sense of a lack of leadership.

A second type of hierarchy problem occurs when a child functions regularly in the parental subsystem. This child assumes an inappropriate level of responsibility within the family and often misses out on age-appropriate experiences and activities. A child in this position is referred to as a parentified child (Minuchin & Fishman, 1981). Parentification occurs in families in which there is a highly inappropriate involvement between a parent and child.

Another hierarchy difficulty is found in families where members repeatedly align together across subsystem boundaries against another family member. An inflexible alignment is known as a coalition. This type of problem is frequently seen in families where parents avoid dealing with their marital conflict by focusing on problems in a child. For example, an adolescent who complains about his mom's nagging is often acting out his father's resistance to what his father perceives as his wife's nagging. Rather than the father confronting his wife, the adolescent, in a coalition with his father, acts out the conflict from across generational boundaries.

In summary, Minuchin used these three constructs to describe family dynamics and to identify the forces that lead to the development of problems in the family system. Subsystems with identified functions serve as the structural elements in the family. Boundaries are the mechanisms by which the family balances between stability and flexibility. Hierarchy is the organizing principle by which subsystems are arranged. By their articulation and extension of these constructs, Minuchin and his collaborators have provided a useful model for applying general systems theory to the problem of family dysfunction.

An Ecostructural Assessment Process

Aponte (1994) described an effective ecostructural assessment process that professionals can use during the family–school interview. The components of the ecostructural assessment process include

- the target issue on which the assessment process is focused;
- diagnostic hypotheses, which are related to structural and functional hypotheses; and
- therapeutic hypotheses that are related to the target issue(s), the client (child, family, and/or community), and the professional.

Aponte made it clear that these components should be seen as dynamic, with the professional revising and gathering new data and testing hypotheses on an ongoing basis. It is important to consider each of the subsystems that influence the target issue when an ecostructural assessment is used as a base for the family–school interview.

Target Issue(s)

The child and, as appropriate, the family and/or community members negotiate the target issue(s) that will be the focus of the intervention process. The target issue(s) should be directly related to the current concerns requiring intervention. When possible, the statement of the target issue(s) should be worded in a way that indicates the possibility for change. Therefore, it is important to include achievable goals. It is also important to consider the whole school–family–community system so that the target statement accurately reflects the degree of control the child has in relation to the situation. A child living with a dying parent or an alcoholic parent, for example, cannot change that situation. For example, the following statement of target issues takes realities into consideration:

> The target of the intervention is Pat's truancy. Pat's absences are nearing the number of days at which a student must repeat the grade, and it is only January. Although nothing can be done to change the fact that Pat's grandfather is dying, it is important for Pat to come to terms with this loss and focus on the job of obtaining the education that will allow her to graduate from high school this year, enroll in college, and pursue her interest in becoming a physician. Mr. and Mrs. Little need to work on refocusing their energies so that they can be available to help Pat focus on her loss in a healthy way instead of being truant.

Diagnostic Hypotheses

The diagnostic hypotheses state tentative explanations concerning the source and nature of the target issue(s) described by the professional and the child as well as family and/or community members (the latter being involved when the problems spill over from the home or school to the community). Diagnostic hypotheses include both structural and functional hypotheses. Together these hypotheses serve as guides for professionals who are working with a child who has a particularly challenging issue.

Structural Hypotheses. This part of the diagnostic hypothesizing process specifies what is going on now in the child's ecosystem in relation to the target issue(s). The professional needs to determine the systems (school, family, and/or community) in which the issues are rooted. Additionally, the structure of the relationships within those systems, as related to the target issue(s), must be identified. Thus, boundaries, alignments, and hierarchies need to be considered.

Boundaries. Boundaries must be considered when determining which systems are involved in the issue. Is it merely school-related, or does it also include home and/or community? As conveyed earlier in this appendix, boundaries are defined by unstated rules for inclusion and for how people participate with one another. It is important to sort out how the interlacing systems within which the child lives and interacts impact one another in terms of the target issue(s). Are the boundaries enmeshed or disengaged, and, if so, where and in what ways? An understanding of the boundaries within which the child functions will allow the professional to speculate and to improve his or her probability of intervening in meaningful and necessary subsystems. In the example of Pat, the truant senior, there is enmeshment in the symbiotic and overprotective relationship between the mother and daughter, and the father is distant and disengaged from his wife as well as his children, spending many evenings at work and golfing on weekends. He functions as an absent father.

Alignments. Only those alliances/coalitions and opposition relating to the people within the subsystems connected to the focal issue are considered. Alignments and opposition are usually thought of as who is "in" and who is "out" of a relationship. For example, the paternal grandfather and Pat are positively aligned with one another. The father is left out of the family relationship and spends most of his time at work; the mother and daughter keep secrets from the father and do not invite him on outings.

Hierarchy. Influence-wielding related to the issue must also be considered. Important questions are who has the power, how is the power wielded, and what transactional patterns occur related to the focal issue. Order and balance are influenced by hierarchy. Order is established by the natural pecking order of parents being on top in terms of power and, in their absence, by the oldest sibling taking that position. Balance is established or maintained by the degree of shared power in decision making. If the youngest child independently makes all of the important decisions and dictates family direction, there is a problem related to balance. If the marital dyad shares equally in decision making, there is balance. An example of a hierarchy problem is Pat calling the shots in her school attendance. The spouses do not have balance in terms of decision making because Pat and her mother collude to steer the direction of the family.

Together, the statement of boundary, alignment, and power structures constitutes the structural hypothesis. An example of a well-stated structural hypothesis is: The school unwittingly has colluded with the symbiotic relationship of the mother and Pat, thus supporting the ongoing dysfunction. This situation has developed because the school has not followed through on Pat's truancy and was overly lenient because her grandfather is dying.

Functional hypotheses. In relationship to the target issue(s), functional hypotheses speak to the meaning and significance of what is occurring. These hypotheses explain "why" the issue is transpiring. Specifically, they relate to "history, social conditions, culture, family relationships, individual psychology, motivation, etc." (Aponte, 1994, p. 36). They include value, motivational, and historical hypotheses.

Value hypotheses. Value hypotheses are related to the meaning and purpose of the underlying issue. For Aponte (1994), values pertain to "ethnicity, culture, race, gender, religion, spirituality, and any other influence on principles, standards, morality, and priorities giving personal significance to life and its problems" (p. 36). Pat, the truant senior, has an absence of spiritual or religious roots to guide her in dealing with the death of the grandfather.

Motivational hypotheses. The motivational hypotheses explain behaviors based on social conditions, family relationships, and individual psychology. They involve such catalysts as the mission of social institutions and family needs as well as individual drives and defenses.

The professional working with Pat would see that she has been unable to deal with the loss of her grandfather and as a result has checked out from school on a regular basis. Having grown up close to her grandfather and distant from her father, she has been angry at her father for not being more like his father. There has been continued strain between Pat's father and grandfather, and the problems of the past remain unresolved. Pat's truancy appears to take the pressure off her father and grandfather, relieving both of them from dealing straightforwardly with one another.

Historical hypotheses. Historical hypotheses focus on the past. They describe sources and antecedents of the target issue(s) that are of a social, family, and personal nature. Events, family stories and legacies, as well as individual emotional struggles are considered.

The maxim that one who does not know the past is condemned to repeat it is true of family history. The intensity or force of the multigenerational transmission of dysfunctional interaction patterns is an important focus of family systems perspectives. Realizing that the past is prologue, professionals are wise to ascertain historical information so that they will reach conclusions more quickly and be able to plan more effective interventions. Without knowing the history, it is easy to simply treat the symptom rather than work on the underlying cause of the problem. If professionals ignore history, their interventions may not work and frustration will likely result.

Therapeutic Hypotheses

Therapeutic hypotheses relate to the planned intervention strategies. For the purposes of this text, this discussion is limited to hypotheses about the issue(s) and hypotheses about the child, family, and community. Goals of the intervention, available resources, and the potential of the child and subsystems for change are taken into account.

Hypotheses about issue(s). School and community professionals look at the key issues that need to be considered to help the child. The professionals work with the child, family, and/or community in this process and focus the issue(s) so that the goals of the intervention are a natural outgrowth of their work.

Hypotheses about child, family, and community. Available resources must also be considered when establishing an intervention strategy. These resources include the motivation, commitment, and freedom to change on the part of the child, the family, and sometimes the community.

Together, these three types of hypotheses—functional, diagnostic, and therapeutic—form an assessment process that is continually updated and revised as new data are gathered. This kind of assessment process informs the therapeutic process directly and dramatically increases the likelihood that an intervention will be successful. In haste, school and community personnel frequently try to solve problems by applying Band-Aids and treating surface symptoms. If, however, professionals can discipline themselves to use this assessment process with cases that are particularly difficult or long standing, they will improve the likelihood of meeting with greater success.

On Postmodern Social Constructionism and Family Systems Therapy

I am inserting a postscript on structural family therapy that could be reproduced in different words to reflect the model of Satir and theory of Bowen. I see much value from the changes in the field that spring from multiculturalism, feminism, and postmodern thinking. I assume that I am like others who reflect deeply; sometimes I co-exist peacefully with the postmodern view with its social constructionism, and other times I embrace its direction. It goes without saying that it is important for professionals to continue to evolve and choose their professional direction based on considered knowledge and reflection. We need to be cognizant of the theoretical and philosophical guides we choose lest we lose track of True North. I found the reflections in the remainder of this section to speak deeply to me and have quoted what I consider to be sacred from what I have read in the last decade. I share it in the hope that it will speak to you also, and if not, that you know your professional compass leads in the directions of "home."

Reflecting on the influence of postmodern thinking, social constructionism, and the field of structural family systems therapy in this early part of the 21st century, Aponte and DiCesare (2002) stated:

> The postmodern world is critical of traditional therapy's notions of the "expert" therapist who can "understand" and has the "power" to "fix." … There is a postmodern reaction in the world of therapy against hierarchy, power, and the assumption of the ability to know reality. Structural theory's emphasis on structure, concrete issues, and an active, interventionist therapist, all seem to buck the modern trend. However, while the differences in philosophy are quite real, today's SFT speaks amicably to the spirit of modern society's concerns through its deepening and developing of the human and spiritual dimensions of structural family [therapy]." (p. 3-4)

Aponte and DiCesare went on to point out some kinship in postmodern social constructionism and structural family therapy. The structural family therapist of today works with the client/family to construct a perspective shared by both that "begins with an agreement on the values platform of the therapy" (p.4). The structural family therapist is cast as working from "personally colored values, and the worldviews of client and therapist meet in therapy" (p. 4). The authors clearly and eloquently elaborate on what I call the kinship of the structural family therapy tenets and the ways they meet in a world of postmodern social constructionism, while remaining true to the theory that guides the structural family therapist. The social constructivist theory refers to choice by sacrificing moral as well as scientific absolutes, whereas structural therapists "hold to a moral and scientific reality, but at the same time, recognize the essential freedom of the human will and base [their] approach to change on that ability to make a free moral choice" (Aponte, 1999, p.4). One side of the prism views change by therapists as critical and the structural therapist "speaks of the 'intimacy' of the therapist's relationship with the client" (Aponte, 1998a, p. 4).

Aponte and DiCesare explained that structural family therapy

> acknowledges a soul to the therapeutic process that lies in the human bond between therapist and client. It recognizes the ultimate mystery of the human spirit, and bases its work on the free will of the human being that can, must, and will choose its own path. The therapist's power is powerless in the face of the client's free will. The therapist's knowledge meets the unknowable of the human soul. The therapist who is expert in the professional sphere is quite humbly nonexpert in the human dimension of the therapeutic encounter. (p. 4)

What you read in this quotation is the reason I chose to invest six years of my family systems training with Harry Aponte. In my experience in the training group, Aponte was always deeply respectful of the sacred relationship shared with those who entrust their souls to be known in a therapeutic context. His ability to hold sacred the deepest aspects of the self is exquisite, and I learned that in trusting I could outgrow my self-limitations and be who I am where I am on the journey. To me this seems only true and possible when we share our deepest self with other human beings. I am confident that Harry Aponte was the same in a therapy context with clients. A therapist of honor and integrity can, together with the client, become the bridge to deeper and more meaningful relationships in the future. This is what I believe schools and communities should take into consideration when locating consultants and guides to further their work with at-risk and special-needs children/youth and their families.

Strategic Family Therapy

This section describes the general theoretical principles underlying the practice of strategic therapy.[1] A brief historical account of the development of this model is followed by a discussion of the basic theory of change from a strategic perspective. It is the approach

---

[1] The co-author of the first edition of this book, Debbie Bragga, was the original author of this section of the appendix.

with which I am least familiar of the four covered in the appendix. I attended training with Virginia Satir, including a month-long seminar one summer. I attended Bowen seminars for a year. I had six years of training in structural family therapy, attending seminars two days a month during the academic year. During the first decade that I studied family systems theories and approaches, I avoided the strategic approach because I felt that it was disrespectful of family members. Of the four approaches described, it is the only one in which I have not been directly involved. In reading, it is clear that, as the field of family systems has continued to evolve, other approaches/models in the field have borrowed from strategic family therapy, and certainly the field has leaned toward the "brief" aspect adopted by strategic family therapy. Nichols and Schwartz (2005) indicated that the approach has evolved over time. The remaining founding presence in the strategic approach has also evolved in relation to working with families, and the manner of working with families has changed with the natural evolution of any approach. Nichols and Schwartz also note that there is always room for "thoughtful problem-solving strategies and therapeutic direction" (p. 121). I concur and am heartened by their balanced view of the evolution of strategic family therapy, their congruent stance (Satir would approve), as well as non-reactivity (Bowen would approve) to some of the past practices of strategic family therapy.

I have, however, been highly influenced by the work of two of the professionals integrally involved in the early development of the approach, Gregory Bateson and Milton Erickson. I also strongly concur with some of the theoretical tenets, in particular the importance of understanding and working with "hierarchy" and "coalitions" within families, or for that matter, within organizational systems. Sharing a systemic view with the other family systems approaches already covered in this appendix, there are many overlapping tenets. If you would like more depth on the strategic approach, I recommend reading chapters devoted to Strategic Family Therapy in Nichols and Schwartz (2004, 2005), Carlson and Kjos (2002), Goldenberg and Goldenberg (2004), Corey (2005), and Walsh and McGraw (2002).

Historical Information

The term strategic is most often used to describe family therapy approaches that focus on identifying the function served by psychiatric symptoms within the family system. Further, the strategic therapist assumes responsibility for directly intervening in the system to effect change. Finally, the focus of strategic therapy is on here-and-now behaviors, with little or no attention paid to historical events. This focus contrasts with that of Bowen's and Satir's approaches, which treat the individual within a context of family history. The main goal of treatment is find how family identifies or views the problem and address it (Walsh & McGraw, 2002).

The two settings historically associated with the strategic approach are the Mental Research Institute (MRI) in Palo Alto, California, and the Family Therapy Institute in Washington, DC. Although each setting is known for its use of particular strategic therapy techniques, this discussion focuses on the commonalities in theory rather than the differences between their approaches. For a more detailed discussion of strategic therapy techniques, consult the relevant sources included in the reference list at the end of this book.

Many of the clinicians who have been important in the strategic therapy movement were originally trained and influenced by two men, Gregory Bateson (1972) and Milton Erickson. Bateson, an anthropologist, directed a 10-year grant project in the 1950s to investigate communication among both animals and people. Jay Haley, John Weakland, and Don Jackson, all of whom made major contributions to strategic therapy, worked on Bateson's grant project.

Milton Erickson, a physician, developed a unique brand of psychotherapy techniques based on hypnosis and paradoxical instruction. As Haley (1985) stated:

> Erickson had one major concern in his professional life—finding ways to influence people. ... He seems to have been the first major therapist to expect clinicians to innovate ways to solve ... problems and to say that the responsibility for ... change lies with the therapist. (p. vii)

Haley, Jackson, and Weakland all studied extensively with Erickson; the influence of his beliefs can be seen in their later work as advocates of the strategic approach.

In 1959, Jackson left Bateson's research project and formed the Mental Research Institute. Several important contributions to strategic therapy have evolved from the MRI group, including brief therapy techniques designed to effect change in families in 10 sessions. In addition, this group maintained that therapeutic change could occur whether or not the entire family was involved in treatment. At MRI, motivated members of the family are advised how to change their own behavior so that the dysfunctional family patterns would then change.

Jay Haley moved from Bateson's project in 1967 to the Philadelphia Child Guidance Clinic, where he worked for 9 years with Minuchin and his colleagues. Haley then moved to Washington, DC and began the Family Therapy Institute. Haley has contributed to the field of family therapy by training therapists in specific interviewing techniques designed to discover behavioral and communicational patterns within the family. He has also developed a model for treating severely disturbed young adults that focuses on the family's failure to allow the person to leave home and become independent.

Although Jackson, Bateson, and Erickson have all died, the ideas that they germinated continue to grow in the field of family therapy. The Mental Research Institute continues to provide training and therapy. The Washington School begun by Haley and Madanes on the East Coast also continues to thrive (Nichols & Schwartz, 2005).

Theoretical Concepts

Strategic therapy is grounded primarily on the general systems principles of homeostasis and levels of interaction (Nichols & Schwartz, 2005). Probably the best-known concepts arising from the strategic therapy movement are those of family homeostasis and the double bind as a communication pattern in the etiology or cause of schizophrenia. The concept of the double bind was the first theory in the area of paradoxical communication. The double bind communication pattern occurs when an individual appears to offer a choice to another; however, no matter which option is chosen by the respondent, he or she ends up in a bind.

An example of a bind is when a mother buys a red sweater and a blue sweater for her son's birthday and presents them both to him with the question, "Which one will you wear to the party?" The boy answers that either sweater will be fine. The mother then insists that the boy choose one of the sweaters. If the boy asks for the red sweater, she responds, "You don't like the blue one?" If he chooses the blue one, she asks why he does not like the red one. In other words, he is given the illusion of choice, but he will lose in this communication no matter which "choice" he makes. The study of this type of communication pattern within families led strategic therapists to develop general theoretical concepts regarding family homeostasis and the importance of family development and problem definition.

Over time, with the movement toward families being co-authors of their therapeutic process, it would seem that "using" such techniques "on" family members would wane. Furthermore, Nichols and Schwartz (2005) indicated that research on the approach found that some families experienced their therapists as distant and impersonal and had difficulty changing as a result of a sense of being cared for by the therapist. These were mostly from the Milan approach to strategic family systems therapy.

Family Homeostasis and Symptom Development

In 1957, Jackson first discussed the idea of psychiatric symptoms in an individual as systemic responses to family communication. In other words, people within a family govern one another's behavior by their responses to each another. Jackson believed that families have a natural movement toward stability or homeostasis, just as other living systems do.

According to strategic therapy (Watzlawick et al., 1974), psychiatric symptoms result from attempts by family members to change an existing difficulty. When difficulties arise in daily living, parents or spouses usually attempt to apply a solution to make things better. For example, if someone is depressed, family members try to cheer up the individual. If initial attempts at cheering up do not work, the family members increase their efforts. Once a symptom is present and a family attempts to treat the symptom, however, they often only succeed in making it worse. The solution then becomes entrenched as the family's behavior for dealing with the problem. The symptom is maintained by a particular sequence of behaviors within the family.

Consider the following scenario: Johnny looks depressed, so his family tries to cheer him up. If their efforts are not successful, they try harder. Johnny sees his family working hard to make him feel better, but he still feels depressed. Only now he also feels guilty about being depressed and taking so much family energy. In addition, his family is angry that they are trying so hard and Johnny is not responding, so they begin to withdraw from Johnny. Johnny then becomes more depressed. This sequence of behaviors is circular. If the therapist can discover this circular sequence and help change the family's reactions at any point along that circle, strategic therapy proponents maintain that the symptomatic behavior will then change.

Life Cycle

Strategic therapists look at the family's stage of development as an important factor in understanding the etiology of symptoms. Families are seen as prone to developing problems at transitional points, such as the birth of a child or a family relocation. At these times, due to the stress of transition, families are less able to adjust their interactions to accommodate necessary changes. In other words, the forces for homeostasis outweigh the forces for flexibility. Haley (1980) related this phenomenon to movement on a stairway. The family must make adjustments to move from one step to the next. Families with a symptomatic member have become "stuck" on one step and cannot move on to the next step in the life cycle. It is the therapist's job to help the family introduce new behaviors that will help them move on up the stairway.

All families become unbalanced at times and react to stress with nonproductive inter-personal cycles. Many people understand this process as a "button-pushing" phenomenon. Once a particular topic is broached or once a particular action takes place, each family member can predict how the other family members will react. It is as if the family is watching a very familiar one-act play, but they cannot seem to change their lines to come up with a more productive outcome. In healthy families, there comes a point when someone does "change his or her lines," and the nonproductive cycle is broken. In pathological families, these cycles continue to repeat over and over for months or years at a time. In these families, the cycles repeat until a crisis ensues. Even then the system does not change, because family members develop symptoms to provide a stabilizing force toward resolving family stress.

Just as the saying goes that people will pull together in times of crisis, the family tends to pull together around the symptomatic member, who is usually a child, and thus avoids making any real changes in the family patterns that caused the initial crisis. This pulling together around the symptom-bearing member might make it look to observers as though the family had changed its dysfunctional patterns and was functioning better. The essence of the system, however, has not changed, and the dysfunctional process will resurface as the problematic family member begins to function more healthily.

Haley (1980) viewed many severely disturbed young people as being stuck at the leaving-home stage of the family life cycle. In these families, the parents need to have their own lives and identities oriented around something other than child-rearing. If child-rearing is a mother's only purpose in life, then the underlying fear of the child leaving home is that the mother will no longer have a job. A strategic therapist would identify the young person as suffering from problems in maturity and independence. He or she would then work to have the parents in this situation become more controlling and demanding of their symptomatic child to help the child mature. As the parents effectively assert their control, the child's concern becomes how to get out from under this structure. The child then begins to work toward gaining independence and leaving home rather than on maintaining the parent's symptom. Once the child has given up the symptom, the family is then unstuck and can begin to introduce more adaptive behaviors. The mother can then give up her focus on the young person and devote her energy to managing her own needs as her role naturally changes.

Problem Definition

According to the underlying assumptions of strategic therapy, there is no objective reality. How one looks at things determines what one sees. This seems to fit with contemporary social constructivism. At the same time, the means used in working with families was not consistent with other tenets of the postmodern thinking of later years in the evolution of family systems therapy. Returning back to the tenet, "how one looks at things determines what one sees" leads the strategic family therapist further down the road. What one sees determines how one behaves. How one behaves determines how others respond.

Families usually seek help from a therapist long after symptoms have developed in a family member. The family has already applied its solution to the problem, and no change has occurred. The family members are demoralized by their maladaptive solution but cannot see how to approach the problem differently. They see the symptom as beyond their control and resistant to change.

In strategic therapy, it is the therapist's job to help the family define the problem in a way that a solution is possible. How one defines the problem determines what one will do about it. Therefore, much of the skill in strategic therapy lies in asking questions that help the family begin to entertain alternative views of the symptom. The therapeutic process of expanding the family's definition of the problem is known as reframing. When family members begin to view the problem differently, the therapist then gives directives concerning how individuals can begin to behave differently. In this model, action or strategy replaces traditional interpretation and insight therapy.

Different ways in which reality can be defined will be seen in the following classroom example: A first-grader has begun to destroy property in the classroom and to hit other students. At first, the teacher views this behavior as angry and aggressive. She responds by setting limits on the child and using time-outs. The teacher later finds out from the social worker or counselor that the child's parents have recently decided to get a divorce. At this point, she views the same behavior as depressed in nature. The next time the child acts-out, she takes him aside and asks him about his feelings about the divorce. In each case, the teacher's perspective on reality governed her behavior.

Current Example of Research

The Center for Family Studies in Miami, Florida conducted research on brief strategic family therapy working with Latino and African American adolescents having behavior and drug abuse problems (Szapocznik & Williams, 2000). Over the course of 30 years, they have conducted systematic research that used elements from strategic and structural approaches. In seven randomized clinical trials, they engaged families in treatment, reduced drug abuse as well as behavior problems, and improved family functioning. They developed the first family-based, minority-focused program treating adolescent for drug abuse that received national recognition. Their work has been recommended as a model by many federal agencies. The Surgeon General commended their work for keeping families engaged in the therapeutic context. Their work involved joining families with therapists from the same culture and working within the cultural value system of the families, thus removing a major barrier to effective engagement and treatment. The work of this center is well worth studying, especially for those who serve minority groups. They maintain a future oriented agenda and work to bridge the research–practice gap.

The three theoretical concepts discussed here—family homeostasis, life cycle, and problem definition—are used to help the therapist determine where to direct his or her efforts toward change. The strategic family therapy approach was developing on the West Coast at about the same time that the structural family therapy approach was developing on the East Coast. Both approaches differ from those of Bowen and Satir, in that their focus is on the behavior and communication of the family in the present. Structural thera-pists tend to develop goals aimed at helping the family members change roles and behav-iors in the here and now. Much of strategic therapy is oriented to techniques used by the therapist to induce change in communication patterns in the family system. In fact, the strategic therapy approach is known for being long on technique and short on theory.

Family Evaluation/Assessment

Assessing family functioning through a family systems lens is a complex and multifaceted process. While many of the different facets have been investigated, in my experience using family systems assessment instruments, none has completely met my needs. I have, how-ever, found the use of genograms (McGoldrick, 1999c; McGoldrick, Gerson, & Schellenberger, 1998) very helpful in describing and remembering the different family systems with which I have worked. The genogram, briefly described earlier in this book, organizes family data and tracks relationship processes and key triangles during treatment. *Genograms: Assessment and Intervention,* by McGoldrick, Gerson, and Schellengerber (1999), provides a useful guide to working with genograms. I provide a sample genogram in the last chapter of this book that is associated with the case study. The development of genograms is also described in chapter 4 of this textbook.

Beyond genograms within the field of family systems therapy, I have found ecostruc-tural assessment (Aponte, 1994) useful. Aponte (1994) provided a clear description of this model, which expands structural family therapy to include the individual, the family, and the community, which can include schools. The focus of Aponte's book is on the poor, and, thus, his model speaks in particular to at-risk children and their families. Though Aponte's book is written for therapists, it is useful for all professionals working in school and com-munity contexts.

Although most professionals working within schools and communities will not be involved in the assessment of family functioning, it is helpful for social workers, profes-sional and school counselors, and psychologists to have some knowledge of this area within family studies. Kerr and Bowen (1988) wrote a text that focuses on family evalua-tion as it relates to Bowen theory. Bowen's concepts, described earlier in this appendix, are used as a means for measurement. The text by L'Abate and Bagarozzi (1993) is an excel-lent sourcebook for marriage and family evaluation, which trained professionals will find useful for selecting appropriate instruments. Others will find it useful for learning more about what each instrument covers and how the different strands are evaluated.

The general field of family studies and therapy has five well-known models of family therapy with which assessment instrumentation is included. In the 22nd volume of *The Journal of Family Therapy* (2000), an issue was devoted to empirical approaches to fam-ily assessment. As the editor, Carr had invited five papers by "originators of major empir-ically based models of family assessment from both sides of the Atlantic" (p.121). The Beavers Family Systems Model (Beavers & Hampson, 2000), Circumplex Model (Olson, 2000), McMaster Model (Miller, Ryan, Keitner, Bishop, & Epstein, 2000), Family Process Model (Skinner, Steinhauer, & Sitarenios, 2000) and (DFAS) Darlington Family Assessment System (Wilkinson, 2000) each outline their conceptual framework or model that was the basis for their instruments. The instruments were described and research findings were summarized as well as implications for their clinical practice.

Like the underlying focus on family strengths in this textbook, all five models were based on strengths and competence, including family resources and competencies to be assessed. All five models also view lack of the competencies and strengths as signaling dysfunction. The editor (Carr, 2000) indicated that it is best to view the models of family functioning as social constructions and realize that different assessment systems were able to solve different problems.

According to Drumm, Carr, and Fitzgerald (2000), the Beavers and McMaster models were found to have particularly high levels of sensitivity in detecting clinical cases, whereas the Circumplex rating scale was particularly good at accurately classifying nonclinical cases. The (FAM) Family Assessment Measure (Carr, 2000) was found to provide "a rich source of information on family functioning" (p. 190). On an overall basis, FAM was found to effectively and efficiently asses functioning of families and gave strong explanatory and predictive utility. According to Wilkinson (2000), the DFAS "can be used to teach family interviewing to trainees in the helping professions, and combined with other assessment methods in a flexible way" (p. 211). As well, it can inform choices about interventions that would be more likely to be successful. Beavers and Hampson (2000) view their model and assessment as useful in training, research and clinical work. Olson (2000) wrote on the Family Adaptability and Cohesion Scales (FACES), a self-report measure, and the Clinical Rating Scale (CRS) supports the hypothesis that "balanced couple and family systems tend to be more functional compared to unbalanced systems" (p. 144). Miller and colleagues (2000) reported on the McMaster approach and three instruments. They view it as an empirically validated approach for assessment and treatment of families.

A description of these five models and their accompanying instrumentation is not included in this appendix. If you are interested in more information on the models and their instruments, reading the 22nd volume of the Journal of Family Therapy from pages 121-238 will provide you with considerable information and insight. I believe you will find each approach and instrumentation well worth you time to familiarize yourself with them, if assessment is of interest to you and it is required of your position. I also believe anyone who is entering the field of social work, counseling, or any form of direct work with families would learn much from reading about these five models in the Journal of Family Therapy.

Being used by family therapists since the 1970s, and translated into eleven languages, is Moos' Family Environment Scale (Moos, 1974) described by Goldenberg and Goldenberg (2004. The instrument was developed to assess the impact of the family environment on both individual and family functioning. This instrument has strong technical characteristics in terms of reliability. Moos' scale includes 10 subscales within the three dimensions of Relationship, Personal Growth, and System Maintenance. The subscales are: cohesion, expressiveness, conflict that examine relationships; independence, achievement orientation, intellectual-cultural orientation, active recreational orientation, moral-religious emphasis that relate to interpersonal development and growth; and the last two subscales, organization and control, refer to system maintenance dimensions that provide information about family structure and its roles.

References

Abbott, D. A., & Meridith, W. H. (1986). Strengths of parents with retarded children. *Family Relations, 35,* 371–375.

Abramovitch, R., Corter, D., & Lando, B. (1979). Sibling interaction in the home. *Child Development, 50,* 997–1003.

Abramovitch, R., & Strayer, F. F. (1977). Preschool social organization: Agonistic, spacing and attentional behaviors. In P. Pliner, T. Kramer, & T. Alloway (Eds.), *Recent advances in the study of communication and affect* (Vol. 6). New York: Academic Press.

Abrams, K. A., Theberge, S. K., & Karan, O. C. (2005). Children and adolescents who are depressed: An ecological approach. *Professional School Counseling, 8,* 284–292.

Ackerman, R. J. (1989). *Perfect daughters: Adult daughters of alcoholics.* Deerfield Beach, FL: Health Communications.

Ackerman, R. J., & Graham, D. (1990). *Too old to cry: Abused teens in today's America.* Blue Ridge Summit, PA: Tab Books.

Adkins, P. G., & Young, R. G. (1976). Cultural perceptions in the treatment of handicapped school children of Mexican-American parentage. *Journal of Research and Development in Education, 9*(4), 83–90.

Adler, A. (1959). *Understanding human nature.* New York: Fawcett.

AFCARS. (2005). *Trends in foster care and adoption—FY 2000–FY2004.* Retrieved November 30, 2007 from http://www.acf.hhs.gov/programs/cb/stats_research/afcars/trends.htm

Ahrons, C. R. (1999). Divorce: An unscheduled family transition. In B. Carter & M. McGoldrick (Eds.), *The expanded family life cycle: Individual, family, and social perspectives* (3rd ed., pp. 381-398). Boston: Allyn & Bacon.

Ahrons, C. R., & Tanner, J. L. (2003). Adult children and their fathers: Relationship changes 20 years after parental divorce. *Family Relations, 52,* 340-351.

Akbar, N. (1985). Nile Valley origins of the science of the mind. In I. Van Sertima (Ed.), *Nile Valley civilizations.* New York: Journal of African Civilization.

Alder, N. (2002). Interpretations of the meaning of care: Creating caring relationships in urban middle school classrooms. *Urban Education, 37,* 241–266.

Aldous, J. (1978). *Family careers: Developmental change in families.* New York: Wiley.

Alexander, K. L., & Entwisle, D. R. (1996). Schools and children at risk. In A. Booth & J. F. Dunn (Eds.), *Family-school links: How do they affect educational outcomes?* (pp. 67–88). Mahwah, NJ: Erlbaum.

Alexander, L. B., Hollingsworth, L. D., Dore, M. M., & Hoopes, J. W., (2004). A family of trust: African American parents' stories of adoption disclosure. *American Journal of Orthopsychiatry, 74,* 448-455.

Algozzine, B., & Ysseldyke, J. (1992). *Strategies and tactics for effective instruction.* Longmont, CO: Sopris West.

Allen, M., Brown, P., & Finlay, B. (1992). *Helping children by strengthening families: A look at family support programs.* Washington, DC: Children's Defense Fund.

Allison, S., Stacey, K. Dadds, V., Roeger, L., Wood, A., & Martin, G. (2003). What the family brings: Gathering evidence for strengths-based work. *Journal of Family Therapy, 25,* 263–284.

Alvarez, K. M., Donohue, B., Kenny, M. C., Cavanagh, N., & Romero, V. (2005). The process and consequence of reporting child maltreatment: A brief overview for professionals in the mental health field. *Aggression and Violent Behavior, 10,* 311–331.

Alvarez, K. M., Kenny, M. C., Donohue, B., & Carpin, K. M. (2004). Why are professionals failing to initiate mandated reports of child maltreatment, and are there any empirically based training programs to assist professionals in the reporting process? *Aggression and Violent Behavior, 9,* 563–578.

Amatea, E. S., Smith-Adcock, S., & Villares, E. (2006). From family deficit to family strength: Viewing families' contributions to children's learning from a family resilience perspective. *Professional School Counseling, 9,* 177–189.

Amato, P. R. (2001). Children of divorce in the 1990s: An update of the Amato and Keith (1991) meta-analysis. *Journal of Family Psychology, 15,* 355–370.

Amato, P. R. (2003). Reconciling divergent perspectives: Judith Wallerstein, quantitative family research, and children of divorce. *Family Relations, 52,* 332–339.

American Academy of Pediatrics, Committee on Child Abuse and Neglect and Committee on Children with Disabilities. (2001). Assessment of maltreatment of children with disabilities. *Pediatrics, 108,* 508–512.

American Academy of Pediatrics, Committee on Children with Disabilities and Committee on School Health. (1990). Children with health impairments in schools. *Pediatrics, 86,* 636–638.

American Academy of Pediatrics, Committee on Psychosocial Aspects of Child and Family Health. (2002). Coparent or second-parent adoption by same-sex parents. *Pediatrics, 109,* 339–340.

Ammerman, R. T., & Hersen, M. (Eds.). (1990a). *Children at risk: An evaluation of factors contributing to child abuse and neglect.* New York: Plenum Press.

Ammerman, R. T., & Hersen, M. (1990b). Issues in the assessment and treatment of family violence. In R. T. Ammerman & M. Hersen (Eds.), *Treatment of family violence: A sourcebook* (pp. 3–14). New York: Wiley.

Ammerman, R. T., & Hersen, M. (Eds.). (1990c). *Treatment of family violence: A sourcebook.* New York: Wiley.

Ammerman, R. T., & Hersen, M. (Eds.). (1991). *Case studies in family violence.* New York: Plenum Press.

Ammerman, R. T., Lubetsky, M. J., & Drudy, K. F. (1991). Maltreatment of handicapped children. In R. T. Ammerman & M. Hersen (Eds.), Case studies in family violence (pp. 209–230). New York: Plenum Press.

Anderson, C. (2003). The diversity, strength, and challenges of single-parent households. In F. Walsh (Ed.). *Normal family processes: Growing diversity and complexity* (3rd ed., pp. 121–152). New York: Guilford.

Anderson, J. A. (1988). Cognitive styles and multicultural populations. *Journal of Teacher Education, 29,* 2–9.

Anhalt, K., & Morris, T. L. (1998). Developmental and adjustment issues of gay, lesbian, and bisexual adolescents: A review of the empirical literature. *Clinical Child and Family Psychology Review, 1*(4), 215–230.

Aponte, H. J. (1976a). The family-school interview: An eco-structural approach. *Family Process, 15,* 303–311.

Aponte, H. J. (1976b). Underorganization in the poor family. In P. Guerin (Ed.), *Family therapy: Theory and practice* (pp. 432–448). New York: Gardner Press.

Aponte, H. J. (1994). *Bread and spirit: Therapy with the new poor.* New York: Norton.

Aponte, H. J. (1998). Love, the spiritual wellspring of forgiveness: An example of spirituality in therapy. *Journal of Family Therapy, 20,* 37–58.

Aponte, H. J, & DiCesare, E. J. (2002). Structural Family Therapy. In J. Carlson & D. Kjos (Eds.). *Theories and strategies of family therapy* (pp. 1–18). Boston: Allyn & Bacon.

Aponte, H. J., & Hoffman, L. (1973). The open door: A structural approach to a family with an anorectic child. *Family Process, 12,* 1–44.

Aponte, H. J., & Van Deusen, J. M. (1981). Structural family therapy. In A. S. Gurman & D. P. Kniskern (Eds.), *Handbook of family therapy* (pp. 310–361). New York: Brunner/Mazel.

Arditti, J. A., & Keith, T. Z. (1992). Visitation frequency, child support payment, and the father-child relationship postdivorce. *Journal of Marriage and the Family, 55,* 699–712.

Arends, R. I. (1990). Connecting the university to the school. In B. Joyce (Ed.), *Changing school culture through staff development* (pp. 117– 143). Alexandria, VA: Association for Supervision and Curriculum Development.

Armstrong, D. (1995). *Power and partnership in education: Parents, children and special educational needs.* New York: Routledge.

Arnold, M. S. (2002). Culture-sensitive family therapy. In J. Carlson & D. Kjos *Theories and strategies of family therapy* (pp. 19–40). Boston: Allyn & Bacon.

Arnowitz, T., & Morrison-Beedy, D. (2004). Resilience to risk-taking behaviors in impoverished African American girls: The role of mother-daughter connectedness. *Research in Nursing and Health, 27,* 29-39.

Aspy, C. B., Spy, C. B., Oman, R. F., Vesely, S. K., McLeroy, K., Rodine, S., & Marshall, L. (2004). Adolescent violence: The protective effects of youth assets. *Journal of Counseling and Development, 82,* 268–276.

Attneave, C. (1982). American Indians and Alaska Native families: Emigrants in their own homeland. In M. McGoldrick, J. K. Pearce, & J. Giordano (Eds.), *Ethnicity and family therapy* (pp. 55–82). New York: Guilford Press.

Attneave, C. L., & Verhulst, J. (1986). Teaching mental health professionals to see family strengths: Core network interventions in a hospital setting. In M. Karpel (Ed.), *Family resources: The hidden partner in family therapy* (pp. 259–271). New York: Guilford Press.

Austin, T. (1994). *Changing the view: Student-led parent conferences.* Portsmouth, NH: Heinemann.

Azpeitia, L. M., & Zahnd, W. F. (1991). Increasing couple intimacy using Virginia Satir's temperature reading. In B. J. Brothers (Ed.), *Virginia Satir: Foundational ideas* (pp. 83–101). New York: Haworth Press.

Baber, K. M., & Allen, K. R. (1992). *Women and families: Feminist reconstructions.* New York: Guilford Press.

Bagley, C. & Tremblay, P. (2000). Elevated rates of suicidal behavior in gay, lesbian, and bisexual youth. *Crisis, 21*(3) 111–117.

Bagnall, G. (1991). *Educating young drinkers.* New York: Routledge.

Bahr, M. W., et al. (2006). Creative problem solving for general education intervention teams. *Remedial and Special Education, 27,* 27–41.

Bailey, D. (1984). A triaxial model of the interdisciplinary team and group process. *Exceptional Children, 51,* 17–25.

Bailey, D. (1987). Collaborative goal-setting with families: Resolving differences in values and priorities for services. *Topics in Early Childhood Special Education, 7*(2), 59–71.

Bailey, D. B., Jr., et al. (1988). Inservice training in family assessment and goal-setting for early interventionists: Outcomes and issues. *Journal of the Division for Early Childhood, 12,* 126–136.

Bailey, D. B., Skinner, D., Rodriguez, D., Gut, D. & Correa, V. (1999). Awareness, use, and satisfaction with services for Latino parents of young children with disabilities. *Exceptional Children, 65,* 367–386.

Bailey, J. M., & Guskey, T. R. (2000) *Implementing student-led conferences.* Thousand Oaks, CA: Corwin.

Bainbridge, W. L., Lasley II, T. J. (2002). Demographics, diversity, and K-12 Accountability: The challenge of closing the achievement gap. *Education and Urban Society, 34,* 422–437.

Bandler, R., & Grinder, J. (1979). *Frogs into princes: Neurolinguistic programming.* Moab, UT: Real People Press.

Bandura, A. (1997). *Self-efficacy: The exercise of control.* New York: W. H. Freeman.

Bandura, A., Barbaranelli, C., Caprara, G. V., & Pastorelli, C. (2001). Self-efficacy beliefs as shapers of children's aspirations and career trajectories. *Child Development, 71,* 187–206.

Bank, S. P., & Kahn, M. D. (1975). Sisterhood-brotherhood is powerful: Sibling subsystems and family therapy. *Family Process, 14,* 311–337.

Bank, S. P., & Kahn, M. D. (1982). *The sibling bond.* New York: Basic Books.

Bardill, D. R. (1997). The relational systems model for family therapy: Living in the four realities. New York: Haworth Press.

Barlow, K. M., Thomson, E., Johnson, D., & Minns, R. A. (2005). Late neurologic and cognitive sequelae of inflicted traumatic brain injury in infancy. *Pediatrics, 116,* 174–185.

Barney, J. (1990). Stepfamilies: Second chance or second-rate? *Phi Delta Kappan, 72,* 144–148.

Barnhill, L. R., & Longo, D. (1978). Fixation and regression in the family life cycle. *Family Process, 17,* 469–478.

Barone, D. (Ed.). (1999). *Resilient children: Stories of poverty, drug exposure, and literacy development.* Newark, DE: International Reading Association and National Reading Conference.

Bartfeld, J. (2000). Child support and the postdivorce economic well-being of mothers, fathers, and children. *Demography, 37,* 203–213.

Barth, R. P., Berrick, J. D., Courtney, M., & Albert, V. (1994). *From child abuse to permanency planning.* New York: Aldine De Gruyder.

Barth, R., Berrick, J. D., & Gilbert, N. (Eds.). (1994). *Child welfare research review* (Vol. 1). New York: Columbia University Press.

Barth, R. P., & Berry, M. (1988). *Adoption and disruption: Rates, risks, and responses.* New York: Aldine De Gruyter.

Barth, R. P., & Miller, J. M. (2000). Building effective post-adoption services: What is the empirical foundation? *Family Relations, 49,* 447–455.

Bates, C., & Wigtil, J. (1994). *Skill building activities for alcohol and drug education.* Boston: Jones & Bartlett.

Bateson, G. (1972). *Steps to an ecology of the mind.* New York: Ballantine Books.

Bauer, A.M., & Shea, T. M. (2003). *Parents and schools: Creating a successful partnership for students with special needs.* Upper Saddle River, NJ: Pearson Education.

Baumeister, R., & Leary, M. (1995). The need to belong: Desire for interpersonal attachments as a fundamental human motivation. *Psychological Bulletin, 117,* 497–529.

Beattie, M. (1987). *Codependent no more.* New York: Harper/Hazelden.

Beavers, R., & Hampson, R. B. (2000). The Beavers systems model of family functioning. *Journal of Family Therapy, 22*(2) 128–143.

Beck, V. (1994). "Opportunity plus": A school and community based tutorial program for elementary students. *Elementary School Guidance and Counseling, 29,* 156–159.

Becker, B. E., & Luthar, S. S. (2002). Social-emotional factors affecting achievement outcomes among disadvantaged students: Closing the achievement gap. *Educational Psychologist, 37*(4), 197–214.

Beckman, P. J. (1983). Influence of selected child characteristics on stress in families of handicapped infants. *American Journal of Mental Deficiency, 88,* 150–156.

Beers, S. R., & DeBellis, M. D. (2004). Neuropsychological function in children with maltreatment-related posttraumatic stress disorder. In C. M. Shore (Ed.). *The many faces of childhood: Diversity in development* (pp. 167–170). Boston, MA: Pearson.

Belisto, L., Ryan, B. A., & Brophy, K. (2005). Using behavioral and academic indicators in the classroom to screen for at-risk status. *Psychology in the Schools, 42,* 151–158.

Belsey, B . (2004). *Cyberbullying.ca.* Retrieved July 31, 2004, from www.cyberbullying.ca

Bemak, F. (2005). Reflections on multiculturalism, social justice, and empowerment groups for academic success: A critical discourse for contemporary schools. *Professional School Counseling, 8,* 401–406.

Benard, B. (August, 1995). *Fostering resilience in children and youth.* Retrieved June 23, 2000, from www.parenthoodweb.com/Library/ERIC Resilience Children and youth.htm

Benard, B. (2004). Resiliency: What we have learned. San Francisco, CA: WestEd.

Benedek, E. P., & Brown, C. F. (1995). *How to help your child overcome your divorce.* Washington, DC: American Psychiatric Press.

Benne, K. D., & Sheats, P. (1948). Functional roles of group members. *Journal of Social Issues, 2,* 42–47.

Bennett, C. I. (1990). *Comprehensive multicultural education: Theory and practice.* Boston: Allyn & Bacon.

Bennett, F. (1982). The pediatrician and the interdisciplinary process. *Exceptional Children, 48,* 306–314.

Benshoff, J. J., & Janikowski, T. P. (2000). *The rehabilitation model of substance abuse counseling.* Belmont, CA: Brooks-Cole/Thomson.

Benson, B. P., & Barnett, S. P. (2005). *Student-led conferencing using showcase portfolios.* Thousand Oaks, CA: Corwin.

Benson, P. L. (1996). *Developmental assets among Minneapolis youth: The urgency of promoting healthy community.* Minneapolis, MN: Search Institute.

Benson, P. L., Galbraith, J., & Espeland, P. (1998) *What kids need to succeed.* Minneapolis, MN: Free Spirit.

Bentovim, A. (2002). Preventing sexually abused young people from becoming abusers, and treating the victimization experiences of young people who offend sexually. *Child Abuse and Neglect, 26,* 661–678.

Berardo, F. M. (1980). Decade preview: Some trends and directions for family research and theory in the 1980s. *Journal of Marriage and the Family, 42,* 723–728.

Berger, A. (1985). Characteristics of abusing families. In L. L'Abate (Ed.), *The handbook of family psychology and therapy* (Vol. 2, pp. 900–936). Homewood, IL: Dorsey Press.

Berger, E. H. (2003). *Parents as partners in education: Families and schools working together* (6th ed.). Englewoood Cliffs, NJ: Prentice Hall.

Berger, M. (1984a). Social network interventions for families that have a handicapped child. In J. C. Hansen & E. I. Coppersmith (Eds.), *Families with handicapped members* (pp. 127–136). Rockville, MD: Aspen.

Bergquist, K. I. (2003). Exploring the impact of birth country travel on Korean adoptees. *Journal of Family Social Work, 7*(4), 45–61.

Berman, W. H., & Turk, D. C. (1981). Adaptation to divorce: Problems and coping strategies. *Journal of Marriage and the Family, 27,* 179–189.

Bernheimer, L. P, Weisner, T. S., & Lowe, E. D. (2003). Impact of children with troubles on working poor families: Mixed-method and experimental evidence. *Mental Retardation, 41,* 403–419.

Bernstein, J., & Watson, M. (1997). Children and youth who are targets of bullying: A victim pattern. *Journal of Interpersonal Violence, 12,* 483–498.

Bevin, T. (2001). Parenting in Cuban American families. In N. B. Webb (Ed.), *Culturally diverse parent-child and family relationship* (pp. 181–201). New York: Columbia University Press.

Billingsley, A. (1992). *Climbing Jacob's ladder: The enduring legacy of African-American families.* New York: Simon and Schuster.

Birenbaum, A. (2002). Poverty, welfare reform, and disproportionate rates of disability among children. *Mental Retardation, 40,* 212–218.

Bitter, J. (1993). Satir's parts party with couples. In T. S. Nelson & T. S. Trepper (Eds.), *101 interventions in family therapy* (pp. 132–136). New York: Haworth Press.

Bitter, J. R., Roberts, A., & Sonstegard, M. A. (2002). Adlerian Family Therapy. In J. Carlson & D. Kjos (Eds.). *Theories and Strategies of family therapy* (pp. 41–79). Boston: Allyn & Bacon.

Björck-Åkesson, E., & Granlund, M. (1995). Family involvement in assessment and intervention: Perceptions of professionals and parents in Sweden. *Exceptional Children, 61,* 520–535.

Blacher, J. (1984). Sequential stages of parental adjustment to the birth of a child with handicaps: Fact or artifact? *Mental Retardation, 22*(2), 55–68.

Blacher, J., Lopez, S., Shapiro, J., & Fusco, J. (1997) Contributions to depression in Latina mothers with and without children with retardation: Implications for caregiving. *Family Relations, 46,* 325–334.

Black, L., & Jackson, V. (2005). Families of African origin: An overview. In M. McGoldrick, J. Giordano, & N. Garcia-Preto (Eds.), *Ethnicity and family therapy* (3rd ed., pp. 77–86). New York: Guilford Press.

Blacker, L. (1999). The launching phase of the life cycle. In B. Carter & M. McGoldrick (Eds.). *The expanded family life cycle: Individual, family, and social perspectives* (3rd ed., pp. 287–306). Boston: Allyn & Bacon.

Blanchard, K., Lacinak, T. H., Thompkins, C., & Ballard, J. (2002). *Whale done! The power of positive relationships.* New York: Free Press.

Blue-Banning, M., Summers, J. A., Frankland, H. C., Nelson, L. L., & Beegle, G. (2004). Dimensions of family and professional partnerships: Constructive guidelines for collaboration. *Exceptional Children, 70,* 167–184.

Blumberg, B. D., Lewis, M. J., & Susman, E. J. (1984). Adolescence: A time of transition. In M. Eisenberg, L. Sutkin, & M. Jansen (Eds.), *Chronic illness and disability through the life span: Effects on self and family* (pp. 133–149). New York: Springer.

Boettcher, M., Koegel, R. L., McNerney, E. K., & Koegel, L. K. (2003). A family-centered prevention approach to PBS in a time of crisis. *Journal of Positive Behavior Interventions, 5*(1), 55–59.

Bogolub, E. B. (1995). *Helping families through divorce: An eclectic approach.* New York: Springer.

Bolger, K. E., & Patterson, C. J. (2003). Sequelae of child maltreatment: Vulnerability and resilience. In

S. Luthar (Ed.). *Resilience and vulnerability: Adaptation in the context of childhood adversities* (pp. 156–181). Cambridge, UK: Cambridge University Press.

Bolman, L. G. & Deal, T. (2003). *Reframing organizations: Artistry, choice, and leadership* (3rd ed.). San Francisco: JosseyBass.

Bonnier, C., Nassogne, M., Saint-Martin, C., Mesples, B., Kadhim, H., & Sebire, G. (2003). Neuroimaging of intraparenchymal lesions predicts outcome in shaken baby syndrome. *Pediatrics, 112,* 808–814.

Booth, A., & Dunn, J. F. (Eds.). (1996). *Family-school links: How do they affect educational outcomes?* Mahwah, NJ: Erlbaum.

Borders, L. D, Penny, J. M., & Portnoy, F. (2000). Adult adoptees and their friends: Current functioning and psychosocial well-being. *Family Relations, 49,* 407–418.

Boswell, J. (1998). *The kindness of strangers: The abandonment of children in Western Europe from late antiquity to the Renaissance.* Chicago: University of Chicago Press.

Bosworth, K., & Earthman, E. (2002). From theory to practice: School leaders' perspectives on resiliency. *Journal of Clinical Psychology, 58,* 299–306.

Boszormenyi-Nagy, I., & Spark, G. M. (1973). *Invisible loyalties.* New York: Harper & Row.

Bowen, M. (1966). The use of family theory in clinical practice. *Comprehensive Psychiatry, 7,* 345–374.

Bowen, M. (1976). Theory in the practice of psychotherapy. In P. J. Guerin, Jr. (Ed.), *Family therapy: Theory and practice* (pp. 42–90). New York: Gardner Press.

Bowen, M. (1978). *Family therapy in clinical practice.* Northvale, NJ: Jason Aronson.

Bowen, M. (1985). *Family therapy in clinical practice* (3rd ed.). Northvale, NJ: Jason Aronson.

Bowlby, J. (1988). Developmental psychiatry comes of age. *American Journal of Psychiatry, 145,* 1–10.

Boyd-Franklin, N. (1989). *Black families in therapy: Multisystems approach.* New York: Guilford Press.

Boyd-Franklin, N. (2003). *Black families in therapy: Understanding the African American experience* (2nd ed.). New York: Guilford Press.

Boyd-Franklin, N., & Bry, B. H. (2000). *Reaching out in family therapy: Home-based, school, and community interventions.* New York: Guilford.

Bradley, C., Johnson, P., Rawls, G., & Dodson-Sims, A. (2005) School counselors collaborating with African American parents. *Professional School Counseling, 8,* 424–427.

Bradley, D. F., & Switlick, D. M. (1997). From isolation to cooperation in teaching. In D. F. Bradley, M. E. King-Sears, & D. M. Tessier-Switlick (Eds.), *Teaching students in inclusive settings: From theory to practice* (pp. 109–128). Boston: Allyn & Bacon.

Bradley, L. J., Gould, L. J., & Hendricks, C. B. (2004). Using innovative techniques for counseling children and adolescents. In A. Vernon (Ed.). *Counseling children and adolescents* (3rd ed., pp. 75-110). Denver: Love.

Bramlett, M. D., & Mosher, W. D. (2002). *Cohabitation, marriage, divorce, and remarriage in the United States*. Hyattsville, MD: National Center for Health Statistics. Vital Health Statistics Series 23, Number 22.

Braver, S. L., & Cookston, J. T. (2003). Controversies, clarifications, and consequences of divorce's legacy: Introduction to the special collection. *Family Relations, 52*, 314–317.

Brazelton, T. B. (1992). *Touchpoints: Your child's emotional and behavioral development*. Reading, MA: Addison-Wesley.

Brendtro, L., & Bacon, J. (1994). Youth empowerment and teamwork. In H. G. Garner & F. P. Orelove (Eds.), *Teamwork in human services: Models and applications across the life span* (pp. 55–71). Boston: Butterworth-Heinemann.

Brendtro, L., Brokenleg, M., & Van Bockern, S. (1990). *Reclaiming youth at risk: Our hope for the future*. Bloomington, IN: National Educational Service.

Brendtro, L., Brokenleg, M., & Van Bockern, S. (2002). *Reclaiming youth at risk: Our hope for the future* (Rev. ed.). Bloomington, IN: National Educational Service.

Breslau, N. (1982). Siblings of disabled children: Birth order and age-spacing effects. *Journal of Abnormal Child Psychology, 10*(1), 85–96.

Breulin, D. C., Schwartz, R. C., & Kune-Karrer, B. (1992). *Metaframeworks: Transcending the models of family therapy*. San Francisco: Jossey-Bass.

Briggs, M. H. (1997). *Building early intervention teams*. Gaithersburg, MD: Aspen.

Brody, E. M. (1974). Aging and family personality: A developmental view. *Family Process, 13*(1), 23–37.

Brody, G. H., & Stoneman, Z. (1983, September). *Contextual issues in the study of sibling socialization*. Paper presented at the National Institute on Child Health and Development Conference on Research on Families With Retarded Persons, Baltimore, MD.

Brodzinsky, D. M. (1990). A stress and coping model of adoption adjustment. In D. M. Brodzinsky & M. D. Schechter (Eds.), *The psychology of adoption* (pp. 3–24). New York: Oxford University Press.

Brodzinsky, D. M., Schechter, M. D., & Henig, R. M. (1992). *Being adopted: The lifelong search for self*. New York: Doubleday.

Brodzinsky, D. M., Smith, D. W., & Brodzinsky. A. B. (1998). *Children's adjustment to adoption: Developmental and clinical issues*. Thousand Oaks, CA: Sage.

Bronfenbrenner, U. (1977). Toward an experimental ecology of human development. *American Psychologist, 32*, 513–531.

Bronfenbrenner, U. (1979). *The ecology of human development*. Cambridge, MA: Harvard University Press.

Bronfenbrenner, U. (1986). Alienation and the four worlds of childhood. *Phi Delta Kappan, 67*, 430–436.

Bronfenbrenner, U. (1988). Interacting systems in human development. Research paradigms: Present and future. In N. Bolger, A. Caspi, G. Downey, & M. Moorehouse (Eds.), *Persons in context: Developmental processes* (pp. 25–49). Cambridge, MA: Cambridge University Press.

Bronfenbrenner, U., & Morris, P. A. (1998). The ecology of developmental processes. In W. Damon (editor-in-chief) & R. M. Lerner (vol. ed.), *Handbook of child psychology: v.1. Theoretical model of human development* (pp. 993–1028. New York: Wiley.

Brooks, C. S., & Rice, K. F. (1997). *Families in recovery: Coming full circle*. Baltimore, MD: Brookes.

Brooks, R. B., & Goldstein, S. (2001). *Raising resilient children: Fostering strength, hope, and optimism in your child*. NY: McGraw-Hill.

Brooks, R., & Goldstein, S. (2003). *Nurturing resilience in our children: Answers to the most important parenting questions*. New York: McGraw-Hill.

Brooks, R., & Goldstein, S. (2004). *The power of resilience: Achieving balance, confidence, and personal strength in your life*. New York: McGraw-Hill.

Brooks-McNamara, V., & Pederson, L. (2006). Practitioner inquiry: A method to advocate for systemic change. *Professional School Counseling, 9*, 257–260.

Brown, B., & Merritt, R. (2002). *No easy answers: The truth behind death to Columbine*. New York: Lantern Books.

Brown, F. H. (1989). The impact of death and serious illness on the family life cycle. In B. Carter & M. McGoldrick (Eds.), *The changing family life cycle: A framework for family therapy* (pp. 457–482). Boston: Allyn & Bacon.

Brown, J. H., D'Emidio-Caston, J., & Benard, B. (2001). *Resilience education*. Thousand Oaks, CA: Corwin Press.

Brown, R. & Evans, W. P. (2002). Extracurricular activity and ethnicity: Creating greater school connections among diverse student populations. *Urban Education, 37*, 41–58.

Brown, S., & Lewis, V. M. (2002). *The alcoholic family in recovery: A developmental model*. New York: Guilford.

Bryan, J. (2005). Fostering educational resilience and achievement in urban schools through school-family-community partnerships. *Professional School Counselors, 8*, 219–227.

Buck, G. H., Polloway, E. A., Smith-Thomas, A., & Cook, K. W. (2003). Prereferral intervention processes: A survey of state practices. *Exceptional Children, 69*(3), 349–360.

Burgess, E. W. (1926) The family as a unity of interacting personalities. *The Family, 7,* 3–9.

Burgess, E. W. (1969) *Personality and the social group* (reprint of the 1929 ed.). Freeport, NY: Books for Libraries Press.

Burke, P., & Cigno, K. (1996). *Support for families: Helping children with learning disabilities.* Brookfield, VT: Ashgate.

Burleson, B. R. (1994). Comforting messages: Significance, approaches, and effects. In B. R. Burleson, T. L. Albrecht, & I. G. Sarason (Eds.), *Communication of social support: Messages, interactions, relationships, and community* (pp. 3–28). Thousand Oaks, CA: Sage.

Burleson, B. R., Albrecht, T. L., & Sarason, I. G. (Eds.). (1994). *Communication of social support: Messages, interactions, relationships, and community.* Thousand Oaks, CA: Sage.

Burns, M. K., & Symington, T. (2002). A meta-analysis of prereferral intervention teams: Student and systemic outcomes. *Journal of School Psychology, 40,* 437–447.

Burrow, A. L., & Finley, G. E. (2004). Transracial, same-race adoptions, and the need for multiple measures of adolescent adjustment. *American Journal of Orthopsychiatry, 74,* 577–583.

Byers, P. (1992). The spiritual in the classroom. *Holistic Education Review, 5,* 6–11.

Byng-Hall, J. (1995). Creating a secure family base: Some implications of attachment theory for family therapy. *Family Process, 34,* 45–58.

Byrne, M., Edmundson, R., & Rankin, E. D. (2005). Symptom reduction and enhancement of psychosocial functioning utilizing a relational group treatment program for dependent/codependent population. *Alcoholism Treatment Quarterly, 23, 4,* 69–85.

Caine, R. N., & Caine, G. (1997). *Education on the edge of possibility.* Alexandria, VA: Association for Supervision and Curriculum Development.

Cameron, G., & Vanderwoerd, J. (1997). *Protecting children and supporting families: Promising programs and organizational realities.* Hawthorne, NY: Aldine.

Campbell, C. (1993). Strategies for reducing parent resistance to consultation in the schools. *Elementary School Guidance and Counseling, 28,* 83–91.

Carney, I., & Gamel-McCormick, M. (1996). Working with families. In F. P. Orelove & D. Sobsey (Eds.), *Educating children with multiple disabilities: A transdisciplinary approach* (3rd ed., pp. 451–476). Baltimore, MD: Paul H. Brookes.

Carroll, C. (Ed.). (1970). *Adoption in eastern Oceania.* Honolulu: University of Hawaii Press.

Carter, B. (1999). Becoming parents: The family with young children. In B. Carter and M McGoldrick (Eds.), *The expanded family life cycle: Individual, family, and social perspectives* (3rd ed., pp. 249–273). Boston: Allyn & Bacon.

Carter, B., & McGoldrick, M. (Eds.). (1989a). *The changing family life cycle: A framework for family therapy* (2nd ed.). Boston: Allyn & Bacon.

Carter, B., & McGoldrick, M. (1989b). Overview: The changing family life cycle—A framework for family therapy. In B. Carter & M. McGoldrick (Eds.), *The changing family life cycle: A framework for family therapy* (2nd ed., pp. 3–28). Boston: Allyn & Bacon.

Carter, B. & McGoldrick, M. (Eds.). (1999a). The divorce cycle: A major variation in the American family life cycle. In B. Carter and M McGoldrick (Eds.), *The expanded family life cycle: Individual, family, and social perspectives* (3rd ed., pp. 373–380). Boston: Allyn & Bacon.

Carter, B. & McGoldrick, M. (Eds.). (1999b). *The expanded family life cycle: Individual, family, and social perspectives* (3rd ed.). Boston: Allyn & Bacon.

Carter, B. & McGoldrick, M. (Eds.). (1999c). Overview: The expanded family life cycle—individual, family, and social perspectives. In B. Carter & M. McGoldrick (Eds.), *The expanded family life cycle: Individual, family, and social perspectives* (3rd ed., pp. 1–26). Boston: Allyn & Bacon.

Carter, B., & Peters, J. (1997). *Love, honor and negotiate: Building partnerships that last a lifetime.* New York: Pocket Books.

Carter, E. A., & McGoldrick, M. (1980). *The family life cycle: A framework for family therapy.* New York: Gardner Press.

Carter, J., & Sugai, G. (1989). Survey on prereferral practices: Responses from state departments of education. *Exceptional Children, 55,* 298–302.

Carter, L. S., Weithorn, L. A., Behrman, R. E. (Winter 1999). Domestic violence and children and youth: Analysis and recommendations. *Domestic Violence And Children And Youth, 9*(3), 3-19.

Carter, R. T. (1995). *The influence of race and racial identity in psychotherapy: Toward a racially inclusive model.* New York: Wiley.

Carter, R. T. (2005). *Handbook of racial-cultural psychology and counseling, theory and research.* Hoboken, NJ: Wiley.

Casper, V., & Schultz, S. R. (1999). *Gay parents/ straight schools: Building communication and trust.* New York: Teachers College Press.

Caspi, A., Elder, G. H., Jr., & Herbeno, E. S. (1990). Childhood personality and the prediction of life-course patterns. In L. N. Robbins & McRutter (Eds.), *Straight and devious pathways from childhood to adulthood* (pp. 13–35). Cambridge, UK: Cambridge University Press.

Chalk, R., Gibbons, A., & Scarupa, H. J. (May, 2002). *Child trends research brief: The multiple dimensions of child abuse and neglect: New insights into an old problem.* Washington, DC: Child Trends.

Chase, A. (2001, July 9). *Violent reaction: What do teen killers have in common? These Times.* Retrieved September 28, 2005, from www.inthese-times.come/issue/25/16/chase2516.html

Chase-Lansdale, P. L., & Hetherington, E. M. (1990). The impact of divorce on life-span development: Short and long term effects. In P. B. Baltes, D. L. Featherman, & R. M. Lerner (Eds.), *Life span development and behavior* (Vol. 10, pp. 105–150). Hillsdale, NJ: Earlbaum.

Chen, D., & Miles, C. (2004). Working with families. In F. P. Orelove, D. Sobsey, & R. K. Silberman (Eds.), *Educating children with multiple disabilities: A collaborative approach* (4th ed., pp. 31–65). Baltimore: Paul H Brookes.

Cherlin, A. J. (2004). The deinstitutionalization of American marriage. *Journal of Marriage and Family, 66,* 848–861.

Child Welfare Information Gateway. (2006a). *Long-term consequences of child abuse and neglect.* Washington, DC: Children's Bureau. [www.child-welfare.gov/pubs/factsheets/long_term_conse-quences.cfm]

Child Welfare Information Gateway. (2006b). *Recognizing child abuse and neglect: Signs and symptoms.* Washington, DC: Children's Bureau. [www.childwelfare.gov/pubs/factsheets/signs.cfm]

Child Welfare Information Gateway. (2006c). *What is child abuse and neglect.* Washington, DC: Children's Bureau. [www.childwelfare.gov/pubs/factsheets/whatiscan.cfm]

Child Welfare Information Gateway. (July, 2005). *Foster care: Numbers and trends.* Washington, DC: Author. [www.childwelfare.gov/pubs/factsheets/foster.cfm]

Child Welfare Information Gateway. (December, 2004). *Adoption disruption and dissolution: Numbers and trends.* Washington, DC: Author. [www.childwelfare.gov/pubs/s_disrup.cfm]

Child Witness to Violence Project, (n.d.). Retrieved September 28, 2005, from Boston Medical Pediatric Center www.childwitnesstoviolence.org/care_givers/for caregivers facts.html

Children's Bureau of the Administration for Children and Families (2004). *Child maltreatment 2004.* Washington, DC: U.S. Department of Health and Human Services. [www.acf.hhs.gov/programs/cb/publications/cm04]

Chopra, R. V., Sandoval-Lucero, E., Aragon, L., Bernal, C., De Balderas, H. B., & Carroll, D. (2004). The paraprofessional role of connector. *Remedial and special education, 25*(4), 219–231

Christenbury, L., Beale, A. V., & Patch, S. S. (1996). Interactive bibliocounseling: Recent fiction and nonfiction for adolescents and their counselors. *The School Counselor, 44*(2), 133–145.

Christenson, S. L. (2004). The family-school partnership: An opportunity to promote the learning competence of all students. *School Psychology Review, 33*(1), 83–104.

Cicchetti, D. (2003). Foreword. In S. S. Luthar (Ed.), *Resilience and vulnerability: Adaptation in the context of childhood adversities* (pp. ix–xxiii). New York: Cambridge University Press.

Cicchetti, D., & Toth, S. L. (2005). Child maltreatment. *Annual Review of Clinical Psychology, 1,* 409–438.

Cicirelli, V. G. (1972). The effect of sibling relationships on concept learning of young children taught by child teachers. *Child Development, 43,* 282–287.

Cicirelli, V. G. (1995). *Sibling relationships across the life span.* New York: Plenum Press.

Clapton, G. (1997). Birth fathers, the adoption process, and fatherhood. *Adoption and Fostering, 21*(1), 29–36.

Clarke-Stewart, K., Vandell, D., McCartney, K., Owen, M., & Booth, C. (2000). Effects of parent separation and divorce on very young children. *Journal of Family Psychology, 14,* 304–326.

Cleveland, D. W., & Miller, N. (1977). Attitudes and life commitments of older siblings of mentally retarded adults: An exploratory study. *Mental Retardation, 15*(3), 38–41.

Cloninger, C, G, (2004). Designing collaborative educational services. In F. Orelove, D. Sobsey, & R. K. Silberman (Eds.). Educating Children with multiple disabilities: A collaborative approach (4th ed.; pp. 1-29). Baltimore: Paul H Brookes.

Cloud, R. N., McKiernan, P., & Cooper, L. (2003). Controlled drinking as an appropriate treatment goal: A critique of current approaches. *Alcoholism Treatment Quarterly, 21*(4), 67–82.

Coates, D. L. (1990). Social network analysis as mental health intervention with African-American adolescents. In F. C. Serafica, A. I. Schwebel, R. K. Russell, P. D. Isaac, & L. B. Myers (Eds.), *Mental health of ethnic minorities* (pp. 230–253). New York: Praeger.

Cobb, S. (1976). Social support as a moderator of life stress. *Psychosomatic Medicine, 38,* 301–314.

Coburn, J., & Nelson, S. (1989). *Teachers do make a difference: What Indian graduates say about their school experience.* ERIC Document Reproduction Service No. ED 306 071.

Cohen, R. (1969). Conceptual styles, culture conflict, and nonverbal tests of intelligence. *American Anthropologist, 71,* 828–856.

Colapinto, J. (1991). Structural family therapy. In A. S. Gurman & D. P. Kniskern (Eds.), *Handbook of family therapy* (Vol. 2, pp. 417–443). New York: Brunner/Mazel.

Colapinto, J. (1982). Structural family therapy. In A. Horne & B. Ohlsen (Eds.), *Family counseling and therapy* (pp. 112–140). Itasca, IL: Peacock.

Coleman, J. S. (1987). Families and schools. *Educational Researcher, 16*(6), 32–38.

Coltrane, S., & Adams, M. (2003). The social construction of the divorce "problem": Morality, child victims, and the politics of gender. *Family Relations, 52,* 363–372.

Combrinck-Graham, L. (1983). The family life cycle and families with young children. In J. Hansen & H. Liddle (Eds.), *Clinical implications of the family life cycle* (pp. 35–53). Rockville, MD: Aspen.

Comer, J. P. (1996). *Rallying the whole village: The Comer process for reforming education.* New York: Teachers College Press.

Comer, J. P. (2001). Schools that develop children. *The American Prospect, 12*(7), 30–35.

Comer, J. P., & Haynes, N. M. (1991). Parent involvement in schools: An ecological

Coppersmith, E. I. (1983). The family and public service systems: An assessment method. In J. Hansen & E. Keene (Eds.), *Diagnosis and assessment in family therapy* (pp. 83–100). Rockville, MD: Aspen.

Corcoran, J. (2000). *Evidence-based social work practice with families: A lifespan approach.* New York: Springer.

Corcoran, J. (2003). *Clinical applications of evidence-based family interventions.* New York: Oxford University Press.

Corey, G. (1996). *Theory and practice of counseling and psychotherapy* (5th ed.). New York: Brooks/Cole.

Corey, G. (2005). *Theory and practice of counseling and psychotherapy* (7th ed.). New York: Brooks/Cole.

Courtnage, L., & Smith-Davis, J. (1987). Interdisciplinary team training: A national survey of special education teacher training programs. *Exceptional Children, 53,* 451–458.

Cowan, P. A., Cowan, C. P., & Schulz, M. S. (1996). Thinking about risk and resilience in families. In E. M. Hetherington & E. A. Blechman, (Eds.), *Stress, coping, and resiliency in children and families* (pp. 1–38). Mahwah, NJ: Erlbaum.

Cuban, L. (1989). The "at-risk" label and the problem of urban school reform. *Phi Delta Kappan, 70,* 780–784.

Cullen, J. C., MacLeod, J. A., Williams, P. D., & Williams, A. R. (1991). Coping, satisfaction, and the life cycle in families with mentally retarded persons. *Issues in Comprehensive Pediatric Nursing, 14,* 193–207.

Cummins, J. (1989). A theoretical framework for bilingual special education. *Exceptional Children, 56,* 111–119.

Cusinato, M. (1994). Parenting over the family life cycle. In L. L'Abate (Ed.), *Handbook of developmental family psychology and psychopathology* (pp. 83–115). New York: Wiley.

Cuskelly, M., & Gunn, P. (2003). Sibling relationships of children with Down syndrome: Perspectives of mothers, fathers, and siblings. *American Journal on Mental Retardations, 108,* 234–244.

Daly, K. (1988). Reshaped parenthood identity: The transition to adoptive parenthood. *Journal of Contemporary Ethnography, 17*(1), 40–66.

Daniels-Mohring, D. (1986). *Sibling relationships with an older sibling as identified patient.* Unpublished manuscript, Georgia State University, Atlanta.

Daro et al. (1990). *Reducing Child Abuse 20% by 1990: Preliminary Assessment. Working Paper Number 843.* Chicago: National Committee for Prevention of Child Abuse.

Day, R., Lewis, C., O'Brien, M., & Lamb, M. (2005). Fatherhood and father involvement: Emerging constructs and theoretical orientations. In V. Bengston, A. Acock, K. Allen, P. Dilworth-Anderson, & D. Klein (Eds.), *Sourcebook of family theory and research* (pp. 341–351). Thousand Oaks, CA: Sage.

DePaepe, P., Garrison-Kane, J., Doelling, J. (2005). Supporting students with health needs in schools. In T. M. Skrtic, K. R. Harris, & J. G. Shriner (Eds.), *Special education policy and practice: Accountability, instruction, and social challenges* (pp. 432–470). Denver: Love.

Darling, R. B. (1991). Initial and continuing adaptation to the birth of a disabled child. In M. Seligman (Ed.), *The family with a handicapped child* (2nd ed., pp. 55–89). Boston: Allyn & Bacon.

D'Augelli, A. R., Grossman, A. H., & Starks, M. T. (2005). Parents' awareness of lesbian, gay, and bisexual youths' sexual orientation. *Journal of Marriage and Family, 67,* 474–482.

D'Augelli, A. R., Pilkington, N. W., & Hershberger, S. L. (2002). Incidence and mental health impact of sexual orientation victimization of lesbian, gay, and bisexual youths in high school. *School Psychology Quarterly, 17,* 148–167.

Dave Thomas Foundation for Adoption (in cooperation with) The Evan B. Donaldson Adoption Institute. (2002, June). *National adoption attitudes survey: Research report.* Dublin, OH: Author, Harris Interactive Market Research. [www.adoptioninstitute.org/survey/Adoption_Attitudes_Survey.pdf]

Davis, L. (1987). *Rivers of pain, bridges of hope.* Hong Kong: Writers' and Publishers' Cooperative.

Dawson, C. A. (2003, Winter). A study of the effectiveness of Life Space Interviewing Intervention for students identified with emotional disturbance. *Reclaiming Children And Youth, 11*(4), 223–230.

Deater-Deckard, K., Petrill, S. A., & Wilkerson, B. (2001). The Northeast-Northwest collaborative adoption project: Identifying family environmental influences on cognitive and social development. *Marriage and Family Review, 33(2/3)* 157–178.

Deegan, P. E. (1996). *Recovery and the conspiracy of hope.* Retrieved December 2, 2003, from http://www.bu.edu/resilience/examples/deegan-recovery-hope.pdf

Delaney, A. J. (Ed.). (1979). *Black task force report: Project on ethnicity.* New York: Family Service Association of America.

del Carmen, R. (1990). Assessment of Asian-Americans for family therapy. In F. C. Serafica, A. I. Schwebel, R. K. Russell, P. D. Isaac, & L. B. Myers (Eds.), *Mental health of ethnic minorities* (pp. 24–68). New York: Praeger.

Delsing, M. J. M. H., van Aken, M. A. G.; Oud, J. H. L.; De Bruyn, E. E. J.; Scholte, R. H. J. (2005). Family loyalty and adolescent problem behavior: The validity of the family group effect. *Journal of Research on Adolescence, 15(2)* p.127–150.

Demick, J., & Wapner, S. (1988). Open and closed adoption: A developmental conceptualization. *Family Process, 27,* 229–249.

Dennis, R. E., & Giangreco, M. F. (1996). Creating conversation: Reflections on cultural sensitivity in family interviewing. *Exceptional Children, 63,* 103–116.

De Voe, J.F., Peter, K., Kaufman, P., Miller, A., Noonan, M., Snyder, T.D., & Burn, K. (2004). *Indicators of school crime and safety: 2004 (NCES 2005-002/NCJ 205290).* U.S. Departments of Education and Justice. Washington, D.C.: U.S. Government Printing Office.

Dienhart, A., & Daly, K. (1997). Men and women cocreating father involvement in a nongeneratative culture. In A. J. Hawkins & D. C. Dollahite (Eds.), *Generative fathering: Beyond deficit perspectives* (pp. 147-164). Thousand Oaks, CA: Sage.

Diffily, D. (2004). *Teachers and families working together.* Boston: Allyn & Bacon.

Dodson, L. S. (1991). Virginia Satir's process of change. In B. J. Brothers (Ed.), *Virginia Satir: Foundational ideas* (pp. 119–142). New York: Haworth Press.

Dong, M., Anda, R. F., Dube, S. R., Giles, W. H., & Felitti, V. J. (2003). The relationship of exposure to childhood sexual abuse to other forms of abuse, neglect, and household dysfunction during childhood. *Child Abuse and Neglect, 27,* 625–639.

Donovan, M. S., & Cross, C. T., *Minority Students in Special and Gifted Education.* Washington, DC: National Academies Press.

Drame, E. R. (2002). Sociocultural context effects on teachers' readiness to refer for learning disabilities. *Exceptional Children, 69,* 41–53.

Dryfoos, J. G. (1994). *Full-service schools: A revolution in health and social services for children, youth, and families.* San Francisco: Jossey-Bass.

Dube, J. (1999). High school hell. *ABC NEWS.com,* April 25, 1999, p. 1.

Duke, D. (2004). *The challenges of educational change.* Boston: Pearson.

Dulfano, C. (1992). *Families, alcoholism, & recovery.* San Francisco: Jossey-Bass.

Dunlap, W. R., & Hollinsworth, J. S. (1977). How does a handicapped child affect the family? Implications for practitioners. *The Family Coordinator, 26,* 286–293.

Dunn, J., & Kendrick, C. (1982). *Siblings.* Cambridge. MA: Harvard University Press.

Dunn, N. A., & Baker, S. B. (2002). Readiness to serve students with disabilities: A survey of elementary school counselors. *Professional School Counseling, 5,* 277–284.

Dunst, C. J., (2002). Family-centered practices: Birth through high school. *Journal of Special Education, 36(3),* 139–147.

Dunst, C. J., & Deal, A. G. (1994). A family-centered approach to developing individualized family support plans. In C. J. Dunst, C. M. Trivette, & A. G. Deal (Eds.), *Supporting and strengthening families: Vol. 1. Methods, strategies and practices* (pp. 73–88). Cambridge, MA: Brookline Books.

Dunst, C. J., Trivette, C. M., & Deal, A. G. (1988). *Enabling and empowering families: Principles and guidelines.* Cambridge, MA: Brookline Books.

Dunst, C. J., Trivette, C. M., & Deal, A. G. (1994a). Enabling and empowering families. In C. J. Dunst, C. M. Trivette, & A. G. Deal (Eds.), *Supporting and strengthening families: Vol. 1. Methods, strategies and practices* (pp. 2–11). Cambridge, MA: Brookline Books.

Dunst, C. J., Trivette, C. M., & Deal, A. G. (1994b). Resource-based family-centered intervention practices. In C. J. Dunst, C. M. Trivette, & A. G. Deal (Eds.), *Supporting and strengthening families: Vol. 1. Methods, strategies and practices (pp. 140–151).* Cambridge, MA: Brookline Books.

Dunst, C. J., Trivette, C. M., & Deal, A. G. (Eds.). (1994c). *Supporting and strengthening families: Vol. 1. Methods, strategies and practices.* Cambridge, MA: Brookline Books.

Dunst, C. J., Trivette, C. M., & Cross, A. H. (1986). Mediating influences of social support: Personal, family, and child outcomes. *American Journal of Mental Deficiency, 90,* 403–417.

Duvall, E. M. (1977). *Marriage and family development* (5th ed.). Philadelphia, PA: Lippincott.

Dyson, L., & Fewell, R. R. (1985). Stress and adaptation in parents of young handicapped and nonhandicapped children: A comparative study. *Journal of the Division for Early Childhood, 10,* 25–34.

Dyson, L., & Fewell, R. (1989). The self-concept of siblings of handicapped children: A comparison. *Journal of Early Intervention, 13,* 230–238.

Dyson, L.L. (1998). A support program for siblings of children with disabilities: What siblings learn and what they like. *Psychology in the Schools, 35,* 57–65.

Eckenrode, J., Powers, J., & Garbarino, J. (1997). Youth in trouble are youth who have been hurt. In J. Garbarino & J. Eckenrode (Eds.), *Understanding abusive families* (pp. 166–193). San Francisco: Jossey-Bass.

Edleson, J.L. (1999). Children and youth's witnessing of adult domestic violence. *Journal of Interpersonal Violence, 14,* 839–870.

Edmond, T., Auslander, W., Elize, D., & Bowland, S. (2006). Signs of resilience in sexually abused adolescent girls in the foster care system. *Journal of Child Sexual Abuse, 15*(1), 1–28.

Edwards, D. L., & Mullis, F. (2003). Classroom meetings: Encouraging a climate of cooperation. *Professional School Counseling, 7,* 20–28.

Egeland, B. (1993). A history of abuse is a major risk factor for abusing the next generation. In R. J. Gelles & D. R. Loseke (Eds.), *Current controversies on family violence* (pp. 197–208). Newbury Park, CA: Sage.

Eheart, B. K., & Ciccone, J. (1982). Special needs of low-income mothers of developmentally delayed children. *American Journal of Mental Deficiency, 87,* 26–33.

Emery, R. E., Sbarra, D., & Grover, T. (2005). Divorce mediation: Research and reflections. *Family Court Review, 43*(1) 22–37.

Entwisle, D. R. (1994). Subcultural diversity in American families. In L. L'Abate (Ed.), *Handbook of developmental family psychology and psychopathology* (pp. 132–156). New York: Wiley.

Epstein, J. L. (1995). School/family/community partnerships: Caring for the children we share. *Phi Delta Kappan, 76,* 701–712.

Epstein, J. L. (1996). Perspectives and previews on research and policy for school, family, and community partnerships. In A. Booth & J. F. Dunn (Eds.), *Family-school links: How do they affect educational outcomes?* (pp. 209–246). Mahwah, NJ: Erlbaum.

Epstein, J. L. (2001). *School, family, and community partnerships: Preparing educators and improving schools.* Boulder, CO: Westview Press.

Epstein, M. H., Rudolph, S., & Epstein, A. A. (2000). Strengths-based assessment. *Teaching Exceptional Children, 32*(6), 50–54.

Epstein, M. H., & Sharma, J. M. (1998). *Behavioral and emotional rating scale: A strength-based approach to assessment.* Austin, TX: Pro-Ed.

Epstein, N. B., Ryan, C. E., Bishop, D. S., Miller, I. W., & Keitner, G. I. (2003). The McMaster model: A view of healthy family functioning. In F. Walsh (Ed.), *Normal family processes: Growing diversity and complexity* (3rd ed., pp. 582–607). New York: Guilford.

Erb, T. O. (1995). Teamwork in middle school education. In H. G. Garner (Ed.), *Teamwork models and experience in education* (pp. 175–198). Boston: Allyn & Bacon.

Erich, S., Leung, P., Kindle, P., & Carter, S. (2005). Gay and lesbian adoptive families: An exploratory study of family functioning, adoptive child's behavior, and familial support networks. *Journal of Family Social Work, 9,* 17–32.

Ericson, N. (2001). Addressing the problem of juvenile bullying. *OJJDP Fact Sheet #27.* U.S. Department of Justice, Office of Justice Programs, Office of Juvenile Justice and Delinquency Prevention, Washington, DC: U.S. Printing Office.

Erikson, E. H. (1959). *Identity, youth, and crisis.* New York, NY: W. W. Norton.

Erikson, E. (1963). *Childhood and society.* New York: Norton.

Ernst, J. W. (2001). Community-level factors and child maltreatment in a suburban county. *Social Work Research, 25*(3) 133–142.

Ethier, L. S., Lemelin, J-P, & Lacharite, C. (2004). A longitudinal study of the effects of chronic maltreatment on children's behavioral and emotional problems. *Child Abuse and Neglect, 28,* 1265–1278.

Evan B. Donaldson Adoption Institute. (2004, November) *What's working for children: A policy study of adoption stability and termination.* New York: Author. [http://www.adoptioninstitute.org/publications/Disruption_Report.pdf]

Evans, E., Spear, S. E., Huang, Y-C., & Hser, H-I. (2006). Outcomes of drug and alcohol treatment programs among American Indians in California. *American Journal of Public Health, 96,* 889–896.

Falicov, C. J. (1999). The Latino family life cycle. In B. Carter and M McGoldrick (Eds.), *The expanded family life cycle: Individual, family, and social perspectives* (3rd ed., pp. 141-152). Boston: Allyn & Bacon.

Falik, L. H. (1995). Family patterns of reaction to a child with a learning disability: A mediational perspective. *Journal of Learning Disabilities, 28,* 335–341.

Family Pediatrics. (2003). Report of the task force on the family. *Pediatrics, 111,* 1541–1571.

Farrington, D. (1993). Understanding and preventing bullying. In M. Tonry (Ed.), *Crime and justice: A review of research, Vol. 17.* Chicago: University of Chicago Press.

Fashola, O. S. (2003). Developing the talents of African American male students during the nonschool hours. *Urban Education, 38,* 398–430.

Featherstone, H. (1980). *A difference in the family.* New York: Basics Books.

Feldman, L. B. (1992). *Integrating individual and family therapy*. New York: Brunner/Mazel.

Fenell, D. L., & Weinhold, B. K. (2003). *Counseling families: An introduction to marriage and family therapy*. Denver: Love.

Ferguson, P. M. (2001) Mapping the family: Disability studies and the exploration of parental response to disability. In G. L. Albrecht, K. D. Seelman, & M. Bury (Eds.), *Handbook of disability study* (pp. 373–395). Thousand Oaks, CA: Sage.

Ferrari, M. (1984). Chronic illness: Psychosocial effects on siblings of chronically ill boys. *Journal of Child Psychology and Psychiatry, 25,* 459–476.

Ferreiro, B. (1990). Presumption of joint custody: A family policy dilemma. *Family Relations, 39,* 420–426.

Festinger, T. (2002). After adoption: Dissolution or permanence? *Child Welfare, 81,* 515–533.

Field, S. (1996). Self-determination instructional strategies for youth with learning disabilities. *Journal of Learning Disabilities, 29,* 40–52.

Figley, C. R., & McCubbin, H. I. (Eds.). (1983). *Stress and the family: Vol. 2. Coping with catastrophe*. New York: Brunner/Mazel.

Fine, M. J., & Carlson, C. (Eds.). (1992). *The handbook of family-school intervention: A systems perspective*. Boston: Allyn & Bacon.

Finkelstein, N., & Markoff, L. S. (2004). The women embracing life and living (WELL) project: Using the relational model to develop integrated systems of care for women with alcohol/drug use and mental health disorders with histories of violence. *Alcoholism Treatment Quarterly, 22, (3/4)* 63–80.

Fischgrund, J. E., Cohen, O. P., & Clarkson, R. L. (1987). Hearing-impaired children in black and Hispanic families. *Volta Review, 89*(5), 59–67.

Fisher, A. P. (2003a). A critique and portrayal of adoption in college textbooks and readers on families, 1998-2001. *Family Relations, 52*(2), 154–160.

Fisher, A. P. (2003b). Still "not quite as good as having your own?" Toward a sociology of adoption. *Annual Review of Sociology, 29,* 335–361.

Fisher, B. A. (1980). *Small group decision making* (2nd ed.). New York: McGraw-Hill.

Fisher, D., & Frey, N. (Eds.). (2003). *Inclusive urban schools*. Baltimore, MD: Brookes.

Fishman, H. C. (1993). *Intensive Structural Therapy: Treating families in their social context*. New York: HarperCollins.

Flores, E., Cicchetti, D., & Rogosch, F. A. (2005). Predictors of resilience in maltreated and nonmaltreated Latino children. *Developmental Psychology, 41,* 338–351.

Fogarty, T. (1976). On emptiness and closeness, Part II. *The Family, 3*(2), 3–17.

Fontana, V. J., & Moolman, V. (1991). *Save the family, save the child: What we can do to help children at risk*. New York: Penguin Group.

Ford, B. A., & Jones, C. (1990). Ethnic feelings book: Created by students with developmental handicaps. *Teaching Exceptional Children, 33*(4), 36–39.

Ford, D. Y., & Harris, J. J. (1995). Underachievement among gifted African American students: Implications for school counselors. *The School Counselor, 42,* 196–203.

Fordyce, W. (1981). On interdisciplinary peers. *Archives of Physical Medicine and Rehabilitation, 62*(2), 51–53.

Forest, M., & Pearpoint, J. (1992). Common sense tools: MAPS and CIRCLES: for inclusive education. In J. Pearpoint, M. Forest, & J. Snow (Eds.), *The Inclusion papers: Strategies to make inclusion work* (pp. 40–51). Toronto: Inclusion Press.

Foster, M. (1986). Families with young disabled children in family therapy. In J. C. Hansen & L. Combrinck-Graham (Eds.), *Treating young children in family therapy* (pp. 62–72). Rockville, MD: Aspen.

Foster, M., Berger, M., & McLean, M. (1981). Rethinking a good idea: A reassessment of parent involvement. *Topics in Early Childhood Special Education, 1,* 56–65.

Four Arrows (2003). *Shifting attention from 'discipline problems' to 'virtue awareness' in American Indian and Alaska Native education*. ERIC Document Reproduction Service No. ED 480 732) Retrieved October, 2005

Fowler, R. C., & Corley, K. K. (1996). Linking families, building community. *Educational Leadership, 53*(7), 24–26.

Fraenkel, P. (2006). Engaging families as experts: Collaborative family program development. *Family Process, 45,* 237–257.

Framo, J. L. (1981). The integration of marital therapy with sessions with family of origin. In A. S. Gurman & D. P. Kniskern (Eds.), *Handbook of family therapy* (pp. 133–158). New York: Brunner/Mazel.

Framo, M. D. (1981). Common issues in recoupled families and therapy interventions. In A. S. Gurman (Ed.), *Questions and answers in the practice of family therapy* (pp. 333–337). New York: Brunner/Mazel.

Frank, D. A., Klass, P. E., Earls, F., & Eisenberg, L. (1996). Infants and young children in orphanages: One view from pediatrics and child psychiatry. *Pediatrics, 4,* 569–578.

Franklin, M. (1992). Culturally sensitive instructional practices for African-American learners with disabilities. *Exceptional Children, 59,* 115–122.

Fraser, M. W. (Ed.). (2004a). *Risk and resilience in childhood: An ecological perspective* (2nd ed.). Washington, D.C.: NASW Press.

Fraser, M. W. (2004b). The ecology of childhood: A multisystems perspective. In M. W. Fraser (Ed.), *Risk and resilience in childhood: An ecological perspective* (2nd ed; pp. 1-12). Washington, D.C.: NASW Press.

Fraser, M. W., Kirby, L. D., & Smokowski, P. R. (2004). Risk and resilience in childhood. In M. W. Fraser (Ed.), *Risk and resilience in childhood: An ecological perspective* (2nd ed.; pp. 13–66). Washington, DC: NASW Press.

Fravel, D. L., McRoy, R. G., & Grotevant, H. D. (2000). Birthmother perceptions of the psychologically present adopted child: Adoption openness and boundary ambiguity. *Family Relations, 49,* 425–433.

Freeark, K., Rosenberg, E. B., Bornstein, J., Jozefowicz-Simbeni, D., Linkevich, M., & Lohnes, K. (2005). Gender differences and dynamics shaping the adoption life cycle: Review of the literature and recommendations. *American Journal of Orthopsychiatry, 74,* 86–101.

Freedman, M. (1993). *The kindness of strangers: Adult mentors, urban youth, and the new volunteerism.* San Francisco: Jossey-Bass.

Freeman, E. M. (2001). *Substance abuse intervention, prevention rehabilitation, and systems change strategies: Helping individuals, families, and groups to empower themselves.* New York: Columbia Press.

French, L. A., (2004). Alcohol and other drug addictions among Native Americans: The movement toward tribal-centric treatment programs. *Alcoholism Treatment Quarterly, 22*(1) 81–91.

French, N. K. (2001). Supervising paraprofessionals: A survey of teacher practices. *Journal of Special Education, 35,* 41–53.

Freshman, A. (2004). Assessment and treatment of adolescent substance abusers. In S. Straussner (Ed.), *Clinical work with substance-abusing clients* (2nd ed., pp. 305–329). New York: Guilford.

Friedlander, M. L. (2003). Adoption: Misunderstood, mythologized, marginalized. *The Counseling Psychologist, 31,* 745–752.

Friedlander, M. L., Larney, L. C., Skau, M., Hotaling, M., Cutting, M. L., & Schwam, M. (2000). Bicultural identification: Experiences of internationally adopted children and their parents. *Journal of Counseling Psychology, 47,* 187–198.

Friedman, E. H. (1986). Emotional process in the marketplace: The family therapist as consultant to work systems. In L. C. Wynne, S. H. McDaniel, & T. T. Weber (Eds.), *Systems consultation: A new perspective for family therapy* (pp. 398–422). New York: Guilford Press.

Friedman, I. A. (2004). Directions in teacher training for low-burnout teaching. In E. Frydenberg (Ed.), *Thriving, surviving or going under: Coping with everyday lives* (pp. 305–326). Greenwich, CT: Information Age Publishing.

Friedman, L. J. (1981). Common problems in stepfamilies. In A. S. Gurman (Ed.), *Questions and answers in the practice of family therapy* (pp. 329–332). New York: Brunner/Mazel.

Friedrich, W. N. (1979). Predictors of the coping behavior of mothers of handicapped children. *Journal of Consulting and Clinical Psychology, 47,* 1140–1141.

Friedrich, W. N., & Friedrich, W. L. (1981). Psychosocial assets of parents of handicapped and nonhandicapped children. *American Journal of Mental Deficiency, 85,* 551–553.

Friedrich, W. N., Wilturner, L. G., & Cohen, D. S. (1985). Coping resources and parenting mentally retarded children. *American Journal of Mental Deficiency, 90,* 130–139.

Friend, M. (2005). *Special education: Contemporary perspectives for school professionals.* Boston: Pearson.

Friend, M., & Cook, L. (2003). *Interactions: Collaboration skills for school professionals* (4th ed.). Boston: Allyn & Bacon.

Friend, M., & Cook, L. (2004). Collaborating with parents and other teachers without being overwhelmed: Building partnerships and teams. In J. Burnette & C. Peters-Johnson (Eds.), *Thriving as a special education teacher.* Alexandria, VA: Council for Exceptional Children.

Frymier, J., & Gansneder, B. (1989). The Phi Delta Kappan study of students at risk. *Phi Delta Kappan, 71,* 142–146.

Fuchs, D., Fuchs, L., & Bahr, M. (1990). Mainstream assistance teams: A scientific basis for the art of consultation. *Exceptional Children, 57,* 128–139.

Fuchs, D., Fuchs, L., Bahr, M., Fernstrom, P., & Stecker, P. (1990). Prereferral intervention: A prescriptive approach. *Exceptional Children, 56,* 493–513.

Fujiura, G., & Yamaki, K. (2000). Trends in demography of childhood poverty and disability. *Exceptional Children, 66,* 187–199.

Fuligni, A., Tseng, V., & Lam, M. (1999). Attitudes towards family obligations among American adolescents with Asian, Latin American, and European backgrounds. *Child Development, 70,* 1030–1044.

Gallagher, J. J., Cross, A., & Scharfman, W. (1981). Paternal adaptation to a young handicapped child: The father's role. *Journal of the Division for Early Childhood, 3,* 3–14.

Gamel-McCormick, M. (1995). Inclusive teams serving included students: Regular and special education teams working in integrated settings. In H. G. Garner (Ed.), *Teamwork models and experience in education* (pp. 157–174). Boston: Allyn & Bacon.

Garbarino, J., & Eckenrode, J. (1997a). The meaning of maltreatment. In J. Garbarino & J. Eckenrode (Eds.), *Understanding abusive families.* San Francisco: Jossey-Bass.

Garcia-Preto, N. (1999). Transformation of the family system during adolescence. In B. Carter & M. McGoldrick (Eds.). *The expanded family life cycle: Individual, family, and social perspectives* (3rd ed., pp. 274–286). Boston: Allyn & Bacon.

Garcia-Preto, N. (2005). Latino families: An overview. In M. McGoldrick, J. Giordano, & N. Garcia-Preto (Eds.), *Ethnicity and family therapy* (3rd ed., pp. 153–165). New York: Guilford Press.

Gargiulo, R. M. (2006). *Special education in contemporary society* (2nd ed.). Belmont, CA: Thomson Wadsworth.

Garland, C. W. (1994). World of practice: Early intervention programs. In H. G. Garner & F. P. Orelove (Eds.), *Teamwork in human services: Models and applications across the life span* (pp. 89–116). Boston: Butterworth-Heinemann.

Garland, C. W. (1995). Moving toward teamwork in early intervention: Adapting models to meet program needs. In H. G. Garner (Ed.), *Teamwork models and experience in education* (pp. 139–155). Boston: Allyn & Bacon.

Garmezy, N. (1991). Resiliency and vulnerability to adverse developmental outcomes associated with poverty. *American Behavioral Scientist, 34,* 416–430.

Garner, H. G. (1994). Critical issues in teamwork. In H. G. Garner & F. P. Orelove (Eds.), *Teamwork in human services: Models and applications across the life span* (pp. 1–18). Boston: Butterworth-Heinemann Publishers.

Garner, H. G. (1995). Teamwork in education and child care. In H. G. Garner (Ed.), *Teamwork models and experience in education* (pp. 1–16). Boston: Allyn & Bacon.

Garofalo, R., Wolf, R. C., Kessel, S., & Palfrey, J. (1998). The association between health risk behaviors and sexual orientation among a school-based sample of adolescents. *Pediatrics, 10*(5), 895–902.

Garrett, M. W. (1995). Between two worlds: Cultural discontinuity in the dropout of Native American youth. *The School Counselor, 42,* 186–195.

Gartin, B. & Murdick, N. L. (2005). IDEA 2004: The IEP. *Remedial and Special Education, 26*(6), 327–331.

Gartrell, N., Deck, A., Rodas, C., & Peyser, H. (2005). The national lesbian family study: 4. Interviews with the 10-year-old children. *American Journal of Orthopsychiatry, 75,* 518–534.

Geary, P. A. (1988). *"Defying the odds?": Academic success among at-risk minority teenagers in an urban high school.* ERIC Document Reproduction Service No. ED 296 055.

Gee, K. (2004). Developing curriculum and instruction. In F. Orelove, D Sobsey, & R. K. Silberman (Ed.), *Educating children with multiple disabilities: A collaborative approach* (4th ed, pp. 67–114). Baltimore, MD: Brookes.

Gergen, K. J. (1991). *The saturated self: Dilemmas of identity in contemporary life.* New York: Basic Books/Harper Collins.

Gerstein, L. H. (2006). Counseling Psychology's Commitment to Strengths: Rhetoric or Reality? *Counseling Psychologist, 34*(2) p. 276–292.

Gesell, A., Ilg, F.L., & Ames, L.B. (1974). *Infant and child in the culture of today: The guidance of development in home and nursery school.* NY: Harper Row.

Giangreco, M. F., & Doyle, M. B. (2005). Students with disabilities and paraprofessional supports: Benefits, balance, and band-aids, In T. M. Skrtic, K. R. Harris, & J. G. Shriner (Eds.) *Special education policy and practice: Accountability, instruction, and social challenges* (pp. 212–241). Denver: Love.

Giangreco, M. F., Edelman, S. W., & Broer, S. M. (2003). Schoolwide planning to improve paraeducator supports. *Exceptional Children, 70,* 63–79.

Gibbs, J. C., Potter, G. B., & Goldstein, A. P. (1995). *The EQUIP program: Teaching youth to think and act responsibly through a peer-helping approach.* Champaign, IL: Research Press.

Gibran, K. (1923). *The prophet.* New York: Knopf.

Gibson, J. G. (1999). Lesbian and gay prospective adoptive parents: The legal battle. *Human Rights, 28*(2) 7–11.

Gil, E. (1996). *Systematic treatment of families who abuse.* San Francisco: Jossey-Bass.

Giles-Sims, J. (1997). Current knowledge about child abuse in stepfamilies. *Marriage and Family Review, 26, (3/4)* 215–230.

Gilligan, C. (1982). *In a different voice: Psychological theory and women's development.* Cambridge: Harvard University Press.

Gilligan, R. (2000). Adversity, resilience and young people: The protective value of positive school and spare time experiences. *Children and Society, 14,* 37–47.

Giordano, J., & McGoldrick, M., & Klages, J. G. (2005). In M. McGoldrick, J. Giordano, & Garcia-Preto (Eds.). *Ethnicity and family therapy* (3rd ed., pp. 616–628). New York: Guilford.

Glidden, L. M. (1989). *Parents for children, children for parents: The adoption alternative.* Washington, DC: American Association on Mental Retardation.

Glidden, L. M. (1994). Not under my heart, but in it. In J. Blacher (Ed.), *When there's no place like home: Options for children living apart from their natural families* (pp. 181–209). Baltimore, MD: Brookes.

Glidden, L. M. (2000). Adopting children with developmental disabilities: A long-term perspective. *Family Relations, 2000,* 397–405.

Glover, G. L. (1994). The hero child in the alcoholic home: Recommendations for counselors. *The School Counselor, 41,* 185–190.

Glover, G. (2001). Parenting in Native American families. In N. B. Webb (Ed.), *Culturally diverse parent–child and family relationships* (pp. 205–231). New York: Columbia University Press.

Golden, O. (2000). The Federal response to child abuse and neglect. *American Psychologist, 55,* 1050–1053.

Goldenberg, I. & Goldenberg, H. (1991). *Family therapy: An overview* (3rd ed.). Monterey, CA: Brooks/Cole.

Goldenberg, I. & Goldenberg, H. (2000). *Family therapy: An overview* (5th ed.). Belmont, CA: Brooks/Cole.

Goldenberg, I. & Goldenberg, H. (2004). *Family therapy: An overview* (6th ed.). Pacific Grove, CA: Brooks/Cole.

Goldsmith, D., & Albrecht, T. L. (1993). The impact of supportive communication networks on test anxiety and performance. *Communication Education, 42,* 142–158.

Goldstein, A., & Conoley, J. C. (1997). *School violence intervention: A practical handbook.* New York: Guilford Press.

Goldstein, A. P., & Soriano, F. I. (1994). Juvenile gangs. In L. D. Eron, J. H. Gentry, & P. Schlegel (Eds.), *Reason to hope: A psychosocial perspective on violence and youth* (pp. 315–333). Washington, DC: American Psychological Association.

Golombok, S., Perry, B., Burston, A., Murray, C., Mooney-Somers, J., Stevens, M., & Golding, J. (2003). Children with lesbian parents: A community study. *American Psychological Association, 39*(1) 20–33.

Gonzalez, J. (2001). *A history of Latinos in America: Harvest of empire.* New York; Viking.

Gonzales, R., & Padilla, A. M. (1997). The academic resilience of Mexican American high school students. *Hispanic Journal of Behavioral Sciences, 19,* 301–318.

Gorman-Smith, D., Henry, D. B., & Tolan, P. H. (2004). Exposure to community violence and violence perpetration: The protective effects of family functioning. *Journal of Clinical and Adolescent Psychology, 33,* 439–449.

Gorman, J. C., & Balter, L. (1997). Culturally sensitive parent education: A critical review of quantitative research. *Review of Educational Research, 67,* 339–369.

Gould, J. (1970). The phases of adult life: A study in developmental psychology. *American Journal of Psychiatry,129*(5), 35–79.

Graden, J. (1989). Redefining "prereferral" intervention as intervention assistance: Collaboration between general and special education. *Exceptional Children, 56,* 227–231.

Grant, B. F. (2000). Estimates of US children exposed to alcohol abuse and dependence in the family. *American Journal of Public Health, 90*(1) 112–126.

Gray, M., & Gibson, S. (2004). Relapse prevention. In S. Straussner (Ed.), *Clinical work with substance-abusing clients* (2nd ed.; pp. 146–168). New York: Guilford.

Green, A. H. (1991). Child neglect. In R. T. Ammerman & M. Hersen (Eds.), *Case studies in family violence* (pp. 135–152). New York: Plenum Press.

Green, R. J. (1995). High achievement, underachievement, and learning disabilities: A family systems model. In B. A. Ryan, G. R. Adams, T. P. Gullotta, R. P. Weissberg, & R. L. Hampton (Eds.), *The family–school connection: Theory, research and practice* (pp. 207–249). Thousand Oaks, CA: Sage.

Greenawalt, C. E., II. (Ed.). (1994a). *Educational innovation: An agenda to frame the future.* Lanham, MD: University Press of America.

Greenawalt, C. E., II. (1994b). Educational outreach programs. In C. E. Greenawalt (Ed.), *Educational innovation: An agenda to frame the future* (pp. 413–433). Lanham, MD: University Press of America.

Greer, J. (1989). Another perspective and some immoderate proposals on "teacher empowerment." *Exceptional Children, 55,* 294–297.

Gresham, F. M., Sugai, G., & Horner, R. H. (2001). Interpreting outcomes of social skills training for students with high-incidence disabilities. *Exceptional Children, 67,* 331–344.

Grigal, M., Test, D. W., Beattie, J., & Wood, W. M. (1997). An evaluation of transition components of individualized education programs. *Exceptional Children, 63,* 357–372.

Grissom, M. O., & Borkowski, J. G. (2002). Self-efficacy in adolescents who have siblings with or without disabilities. *American Journal on Mental Retardation, 107,* 79–90.

Grossman, F. (1972). *Brothers and sisters of retarded children: An exploratory study.* Syracuse, NY: Syracuse University Press.

Grotberg, E. H. (Ed.). (2003a). *Resilience for today: Gaining strength from adversity.* Westport, CN: Praeger.

Grotberg, E. H. (2003b). What is resilience? How do you promote it? How do you use it? In E. H. Grotberg (Ed.), *Resilience for today: Gaining strength from adversity* (pp. 1–29). Westport, CN: Praeger.

Grotevant, H. D. (1998). Adolescent development in family context. In W. Damon & N. Eisenberg (Eds.), *Social, emotional, and personality development: Volume 3, Handbook of child psychology* (5th ed; pp. 1097–1149). New York Wiley

Grotevant, H. D. (2003). Counseling psychology meets the complex world of adoption. *The Counseling Psychologist, 31,* 753–762.

Grotevant, H. D., & McRoy, R. G. (1998). *Openness in adoption : Exploring family connections.* Thousand Oaks, CA: Sage.

Groves, B. M. (2003). When home isn't safe: Children and youth and domestic violence. In J. Miller, I. R. Martin, G. Schamess (Eds.), *School violence and children in crisis* (pp. 15–36). Denver: Love.

Grskovic, J. A., & Goetze, H. (2005, Winter). An evaluation of Life Space Crisis Intervention on the challenging behavior of individual students. *Reclaiming Children and Youth, 13*(4), 231–235.

Guerin, K., & Guerin, P. (2002). Bowenian family therapy. In J. Carlson & D. Kjos (Eds.). *Theories and strategies of family therapy* (pp. 126–157). Boston: Allyn & Bacon.

Guerin, P. J. (Ed.). (1976). *Family therapy: Theory and practice.* New York: Gardner Press.

Guerin, P. J., & Chabot, D. R. (1992). Development of family systems theory. In D. K. Freedheim (Ed.), *History of psychotherapy: A century of change* (pp. 225–260). Washington, DC: American Psychological Association.

Guidubaldi, J., & Cleminshaw, H. (1985). Divorce, family health, and child adjustment. *Family Relations, 34,* 35–41.

Gustafson, C. (1997). For a champion of racial harmony. *Educational Leadership, 54*(5), 67–69.

Guterman, N. B. (2001). *Stopping child maltreatment before it starts: Emerging horizons in early home visitation services.* Thousand Oaks, CA: Sage.

Guterman, B. R. (1995). The validity of categorical learning disabilities services: The consumer's view. *Exceptional Children, 62,* 111–124.

Guthrie, L. F., & Guthrie, G. P. (1993). Linking classrooms and communities: The health and media academies in Oakland. In G. A. Smith (Ed.), *Public schools that work: Creating community* (pp. 155–177). New York: Routledge.

Gutierres, S. E., & Van Puymbroeck, C. (2006). Childhood and adult violence in the lives of women who misuse substances. *Aggression and Violent Behavior, 11,* 497–513.

Haas, T. (1993). School in communities: New ways to work together. In G. A. Smith (Ed.), *Public schools that work: Creating community* (pp. 215–245). New York: Routledge.

Hadley, T., Jacob, T., Miliones, J., Caplan, J., & Spitz, D. (1974). The relationship between family developmental crisis and the appearance of symptoms in a family member. *Family Process, 13,* 207–214.

Haggerty, R. J., Sherrod, L. R., Garmezy, N., & Rutter, M. (1994). *Stress, risk, and resilience in children and adolescents: Processes, mechanisms, and interventions.* Cambridge, UK: Cambridge University.

Haimes, R. (1995). Planning for change. In H. G. Garner (Ed.), *Teamwork models and experience in education* (pp. 73–83). Boston: Allyn & Bacon.

Haine, R. A., Sandler, I. N., Wolchik, S. A., Tein, J-Y., & Dawson-McClure, S. R. (2003). Changing the legacy of divorce: Evidence from prevention programs and future directions. *Family Relations, 52,* 397–405.

Hajal, F., & Rosenberg, E. B. (1991). The family life cycle in adoptive families. *American Orthopsychiatric Association, 61,* 78–85.

Hale-Benson, J. E. (1982). *Black children: Their roots, culture, and learning styles* (rev. ed.). Baltimore, MD: Johns Hopkins University Press.

Haley, J. (1980). *Leaving home: The therapy of disturbed young people.* New York: McGraw-Hill.

Haley, J. (Ed.). (1985). *Changing individuals: Conversations with Milton H. Erickson, M.D.* (Vol. 1). New York: Triangle Press.

Haley, J. (1987). *Problem-solving therapy* (2nd ed.). San Francisco: Jossey-Bass.

Haley, J., & Hoffman, L. (1967). *Techniques of family therapy.* New York: Basic Books.

Hall, C. S., & Lindzey, G. (1978). *Theories of personality* (3rd ed.). New York: John Wiley.

Hall, G. E., & Hord, S. M. (1987). *Change in schools: Facilitating the process.* Albany: State University of New York Press.

Hall, G. E., & Hord, S. M. (2001). *Implementing change: Patterns, principles, and potholes.* Boston: Pearson/Allyn & Bacon.

Hall, G. E., Wallace, R. C., Jr., & Dossett, W. (1973). *A developmental conceptualization of the adoption process within educational institutions.* Austin: The University of Texas at Austin, Research and Development Center for Teacher Education. (ERIC Document Reproduction Service No. ED 095 126).

Hall, J. A., & Maza, P. L. (1990). No fixed address: The effects of homelessness on families and children. *Child and Youth Services, 14*(1), 35–47.

Halsall, P. (1998). *Ancient history sourcebook: Code of Hammurabi, c. 1780 BCE.* Retrieved July 21, 2006 from www.fordham.edu/halsall/ancient/ham code.html

Hamilton, B. E., Martin, J. A., & Sutton, P. D. (2004). Births: Preliminary data for 2003. *National Vital Statistics Report, 53*(9). Centers for Disease Control and Prevention. Retrieved November 28, 2005, from http://www.cdc.gov/nchs/data/nvsr/nvsr53/nvsr53_09.pdf

Hampton, R. L., & Gelles, R. J. (1991). A profile of violence toward black children. In R. L. Hampton (Ed.), *Black family violence: Current research and theory* (pp. 21–34). Lexington, MA: D.C. Heath.

Hanline, M. F. (1991). Transitions and critical events in the family life cycle: Implications for providing support to families of children with disabilities. *Psychology in the Schools, 28,* 53–59.

Hannah, M. E., & Midlarsky, E. (2005). Helping by siblings of children with mental retardation.

American Journal on Mental Retardation, 110(2) 87–99.

Hansen, J. C., & Coppersmith, E. I. (Eds.). (1984). *Families with handicapped members.* Rockville, MD: Aspen.

Hansen, J. C., & Falicov, C. J. (Eds.). (1983). *Cultural perspectives in family therapy.* Rockville, MD: Aspen.

Hanson, D. J. (1996). *Alcohol education: What we must do.* Westport, CT: Praeger.

Harry, B. (1992). Making sense of disability: Low-income, Puerto Rican parents' theories of the problem. *Exceptional Children, 59,* 27–40.

Harry, B. (2002). Trends and issues in serving culturally diverse families of children with disabilities. *Journal of Special Education, 36,* 131–138.

Harry, B., Rueda, R., & Kalyanpur, M. (1999). Cultural reciprocity in sociocultural perspective: Adapting the normalization principle for family collaboration. *Exceptional Children, 66,* 123–136.

Hart, P. J., & Jacobi, M. (1992). *From gatekeepers to advocate: Transforming the role of the school counselor.* New York: College Entrance Examination Board.

Hartman, A. (2003). Family policy: Dilemmas, controversies, and opportunities. In F. Walsh (Ed.). *Normal family processes: Growing diversity and complexity* (3rd ed., pp. 635–662). New York: Guilford.

Harvard Family Research Project. (1995). *Raising our future: Families, schools, and communities joining together.* Cambridge, MA: Author.

Hastings, R. P., & Taunt, H. M. (2002). Positive perceptions in families of children with developmental disabilities. *American Journal of Mental Retardations, 2,* 116–127.

Haugaard, J. J. (1998). Is adoption a risk factor for the development of adjustment problems? *Clinical Psychology Review, 18,* 47–69.

Havinghurst, R. J. (1952). *Developmental tasks and education.* New York: Longmans, Green.

Hawley, D. R., & DeHaan, L. (1996), Toward a definition of family resilience: Integrating life-span and family perspectives. *Family Process, 35,* 283–298.

Hayes, S. A. (1996). Cross-cultural learning in elementary guidance activities. *Elementary School Guidance and Counseling, 30,* 264–274.

Hazzard, A. P. (1990). Prevention of child sexual abuse. In R. T. Ammerman & M. Hersen (Eds.), *Treatment of family violence: A sourcebook* (pp. 354–384). New York: Wiley.

Heavey, C. L., Shenk, J. L., & Christensen, A. (1994). Marital conflict and divorce: A developmental family psychology perspective. In L. L'Abate (Ed.), *Handbook of developmental family psychology and psychopathology* (pp. 221–242). New York: Wiley.

Henderson, A. T., & Mapp, K. L. (2002). *A new wave of evidence: The impact of school, family, and community connections on student achievement.* Austin: Southwest Educational Development Laboratory.

Henderson, H. (Ed.). (2000). *Domestic Violence and child abuse: Sourcebook.* Detroit, MI: Omnigraphics.

Henderson, N., & Milstein, M. M. (1996). *Resilience in schools: Making it happen for students and educators.* Thousand Oaks, CA: Corwin Press.

Hendrick, J. (1984). *The whole child: Early education for the eighties.* St. Louis, MO: C.V. Mosby.

Henry, C. S., Robinson, L. C., Neal, R. A., & Huey, E. L. (2006). Adolescent perceptions of overall family system functioning and parental behaviors. *Journal of Child and Family Studies, 15,* 319–329.

Hernandez, M. & McGoldrick, M. (1999). Migration and the life cycle. In B. Carter and M McGoldrick (Eds.), *The expanded family life cycle: Individual, family, and social perspectives* (3rd ed., pp. 169–185). Boston: Allyn & Bacon.

Herring, R. D., & Meggert, S. S. (1994). The use of humor as a counselor strategy with Native American Indian children. *Elementary School Guidance & Counseling, 29,* 67–76.

Hess, B. B., & Waring, J. M. (1978). Parent and child in later life: Rethinking the relationship. In R. Lerner & G. Spanier (Eds.), *Child influences on marital and family interaction: A life-span perspective* (pp. 241–275). New York: Academic Press.

Hetherington, E. M. (1999a). Introduction and overview. In E. M. Hetherington (Ed.), *Coping with divorce, single parenting, and remarriage* (pp. vii-x). Mahwah, NJ: Erlbaum.

Hetherington, E. M. (1999b). Should we stay together for the sake of the children? In E. M. Hetherington (Ed.), *Coping with divorce, single parenting, and remarriage* (pp. 93–116). Mahwah, NJ: Erlbaum.

Hetherington, E. M. (2003). Intimate pathways: Changing patterns in close personal relationships across time. *Family Relations, 52,* 318–331.

Hetherington, E. M., & Blechman, E. A. (Eds.). (1996). *Stress, coping, and resiliency in children and families.* Mahwah, NJ: Erlbaum.

Hilarski, C. (Ed.). (2005). *Addiction, assessment, and treatment with adolescents, adults, and families.* Binghamton, NY: Haworth Social Work Press.

Hill, J., Fonagy, P., Safier, E., & Sargent, J. (2003). The ecology of attachment in the family. *Family Process, 42,* 205 (electronic version).

Hindley, N., Ramchandani, P. G., & Jones, D. P. H. (2006). Risk factors for recurrence of maltreatment: A systematic review. *Achieves of Disease in Childhood, 91,* 744–752.

Hines, P. M. (1990). African-American mothers. *Journal of Feminist Family Therapy, 2*(2), 23–32.

Hines, P. M. (1999). The family life cycle of African American families living in poverty. In M.

McGoldrick, J. Giordano, & N. Garcia-Preto (Eds.), *Ethnicity and family therapy* (3rd ed., pp. 327–345). New York: Guilford Press.

Hines, P. M., & Boyd-Franklin, N. (1996). African American families. In M. McGoldrick, J. Giordano, & J. Pearce (Eds.), *Ethnicity and family therapy* (2nd ed., pp. 66–84). New York: Guilford Press.

Hines, P. M., & Boyd-Franklin, N. (2005). African American families. In M. McGoldrick, J. Giordano, & N. Garcia-Preto (Eds.), *Ethnicity and family therapy* (3rd ed., pp. 87–100). New York: Guilford Press.

Hines, P. M., Garcia-Preto, N. G., McGoldrick, M., Almeida, R., & Weltman, S. (1999). Culture and the family life cycle. In B. Carter and M McGoldrick (Eds.), *The expanded family life cycle: Individual, family, and social perspectives* (3rd ed., pp. 69–87). Boston: Allyn & Bacon.

Hipke, K. N., Wolchik, S. A., Sandler, I. N., & Braver, S. L. (2002). Predictors of children's intervention-induced resilience in a parenting program for divorced mothers. *Family Relations, 51,* 121–129.

Ho, M. K. (1992). *Minority children and adolescents in therapy.* Newbury Park, CA: Sage.

Hobbs, N. (1975). *Futures of children.* San Francisco: Jossey-Bass.

Hobfoll, S. E., & Stephens, M. A. P. (1990). Social support during extreme stress: Consequences and intervention. In B. R. Sarason, I. G. Sarason, & G. R. Pierce (Eds.), *Social support: An interactional view* (pp. 454–481). New York: Wiley.

Hodapp, R., & Krasner, D. (1995). Families of children with disabilities: Findings from a national sample of eighth-grade students. *Exceptionality, 5*(2), 71–81.

Hodapp, R. M., Glidden, L. M., & Kaiser, A. P. (2005) Sibling of persons with disabilities: Toward a research agenda. *Mental Retardation, 43,* 334–338.

Hodges, E. M., Malone, M., & Perry, D. (1997). Individual risk and social risk as interacting determinants of victimization of the peer group. *Developmental Psychology, 33*(6), 1032–1036.

Hodgkinson, H. L. (1990). *The demographics of American Indians: One percent of the people; fifty percent of the diversity.* Washington, DC: Institute for Educational Leadership.

Hoffman, L. (1981). *Foundations of family therapy.* New York: Basic Books.

Hoffman-Riem, C. (1990). *The adopted child: Family life with double parenthood.* New Brunswick, NJ: Transaction.

Hogan, J., Gabrielsen, K., Luna, N., & Grothaus, D. (2003). *Substance abuse prevention: The intersection of science and practice.* Boston: Allyn & Bacon.

Holcomb-McCoy, C. (2005). Professional school counseling in urban settings: Introduction to special issue. *Professional School Counselor, 8,* 182–183.

Hollingsworth, L. D. (2000). Who seeks to adopt a child? Findings from the national survey of family growth. *Adoption Quarterly, 3,* 1–23.

Holman, T. B., & Burr, W. R. (1980). Beyond the beyond: The growth of family theories in the 1970s. *Journal of Marriage and the Family, 42,* 729–740.

Hoopes, J. L. (1990). Adoption and identity formation. In D. M. Brodzinsky & M. D. Schechter (Eds.), *The psychology of adoption* (pp. 144–166). New York: Oxford University Press.

Hosp, J. L., & Reschly, D. J. (2002). Predictors of restrictiveness of placement for African-American and Caucasian students. *Exceptional Children, 69,* 225–238.

Howard, J. (1978). The influence of children's developmental dysfunctions on marital quality and family interaction. In R. Lerner & G. Spanier (Eds.), *Child influences on marital and family interaction: A life-span perspective* (pp. 275–298). New York: Academic Press.

Hoy, W. K., & Miskel, C. (2005). *Educational administration: Theory, research, and practice* (7th ed.). Boston: McGraw-Hill.

Hudak, J., Krestan, J. A., & Bepko, C. (1999). Alcohol problems and the family life cycle. In B. Carter and M McGoldrick (Eds.), *The expanded family life cycle: Individual, family, and social perspectives* (3rd ed., pp. 455–469). Boston: Allyn & Bacon.

Hunt, P., Soto, G., Maier, J., & Doering, K. (2003). Collaborative teaming to support students as risk and students with severe disabilities in general education classrooms. *Exceptional Children, 69,* 315–332.

Hurtig, A. L. (1994). Chronic illness and developmental family psychology. In L. L'Abate (Ed.), *Handbook of developmental family psychology and psychopathology* (pp. 265–283). New York: Wiley.

Individuals with Disabilities Education Act of 1997, Pub. L. No. 105-17 (1997).

Idol, L., Nevin, A., & Paolucci-Whitcomb, P. (1994). *Collaborative consultation* (2nd ed.). Austin, TX: Pro-Ed.

Imber-Black, E. (1986). Toward a resource model in systemic family therapy. In M. Karpel (Ed.), *Family resources: The hidden partner in family therapy* (pp. 148–174). New York: Guilford Press.

Imber-Black, E. (1989). Idiosyncratic life cycle transitions and therapeutic rituals. In B. Carter & M. McGoldrick (Eds.), *The changing family life cycle: A framework for family therapy* (pp. 149–163). Boston: Allyn & Bacon.

Individuals with Disabilities Education Act of 1997. P.L. 105-17, 20 U.S.C. §1400 *et seq.*

Individuals with Disabilities Education Improvement Act of 2004. P.L. 108-446, 20 U.S.C. §1400 *et seq.*

Intagliata, J., & Doyle, N. (1984). Enhancing social support for parents of developmentally disabled children: Training in interpersonal problem solving skills. *Mental Retardation, 22*(1), 4–11.

Isaacs, M. (1992). *Impact of community violence on African American children and youth and families: Collaborative approaches to prevention and intervention, workshop summary.* Arlington, VA: National Center for Education in Maternal and Child Health.

Isaacs, M. L., & Duffus, L. R. (1995). Scholars' club: A culture of achievement among minority students. *The School Counselor, 42,* 204–210.

Jacobson, N. S., & Gurman, A. S. (Eds.). (1995). *Clinical handbook of couple therapy.* New York: Guilford Press.

Jalali, B. (1996). Iranian families. In M. McGoldrick, J. Giordano, & J. Pearce (Eds.), *Ethnicity and family therapy* (2nd ed., pp. 347–363). New York: Guilford Press.

Jalali, B. (2005). Iranian Families. In M. McGoldrick, J. Giordano, & Garcia-Preto, N. (Eds.), *Ethnicity and family therapy* (3rd ed., pp. 451–467). New York: Guilford.

James, S. H., & DeVaney, S. B. (1994). Reporting suspected sexual abuse: a study of counselor and counselor trainee responses. *Elementary School Guidance and Counseling, 28,* 257–263.

James, W. H. (2004). The sexual orientation of men who were brought up in gay or lesbian households. *Journal of Biosocial Science, 36,* 371–374. Cambridge University Press: DOI: 1017/S00219 32004006583

Jameson, P. B., & Alexander, J. F. (1994). Implications of a developmental family systems model for clinical practice. In L. L'Abate (Ed.), *Handbook of developmental family psychology and psychopathology* (pp. 392–412). New York: Wiley.

Jenkins, J. R., Antil, L. R., Wayne, S. K., & Vadasy, P.F. (2003). How cooperative learning works for special education and remedial students. *Exceptional Children, 69,* 279–292.

Jens, K. G., & Gordon, B. N. (1991). Understanding risk: Implications for tracking high-risk infants and making early service decisions. *International Journal of Disability, 38,* 211–224.

Jeynes, W. H. (2002). A meta-analysis of the effects of attending religious schools and religiosity on Black and Hispanic academic achievement. *Education and Urban Society, 35,* 27–49.

Jeynes, W. H. (2003a). The effects of Black and Hispanic 12th graders living in intact families and being religious on their academic achievement. *Urban Education, 38,* 35–37.

Jeynes, W. H. (2003b). A meta-analysis: The effects of parental involvement on minority children's academic achievement. *Education and Urban Society, 35,* 202–218.

Jeynes, W. H. (2005). A meta-analysis of the relations of parental involvement to urban elementary school student academic achievement. *Urban Education, 40,* 237–269.

Jimerson, S., Egeland, B., & Teo, A. (1999). A longitudinal study of achievement trajectories: Factors associated with change. *Journal of Educational Psychology, 91*(1), 116–126.

Johnson, C. L. (1982). Sibling solidarity: Its origin and functioning in Italian-American families. *Journal of Marriage and the Family, 44,* 155–167.

Johnson, D. E. (2002). Adoption and the effect on children's development. *Early Human Development, 68*(1) 39–54.

Johnson, D. (2005). *Reaching out: Interpersonal effectiveness and self-actualization* (9th ed.). Boston: Allyn & Bacon.

Johnson, T. W. & Colucci, P. (1999). Lesbians, gay men, and the family life cycle. In B. Carter and M McGoldrick (Eds.), *The expanded family life cycle: Individual, family, and social perspectives* (3rd ed., pp. 346–361). Boston: Allyn & Bacon.

Jones, R. (2004). *Black psychology* (4th ed.). Hampton, VA: Cobb & Henry Press.

Jordan, L., Reyes-Blanes, M. E., Peel, B. B., Peel, H. A., & Lane, H. B. (1998). Developing teacher-parent partnerships across cultures: Effective parent conferences. *Intervention in School and Clinic, 33,* 141–147.

Josephson Institute on Ethics (2001). *2000 report card: The ethics of American youth.* Retrieved November 3, 2005, from Josephson Institute on Ethics Website: http://www.josephsoninstitute.org/ Survey2000/violence2000-commentary.htm

Judge, S. (2003). Determinants of parental stress in families adopting children from Eastern Europe. *Family Relations, 52,* 241–248.

Junger-Tas, J., & Van Kesteren, J. (1999). *Bullying and delinquency in a Dutch school population.* The Hague, Netherlands: Kugler.

Kahn, M. D., & Lewis, K. G. (Eds.). (1988). *Siblings in therapy: Life span and clinical issues.* New York: Norton.

Kakli, Z., Kreider, H., Little, P., Buck, T., & Coffey, M. (2006). *Focus on families!: How to build and support family-centered practices in after school.* [www.gse.harvard.edu/hfrp].

Kaltman, G. S. (2006). *Help for teachers of young children: 88 tips to develop children's social skills and create teacher-family relationships.* Thousand Oaks, CA: Corwin.

Kanter, R. M. (1995). Managing the human side of change. In D. A. Kolb, J. S. Osland, & I. M. Rubin (Eds.), *The organizational behavior reader* (6th ed., pp. 676–682). Englewood Cliffs, NJ: Prentice-Hall.

Kantor, D. (1983). The structural-analytic approach to the treatment of family developmental crisis. In J.

Hansen & H. Liddle (Eds.), *Clinical implications of the family life cycle* (pp. 12–34). Rockville, MD: Aspen.

Kapinus, C. A. (2004). The effects of parents' attitudes toward divorce on offspring's attitudes: Gender and parental divorce as mediating factors. Journal of *Family Issues, 25,* 112–135.

Kaplan, C. P., Turner, S., Norman, E., & Stillson, K. (1996). Promoting resilience strategies: A modified consultation model. *Social Work in Education, 18*(3), 158–168.

Karp, S. (1997). Educating for a civil society: The core issue is inequality. *Educational Leadership, 54*(4), 40–43.

Karpel, M. (Ed.). (1986a). *Family resources: The hidden partner in family therapy*. New York: Guilford Press.

Karpel, M. (1986b). Testing, promoting, and preserving family resources: Beyond pathology and power. In M. Karpel (Ed.), *Family resources: The hidden partner in family therapy* (pp. 174–234). New York: Guilford Press.

Kaslow, F. W. (2003). Problems, perils, and pleasures of multicultural and biracial adoptions. In L. L. Schwartz & F. W. Kaslow (Eds.), *Welcome home: An international and nontraditional adoption reader* (pp. 237–256). New York: Haworth Clinical Practice Press.

Katsiyannis, A., Hodge, J., & Lanford, A. (2000). Paraeducators: Legal and practice considerations. *Remedial and Special Education, 21,* 297–304.

Kaufman, E., & Kaufmann, P. (Eds.). (1992). *Family therapy of drug and alcohol abuse* (2nd ed.). Boston: Allyn & Bacon.

Kaufman, J., & Zigler, E. (1993). The intergenerational transmission of abuse is overstated. In R. J. Gelles & D. R. Loseke (Eds.), *Current controversies on family violence* (pp. 209–221). Newbury Park, CA: Sage.

Kay, P. J., Fitzgerald, M., Paradee, C., & Mellencamp, A. (1994). Making homework work at home: The parent's perspective. *Journal of Learning Disabilities, 27,* 550–561.

Kazak, A. E. (1987). Families with disabled children: Stress and social networks in three samples. *Journal of Abnormal Child Psychology, 15,* 137–146.

Kazak, A. E., & Marvin, R. S. (1984). Differences, difficulties and adaptation: Stress and social networks in families with a handicapped child. *Family Relations, 33,* 66–77.

Kazak, A. E., & Wilcox, B. (1984). The structure and function of social support networks in families with handicapped children. *American Journal of Community Psychology, 12,* 645–661.

Keith, N. Z. (1997). Doing service projects in urban settings. In A. S. Waterman (Ed.), *Service-learning: Applications from the research*. Mahwah, NJ: Erlbaum.

Keith, V. M., & Finlay, B. (1988). The impact of parental divorce on children's educational attainment, marital timing, and probability of divorce. *Journal of Marriage and the Family, 50,* 797–809.

Kelley, B. T., Thornberry, T. P., & Smith, C. A. (1997). *In the wake of childhood maltreatment*. Washington, DC. National Institute for Justice. [www.ncjrs.gov/pdffiles1/165257.pdf]

Kelly, J. B., & Emery, R. E. (2003). Children's adjustment following divorce: Risk and resilience perspectives. *Family Relations, 52,* 352–362.

Kelso, D. R., & Attneave, C. L. (1981). *Bibliography of North American Indian mental health*. Westport, CT: Greenwood Press.

Kennedy, S., Kiecolt-Glaser, J. K., & Glaser, R. (1990). Social support, stress and the immune system. In B. R. Sarason, I. G. Sarason, & G. R. Pierce (Eds.), *Social support: An interactional view* (pp. 253–266). New York: Wiley.

Kerr, M. (1988, September). Chronic anxiety and defining a self. *Atlantic Monthly,* pp. 35–58.

Kesner, J. E., & Robinson, M. (2002). Teachers as mandated reporters of child maltreatment: Comparison with legal, medical, and social services reporters. *Children and Schools, 24,* 222–231.

Kerr, M., & Bowen, M. (1988). *Family evaluation: An approach based on Bowen theory*. New York: Norton.

Keys, S. G., Bemak, F., Carpenter, S. L., & King-Sears, M. (1998). Collaborative consultant: A new role for counselors serving at-risk youths. *Journal of Counseling & Development, 76,* 123–133.

Keyton, J. (2005). *Communication and organizational culture: A key to understanding work experiences*. Thousand Oaks, CA: Sage.

Kidd, S. A., & Scrimenti, K. (2004). Evaluating child and youth homelessness. *Evaluation Review, 28,* 325–341.

King, G. A., Brown, E. G., & Smith, L. K. (Eds.). (2003). *Resilience: Learning from people with disabilities and the turning points in their lives*. Westport, CN: Praeger.

King-Sears, M. E. (1997). Disability: Legalities and labels. In D. F. Bradley, M. E. King-Sears, & D. M. Tessier-Switlick (Eds.), *Teaching students in inclusive settings: From theory to practice* (pp. 21–55). Boston: Allyn & Bacon.

Kjos, D. (2002). Feminist family therapy. In J. Carlson, & D. Kjos (Eds.), *Theories and strategies of family therapy* (pp. 158–169). Boston: Allyn & Bacon.

Kliewer, W., et al. (2004). Violence exposure and adjustment in inner-city youth: Child and caregiver emotion regulation skill, caregiver-child relationship quality, and neighborhood cohesion as protective factors. *Journal of Clinical Child and Adolescent Psychology, 33*(3), 477–487.

Kliman, J., & Madsen, W. (1999). Social class and the family life cycle. In B. Carter & M. McGoldrick (Eds.), *The expanded family life cycle: Individual, family, and social perspectives* (3rd ed., pp. 88–105). Boston: Allyn & Bacon.

Knight, S. M. (1994). Elementary-age children of substance abusers: issues associated with identification and labeling. *Elementary School Guidance and Counseling, 28,* 274–284.

Knotek, S. (2003). Bias in problem solving and the social process of student study teams. *Journal of Special Education, 37,* 2–14.

Koch, A. (1985). "If only it could be me": The families of pediatric cancer patients. *Family Relations, 34,* 63–70.

Koerner, S. S., Wallace, S., Lehman, S. J., Lee, S-A., & Escalante, K. A. (2004). Sensitive mother-to-adolescent disclosures after divorce: Is the experience of sons different from that of daughters? *Journal of Family Psychology, 18,* 46–57.

Koh, M-S., & Robertson, J. S. (2003). School reform models and special education. *Education and Urban Society, 35,* 421–442.

Komoski, P. K. (1990). Needed: A whole-curriculum approach. *Educational Leadership, 47*(5), 72–78.

Kornfield, J. (1993). *A path with heart.* NY: Bantam.

Kottler, J. A. (2001). *Making changes last.* London: Brunner-Routledge.

Kottman, T. (2004). Play therapy. In A. Vernon (Ed.). *Counseling children and adolescents* (3rd ed., pp. 111–136). Denver: Love.

Kreider, R. M. (2003). *Adopted children and stepchildren: 2000, Census 2000 Special reports.* Washington, DC: U.S. Department of Commerce Economics and Statistics Administration, U. S. Census Bureau. [www.census.gov/prod/2003pubs/censr-6.pdf]

Kreider, R. M. (2005). *Number, timing, and duration of marriages and divorces: 2001. Current population reports, P70-97.* Washington, D.C.: U.S. Census Bureau. [www.census.gov/prod/2005pubs/p70-97.pdf]

Kreider, R. M., & Fields, J. (2005). Living arrangements of children: 2001. *Current population reports, P70-104.* Washington, D.C.: U.S. Census Bureau. [www.census.gov/prod/2005pubs/p70-104.pdf]

Kreppner, K., & Lerner, R. M. (Eds.). (1989). *Family systems and life span development.* Hillsdale, NJ: Erlbaum.

Kroth, R., & Edge, D. (1997). *Strategies for communicating with parents and families of exceptional children.* Denver, CO: Love.

Krovetz, M. L. (1999). *Fostering resiliency: Expecting all students to use their minds and hearts well.* Thousand Oaks, CA: Corwin Press.

Kuo, W. (1984). Prevalence of depression among Asian Americans. *Journal of Nervous and Mental Diseases, 172,* 449–457.

Kubler-Ross, E. (1997, reprinted.). *On death and dying.* New York: Scribner.

Kupersmidt, J. B., Coie, J. D., & Howell, J. C. (2004). Resilience in children exposed to negative peer influences. In K. I. Maton, C. J. Schellenbach, B. J. Leadbeater, & Solarz, A. L. (Eds.), *Investing in children, youth, families, and communities: Strengths-based research and policy* (pp. 251–268). Washington, DC: American Psychological Association.

Kurtz, E. (2002). Alcoholics anonymous and the disease concept of alcoholism. *Alcoholism Treatment Quarterly, 20(3/4)* 5–40.

Kyle, D. W., McIntyre, E., Miller, K. B., & Moore, G. H. (2002). *Reaching Out: A K-8 resource for connecting families and schools.* Thousand Oaks, CA: Corwin.

L'Abate, L. (Ed.). (1994a). *Handbook of developmental family psychology and psychopathology.* New York: Wiley.

L'Abate, L. (1994b). What is developmental family psychology? In L. L'Abate (Ed.), *Handbook of developmental family psychology and psychopathology* (pp. 3–23). New York: Wiley.

L'Abate, L., & Bagarozzi, D. A. (1993). *Sourcebook of marriage and family evaluation.* New York: Brunner/Mazel.

Lago-Dellelo, E. (1998). Classroom dynamics and the development of serious emotional disturbance. *Exceptional Children, 64,* 479–492.

Laird, J. (2003). Lesbian and gay families. In F. Walsh (Ed.). *Normal family processes: Growing diversity and complexity* (3rd ed., pp. 176–209. New York: Guilford.

Lake, J. F., & Billingsley, B. S. (2000). An analysis of factors that contribute to parent-school conflict in special education [Electronic version]. *Remedial and Special Education, 21,* 240–251.

Lambie, G. W. (2005). Child abuse and neglect: A practical guide for professional school counselors. *Professional School Counseling, 8,* 249–258.

Lansford, J. E., Malone, P. S., Castellino, D. R., Dodge, K. A., Pettit, G. S., & Bates, J. E. (2006). Trajectories of internalizing and externalizing, and grades for children who have and have not experienced their parent's divorce or separation. *Journal of Family Psychology, 20,* 292–301.

Lardieri, L. A., Blacher, J., & Swanson, H. L. (2000). Sibling relationships and parent stress in families of children with and without learning disabilities. *Learning Disability Quarterly, 23,* 105–121.

Larson, C. E., & LaFasto, F. M. (1989). *Teamwork: What must go right—what can go wrong.* Newbury Park, CA: Sage.

Laursen, E. K. (2002). Seven habits of reclaiming relationship. *Reclaiming Children and Youth, 11*(1), 95–99.

Laursen, E. K., & Birmingham, S. M. (2003). Caring relationships as a protective factor for at risk youth: An ethnographic study. *Families in Society, 84*, 240–246.

Lawler, S. D. (1991). *Parent-teacher conferencing in early childhood education*. Washington, DC: National Education Association.

Lawrence-Lightfoot, S. (2003). *The essential conversation: What parents and teachers can learn about each other*. New York: Random House.

Lawson, H. A., & Sailor, W. (2005). Integrating services, collaborating, and developing connections with schools. In T. M. Skrtic, K. R. Harris, & J. G. Shriner (Eds.), *Special education policy and practice: Accountability, Instruction, and social challenges* (pp. 526–564). Denver: Love.

Lawyer, S. R., Ruggiero, K. J., Resnick, H. S., Kilpatrick, D. G., & Saunders, B. E. (2006). Mental health correlates of the victim-perpetrator relationship among interpersonally victimized adolescents. *Journal of Interpersonal Violence, 21*(10) 1333–1354.

Lebner, A. (2000). Genetic "mysteries" and international adoption: The cultural impact of biomedical technologies on the adoptive family experience. *Family Relations, 49*, 371–377.

Lee, C. (2005). Urban school counseling: Context, characteristics, and competencies. *Professional School Counseling, 8*, 184–188.

Lee, E. (1996). Asian American families: An overview. In M. McGoldrick, J. Giordano, & J. Pearce (Eds.), *Ethnicity and family therapy* (2nd ed., pp. 227–248). New York: Guilford Press.

Lee, E., & Mock, M. R. (2005a). Asian families: An overview. In M. McGoldrick, J. Giordano, & N. Garcia-Preto (Eds.), *Ethnicity and family therapy* (3rd ed., pp. 269–289). New York: Guilford Press.

Lee, E., & Mock, M. R. (2005b). Chinese families. In M. McGoldrick, J. Giordano, & N. Garcia-Preto (Eds.), *Ethnicity and family therapy* (3rd ed., pp. 302–318). New York: Guilford Press.

Leigh, I. W. (1987). Parenting and the hearing impaired: Attachment and coping. *Volta Review, 89*(5), 11–21.

Leithwood, K. (1997). *Presentation made at Virginia Commonwealth University School of Education annual Scholar in Residence seminar*.

Leman, K. (1989). *Growing up firstborn: The pressure and the privilege of being number one*. New York: Delacorte.

Leon, I. G. (2002). Adoption losses: Naturally occurring or socially constructed? [Electronic version]. *Child Development, 73*, 652–664.

Leone, P. E., Mayer, M. J., Malmgren, K., & Meisel, S. M. (2003). School violence and disruption: Rhetoric, reality, and reasonable balance. In J. Miller, I. R. Martin, & G. Schamess (Eds.), *School violence and children and youth in crisis* (pp. 51–84). Denver: Love.

LePere, D. W. (1988). Vulnerability to crises during the life cycle of the adoptive family. In D. Valentine (Ed.), *Infertility and adoption: A guide for social work practice* (pp. 73–85). New York: Haworth Press.

Lerner, R.M. (2002). *Adolescence: development, diversity, context, and application*. Upper Saddle Rive, NJ: Prentice Hall.

Lerner, R. M. (2004). *Liberty: Thriving and civic engagement among America's youth*. Thousand Oaks, CA: Sage.

Leung, P., & Erich, S. (2002). Family functioning of adoptive children with special needs: Implications of familial supports and child characteristics. *Children and Youth Services Review, 24*, 799–816.

Levin, D. E., & Carlsson-Paige, N. (2003). Marketing violence: The special toll on youth children and youth of color. *Journal of Negro Education, 72*(4), 427–437.

Levine, M. (1982). The child with school problems: An analysis of physician participation. *Exceptional Children, 48*, 296–304.

Levine, M. (2002). *A mind at a time*. New York: Simon & Schuster.

Lewis, C. C., Schaps, R., & Watson, M. (1995). Beyond the pendulum: Creating challenging and caring schools. *Phi Delta Kappan, 76*, 547–554.

Lewis, J. A., Dana, R. Q., & Blevins, G. A. (2002). *Substance abuse counseling* (3rd ed.). Pacific Grove, CA: Brooks/Cole.

Lidz, T., Cornelison, A., Fleck, S., & Terry, D. (1957a). The intrafamilial environment of the schizophrenic patient I. The father. *Psychiatry, 20*, 329–342.

Lin, K. M., Inui, T. S., Kleinman, A. M., & Womack, W. M. (1982). Sociocultural determinants of the helpseeking behavior of patients with mental illness. *Journal of Nervous and Mental Disease, 170*, 78–84.

Linnekin, J., & Poyer, L. (Eds.). (1990). *Cultural identity and ethnicity in the Pacific*. Honolulu: University of Hawaii Press.

Liontos, L.B. (1991). *Involving the families of at-risk youth in the educational process*. ERIC Document Reproduction Service No. ED 328946).

Liptak, K. (1993). *Adoption controversies*. New York: Franklin Watts.

Little Soldier, L. (1985). To soar with the eagles: Enculturation and acculturation of Indian children. *Childhood Education, 61*(3) p. 185–191.

Loman, L.A. (2006). *Families frequently encountered by Child Protective Services: A report on chronic child abuse and neglect*. St. Louis, MO: Institute of

Applied Research. [www.iarstl.org/papers/FE families Chronic CAN.pdf]

Long, N. J., Wood, M. M., & Fecser, F. A., (2001). *Life space crisis intervention: Talking with students in crisis*. Austin, TX: Pro-Ed.

Longo, D. C., & Bond, L. (1984). Families of the handicapped child: Research and practice. *Family Relations, 33,* 57–65.

Lopez, M. E., Kreider, H., & Coffman, J. (2005). Intermediary organizations as capacity builders in family educational involvement. *Urban Education, 40,* 78–105.

Lopez, R. I., & Kelly, K. (Eds.). (2003). *The teen health book: A parents' guide to adolescent health and well-being*. New York: W.W. Norton.

Losen, S., & Losen, J. (1985). *The special education team*. Boston: Allyn & Bacon.

Losen, S. M., & Losen, J. G. (1994). Teamwork and the involvement of parents in special education programming. In H. G. Garner & F. P. Orelove (Eds.), *Teamwork in human services: Models and applications across the life span* (pp. 117–141). Boston: Butterworth-Heinemann.

Love, H. D. (1973). *The mentally retarded child and his family*. Springfield, IL: Charles C. Thomas.

Lowe, J. I., & Herranen, M. (1981). Understanding teamwork: Another look at the concepts. *Social Work in Health Care, 7*(2), 1–10.

Lugalia, T, & Overturf, J. (2004). Children and the households they live in: 2000. Census Special Reports. Washington, DC: U.S. Department of Commerce, U. S. Census Bureau. [www.census.gov/prod/2004pubs/censr-14.pdf]

Lusthaus, E., & Lusthaus, C. (1993). A "normal" life for Hannah. In A. P. Turnbull, J. M. Patterson, S. K. Behr, D. L. Murphy, J. G. Marquis, & M. J. Blue-Banning (Eds.), *Cognitive coping, families, and disability* (pp. 43–50). Baltimore, MD: Brookes.

Luthar, S. S. (Ed.). (2003). *Resilience and vulnerability: Adaptation in the context of childhood adversities*. Cambridge, UK: Cambridge University Press.

Luthar, S. S., & D'Avanzo, K. (1999). Contextual factors in substance abuse: A study of suburban and inner-city adolescents. *Development and Psychopathology, 11,* 845–867.

Luthar, S. S., & Latendresse, S. J. (2005). Comparable "risks" at the socioeconomic status extremes: Preadolescents' perceptions of parenting. *Development and Psychopathology, 17,* 207–230.

Luthar, S. S., & Zelazo, L. B. (2003). Research on resilience: An integrative review. In S. Luthar (Ed.), *Resilience and vulnerability: Adaptation in the context of childhood adversities* (pp. 510–549). Cambridge, UK: Cambridge University Press.

Lutzker, J. R., & Bigelow, K. M. (2002). *Reducing child maltreatment: A guidebook for parent services*. New York: Guilford.

Lynch, E. W., & Stein, R. C. (1987). Parent participation by ethnicity: A comparison of Hispanic, Black, and Anglo families. *Exceptional Children, 54,* 105–111.

Mack, C. C., Jr. (1981). Racism, educational models, and black children. In D. Claerbaut (Ed.), *New directions in ethnic studies: Minorities in America* (pp. 84–94). Saratoga, CA: Century Twenty-One.

Macy, R. D., Barry, S., Noam. G. G. (2003). Threat and trauma: An overview. *New Directions for Youth Development, 98,* 11–28.

Madanes, C., Keim, J. P., & Smelser, D. (1995). *The violence of men: New techniques for working with abusive families: A therapy of social action*. San Francisco, CA: Jossey-Bass.

Mainzer, R. W., Deshler, D., Coleman, M. R., Kozleski, E., & Rodriguez-Walling, M. (2005). To ensure the learning of every child with a disability. In T. M. Skrtic, H. R. Harris, & J. G. Shriner (Eds.), *Special education policy and practice: Accountability, Instruction, and social challenges* (pp. 83–102). Denver: Love.

Malatchi, A. (1997). Family partnerships, belonging, and diversity. In L. A. Power-deFur & F. P. Orelove (Eds.), *Inclusive education: Practical implementation of the least restrictive environment* (pp. 91–115). Gaithersburg, MD: Aspen.

Mangham, C., McGrath, P., Reid, G., & Stewart, M. (1995). *Resiliency: Relevance to health promotion discussion paper*. Retrieved June 24, 2000, from http://www.hc-sc.gc.ca/ahc-asc/pubs/drugs-drogues/resiliency-ressortpsycholoique/indexe.html

Markowitz, R. (2004). Dynamics and treatment issues with children of drug and alcohol abusers. In S. Straussner (Ed.), *Clinical work with substance-abusing clients* (2nd ed., pp. 284–302). New York: Guilford.

Marshall, S. (1992). *Teenage addicts can recover: Treating the addict, not the age*. Littleton, CO: Gylantic.

Martin, H. P. (1980). Working with parents of abused and neglected children. In R. R. Abidin (Ed.), *Parent education and intervention handbook* (pp. 252–271). Springfield, IL: Charles C. Thomas.

Martin, J. E., Marshall, L., & Sale, P. (2004). A 3-year study of middle, junior high, and high school IEP meetings. *Exceptional Children, 70,* 285–297.

Martin, J. E., vanDycke, J. L., Christensen, W. R., Greene, B. A., Gardner, J. E., & Lovett, D. L. (2006a). *Exceptional Children, 72,* 299–317.

Martinez, P., & Richters, J. (1993). The NIMH community violence project: II children and youth's distress symptoms associated with violence exposure. *Psychiatry, 56*(1), 22–35.

Maslow, A. (1970). *Motivation and personality*. New York: Harper & Row.

Mason, C., Field, S., & Sawilowsky, S. (2004). Implementation of self-determination activities and student participation in IEPs. *Exceptional Children, 70,* 441–451.

Masten, A. S., Best, K. M., & Garmezy, N. (1990). Resilience and development: Contributions from the study of children who overcome adversity. *Development and Psychopathology, 2,* 425–444.

Masten, A. S., & Coatsworth, J. D. (1998). The development of competence in favorable and unfavorable environments. *American Psychologist, 53,* 205–220.

Maton,K. I, Schellenbach, C. J., Leadbeater, B. J., & Solarz, A. L. (2004). *Investing in children, youth, families, and communities.* Washington, DC: American Psychological Association.

Maxwell, M. G., & Widom, C. S. (1996). The cycle of violence revisited 6 years later. *Archives of Pediatric and Adolescent Medicine, 150,* 390–395.

Mayer, M. J., & Leone, P. E. (1999). A structural analysis of school violence and disruption: Implications for creating safer schools. *Education and Treatment of Children and Youth, 22,* 333–358.

McAdoo, H.P., (2001). Parent and child relationships in African American families. In N. B. Webb (Ed.), *Culturally diverse parent-child and family relationships* (pp. 89-105). New York: Columbia University Press.

McCallion, P., Janicki, ,M., & Grant-Griffin, L. (1997). Exploring the impact of culture and acculturation on older families caregiving for persons with developmental disabilities. *Family Relations, 46,* 347–357.

McCarty, H., & Chalmers, L. (1997). Bibliotherapy: Intervention and prevention. *Teaching Exceptional Children, 29*(6), 12–13, 16–17.

McConville, D. W., & Cornell, D. G. (2003). Aggressive attitudes predict aggressive behavior in middle school students. *Journal of Emotional and Behavioral Disorders, 11*(13), 179–187.

McCubbin, H. I., McCubbin, M. A., Thompson, A. I., & Thompson, E. A. (1995). Resiliency in ethnic families: A conceptual model for predicting family adjustment and adaptation. In H. I. McCubbin, E. A. Thompson, A. I. Thompson, & J. E. Fromer (Eds.), *Resiliency in ethnic minority families, Vol. 1: Native and immigrant American families* (pp. 3–48). Madison, WI: University of Wisconsin System, Center for Excellence in Family Studies.

McCubbin, H. I., Thompson, E. A., Thompson, A. I., & Fromer, J. E. (Eds.). (1998). *Resiliency in Native American and immigrant families: Resiliency in family series.* Thousand Oaks, CA: Sage.

McCubbin, H. I., & Patterson, J. (1982). Family adaptation to crises. In H. McCubbin, A. Cauble, & J. Patterson (Eds.), *Family stress, coping and social support* (pp. 26–47). Springfield, IL: C. C. Thomas.

McCurdy, B. L., Mannella, M. C., & Eldridge, N. (2003). Positive behavior support in urban schools: Can we prevent the escalation of antisocial behavior? *Journal of Positive Behavior Interventions, 5*(3), 158–170.

McEwan, E. K. (2004). *How to deal with parents who are angry, troubled, afraid, or just plain crazy* (2nd ed.). Thousand Oaks, CA: Corwin.

McFadden, V. M., & Doub, G. (1983). The therapist's new role: Training families for healthy survival. In J. Hansen & H. Liddle (Eds.), *Clinical implications of the family life cycle* (pp. 134–160). Rockville, MD: Aspen.

McFarland, B. H., Gabriel, R. M., Bigelow, D. A., & Walker, R. D. (2006). Organization and financing of alcohol and substance abuse programs for American Indians and Alaska Natives. *American Journal of Public Health, 96,* 1469–1477.

McFarland, W. P., & Tollerud, T. R., (2004). Counseling children and adolescents with special needs. In A. Vernon (Ed.). *Counseling children and adolescents* (3rd ed., pp. 257–309). Denver: Love.

McGill, D. W., & Pearce, J. K. (2005). American families with English ancestors from the colonial era. In M. McGoldrick, J. Giordano, & N. Garcia-Preto (Eds.), *Ethnicity and Family Therapy* (pp. 520–554). New York: Guilford.

McGoldrick, M. (1999a). Becoming a couple. In B. Carter and M. McGoldrick (Eds.). *The expanded family life cycle: Individual, family, and social perspectives* (3rd ed., pp. 231–248). Boston: Allyn & Bacon.

McGoldrick, M. (1999b). History, genograms, and the family life cycle. In B. Carter and M. McGoldrick (Eds.). *The expanded family life cycle: Individual, family, and social perspectives* (3rd ed., pp. 47–68). Boston: Allyn & Bacon.

McGoldrick, M. (1999c). Women in the family life cycle. In B. Carter and M McGoldrick (Eds.), *The expanded family life cycle: Individual, family, and social perspectives* (3rd ed., pp. 106–123). Boston: Allyn & Bacon.

McGoldrick, M. (2005). Irish families. In M. McGoldrick, J. Giordano, & N. Garcia-Preto (Eds.), *Ethnicity and family therapy* (3rd ed., pp. 595–615). New York: Guilford Press.

McGoldrick, M., Broken Nose, M. A., & Potenza, M. (1999). In B. Carter and M McGoldrick (Eds.). *The expanded family life cycle: Individual, family, and social perspectives* (3rd ed., pp. 470–491). Boston: Allyn & Bacon.

McGoldrick, M., & Carter, B. (1989). Forming a remarried family. In B. Carter & M. McGoldrick (Eds.), *The changing family life cycle: A framework for family therapy* (2nd ed., pp. 399–429). Boston: Allyn & Bacon.

McGoldrick, M. & Carter, B. (1999). Remarried families. In B. Carter and M McGoldrick (Eds.). *The expanded family life cycle: Individual, family, and social perspectives* (3rd ed., pp. 417–435). Boston: Allyn & Bacon.

McGoldrick, M., & Gerson, R. (1985). *Genograms in family assessment.* New York: Norton.

McGoldrick, M., & Gerson, R. (1989). Genograms in the family life cycle. In B. Carter & M. McGoldrick (Eds.), *The changing family life cycle: A framework for family therapy* (2nd ed., pp. 164–189). Boston, Allyn & Bacon.

McGoldrick, M., & Gerson, R. (1999). *Genograms: Assessment and intervention* (2nd ed.). New York: Norton.

McGoldrick, M., Gerson, R., & Shellenberger, S. (1999). *Genograms in family assessment* (2nd ed.). New York: Norton.

McGoldrick, M., & Giordano, J. (1996). Overview: Ethnicity and family therapy. In M. McGoldrick, J. Giordano, & J. Pearce (Eds.), *Ethnicity and family therapy* (2nd ed., pp. 1–27). New York: Guilford Press.

McGoldrick, M., Giordano, J., & Pearce, J. (Eds.). (1996). *Ethnicity and family therapy* (2nd ed.). New York: Guilford Press.

McGoldrick, M., Giordano, J. & Garcia-Preto, N. (Eds.). (2005a). *Ethnicity and Family Therapy* (3rd ed.). New York: Guilford Press.

McGoldrick, M., Giordano, J., & Garcia-Preto, N. (2005b) Overview: Ethnicity and Family Therapy. In M. McGoldrick, J. Giordano, & N. Garcia-Preto (Eds.), *Ethnicity and Family Therapy* (3rd ed., pp. 1–40). New York: Guilford Press.

McGoldrick, M., Pearce, J. K., & Giordano, J. (Eds.). (1982). *Ethnicity and family therapy.* New York: Guilford Press.

McGoldrick, M., Watson, M., & Benton, W. (1999). Siblings through the life cycle. In B. Carter and M McGoldrick (Eds.), *The expanded family life cycle: Individual, family, and social perspectives* (3rd ed., pp. 153–168). Boston: Allyn & Bacon.

McGrath, M., & Grant, G. (1993). The life cycle and support networks of families with a person with a learning difficulty. *Disability, Handicap & Society, 8*(1), 25–41.

McGuigan, W. M., & Pratt, C. C. (2001). The predictive impact of domestic violence on three types of child maltreatment. *Child Abuse and Neglect, 25,* 869–883.

McHale, S. M., Sloan, J., & Simeonsson, R. J. (1986). Sibling relationships of children with autistic, mentally retarded, and nonhandicapped brothers and sisters. *Journal of Autism and Developmental Disorders, 16,* 399–413.

McIntyre, J. R. (2004). Family treatment of substance abuse. In S. Straussner (Ed.), *Clinical work with substance-abusing clients* (2nd ed., pp. 237–263). New York: Guilford.

McIntyre, T. (1996). Guidelines for providing appropriate services to culturally diverse students with emotional and/or behavioral disorders. *Behavioral Disorders, 21,* 137–144.

McLanahan, S., & Sandefur, G. (1994). *Growing up with a single parent: What hurts, what helps.* Cambridge, MA: Harvard University Press.

McLendon, J., & Davis, B. (2002). The Satir system. In J. Carlson & D. Kjos (Eds.), *Theories and strategies of family therapy* (pp. 170–189). Boston: Allyn & Bacon.

McLoughlin, J. A. (1981). Training together to work together. *Teacher Education and Special Education, 4*(4), 45–54.

McLuhan, M. (1967). *The medium is the message.* New York: Touchstone.

McMillan, D. L., & Turnbull, A. P. (1983). Parent involvement with special education. *Education and Training of the Mentally Retarded, 18,* 5–9.

McMillan, J., & Reed, D. (1994). *Defying the odds: A study of resilient at-risk students.* Richmond: Virginia Commonwealth University.

McNeece, C. A., & DiNitto, D. M. (2005). *Chemical dependency: A systems approach* (3rd ed.). Boston, MA: Allyn & Bacon.

McNeely, C. A., Nonnemaker, J. M., & Blum, R. W. (2002). Promoting school connectedness. *Journal of School Health, 72*(4), 138–146.

McRoy, G. G. (1999). *Special needs adoptions: Practice issues.* New York: Garland.

McWilliam, P. J. (1996). Family-centered practices in early intervention. In P. J. McWilliam, P. J. Winton, & E. R. Crais (Eds.), *Practical strategies for family-centered early intervention* (pp. 1–13). San Diego, CA: Singular.

Meier, J. H., & Sloan, M. P. (1984). The severely handicapped and child abuse. In J. Blacher (Ed.), *Severely handicapped young children and their families* (pp. 247–274). New York: Academic Press.

Mercier, L. R., & Harold, R. D. (2003). At the interface: Lesbian-parent families and their children's schools. *Children and Schools, 25*(1) 35–47.

Meyer, D. J., & Vadasy, P. F. (1994). *Sibshops: Workshops for siblings of children with special needs.* Baltimore, MD: Brookes.

Miall, C. E. (1998). Community assessments of adoption issues: Open adoption, birth reunions, and the disclosure of confidential information [Electronic version]. *Journal of Family Issues, 19,* 556–578.

Miall, C. E., & March, K. (2005a). Community attitudes toward birth fathers' motives for adoption placement and single parenting. *Family Relations, 54,* 535–546.

Miall, C. E., & March, K. (2005b). Open adoption as a family form: Community assessments and social support. *Journal of Family Issues, 26,* 380–419.

Miall, C. E., & March, K. (2005c). Social support for changes in adoption practice: Gay adoption, open adoption, birth reunions, and the release of confidential identifying information. *Families in Society. 86,* 83–92.

Miedel, W. T., & Reynolds, A. J. (1999). Parent involvement in early intervention for disadvantaged children: Does it matter? *Journal of School Psychology, 37,* 379–402.

Miller, B. C., Fan, X., Christensen, M., Grotevant, H. D., & van Dulmen, J. (2000). Comparisons of adopted and nonadopted adolescents in a large nationally representative sample. *Child Development, 71,* 1458–1473.

Miller, I. W., Ryan, C. E., Keitner, G. I., Bishop, D. S., & Epstein, N. B. (2000). The McMaster approach to families: Theory, assessment, treatment and research. *Journal of Family Therapy, 22*(2) 168–189.

Miller, J. B. (1986). *Toward a new psychology of women* (2nd ed.). Boston: Beacon Press.

Miller, L., Wasserman, G., Neugebauer, R., Gorman-Smith, D., & Kamboukos, D. (1999). Witnessed community violence and anti-social behavior in high-risk urban boys. *Journal of Community Psychology, 28,* 417–425.

Miller, R. (1996). *The developmentally appropriate inclusive classroom in early education.* Albany, NY: Delmar.

Miller, S. P. (2002). *Validated practices for teaching students with diverse needs and abilities.* Boston: Allyn & Bacon.

Mills, J., & Crowley, R. (1986). *Therapeutic metaphors for children and the child within.* New York: Brunner/Mazel.

Milsom, A. S. (2002). Students with disabilities: School counselor involvement and preparation. *Professional School Counseling, 5,* 331–338.

Minke, K. M., & Anderson, K. J. (2005). Family-school collaboration and positive behavior support. *Journal of Positive Behavior Interventions, 7*(5), 181–185.

Minnard, C. V. (2002). A strong building: Foundation of protective factors in schools. *Children in Schools, 24*(4), 233–243.

Minshew, D. H., & Hooper, C. (1990). *The adoptive family as a healing resource for the sexually abused child: A training manual.* Washington, DC: Child Welfare League of America.

Minuchin, P., Colapinto, J., & Minuchin, S. (1998). *Working with families of the poor.* New York: Guilford.

Minuchin, S. (1974). *Families and family therapy.* Cambridge, MA: Harvard University Press.

Minuchin, S. (1992). Constructing a therapeutic reality. In E. Kaufman & P. Kaufman (Eds.), *Family therapy of drug and alcohol abuse* (2nd ed., pp. 1–14). Boston: Allyn & Bacon.

Minuchin, S., & Fishman, H. (1981). *Family therapy techniques.* Cambridge, MA: Harvard University Press.

Minuchin, S., Montalvo, B., Guerney, B. G., Jr., Rosman, B. L., & Schumer, F. (1967). *Families of the slums: An exploration of their structure and treatment.* New York: Basic Books.

Minuchin, S., & Nichols, M. P. (1993). *Family healing: Tales of hope and renewal from family therapy.* New York: The Free Press.

Minuchin, S., Rosman, B., & Baker, L. (1978). *Psychosomatic families: Anorexia nervosa in context.* Cambridge, MA: Harvard University Press.

Mirowsky, J., & Ross, C. (2003). *Social causes of psychological distress* (2nd ed.). New York: Aldine de Gruyter.

Moles, O. C. (1993). Collaboration between schools and disadvantaged parents: Obstacles and openings. In N. F. Chavkin (Ed.), *Families and schools in a pluralistic society* (pp. 1–49). Albany: State University of New York Press.

Modell, J. S. (1994). *Kinship with strangers: Adoption and interpretations of kinship in American culture.* Berkley: University of California Press.

Moe, B. K., King, A. R., & Bailly, M. D. (2004). Retrospective accounts of recurrent parental physical abuse as a predicator of adult laboratory-induced aggression. *Aggressive Behavior, 30,* 217–228.

Molnar, B. E., Buka, S. L., Brennan, R. T., Holton, J. K., & Earls, F. (2003). A multilevel study of neighborhoods and parent-to-child physical aggression: Results from the project on human development in Chicago neighborhoods. *Child Maltreatment, 8*(2), 84–97.

Momeni, J. A. (Ed.). (1984). *Demography of racial and ethnic minorities in the United States.* Westport, CT: Greenwood Press.

Monkman, K., Ronald, M., & Theramene, F. D. (2005). Social and cultural capital in an urban Latino school community. *Urban Education, 14,* 4–33.

Montague, M., & Rinaldi, C. (2001). Classroom dynamics and children at risk: A followup. *Learning Disability Quarterly, 24,* 75–83.

Montalvo, B., & Guitierrez, M. (1983). A perspective for the use of the cultural dimension in family therapy. In J. C. Hansen & C. J. Falicov (Eds.), *Cultural perspectives in family therapy* (pp. 15–32). Rockville, MD: Aspen.

Montgomery, R., Gonyea, J., & Hooyman, N. (1985). Caregiving and the experience of subjective and objective burden. *Family Relations, 34,* 19–26.

Moos, R. H. (1974). *Family environment scale: Preliminary manual.* Palo Alto: Consulting Psychologists Press.

Moran, M. (1978). *Assessment of the exceptional learner in the regular classroom.* Denver, CO: Love.

Morgan, A. (2000). *What is narrative therapy? An easy-to-read introduction.* Adelaide, Australia: Dulwich Centre.

Morgan, O. (2002). Spirituality, alcohol and other drug problems: Where have we been? Where are we going? *Alcoholism Treatment Quarterly, 20, (3/4)* 5–40.

Morsink, C. V., Thomas, C. C., & Correa, V. I. (1991). *Interactive teaming: Consultation and collaboration in special programs.* New York: Macmillan.

Mullins, J. B. (1983). The uses of bibliotherapy in counseling families confronted with handicaps. In M. Seligman (Ed.), *The family with a handicapped child: Understanding and treatment* (pp. 235–260). New York: Grune & Stratton.

Mullis, F., & Edwards, D. (2001). Consulting with parents: Applying family systems concepts and techniques. *Professional School Counseling, 5,* 116–123.

Murdock, T. B., & Bolch, M. B. (2005). Risk and protective factors for poor school adjustment in lesbian, gay, and bisexual (LGB) high school youth: Variable and person-centered analyses. *Psychology in the Schools, 42*(2), 159–172.

Murphy, J., & Forsyth, P. B. (1999). *Educational administration: A decade of reform.* Thousand Oaks, CA: Corwin Press.

Murray, C., & Malmgren, K. (2005). Implementing a teacher-student relationship program in a high-poverty urban school: Effects on social, emotional, and academic adjustment and lessons learned. *Journal of School Psychology, 43,* 137–152.

Muuss, R. E. (1996). *Theories of adolescence.* New York: McGraw-Hill.

Nabozyne v Podlesny, 92 F.3rd 446 (7th Cir. 1996).

Nansel, T., Overpeck, M., Pilla, R., Ruan, W., Simons-Morton, B., & Scheidt, P. (2001). Bullying behavior among US youth: Prevalence and association with psychosocial adjustment. *Journal of the American Medical Association, 285*(16), 2094-2100.

National i-SAFE Survey. (2004, June 28). *National i-SAFE survey finds over half of students are being harassed online.* Retrieved July 21, 2004, from www.isafe.org

Nardone, G., & Watzlawick, P. (1993). *The art of change: Strategic therapy and hypnotherapy without trance.* San Francisco: Jossey-Bass.

Nash, J. K., & Bowen, G. L. (1999). Perceived crime and informal social control in the neighborhood as a context for adolescent behavior: A risk and resilience perspective. *Social Work Research, 23,* 171–186.

Nastasi, B. K., & DeZolt, D. M. (1994). *School interventions for children of alcoholics.* New York: Guilford Press.

Nastasi, B. K., Moore, R. B., & Varjas, K. M. (2004). *School-based mental health services: Creating comprehensive and culturally specific programs.* Washington, DC: American Psychological Association.

National Adoption Information Clearinghouse [NAIC] (1996). *Factsheet.* [www.calib.com/halc]

National Center for Education Statistics. (2005). *Student dropout rates by race/ethnicity.* Retrieved November 16, 2005 from www.nces.ed.gov/quicktables

National Committee for the Prevention of Child Abuse, NCPCA. (1998). *Twelve alternatives to lashing out at your child.* [www.childabuse.org/alterntv.html]

National Children's Advocacy Center. (2006). *Physical and behavioral indicators of abuse.* Huntsville, AL: NCAC. [www.nationalcac.org/families/for_workers/abuse_indicators.htm.]

National Institute on Alcohol Abuse and Alcoholism. (1994). *Alcohol Health and Research World, 18,* 243–245. See Internet web site for NCADD (National Council on Alcoholism and Drug Dependency) Alcoholism and Alcohol-Related Problems: A Sobering Look.

Nazzaro, J. N. (Ed.). (1981). *Culturally diverse exceptional children in school.* Washington, DC: National Institute of Education.

Neely-Barnes, S., & Marcenko, M. (2004). Predicting Impact of Childhood Disability on Families: Results from the 1995 National Health Interview Survey Disability Supplement. *Mental Retardation: A Journal of Practices, Policy and Perspectives, 42*(4) p. 284–293.

Nelson, L. G., Summers, J. A., & Turnbull, A. P. (2004). Boundaries in family-professional relationships: Implications for special education. *Remedial and Special Education, 25*(3), 153–165.

Newcomb, M. D., & Locke, T. F. (2005). Childhood adversity and poor mothering: Consequences of polydrug use as a moderator. *Addictive Behavior, 30,* 1061–1064.

Newman, K. S. (2004). *Rampage: The social roots of school shootings.* New York: Basic Books.

Newsome, W. S. (2005). The impact of solution-focused brief therapy with at-risk junior high school students. *Children in Schools, 27,* 83–90.

Nichols, M. P., & Schwartz, R. C. (2004). *Family therapy: Concepts and methods* (6th ed.). Boston: Allyn & Bacon.

Nichols, M. P., & Schwartz, R. C. (2005). *The essentials of family therapy* (2nd ed.). Boston: Allyn & Bacon.

Nichols, W. C. (1996). *Treating people in families: An integrative framework.* New York: Guilford Press.

Nickman, S. L, Rosenfeld, A. A., Fine, P., MacIntyre, J. C., Pilowsky, D. J., Howe, R-A., et al. (2005).

Children in adoptive families: Overview and update. *Child and Adolescent Psychiatry, 44,* 987–995.

Niels, J. B. (1980). *A study of birth order and family constellation among high school and delinquent students.* Ann Arbor, MI: Xerox University Microfilms.

Nihira, K., Meyers, C. E., & Mink, I. T. (1983). Reciprocal relationship between home environment and development of TMR adolescents. *American Journal of Mental Deficiency, 88,* 139–149.

Nihira, K., Mink, I. T., & Meyers, C. E. (1985). Home environment and development of slow-learning adolescents: Reciprocal relations. *Developmental Psychology, 21,* 784–794.

No Child Left Behind Act of 2001. P.L. 107-110, 20 U.S.C. § 6301 *et seq.*

Nobles, W. (2004). African philosophy: Foundations for Black psychology. In R. Jones (Ed.), *Black psychology* (4th ed.; pp. 280–292). New York: Harper & Row.

Nock, S. (1998). The consequences of premarital fatherhood. *American Sociological Review, 63,* 250–263.

Noddings, N. (1984). *Caring: A feminine approach to ethics and moral education.* Berkeley: University of California Press.

Noddings, N. (1995). Teaching themes of care. *Phi Delta Kappan, 76*(9), 675–679.

Noddings, N. (2002). *Educating moral people: A caring alternative to character education.* New York: Teacher's College Press.

Noddings, N. (2003). *Happiness and education.* New York: Cambridge University Press.

Noddings, N. (Ed.). (2005a). *Educating citizens for global awareness.* New York: Teachers College Press

Noddings, N. (2005b). *The challenge to care in schools: An alternative approach to education* (2nd ed.). New York: Teachers College Press.

Noller, P. (1994). Relationships with parents in adolescence: Process and outcome. In R. Montemayor, G. R. Adams, & T. P. Gullotta (Eds.), *Personal relationships during adolescence* (pp. 37–77). Thousand Oaks, CA: Sage.

Oates, R. K. (1991). Child physical abuse. In R. T. Ammerman & M. Hersen (Eds.), *Case studies in family violence* (pp. 113–134). New York: Plenum Press.

Obama, B. (2006). *The audacity of hope: Thoughts on reclaiming the American dream.* New York: Crown.

Obiakor, F. E., Utley, C. A., Smith, R., & Harris-Obiakor, P. (2002). The comprehensive support model for culturally diverse exceptional learners: Intervention in an age of change. *Intervention in School and Clinic, 38,* 14–27.

O'Brien, K. M., & Zamostny, K. P. (2003). *The Counseling Psychologist, 31,* 679–710.

Oddone, A. (2002). Promoting resilience in an "At Risk" world. *Childhood Education, 78,* 274–278.

O'Dell, S. (2000). Psychotherapy with gay and lesbian families: Opportunities for cultural inclusion and clinical challenge. *Clinical Social Work Journal, 28,* 171–182.

O'Keefe, E. M. (2004). *Tools for conflict resolution: A practical K-12 Program based on Peter Senge's 5th discipline.* Lanham, MD: Scarecrow Education.

Olsen, G., & Fuller, M. L. (2003). *Home-school relations: Working successfully with parents and families* (2nd ed.). Boston: Allyn & Bacon.

Olson, D. H. (1988). Family types, family stress, and family satisfaction: A family developmental perspective. In C. J. Falicov (Ed.), *Family transitions: Continuity and change over the life cycle* (pp. 55–79). New York: Guilford Press.

Olson, D. H. (2000). Circumplex model of marital and family systems. *Journal of Family Therapy, 22*(2) 144–167.

Olson, D., McCubbin, H., Barnes, H., Larsen, A., Muxen, M., & Wilson, M. (1983). *Families: What makes them work.* Beverly Hills, CA: Sage.

Olson, D. H., McCubbin, H. I., Barnes, H., Larsen, A., Muxen, M., & Wilson, M. (1984). *One thousand families: A national survey.* Beverly Hills, CA: Sage.

Olweus, D. (2003). A profile of bullying at school. *Educational Leadership, 60*(6), 12–17.

Olweus, D., Limber, S. & Mihalic, S.F. (1999). *Bullying Prevention Program: Blueprints for Violence Prevention, Book Nine.* Blueprints for Violence Prevention Series (D.S. Elliott, Series Editor). Boulder, CO: Center for the Study and Prevention of Violence, Institute of Behavioral Science, University of Colorado.

Orelove, F. P. (1995). The transdisciplinary model in educational programs for students with severe disabilities. In H. G. Garner (Ed.), *Teamwork models and experience in education* (pp. 31–42). Boston: Allyn & Bacon.

Orelove, F. P., & Malatchi, A. (1996). Curriculum and instruction. In F. P. Orelove & D. Sobsey, *Educating children with multiple disabilities: A transdisciplinary approach* (3rd ed., pp. 377–409). Baltimore, MD: Brookes.

Orelove, F., & Sobsey, D. (1991). *Educating children with multiple disabilities: A transdisciplinary approach* (2nd ed.). Baltimore, MD: Brookes.

Orelove, F. P., & Sobsey, D. (Eds.). (1996). *Educating children with multiple disabilities: A transdisciplinary approach* (3rd ed.). Baltimore, MD: Brookes.

Orelove, F. P., Sobsey, D., & Silberman, R. K. (Eds.). (2004). *Educating children with multiple disabilities: A collaborative approach* (4th ed.). Baltimore, MD: Brookes.

Ortega, R., & Lera, M. (2000). The Seville anti-bullying school project. *Aggressive Behavior, 26,* 113–123.

Orthner, D. K., Jones-Sanpei, H., & Williamson, S. (2004). The resilience and strengths of low-income families. *Family Relations, 53,* 159–167.

Orr, L., Craig, G., Best, J., Borland, A., Holland, D., Knodel, H., Lehman, A., Matthewson, C., Miller, M., & Pequignot, M. (1997). Exploring developmental disabilities through literature: An annotated bibliography. *Teaching Exceptional Children, 29*(6), 14–15.

OSERS (1999). Grant applications under Part D. Subpart 2 of the Individuals with Disabilities Education Act Amendments of 1997. *Federal Register,* pp. 352–362.

Osher, T. W., & Osher, D. M. (2002). The paradigm shift to true collaboration with families. *Journal of Child and Family Studies, 11,* 47-60.

Osofsky, J. D. (Winter, 1999). The impact of violence on children and youth. *Domestic Violence and Children and Youth, 9*(3), 33-49.

O'Toole, T. J., & Switlick, D. M. (1997). Integrated therapies. In D. F. Bradley, M. E. King-Sears, & D. M. Tessier-Switlick (Eds.), *Teaching students in inclusive settings: From theory to practice* (pp. 202–224). Boston: Allyn & Bacon.

Otto, M. L., & Smith, D. G. (1980). Child abuse: A cognitive behavioral intervention model. *Journal of Marital and Family Therapy, 6,* 425–430.

Ozer, E. J., & Weinstein, R. S. (2004). Urban adolescents' exposure to community violence: The roles of support, school safety, and social constraints in a school-based sample of boys and girls. *Journal of Clinical Child and Adolescent Psychology, 33*(3), 463–476.

Pan, E., & Farrell, M. P. (2006). Ethnic differences in the effects of intergenerational relations on adolescent problem behavior in U.S. single-mother families. *Journal of Family Issues, 27,* 1137–1158.

Park, J., & Turnbull, A. (2002). Quality indicators of professionals who work with children with problem behavior. *Journal of Positive Behavior Interventions, 4,* 118–122.

Park J., Turnbull, A. P., & Turnbull, H. R. (2002). Impacts of poverty on quality of life in families of children with disabilities. *Exceptional Children, 68,* 151–170.

Parke, R. D. (2004). Development in the family. Annual Review of Psychology, 55, 365-399.

Pasley, K. (2003). Editorial. *Family Relations, 52,* 313.

Patterson, J. M. (1985). Critical factors affecting family compliance with home treatment for children with cystic fibrosis. *Family Relations, 34,* 79–89.

Patterson, J. M. (1997). Promoting resilience in families. *Resiliency in Action, 2*(2), 8–16.

Patterson, J.M. (2002). Understanding family resilience. *Journal of Clinical Psychology, 58*(3), 233–246.

Patterson, J. M., & McCubbin, H. I. (1983). Chronic illness: Family stress and coping. In C. R. Figley & H. I. McCubbin (Eds.), *Stress and the family: Vol. 2. Coping with catastrophe* (pp. 21–36). New York: Brunner/Mazel.

Pearpoint, J., O'Brien, J., & Forest, M. (1995). *Planning alternative tomorrows with hope* (2nd ed.). Toronto, Ontario, Canada: Inclusion Press.

Pearpoint, J, Forest, M., & ., O'Brien, J. (1996). MAPS, CIRCLES of Friends and PATH: Powerful tools to help build caring communities. In S. Stainback, & W. Stainback (Eds.), *Inclusion: A guide for educators* (pp. 67–86). Baltimore, MD: Brookes.

Peck, M. S. (1978). *The road less traveled.* New York: Simon & Schuster.

Pedersen, F. A. (1983). Differentiation of the father's role in the infancy period. In J. Vincent (Ed.), *Advances in family intervention, assessment, and theory* (Vol. 3, pp. 185–208). New York: JAI Press.

Peeks, B. (1993). Revolutions in counseling and education: A systems perspective in the schools. *Elementary School Guidance and Counseling, 27,* 245–251.

Peeks, B. (1997). Revolutions in counseling and education: A systems perspective in the schools. In W. M. Walsh & G. R. Williams (Eds.), *Schools and family therapy: Using systems theory and family therapy in the resolution of school problems* (pp. 5–12). Springfield, IL: C. C. Thomas.

Peled, E., Jaffe, P. G., & Edleson, J. (Eds.). (1995). *Ending the cycle of violence: Community responses to children of battered women.* Thousand Oaks, CA: Sage.

Peng, S. S., Wang, M. C., & Walberg, H. J. (1992, April). *Resilient students in urban settings.* Paper presented at the annual meeting of the American Educational Research Association, San Francisco, CA.

Perry, B. D. (2001). The neuroarcheology of childhood maltreatment: The neurodevelopmental costs of adverse childhood events. In K. Franey, R. Geffner, & R. Falconer (Eds.), *The cost of maltreatment: Who pays? We all do* (pp. 15–37). San Diego, CA: Family Violence and Sexual Assault Institute. [www.childtrauma.org/ctamaterials/neuroarcheology.asp]

Peterson, C., & Seligman, M. E. P. (2004). *Character strengths and virtues: A handbook and classification.* Washington, DC: American Psychological Association and New York: Oxford University Press.

Pertman, A. (2000). *Adoption nation: How the adoption revolution is transforming America.* New York: Basic Books.

Peters, B. R., Atkins, M. S., & McKay, M. M. (1999). Adopted children's behavior problems: A review of five explanatory models. *Clinical Psychology Review, 19,* 297–328.

Peterson, E. T., & Kunz, P. R. (1975). Parental control over adolescents according to family size. *Adolescence, 10,* 419–427.

Pfeiffer, S. (1980). The school-based interprofessional team: Recurring problems and some possible solutions. *Journal of School Psychology, 18,* 388–394.

Phillips, V., & McCullough, L. (1990). Consultation-based programming: Instituting the collaborative ethic in schools. *Exceptional Children, 56,* 291–304.

Phillips-Hershey, E. H., & Ridley, L. L. (1996). Strategies for acceptance of diversity of students with mental retardation. *Elementary School Guidance & Counseling, 30,* 282–291.

Phinney, J. S., & Ong, A. D. (2002). Adolescent-parent disagreements and life satisfaction in families from Vietnamese- and European-American backgrounds. *International Journal of Behavioral Development, 26,* 556–561.

Piaget, J. (1952). *The origins of intelligence in children.* New York: International Universities Press.

Piaget, J., & Inhelder, B. (1958). *The growth of logical thinking from childhood to adolescence* (A. Parsons & S. Milgram, Trans.). New York: Basic Books.

Piaget, J., & Inhelder, B. (1969). *The psychology of the child.* New York: Basic Books.

Pianta, R. C. (2000). *Enhancing relationships between children and teachers.* Washington, DC: American Psychological Association.

Pinkney, A. (1975). *Black Americans.* Englewood Cliffs, NJ: Prentice-Hall.

Plomin, R. & Asbury, K. (2001). Nature and nurture in the family. *Marriage and Family Review, 33(2/3)* 273–281.

Pollard, J. A., Hawkins, J. D., & Arthur, M. W. (1999). Risk and protection: Are both necessary to understand diverse behavioral outcomes in adolescence? *Social Work Research, 23,* 145–158.

Powell, T. H., & Gallagher, P. A. (1993). *Brothers and sisters: A special part of exceptional families* (2nd ed.). Baltimore, MD: Brookes.

President & Fellows of Harvard College. (2002). Beyond the head count: Evaluating family involvement in out-of-school time. *Issues and Opportunities in Out-of-School Time Evaluations, 4*(March), 1–15.

President & Fellows of Harvard College. (2003a). A review of out-of-school time program quasi-experimental and experimental evaluation results. *Out-of-School Time Evaluation Snapshot, 1*(July), 1–12.

President & Fellows of Harvard College. (2003b). A review of activity implementation in out-of-school time programs. *Out-of-School Snapshot, 2*(August), 1–4.

President & Fellows of Harvard College. (2004a). Engaging with families in out-of-school time learning. *Out-of-School Time Evaluation Snapshot, 4*(April), 1–8.

President & Fellows of Harvard College. (2004b). Moving beyond the barriers: Attracting and sustaining youth participation in out-of-school time programs. *Issues and Opportunities in Out-of-School Time Evaluation, 6*(July), 1–16.

Proctor, B. D., & Dalaker, J., (2003). *U.S. Census Bureau, Current Population Reports, P60-222, Poverty in the United States: 2002.* Washington, DC: U.S. Government Printing Office.

Prosen, H., Toews, J., & Martin, R. (1981). The life cycle of the family: I. Parental midlife crisis and adolescent rebellion. *Adolescent Psychiatry, 9,* 170–179.

Pugach, M. C. (2001). The stories we choose to tell: Fulfilling the promise of qualitative research for special education. *Exceptional Children, 67,* 439–453.

Pugach, M. C., & Johnson, L. J. (2002). *Collaborative practitioners: Collaborative schools* (2nd ed.). Denver: Love.

Purvis, M., & Ward, T. (2006). The role of culture in understanding child sexual offending: Examining feminist perspectives. *Aggression and Violent Behavior, 11,* 298–312.

Quinn, W. H., Newfield, N. A., & Protinsky, H. O. (1985). Rites of passage in families with adolescents. *Family Process, 24,* 101–111.

Raines, J. C. (2004). Evidence-based practice in school social work: A process in perspective. *Children in Schools, 26*(2), 71–85.

Rainforth, B., York, J., & Macdonald, C. (1992). *Collaborative teams for students with severe disabilities: Integrating therapy and educational services.* Baltimore, MD: Brookes.

Rak, C. F., & Patterson, L. W. (1996). Promoting resilience in at-risk children. *Journal of Counseling & Development, 74*(4), 368–373.

Ralph, J. (1989). Improving education for the disadvantaged: Do we know whom to help? *Phi Delta Kappan, 70,* 385–401.

Raychaba, B. (1993). *Pain...lots of pain.* Ottawa, ON: National Youth in Care Network.

Raynor, L. (1980). *The adopted child comes of age.* London: Allen & Unwin.

Reed, D. F. (1993). Culturally diverse students. In J. Wood (Ed.), *Mainstreaming: A practical approach for teachers* (pp. 122–154). Columbus, OH: Merrill.

Reilly, T, & Platz, L. (2004). Post-adoption service needs of families with special needs children: Use, helpfulness, and unmet needs. *Journal of Social Service Research, 30*(4), 51–67.

Reimers, S., & Street, E. (1993). Using family therapy in child and adolescent services. In J. Carpenter

& A. Treacher (Eds.), *Using family therapy in the 90s* (pp. 32–56). Cambridge, MA: Blackwell.

Reinsmith, W. A. (1989). The whole in every part: Steiner and Waldorf schooling. *Educational Forum, 54,* 79–91.

Reis, B. (1996). *Safe schools anti-violence documentation project: Third annual report.* Seattle: Safe Schools Coalition.

Reiss, D., & Oliveri, M. E. (1980). Family paradigm and family coping: A proposal for linking the family's intrinsic adaptive capacities to its responses to stress. *Family Relations, 29,* 431–444.

Reitz, M., & Watson, K. W. (1992). *Adoption and the family system: Strategies for treatment.* New York: Guilford Press.

Rhodes, W. A., & Brown, W. K. (1991). *Why some children succeed despite the odds.* New York: Praeger.

Rich, C. L., Warsradt, G. M., Nemiroff, R. A., Fowler, R. C., & Young, D. (1991). Suicide, stressors, and the life cycle. *American Journal of Psychiatry, 148,* 524–527.

Rich, S. (1986, November 12). Parental fighting hurts even after divorce. *The Washington Post,* p. H–12.

Richardson, G. E. (2002). The metatheory of resilience and resiliency. *Journal of Clinical Psychology, 58*(3), 307–321.

Richardson, G. E., & Hawks, S. R. (1995). A practical approach for enhancing resilience within families. *Family Perspective, 29,* 235–250.

Richardson, R. A. (2004). Early adolescence talking points: Questions that middle school students want to ask their parents. *Family Relations, 53,* 87–94.

Richman, J. M., Bowen, G. L., & Woolley, M. E., (2004). School failure: An eco-interactional developmental perspective. In M. W. Fraser (Ed.), *Risk and resilience in childhood: An ecological perspective* (2nd, ed.; pp. 133–160). Washington, DC: NASW Press.

Rigby, K., & Slee, P. (1999). Australia. In P. Smith, Y. Morita, J. Junger-Tas, D. Olweus, R. Catalano, & P. Slee (Eds.), *The nature of school bullying: A cross-national perspective* (pp. 324–339). London and NY: Routledge.

Ripple, C. H. & Luthar, S. S. (2000). Academic risk among inner-city adolescents: The role of personal attributes. *Journal of School Psychology, 38,* 277–298.

Roberto, L. G. (1992). *Transgenerational family therapies.* New York: Guilford Press.

Roberts, S. (2004). *Who are we now: The changing face of America in the twenty-first century.* New York: Times Books.

Robinson, T. N., Wilde, M. L., Navracruz, L. C., Haydel, K. F., & Varady, A. (2001). Effects of reducing children and youth's television and video game use on aggressive behavior: A randomized controlled trial. *Archives of Pediatrics and Adolescent Medicine, 155*(1), 17–23.

Rodriguez, D., Parmar, R. S., & Signer, B. R. (2001). Fourth-grade culturally and linguistically diverse exceptional students' concepts of number line. *Exceptional Children, 67,* 199–210.

Rolland, J. S. (1999). Chronic illness and the family life cycle. In B. Carter and M. McGoldrick (Eds.), *The expanded family life cycle: Individual, family, and social perspectives* (3rd ed., pp. 492–511). Boston: Allyn & Bacon.

Rolland, J. S. (2003). Mastering family challenges in illness and disability. In F. Walsh (Ed.), *Normal family processes: Growing diversity and complexity* (3rd ed., pp. 460–489). New York: Guilford.

Rompf, E. R., (1993). Open Adoption: What Does the "Average Person" Think? *Child Welfare, 72*(3) p. 219–30.

Rosen, E. J. (1999). Men in transition: The "new man." In B. Carter and M McGoldrick (Eds.), *The expanded family life cycle: Individual, family, and social perspectives* (3rd ed., pp. 124–140). Boston: Allyn & Bacon.

Rosenberg, E. B. (1992). *The adoption life cycle: The children and their families through the years.* New York: Free Press.

Rossi, A. S., & Rossi, P. H. (1990). *Of human bonding: Parent-child relations across the life course.* Hawthorne, NY: Aldine.

Roy, S. A. (1995). The process of reorganization. In H. G. Garner (Ed.), *Teamwork models and experience in education* (pp. 85–101). Boston: Allyn & Bacon.

Rubin, K. H. (1985). Socially withdrawn children: An "at risk" population? In B. H. Schneider, K. H. Rubin, & J. E. Kedingham (Eds.), *Children's peer relations: Issues in assessment and intervention* (pp. 125–140). New York: Springer-Verlag.

Rueveni, U. (1979). *Networking families in crisis: Intervention strategies with families and social networks.* New York: Human Sciences Press.

Russell, B. S., & Britner, P. A. (2006). Measuring shaken baby syndrome awareness: Preliminary reliability of a caregiver attitudes and beliefs survey. *Journal of Child and Family Studies, 15,* 765–778.

Rutter, M. (1987). Psychological resilience and protective mechanisms. *American Journal of Orthopsychiatry, 57,* 316–331.

Ryan, G. (1997). A developmental-contextual view. In G. Ryan & S. Lane (Eds.), *Juvenile sexual offending* (pp. 122–135). San Francisco: Jossey-Bass.

Safren, S. A., & Heimberg, R. G. (1999). Depression, hopelessness, suicidality, and related factors in sexual minority and heterosexual adolescents. *Journal of Consulting and Clinical Psychology, 67,* 859–866.

Sagor, R. (1996). Building resiliency in students. *Educational Leadership, 54*(1), 38–43.

Saitoh, S., Steinglass, P., & Schuckit, M. A. (Eds.). (1992). *Alcoholism and the family*. New York: Brunner/Mazel.

Salmivalli, C. (1999). Participant role approach to school bullying: Implications for interventions. *Journal of Adolescence, 22,* 453–459.

Samuels, S. C. (1990). *Ideal adoption: A comprehensive guide to forming an adoptive family*. New York: Plenum.

Sanders, D. (1987). Cultural Conflicts: An Important Factor in the Academic Failures of American Indian Students. *Journal of Multicultural Counseling and Development, 15*(2) p. 81–90.

Satir, V. (1972). *Peoplemaking*. Palo Alto, CA: Science and Behavior Books.

Satir, V. (1978). *Your many faces*. Millbrae, CA: Celestial Arts.

Satir, V. (1983a). *AVANTA Process Community III. The Third International Summer Institute*. Crested Butte, CO: AVANTA Process Community.

Satir, V. (1983b). *Conjoint family therapy* (3rd ed.). Palo Alto, CA: Science and Behavior Books.

Satir, V. (1988). *The new peoplemaking*. Mountain View, CA: Science and Behavior Books.

Satir, V., & Baldwin, M. (1983). *Satir, step by step*. Palo Alto, CA: Science and Behavior Books.

Satir, V., & Bitter, J. R. (2000). The therapist and family therapy: Satir's human validation model. In A. M. Horne & J. L. Passmore (Eds.), *Family counseling and therapy* (3rd ed., pp. 62–101). Itasca, IL: F. E. Peacock.

Satir, V., Stachowiak, J., & Taschman, H. (1975). *Helping families to change*. New York: Jason Aronson.

Saunders, D. (1987). Cultural conflicts: An important factor in the academic failure of American Indian students. *Journal of Multicultural Counseling & Development, 15,* 81–90.

Scanlon, D., & Mellard, D. F. (2002). Academic and participation profiles of school-age dropouts with and without disabilities. *Exceptional Children, 68,* 239–258.

Scannapieco, M., & Carrick, K. C. (2003). Families in poverty: Those who maltreat their infants and toddlers and those who do not. *Journal of Family Social Work, 73*(3) 49–40.

Scarpa, A. (2001). Community violence exposure in a young adult sample. *Journal of Interpersonal Violence, 16,* 36–53.

Schechter, S., & Edleson, J. L. (1999). *Effective intervention in domestic violence and child maltreatment cases: Guidelines for policy and practice*. Reno, NV: National Council of Juvenile and Family Court Judges

Schell, G. (1981). The young handicapped child: A family perspective. *Topics in Early Childhood Special Education, 1*(3), 21–27.

Scher, C. D., Forde, D. R., McQuaid, J. R., & Stein, M. B. (2004). Prevalence and demographic correlates of childhood maltreatment in an adult community sample. *Child Abuse and Neglect, 28,* 167–180.

Schlesinger, S. E., & Horberg, L. K. (1988). *Taking charge: How families can climb out of the chaos of addiction and flourish*. New York: Simon & Schuster.

Schniedewind, N., & Davidson, E. (1998). *Open minds to equality: A sourcebook of learning activities to affirm diversity and promote equity*. Boston: Allyn & Bacon.

Schoon, I. & Parsons, S. (2002) Competence in the face of adversity: The influence of early family environment and long-term consequences. *Children and Society, 16,* 260–272.

Schuck, A. M. (2002). *Understanding the role of neighborhood in the long-term criminal consequences of childhood maltreatment*. Washington, DC: US Department of Justice. Unpublished dissertation manuscript [www.ncjrs.gov/pdffiles1/nij/grants/197049.pdf]

Schweiger, W. K., & O'Brien, M. (2005). Special needs adoption: An ecological systems approach. *Family Relations, 54,* 512–522.

Scott, T. M. (2001). A schoolwide example of positive behavioral support. *Journal of Positive Behavior Interventions, 3*(2), 88–94.

Scott, T. M., & Eber, L. (2003). Functional assessment and wraparound as systemic school processes: Primary, secondary, and tertiary systems examples. *Journal of Positive Behavior Interventions, 5*(3), 131–143.

Schulman, G. L. (1984). Transitions in family structure. In C. E. Schaefer, J. M. Briesmeister, & M. E. Fitton (Eds.), *Family therapy techniques for problem behaviors of children and teenagers* (pp. 337–340). San Francisco: Jossey-Bass.

Schumacher, J. A., Slep, A. M. S., & Heyman, R. E. (2001). Risk factors for child neglect. *Aggression and Violent Behavior, 6,* 231–254.

Schuster, M. A., Franke, M. F., Bastian, A. M., Sor, S., & Halfon, N. (2000) Firearm storage patterns in US homes with children and youth. *American Journal of Public Health, 90*(4), 588–594.

Schvaneveldt, J. D., & Ihinger, M. (1979). Sibling relationships in the family. In W. R. Burr, R. Hill, F. J. Nye, & I. L. Reiss (Eds.), *Contemporary theories about the family* (Vol. 1, pp. 96–97). New York: Free Press.

Schwab, J. (1990). *A resource handbook for Satir concepts*. Palo Alto, CA: Science and Behavior Books.

Schwartz, L. L., & Kaslow, F. W. (1997). *Painful partings: Divorce and its aftermath*. New York: Wiley.

Schwartz, L. L., & Kaslow, F. W. (Eds.). (2003). *Welcome home: An international and nontraditional adoption reader*. New York: Haworth Clinical Practice Press.

Schweiger, W. K., & O'Brien, M. (2005). Special needs adoption: An ecological systems approach. *Family Relations, 54,* 512–522.

Scorgie, K. & Sobsey, D. (2000). Transformational outcomes associated with parenting children who have disabilities. *Mental Retardation, 38,* 195–206.

Scorgie, K., Wilgosh, L., & McDonald, L. (1998). Stress and coping in families of children with disabilities: An examination of recent literature. *Developmental Disabilities Bulletin, 26,* 22–42.

Seligman, M. (1991a). Family systems and beyond: Conceptual issues. In M. Seligman (Ed.), *The family with a handicapped child* (2nd ed., pp. 27–53). Boston: Allyn and Bacon.

Seligman, M. (1991c). Siblings of disabled brothers and sisters. In M. Seligman (Ed.), *The family with a handicapped child* (2nd ed., pp. 181–201). Boston: Allyn & Bacon.

Seligman, M. (2000). *Conducting effective conferences with parents of children with disabilities: A guide for teachers*. New York: Guilford.

Seltzer, M.M., Greenberg, J.S., Orsmond, G.I., & Lounds, J. (2005). Life course studies of siblings of individuals with developmental disabilities. *Mental Retardation, 43*(5), 354–359.

Seltzer, M. M., Greenberg, J. S., Floyd, F. J., Pettee, Y., & Hong, J. (2001). Life course impacts of parenting a child with a disability. *American Journal on Mental Retardation, 106,* 265–286.

Senge, P. M. (1990). *The fifth discipline: The art and practice of the learning organization*. New York: Doubleday.

Serafica, F. C. (1990). Counseling Asian-American parents: A cultural-developmental approach. In F. C. Serafica, A. I. Schwebel, R. K. Russell, P. D. Isaac, & L. B. Myers (Eds.), *Mental health of ethnic minorities* (pp. 222–244). New York: Praeger.

Sexton, D., Lobman, M., Constans, T., Snyder, P., & Ernest, J. (1997). Early interventionists' perspectives of multicultural practices with African-American families. *Exceptional Children, 63,* 313–328.

Shapiro, J. (1983). Family reactions and coping strategies in response to the physically ill or handicapped child: A review. *Social Science Medicine, 17,* 913–931.

Sheehy, G. (1976). *Passages: Predictable crises of adult life*. New York: Dutton.

Sheehy, G. (1995). *New passages: Mapping your life across time*. New York: Random House.

Shepard, H. A. (1995). On the realization of human potential: A path with a heart. In D. Kolb, J. Osland, & I. Rubin (Eds.), *The organizational behavior reader* (6th ed., pp. 168–178), Englewood Cliffs, NJ: Prentice Hall.

Shepard, H. A. (2001). Rules of thumb for change agents. In J. Osland, D. Kolb, & I. Rubin (Eds.), *The organizational behavior reader* (7th ed., pp. 589–594). Upper Saddle River, NJ: Prentice Hall.

Sheridan, S. M., Warnes, E. D., Cowan, R. J., Schemm, A. V., & Clarke, B. L. (2004). Family-centered positive psychology: Focusing on strengths to build student success. *Psychology in the Schools, 41,* 7–17.

Shields, A., & Cicchetti, D. (2001). Parental maltreatment and emotion dysregulation as risk factors for bullying and victimization in middle childhood. *Journal of Clinical Child Psychology, 30,* 349–363.

Shipman, K., Edwards, A., Brown, A., Swisher, L., & Jennings, E. (2005). Managing emotion in a maltreating context: A pilot study examining child neglect. *Child Abuse and Neglect, 29,* 1015–1029.

Shore, C. M. (2004). *The many faces of childhood: Diversity in development*. Boston: Pearson Education.

Shulman, B., & Mosak H. (1977). Birth order and ordinal position: Two Adlerian views. *Journal of Individual Psychology, 33,* 114–121.

Silverstein, D. R., & Demick, J. (1994). Toward an organizational-relational model of open adoption. *Family Process, 33,* 111–124.

Simcox, A. G., Nuijens, K. L., Lee, C. C. (2006). School counselors and school psychologists: Collaborative partners in promoting culturally competent schools. *Professional School Counseling, 9,* 272–277.

Simon, B. S. (2004). High school outreach and family involvement. *Social Psychology of Education, 7,* 185–209.

Simon, R. J., & Altstein, H. (2002). *Adoption, race, and identity: From infancy to young adulthood* (2nd ed.). New Brunswick, NJ: Transaction.

Simpson, R. (1990). *Conferencing parents of exceptional children* (2nd ed.). Austin, TX: Pro-Ed.

Simpson, R. (1996). *Working with parents and families of exceptional children and youth: Techniques for successful conferencing and collaboration* (3rd ed.). Austin, TX: Pro-Ed.

Singer, G. H. S. (2002). Suggestions for a pragmatic program of research on families and disability. *Journal of Special Education, 36,* 148–154.

Singer, M. I., Miller, D. B., Guo, S., Slovak, K., & Frieson, T. (1998). *The mental health consequences of children and youth's exposure to violence*. Cleveland, OH: Cuyahoga County Community Health Research Institute, Mandel School of Applied Social Sciences, Case Western Reserve University.

Sink, C. A., & Richmond, L. J., (2004). Introducing Spirituality to Professional Counseling [Special Issue]. *Professional School Counseling, 7*(5).

Skinner, D., Bailey, D. B., Correa, V., & Rodriguez, P. (1999). Narrating self and disability: Latino mothers' construction of identities vis-`a-vis their child with special needs. *Exceptional Children, 65,* 481–495.

Skinner, H. Steinhauer, P., & Sitarenios, G. (2000). Family assessment measure (FAM) and process model of family functioning. *Journal of Family Therapy, 22*(2) 190–210.

Skovholt, T. M. (2001). *The resilient practitioner: Burnout prevention and self-care strategies for counselors, therapists, teachers, and health professionals.* Needham Heights, MA: Allyn & Bacon.

Skowron, E. A. (2005). Parent differentiation of self and child competence of self in low-income urban families. *Journal of Counseling Psychology, 52,* 337–346.

Skowron, E., & Reinemann, D. H. S. (2005). Effectiveness of psychological interventions for child maltreatment: A meta-analysis. *Psychotherapy: Theory, Research, Practice, Training, 42*(1) 52–71.

Skrtic, T. (1991). *Behind special education: A critical analysis of professional culture and school organization.* Denver, CO: Love.

Slavin, R., & Madden, N. (1989). What works for student at risk: A research synthesis. *Educational Leadership, 46*(5), 4–13.

Slavin, R. E., Madden, N. A., Dolan, L. J., & Wasik, B. A. (1996). *Every child, every school: Success for all.* Thousand Oaks, CA: Corwin Press.

Sluckin, A., & Smith, P. (1977). Two approaches to the concept of dominance in preschool children. *Child Development, 48,* 911–923.

Smith, A. H. (1978). Encountering the family system in school-related behavior problems. *Psychology in the Schools, 15,* 379–386.

Smith, E. P., Boutte, G. S., Zigler, E., & Finn-Stevenson, M. (2004). Opportunities for schools to promote resilience in children and youth. In K. I. Maton, C. J. Schellenbach, B. J. Leadbeater, & Solarz, A. L. (Eds.), *Investing in children, youth, families, and communities: Strengths-based research and policy* (pp. 213–231). Washington, DC: American Psychological Association.

Smith-Bird, E., & Turnbull, A. P. (2005). Linking positive behavior support to family quality-of-life outcomes. *Journal of Positive Behavior Interventions, 7*(3), 174–180.

Smith, P., & Sharp, S. (1994). *School bullying: Insights and perspectives.* London and New York: Routledge.

Smith, T. E. C. (2005). IDEA 2004: Another round in the reauthorization process. *Remedial and special education, 26,* 314–319.

Smith, T. E. C., Polloway, E. A., Patton, J. R., & Dowdy, C. A. (2006) *Teaching students with special needs in inclusive settings, IDEA update edition.* Boston: Allyn & Bacon.

Sobol, M. P., Daly, K. J., & Kelloway, E. K. (2000). Paths to the facilitation of open adoption. *Family Relations, 49,* 419–424.

Sobolewski, J. M., & King, V. (2005). The importance of the coparental relationship for nonresident fathers' ties to children. *Journal of Marriage and Family, 67,* 1196–1212.

Sobsey, D. (1994). *Violence and abuse in the lives of people with disabilities: The end of silent acceptance?* Baltimore, MD: Brookes.

Sobsey, D. (2002). Exceptionality, education, & maltreatment. *Exceptionality, 10*(1) 29–46.

Solomon, M. (2005). *AA – Not the only way: Your one stop resource guide to 12-step alternatives.* Venice, CA: Capalo Press.

Solomon, Z. P. (1991). California's policy on parent involvement: State leadership for local initiatives. *Phi Delta Kappan, 72,* 359–362.

Somit, A., Arwine, A., & Peterson, S. A. (1996). *Birth order and political behavior.* New York: University Press of America.

Sontag, J. C., & Schacht, R. (1994). An ethnic comparison of parent participation and information needs in early intervention. *Exceptional Children, 60,* 422–433.

Spark, G. M., & Brody, E. M. (1970). The aged are family members. *Family Process, 9,* 195–210.

Spinelli, C. G. (1999). Breaking down barriers—Building strong foundations: Parents and teachers of exceptional students working together. *Learning Disabilities: A Multidisciplinary Journal, 9*(3), 123–129.

Stanton, M. D., Todd, T. C. (1982). *The family therapy of drug abuse and addiction.* New York: Guilford Press.

Staples, R. (1994). *Black family: Essays and studies* (5th ed.). New York: Van Nostrand Reinhold.

Steel, J., Sanna, L., Hammond, B., Whipple, J., & Cross, H. (2004). Psychological sequelae of childhood sexual abuse: Abuse-related characteristics, coping strategies, and attributional style. *Child Abuse and Neglect, 28,* 785–801.

Stemmler, M., & Peterson, A. C. (1999). Reciprocity and change within the affective family environment in early adolescence. *International Journal of Behavioral Development, 23,* 185–198.

Stepp, L. S. (2001, June 19). A lesson in cruelty: Antigay slurs common at school. *The Washington Post,* p. A01.

Stevens, M., & Higgins, D. J. (2002). The influence of risk and protective factors on burnout experienced by those who work with maltreated children. *Child Abuse Review, 11,* 313–331.

Stinson, K. M. (1991). *Adolescents, family, and friends: Social support after parents' divorce or remarriage.* New York: Praeger.

Stoneman, Z. (2005). Siblings of children with disabilities: Research themes. *Mental Retardation, 43,* 339–350.

Straussner, S. L. A. (2001b). Ethnocultural issues in substance abuse treatment: An overview. In S. Straussner (Ed.), *Ethnocultural factors in substance abuse treatment* (pp. 3–28). New York: Guilford.

Stutman, S. S. (1984). *Family life cycle development: Examination of the pathway linking differentiation from the family of origin, marital adjustment, child-focused triangulation, and adolescent adjustment.* Los Angeles: California School of Professional Psychology.

Suelzle, M., & Keenan, V. (1981). Changes in family support networks over the life cycle of mentally retarded persons. *American Journal of Mental Deficiency, 86,* 267–274.

Sullivan, P. M., & Knutson, J. F. (2000). Maltreatment and disabilities: A population-based epidemiological study. *Child Abuse and Neglect, 24*(10) 1257–1273.

Sullivan, T. N., Kung, E.M., & Farrell, A. D. (Eds.). (2004). Relation between witnessing violence and drug use initiation among rural adolescents" Parental monitoring and family support as protective factors. *Journal of Clinical Child and Adolescent Psychology, 33*(3), 488–498.

Sulloway, F, (1996). *Born to rebel.* NY: Pantheon.

Sussell, A., Carr, S., & Hartman, A. (1996). Families R Us: Building a parent/school partnership. *Teaching Exceptional Children, 28*(4), 53–57.

Sutton, C. T., & Broken Nose, M. A. (1996). American Indian families: An overview. In M. McGoldrick, J. Giordano, & J. Pearce (Eds.), *Ethnicity and family therapy* (2nd ed., pp. 31–44). New York: Guilford Press.

Sutton, C. T., & Broken Nose, M. A. (2005). American Indian families: An overview. In M. McGoldrick, J. Giordano, & N. Garcia-Preto (Eds.), *Ethnicity and family therapy* (3rd ed., pp. 43–54). New York: Guilford Press.

Suzuki, L. A., & Kugler, J. F. (1995). Intelligence and personality assessment. In J. G. Ponterotto, J. M. Casas, L. A. Suzuki, & C. M. Alexander (Eds.), *Handbook of multicultural counseling* (pp. 493–515). Thousand Oaks, CA: Sage.

Switlick, D. M. (1996). Curriculum modifications and adaptations. In D. F. Bradley, M. E. King-Sears, & D. M. Tessier-Switlick (Eds.), *Teaching students in inclusive settings: From theory to practice* (pp. 225–251). Boston: Allyn & Bacon.

Switlick, D. M. (1997b). Integrating specialized curricula. In D. F., Bradley, M. E. King-Sears, & D. M. Terrier-Switlick (Eds.), *Teaching students in inclusive setting: From theory to practice* (pp. 252–282). Boston: Allyn & Bacon.

Sykes, M. R. (2001). Adoption with contact: A study of adoptive parents and the impact of continuing contact with families of origin. *Journal of Family Therapy, 23,* 296–316.

Syverson, M. A. (2005). *Student-led conferences: Fourth-grade students and their parents' perceptions.* Ann Arbor, MI: ProQuest.

Szapocznik, J., & Williams, R. A. (2000). Brief strategic family therapy: Twenty-five years of interplay among theory, research and practice in adolescent behavior problems and drug abuse. *Clinical Child and Family Psychology Review, 3*(2) 117–134.

Tarver-Behring, S., & Spagna, M. E. (2004). Counseling with exceptional children. In A. Verson (Ed.). *Counseling children and adolescents* (3rd ed., pp. 189–226). Denver: Love.

Tashima, N. (1981). Asian Americans in psychiatric systems. In D. Claerbaut (Ed.), *New directions in ethnic studies: Minorities in America* (pp. 95–106). Saratoga, CA: Century Twenty One.

Teachman, J. D., Tedrow, L. M., & Crowder, K. D. (2000). The changing demography of America's families. *Journal of Marriage and the Family, 62,* 1234–1246.

Terrell, J. E. (Ed.). (2001). *Archaeology, language, and history: Essays on culture and ethnicity.* Bergin & Garvey

Terrell, J. & Modell, J. S. (1994). Anthropology and adoption. *American Anthropologist, 96,* 155–161.

Test, D. W., Mason, C., Hughes, C., Konrad, M., Neale, M., & Wood, W. M. (2004). Student involvement in individualized education program meetings. *Exceptional Children, 20,* 391–412.

Teyber, E. (1994). *Helping children cope with divorce.* New York: Lexington Books.

Thaxton, L. (1985). Wife abuse. In L. L'Abate (Ed.), *The handbook of family psychology and therapy* (Vol. 2, pp. 876–899). Homewood, IL: Dorsey Press.

Thomas, C. (2000). Family treatment with adult substance abuse. In J. Corcoran (Ed.), *Evidence-based social work practice with families: A lifespan approach* (pp. 369–394). New York: Springer.

Thomlison, B. (2004). Child maltreatment: A risk and protective factor perspective. In M. W. Fraser (Ed.). *Risk and resilience in childhood: An ecological perspective* (2nd ed., pp. 89–131). Washington, D.C.: NASW Press.

Thorin, E. J., & Irvin, L. K. (1992). Family stress associated with transition to adulthood of young people with severe disabilities. *Journal for Association of Severe Handicaps, 17,* 31–39.

Thousand, J. S., Villa, R. A., & Nevin, A. I. (1994). *Creativity and collaborative learning: A practical guide to empowering students and teachers.* Baltimore, MD: Brookes.

Thousand, J. S., Villa, R. A., & Nevin, A. I. (Eds.). (2003). *Creativity and collaborative learning: A practical guide to empowering students, teachers, and families* (2nd ed.). Baltimore, MD: Brookes.

Thuppal, M., & Sobsey, D. (2004). Children with special health care needs. In F. P. Orelove, D. Sobsey, & R. K. Silberman (Eds.). *Educating children with multiple disabilities: A collaborative approach* (4th ed.; pp. 311–377). Baltimore, MD: Brookes.

Tindal, G., Shinn, M., & Rodden-Nord, K. (1990). Contextually based school consultation: Influential variables. *Exceptional Children, 56,* 324–336.

Tittler, B., Friedman, S., Blotcky, A., & Stedrak, J. (1982). The influence of family variables on an ecologically-based treatment program for emotionally disturbed children. *American Journal of Orthopsychiatry, 52,* 123–130.

Toews, M. L., & Cerny, J. M. (2005). The impact of service-learning on student development: Students' reflections in a family diversity course. *Marriage and Family Review, 38, 4/5,* 79–96.

Tolan, P. H., Guerra, N. G., & Kendall, P. C. (1995). Introduction to special section: Predictions and prevention of antisocial behavior in children and youth and adolescents. *Journal of Consulting & Clinical Psychology, 63,* 515–517.

Toman, W. (1969). *Family constellation: Its effect on personality and social behavior.* (2nd ed.). New York: Springer.

Toman, W. (1976). *Family constellation: Its effect on personality and social behavior.* (3rd ed.). New York: Springer.

Toman, W. (1993). *Family constellation: Its effect on personality and social behavior* (4th ed.). New York: Springer.

Topper, M. D. (1992). Multidimensional therapy: A case study of a Navajo adolescent with multiple problems. In L. A. Vargas & J. D. Koss-Chioino (Eds.), *Working with culture: Psychotherapeutic interventions with ethnic minority children and adolescents* (pp. 225–245). San Francisco: Jossey-Bass.

Treadway, D. (1987, July/August). The ties that bind: Both alcoholics and their families are bound to the bottle. *Family Networker,* pp. 17–23.

Trimble, J. E. (1992). A cognitive-behavioral approach to drug abuse prevention and intervention with American Indian youth. In L. A. Vargas & J. D. Koss-Chioino (Eds.), *Working with culture: Psychotherapeutic interventions with ethnic minority children and adolescents* (pp. 246–275). San Francisco: Jossey-Bass.

Trinke, S. F., & Bartholomew, K. (1997). Hierarchies of attachment relationships in young adulthood. *Journal of Social and Personal Relationships, 14,* 603–625.

Trout, M. D. (1983). Birth of a sick or handicapped infant: Impact on the family. *Child Welfare, 62,* 337–347.

Truscott, S. D., Cohen, C. E., Sams, D. P., Sanborn, K. J., & Frank, A. J. (2005). The currents state(s) of prereferral intervention teams: A report from two national surveys. *Remedial and Special Education, 26*(3), 130–140.

Tseng, W., & McDermott, J. (1979). Triaxial family classification. *Journal of the American Academy of Child Psychiatry, 18,* 22–43.

Tuckman, B. W. (1965). Developmental sequences in small groups. *Psychological Bulletin, 63,* 384–399.

Turnbull, A. P., & Turnbull, H. R. (2001). *Families, professionals, and exceptionality: A special partnership* (4th ed.). Upper Saddle River, NJ: Merrill.

Turnbull, H. R. (2005). Individuals with disabilities education act reauthorization: Accountability and personal responsibility. *Remedial and Special Education, 26,* 320-326.

Turnbull, H. R., & Turnbull, A. P. (2000). *Free appropriate public education: The law and children with disabilities* (6th ed.). Denver: Love.

Turnbull, R., Huerta, N., & Stowe, M. (2006). *The Individuals With Disabilities Education Act as amended in 2004.* Upper Saddle River, NJ: Pearson/Merrill.

Turnbull, R., Turnbull, A., Shank, M., Smith, S., & Leal, D. (2002). *Exceptional lives: Special education in today's schools* (3rd ed.). Upper Saddle River, NJ: Merrill.

Turner, R. (1981). Social support as a contingency in psychological well-being. *Journal of Health and Social Behavior, 22,* 357–367.

Ungar, M. The importance of parents and other caregivers to the resilience of high-risk adolescents. *Family Process, 43,* 23–41.

Unger, D., Tressell, P. A., Jones, C. W., & Park, E. (2004). Involvement of low-income single caregivers in child-focused early intervention services: Implication for caregiver-child interaction. *Family Relations, 53,* 210–218.

U.S. Bureau of the Census (2000). *Census 2000.* Retrieved November 28, 2007, from http://www.census.gov/main/www/cen2000.html

U.S. Bureau of the Census (2005). *2005 American Community Survey.* Retrieved November 28, 2007, from http://factfinder.census.gov/servlet/DatasetMainPageServlet?_program=ACS

U.S. Conference of Mayors. (2002). *A status report on hunger and homelessness in America's cities.* Retrieved on November 28, 2007 from http://www.usmayors.org/USCM/news/publications/

U.S. Department of Education. (2001). *Twenty-third annual report to Congress on the implementation of IDEA.* Department of Education: Washington, DC: Author.

U.S. Department of Education. (2002). *Twenty-fourth annual report to Congress in the implementation of the Individuals with Disabilities Act.* Washington, DC: US Government Printing Office.

U.S. Department of Health and Human Services. (2004a). *How many children were adopted in 2000 and 2001?* Washington, D. C.: National Adoption Information Clearinghouse. [http://childwelfare. gov/pubs/s_adopted/index.cfm]

U. S. Department of Health and Human Services (2004b). *15+ make time to listen, take time to talk.... About bullying.* Retrieved on October 11, 2005, from SAMHSA, www.mentalhealth.samhas. gov/publications/allpubs/SVP%2D0051

U.S. Department of Interior. (2005). *Bureau of Indian Affairs.* Retrieved October 21, 2005, from www.doi.gov/bureau-indian-affairs.html

Vadasy, P. F., Fewell, R. R., Meyer, D. J., & Schell, G. (1984). Siblings of handicapped children: A developmental perspective on family interactions. *Family Relations, 33,* 155–167.

Vail-Smith, K., Knight, S. M., & White, D. M. (1995). Children of substance abusers in the elementary school: A survey of counselor perceptions. *Elementary School Guidance and Counseling, 29,* 163–176.

Vanfraussen, K., Ponjaert-Kristoffersen, & Brewaeys, A. (2003). Family functioning in lesbian families created by donor insemination. *American Journal of Orthopsychiatry, 73,* 78–90.

Vaughn, B. J., White, R., Johnston, S., & Dunlap, G. (2005), Positive behavior support as a family-centered endeavor. *Journal of Positive Behavior Interventions, 7*(1), 55–58.

Vaughn, S., Gersten, R., Chard, D. J. (2000). The underlying message in LD intervention research: Findings from research syntheses. *Exceptional Children, 67,* 99–114.

Vernon, A. (2004). *Counseling children and adolescents* (3rd ed.). Denver: Love.

Viadero, D. (2000, March 28). Lags in minority achievement defy traditional explanations. *Education Week, 19*(28), 1.

Vickers, H. S., & Minke, K. M. (1997). Family systems and family–school connection. In G. G. Bear, K. M. Minke, & A. Thomas (Eds.). *Children and youth's needs: Development, problems and alternatives.* Bethesda, MD: National Associations of School Psychologists.

Virginia Best Practices in School-based Violence Prevention (2005). Retrieved October 17, 2005 from www.publicinfo.vcu.edu/vabp/default.asp

Visher, E. B., & Visher, J. S. (1991). *How to win as a stepfamily* (2nd ed.). New York: Brunner/Mazel.

Visher, E. B., & Visher, J. S. (1996). *Therapy with stepfamilies.* New York: Brunner/Mazel.

Visher, E. B., Visher, J. S., & Pasley, K. (1997). Stepfamily therapy from the client's perspective. *Marriage and Family Review, 26(1/2)* 191–213.

Visher, E. B., & Visher, J. S., & Pasley, K. (2003). Remarriage families and stepparenting. In F. Walsh

(Ed.). Normal family processes: Growing diversity and complexity (3rd ed., pp. 153-175). New York: Guilford.

Volkman, T. A. (2003). Introduction: Transnational adoption [Electronic version]. *Social Text, 21,* 1–5.

Vondra, J. I. (1990). Sociological and ecological factors. In R. T. Ammerman & M. Hersen (Eds.), *Children at risk: An evaluation of factors contributing to child abuse and neglect* (pp. 149–170). New York: Plenum Press.

Vorrath, H. H., & Brendtro, L. K. (1985). *Positive peer culture* (2nd ed.). New York: Aldine.

Waddington, C. H. (1957). *The strategy of the genes: A discussion of some aspects of theoretical biology.* London: George Allen and Unwin LTD.

Waddock, S. A. (1993). The spider's web: Influences on school performance. *Business Horizons, 36*(5), 39–48.

Waddock, S. A. (1995). *Not by schools alone: Sharing responsibility for America's education reform.* Westport, CN: Praeger.

Wallace, T., Shin, J., Bartholomay, M., & Stahl, B. J. (2001). Knowledge and skills for teachers supervising the work of paraprofessionals. *Exceptional Children, 67,* 520–533.

Wallerstein, J. S. (1983). Children of divorce: The psychological tasks of the child. *American Journal of Orthopsychiatry, 53,* 230–243.

Wallerstein, J. S., & Blakeslee, S. (1989). *Second chances: Men, women, and children a decade after divorce.* New York: Ticknor & Fields.

Wallerstein, J. S., & Kelly, J. B. (1980). Divorce counseling: A community service for families in the midst of divorce. In R. R. Abidin (Ed.), *Parent education and intervention handbook* (pp. 272–298). Springfield, IL: C. C. Thomas.

Walsh, F. (1982). *Normal family processes.* New York: Guilford Press.

Walsh, F. (1983). The timing of symptoms and critical events in the family life cycle. In J. Hansen & H. Liddle (Eds.), *Clinical implications of the family life cycle* (pp. 120–132). Rockville, MD: Aspen.

Walsh, F. (1996). The concept of family resilience: Crisis and challenge. *Family Process, 35,* 261–281.

Walsh, F. (1999). Families in later life: Challenges and opportunities. In B. Carter & M. McGoldrick (Eds.), *The expanded family life cycle: Individual, family, and social perspectives* (3rd ed., pp. 307–326). Boston: Allyn & Bacon.

Walsh, F. (2002) A family resilience framework: Innovation practice applications. *Family Relations, 51,* 130–137.

Walsh, F. (2003a). Clinical views of family normality, health, and dysfunction: From deficit to strengths perspective. In F. Walsh (Ed.), *Normal family processes: Growing diversity and complexity* (3rd ed.; pp. 27–57). New York: Guilford.

Walsh, F. (2003b). Family resilience: A framework for clinical practice. *Family Process, 42*(1), 1–18.

Walsh, F. (2003c). Family resilience: strengths forged through adversity. In F. Walsh (Ed.), *Normal family processes* (3rd ed.; pp. 399–423). New York: Guilford.

Walsh, F. (Ed.). (2003d). *Normal family processes: Growing diversity and complexity* (3rd ed.). New York: Guilford.

Walsh, F., & McGoldrick, M. (Eds.). (2004). *Living beyond loss: Death in the family* (3rd ed.). New York: Norton.

Walsh, F., & Pryce, J. (2003). The spiritual dimension of family life. In F. Walsh (Ed.), *Normal family processes: Growing diversity and complexity* (3rd ed., pp. 337–372). New York: Guilford.

Walsh, M.E., & Buckley, M. A. (1994). Children's experiences of homelessness: Implications for school counselors. *Elementary School Guidance & Counseling, 29,* 4–15.

Walsh, M. E., & Galassi, J. P. (2002). An introduction: Counseling psychologists and schools. *The Counseling Psychologist, 20,* 675–681.

Walsh, W. M., & McGraw, J. (2002). *Essentials of family therapy: A structured summary of nine approaches* (2nd Ed.). Denver: Love.

Walsh, W. M., & Williams, G. R. (1997). *Schools and family therapy: Using systems theory and family therapy in the resolution of school problems.* Springfield, IL: C. C. Thomas.

Walters, M. (1972). We became family therapists. In A. Ferber, M. Mendelsohn, & A. Napier (Eds.), *Book of family therapy* (pp. 118–120). New York: Science House.

Walther-Thomas, C., Korinek, L., & McLaughlin, V. (2005). Collaboration to support students' success. In T. M. Skrtic, K. R. Harris, & J. G. Shriner (Eds.). *Special education policy and practice: Accountability, instruction, and social challenges* (pp. 182–211). Denver: Love.

Walton, E., Roby, J., Frandsen, A., & Davidson, R. (2003). Strengthening at-risk families by involving the extended family. *Journal of Social Work, 7*(4), 1–21.

Wang, M. C., & Haertel, G. D. (1995). Educational resilience. In M. C. Wang, M. C. Reynolds, & H. J. Walberg (Eds.), *Handbook of special and remedial education: Research and practice* (2nd ed., pp. 159–200). New York: Elsevier Science.

Wang, M. C., Haertel, G. D., & Walberg, H. J. (1994). Educational resilience in inner cities. In M. C. Wang & E. W. Gordon (Eds.), *Educational resilience in inner-city America: Challenges and prospects* (pp. 45–72). Hillsdale, NJ: Erlbaum.

Warren, J. S., Edmonson, H. M., Griggs, P., Lassen, S. R., McCart, A., Turnbull, A., & Sailor, W. (2003). Urban application of school-wide positive behavior support: Critical issues and lessons learned. *Journal of Positive Behavior Interventions, 5*(2), 80–91.

Watkins, M., & Fisher, S. (1995). *Talking with young children about adoption* (reissue edition). New Haven, CT: Yale University Press.

Watzlawick, P., Weakland, J. H., & Fisch, R. (1974). *Change: Principles of problem formation and problem resolution.* New York: Norton.

Webb, L. D., Brigman, G. A., & Campbell, C. (2005). Linking school counselors and students success: A replication of the student success skills approach targeting the academic and social competence of students. *Professional School Counseling, 8,* 407–413.

Weber, J. L., & Stoneman, Z. (1986). Parental non-participation in program planning for mentally retarded children. An empirical investigation. *Applied Research in Mental Retardation, 7,* 359–369.

Wegar, K. (2000). Adoption, family ideology, and social stigma: Bias in community attitudes, adoption research, and practice. *Family Relations, 49,* 363–370.

Wegscheider-Cruse, S. (1985). *Choicemaking.* Pompano Beach, FL: Health Communications.

Weinberg, R. B., & Mauksch, L. B. (1991). Examining family-of-origin influences in life at work. *Journal of Marital and Family Therapy, 17,* 233–242.

Weisner, T. S. (1982). Sibling interdependence and child caretaking: A cross-cultural view. In M. E. Lamb & B. Sutton-Smith (Eds.), *Sibling relationships* (pp. 305–328). Hillsdale, NJ: Erlbaum.

Weiss, H. B., Faughnan, K., Caspe, M., Wolos, C., Lopez, M. E., & Kreider, H. (2005). *Taking a closer look: A guide to online resources on family involvement.* Cambridge, MA: Harvard Family Research Project/Family Involvement Network of Educators. [www.gse.harvard.edu/hfrp]

Weissbourd, R. (1996). *The vulnerable child: What really hurts America's children and what we can do about it.* Reading, MA: Addison-Wesley.

Wendell, H. V., & Leoni, D. (1986). *Multiethnic/multicultural materials.* Richmond: Virginia State Department of Education.

Wendt, R. N., & Ellenwood, A. E. (1994). From impotence to activation: Conjoint systemic change in the family and school. In M. Andolfi & R. Haber (Eds.), *Please help me with this family: Using consultants as resources in family therapy* (pp. 219–233). New York: Brunner/Mazel.

Werner, E. E. (1984). Resilient children. *Young Children, 40*(1), 68–72.

Werner, E. E. (1986). Resilient offspring of alcoholics: A longitudinal study from birth to age 18. *Journal of Studies on Alcohol, 47,* 34–40.

Werner, E. E. (1989). High risk children in young adulthood: A longitudinal study from birth to 32 years. *American Journal of Orthopsychiatry, 59,* 72–81.

Werner, E. E. (1993). The children of Kauai: Resiliency and recovery in adolescence and adulthood. *Journal of Adolescent Health, 13,* 262–268.

Werner, E. E. (1994). Overcoming the odds. *Journal of Developmental and Behavioral Pediatrics, 15,* 131–136.

Werner, E. E. (1995). Resilience in development. *Current Directions in Psychological Science, 4,* 81–85.

Werner, E. E. (1997). *Conceptual and methodological issues in studying minority children: An international perspective.* Paper presented at the Biennial Meeting of the Society for Research in Child Development (62nd, Washington, DC, April 3–6, 1997). (ERIC Document Reproduction Service No. ED 414 010)

Werner, E. E., & Smith, R. S. (1977). *Kauai's children come of age.* Honolulu: University of Hawaii Press.

Werner, E. E., & Smith, R. S. (1982). *Vulnerable but invincible: A longitudinal study of resilient children and youth.* New York: McGraw Hill.

Werner, E. E., & Smith, R. S. (1992). *Overcoming the odds: High risk children from birth to adulthood.* Ithaca, NY: Cornell University Press.

Werner, E. E. (1993). Risk and resilience in individuals with learning disabilities. *Learning Disabilities Research and Practice, 8*(1), 28–34.

Werner, E. E., & Smith, R. S. (1998). *Vulnerable but invincible: A longitudinal study of resilient children and youth.* New York: Adams, Bannister, Cox.

Werner, E. E., & Smith, R. S. (2001). *Journeys from childhood to midlife: Risk, resilience, and recovery.* Ithaca, NY: Cornell University Press.

Werts, M. G., Harris, S., Tillery, C. Y., & Roark, R. (2004). What parents tell us about paraeducators. *Remedial and special education, 25*(4), 232–239.

Westfall, A., & Pisapia, J. (1994). *Students who defy the odds: A study of resilient at-risk students* (Research Brief No. 18). Richmond, VA: VCU Metropolitan Education Research Consortium.

Whitaker, T., & Fiore, D. J. (2001). *Dealing with difficult parents: And with parents in difficult situations.* Larchmont, NY: Eye on Education.

White, J. M. (1991). *Dynamics of family development.* New York: Guilford Press.

White, J.M. (2004). Towards a black psychology. In R. Jones (Ed.), *Black psychology* (4th ed.). Hampton, VA: Cobb & Henry Press.

White, M., & Epston, D. (1990). *Narrative means to therapeutic ends.* New York: Norton.

White, W., & Savage, B. (2005). All in the family: Alcohol and other drug problems, recovery, advocacy. *Alcoholism Treatment Quarterly, 23*(4) 3–38.

Wikler, L. (1981). Chronic stresses of families of mentally retarded children. *Family Relations, 30,* 281–288.

Wikler, L., Wasow, M., & Hatfield, E. (1981). Chronic sorrow revisited: Parent vs. professional depiction of the adjustment of parents of mentally retarded children. *American Journal of Orthopsychiatry, 51,* 63–70.

Wilcox, D. T., Richards, F., & O'Keefe, Z. C. (2004). Resilience and risk factors associated with experiencing childhood sexual abuse. *Child Abuse Review, 13,* 338–352.

Wilkes, G. (2002a). Abused child to nonabusive parent: Resilience and conceptual change. *Journal of Clinical Psychology, 58,* 261–276.

Wilkes, G. (2002b). Introduction: A second generation of resilience research. *Journal of Clinical Psychology, 58,* 229–232.

Wilkinson, I. (2000). The Darlington family assessment system: clinical guidelines for practitioners. *Journal of Family Therapy, 22*(2) 211–224.

Williams, J. H., Ayers, C. D., Van Dorn, R. A., & Arthur, M. W. (2004). Risk and protective factors in the development of delinquency and conduct disorder. In M. W. Fraser (Ed.), *Risk and resilience in childhood: An ecological perspective* (2nd ed., pp. 209–249). Washington, D.C.: NASW Press.

Williams, T. R., Davis, L. E., Cribbs, J. M., Saunders, J., & Williams, J. H. (2002). Friends, family and neighborhood: Understanding academic outcomes of African American youth. *Urban Education, 37,* 408–431.

Willie, C. V. (1991). *A new look at black families.* (4th ed.). Bayside, NY: General Hall.

Willis, D. J., Dobrec, A., & Sipes, D. S. B. (1992). Treating American Indian victims of abuse and neglect. In L. A. Vargas & J. D. Koss-Chioino (Eds.), *Working with culture: Psychotherapeutic interventions with ethnic minority children and adolescents* (pp. 276–299). San Francisco: Jossey-Bass.

Wilson, R. F. (2004a). Recognizing the threat posed by an incestuous parent to the victim's siblings. Part I: Appraising the risk. *Journal of Child and Family Studies, 13,* 143–162.

Wilson, R. F. (2004b). Recognizing the threat posed by an incestuous parent to the victim's siblings. Part II: Improving legal responses. *Journal of Child and Family Studies, 13,* 263–276.

Wilson, W. J. (1982). The declining significance of race. In N. R. Yetman & C. H. Steele (Eds.), *Majority and minority: The dynamics of race and ethnicity in American life* (3rd ed., pp. 385–392). Boston: Allyn & Bacon.

Winton, P. J. (1996). Understanding family concerns, priorities, and resources. In P. J. McWilliam, P. J. Winton, & E. R. Crais (Eds.), *Practical strategies for family-centered early intervention* (pp. 31–53). San Diego, CA: Singular.

Wise, L. A., Zierler, S., Krieger, N., & Harlow, B. L. (2001). Adult onset of major depressive disorder in relation to early life violent victimisation: A case-control study. *The Lancet, 358,* 881–887.

Wlodkowski, R. J., & Ginsberg, M. B. (1995). A framework for culturally responsive teaching. *Educational Leadership, 53*(1), 17–21.

Wolin, S. J., & Wolin, S. (1993). *The resilient self: How survivors of troubled families rise above adversity.* New York: Villard.

Wolin, S., & Wolin, S. J. (1996). Beating the odds: Some kids who have been dealt a losing hand end up winning the game. What can we learn from them? *Learning, 25*(1), 66–68.

Woititz, J. (2002). *The complete ACOA sourcebook: Adult children of alcoholics at home, at work and in love.* Deerfield Beach, FL: Health Communications, Inc.

Wu, S. J. (2001). Parenting in Chinese American families. In N. B. Webb (Ed.), *Culturally diverse parent-child and family relationships* (pp. 235–260). New York: Columbia University Press.

Wynne, E. A., & Walberg, H. J. (1995). The virtues of intimacy in education. *Educational Leadership, 53*(3), 53–54.

Yalisove, D. L. (2004). *Introduction to alcohol research: Implications for treatment, prevention, and policy.* Boston: Allyn & Bacon.

Yell, M. L., & Shriner, J. G. (2005) The IDEA amendments of 1997: Implications for special and general education teachers, administrators, and teacher trainers. In T. M. Skrtic, K. R. Harris, & J. G. Shriner (Eds.). *Special education policy and practice: Accountability, instruction, and social challenges* (pp. 29–57). Denver: Love.

Young-Eisendrath, P. (1996). *The gifts of suffering: Finding insight, compassion, and renewal.* Reading, MA: Addison-Wesley.

Ysseldyke, J. E., Christenson, S., & Kovaleski, J. F. (1994). Identifying students' instructional needs in the context of classroom and home environments. *Teaching Exceptional Children, 26*(3), 37–41.

Zamostny, K. P., O'Brien, K. M., Baden, A. L., & Wiley, M. O. (2003). The practice of adoption: History, trends, and social context. *The Counseling Psychologist, 31,* 651–678.

Zamostny, K. P., Wiley, M. O., O'Brien, K. M., Lee, R. M., & Baden, A. L. (2003). *The Counseling Psychologist, 31,* 647–650.

Zayaz, L. H., Canino, I., & Suarez, Z. E. (2001). Parenting in mainland Puerto Rican families. In N. B. Webb (Ed.), *Culturally diverse parent-child and family relationships: A guide for social workers and other practitioners* (pp. 133–156). New York: Columbia University Press.

Zetlin, A. G. (1985). Mentally retarded teenagers: Adolescent behavior disturbance and its relation to family environment. *Child Psychiatry and Human Development, 15,* 243–254.

Zelvin, E. (2004). Treating the partners of substance abusers. In S. Straussner (Ed.), *Clinical work with substance-abusing clients* (2nd ed., pp. 264–283). New York: Guilford.

Zill, N., & Nord, C. W. (1994). *Running in place: How American families are faring in a changing economy and an individualistic society.* Washington, DC: Child Trends.

Zimet, D. M., & Jacob, T. (2001). Influences of marital conflict on child adjustment: Review of theory and research. *Clinical Child and Family Psychology Review, 4,* 319–335.

Zmuda, A., Kuklis, R., & Kline, E. (2004). *Transforming schools: Creating a culture of continuous improvement.* Alexandria, VA: Association for Supervision and Curriculum Development.

Zuvarin, S. J., & Starr, R. H. (1991). Psychosocial characteristics of mothers of physically abused and neglected children: Do they differ by race? In R. L. Hampton (Ed.), *Black family violence: Current research and theory* (pp. 35–70). Lexington, MA: D.C. Heath.

NAME INDEX

A

Abbott, D. A., 65
Abramovitch, R., 73, 95
Abrams, K. A., 3, 6
Ackerman, R. J., 235, 244, 249
Adams, M., 202
Adkins, P. G., 133, 134
Adler, A., 19, 92, 93, 94, 104
Ahrons, C. R., 23, 205
Akbar, N., 156, 165, 169
Albert, V., 192
Albrecht, T. L., 311–312
Alder, N., 219, 299, 307–308
Aldous, J., 28
Alexander, J. F., 24, 31
Alexander, K. L., 3
Alexander, L. B., 170, 177
Algozzine, B., 386
Allen, K. R., 20
Allen, M., 315
Allison, S., 5, 115, 381
Almeida, R., 133
Altstein, H., 182, 192
Alvarez, K. M., 243, 256
Amatea, E. S., 306–307, 311, 406
Amato, P. R., 202, 204, 206, 303
Ames, L. B., 19
Ammerman, R. G., 91
Ammerman, R. T., 251–252
Anda, R. F., 259
Anderson, C., 209–210, 303
Anderson, J. A., 138
Anderson, K. J., 352
Anhalt, K., 222
Antil, L. R., 435
Aponte, H. J., 7, 53, 59, 116, 117, 126, 233, 417, 487, 506, 510, 511, 513, 514, 515, 521
Arditti, J. A., 207
Arends, R. I., 471
Armstrong, D., 358
Arnold, M. S., 120
Arnowitz, T., 304
Arthur, M. W., 204, 298–299
Arwine, A., 92, 93

Asbury, K., 232
Aspy, C. B., 280
Atkins, M. S., 171
Attneave, C. L., 125, 136, 309
Auslander, W., 297
Austin, T., 379
Ayers, C. D., 204, 298
Azpeitia, L. M., 443–444

B

Baber, K. M., 20
Bacon, J., 335, 371
Baden, A. L., 192
Bagarozzi, D. A., 521
Bagley, C., 222
Bagnall, G., 239
Bahr, M., 368, 386–387
Bailey, D. B., 123, 134, 135, 355, 398, 414
Bailey, J. M., 371, 379
Bailly, M. D., 242
Bainbridge, W. L., 128
Baker, L., 76, 507
Baker, S. B., 15, 402
Baldwin, M., 88, 97, 372, 374, 386, 406, 428, 440, 490, 491, 492, 493, 494
Ballard, J., 288
Balter, L., 143
Bandler, R., 381
Bandura, A., 300
Bank, S. P., 67, 509
Barbaranelli, C., 300
Bardill, D. R., 25, 28, 409
Barlow, K. M., 253
Barnes, H., 35
Barnett, S. P., 371, 379
Barney, J., 216, 218
Barnhill, L. R., 26, 33
Barone, D., 296–297
Barry, S., 242, 253
Bartfeld, J., 204
Barth, R. P., 170, 181, 192
Bartholomay, M., 337, 351
Bartholomew, K., 302
Bastian, A. M., 273
Bates, C., 239
Bateson, G., 296, 517
Bauer, A. M., 379, 396–397, 454–455
Baumeister, R., 282

Beattie, J., 415
Beattie, M., 86
Beavers, R., 521, 522
Beck, V., 308
Becker, B. E., 121, 296, 303, 305
Beckman, P. J., 36
Beegle, G., 351
Beers, S. R., 242, 255
Behrman, R. E., 270, 280
Belisto, L., 15
Belsey, B ., 276
Bemak, F., 307
Benard, B., 282, 295, 297–299, 301–302, 305–306
Benedek, E. P., 211–213, 216
Benne, K. D., 348
Bennett, C. I., 134
Bennett, F., 333
Benshoff, J. J., 233, 236
Benson, B. P., 371, 379
Benson, P. L., 187, 282
Benton, W., 23, 32, 35, 36, 37, 38, 41, 67
Bentovim, A., 259
Bepko, C., 23
Berardo, F. M., 9
Berger, A., 249, 251
Berger, E. H., 382
Berger, M., 74, 312, 314
Bergquist, K. I., 187, 188
Berman, W. H., 211
Bernhard, Y. M., 493
Bernheimer, L. P., 120
Bernstein, A. C., 278
Bernstein, H., 277
Berrick, J. D., 192
Berry, M., 181
Bertolino, B., 286
Best, K. M., 296
Bevin, T., 135
Bigelow, D. A., 240
Bigelow, K. M., 242
Billingsley, A., 156, 165, 169
Billingsley, B. S., 352
Birenbaum, A., 116
Birmingham, S. M., 282
Bishop, D. S., 309, 521
Bitter, J. R., 92, 428, 440, 488, 489, 494, 496

Björck-Åkesson, E., 465
Blacher, J., 34, 36, 68, 138
Black, L., 129
Blacker, L., 28
Blakeslee, S., 206
Blanchard, K., 288
Blechman, E. A., 303, 305
Blevins, G. A., 239
Blotcky, A., 396
Blue-Banning, M., 351–352, 359, 362, 365, 371, 385, 454
Blum, R. W., 282
Blumberg, B. D., 41
Boettcher, M., 411
Bogolub, E. B., 206, 210, 213
Bolch, M. B., 223
Bolger, K. E., 242, 253–255
Bolman, L. G., 474
Bond, L., 65
Bonnier, C., 253
Booth, A., 308, 407
Booth, C., 206
Borders, L. D., 188, 195
Borkowski, J. G., 68
Boswell, J., 156
Bosworth, K., 298
Boszormenyi-Nagy, I., 76
Boutte, G. S., 307, 315
Bowen, G. L., 298, 305–306
Bowen, M., 32, 83, 84, 85, 87, 88, 89, 92, 95, 96, 101, 104, 231, 498, 500, 501, 502, 503, 505, 521
Bowland, S., 298
Bowlby, J., 302
Boyd-Franklin, N., 128, 129, 130, 143, 156, 165, 169, 311, 466, 469–470, 474
Bradley, C., 5
Bradley, D. F., 360
Bradley, L. J., 186, 409, 438
Bramlett, M. D., 205
Braver, S. L., 204, 212
Brazelton, T. B., 341
Brendtro, L., 14, 284, 286, 335, 371
Brennan, R. T., 249
Breslau, N., 95
Breulin, D. C., 46, 488

563

SUBJECT INDEX